ACCOUNTING AND FINANCE PRACTICE SERIES

Handbook of Sampling for Auditing and Accounting

Third Edition

ACCOUNTING AND FINANCE PRACTICE SERIES

Handbook of Sampling for Auditing and Accounting

Third Edition

Herbert Arkin
Professor Emeritus
Bernard M. Baruch College
City University of New York

SHEPARD'S/McGRAW-HILL, INC.
P.O. Box 1235
Colorado Springs, Colorado 80901

McGRAW-HILL BOOK COMPANY

New York • St. Louis • San Francisco • Auckland • Bogotá
Caracas • Colorado Springs • Hamburg • Lisbon • London
Madrid • Mexico • Milan • Montreal • New Delhi
Oklahoma City • Panama • Paris • San Juan • São Paulo
Singapore • Sydney • Tokyo • Toronto

34567890 SHCU 898

Library of Congress Cataloging in Publication Data

Arkin, Herbert, 1906–
Handbook of sampling for auditing and accounting.

Includes index.
1. Accounting. 2. Auditing. 3. Sampling (Statistics)
I. Title.
HF5657.A73 1984 519.5'2'024657 83-9830
ISBN 0-07-002245-3

ISBN 0-07-002245-3

Contents

PREFACE TO THE THIRD EDITION xi
PREFACE TO THE SECOND EDITION xiii

1. The Place of Sampling in Auditing *1*

Sampling in Accounting
Sampling and the Auditor
The Auditor's Test
Test Objectives and Sampling
Objective Sampling
The Statistical Sample
The Advantages of the Statistical Sample
Types of Statistical Samples
The Sampling Plan
Estimation Sampling
Acceptance Sampling
Discovery (Exploratory) Sampling
Test Objectives and the Sampling Plan
When to Use Statistical Sampling

2. Selecting the Sample *18*

Sampling Problems
What Is to Be Sampled?
The Field or Universe
Nonsampling Errors
Multiple Purpose Samples

3. The Mechanics of Sampling *25*

The Probability Sample
Methods of Obtaining a Probability Sample
Random Number Sampling
Random Number Tables
Mechanics of Random Number Sampling
Computer Random Number Generation
Special Problems in Random Number Sampling
Sampling Unnumbered Documents
Systematic Sampling
The Mechanics of Systematic Sampling
Special Sampling Methods
  Stratified Random Samples
  Cluster Samples
  Multistage Samples
Sampling Selection and Costs

4. Elementary Statistical Concepts *50*

Statistical Theory and the Auditor
Basic Statistical Measures
  1. Averages
  2. Measures of Dispersion
  3. The Standard Deviation
Sampling Concepts
Attributes Sampling
Variables Sampling
General

5. Determining Sample Size (Estimation Sampling) *75*

Selection of Sample Size
Sample Precision
The Confidence Level
Attributes Sampling—Sample Size
  Concepts
  Tables for Attribute Sample Size
Steps in Determining Sample Size—Attributes
General Sample Size Considerations—Attributes Sampling
  General Considerations
Variables Sampling—Sample Size
  Concepts
  Tables for Variables Sample Size
Steps in Determining Sample Sizes—Estimation Sampling—Variables
General Sample Size Considerations—Variables
Sample Size Estimation for Multipurpose Tests
Other Sampling Methods—Estimation Sampling

6. Appraisal of Sample Results (Attributes) *100*

The Need for Post-sampling Appraisal
Principles of Sample Appraisal
The Tables (Sample Precision for Relative Frequencies)
Values Not Covered by Tables
Missing Field Sizes
Missing Percentages in Sample
Missing Sample Sizes
One-sided Confidence Limits
Interim Appraisals
Another Approach to Sample Size Estimation

7. Appraisal of Sample Results (Variables) *116*

The Need for Post-sampling Appraisal
Estimating Variability
The Tables
Values Not Covered by Tables
One-sided Confidence Limits
General Considerations
Estimating Total Values When Population Size Is Unknown

8. Discovery Sampling *132*

The Place of Discovery Sampling in Auditing
Principles of Discovery Sampling
Tables for Discovery Sampling
General Considerations
Discovery Sampling and Estimation Sampling

9. Acceptance Sampling *141*

Objectives
Advantages and Limitations
Statistical Principles
Selection of a Plan
1. Rejection of Bad Fields
2. Acceptance of Good Fields
Use of the Tables
Average Error Rates
Multiple Sampling Plans
Other Tables
Applications

10. *Stratified Sampling* **158**

The Reasons for Special Sampling Plans
Stratified Random Sampling
Sampling Efficiency—Stratified Samples
Sample Appraisal—Stratified Sampling—Variables
Allocation of Sample Items to Strata—Variables Sampling—Arbitrary Sample Size
Other Allocation Methods
Proportional Allocation (Stratum Population Sizes)
Proportional Allocation (Stratum Dollar Totals)
Sample Size Determination—Stratified Samples—Variables
Stratified Sampling—Attributes
General Considerations

11. *Cluster Sampling* **182**

The Reason for Cluster Sampling
The Cluster Sample
Drawing a Cluster Sample
Appraising the Determination—A Cluster Sample—Variables
Sample Size Determination—Cluster Samples—Variables
Appraising the Precision of Cluster Samples—Attributes
Sample Size Determination—Cluster Samples—Attributes
General Comment on Cluster Sampling

12. *Difference and Ratio Estimates* **195**

The Reason for Difference and Ratio Estimates
Difference Estimates
Ratio Estimates
General Comments on Difference and Ratio Estimates

13. *Multistage Sampling* **210**

The Reason for Multistage Sampling
Limitations
Sample Precision
An Illustration
General

14. *Other Sampling Plans* **218**

Post Stratification (Stratification after Sample Selection)
Ratio Estimate of a Ratio
Sampling with Unequal Size Clusters
The Replicated Sample
Combinations of Sampling Plans

APPENDIXES

A Table of Random Numbers *235* **A**

B Table of Random Letters of the Alphabet *296* **B**

C Table of Random Months *298* **C**

D Tables for Estimating Sample Size—Attributes *310* **D**

E Tables for Estimating Sample Size—Variables *376* **E**

F Tables for Sample Precision for Relative Frequencies *388* **F**

G Tables for Sample Precision for Average Values for Random Samples Only *470* **G**

H Table for Sample Precision for Average Values for Random Samples Only When Field Size Is Infinite *475* **H**

I Table for Finite Population Correction Factor *481* **I**

J Tables for Probabilities of Incuding at Least One Occurrence in a Sample (Discovery Sampling) *485* **J**

K Tables of Acceptance Sampling Plans *489* **K**

L Table for Cluster Sampling *504* **L**

TECHNICAL APPENDIXES

I An Alternative Method for Computation of Standard Deviation *507*

II Standard Error of Arithmetic Mean *509*

III Cluster Sampling *511*

IV Multistage Sampling *514*

V Basis of Computation of Tables for Estimating Sample Size for Variables *516*

VI Basis of Computation of Tables for Estimating Sample Size for Attributes (Appendix D) *518*

VII Basis of Computation of Tables for Appraising the Sample of Relative Frequencies (Appendix F) *519*

VIII Post Stratification *521*

INDEX *523*

Preface to the Third Edition

Since the publication of the second edition of this volume, the use of statistical sampling in auditing has increased greatly, especially in government audits. This development, plus the use of such samples to obtain reimbursement for improperly expended funds or improperly claimed amounts, has attracted considerable attention to the method. The U.S. Internal Revenue Service has made extensive use of these techniques in the audits of business tax returns, with the resulting collection of many millions of dollars of disallowances based on sample projections.

In consequence of the increased use of sampling methods, techniques have become more sophisticated. In recognition of this trend, several new topics have been included in this new edition. Among these new sampling plans are included post-stratification methods, sampling of unequal clusters, and ratio estimates of a ratio (such as the LIFO index), as well as additional methods of sample allocation in stratified samples and combinations of sampling plans.

The development of inexpensive but powerful pocket electronic calculators as well as small-scale and personal computers have reduced the burden of calculations imposed by statistical sampling methods of the more complex types. Although the tables included in this book have long encouraged the use of the basic methods, use of the more efficient sampling plans has been limited by the complexity of the calculations involved. In recognition of this development, discussions of the uses of these devices have been included at appropriate points. A brief section on random number generators for computers is included to acquaint the reader with the impact of the technique upon sampling requirements. To further this trend, the author has in preparation a software package of programs for small personal computers, which will be published by McGraw-Hill Book Company, to encourage further the use of the more complex plans as well as to facilitate computations in the basic methods.

Finally, experience over the nearly 10 years since the publication of the second edition has revealed areas of discussion that were in need of expansion or clarification.

Herbert Arkin

Preface to the Second Edition

This volume is designed to bridge the gap between the current interest in the accounting applications of sampling theory and the dearth of concise, understandable reference material which explains sampling theory and demonstrates how it may be used effectively in practical situations. An outgrowth of materials developed for Price Waterhouse and Company and the Army Audit Agency for use in their staff training programs, this book is a working manual and not an academic treatment of the theory of sampling. It is intended not to satisfy the professional statistician looking for new theory or rigorous mathematical development but to meet the practical need of accounting practitioners to understand and use efficiently statistical sampling techniques.

The spread of the application of statistical sampling in auditing and accounting has been severely hampered by a lack of materials useful for training the accountant in this area.

The literature of statistical sampling is usually directed toward problems of survey sampling, industrial quality control, and sampling in scientific research. It is often difficult to read. Many books in the field presume the reader has a considerable prior statistical background and a good grasp of mathematics. Unfortunately, most accountants have neither. Confronted with incomprehensible statistical terminology and forbidding formulas full of Greek letters and involved mathematics, the accountant seeking the means of solving a practical sampling problem often finds an extremely useful statistical approach beyond his grasp.

In this handbook, the basic concepts of the theory of sampling are examined briefly and explained clearly to provide the accountant with the necessary background to enable him to apply sampling methods. Necessary formulas are explained and cited, but in most cases tables are provided which make the solution of formulas unnecessary in actual field work. Proofs, when given, are relegated to a technical appendix. Major attention is directed toward all forms of sampling useful in the field of accounting and auditing. The way in which they may be used and specific instructions as to the method of application are treated in detail.

Effective shortcuts, which cost little in ultimate accuracy, are described. For example, the use of a simple technique for estimating the standard deviation based on the average range to eliminate the direct computation of that measure, a method widely used in statistical quality control, is presented. Sampling to answer the questions how much or how many, estimation sampling of both attributes and variables, discovery sampling, and acceptance sampling—all are thoroughly discussed in "how-to-do-it" terms. Advanced forms of sampling methods which make possible considerable savings in sample size are described, and new methods of applying sampling techniques to accounting and auditing problems are included. Suggestions are given for dealing with the practical problems that arise in applying probability samples when sampling from accounting records.

One who uses statistical methods should always be careful in sacrificing rigor on the altar of practical necessity. Approximations are useful only when the margin of error is not significant. Some approximate methods, generally used even by competent statisticians, may be refined. For example, in establishing confidence limits for proportions, the normal curve deviates are often used in place of the actual solution of the binomial or hypergeometric distribution, because a large amount of effort is required to obtain more precise confidence limits. In Chapter 6 the use of tables (contained in the appendix) to overcome this difficulty and get the precise limits is explained. In the problems usually encountered by the accountant, where both population and sample size are relatively small, the difference between the results obtained under the two methods can be quite important.

An extensive set of practical tables is provided to make this handbook a useful working tool for the accountant. Many of these tables have not previously been available to the practitioner in a form in which they can be used with ease and confidence. These tables enable the auditor to develop sampling plans for acceptance and discovery sampling and to determine quickly sample size requirements and sample reliability for estimation sampling.

The widespread interest by accountants in statistical sampling is evidenced by the fact that many accounting associations have established committees to investigate this area. An increasing number of articles on the subject appear in the recent accounting literature. Numerous meetings and seminars on the subject have been held. There is little doubt that the future will see an ever-growing use of statistical sampling methods by auditors and accountants and a demand in the profession for persons conversant with this statistical tool. The author hopes that the approach following in this book, which explains sampling in terms of the practical problems faced by the accountant, will contribute to the current effort to apply effectively in this area the scientific concepts of statistical sampling theory.

Since the publication of the first edition of this book in 1963, the prediction of an ever-growing application of statistical sampling in the field of auditing has been definitely fulfilled. The use of this technique is actually accelerating with the increasing prospect of the future requirement of statistical sampling as the generally accepted standard test method.

Herbert Arkin

ONE

The Place of Sampling in Auditing

SAMPLING IN ACCOUNTING

Although the primary objective of this book is to discuss the application of statistical sampling techniques in auditing, by either independent or internal auditors, it must be recognized that statistical sampling methods are used for a variety of purposes in the field of accounting in general.

These applications include:

1. The audit test
2. Direct estimates of values in accounting operations in place of 100 per cent detailing, as in establishing dollar values of inventories and aging of accounts receivable by sampling
3. Transaction accounting by sampling, such as settlement of intercompany balances
4. Control of bookkeeping and clerical errors
5. Cost accounting operations
6. Establishment of appropriate values for reserves by sampling, such as reserves for bad debts, reserves for obsolescence of inventory items, and reserves for unexpended subscriptions
7. Establishing total amounts of improper or illegal payments or payments made not in accordance with prescribed regulations, especially in governmental accounting, e.g., welfare payments to ineligibles

Thus, although this discussion is directed primarily toward the auditor, it is necessary to note these other accounting applications since, to an increasing degree, they comprise part of the material examined by the auditor when these methods are used by his client and may even become part of the internal control system he relies upon.

The principles upon which these sampling techniques are based when used for purposes other than the test are the same as those for the test sample. The discussions relating to test samples serve the purpose of providing the background. Some nonaudit applications are given in this volume. However, the sampling techniques discussed here cover the needs of the accountant in any area of sampling accounting data.

SAMPLING AND THE AUDITOR

In the early stages of the development of the independent audit, which culminated in its widespread acceptance in our modern economy, it was not uncommon practice for an auditor to perform a 100 per cent examination of the entries and records of the company audited. As our economy grew and large-scale enterprise put in its appearance, however, it quickly became apparent that a 100 per cent examination of the tremendous volume of entries was unwarranted and uneconomical. The auditor's only recourse, which would provide him with reasonable assurance as to the validity of the entries in the books of account, was to examine a portion of the entries or records—in effect a spot check. This developed into the *test* or *test check approach*, which is both widely accepted and widely used in auditing.

It is quite obvious that such a method, involving the examination of a portion of a larger mass of entries in order to draw conclusions about that larger group, is a sampling operation, even though the word "sample" is not generally used in connection with a test.

THE AUDITOR'S TEST

The American Institute of Certified Public Accountants defines the auditor's objective by stating, "The objective of the ordinary examination of financial statements by the independent auditor is the expression of an opinion on the fairness with which they present financial position and results of operations."[1]

Alden C. Smith[2] notes that "the larger enterprise has made it possible to establish internal accounting controls, so it is no longer necessary to employ outside auditors to balance the books and check all detail postings."

Thus, heavy reliance is commonly placed on the determined adequacy of the client's internal control system. In fact, as defined in *Auditing Standards and Procedures*,[3] the auditing process, from the viewpoint of the independent auditor, calls

[1]*Codification of Statements on Auditing Standards, Numbers 1 to 39*, American Institute of Certified Public Accountants, Commerce Clearing House, Chicago, 1982, p. 5.

[2]Alden C. Smith, "The Accounting Profession's Growing Interest in Statistical Methods." *The New York Certified Public Accountant*, vol. 27, p. 451, July 1957.

[3]*Codification of Statements on Auditing Standards, op. cit.*, p. 47, ¶320.01. This refers to the second standard of field work.

for a study of and evaluation of the existing internal control system as a basis for the determination of the extent of testing, followed by the examination of evidential matter in support of the opinion.

The existence of an internal control system subjectively evaluated to be satisfactory does lend considerable confidence to the auditor, whether he is an independent auditor or an internal auditor, but there still remains the basic concern that although such a system exists, it may exist on paper only.

It is necessary that the auditor guard against the possibility that although an adequate protective system is prescribed, it may not actually be executed fully, either by design, accident, or carelessness. The auditor must assure himself that, in fact, the internal control system is effectively operative.

Further, although the internal control system may give every appearance of effectively protecting the records of the business, experience has indicated that there are always those who manage to evade the restrictions of even the best of systems.

To gain a confidence that the system does provide the desired protection and that the records are reasonably accurate, the auditor must examine the records and entries that constitute the evidence of the effectiveness of the control system.

However, the auditor is frequently confronted by tremendous masses of documentation or, in many instances, smaller numbers of entries but still too many for him to perform a 100 per cent detailed examination in the available time or at reasonable cost. He must then examine a portion of the documentation in such a situation and base his decision as to whether there is evidence of effective operation of the system on conclusions drawn from this portion of the data.

The examination of a portion of the documentation by the auditor as a means of judging the whole is known as a *selective test* or *test check* or simply a "test."

The publication *Auditing Standards and Procedures* states that "the well established practice of the independent auditor of evaluating the adequacy and effectiveness of the system of internal control by testing the accounting records and related data . . . has generally proved sufficient for making an adequate examination."[4]

It is apparent that the examination of evidential matter through such tests is concerned with the validity of the conclusion drawn from the study of the internal control system as well as the desire to create a reasonable basis for an opinion regarding the financial statements under question.

Evidence of numerous clerical errors, widespread carelessness, frequent violations of accepted accounting principles, or evidence of manipulation or fraud will render the previously drawn conclusions as to the effectiveness of the prescribed internal control system of little value in assessing the financial statements.

Tests designed to accomplish this purpose are called *tests of compliance.* The AICPA publication *Statements on Auditing Standards* states that "the purpose of

[4] *Auditing Standards and Procedures,* Statements on Auditing Procedures, no. 33, American Institute of Certified Public Accountants, New York, 1963, p. 11.

tests of compliance is to provide reasonable assurance that the accounting controls are being applied as prescribed."[5]

In addition, the auditor is directly concerned with the reasonableness of the account balances indicated in the financial statements. The reasonableness of these account balances can be confirmed by projections of sampled (and audited) entries or records comprising the values constituting such account balances.

While direct projections of sample results to validate stated account balances could not be accomplished with the judgment (selective samples) of the past, the advent of statistical sampling with such an ability has resulted in the rapidly increasing use of such approaches. Such tests are referred to as *substantive tests.*[6]

To the extent that the auditor projects his test findings as a generalization about the state of affairs in the entire field of documents or entries examined, the test executed by the auditor is a *sampling* operation. If he is to generalize about the field from the test data, he is dealing with a sample. If he is interested only in discussing or observing any instances that he may accidentally encounter in a haphazard examination of some entries, without considering their impact on the books of record in terms of the frequency of their occurrence or their magnitude, he has no sampling problem. If he wishes to follow through one or two documents in order to observe whether an understanding of the system exists, he has no sampling problem. It matters little what documents he selects or how many he looks at, since one or two may well suffice for this purpose. However, as soon as he starts talking about the impact of his test findings or generalizes as a result of his findings as to the state of all of the documents, then a sampling problem will arise.

Scientific sampling techniques have long been widely used in business, industry, and science. It is only recently that the use of these techniques in auditing has attracted much interest.

The unique feature of the scientific or statistical sampling method is the ability to project sample results to state the condition of the field examined with a known reliability.

Thus, from the sample results (test data), statements may be made as to the frequency of clerical errors, evasions of internal control, etc., as well as their dollar-value impact on the financial statement. In addition, the method places new tools in the hands of the auditor. The ability to project from the sample makes possible the direct determination of the reasonableness of dollar values reflected in the financial statements, such as the dollar values of inventories and groups of accounts. This process is often referred to as the *validation of account balances.*

Further, other devices become possible, such as fixing sample sizes to assure the finding of certain events if they occur in the field examined with a certain minimum

[5]*Codification of Statements on Auditing Standards, op. cit.*, p. 62, ¶320.55.

[6]*Statements on Auditing Standards and Procedures, op. cit.* (p. 49), states that "the feature of audit interest in performing substantive tests is the monetary amount of errors. . . ."

frequency. In other words, in addition to providing the auditor with an objective approach to the test operation, certain new approaches which will be discussed in detail in later sections of this book become available.

However, in considering the use of statistical sampling approaches by the auditor, it must be remembered that he is in a somewhat different position from that of the sampler in most other fields. He normally does not place total reliance on the results of a single sample (test) in arriving at his decision but usually performs other examinations and a variety of other tests and analyses in evaluating the condition of the records and their impact on the accuracy of the financial statement.

The sampler in industry will often decide to accept or reject a lot on the basis of the results of one sample drawn from that lot. The market researcher or public opinion surveyer will base his conclusions on the outcome of a survey based on one large sample. The auditor, on the other hand, uses the sample (test) result as only one component of a variety of examinations and tests. Often the test result plays a relatively minor part in his considerations unless it discloses a very bad situation. Thus, the auditor must look at the sampling problem in a somewhat different way.

TEST OBJECTIVES AND SAMPLING

As noted previously, the independent auditor's audit objective is to express an opinion as to the reasonableness of the financial statements and their compliance with generally accepted accounting principles.

To this end the auditor examines a variety of accounting evidence, possibly including data compiled by a variety of tests of specific areas selected to provide him the assurance he requires. He is primarily concerned with the impact of his findings on his decision as to the reasonableness of the financial statements.

The objective of the independent public accountant's use of the audit test relates to the prescription that he will, as part of his examination, evaluate the internal control system in use by his client. This evaluation includes a subjective evaluation of the protection afforded by the system followed by a test of the extent of compliance with the system. This test of compliance can be accomplished effectively by the use of statistical sampling, which also makes it possible to establish directly the reasonableness of the stated account balances.

The independent public auditor's objective in the use of an audit test, and thus statistical sampling, may be summarized to be

1. Tests of compliance with internal controls, sometimes referred to as a *test of transactions.*

2. Tests to validate the reasonableness of account balances (substantive tests).

The internal auditor's objective is somewhat different and has been defined as follows: "Internal auditing is an independent appraisal activity within an organization for the review of accounting, financial and other operations as a basis for service to management."[7] This covers an area beyond the question of the accuracy of the records and includes "appraising the quality of performance in carrying out assigned responsibilities."[8] Thus, in addition to assuring himself as to the accuracy of the company's records and endeavoring to safeguard the company against losses of all kinds, he is charged with an audit of operations. This management audit activity is especially important to government auditors.

From either viewpoint, each test used as part of the approach toward meeting the overall objective has in turn a specific detailed objective all its own. It is designed to produce data related to some specific point of investigation which the auditor has in mind.

The emphasis on audit objectives arises from the impact that the specific goal in the test at hand has upon the sampling plan to be used. As will be seen, no single universal sampling method will achieve the objectives of all possible audit tests, and a particular method must therefore be chosen to meet a given set of needs.

In consideration of this fact, *it is essential that the objective of a particular test be fully and explicitly stated before a sampling plan is selected.* This is especially true when statistical sampling methods are used. Vague and nonpurposeful objectives do not permit the design of an effective test.

OBJECTIVE SAMPLING

Auditors have been using the selective test approach to their problems for decades. The use of the test or sample has not been a matter of choice but one forced upon them by the increasing mass of documentation confronting them as business and government have grown in size and complexity.

However, unlike other fields, where sampling has long been recognized as a scientific problem, the choice of the sampling plan as well as the interpretation of the results has largely been one of judgment of the auditor.

The literature on this subject, including published standards of auditing, has dealt with it in a general fashion. For instance, an earlier publication of the American Institute of Certified Public Accountants, *Generally Accepted Auditing Standards,*[9] stated merely that "the appropriate degree of testing will be that which may reasonably be relied upon to bring to light errors in about the same proportion as that which would exist in the whole of the record being tested," and that "the testing technique thus rests for its justification upon its reasonableness, which in turn involves a variety of circumstances."

[7] Statement approved by Directors of Institute of Internal Auditors on May 30, 1957, as published in J. T. Johnson and J. H. Brasseaux, *Readings in Auditing,* South-Western Publishing Company, Cincinnati, 1960, p. 322.

[8] *Ibid.*

[9] *Generally Accepted Auditing Standards, Their Significance and Scope,* American Institute of Certified Public Accountants, New York, 1954, pp. 37 and 35.

Since it is recognized that the judgment of no individual is infallible and that ability in effective judgments varies widely from individual to individual and even for the same individual from time to time, it would seem that objective and scientific methods would be desirable in devising a test and evaluating its results. To be truly scientific, a sampling technique, once the test objective is definitely established, should lead to the same factual conclusions even if designed by different auditors and should not vary from time to time depending on the condition of mind of the auditor.

Yet in spite of the fact that the need for scientific sampling methods was recognized by other divisions of a business or governmental agency, it has not reached full acceptance by the auditor. For instance, the Department of Defense has for many years been using the principles of statistical sampling in accepting procured material (see Military Standard 105D, *Sampling Procedures and Tables for Inspection by Attributes*, Department of Defense, Washington, D.C., April 29, 1963).

It is only during the last two decades that interest in the application of statistical sampling to the problem of the auditor's test has developed and only very recently that any widespread interest or activity has become apparent. All major accounting societies, including the American Institute of Certified Public Accountants and the Federal Government Accountants Association, have now established committees to investigate this area. The large accounting firms have developed training programs, as have a goodly number of the accounting departments of commercial organizations in other fields.

More recently, the publications of the American Institute of Certified Public Accountants and its committees have recognized the place of statistical sampling in the audit test. In one of the publications of that organization, it is noted, "In determining the extent of a particular audit test and the method of selecting items to be examined, the auditor might consider using statistical sampling techniques which have been found to be advantageous in certain instances."[10]

Further evidence of such recognition can be found in the inclusion of questions on this subject in the CPA examinations, as well as the publication of a series of self-programmed lessons on this subject by the American Institute of Certified Public Accountants.[11] The Institute of Internal Auditors published a manual on statistical sampling entitled *Sampling Manual for Auditors* (Lockheed Aircraft Corporation, 1967).

There is no doubt that the qualified auditor of the future will be required to have a good grasp of the principles of statistical sampling for use in his tests, although this does *not* mean he will have to be a statistician.

[10]*Auditing Standards and Procedures*, *op. cit.*, p. 37.

[11]*An Auditor's Approach to Statistical Sampling* (5 vols.), American Institute of Certified Public Accountants, New York, 1967–1972.

THE STATISTICAL SAMPLE

Any sample for which the selection of the items to be included is independent of the sampler may be termed an "objective sample." However, an effective sampling method also requires a means of establishing the required sample size objectively and a means of appraising the sample results objectively. The only type of sample that accomplishes such objectives is the *statistical sample,* more properly called a *probability* or *random sample.*

The term "probability" sample arises from the fact that a sample drawn in this manner will have a behavior which is predictable in terms of the laws of the theory of probability. This type of sample must be obtained in a certain way.

It is emphasized that a haphazard sample or one obtained by any method other than those described in detail in the next chapter will not meet those requirements.

Samples obtained by *other* than the methods to be described later which result in a probability sample are considered together under the term "judgment" sample. This does not confine this type of sample to those in which the auditor actually exercised his judgment in the selection of items but broadly includes all samples which are obtained by nonprobability sample methods. For instance, drawing documents out of a file on a haphazard basis does not of necessity result in a probability sample.

Judgment samples, though not necessarily less accurate than probability samples as a description of a field of documents or entries from which they are drawn, do not have two important characteristics—estimation of the required sample size and of objective projection or evaluation of the sample results.

In other words, while the judgment sample may provide an excellent description of the field investigated, there is no way of establishing this fact objectively. The statistical sample result, on the other hand, may be evaluated as being no further away from the true result (which would have been obtained if *all* items in the field had been examined) than some given amount, based on widely accepted and mathematically provable statistical principles. Thus, the tables and methods outlined in this book to be used in fixing required sample sizes and in evaluating the results should be used *only* in conjunction with probability or random samples.

THE ADVANTAGES OF THE STATISTICAL SAMPLE

As observed above, the statistical sample provides a means for an advance estimate of the sample size required for a given objective and an ability to appraise sample results. Further, when a sample is obtained by this method, it is possible to state, with any desired degree of confidence, that the sample result is no further away from the result obtainable from a similar complete examination of all items than some calculable amount. This provides a whole series of advantages:

1. *The sample result is objective and defensible*

Since the interpretation of the results is based on demonstrable statistical principles, the test is not only objective, but defensible, even before a court of law and certainly before one's superiors or, even more important, before one's own conscience.

Since the sample is objective and unbiased, it is not subject to the questions that might be raised relative to a judgment sample. Certainly a complaint that the auditor had looked only at the worst items and therefore has biased the results would have no standing. This results from the fact that an important feature of this method of sampling is that all entries or documents have an equal opportunity for inclusion in the sample.[12]

2. *The method provides a means of advance estimation of sample size on the objective basis*

The size of the sample used in a test need not depend upon the caprice of the moment, consideration of expediency, mere tradition, or guesswork if the statistical approach is used. This provides both a defense for the reasonableness of the sample size used and a justification for the expenditure involved. It lifts the burden of arbitrary sample size determination from the shoulders of the auditor. Nevertheless, sample size determination is not mechanical and will call for good judgment and decisions by the auditor.

Although the auditor certifies that his examination is "in accordance with generally accepted auditing standards," such standards do not exist with reference to the proper sample size for an audit test. In an earlier publication, *Audits by Certified Public Accountants*, the American Institute of Certified Public Accountants avoids the problem by stating that "the extent of testing in any audit is decided by the CPA in the light of his best independent judgment required to constitute a fair sampling of the records being tested."[13]

This general statement and those cited previously merely shift the responsibility to the individual auditor without providing any actual guidance or standards. The statistical sample approach provides the appropriate technique.

Nevertheless, as will be seen later (p. 101), any sample size, no matter how determined, as long as it is drawn in accordance with probability sampling principles, will provide a *valid* projected result, although perhaps not a *useful* projection because of the magnitude of the resulting sampling error.

[12] For stratified samples, this statement must be modified to indicate that the probability of inclusion of all entries or records *within each stratum* is equal.

There are other sampling techniques not discussed in this volume for which there is a known but unequal probability of selection for each sampling unit.

[13] *Audits by Certified Public Accountants*, American Institute of Certified Public Accountants, New York, 1950, p. 23.

3. *The method provides an estimate of the sampling error*

As noted above, when a probability sample is used, the results may be evaluated in terms of how far the sample projection might deviate from the value that could be obtained by a 100 per cent check.

The challenge of a judgment sample on the grounds that another sample might disclose an entire different result would not be valid for this type of sampling. For instance, if a sample of 300 items drawn from a population of 20,000 such items discloses that 3% of the sample items contained a certain type of error, then it may be said that there are 95 chances in 100 that the actual proportion of this kind of error obtainable by a complete check would have been between 1.5 and 5.5%. Further, there are 99 chances in 100, or almost certainty, that it would have been somewhere between 1.2 and 6.4%. There is no way of knowing how far wrong any other type of sample might be because of sampling variations.

4. *The statistical sampling approach may provide a more accurate method of drawing conclusions about a large mass of data than the examination of all the data*

The mountainous task of examining huge quantities of data may require large staffs and long periods of time. For instance, in evaluating the accuracy of inventory records, a complete count would require a large number of persons, some of whom might have doubtful qualifications for the task, resulting in errors in counting and identification. On the other hand, a relatively small sample carefully and accurately accomplished by a small group of selected qualified persons would be subject only to the computable sampling error rather than the indeterminable effect of numerous clerical errors.

Even when qualified personnel are available, tackling huge masses of documents results in boredom and loss of interest that may cause inaccuracies in the tabulations. The known sampling error is preferable to the unknown errors arising from this source.

In fact, some commercial organizations that have used statistical sampling to estimate the total inventory value claim that the sample result is actually more accurate when projected than a 100 per cent count and valuation.

5. *Statistical sampling may save time and money*

Owing to a popular, but *incorrect*, intuitive feeling that adequate and consistent protection will be provided by taking some fixed percentage (say 5 or 10 or some other per cent) of the field as a sample, *oversampling* is quite frequent in auditing when sampling from a large mass of data. This assumption will be demonstrated to be incorrect in later discussions.

Thus, the statistical sampling approach may then result in a smaller sample size than might be used on the basis of a "common sense" approach, with resultant savings. However, it may, in other instances, demonstrate the inadequacy of the size of the sample taken in prior checks and result in a higher cost if adequate protection is desired.

Any decreased cost resulting from the use of statistical sampling, as contrasted with traditional test methods, can be established only by comparison with the cost of such past methods. It must be recognized that if past tests have relied on inadequate sample sizes, which have really served no useful purpose, the requirement of an adequate sample size in statistical samples may result in higher costs.

On the other hand, there have been many examples of unnecessarily large test samples being used in order to achieve a 5 or 10% sample or because the auditor otherwise felt it necessary, on an intuitional basis, to achieve the protection he desired.

6. *Statistical samples may be combined and evaluated, even though accomplished by different auditors*

That the entire test operation has an objective and scientific basis makes it possible for different auditors to participate independently in the same test and for the results to be combined as though accomplished by one auditor.[14]

For instance, in an audit covering a number of locations, the audit can be accomplished independently and separately at the different locations and the results combined for an overall evaluation of all localities if statistical sampling techniques have been applied.

When the statistical sampling method is used, an audit started by one auditor can be continued by another without difficulty and the results combined. Further, if an audit test is accomplished and it is decided to extend the sampling, this can be achieved without difficulty and with the assurance that the two audit results can be combined.

7. *Objective evaluation of test results is possible*

If an audit test discloses a certain percentage of error when a judgment sample has been used, there is no way of projecting the results to describe the situation in the whole field with any degree of assurance.

If the statistical method is used, the audit test result can be projected to be within not more than a known interval from the result that would have been obtained if the whole field had been subjected to a 100 per cent check with a stated probability confidence.

Thus, all auditors performing this test would be brought to the same conclusion about the numerical extent of error existing in the field. While the impact of these

[14]The techniques of stratified sampling described in Chapter 10 must be used to combine the results of such independent tests.

errors might be interpreted differently, there can be no question of the facts obtained here, since the method for the determination of their frequency in the field is objective.

TYPES OF STATISTICAL SAMPLES

A broad distinction has been made above with reference to judgment and probability or random samples. However, this does *not* imply that a valid probability sample can be obtained in only one way, or that there is only one type of valid statistical sample.

Probability or random samples may be drawn in a variety of forms, depending on a number of conditions. These methods of drawing samples include:[15]

1. Unrestricted random samples
2. Stratified random samples
3. Cluster samples
4. Multistage samples

The *unrestricted random sample* is obtained by using the later-described method to draw individual items from the entire field (population or universe) without segregating or separating any portion of it and thus by drawing individual items (sampling units) with an equal probability that any unit will be included in the sample. This is the most common method of sampling but is sometimes less efficient than other methods.

In the *stratified random sample* the sampling units or values to be included in the sample are obtained by the random methods to be described later, but the items are drawn from separate sections of the field independently, perhaps not in proportion to the number of items in that section of the population. However, within that segment (or stratum) of the field, the probability that any one sampling unit is included in the sample will be the same as for any other in that stratum.

This technique is a very common and valid practice among auditors when it is desirable to separate and sample certain types of documents or entries separately, as, for instance, when all large-value items are examined or when a larger proportion of these items are covered than smaller-value items. Other instances of this type of sampling arise when special samplings are provided to check on sensitive items, entries especially susceptible to fraud, or suspicious types of entries.

It is characteristic of the stratified random sample that for each separate section or portion of the field tested, the sample is drawn by unrestricted random methods. The stratified random sample is often more efficient than the unrestricted random sample as well as providing special attention to portions of the field of particular interest.

[15] There are other methods of sample selection but these are not covered in this volume, since they are not especially relevant to the audit situation.

The *cluster sample* is a special form of either of the above two sample types in which, instead of drawing individual items or sampling units (such as documents or entries), *groups* of items are drawn at random points. For instance, in sampling a file it is possible to draw several records at a selected random point. This method obviously saves time in cumulating the sample, since many fewer points in the file are sought, but often this saving in time is a delusion since a loss in sampling efficiency may result and a larger sample size may be necessary. This point will be developed more completely in a later chapter.

Multistage sampling involves sampling on several levels. For instance, in determining some characteristics of data at various stores or branch offices, it may be possible to take a random sample of such stores or branch offices and then to take a random sample of the records at each of these points. The pros and cons of this type of sampling will be discussed in detail in a later chapter.

Post stratification is based on the simple or unrestricted method of selection of the sample, but the distribution of the sample results to a stratified approach. The method may be used when the auditor decides to stratify after drawing the sample as an unrestricted random sample and completing the audit examination of the sampling units. The advantages and disadvantages of the method are discussed later.

THE SAMPLING PLAN

The approach to a test through a sampling plan is a function of the objective of the test itself or that which the auditor hopes to achieve. A variety of possible approaches may be classified as shown below:

1. Estimation sampling
2. Acceptance sampling
3. Discovery sampling

Because of the wide choice of plans which may be used to approach a given test, it is essential first that a very specific objective be formulated for each test proposed.

ESTIMATION SAMPLING

Estimation sampling is the most widely used approach to audit tests. It provides the answer to the question of how many or how much. When this method is used, a random sample of a special size is obtained, and either the number of some specified type of item or event (such as errors) appearing in the sample is counted and the proportion of these items determined, or the average (or total) value of some characteristic (such as dollar value, etc.) is obtained.

If the sample is used as a means of establishing the frequency of occurrence of some kind of event or type of item, the process is referred to as *attributes sampling.* The result of such a sampling operation is commonly expressed as the *per cent* of the type of event specified.

In statistical terminology, any measurement obtained by counting the number of items falling in a given category is called an *attribute measurement.* The categories established for this purpose must be mutually exclusive; that is, an observation is counted in one category only, and it cannot fall in another. Examples of attribute categories include errors versus nonerrors, missing documentation versus nonmissing documentation, improperly completed requisitions versus properly completed requisitions, etc.

When attributes measurement, or the answer to how many, is the proper approach to an audit test, the type of sampling calculations is different from the situation in which it is desired to know how much. For this reason, in all following discussions, for all types of sampling problems, a distinction will be made between attributes sampling (how many) and the other type of sampling, known as variables sampling (how much).

From the prior discussion, it will be noted that tests of compliance with internal controls (tests of transactions) are examples of attributes tests, since it is desired to establish the frequency of deviation from the requirements of the internal control system.

Variables measurements are designed to provide an estimate of an *average* or *total* value. Each observation, instead of being counted as falling in a given category, provides a value (say dollar amount, period of time, etc.) which is totaled or averaged for the sample. Examples of variables measurements include the dollar value of an inventory, the average length of time required to fill a requisition, the average or total dollar value of errors of a certain type, the total dollar amount of expenses of a certain kind, etc.

Tests to validate the reasonableness of account balances may be recognized as variable measurement tests and are sometimes termed "dollar-value" samples in the literature.

The estimation sampling approach provides the auditor with an estimate of the frequency of occurrence of an event in the field (such as errors) or an estimate of an average or total value. In addition, it provides an estimate of the sampling error which must be considered when relying on the sample result; this sampling error is a statement of how far from the value obtainable from a 100 per cent check the sample result might be.

Thus, the auditor is provided with a range (interval estimate) rather than a single value (point estimate). For instance, the result might be a statement, based on the test, that the field contained between 6 and 8% of errors or that the dollar value of an inventory is between $1,650,000.00 and $1,660,000.00. The interpretation of the audit impact or the audit finding then rests upon the auditor, who must, in light of other tests and information available to him, come to a determination of the importance of a rate of error in this range for this field or of a departure of the book record value of the inventory from the interval estimate.

ACCEPTANCE SAMPLING

Acceptance sampling provides another possible approach for the auditor, although generally speaking it is more useful for the control of error than for the auditor's test purposes.

When acceptance sampling is used, a sampling of a given size is drawn by probability or random sampling methods, and if not more than a certain number of errors are found in the sample, the field examined is considered acceptable, and if more than that number are found, the field is rejected as unacceptable.

The sampling plan for acceptance sampling contains a statement of the field (lot) size, an indication of the sample size to be used, and an acceptance number or maximum number of errors which may be included in the sample for the field to be considered acceptable.

The particular sampling plan to be used in a given situation depends on the objectives of the plan. A later chapter will discuss the criteria for the selection of an acceptance sampling plan.

The acceptance sampling method provides only an accept-or-reject decision. In itself it provides no information as to how good or how bad the field is nor any estimate of the rate of occurrence of errors in the field. There still remains the problem of what to do about the situation when the test calls for rejection.

Further, it requires a precise advance decision as to the rate of error for which rejection is necessary. This type of advance decision is often difficult, if not impossible for the auditor, since the rate of error existent must be considered together with other tests and examinations perhaps not accomplished at the time the decision is to be made. The limitations of this method, together with its advantages and some examples of its uses, will be discussed fully in a later chapter.

There are several types of acceptance sampling plans, including *single*, *double*, *multiple*, and *sequential*. Each of these types will be described later.

DISCOVERY (EXPLORATORY) SAMPLING

There are areas within which the auditor's objective may not be achieved by either estimation or acceptance sampling. He may not be interested in determining how many or how much or in a simple accept-or-reject decision.

When there is a possibility of fraud, avoidance of the internal control system, evasion of regulation, or other critical departures, it may be sufficient to disclose only one such example to precipitate further action or investigation.

It is recognized that no sampling method, and for that matter not even a 100 per cent check, is likely to disclose a "needle-in-the-haystack" type of situation, such as one instance of fraud in a million entries. If several are included in a field, it is possible to determine a sample size which will give any desired degree of assurance that *at least one* occurrence of this type would be included in the sample when it happens with at least that frequency in the field.

This type of sampling is known as *discovery* or *exploratory sampling.* This method will be fully discussed in a later section of this book and provides a new and very useful tool for the auditor.

TEST OBJECTIVES AND THE SAMPLING PLAN

It is apparent now that there are several different approaches which may be used in developing a sampling plan to meet the needs of an audit test. It will be seen later that a number of other decisions are necessary in order to develop and execute the sample.

The particular approach to be used, as well as the other decisions which must be reached, will be determined by the objectives of the particular test at hand. However, to make these decisions possible, the objectives must be known in specific terms and not be vague, with fuzzy purposes.

For instance, if attributes sampling methods are to be used, it is necessary to define the categories very specifically. In the case of a count of errors, advance determination must be made as to what constitutes an error or, if desired, a significant error. If the errors are to be analyzed by type, the categories for the different types of errors must be carefully defined. Of course, if a new and unexpected type of error is encountered during the test, there is nothing to preclude the inclusion of a new category.

If a decision is to be made as to an estimation, acceptance, or discovery sampling type of plan, the auditor must have his test purpose firmly in mind in very explicit terms. This is one of the considerable advantages of the statistical sampling approach: it forces advance and specific determination of test purposes. On the other hand, the same sample can be used for several approaches, for instance, as will be seen later, for both discovery and estimation sampling. In addition, the same sample can be used for several different and independent test purposes. For instance, a sample of items counted at a warehouse can be used to estimate the frequency of errors in the warehouse records, the proportion of slow-moving items at the warehouse, the proportion of the items which are overstocked, the dollar value of the warehouse inventory, etc., by securing the necessary information about each item selected for inclusion in the sample.

WHEN TO USE STATISTICAL SAMPLING

Statistical sampling is appropriate whenever it is desired to generalize about the field from which the sample was drawn on the basis of sample results. However, this does not mean that the sampling must be performed against the better judgment of the auditor as to the type of entry in which he is interested. For instance, in testing expense vouchers, many of these vouchers may represent very small sums of money. There is nothing in the statistical sampling approach that dictates that the sampling must be of all items when only the larger dollar-value items are of interest. On the other hand, it must be remembered that the conclusions thus obtained can be projected then to describe only the field of higher-value items.

Further, nothing in statistical sampling restricts the auditor from making any additional examinations of items not included in the sample, which because of their susceptibility or for other reasons are of special interest. Of course, such items do not become part of the sample projection. Nevertheless, if he desires, he may sample only the suspicious type of item; however, he should use statistical sampling for these items.

A common fallacy in the thinking of many auditors relative to the use of statistical sampling is believing it applies only to large fields containing many records. It is to be recognized that whenever less than the totality of the records are examined, a sample has been taken. There is no way of projecting or otherwise generalizing the result obtained from a partial examination of a group of records (a sample) other than by the use of statistical (probability) sampling techniques *regardless of the field size.*

Thus, if it is desired to interpret the results of a test based on an examination of less than all of the records, this is the only method available.

Of course, it may develop that the sample size required for this purpose is very large and perhaps, from an audit viewpoint, prohibitive. If so, this is merely a recognition that such a test is useless if performed on a smaller scale. The use of a smaller and more expedient sample size is then a waste of time, money, and resources. It should be obvious that an inadequate test which does not meet its own objectives is useless.

Thus, the idea that one may avoid the larger sample size indicated as necessary in a statistical sample by reverting to judgment sampling is a delusion, and the attempt to do so is likely to do more harm than good.

TWO

Selecting the Sample

SAMPLING PROBLEMS

Whether statistical sampling or judgment sampling is used, certain problems must be resolved for the auditor's test to be properly executed. These problems include:

1. What is to be sampled?
2. How is it to be sampled?
3. How much is to be sampled?
4. What do the sample results mean?

With a nonstatistical approach it is sometimes possible that these problems are not clearly resolved. The approach may be vague and indefinite. There may be little or no attempt to define specifically the field from which the observations are to be drawn or any careful consideration as to how they are to be selected. The determination of how many observations are to be included in the sample may be arbitrary under these circumstances. As to the meaning of the sample results, the auditor can speak only about the instances disclosed by the sample and is not in a position to interpret his results in terms of the entire field investigated.

However, when statistical sampling is used, the problems listed above must be carefully and precisely resolved. This preciseness is one of the major advantages of the statistical approach. This method requires incisive thinking and very careful planning.

WHAT IS TO BE SAMPLED?

The tests to be performed and their specific objectives are an audit decision to be reached by the auditor. This decision is reached independently of the method of sampling and will be the same whether or not statistical sampling is used. However, as seen previously, the requirements of statistical sampling may result in a more precise definition of these objectives. The specific goal of a given test will determine the nature of the items to be sampled.

THE FIELD OR UNIVERSE

If statistical sampling is used, the field of entries or documents from which the sampling is to be made *must* be defined carefully. In statistical parlance, the field is called a *universe* or *population.*[1]

The field (universe or population) is comprised of *sampling units.* The *sampling units* consist of the individual elements from which the sample will be drawn, consisting of such elements as documents, entries, etc., each comprising one unit in the sample. More specifically, the sampling unit consists of those elements in the population whose characteristics are to be measured or determined in order to estimate the distribution of those characteristics for the population. For instance, the sampling units may be the items of an inventory for which dollar values are to be established in order to estimate the total dollar value of an inventory. The sampling unit may be individual extensions which are to be established as correct or incorrect in order to determine the percentage of error in the field. The sampling unit may be an accounts-receivable for which the age is to be determined in order that the age distribution of the balances may be estimated.

However, the definition of the sampling unit must be considered in the light of the test objective. For instance, if the objective of the test is to determine the frequency with which disbursement vouchers occur without proper authorizing signature, the *voucher* itself becomes the sampling unit, and the presence or absence of the signature, the characteristic measured.

On the other hand, if the object is to determine whether the items on the voucher, of which there may be several, are authorized items, the *line item* on the voucher becomes the sampling unit, and there may be several sampling units on a single voucher. Again, if the accuracy of the footing of these vouchers is being tested, the voucher is again the sampling unit, since the footing is either right or wrong (or perhaps is in error by some amount), and only one such measurement can be made per voucher.

Therefore the sampling unit may comprise a single physical unit such as a voucher or may be part of a physical unit such as a line item on a voucher, an entry in a ledger, etc. Thus, it is apparent that the object of the test determines the sampling unit as well as the characteristic of the sampling unit which is to be measured.

As previously observed, the field or universe is a collection of sampling units. Statisticians sometimes refer to a listing of all the sampling units in the universe as a

[1]Some authors distinguish between the term "population" and the term "universe," where the term "universe" is used to describe a hypothetical infinite underlying population. This concept has no relevance in auditing, and thus no distinction is made here.

frame. While it is not essential that a frame exist when sampling is performed, it is helpful. In addition, the concept of the frame, whether it physically exists or not, is useful in studying sampling. The auditor may have such a frame in the form of an IBM listing, a trial balance, or a tape produced for some other purpose.

The precise definition of the universe or population in light of the test objective is of maximum importance. When statistical sampling is applied to an improperly defined field, unsatisfactory results may be obtained.

In one test where statistical sampling was used, the auditor condemned the method because many vouchers, each amounting to less than $1.00, had turned up in the sample. This was to be expected in consideration of the fact that a large proportion of the vouchers were in this value range. If the auditor had desired to test vouchers with a value in excess of $1.00 only, he should have so defined his population and there would have been no problem.

Statistical sampling does *not* automatically require the sampling of all possible documents, as some seem to think.

Nevertheless, no matter how the field is defined, the results obtained from the sampling of this population may be projected to represent only the field sampled. Thus, the test objective determines the definition of the field.

A specific test might be directed only to a specified group of items, accounts, or vouchers, depending on the purpose of the test. If a test is to be performed to determine whether there is any extensive pilferage of items such as small tools, it is not necessary to include cranes and steam rollers in the population to be sampled. A test of accuracy of payment for loading ships does not require that the field include documents for loading items handled by the ship's equipment where no payment is made to the contractor.

A frequent argument advanced by some auditors against the possible use of statistical sampling in tests is that they would rather examine certain types of entries, documents, etc., about which they have greatest concern or suspicion as a possible source of error or deviation.

Actually this is not an argument against statistical sampling at all but merely a point to consider in defining the universe from which the sampling is to be done. If these entries or documents are those of concern and these auditors do not wish to test others, in effect all they have done is to define their field to include these documents only. They may then use statistical sampling methods to approach *the area in which they are interested.*

Since a sample result is used in lieu of an equally complete coverage which represents the results of a 100 per cent sample carried out by the same method,[2] the sample result may be projected *to represent only the field from which the sample was drawn.* Thus, it is of utmost importance that the documents or entries from

[2] See *Standards of Probability Sampling for Legal Evidence, Admission of Data from Probability Samples,* The Society of Business Advisory Professions, Graduate School of Business Administration, New York University, undated, p. 3.

which the entries are drawn be complete and that all sampling units be provided with an equal probability of being included in the sample.[3]

If the concept of the *frame* is defined as constituting all of the sampling units actually available to be sampled, it is evident that the sample projection applies to the frame and not to the population unless the frame and the population are the same or substantially the same.

This situation places an additional responsibility on the auditor, which applies regardless of whether a statistical sampling is performed, to take such steps as necessary to assure himself that the frame and population are at least substantially the same.

For instance, if the sampling is from a file, it may be possible that certain documents have been removed from the file for processing or special study. Unless these documents are made available for the sample, any projection of the sample results applies only to that portion of the field included in the file. The impact of this consideration becomes clear if the missing documents have been removed for trouble shooting because of errors, violations, or special problems and perhaps are those of most interest to the auditor.

It is not sufficient in the case of a document missing from the field for an auditor to take another sample item in its place without running down the missing document, unless he is willing to restrict his conclusions only to those items remaining in the file and to recognize the deficiency.

Failure to locate missing sampling units and to give them equal opportunity for inclusion in the sample because of difficulties in making these documents available (because some are at remote locations or inconvenient to secure) may bias a sample result, and the projection becomes an estimate of the character of the readily available documents only.

If part of the field was not made available for sampling, the sample results may be projected to represent *only* that portion of the field available for sample selection and *not* the whole field.

For instance, if an auditor decides to test only high-value items since they comprise the bulk of the dollar values involved and these are most important in their impact on the financial statements, there is no basic objection to such an approach, but it means that conclusions reached on the basis of such a test relating to the frequency of certain types of errors or their magnitude apply only to these high-value items. No conclusion may be drawn as to the frequency or magnitude of errors among the small-value items not made available for inclusion in the sample. While this same restriction applies to samples drawn by other than statistical methods (judgment samples), unfortunately, this fact frequently is not recognized.

A case in point is the often-used practice in audit tests of selecting documents for a limited period of time for a test. For example, in testing payrolls, it is not uncommon for the auditor to select a payroll for one period, perhaps for a specified week

[3] In a stratified sample, the equality of probability applies within each stratum.

or a month, and to test that payroll in its entirety or on a sampling basis. The inherent assumption in this practice is that if the test for that period discloses a satisfactory state of affairs, all the rest of the payrolls for the balance of the year are satisfactory.

It is seen from the previous discussions that sampling of a single payroll or even examination of the entire payroll can lead only to a conclusion about that payroll. Since no sampling units were drawn from other payrolls, there is no way of drawing a conclusion or making a projection to the rest of the year. If the purpose is to test the accuracy of the pay rates or computations for individuals on the payrolls, and this is part of an examination covering a year's operations, it is evident that the field comprises not only the line items on the payroll examined but consists of all line items on all payrolls for the period. Of course, if the auditor is satisfied with conclusions about that one week only and feels that other tests and examinations will provide protection, no objection can be proffered to such an approach. However, he must realize the limited nature of his test.

On the other hand, if the purpose of the test is to verify the situation as of some given date, for instance, the balance of the accounts receivable as of December 31, then sampling at one point in time is entirely appropriate.

The same note of caution must be sounded with reference to location sampling. If it is desired to test locations in a chain-store system to determine whether the store managers are "putting their fingers into the till," it would be of little value to test one or two locations out of 100 or 1,000. It may be that the event of interest is happening at other stores. Nor should any auditor test for anything at only one or two stores in the chain and draw conclusions about all the stores.

Again, one cannot draw conclusions about a field from which the sample was not drawn. However, remember that this is true of both the statistical and judgment sample or test.

Of course, the independent auditor may be confronted with some severe obstacles in this respect. For instance, it may be necessary to perform the test on an interim basis. At best he can then sample only from that portion of the fiscal period which has elapsed. In such circumstances, his sample results can only be interpreted to apply to that part of the period which has expired. Obviously, he cannot draw conclusions about documents or entries which have not yet been created![4]

It is within the province of the auditor's judgment to accept such limited results, particularly since it is a practical necessity, in some cases. The audit judgment that such a test is adequate or the best that can be accomplished under the circumstances is a matter for decision by the auditor. However, the practice of drawing a conclusion about the whole period from a test of part of it cannot be defended statistically or for that matter in any other way.

[4] It is to be noted that this difficulty can be validly overcome by either drawing the sample item numbers in advance and auditing those created subsequent to the interim test at the end of the period or sampling the period prior to the interim period and that after, separately and combining the results by use of stratified sampling techniques.

In the *Codification of Statements on Auditing Standards* (American Institute of Certified Public Accountants, Commerce Clearing House, Chicago, 1982, ¶320.61), with reference to interim audit tests, it is noted that such tests "ideally should be applied to transactions executed throughout the period under audit. . . ."[5]

Considerations of practicality or cost actually constitute no defense or comfort at all, especially when it is subsequently determined that the test failed in its purpose.

In summary, the important point to remember is that if a sample is taken from a given field, it can be projected or used to represent that field only. If any of the sampling units have been left out of the field when sampled, the sample results do not apply to that section of the field which is omitted.

Finally, the random selection of one or two days, weeks, or months out of a year, even though valid statistical techniques are used in the random selections, does not alter this situation.

NONSAMPLING ERRORS

As previously indicated, the primary advantage of statistical sampling is the resultant ability to project the sample results to represent the field with a known sampling error. In other words, the results obtained from a sample may be used to represent an estimate of the result which would have been obtained if the entire field had been examined *in the same manner* and with a known sampling precision.

In a publication on the use of sampling data as legal evidence previously cited,[6] it is noted that, providing the sampling error is innocuous, the numerical result of a sample should be accepted as legal evidence "on the same status as the result of an equal complete coverage of all units . . ." where equal complete coverage is defined as "a coverage of all the sampling units (100% sample) in the same frame as was used for the sample, *under the stipulation that the complete coverage was carried out with the same procedure as was used for the sample for eliciting the information*, with the same thoroughness. . . ." The importance of this statement lies in the fact that if the sample measurements or determinations are erroneously made, the projection would be to estimate the result of a 100 per cent examination *with the same carelessness.*

Thus, if an auditor performs a test using statistical sampling techniques, or for that matter any other sampling methods, and fails to recognize errors or makes mis-

[5]It is also stated in the same publication, however, that tests undertaken during the interim period need not require any testing of the remaining period, if the auditor takes into consideration certain factors, including the interim test results, the length of that period, the nature and amount of the remaining transactions, other evidence of compliance during the remaining period, and "other matters the auditor considers relevant in the circumstances." Nevertheless, the fact remains that the interim test results have no application to the balance of the period.

[6]*Standards of Probability Sampling for Legal Evidence, Admission of Data from Probability Samples*, p. 3.

takes of his own in the audit, the projection obtained will *not* be for an equivalent 100 per cent examination *carried out correctly.*

The sampling error determination, the methods for which will be explored later, does not allow for errors made by the auditor but rather reflects them.

Of course, great care must be exercised in any audit test that the audit examination be done correctly, and it is presumed that this applies to a statistically conducted audit test as well. However, there is no magic in the statistical sampling approach that will allow for these errors.

Thus, a distinction may be made between the "true" value for the population, assuming a completely correct audit examination, and a value obtained by the kind of audit examination actually accomplished. These two different values may not coincide even when 100 per cent coverage is used.

As a case in point, a confirmation of accounts receivable will fail in its purpose if negative confirmations are used and a nonresponse is interpreted as meaning no error when in fact nonresponse may have arisen in part from mere failure to answer where such errors do exist. The projection from a statistical sample here can be interpreted as representing the state of affairs only of the unknown proportion of the customers who actually made a determination that the balance was correct or responded that it was not and not that unknown proportion who did not bother to check their balances or did not care to do so and therefore did not respond for this reason.

MULTIPLE PURPOSE SAMPLES

It is recognized that one probability sample may be used to estimate several characteristics of the field to be tested.

Thus, a single statistical (probability) sample of items from physical inventories may be used to estimate the frequency of errors in counting, pricing, and extending the values as well as to estimate the total value of the inventory in order to establish the reasonableness of the book value.

The sample, if it is truly random, will be random with respect to all of these characteristics, and it is not necessary to resort to separate samples for each purpose.

In fact, the same sample may be used if desired to effectuate all three approaches, estimation, acceptance, and discovery sampling, at one time or any combination thereof.

THREE

The Mechanics of Sampling

THE PROBABILITY SAMPLE

If the advantages of the statistical sampling method, including the ability to project from the sample to the field, the ability to determine the sample size in advance, and the ability to appraise the reliability of the sample result after it has been achieved, are to be obtained, a probability (random) sample must be achieved.

If the sampling is correctly carried out, not only will these advantages be secured, but the auditor can be assured that the statistical approach eliminates any possible bias (deliberate or unconscious) in his selection of items examined. Some auditors who use the statistical approach for the first time express considerable astonishment as to the adequacy of the cross section of items obtained for examination when this method is used. In fact they have complained that at times the method has forced the use of documents in inaccessible places or documents which because of their bulk or nature were particularly difficult to examine. These awkward items cannot be avoided in the statistical sampling method, and thus a broad cross section of test documents must be examined.

However, satisfactory results cannot be achieved unless a true probability sample is drawn, since only then are the laws of probability, which are used in obtaining a sample size estimate or in appraising the reliability of a sample projection, operative. Mere avoidance of personal subjectivity through a haphazard choice of items does not provide a probability sample. The auditor must be careful in compiling a sample to use methods which will ensure that the laws of probability are operative so that the computations based on these laws can be executed.

It is important to remember that unless the methods described in this chapter are used in selecting the sampling units included in the test, the methods for estimating the sample size or for appraising the reliability of sample results as well as all other techniques described in this book simply have no application or meaning. The auditor is warned not to attempt to apply the tables or formulas described later to any test in which judgment or haphazard methods were used in selecting the items to be examined.

The basic requirement for a probability sample is that each sampling unit in the field has an equal (or known) probability of being included in the sample. This requirement is not easily met. Unless the sampling is accomplished in a certain way, a probability sample will not result.

METHODS OF OBTAINING A PROBABILITY SAMPLE

While a variety of probability sampling plans are available, many of which will be discussed later, the most widely used is unrestricted random sampling, sometimes called *simple random sampling.*[1] To simplify the discussion of the manner of selection of the sampling units, the unrestricted random sampling plan will be used as the basis of the description. It will be recalled that for unrestricted random sampling plans the choice of sampling units must be made from the entire field without special treatment or segregation of any portion of the field and with equal probability of selection of all sampling units in the sample.

Theoretically, an unrestricted random sample can be obtained by a thorough mixing of the items to be sampled, as in a shuffling operation, and by a random selection of a group of these items after they have been mixed. The mixing required for such a purpose would have to be very thorough and extensive.

However, this approach is impractical since vouchers, payroll items, cards in a file, etc., cannot be shuffled for this purpose. In addition, a truly thorough mixing or shuffling sufficient to create a random sample is difficult if not impossible to achieve by ordinary methods. In addition, methods of sampling selection must be used which will not extensively disturb the records or items to be sampled.

The two basic methods for effectively achieving an unrestricted random sample of individual sampling units are:

1. Random number sampling
2. Systematic sampling

RANDOM NUMBER SAMPLING

Since it is not feasible to shuffle the basic records, an alternative is numbering the items to be sampled and shuffling the numbers rather than the documents.

[1]Some writers distinguish between an unrestricted random sample and a simple random sample, applying the term "unrestricted random sampling" to sampling with replacement (in effect for an infinite population) and the term "simple random sampling" when sampling without replacement (in effect a finite population).

The documents corresponding to the selected numbers are then included in the sample.

In principle, this is the same as placing numbers equivalent to those on the sampling units on slips of paper and drawing the required number of slips out of a hat after they have been thoroughly mixed. However, such a technique is not practical for any considerable number of sampling units and, further, it is unlikely that sufficient mixing can be secured.

RANDOM NUMBER TABLES

On the other hand, the inherent difficulties in mixing can be eliminated by resorting to available tables of thoroughly mixed (random) numbers. These random number, or more properly random digit tables, which have been created by various means, have been tested according to statistical techniques to certify their randomness. The best known of these tables are[2]

1. *Table of* 240,000 *Random Decimal Digits,* Herbert Arkin, New York, 1961.
2. *Table of* 105,000 *Random Decimal Digits,* Interstate Commerce Commission, Bureau of Transport Economics and Statistics, Washington, D.C., 1949.
3. *A Million Random Digits,* The RAND Corporation, The Free Press of Glencoe, New York, 1955. (Also available in punched-card form from the RAND Corporation, Santa Monica, California.)

Sample pages of each of these publications are shown in Figures 3-1, 3-2, and 3-3. One-half of the *Table of* 240,000 *Random Decimal Digits,* containing 120,000 digits is included in Appendix A of this book.

It is to be noted that in the first table the digits are arranged in blocks of four digits in width and five digits in length, while in both of the other tables, the random digits are arranged in blocks of five digits in width and five digits in length. This arrangement *is for convenience in reading only and has no bearing on the random digits themselves.* Thus, a random number may be created from these digits by extending (horizontally) the number of digits used to complete a number of any length.

Any indicated point in the tables of random digits can be specified by referring to the page number, line number, and column number. In the tables every line has a reference number in the first column so that a given point in the table can be located by referring to that line number and the column number.

When the sampling units are or can be numbered, or can readily be construed

[2]Other earlier but more limited random number tables include:

a. L. H. C. Tippett, *Random Sampling Numbers,* Tracts for Computers no. XV, Cambridge University Press, New York, 1927. (Contains 40,000 digits.)
b. R. A. Fisher and F. Yates, *Statistical Tables for Biological, Agricultural and Medical Research,* Oliver & Boyd Ltd., Edinburgh and London, 1938. (Contains 15,000 digits.)
c. M. G. Kendall and B. Babington-Smith, *Tables of Random Sampling Numbers,* Tracts for Computers no. XXIV, Cambridge University Press, New York, 1939. (Contains 100,000 digits.)

	(01)	(02)	(03)	(04)	(05)	(06)	(07)	(08)	(09)	(10)
(0801)	3116	1400	5277	8522	2155	6305	8549	8693	5699	9795
(0802)	3137	5970	9837	0026	7407	8780	8063	7477	7329	3495
(0803)	4217	0434	6702	8747	8524	3093	5107	3734	6608	2124
(0804)	0295	7860	1202	7786	8865	3137	3779	8132	0880	4350
(0805)	9299	4686	1880	7537	9438	2071	9576	8590	0983	9663
(0806)	8888	3589	3813	9911	6808	7730	5361	6022	4617	9723
(0807)	1299	3551	5447	9755	4777	1545	5109	6274	9595	6374
(0808)	2380	2854	7563	7040	7324	3512	0747	0099	1276	6490
(0809)	6815	1785	9059	7875	0439	5494	8792	1799	1622	7361
(0810)	3053	2650	7918	6947	3666	3087	4794	8370	4007	5401
(0811)	7257	1315	1105	2874	3074	1833	1738	1365	4286	8386
(0812)	2957	4380	4779	2441	1325	6259	5898	8752	7128	5525
(0813)	5955	0701	0293	6332	7297	1250	5095	5638	5364	2864
(0814)	0190	9213	9307	4453	8318	6934	9277	9636	8068	8426
(0815)	0586	3247	0180	6782	9098	1187	5589	7132	8274	6896
(0816)	1142	6778	3882	4992	0609	9008	2623	1647	7739	2197
(0817)	4549	9224	9583	6316	8879	4913	6421	9186	8918	4245
(0818)	0469	2882	4560	5123	1599	3294	5277	8499	1948	8513
(0819)	1600	0716	3679	4540	6905	0401	5311	2678	2137	9894
(0820)	7519	6867	8359	6636	7603	9126	4313	0724	1195	0162
(0821)	2859	2601	5332	5435	6703	6507	7500	0565	4098	2848
(0822)	4716	9195	0826	9017	1733	2031	0505	6993	5393	2843
(0823)	2313	7496	4246	0255	0927	3130	9764	9965	6047	5607
(0824)	4605	9784	6546	7678	7295	9611	8505	4811	6035	3349
(0825)	8961	1939	8390	1286	2757	0918	6222	9735	3709	2941
(0826)	3925	1915	0612	3367	9544	4905	8853	7399	4043	7354
(0827)	2720	0049	8888	3627	2009	8354	1424	4569	4600	7043
(0828)	9290	9394	2931	8414	2523	0429	9186	3512	8424	9058
(0829)	9991	9094	2421	3651	2947	6690	3936	2836	4942	8911
(0830)	0752	1913	4936	7317	4295	4784	2938	1191	5741	6791

FIGURE 3-1 *From* Table of 240,000 Random Decimal Digits. *(Herbert Arkin, New York, 1961.)*

as being numbered, the random number tables can be used to select items for a random sample.

Preliminary to the use of random number sampling methods, the auditor must establish a one-to-one correspondence between any possible random number that might be drawn and the sampling units (accounting records). Such a correspondence must be unambiguous so that a given number specifies a given sampling unit and only that sampling unit. Accounting documents or records which are numbered serially from 1 on are the simplest situation. Here the drawing of a random number will specify without equivocation one specific sampling unit. Since no other record has the same number, there can be no ambiguity.

If this sample situation does not exist, there are other methods of achieving the desired correspondence. These techniques will be discussed in detail later.

Line \ Col.	(1)	(2)	(3)	(4)	(5)	(6)	(7)	(8)	(9)	(10)	(11)	(12)	(13)	(14)
1	10480	15011	01536	02011	81647	91646	69179	14194	62590	36207	20969	99570	91291	90700
2	22368	46573	25595	85393	30995	89198	27982	53402	93965	34095	52666	19174	39615	99505
3	24130	48360	22527	97265	76393	64809	15179	24830	49340	32081	30680	19655	63348	58629
4	42167	93093	06243	61680	07856	16376	39440	53537	71341	57004	00849	74917	97758	16379
5	37570	39975	81837	16656	06121	91782	60468	81305	49684	60672	14110	06927	01263	54613
6	77921	06907	11008	42751	27756	53498	18602	70659	90655	15053	21916	81825	44394	42880
7	99562	72905	56420	69994	98872	31016	71194	18738	44013	48840	63213	21069	10634	12952
8	96301	91977	05463	07972	18876	20922	94595	56869	69014	60045	18425	84903	42508	32307
9	89579	14342	63661	10281	17453	18103	57740	84378	25331	12566	58678	44947	05585	56941
10	85475	36857	53342	53988	53060	59533	38867	62300	08158	17983	16439	11458	18593	64952
11	28918	69578	88231	33276	70997	79936	56865	05859	90106	31595	01547	85590	91610	78188
12	63553	40961	48235	03427	49626	69445	18663	72695	52180	20847	12234	90511	33703	90322
13	09429	93969	52636	92737	88974	33488	36320	17617	30015	08272	84115	27156	30613	74952
14	10365	61129	87529	85689	48237	52267	67689	93394	01511	26358	85104	20285	29975	89868
15	07119	97336	71048	08178	77233	13916	47564	81056	97735	85977	29372	74461	28551	90707
16	51085	12765	51821	51259	77452	16308	60756	92144	49442	53900	70960	63990	75601	40719
17	02368	21382	52404	60268	89368	19885	55322	44819	01188	65255	64835	44919	05944	55157
18	01011	54092	33362	94904	31273	04146	18594	29852	71585	85030	51132	01915	92747	64951
19	52162	53916	46369	58586	23216	14513	83149	98736	23495	64350	94738	17752	35156	35749
20	07056	97628	33787	09998	42698	06691	76988	13602	51851	46104	88916	19509	25625	58104
21	48663	91245	85828	14346	09172	30168	90229	04734	59193	22178	30421	61666	99904	32812
22	54164	58492	22421	74103	47070	25306	76468	26384	58151	06646	21524	15227	96909	44592
23	32639	32363	05597	24200	13363	38005	94342	28728	35806	06912	17012	64161	18296	22851
24	29334	27001	87637	87308	58731	00256	45834	15398	46557	41135	10367	07684	36188	18510
25	02488	33062	28834	07351	19731	92420	60952	61280	50001	67658	32586	86679	50720	94953
26	81525	72295	04839	96423	24878	82651	66566	14778	76797	14780	13300	87074	79666	95725
27	29676	20591	68086	26432	46901	20849	89768	81536	86645	12659	92259	57102	80428	25280
28	00742	57392	39064	66432	84673	40027	32832	61362	98947	96067	64760	64584	96096	98253
29	05366	04213	25669	26422	44407	44048	37937	63904	45766	66134	75470	66520	34693	90449
30	91921	26418	64117	94305	26766	25940	39972	22209	71500	64568	91402	42416	07844	69618
31	00582	04711	87917	77341	42206	35126	74087	99547	81817	42607	43808	76655	62028	76630
32	00725	69884	62797	56170	86324	88072	76222	36086	84637	93161	76038	65855	77919	88006
33	69011	65795	95876	55293	18988	27354	26575	08625	40801	59920	29841	80150	12777	48501
34	25976	57948	29888	88604	67917	48708	18912	82271	65424	69774	33611	54262	85963	03547
35	09763	83473	73577	12908	30883	18317	28290	35797	05998	41688	34952	37888	38917	88050
36	91567	42595	27958	30134	04024	86385	29880	99730	55536	84855	29080	09250	79656	73211
37	17955	56349	90999	49127	20044	59931	06115	20542	18059	02008	73708	83517	36103	42791
38	46503	18584	18845	49618	02304	51038	20655	58727	28168	15475	56942	53389	20562	87338
39	92157	89634	94824	78171	84610	82834	09922	25417	44137	48413	25555	21246	35509	20468
40	14577	62765	35605	81263	39667	47358	56873	56307	61607	49518	89656	20103	77490	18062
41	98427	07523	33362	64270	01638	92477	66969	98420	04880	45585	46565	04102	46880	45709
42	34914	63976	88720	82765	34476	17032	87589	40836	32427	70002	70663	88863	77775	69348
43	70060	28277	39475	46473	23219	53416	94970	25832	69975	94884	19661	72828	00102	66794
44	53976	54914	06990	67245	68350	82948	11398	42878	80287	88267	47363	46634	06541	97809
45	76072	29515	40980	07391	58745	25774	22987	80059	39911	96189	41151	14222	60697	59583
46	90725	52210	83974	29992	65831	38857	50490	83765	55657	14361	31720	57375	56228	41546
47	64364	67412	33339	31926	14883	24413	59744	92351	97473	89286	35931	04110	23726	51900
48	08962	00358	31662	25388	61642	34072	81249	35648	56891	69352	48373	45578	78547	81788
49	95012	68379	93526	70765	10592	04542	76463	54328	02349	17247	28865	14777	62730	92277
50	15664	10493	20492	38391	91132	21999	59516	81652	27195	48223	46751	22923	32261	85653

FIGURE 3-2 *ICC, Random Digit Table.* (*From* Table of 105,000 Random Decimal Digits, *Interstate Commerce Commission, Bureau of Transport Economics and Statistics, Washington, D.C., 1949.*)

04800	73831	87202	27346	42658	51948	38726	67360	35815	18792	76264
04801	65465	26365	80200	45336	46016	24437	61384	38839	69168	83777
04802	98955	82357	80400	73053	19430	46868	99858	51892	00077	58012
04803	34797	71994	96962	18361	95116	90743	34025	14492	90532	00041
04804	90650	04701	16569	04723	35509	67283	51736	44666	58261	80604
04805	31247	38088	28686	51435	47978	06875	67232	57212	34623	14546
04806	45081	30791	61840	04458	05667	21213	92997	00965	97809	26270
04807	08987	01058	58777	64807	31668	04621	93798	54435	06558	82608
04808	62598	19741	70363	20838	28054	64435	87525	26052	85354	02547
04809	00033	73503	70553	60008	62915	52836	20419	64342	82251	75692
04810	52763	53788	33344	93499	42232	85468	55404	21294	17285	49489
04811	97878	97853	76376	17352	79250	60879	75135	97473	33288	68080
04812	99391	91462	97370	44776	78311	53732	10635	31005	07654	76811
04813	65090	94827	79573	01053	31204	42038	73777	59818	23569	58109
04814	42280	96162	35946	30097	13326	02838	22111	97143	17085	66854
04815	12069	58506	73031	15132	74172	36630	54994	03400	82628	09339
04816	91617	20793	07798	37615	29403	92357	83551	41692	50328	21412
04817	87040	39291	02576	33545	77386	30841	05206	08838	91607	08366
04818	70903	64924	80144	91232	46165	13197	22528	58269	38897	25113
04819	35990	95773	57107	60053	94567	55974	40237	81553	05368	72120
04820	90109	22578	21653	76800	37430	82842	23888	60924	38698	70997
04821	95376	62519	86296	47616	31549	54788	80346	45737	08185	45779
04822	23496	71867	55843	59259	93602	43541	17042	50541	06527	09009
04823	66037	19952	70017	47836	22271	54216	42186	90820	77460	75942
04824	08222	87515	50667	89916	24842	80389	57695	01331	59745	07576

FIGURE 3-3 *Section of page of RAND Corporation Random Digit Table.* (*RAND Corporation,* A Million Random Digits, *The Free Press of Glencoe, New York, 1955, p. 97.*)

MECHANICS OF RANDOM NUMBER SAMPLING

The first step in the use of random number tables consists of establishing the range of numbers to be sampled and thus obtaining the number of digits required for each random number.

For instance, assume that a random sample of 100 vouchers is to be obtained from vouchers numbered from #265 (or 0265) to #9158. This means that four-digit numbers will be required, although in some instances the first digit or digits will be a zero. The number of digits necessary will be that contained in the largest number in the series.

The second step consists of finding a starting point in the table. The usual method of locating a starting point is to open the random number table haphazardly and poke a finger at the page. The number pointed to by the finger constitutes the starting point.

For those who wish to be more technically correct, a six-digit number may be selected at this point, using the first four digits to indicate the line number, and the last two the column number for the starting point.

The third step consists of proceeding vertically down the column,[3] selecting numbers of sufficient digits in order until enough random numbers required by the sample size have been chosen. Since the block (four by five) arrangement is a matter of convenience only, any horizontal grouping of the required number of digits will serve the purpose.

For instance, for the sample selection to be accomplished as outlined above (100 items between #265 and #9158), four-digit numbers will be required. Assuming that the starting point selected haphazardly is that marked in Figure 3-1 by the underlined number (column 2, line 826), the horizontal grouping of four digits may be used. In this case, the four-digit grouping #1915 was the starting point.

The first sample number is #1915. The next line will provide the next sample number in like fashion. The next number vertically is 0049 or #49. The following line gives #9394. It is to be noted that this last number is beyond the range of the numbers to be sampled; therefore this number is discarded, and the next useful number selected.

If more than four digits must be used for each number, the number can be extended by moving the required number of digits beyond the block, horizontally. The same procedure is followed right down the column, including all numbers within the limits of the field and discarding others. When the end of the column is reached, the top of the next column may be used. The next column may include any unused portion of the last column used, or it may start with the next block of digits. Either method may be used provided that it is consistent throughout the sampling operation. When

[3] Alternatively, the sampler may proceed across the table.

the page is exhausted, the first column on the next page may be used, continuing in like fashion until the required group of random numbers is attained.

When the end of the table is reached, the selection will continue from any *unused* portion at the beginning of the table. If the entire table is exhausted in meeting the needs of a large sample, the table should not be used over again. In this case a larger random number table such as the RAND Corporation Table should be used to continue the selection of digits.

If duplicate numbers occur in the selected series of random numbers, they can be discarded and replaced by the next available random number. If duplicate numbers are not discarded but are included in the sample, the result would be the equivalent of auditing the same sampling unit twice or counting it twice. This failure to eliminate duplicates results in sampling *with replacement,* which simulates an infinite population. If duplicates are eliminated, the result is equivalent to sampling without replacement, which recognizes the finite nature of an accounting population. In addition to the lack of logic in auditing or counting the same unit twice in the audit situation, the failure to recognize the finite character of the accounting population means loss of the statistical advantage of a limited population.

The sampling units with numbers corresponding to the random numbers drawn will, then, constitute the sample.

If there are gaps in the series of numbers of the items to be sampled the above procedure may be used, but the numbers missing in the series, which turn up in the random numbers selected, will be discarded and replaced by the next available random number which is useful.

For instance, assume that a series of documents numbered in blocks of 1 to 756, 1256 to 3942, and 5318 to 9142 is to be sampled by random number methods. As usual a starting point is obtained. Four-digit numbers will be required. Assume that the starting point is column 4, line 0811.

The numbers starting at this point are

2874
2441
6332
4453
6782
4992
. . . .

Note that the first number (2874) falls within one of the blocks, and it may be used. The fourth number (4453), however, occurs between the required blocks and is discarded. The process is continued until a group of useful numbers equivalent to the desired sample size has been attained.

It will then be necessary to find these sampling units. If the file or listing of items is consecutive, their location, in the haphazard order in which the random numbers were selected, may be arduous, since their sequence may require reference to widely separated file sections or parts of the listing.

It would be more efficient if the selected random numbers were in numerical sequence. This can be accomplished by writing the numbers on slips of paper or index cards as they are drawn from the random number table and then sorting these slips into numerical order before securing the sampling units. This technique also facilitates the location of duplicate numbers, especially if the random numbers are sorted into numerical sequence as they are drawn.

It is desirable that the slips of paper be serially numbered (i.e., in consecutive order) before entering the selected random numbers so that the numbers can be restored to their original random number sequences if necessary.

An alternative method of effectively dealing with the problem of efficiently handling the random numbers as they are drawn is to make use of a random number grid (see Figure 3-4).

Assume that random numbers are to be drawn for a series of documents numbered from 0001 to 8765. The grid is prepared with columns for the hundreds digits and rows for the thousands. As the numbers are drawn they are entered in the proper cell in the table by reference to the appropriate column and row. Thus random number 3362 would be entered in column 300 (for the hundreds digit) and row

	00	100	200	300	400	500	600	700	800	900
0000	0025	0155			0408					
1000	1063						1648			1908
2000			2210	2304 2382	2406 2401			2717		
3000				3362						
4000			4292			4517		4725	4872 4822	4925
5000		5198		5376					5880	
6000							6623		6802	
7000			7278		7427					
8000	8024		8240	8372		8543				
9000					9456			9792		

FIGURE 3–4 *Random Number Grid.*

3000 (for the thousands digit). Duplicate numbers will be in close proximity and can be identified readily. In addition, numbers can easily be selected in serial sequence to facilitate locating the documents in the file. Care must be taken that the cells of the grid be large enough to accomplish sufficient random numbers. An illustration of how such a random number sequence might appear in preparation is shown in Figure 3-1.

It is to be noted that a disadvantage of the use of a random number grid is the loss of the random sequence of drawing. This order of drawing may be desirable for certain purposes, as described later.

Occasionally, some of the numbers of the sampling units are not useful. For instance, some of the random numbers drawn may correspond to documents (say vouchers) which have been voided or represent some type that is not to be included in the sample. In such an instance, these random numbers should be rejected and replaced by additional random numbers obtained from the next unused random numbers at the point where the random number drawing was terminated.

It is important to emphasize, however, that such sampling units can be eliminated from the sample only if they may properly be excluded from the population as not relevant to that population. Sampling units may not be replaced because of difficulties in performing the audit examination of that unit or because of problems in obtaining the necessary information about that sampling unit. This process may be continued until the required number of sampling units has been obtained.

In good auditing practice, it is essential that the *starting* point and the *terminating* point in the random number table used be noted and included in the working papers as a minimum requirement, although it is preferable to record the random numbers (document numbers) used. In addition, the basis of the correspondence between the accounting record number and the random number should be specified, if the documents were not numbered serially. Further, the route used in drawing random numbers from the table (down, across, etc.) should be specified. The inclusion of this information relative to the sampling process will make it possible for the auditor's work to be verified independently.

When only certain documents or entries are eligible for inclusion in the sample, difficulties may arise. For instance, in testing the validity of special deductions on payrolls, where not all lines contain these deductions, the determination of the number of random numbers to draw initially becomes difficult, particularly if there is no advance knowledge of the proportion of the lines containing such deductions. As a result it is not known in advance how many of the drawn random numbers will be useful. Basically, the most efficient method must ensure that the first drawing of random numbers results in *fewer* usable sampling units than are required by the sample size, with the deficit made up by later drawings. It is easier to increase the sample size than to decrease it.

Sample selection in such a case can be accomplished in several ways. The simplest but least efficient method is to draw a group of random numbers until the required sample size is reached. Since it is certain that not all the numbers drawn will be usable, this will ultimately provide too small a sample. These numbers can then be checked to determine which are useful (i.e., which payroll lines have special deductions). Additional random numbers may now be drawn, starting at the point in the random table where the drawing was previously terminated, to make up the deficit in sample size.

However, in this second drawing, once again not all the numbers will be useful. The replenishment may then be continued until the required sample size is reached by the cumulated usable sampling units. Care must be exercised to eliminate duplicates arising in this process.

A more efficient method consists of estimating the proportion of the usable items in advance by scanning the sampling units or by taking a preliminary sample. On this basis, a rough estimate of the usable proportion may be obtained. This estimate should be deliberately increased to make sure that an oversampling will not result.

For instance, in the payroll example it might be estimated that about 25 per cent of the lines contain special deductions. It might perhaps be wise to raise this estimate to 30 per cent. The required drawing of random numbers is then increased to allow for this. For example, if it is desired to sample 200 of these special deductions, this figure can be *divided* by 30 per cent. This indicates a need for 667 (or 200/.30) random numbers initially.

When the 667 numbers have been checked, there will still be a requirement for additional random numbers because of the underestimate, and the replenishment process outlined above may be used until the required number of sampling units has been secured.

An alternative approach would be to prepare a listing of random numbers equal to the sample size required (in this instance 200) and a supplementary list of random numbers *in their original random sequence,* based on somewhat *less* than the estimated proportion of useful items. For instance, in the case outlined above, where it is estimated that 25 per cent of the lines contain special deductions, an initial listing containing 200 numbers (the required sample size) plus a supplementary listing in random sequence of 800 items (or 200/.25) will be compiled.

The initial list (200 numbers) may be exhausted and numbers drawn *in order* from the supplementary listing until the required number of usable sampling units is secured.

If, for some reason, too many random numbers are obtained in attempting to secure a sample without using the above methods, items may be removed from the sample in the reverse order of their random number sequence. Thus, starting at the terminal point in the random number table and working back, sampling units with numbers corresponding to the random numbers encountered may be removed from the sample until it is reduced to the size required.

If the random numbers drawn have been placed in numerical sequence to facilitate the location of the items, *under no circumstances* will the sample size be reduced by eliminating the last items on this list. This action would be equivalent to eliminating the last section of a file or last group of documents or entries from the sample and may well bias the results.

COMPUTER RANDOM NUMBER GENERATION

The required random numbers for sample selection may also be obtained from a computer. The computer used for this purpose may be a large-scale computer, mini or micro computer, or a time-sharing system.

Programs are available which, using any of the computer types, will provide lists of random numbers in very short periods of time and without any clerical effort by the auditor. Such programs frequently provide lists of random numbers both in the original random selection sequence and in serial sequence as well. Some programs will eliminate duplicate random numbers, some will not.

There are batch processing programs which will not only provide random numbers but when applied to computerized records will actually select and print out the details of the sampling unit record to be audited. Some of these programs will provide pairs or triplets of random numbers for use in situations such as page and line number sampling.

All computer programs which generate random numbers require an initiator number (seed), which assures a random start so that the same series of random numbers will not be obtained each time. In some programs this initiator number is requested of the sampler, while in other programs it is computer-provided, usually from the internal computer clock.

It is important that the auditor know the initiator number used and preserve it among his work papers. If there are legal problems, the manner in which the random numbers were obtained can be demonstrated, since the entry of a given initiator number will always produce the same series of random numbers on the same computer using the same generator program. For this reason, programs that use an internally obtained initiator number, which is not shown in the output, should be avoided.

Since the same initiator number will provide repetition of the same series of random numbers, it is important that the initiator number be chosen randomly and not be the same in all or many tests. Continued use of the same initiator number—for instance, the client's account number, the auditor's phone number, etc.—would mean that the same random number series would be used for all samples. This practice would eliminate the surprise element so important in audit tests as well as violate the basic requirements of probability sampling.

SPECIAL PROBLEMS IN RANDOM NUMBER SAMPLING

There are a number of situations which present special problems in random number sampling. The simplest of these deals with problems arising from the nature of sampling unit identification numbers.

An example of such a situation may be seen when the identification number includes a letter of the alphabet as a suffix or prefix. While at first glance this type of number seems to represent a serious difficulty, the problem vanishes when one considers that the letters of the alphabet can be represented by the numbers from 01 to 26. Thus, the selection of an additional two digits for each number from the random number table to represent a letter of the alphabet will resolve the problem.

However, to simplify the process, Appendix B of this book contains random letters of the alphabet which have been generated from the random number tables. After a random number has been drawn for each sampling unit, random letters of the alphabet may be added as a prefix or suffix to the rest of the number. These random letters may be obtained by using the table in the same manner as the ordinary random number table.

It is important to note that when using this method, employing separate drawings for both the letters of the alphabet and the numerical portion of the identification, duplicates are *not* eliminated. It is only when both the letter of the alphabet and the number it is combined with are identical with another combination that it could be eliminated as a duplicate. There will be numerous duplications of the letters.

This process of selecting random numbers involving a letter of the alphabet is demonstrated for two different situations.

The first situation arises when there are the same number of documents for each letter of the alphabet used. For instance, assume that the following numbering system has been used:

A 0001 to A 7000
B 0001 to B 7000
C 0001 to C 7000
. . . . . to . . . . .
R 0001 to R 7000

Assume that a selection of four-digit random numbers from the random number table in the range 0001 to 7000 results in the following:

2950	2451
1298	5840
4439	6319
1886	5152
5352	4797
2666	6357
5274	. . . .

This process is continued until a sufficient number of random numbers is secured to attain the required sample size. Duplicate numbers are *not* eliminated at this point.

By referring to Appendix B, a series of random letters is obtained in the same manner as the random numbers drawn from the random number table. Since there are no documents in the series to be sampled with letters beyond R, any letters from

S to Z are discarded when encountered. For example, assume a starting point on the first page of Appendix B on row one of the first letter of the second group of five (L). The random letters would then be

L	C
F	P
B	P
G	E
I	E
G	G
J	. . .

Once again, duplicates are *not* eliminated. These letters may now be joined in their random sequence with the previously drawn numbers to form random numbers (with alphabetic prefix) for the sample selection as follows:

L 2950	C 2451
F 1298	P 5840
B 4439	P 6319
G 1886	E 5152
I 5352	E 4797
G 2666	G 6357
J 5274	. . . . .

At this point duplicates are deleted. The duplicate to be deleted must contain *both* the same letter and the same number. For instance, if the first number, L 2950, is duplicated by another L 2950, the second is deleted and an entirely new combination of both letter and number drawn to replace it by continuing from the point at which the drawing was left off in both the table of random letters and the table of random numbers.

A second situation may arise when the number of documents for each letter of the alphabet is not the same. For instance, it may be desired to drawn a random number sample from the following series of documents:

A 0001 to A 4500
B 0001 to B 6392
C 0001 to C 2596
D 0001 to D 6892
E 0001 to E 5561

The random number combination of letter and number is obtained as before. However, here it is evident that letters of the alphabet beyond E are not needed. While some four-digit numbers will not be useful, these are not completely determinable until the final combinations of letter and four-digit number have been created. On the other hand, it is apparent that no four-digit numbers beyond 6892 (the highest number in any of the alphabetic groups) will be needed. Thus all four-digit groups beyond 6892 may be discarded at once.

After the letter-number combinations are formed, some of them will be beyond the useful numbers in the blocks. As an example, if A 5621 is drawn, it cannot be used since there is no document so numbered. Thus A 5621 will be dropped, and *both* a new letter and new four-digit random number will be drawn to replace it. It is important that the new four-digit number must *not* be used in conjunction with the A previously drawn, since this would give a probability of inclusion in the sample for the A block disproportionate to the rest of the items in the block.

Another difficult situation in random number sampling arises when the serial numbering of documents or entries is restarted with number 1 at various periods of time such as every week or month. This generates several series of sampling units with essentially the same identification numbers.

This problem is solved by considering that each month (or week or other designated period of time) may be represented by a number. For instance, it is common practice to record the month of January as 1, February as 2, etc. Thus, the selection of additional digits to represent the period of time, which may be used as a prefix to identify the period of time in which the number is to be found, can be carried out from a random number table.

Since most commonly the period involved is the month, a table of random months is included as Appendix C.

To use this table, a random selection of months would be obtained *(without elimination of duplicates)* in sufficient number to equal the required sample size. A selection of random numbers *(without elimination of duplicates)* from 1 to the largest number found in any month will then be made. The months listed in *random sequence* will then have the item numbers, also in random sequence, listed next to them. If it subsequently develops that the selected number does not exist during a month, another random selection is made to replace the unusable number and month. Duplicates are eliminated only when the month and number combined refer to the same sampling unit.

Random number sampling is most easily applied when the items are actually numbered and filed or cross indexed according to number, making it possible to locate each sampling unit conveniently by number.

However, random number sampling can be used in certain circumstances when these sequence requirements are not met. When the field is relatively small, the sample may be drawn by counting the sampling units until all the items required by the random number are reached. This can be accomplished even if the items are not systematically numbered, are in no special numerical sequence, or have no numerical designation at all. An example of this type might be an unnumbered payroll where the line items can be counted. However, when there are a considerable number of sampling units in the field, the counting approach is not feasible. Other methods may be used.

SAMPLING UNNUMBERED DOCUMENTS

When a listing is available, even if the items are unnumbered or have noncontinuous or nonsystematic numbering systems, the random number sampling can be accomplished by making use of the page and line number.

For instance, it might be desired to obtain a random number sample of items stored at a warehouse for inventory observation purposes. An IBM listing of items at the warehouse is available, consisting of sheets which include perhaps about 20,000 different items. The pages of the listing can be easily numbered or their numbers established by counting. There may be the same number of lines on most pages, with perhaps fewer on some.

Assume that there are 400 pages in the listing with 50 lines on most pages. A sample of 500 items is desired. A random number table may be used to provide 500 three-digit random numbers between 1 and 400. Duplicates are *not* eliminated. These numbers are listed in their *original random sequence* and will indicate the page numbers.

Since there are not more than 50 items per page, 500 two-digit random numbers between 1 and 50 are secured from the random number table and paired in their random sequence with the random page number listing. Again duplicates are *not* deleted.

The first three digits of the resulting five-digit number provide the page number, while the last two digits indicate the line number. Sampling units may now be located by finding the appropriate page and line number.

However, if any five-digit duplicates (reference to the same page and line) are encountered, they must now be eliminated. If the line does not exist on the page because it is incomplete, an *entirely new* five-digit random number (three digits for the page and two for the line) should be selected to replace it.

In this type of sampling, care must be exercised if each line item (sampling unit) has several entries or lines on the listing. In this case, when determining the line item to be selected, each group of entries for each line item will be counted as one item regardless of the number of lines on the page. For instance, a page of inventory listings which has been selected by the random number is as shown in Table 3-1 and the two-digit random number is 04, requiring the fourth line item. Assume further that the selection is of stock items (stock numbers).

The item selected is the fourth *stock number* or 37-100-1 and *not* the item on the fourth line. On the other hand, if the sampling unit is item by location, the item selected would be 36-340-5 *at location* 3, since each location must be counted as a sampling unit.

Similar methods may be used with any paged materials, such as ledgers or even materials in files when there are numerous file drawers. In the latter case, the first number represents the file drawer, and the second, the item number in the file.

In an electronic data-processing system, the computer can be programmed to

TABLE 3-1

Stock number	Location	Quantity
36-126-2	1	100
36-126-2	2	200
36-340-5	1	1,000
36-340-5	3	2,000
36-340-5	4	100
36-590-2	1	10,000
37-100-1	3	50
37-100-1	6	75

select and list the units to be sampled on the basis of the internally generated random numbers.

A number of computer time-sharing systems have been developed with programs which will provide lists of random numbers.

Such programs have been developed by accounting firms and governmental agencies for their own use with terminals available in local or regional offices. Upon request, through the terminal, lists of random numbers are provided within specified ranges, often in both random and numerical sequence.

Similar programs are included on some publicly available time-sharing systems.

In either method, care must be taken that the procedure is as outlined above, including provision for elimination of duplicate random numbers.

SYSTEMATIC SAMPLING

While the random number sampling technique is without question the preferred method, under certain circumstances it is possible to use other methods to achieve the same end.

At first glance, the random number method of obtaining a sample seems complex and time-consuming. Some samplers prefer to use simpler methods, if possible. Actually the random number method is not as difficult nor as time-consuming as it seems, a fact which will become apparent after it has been used a few times. Further, it has definite statistical advantages. The question of the relative costs of the random number method will be discussed more fully later.

To overcome the objections to random number sampling, some samplers resort to a technique known as *systematic sampling.* This method consists of drawing every *k*th item beginning with a random start.

For example, suppose it is desired to draw a sample of 200 items from a file containing 10,000 items. A division of the field size (10,000) by the sample size (200) indicates that a *sampling interval* of 50 is appropriate. As a starting point, a random number between 01 and 50 is obtained from a random number table. Starting with this item, every fiftieth item is selected from the file.

For instance, if the random starting number between 01 and 50 turns out to be 36, the thirty-sixth item, the eighty-sixth item, the 136th item, etc., are pulled from the file to comprise the sample.

Although this is indeed a simple method, eliminating the need for the preparation of lists of random numbers, the method must be used with caution since certain difficulties may arise. It is possible, when this method is used, that the sample result may be biased from the audit viewpoint.

An example of the possibility of introducing a bias in sample results is sampling from a payroll where every tenth line is for an assistant foreman. It is evident in such a case that, depending on the happenstance of the random start, a systematic sample with a sampling interval of 10 or some multiple of 10 will include either all assistant foremen or none.

Another such situation may arise when the common practice of leaving a space at fixed intervals in a card file, say after every 100th card, for new cards is used. If a systematic sampling method is used involving a sampling interval which is a multiple of the spacing of the gap, too many or too few of the new cards in the file will be included in the sample.

In general, if there is any periodic or cyclic arrangement of the items in the file *which is related to the characteristic being measured or tested,* a bias can result.[4] Unfortunately, such a bias is not allowed for in the sampling error computation discussed later. Further, it may not be apparent from the sample that such a bias exists. As an example of the nature of such a bias, consider the listing of amounts in Table 3-2.

Assume that a systematic sample with a sampling interval of four is to be drawn. If the random starting point happens to be #1, then the sample in Table 3-3 is drawn.

If the random starting number happened to be #3, the sample would be that shown in Table 3-4.

It is apparent that the difference in the sample averages arises from the pattern that exists in the original arrangement of the sampling units. The result is biased.

Other patterns or arrangements of the sampling units also may introduce a bias into the results. Thus, the use of systematic sampling methods for obtaining a sample could result in biased samples due to the arrangement of the sampling units.

Of course, if the effect of the sampling unit arrangement were known, it might be possible to draw the sample in such a manner as to avoid such a bias. Unfortunately, such arrangements within the data are usually unknown and unsuspected.

Remember that the arrangement of the sampling units *with reference to the type of information being sought* is the key factor in introducing bias. Thus, if the objective of the sample is to locate errors, any periodic arrangement of errors, arising perhaps

[4]The use of the term "bias" in this context refers to an audit rather than statistical bias in the classical sense.

from the fact that certain blocks of numbers are handled by specified persons, may cause difficulty.

TABLE 3–2

Item number	*Amount*	*Item number*	*Amount*
1	$100.00	21	$110.00
2	50.00	22	60.00
3	10.00	23	20.00
4	80.00	24	90.00
5	110.00	25	100.00
6	60.00	26	50.00
7	20.00	27	10.00
8	90.00	28	80.00
9	100.00	29	110.00
10	50.00	30	60.00
11	10.00	31	20.00
12	80.00	32	90.00
13	110.00	33	100.00
14	60.00	34	50.00
15	20.00	35	10.00
16	90.00	36	80.00
17	100.00	37	110.00
18	50.00	38	60.00
19	10.00	39	20.00
20	80.00	40	90.00

However, if the auditor may have reasonable assurance that no such periodic arrangement exists or that the arrangement of the sampling unit with respect to that characteristic being studied is random, systematic sampling can be used. For instance, if a sampling is to be made of a group of accounts receivable and these are filed alphabetically, it is possible that the arrangement is unrelated to the characteristic being measured and systematic sampling may be used without concern as to bias.

However, the choice of systematic sampling techniques for drawing the sample places the responsibility for the accuracy of the assumption that no pattern exists in the data with respect to the characteristic measured on the shoulders of the accountant.

Another difficulty that arises when systematic sampling is used relates to the computation of the sample precision. A precise calculation of the sampling error of a projection from the sample where a fixed-interval, single systematic selection is used is not possible without some knowledge of the actual distribution of the values in the field. Of course this is not usually known.[5]

[5]One of the methods for overcoming this difficulty is to use several systematic random samples within the same population using several random starts. The method of replicated sampling outlined in Chapter 14 can then be used to compute the sample precision.

TABLE 3-3

Item number	*Amount*
1	$100.00
5	110.00
9	100.00
13	110.00
17	100.00
21	110.00
25	100.00
29	110.00
33	100.00
37	110.00
Average.......	$105.00

TABLE 3-4

Item number	*Amount*
3	$10.00
7	20.00
11	10.00
15	20.00
19	10.00
23	20.00
27	10.00
31	20.00
35	10.00
39	20.00
Average.......	$15.00

If there is a periodic or cyclic pattern in the sampling units of the field, the sample precision of a systematic sample will be poorer than that for a random number sample, and accurate calculation of the sampling error will not be possible by the methods outlined later in this book. However, under other circumstances the precision of a sample result obtained by systematic sampling methods will be as good as or better than that of a random number sample. Thus, if the sampler can reasonably assume that such a pattern does not exist, he can proceed with the assurance that the sampling error computations later described will give him a conservative statement of the sample reliability.

For these reasons, some statisticians frown on the use of systematic samples. Further, in most cases the use of the systematic approach will result in a saving only of the preparation of a random number list; but since the sampling units to be used usually must be found by counting or measuring, the net saving in time by resort to

---

For a mathematical discussion of possible biases arising from systematic sampling and difficulties in computing the sampling precision of such samples see: W. G. Cochran, *Sampling Techniques*, John Wiley & Sons, Inc., New York, 1953, chap. 18; M. H. Hansen, W. M. Hurwitz, and W. G. Madow, *Sample Survey Methods and Theory*, John Wiley & Sons, Inc., New York, 1953, pp. 51–52, 94–97, 503–512.

random number sampling may be largely an illusion or at least may not result in any great reduction in time.

If it is necessary to count the length of the sampling interval, it would require little additional time to prepare the random number list and count the item numbers.

Nevertheless, there are some situations in which, because of purely practical reasons, systematic sampling seems to be the only feasible approach. In such cases, if the sampler has reasonable assurance that no cyclical pattern of the characteristic to be measured exists because of the filing arrangement of the sampling unit, such an approach may be used.

THE MECHANICS OF SYSTEMATIC SAMPLING

As previously observed, a systematic sample is secured by selecting every kth item from the sampling units, starting with a randomly selected sampling unit between 1 and k. The interval k is obtained by dividing the field size N by the sample size n. If the result of this division is not a whole number, the result may be rounded off to the nearest digit.

Once the initial sampling unit has been randomly selected and the sampling interval established, the units to be included in the sample become every kth unit after the initial unit. This is accomplished by counting k units after the first unit included, then the next k, etc. If the sampling units are numbered and are filed in numerical order and none are missing, this selection can be accomplished without actual counting.

When large files are to be sampled, such a counting operation may be quite arduous. If the items in the file are of uniform thickness or are listed on uniform lines, the actual selection of a systematic sample may be made by measurement.

For instance, in sampling an IBM card file, the fact that there are 145 punched cards to the inch when tightly packed may be used. Thus, if the sampling interval required is every 500th card after the randomly selected starting point, a ruler may be used to measure off 3.4 inches, and a card is selected at that point. This will provide an approximate equivalent to counting, and the resultant sample will be the approximate equivalent of, and is generally accepted as, a systematic sample.

However, if the files to be sampled have filing units of varying thickness, location of sampling units by measurement will not provide a systematic sample and will give a greater probability of inclusion of thick folders than thin ones.

An IBM listing usually has 6 lines to the inch. Thus, if a sampling interval of every 300th item is desired, a selection may be made every 50 inches. In this case, by careful measurement the correct sampling unit can be found.

Certain difficulties may be encountered in systematic sampling. For instance, if the accounts receivable are to be sampled from a file of ledger cards and there are varying numbers of cards per account, it will be necessary to locate the sampling units by counting accounts and not cards. Failure to do this will give accounts with a larger number of cards a greater probability of inclusion in the sample and the basic requirement of a random sample, namely, that all sampling units have an equal probability of inclusion in the sample, will not be met. Measurement methods of selection cannot be used in such a case for the same reason.

An identical problem is faced in obtaining a systematic sample from a listing when there may be several lines listed for some sampling units and other numbers of lines for other sampling units.

If a periodic arrangement of the sampling units is suspected and if therefore it is feared that a bias may be introduced into the sample results when systematic sampling is used, several other approaches are possible.

The introduction of a bias due to the arrangement of the items may be eliminated by using systematic sampling with a randomly varying sampling interval. This method requires that after a sampling interval (say $k = 100$) is established and an initial item (say the 70th) is randomly selected, a random number between 1 and $2k$ is obtained after the selection of each sampling unit. For instance, in this case, the starting point is sampling unit #70. A random number between 1 and 200 (or $2k$) is found in the random number table. Assume that this turns out to be #110. The 110th card after the 70th, or the 180th card in the file, would be found. The next random number between 1 and 200 would then be found in the random number table (assume it to be #85). A total of 85 additional cards would then be counted to reach the next (180 + 85 = 265th card in the file). This process will be continued until the end of the file is reached. Since the average of random numbers between 001 and 200 will be 100, a sample with an average number of sampling units of about 200 will result. This sample will be a true random sample.

An alternative approach is to select a random number from a random number table between 1 and k and to use that number within each interval. For example, if the sampling interval is 100, a random number between 1 and 100 would be obtained from a random number table and that item used from among the first 100. A second random number between 1 and 100 (assume it to be #46) is then used to determine which unit among the second hundredth is to be used. This would be the 146th from the beginning of the file. This process is continued until the end of the file is reached.[6]

It may seem that the requirement for the use of random numbers here destroys the practical advantages of systematic sampling. While these alternative methods do require more time than the fixed sampling interval method, no lists of random numbers in numerical sequence are needed and there is no requirement for elimination of duplicate numbers.

Another problem which may be encountered occurs when a proportion of the items selected by the systematic sample are of a category which is not to be sampled or are voided documents. As an example, a systematic sampling of invoices may be confined to sampling only those invoices over $10.00 or only those for a certain type of

[6]This in effect becomes a stratified sample with one sampling unit per stratum. The strata are the k divisions of the field (see Chap. 10).

expense. In such a case, a varying number of these items will have to be rejected when encountered in the systematic sampling process. It is *not* proper to proceed to the next useful voucher adjacent to the one selected. Thus the sampler will secure less than the desired number of sampling units. It is important that the estimate of the field size be reasonably accurate when systematic sampling is used, or an over-sampling or undersampling may result.

As an example, assume that the field size is 50,000 and that a sample size of 500 is desired. This results in a sampling interval of 100 (or 50,000/500). If this is not correct and, in fact, there are 60,000, a sample of 500 will be provided *before* reaching the end of the file or list, in fact when the 50,000th sampling unit has been reached, thus leaving the last 10,000 unsampled.

In such a case, it will be necessary to continue sampling until the end, resulting in a sample of 600. If this is not done, the sample may be biased to the extent that the unsampled portion of the field is different from the rest of the field. Certainly under such circumstance, the requirement that the sample be drawn from the entire field with equal probability of inclusion of *all* sampling units in the field would not be met.

In the event that such a situation arises, several alternatives may be used. If the sample is not too greatly increased by the inaccurate estimate of field size, the larger sample may be used.

If it is desired to reduce the increased sample size to its original level, some sampling units may be deleted from the sample, but this must be done on a *systematic or random number* basis. The simplest way is to delete items systematically, thus deleting each *k*th sampling unit from the sample. For instance, in the case described above where 600 items resulted in the sample rather than the desired 500, every sixth sampling unit (the enlarged sample size divided by the number to be dropped) may be eliminated from the sample *in the order in which they were drawn.* Another method would be to draw 100 random numbers between 1 and 600 and to delete the corresponding sampling units.

On the other hand, if the field size is overestimated, the resulting sample will be too small. For example, if in the case above the field was estimated to contain 50,000 sampling units whereas it actually contained 40,000, the entire file would have been completed with the 400th drawing, and only 400 sampling units would be contained in the sample as compared with the desired 500.

Again, there are alternative possibilities. The smaller sample can be accepted; but if it is desired to increase the sample size, a new systematic sampling starting *from the beginning* will have to be obtained. Since the sample was short 100 sampling units, an additional 100 would be needed. Since the field size is now known to be 40,000, every 400th sampling unit starting with a new random start can be included in the sample.[7]

The location of the sampling units to be included in the sample is simple and effi-

[7]An advantage of the systematic sampling method is that it does provide a measurement of field size when it is otherwise not available.

cient if the items are serially numbered. For example, if every 100th item is to be selected with a random start of say #33, items #33, #133, #233, etc., are found in the file by locating documents with these numbers.

SPECIAL SAMPLING METHODS

As noted in the first chapter, there are a variety of methods of obtaining statistical (probability) samples in addition to the unrestricted random sampling method, including:

1. Stratified random samples
2. Cluster samples
3. Multistage samples

The mechanics of properly drawing samples of these types are discussed below.

Stratified random samples

It will be recalled that this type of sampling requires separation of the field into various segments or strata and independent sampling from each stratum. The method of drawing a stratified random sample is identical with that of unrestricted random samples with the exception that each strata or segment of the field is sampled separately by the techniques outlined above.

Cluster samples

Cluster sampling consists of either an unrestricted random sample or a stratified random sample in which, instead of drawing individual sampling units, groups of contiguous sampling units are drawn.

This method, since it requires location of fewer points at which to sample, reduces the time and cost involved. However, as will be shown later, this method is frequently less efficient than single sample unit drawings and requires larger sample sizes with no net savings in effort and perhaps even an increased overall cost. This point is discussed more fully later.

In the cluster sampling method, a sample of 500 items might be obtained by drawing 10 sampling units at each of 50 points. The points of location of the clusters may be obtained by either random number or systematic sampling, with that unit and the nine sampling units immediately following the selected point being included in the sample.

Multistage samples

As previously described, this method of sampling involves sampling at several levels. Thus a sample of locations may be taken and a further sample of payroll payments (persons) taken at each location to obtain an overall picture for a business organization.

The selection of the first stage or primary sampling units (locations) as well as that of the secondary sampling units (payroll line items) can both be accomplished, using either random number or systematic sampling in accordance with the methods described above.

SAMPLING SELECTION AND COSTS

The use of the random number method for selecting a sample imposes an additional time requirement in the audit test. It is obvious that the selection of items for the test according to *any* planned method requires more time than merely going to a file and without design pulling an item here and there haphazardly. Some auditors have objected to this additional time requirement.

In examining this problem, the first point to be remembered is that in virtually all audit testing, the time necessary to examine the items selected after they have been found by far exceeds that which might be required by this method of obtaining sampling units. Relatively, then, the additional time required will be an unimportant portion of the total audit time. Further, the actual preparation of a random number list does not require the services of an auditor. Any clerk or typist can draw up such lists when the method is explained to them.

The extra time spent in preparing lists of random numbers is the price that must be paid for the privilege of being able to project sample results to describe the entire field investigated as well as for all the other advantages of the statistical approach.

A series of tests employing an experienced clerk has indicated that the preparation of random numbers by writing these numbers on cards or slips, eliminating duplicates, and arranging the resulting numbers in numerical sequence, to facilitate the location of items in a file, is approximately thirty minutes per 100 random numbers when the *entire* block is used. If, however, only a portion of a block of numbers is to be used, this time will be increased proportionately. For instance, if the random number requirement is for 100 random numbers of four digits each from the block 0001 to 5000 (rather than 0001 to 9999), thus using 50 per cent of the block, the time will be doubled.

As explained previously, the time requirement for the selection of large samples can be reduced appreciably by using computer-generated random numbers. Some audit organizations have available programs for random number generation, usually on time-sharing systems. In addition, programs are available for sampling computerized data (on tape or disks) which not only generate the required random numbers but actually select the included sampling units and print out the details of the selected sample records.

However, it is to be expected that the first time a person draws a random number sample, considering the strangeness of the operation, he may need a longer period of time than a practiced sampler. With experience the time requirement will be reduced to about the level indicated above.

Some samplers, to avoid this time requirement, have resorted to systematic sampling. Although this does eliminate such lists, this method may be inadvisable because of the disadvantages of systematic sampling previously discussed.

Considering the fact that the time required for the preparation of such lists is greatly overshadowed by the time required for the examination of the selected documents, this additional time requirement is a small price indeed to pay for the advantages of statistical sampling.

FOUR

Elementary Statistical Concepts

STATISTICAL THEORY AND THE AUDITOR

To the nonstatistician, at first glance the techniques of statistics seem quite formidable. Elaborate statistical formulas involving Greek letters may cause the auditor to hesitate to make use of these scientific techniques. Further, to the uninitiated, the literature of the field of statistical methods is difficult to comprehend, particularly in the area of statistical sampling, since these techniques are often treated as an advanced subject, and the discussion presupposes previous formal training.

However, it is not required that the auditor be a trained statistician in order to apply statistical sampling methods to his tests and other accounting evaluations. To accept this view would result in the assumption that only trained statisticians can use statistical sampling, thus limiting the use of these techniques to a select few. Actual experience, as in the field of industrial quality control, has demonstrated that this is not true. Statistical sampling may be used effectively by those who have an understanding of the principles in spite of a lack of formal or extensive training. Of course, the trained statistician can devise more efficient methods of sampling, and his services may be required in certain complex situations.

The auditor need not be alarmed when confronted by the statistician's complex formulas, since most of these formulas can be reduced to the form of tables from which the sampler can obtain his result without having to solve these formulas. Nevertheless, a basic understanding of his tools will provide the auditor not only with greater facility in using these techniques, but with an understanding of the methods which will enable him to avoid blunders.

For these reasons, this chapter will be devoted to the consideration of some elementary statistical concepts and tools.

BASIC STATISTICAL MEASURES

Statistical techniques have their greatest value when the analyst is confronted by large masses of data. In such instances he is required to interpret the significance of a large number of observations or measurements, generally all differing from one another.

Consider, for instance, a list of 2,000 vouchers. A mere scanning of these data as to the amounts of the vouchers provides little information for the analyst because of the mass of numbers confronting him. An organized approach is essential if any information is to be gleaned from this extensive listing.

The first step in analyzing such data on a complete (nonsampling) basis would be to reduce the mass of the data by arranging the observations in magnitude groupings or size categories. This is accomplished by tallying or counting the number of observations which fall into each dollar-value category. The resulting table (technically called a *frequency distribution*) for the above-mentioned voucher data is shown in Table 4-1.

Now, instead of a listing of values covering many pages, the analyst need deal only with this one short table.

If desired, the data in Table 4-1 may be presented pictorially in a graph by preparing a dollar-value scale for the horizontal axis of the graph and a scale to represent the number of vouchers on the vertical axis. The resulting graph is shown in Figure 4-1.

The general appearance of this graph is typical of many frequency distributions. Note that the curve has a peak and tapers off in both directions.

TABLE 4-1. ***Distribution of Dollar Amounts of Vouchers (From Appendix M)***

Dollar value of vouchers	*Number of vouchers*
0– 49.99	1
50– 99.99	49
100–149.99	252
150–199.99	681
200–249.99	399
250–299.99	301
300–349.99	184
350–399.99	93
400–449.99	28
450–499.99	9
500–549.99	3
Total........................	2,000

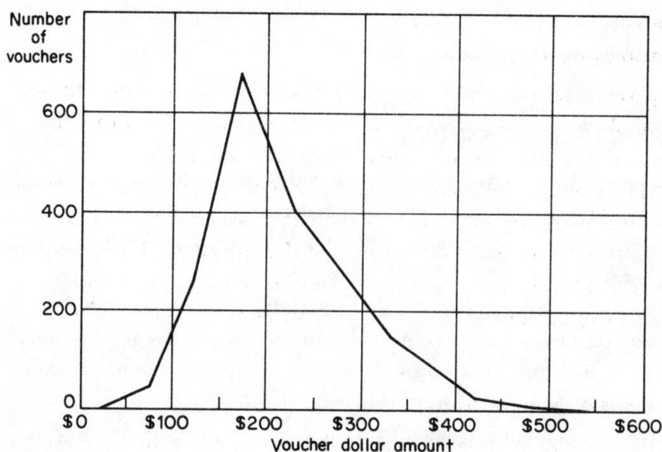

FIGURE 4-1 *Distribution of voucher dollar amounts.*

1. *Averages*

Thus, it appears that the values tend to cluster about the peak point in the distribution. The *location* of this *point of central tendency* about which the values cluster is often used to typify the entire mass of observations. The measure of the location of this point is called an *average.*

Although there are many types of averages, the most useful one for most accounting problems is the *arithmetic mean* or *arithmetic average.* Unless otherwise specified, the word "average" in this book will refer to the arithmetic average. The arithmetic mean is obtained by totaling all the values and then dividing by the number of observations included in the total. The symbol $\overline{X}$ (say "X bar") will represent the arithmetic mean.

For the above list of vouchers the arithmetic mean may be computed to be $220.04. Generally speaking, this indicates that the *typical* amount is $220.04. However, this is a considerable oversimplification of the interpretation of the arithmetic mean.

It is noted that if the arithmetic mean is available, the grand total value of all items can be obtained by multiplying the mean by the number of observations comprising the average.[1]

[1] This is obvious, since the average was obtained by *dividing* the total by the number of observations comprising that total. Symbolically,

$$\overline{X} = \frac{\Sigma X}{n}$$

where Σ means the sum of
X represents each observation
n equals the number of observations

thus $$n\overline{X} = n\frac{\Sigma X}{n} = \Sigma X$$

2. *Measures of dispersion*

It is apparent that, since all the voucher values are not the same, the average alone will not supply complete information about the data, owing to the fact that many of the observations depart considerably from the average.

To provide complete information about the data, in addition to stating the "typical" value, it is necessary to indicate the extent to which the individual values depart from the average by means of some measure of *dispersion*. Thus, the understanding of the data provided by the statistical measures is considerably improved if it is noted that the average (arithmetic mean) voucher value is $220.04 and that the *range* of the values is from $13.48 to $547.53.

3. *The standard deviation*

While this statement about the data is improved, the range is a poor measure of the *dispersion* of the values about the arithmetic mean, since it considers only the two most extreme or freakish values (the highest and the lowest) and does not give any indication as to the behavior or spread of the other items about the average.

A better measure of dispersion of the values would be one which would be dependent upon the spread of all observations about the average. The measure found most useful for this purpose is a peculiar kind of average of the distance of all values from the arithmetic mean called the *standard deviation.*

If the distance of a value from the average is each represented[2] by $X - \overline{X}$, then the standard deviation is obtained by squaring these deviations, $(X - \overline{X})^2$, dividing the sum of these squares by the number of observations, $\Sigma(X - \overline{X})^2/n$, thus obtaining the average square of the deviations from the arithmetic mean, and then taking the square root of the result.

Symbolically, if, as is customary, the Greek lowercase letter sigma, σ, is used to represent the standard deviation, its formula becomes

$$\sigma = \sqrt{\frac{\Sigma(X - \overline{X})^2}{n}}$$

or, when computed from a sample,

$$\sigma = \sqrt{\frac{\Sigma(X - \overline{X})^2}{n - 1}}$$

When the sample is of any considerable size, the difference in the results turns out to be negligible. As a result, the division by the value n rather than $n - 1$ is common. When the sample is less than 40, however, the second version of the formula should be used.

[2]See explanation of symbols on page 52.

While the above calculation may look formidable, there are now available a number of models and makes of pocket electronic calculators with a standard deviation key which require only the entry of the individual values and the pressing of the standard deviation key to obtain the result of the above formulas.

In addition, the value of the standard deviation for a given group of data may be approximated by a method not requiring the solution of the formulas, as will be explained in a later chapter.

If the auditor should later find it desirable to calculate the measure precisely for a large number of observations, methods of facilitating and accomplishing the computations from frequency distributions are covered in elementary statistical texts.[3]

The computation of the standard deviation from a limited number of observations is illustrated below, given the following values:

	$191.10
	251.53
	205.10
	196.86
	192.66
Total	$1,037.25

The average is $207.45 or $1,037.25/5. The deviation or difference between each of the above values and the arithmetic average is secured and squared as shown in Table 4-2.

TABLE 4–2

Value (X)	Deviation from average of $207.45 ($X - \bar{X}$)	Square of deviation $(X - \bar{X})^2$
$191.10	−16.35	267.3225
251.53	+44.08	1,943.0464
205.10	− 2.35	5.5225
196.86	−10.59	112.1481
192.66	−14.79	218.7441
Total.....		2,546.7836

The total of the squared deviations is divided by the number of items (in this case $n = 5$) to give 509.3567. The square root of this figure[4] is the standard deviation, which is $22.57 in this case.[5]

It is apparent that the greater the spread of the individual observations about the

[3] See, for instance, H. Arkin and R. R. Colton, *Statistical Methods*, 5th ed., Barnes & Noble, Inc., New York, 1970, chap. IV.

[4] The value obtained *before* taking the square root is called the *variance.* This is the square of the standard deviation.

[5] See Technical Appendix I for a less laborious method which may be used to calculate the standard deviation.

arithmetic mean, the greater will be the standard deviation. Thus, in comparing two sets of data, if one is found to have a larger standard deviation than the other, that set of data shows greater variability.

At this point, the reader may wonder why such a peculiar measure was resorted to, especially one which is so arduous to compute. There is sound reason for this choice of a measure of dispersion, but to understand this reason it is necessary to return to a general discussion of the nature of frequency distributions.

To facilitate the discussion, it will be assumed that an extremely large number of observations are included in the frequency distribution under discussion and that for this reason the irregularities arising from limited data will vanish in graphs of these distributions. A smooth curve will then be seen in a graph of the distribution. Curves of this type will be used in the discussion below.

A basic and most important type of distribution is pictured in Figure 4-2. It is seen that this graph looks like a cross section of a bell and, in fact, is often called a "bell-shaped" curve. It is properly known as a *normal* distribution.[6] Its origin will be explained later, but it may now be observed that it often arises as a result of random variations.

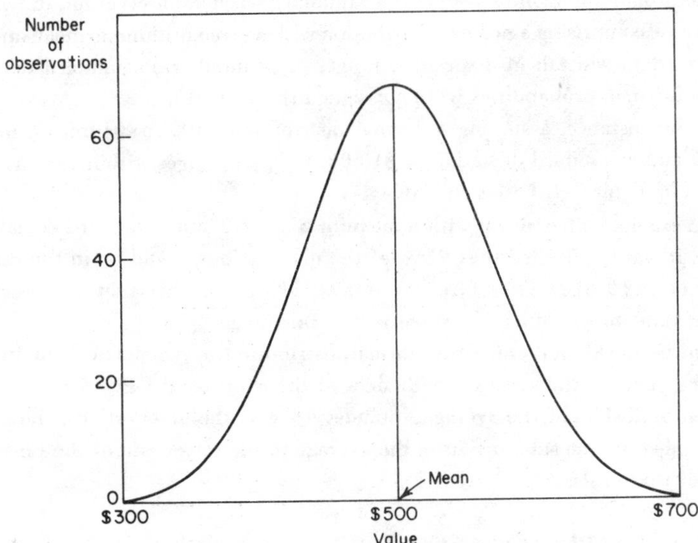

FIGURE 4-2

The formula for the curve is known.[7] The standard deviation is the only variable in this formula. Hence, by mathematical methods it is possible to determine the

[6] Also known as the Gaussian distribution.
[7] For the mathematically trained, the formula is

$$Y = \frac{1}{\sigma\sqrt{2\pi}} e^{-(X-\bar{X})^2/2\sigma^2}$$

where e and π are mathematical constants.

proportion of the area under the curve and thus the percentage of observations contained within any given distance measured from the arithmetic mean. Tables of such values have been compiled. A few of the more important of these values are shown in Table 4-3.

Thus if a set of observations is known to comprise a normal distribution and the distribution has an arithmetic mean of $100 and a standard deviation of $10.00, it may be said that 95% of the observations will fall in the range of $80.40 to $119.60 [$\bar{X} \pm 1.96\sigma$, or in this instance, $100.00 ± 1.96 ($10.00)]. This is illustrated in Figure 4-3.

Conversely, it may be said that if an observation is drawn at random from among those comprising a normal distribution, there are 95 chances in 100 or a 95% probability (confidence) that it will fall within the range established by the arithmetic mean ±1.96 times the standard deviation. In Figure 4-3 there is a 95% probability that it will fall between $80.40 and $119.60. This point is basic to an understanding of sampling variability measurements and thus should be carefully studied and understood by the reader.

In similar fashion, various ranges can be established which will give any desired degree of probability (confidence) that a randomly selected observation, drawn from among those comprising a normal distribution with a given arithmetic mean and standard deviation, will fall in a specified range. The number of standard deviations required for such probabilities will be assigned the symbol t.

Thus, for instance, assuming a normal distribution with an arithmetic mean of $100.00 and a standard deviation of $10.00, the percentages within various ranges are given in Table 4-4, based on Table 4-3.

In the example cited above with a mean of $100.00 and a standard deviation of $10.00, it was established that 95% of the observations would be in the range of $80.40 to $119.60. Therefore, there is a 95% probability that an observation drawn at random would be contained within this range.

It is to be noted that since the normal distribution is symmetrical, or in other words the curve is the same on both sides of the average, if a given range, say of 1.65σ on both sides of the average, includes 90% of the observations, the proportion included on one side, say from the average to the upper end of the range, will be half of that or 45%.

TABLE 4–3. ***Table of t Values***

Distance from arithmetic mean in terms of standard deviation on both sides of the mean ($\pm t\sigma$)	*Percentage of observations included*
$\pm 1.00\sigma$	68.26%
±1.65	90.00
±1.96	95.00
±2.33	98.00
±2.58	99.00
±3.00	99.73
±3.30	99.90

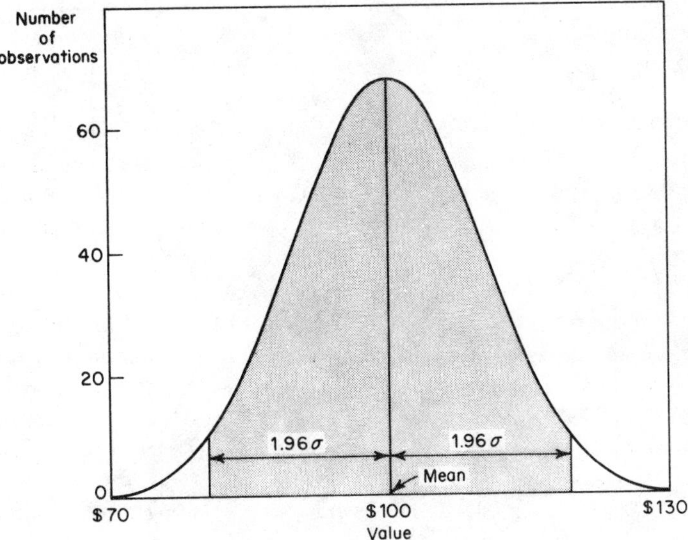

FIGURE 4–3

Likewise, it may now be seen that *below* the upper limit (without reference to a lower range limit) there will be included one-half of the given percentage (in this case 90%/2 = 45%) from that point to the average *plus* the 50% below the average or 95%. A similar calculation may be performed for the percentage above the lower end of the range. For instance, if the mean is $100.00 and the standard deviation is $10.00, the range of $100.00 ± 1.96 ($10.00) or from $80.40 to $119.60 will include 95% of the observations. On the other hand, above $80.40, there will be 97.5% of the observations or 95%/2 + 50%. In similar manner, 97.5% of the observations will be less than $119.60. This is illustrated graphically in Figures 4-4*a* and 4-4*b*.

An examination of the normal distribution pictured in Figure 4-2 discloses that it is symmetrical. The two halves of the distribution on the opposite sides of the arithmetic mean are exactly alike. However, many distributions are not normal nor may they be assumed to be normal. This is especially true of numerous types of accounting data.

When the data contain extreme or unusual values, as when a large group of accounts receivable cluster about some level but relatively few customers have very

TABLE 4–4

Probability	*Range (limits)*
68.26%	$90.00 to $110.00 ($\bar{X} \pm 1\sigma$)
90.00	$83.50 to $116.50 ($\bar{X} \pm 1.65\sigma$)
95.00	$80.40 to $119.60 ($\bar{X} \pm 1.96\sigma$)
99.00	$74.20 to $125.80 ($\bar{X} \pm 2.58\sigma$)

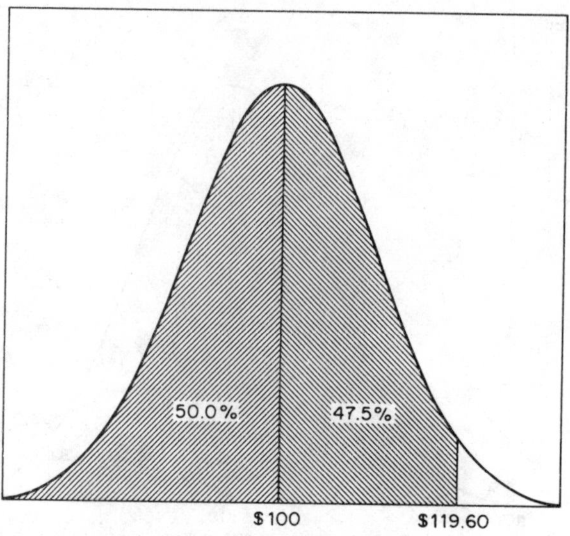

FIGURE 4-4*a*

large accounts, the basic distribution is no longer symmetrical but may look more like the distribution picture in Figure 4-5*a*.

A distribution which is not symmetrical is called a ***skewed*** distribution. The distribution in Figure 4-5*a* has the extreme values on the high side and is called the ***right skewed*** distribution. Figure 4-5*b* pictures a distribution with the extremes on the low side and is called a ***left skewed*** distribution.

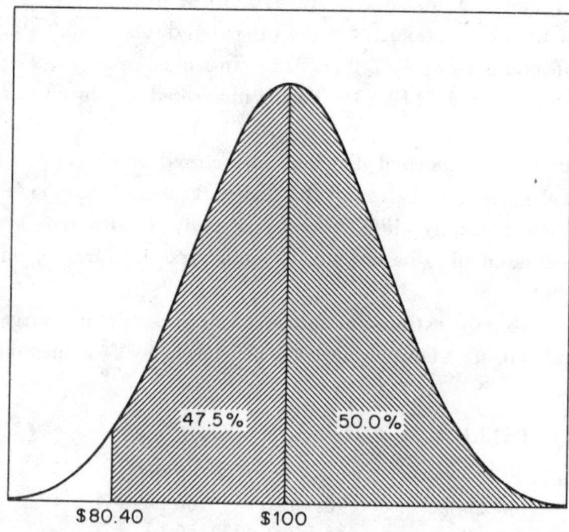

FIGURE 4-4*b*

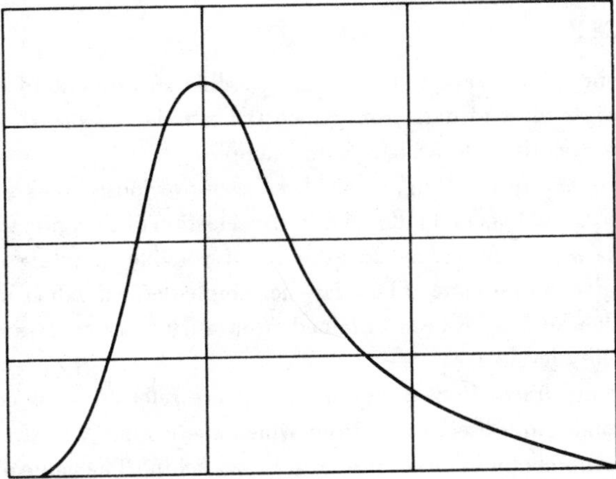

FIGURE 4-5a

Most distributions of the values on accounting records constitute right skewed frequency distributions, characterized by many small or moderate values accompanied by a few very large values.

The table of percentages (Table 4-3) given as being included within a given number of standard deviations from the arithmetic mean (on both sides) applies exactly only to normal distributions.

For distributions which depart only slightly from normality, these values are still good approximations. For badly skewed distributions, the values in the table cannot be used. This is considered in later discussions where special measures are taken to cope with such situations.

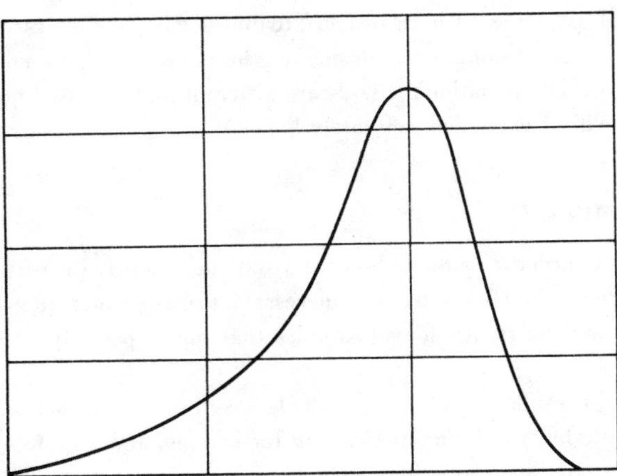

FIGURE 4-5b

SAMPLING CONCEPTS

The object in obtaining a sample is to make possible an estimate of some characteristic of the larger mass of data from which the sample was drawn by use of the value of that characteristic derived from the sample.

The use of probability sampling, as has been seen previously, makes possible the elimination of personal bias and judgment in the selection of the units to be included in the sample as well as providing an estimate of possible sampling errors. This sampling error gives an estimate of how far the sample-derived values might deviate from that which would have been obtained from a 100 per cent sample for any selected probability level.

The observations drawn from the entire group are referred to as constituting a *sample.* The totality of observations from which the sample was drawn is called a *universe* or *population* (or in more familiar terms, a field). The value of the characteristic (average, proportion of some specified type, etc.) derived from the sample is called a *statistic.* The same type of value which might be obtained by a 100 per cent census of the population (100 per cent sample) is called a *parameter.*

Basically, to be able to determine how far a statistic computed from a sample might differ from the population parameter, at a given probability level, the auditor must have some knowledge of the behavior of all the possible sample results that might be drawn from such a population. This is possible if probability sampling methods have been used to select the sampling units.

In Chapter 1 (see pages 13–14) a distinctionn was made between measurements in terms of variables as contrasted with observations expressed as attributes.

Recall that an attributes observation relates to the occurrence of some event, such as an error, a particular type of voucher, etc., or a categorization of the items examined. A variable observation is a measurement obtained from the sampling unit, such as the dollar amount, the number of days an account is overdue, etc.

The theory of sampling as it relates to attributes will be discussed first. The objective of this type of sampling is to answer the question, "How many?" Since the sampling error determination methods are different for these two types of measurements, they will be examined separately below.

ATTRIBUTES SAMPLING

As noted above, in order to estimate how far a statistic might (with reasonable probability) depart from the parameter, it is necessary to have some knowledge of the behavior of all possible results for all samples that might possibly be drawn from the universe.

If probability (or random) sampling methods have been used, each sampling unit has an equal probability of being included in the sample, and therefore all possible groupings of the sampling units (for a sample of a given size) are equally probable.

TABLE 4-5

Coin tossing		Ball drawing	
Coin #1	Coin #2	Ball #1	Ball #2
Tail	Tail	White	White
Head	Tail	Black	White
Tail	Head	White	Black
Head	Head	Black	Black

A very simple example may be developed to illustrate this point. Assume that two coins are tossed and the number of heads resulting are counted. An alternative similar example would be the drawing of two balls from a very large number of such balls, when 50 per cent of the balls from which the drawing is made are black, and the other half white. In this latter case, the number of black balls in the sample are counted.

In either example, the measurement is an attribute (head versus tail, black versus white). Since all possible groupings are equally likely, it would be desirable to list all these groupings. They are shown in Table 4-5 for both examples (for 2 coins and 2 balls).

Since all groupings are equally likely, it is evident that the probability of no heads at all in 2 tosses in only one in four (or ¼ or 25 per cent), since only one of the four groupings (tail-tail) provides this result with the same figure for no black balls. In similar manner, there are 2 out of 4 equally likely ways of obtaining one head (head-tail or tail-head), and thus the probability of one head in tosses of 2 coins is two out of four (²⁄₄ or 50 per cent). The same calculation applies to the probability of 1 black ball in a sample of 2.

Finally, since there is only one way of obtaining 2 heads (head-head) out of four equally likely groupings, the probability of 2 heads in tosses of 2 coins (or 2 black balls in drawings of 2 balls) is one in four (or ¼ or 25 per cent).

Thus, it is now possible to tabulate the various possible sample measurements

TABLE 4-6. *Outcome of Tosses of 2 Coins (or Drawings of 2 Balls*)*

Number of heads (or black balls)	*Probability*
0	25%
1	50
2	25

* When the ball population contains 50% black balls.

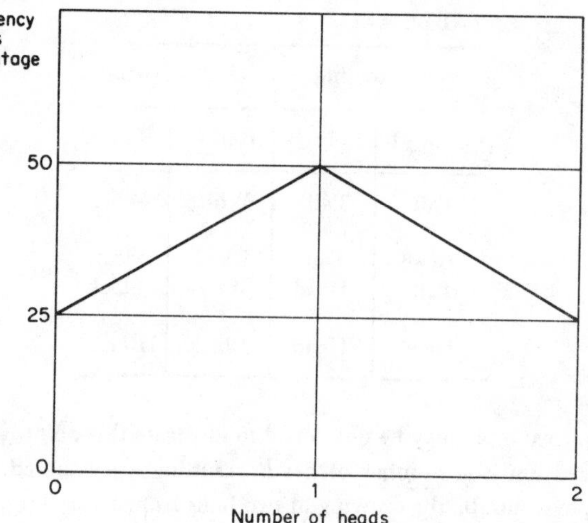

FIGURE 4–6a

(in this case the attribute-number of heads or number of black balls) for all possible sample outcomes together with their probabilities (see Table 4-6).

Table 4-6 is presented graphically as a frequency distribution in Figure 4-6*a*. This type of distribution, which indicates all possible sample outcomes together with their relative frequencies, is called a ***sampling distribution.***

It is apparent from the above data that if 2 coins are tossed, there is a considerable probability of *any* of these outcomes (no heads, 1 head, or 2 heads). If a similar procedure is followed for tosses of 3 coins (or drawings of 3 balls), the probabilities shown in Table 4-7 will result.[8] Figure 4-6*b* is a graphical representation of the information in Table 4-7.

TABLE 4–7. ***Outcome of Tosses of 3 Coins (or Drawings of 3 Balls*)***

Number of heads (or black balls)	*Probability*
0	12.5%
1	37.5
2	37.5
3	12.5

* When the population contains 50% black balls. These data are graphed in Figure 4-6*b*.

[8] The reader can confirm this by listing all the possible sample groupings as was done above for 2 coins.

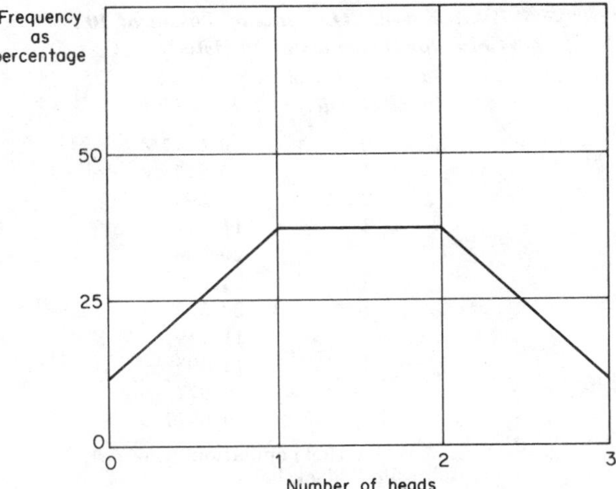

FIGURE 4–6*b*

There is still an appreciable probability of the occurrence of any number of heads (or black balls). A frequency distribution generated in this manner for attributes is called *a binomial distribution.*

When a much larger number of coins are tossed (or balls drawn), the method used above, the enumeration of all possible sample groupings, becomes arduous. However, the values can be found through mathematics.[9]

For tosses of 10 coins (or drawings of 10 balls) the probability of each possible number of heads in 10 tosses is shown in Table 4-8. This is shown graphically in Figure 4-7*a*.

From Table 4-8 it may be seen that if 10 coins are tossed (or 10 balls drawn), it is most unlikely that there will be no heads (or no black balls), since the probability of such an event is less than 1 in 1,000.

Further, the probability of either no heads *or* all heads is also very small (less than 2 in 1,000 or 0.19%, which equals 2 × 0.0977%). Thus, while it is possible for such an event to take place, the probability is very small, and it may be said with a high degree of *confidence* that it will *not* happen in a single sample of 10 coins.

[9]For the mathematically trained, the formula is

$$\frac{n!}{r!(n-r)!}p^r q^{n-r}$$

where ! = factorial
r = specified number of head
n = number of coins tossed
p = percent of characteristic in population (½ for heads)
$q = 1 - p$

TABLE 4–8. *Outcome of Tosses of 10 Coins (or Drawings of 10 Balls*)*

Number of heads (or black balls)	*Probability*
0	0.0977%
1	0.977
2	4.395
3	11.719
4	20.508
5	24.609
6	20.508
7	11.719
8	4.395
9	0.977
10	0.0977

* When the population contains 50% black balls.

On the other hand, this statement can be reversed, and it can be said, with a high degree of confidence, 99.8046% [or 100% − (0.0977% + 0.0977%)], that if 10 coins are tossed (or 10 balls drawn), the outcome will be something between 1 and 9 heads (or black balls). Similarly, there is a 97.8506% [or 100% − (0.0977% + 0.0977% + 0.977% + 0.977%)] probability that the outcome will be between 2 and 8 heads (or black balls).

Expressing this a little differently, if a sample of 10 balls is drawn from a large population of balls of which 50% are black, there is a 97.8506% *confidence level* that the sample will reveal a number of black balls between the confidence limits of 2 and 8 balls or 20 to 80% of black balls. It may also be said that the *confidence*

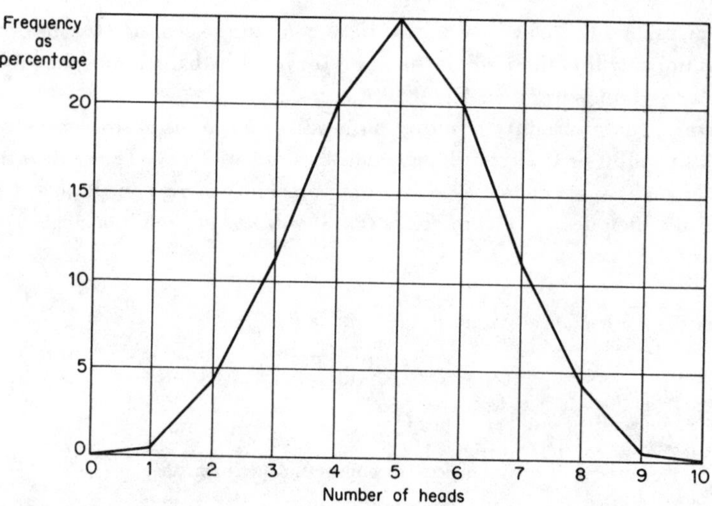

FIGURE 4–7a

interval is 6 (that is, from 2 to 8). Since the spread of these limits on both sides of the expected 50% of black balls is 30% or (50% − 20% and 80% − 50%), the precision of the sample is ±30%. Thus, the result is a sample with a ±30% sampling *precision* and a confidence level of 97.8506%.

To illustrate more practically, assume that an auditor is confronted with a large number of shipment records and that 50% of the shipments required more than a certain number of days to be completed.[10] If the auditor obtains a random sample of 10 of these shipments, he can have a confidence level of 97.8506% that his sample will contain between 20 and 80% of such shipments or that his sampling *precision* will be ±30%.

Conversely, if he should find no such shipments or 1, 9, or 10 in his sample (less than 20% or more than 80%), there is a very high probability that the universe does *not* contain 50% of these late shipments but some other proportion.

This conclusion can be reached since the probability that such a sample would contain no such shipments under these circumstances is so small (0.0977% or less than 1 chance in 1,000) that its occurrence would challenge the assumption that 50% of these shipments were of this type.

Obviously, the wide spread possible within such a limited sample will render it useless. The precision is not good enough. This arises, as will be seen later, from the use of too small a sample.

Of course, the above illustration is not realistic because it assumes that the proportion in the population was known in advance. This is rarely the case. In fact, if it were known, there would be no point to sampling.

However, by inverse reasoning, it is possible, when a sample is at hand containing a given proportion of the studied characteristic, to determine the minimum and maximum proportion that a population would have to contain in order to generate such a sample (with a specified probability), and these values become the sampling limits.

Figure 4-7*b* illustrates the binomial distribution or expected relative frequencies of heads when 1,000 coins are used. It will be noted that this curve is almost identical with that of the normal distribution shown in Figure 4-2. In fact, the normal distribution is a special case of the binomial when n (the number of sampling units—coins or balls—in the example) is equal to infinity.

If the proportion in the population is 50% or fairly close to it or if the sample contains a large number of sampling units, the normal curve is a good approximation of the binomial.

If the standard deviation of the binomial distribution were known, it would then be possible to approach the determination of confidence limits through Table 4-3 (table of t values), which indicates the proportion of the observations that are included within any given number of standard deviations on both sides of the arithmetic mean for a normal distribution.

[10] The reader may think of the shipment records as balls, with half of these balls black to represent the shipments which required more than the indicated number of days.

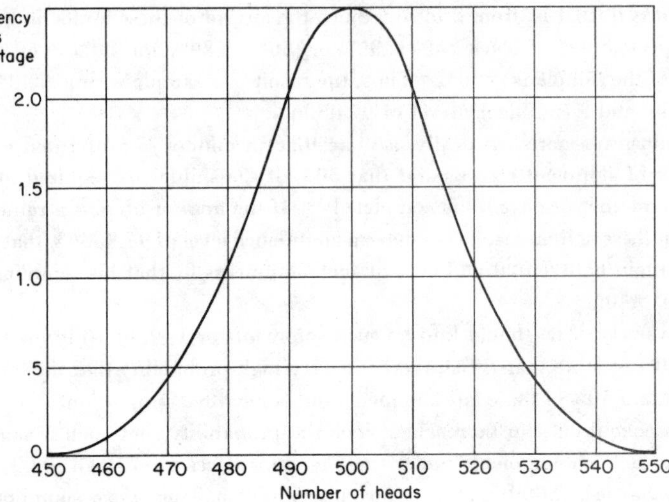

FIGURE 4-7*b*

The standard deviation of the binomial distribution has been derived mathematically and is known to be[11]

$$\sigma_{\%} = \sqrt{\frac{p(1-p)}{n}}$$

where p = proportion of characteristic in population
n = sample size

Thus, for fairly large sample sizes, the sampling distribution of a proportion (all possible occurrences in samples) which occurs in a population containing exactly 50% of a characteristic or close to 50% is normally or approximately normally distributed with the standard deviation given above. The average or expected value will be the overall proportion occurring in the population or

$$\bar{X} = p$$

Given the arithmetic mean and standard deviation of a proportion and the knowledge that this sampling distribution is at least approximately normal, together with the information in Table 4-3, it is now possible to make statements as to the prob-

[11] In absolute form, rather than percentage, the standard deviation of the binomial becomes

$$\sigma = \sqrt{np(1-p)}$$

For proof of these formulas see E. E. Croxton, D. J. Cowden, and S. Klein, eds., *Applied General Statistics,* Prentice-Hall, Inc., Englewood Cliffs, N.J., 1967, app. S25.1.

ability of occurrences of various sample results if the population contains a given proportion of some characteristic.

An illustration of the use of this knowledge is given below. If 100 balls are drawn from a population of balls which are 50% black (representing any given characteristic of the sampling units), this sample will comprise one of the many possible samples of 100 that might be drawn. It is thus one of the samples comprising the sampling distribution.

Since it is now known that all the possible samples of 100 balls that might be drawn constitute a sampling distribution which is the binomial distribution which in turn may be considered at least approximately normal, prior knowledge of the normal distribution may be applied here.

The arithmetic mean of such a distribution has been defined as p. In this situation $p = .50$ or 50% by assumption.

The standard deviation of the sampling distribution may now be computed by

$$\sigma_{\%} = \sqrt{\frac{p(1-p)}{n}}$$

which in this case is

$$\sigma_{\%} = \sqrt{\frac{(.50)(.50)}{100}} = .05 \text{ or } 5\%$$

By referring to Table 4-3 (page 56), it is seen that 99% of the area under the normal curve will be included in a range of the average ± 2.58 standard deviations. Thus, it may be said that there is a 99% probability (confidence level) that this sample will be one of those in the sampling distribution within the range of samples containing between 37.10 and 62.90% of black balls or, since a fraction of a sampling unit is not possible, 38 to 62 black balls, which represents the *confidence limits* [$\overline{X} \pm 2.58\sigma\%$ or $.50 \pm 2.58\,(.05)$]. This gives a sample *precision* $\pm 12.90\%$ [or 2.58 (.05)].

This calculation is an approximation of the results that would have been obtained if the actual probabilities of zero black balls, 1 black ball, 2 black balls, 3 black balls, etc., had been calculated precisely on the basis of the binomial distribution. Thus, this technique makes unnecessary the complex computations involved in solving the binomial distribution, although it does not give precisely the same results.

If the confidence limits had been desired for other confidence levels, other multipliers (t values) from Table 4-3 could have been used as desired to achieve the specified confidence level.

By inverse reasoning, it can be shown that if a random sample of 100 contains 50% black balls, the universe from which it was drawn probably (99% probability) would not have contained less than about 37.1% or more than 62.9% black balls (the measured characteristic).

If the above sample precision is not adequate, the spread of the confidence limits can be reduced by taking a larger sample. This follows from the fact that the sampling precision is obtained from

$$t\sigma_{\%} = t\sqrt{\frac{p(1-p)}{n}}$$

where t is a factor from Table 4-3 (page 56) required for a given confidence level, as for instance 2.58 for a 99% confidence level. It is evident that the larger the value of the divisor n, the smaller the sampling error will be.

The solution to the question of the size of the sample required to accomplish this end can be obtained by the inverse solution of the formula which gave rise to the sampling limits.

$$\bar{X} \pm 2.58\sigma$$

or

$$p \pm 2.58\sigma_{\%}$$

Thus, assume it is desired, in sampling from this large universe of balls containing 50% black balls, to have a 99% probability (confidence level) that the sample would contain between 45 and 55% black balls (sample reliability or precision of ±5%).

The solution is

$$\text{Confidence limits} = p \pm 2.58\sigma_{\%}$$

or

$$\text{Sample precision} = 2.58\sigma_{\%} = \pm 5\%$$

Therefore

$$.05 = 2.58\sqrt{\frac{(.5)(.5)}{n}}$$

and

$$n = 666$$

However, the solution of these formulas will not be required of the auditor since tables will be given which will make possible the determination of the sample size required to achieve a given sample precision at various confidence levels for attributes sampling *without calculations.*

Another set of tables will provide the confidence limits at selected confidence levels for samples containing various proportions of an attribute, again without calculation. Nevertheless, full use of these tables will be achieved only when the auditor has an adequate understanding of the principles outlined above.

A note of caution may be inserted here. In the examples above two assumptions have been made repeatedly, namely, that the universe contained 50% of the characteristic studied (50% heads or 50% black balls) and that the universe was very large. If the universe does not contain 50% of the characteristic, two different effects will be felt. The first of these arises out of the impact of this departure from 50% on the standard deviation (or more properly the *standard error*) of the sampling distribution of percentages.

Since the formula for the standard error is

$$\sigma_{\%} = \sqrt{\frac{p(1-p)}{n}}$$

it is possible to analyze the effect of various proportions p on the standard error $\sigma_{\%}$ at a fixed sample size. This is shown in Table 4-9 for various values of p, assuming a sample size of 100.

TABLE 4–9

Value of p	$p(1-p)$	$\sigma_{\%} = \sqrt{\frac{p(1-p)}{n}}$ (where $n = 100$)	Sample precision at 99% confidence level ($2.58\sigma_{\%}$)
.10	.09	.030	± 7.74%
.20	.16	.040	±10.32
.30	.21	.046	±11.87
.40	.24	.049	±12.64
.50	.25	.050	±12.90
.60	.24	.049	±12.64
.70	.21	.046	±11.87
.80	.16	.040	±10.32
.90	.09	.030	± 7.74

It is to be emphasized that the p value listed in Table 4-9 is the p of the *population.*

From Table 4-9, it may be seen that the greater the departure of p from 50% (in either direction), the better the sample precision (smaller the sampling error) for a sample of a given size and at a given confidence level. Conversely, the sample size required to achieve a given reliability at a specified confidence level will become smaller as p departs from 50%. The effect of this fact on establishing required sample sizes will be studied in detail in the next chapter.

The second effect of the departure of the population p from 50% is felt most severely when the sample size is small. In such an instance, the binomial or sampling distribution becomes skewed (right skewed for values of p of less than 50% and left skewed for values of p over 50%—see Figures 4-5*a* and 4-5*b*).

As was previously observed, the table used in establishing the confidence limits (see Table 4-3) applies exactly only to normal distributions. Thus, the confidence limits established in this way become more and more approximate as p departs from 50% and n grows smaller (np grows smaller). The method for handling this situation will be examined in detail in a later chapter.

Finally, when the second assumption of a very large (actually infinite) population is violated, a further effect is felt. It is apparent that a sample of 100 out of a population of 101 will give a better sample reliability than a sample of 100 out of a population of one million. However, the relationship is not simple. It can be shown mathematically that the reduction in the sample reliability percentage will be equivalent to multiplying that sample reliability by the following finite population correction factor:[12]

$$\sqrt{\frac{N-n}{N-1}} \quad \text{or approximately} \quad \sqrt{1-\frac{n}{N}}$$

where N = population size
n = sample size

The impact of this factor may be illustrated by the example used before in which a sample of 100 was drawn from a very large population of balls containing 50% black balls. It was found that the sampling precision was ±12.9% at the 99% confidence level. Table 4-10 illustrates the effect of the finite correction factor.

Table 4-10 indicates that the precision of a sample of 100 will give a reliability that is virtually the same when drawn from a field (universe) of 10,000 as it will when drawn from a field containing a million sampling units.

This explodes the often believed intuitive feeling that a fixed proportion of the field (say 5 to 10%) will be required to give identical sample precision. This belief is simply not true.

TABLE 4–10

Population or field size	n (sample size)	Finite correction factor	Sample precision (n = 100; p = .50) at 99% confidence level
500	100	.8953	±11.55%
1,000	100	.9492	±12.24
2,000	100	.9749	±12.58
5,000	100	.9901	±12.77
10,000	100	.9950	±12.84
100,000	100	.9995	±12.89
1,000,000	100	.99995	±12.8993
Infinity....	100	1.000	±12.900

In summary, in sampling for attributes, the sample (of a given size) drawn will be one of those contained within the sampling distribution, and there is a given probability (confidence level) that the sample will be contained within a range

[12]The complete formula for the reliability of a proportion from a sample from a finite population then becomes

$$SE = \pm t\sqrt{\frac{p(1-p)}{n}}\sqrt{1-\frac{n}{N}}$$

(confidence limits) defined by the arithmetic mean of the population p plus and minus a given factor (determined by the confidence level—Table 4-3) times the standard deviation (standard error) of the sampling distribution, where that standard error is adjusted by the finite correction factor where necessary.

VARIABLES SAMPLING

In variables sampling, the selected sampling units are measured or evaluated (in terms of dollars, pounds, days, etc.), and some statistical measure (statistic) is computed from these measurements to estimate the universe parameter.

The measure most frequently used by the auditor for this purpose is the arithmetic mean. It will be recalled that the total of a group of values can be obtained by multiplying the arithmetic mean by the number of items. The arithmetic mean of a sample may be multiplied by the number of items N in the *universe* to give an estimate of the universe total.

Once again the approach to evaluating the reliability of a sample mean or average is through study of the behavior of all possible sample results or the sampling distribution of the arithmetic mean.

Assume that a large universe consists of slips of paper on which there are written a wide variety of values (say account balances). A random sample of specified size n is drawn, and the arithmetic mean of the values on the slips selected for the sample is obtained. This process of drawing the sample and computing the arithmetic mean is repeated a very great number of times (say a billion). The resulting arithmetic means are arranged in a frequency distribution. This will be the sampling distribution of the arithmetic mean.

Of course, in an ordinary situation only one sample will be drawn, but that sample will be one of the great many (actually infinite number) contained in the sampling distribution. Alternatively, the same result could have been obtained by determining every possible combination of values for sample size n and by obtaining the average for each combination.

If the universe from which the sample was drawn was "normally" distributed, the sampling distribution of the mean will constitute a normal distribution also. However, if the universe from which the sample was drawn was not normal (for instance, if it was skewed), the sampling distribution of the means will nevertheless approach the normal form as the sample size is increased.

Except for the most extremely skewed universes, the sampling distribution of the mean may then be accepted as being of the normal form or close to it for samples of the size usually used in auditing and for purposes of computation of sample reliability.

However, some accounting data will be extremely skewed, and special methods must be used. This problem and methods for coping with it will be discussed in detail later.

If the sampling distribution of the arithmetic mean of samples drawn by random methods is of the normal form, the sample under consideration is one of the numerous possible samples of the given size that might be drawn from that population, and its arithmetic mean will be contained in this normal sampling distribution.

In previous discussions, it has been shown that if the standard deviation of a normal distribution is known, a great deal can be said about how the observations are distributed about the mean of that distribution (see Table 4-3).

The formula for the standard deviation of the sampling distribution of arithmetic means (standard error of the mean) has been developed mathematically. It is[13]

$$\sigma_{\bar{X}} = \frac{\sigma}{\sqrt{n}}$$

where $\sigma_{\bar{X}}$ = standard deviation of sampling distribution of means or standard error of the mean

σ = standard deviation of universe from which sample was drawn

n = sample size (number of sampling units in sample)

Assume, for instance, that a sample of 100 observations is drawn from a very large normal or near normal universe of which the arithmetic mean is \$200.00 and the standard deviation is \$50.00. The standard deviation of the arithmetic means of all possible samples of 100 that might be drawn from that universe may then be computed as follows:

$$\sigma_{\bar{X}} = \frac{\sigma}{\sqrt{n}} = \frac{\$50.00}{\sqrt{100}} = \$5$$

The resulting sampling distribution may then be seen in Figure 4-8.

It is to be recalled that the single sample of 100 under examination is one of the many possible samples which might be drawn and is one of those comprising the sampling distribution.

By referring to Table 4-3 (page 56), it is seen that there is a 95% probability that if one observation from among those comprising a normal distribution is drawn at random, it will fall within 1.96σ on either side of the arithmetic mean of that distribution. Thus, there is a 95% probability that the sample being studied will be within $1.96\sigma_{\bar{X}}$ or \$9.80 of the mean of the sampling distribution.

It can be shown that the average of the sampling distribution of the mean (average of all possible averages) will be equal to the arithmetic mean of the universe.

It may be then said that if a sample of 100 is drawn by random methods from this large universe of values, with a mean of \$200.00 and a standard deviation of \$50.00, there is a 95% probability (confidence level) that the mean of that sample will be between \$190.20 and \$209.80 (confidence limits). The sample mean will not depart from the universe mean by more than ±\$9.80 (sample precision) at the 95% confidence level.

[13] See Technical Appendix II for proof.

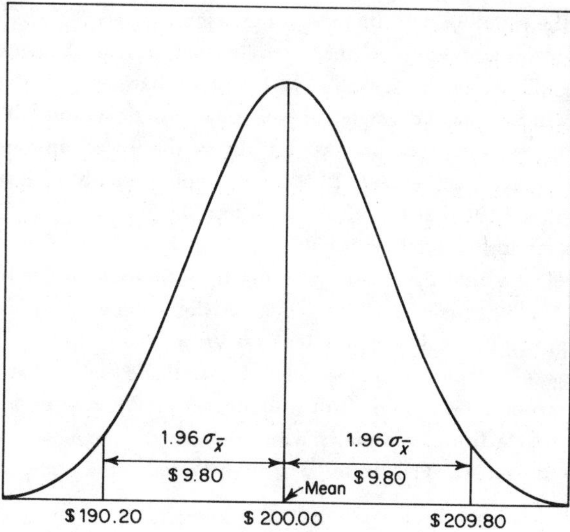

FIGURE 4–8

It is observed that this sample precision is dependent solely upon the standard deviation of the universe and the sample size and is independent of the universe average. Thus the sample precision estimate may be made even when the population mean is unknown, as is usually the case.

In the above example, then, there is a 95% probability that the sample mean will fall within ±$9.80 of the true population mean which might be obtained by 100% enumeration of all observations in the universe. Similarly (using Table 4-3), at the 99% confidence level, the precision of the sample mean will be ±$12.90 (or $2.58\sigma_{\bar{X}}$).

An examination of the formula for the standard error of the mean, through which the sample precision is established, discloses some interesting points. A knowledge of standard deviation of the *population* is necessary for its solution. Since this is commonly unknown, the standard deviation of the *sample* is used as an estimate of the population standard deviation for this purpose. The relative stability of the standard deviation computed from a sample, for samples of a reasonable size, makes this possible without too severe a disturbance to the calculation. Methods of arriving at the standard deviation without complex calculations are discussed in a later chapter.

Since the sample precision of the arithmetic mean of a sample is obtained by multiplying its standard error by a factor t (such as $1.96\sigma_{\bar{X}}$ or $1.96\sigma/\sqrt{n}$), it is apparent that this sampling variability will increase as the standard deviation (variability) of the universe increases.

Further, as the sample size n increases, the sampling spread is reduced, since n is a divisor. However, because of the square root radical in the divisor, doubling the sample size will not cut the sampling variability in half.

For instance, in the above example (universe standard deviation $50.00 and sample size 100), the sample precision was ±$9.80 at the 95% confidence level. If the sample size is doubled (becomes 200), the sample reliability becomes ±$6.94 [or $1.96(\$50.00/\sqrt{200})$] at the 95% confidence level.

To cut the sampling variability in half to 4.90 (or 50% of $9.80) at the 95% confidence level, it would be necessary to multiply the sample size by 4 (or n = 400), since $2\sqrt{100}$ equals $\sqrt{400}$. Thus, as the sample size is increased, the decrease in sampling variability is at a decreased rate.

As in the case of attributes, the assumption was made above that the sampling drawings were from a very large (infinite) universe. A correction is necessary when the universe is finite, especially when the sample comprises an appreciable portion of that universe. The finite correction factor is the same as that used in attributes sampling,

$$\sqrt{\frac{N-n}{N-1}} \quad \text{or approximately} \quad \sqrt{1-\frac{n}{N}}$$

and is used as a multiplier for the standard error of the mean.

GENERAL

It is noted that the actual solution of the formulas given for both attributes and variables will be unnecessary, since the answers will be found in extensive tables in later sections of this book. Nevertheless, the most effective use of these tables will be attained only if there is adequate understanding of the formulas and other concepts outlined in this chapter.

FIVE

Determining Sample Size

(Estimation Sampling)

SELECTION OF SAMPLE SIZE

After establishing the objective of the audit test, defining the universe (field), and determining the sampling unit, the auditor is confronted with the basic problem of fixing the size of the sample necessary to accomplish the test objective.

While three basic sampling techniques are available to the auditor in performing his tests (see Chapter 1), including estimation sampling, acceptance sampling, and discovery sampling, the most widely used method, and generally the most useful to the auditor in his tests, is estimation sampling.[1] This chapter is devoted to the problem of sample size determination in estimation sampling for both attributes and variables involving unrestricted random sampling.[2] The problems of sample size determination when discovery sampling or acceptance sampling is appropriate will be discussed in detail in later chapters.

Statistical techniques provide the method by which the appropriate sample size can be estimated by using the proper statistical formulas or even more simply by resorting to statistical tables such as those included in this book. However, the process of determining sample size is not a mechanical operation. It requires considerable thought and judgment on the part of the auditor.

[1]"Of the available statistical techniques, 'statistical estimation' rather than 'acceptance sampling' has received the most favorable attention from accountants and auditors." R. G. Brown, "Statistical Sampling Tables for Auditors," *The Journal of Accountancy*, May 1961, p. 46.

[2]Unrestricted random sampling applies to sampling individual items from the entire field without any restrictions.

As will be shown later, these methods provide only an approximation of the required sample size which may actually, if desired, be omitted in its entirety. For instance, the test size may be dictated by the availability of audit time or funds. However, if the sample size resulting from such an arbitrary method is not adequate to the test objective, the purpose of the test may be completely defeated. It is better not to test at all than to be misled by the results of an inadequate test. On the other hand, determination of test size on the basis of audit time available may result in appreciable overtesting and resultant waste if advance sample size determination would call for a smaller statistical sample.

Since methods are provided later for evaluating sample results, the auditor may, at his own risk, ship this method of sample size determination and hope for the best with an arbitrarily selected sample size. He will be proved later to be right or wrong.

With the test objective specifically known, the auditor must make certain decisions in order to establish the proper sample size. The first of these is to decide how closely (or with what sampling precision) it is necessary to estimate the characteristic to be tested (such as the percentage of certain types of errors, system failures, or certain dollar or other values). The second decision relates to the probability or assurance (confidence level) that the sample will actually fall within the required distance (sampling error) from the true or universe value.

It is apparent that some risk of being wrong is involved in using the sample value (statistic) from any sample, no matter how large, to estimate the population value (parameter). However, the auditor can limit this risk to any desired level by resorting to appropriate statistical techniques which will indicate a sample size necessary to accomplish his ends.

The mere fact that a sample size was chosen by resorting to a statistical formula or table, however, *is not in itself* a justification for the use of that sample size. When the decisions outlined above as to confidence level and sampling precision have been made, the sample size then proceeds automatically from the formula or table. It is these decisions which must be justifiable, and here the statistical formulas or tables provide no defense. The auditor will find that the resolution of these decisions (as to sample precision and confidence level) is not a simple matter. Actually such decisions cannot be reached casually. Thus, those who feel that the use of statistical techniques eliminates or reduces the exercise of the auditor's judgment in the design of tests will find to their surprise that a new and higher order of judgment is required.

Where statistical techniques have not been used previously, sample sizes for test purposes generally have been established by various means. Analysis of past practices discloses that often the determination of the sample size is fixed on the basis of "cost of audit," traditional usage, some fixed percentage of the field, or even the whim of the auditor, all too often without sufficient consideration of the impact of the sample size selected.

Perhaps the most frequently cited reason for the use of a given sample size, particularly a small one, other than the fact that it has been used before, is the cost of

"A SAMPLE SIZE OF 50 IS USELESS UNLESS THE ERROR RATE IN THE UNIVERSE IS CATASTROPHIC"

the audit test. While undoubtedly cost is a vital consideration confronting the auditor who has a test to perform, it should not be an overriding consideration. After all, the lowest cost is attained by not performing the test at all!

Each test has an objective. If the objective is to be met satisfactorily, a certain sample size is required. If a sample size sufficient to meet the test objective is not used, the test is not adequate. There is little point in performing a test with an inadequate sample size merely to perform "lip service" to the test objectives. From the point of view of tenable conclusions, it is a waste of time and money.

Instances of auditors' tests with sample sizes of 50 or less are not unusual, even though the test objective may be to determine whether or not there is an unduly high error rate existent in the records tested. With a sample size this small, the error rate in the field would have to be catastrophic, or the auditor unusually lucky, to disclose a situation which is bad.

The unfortunate truth is that an inadequate sample may well not disclose a bad situation, but by the mere fact of failing to find such a situation, will tend to instill confidence on the part of the auditor in the validity of the records. Thus the test, because of limited sample size, may provide misleading results. Again, *it would be far better to conduct no test at all than one with an inadequate sample size resulting in misleading conclusions.*

Of course, in considering the question of the sample size to be used in a test, it must be remembered that ordinarily the test is not the total of the auditor's examination. He will ordinarily consider the entire system, evaluating the effectiveness of the internal controls and the quality of the supervision and personnel involved, and will apply other tests and analysis as well. In other words, a single test is part of the fabric of the examination and does not stand alone. To this extent the auditor's test differs from the usual sampling operation, which requires the whole decision or evaluation to be made on the basis of a single sample.

On the other hand, it cannot be construed that since this test is only one of several tests, its validity can be neglected. Such an approach might result in a series of tests, none of which is valid or adequate, but all of which are justified on the basis of the others.

A further word of caution must be entered here. That a good internal control system exists, together with other evidence, such as good supervision, *in itself* is not a justification for inadequate compliance testing.

This point is to be made in spite of the statement in *Statements on Auditing Standards, Codification of Auditing Standards and Procedures,* no. 1 (AICPA, 1973), that "there is to be a proper study and evaluation of existing internal control as a basis for reliance thereon and for the determination of the resultant extent of the tests to which auditing procedures are to be restricted." If this is interpreted to mean that the extent and magnitude of the tests of compliance with internal controls are established by this evaluation, a circular argument results. It is the very purpose of the test to establish the effectiveness of the internal control in operation and thus the dependability of the resulting financial data.

It is the evident intent that the extent of the testing referred to above applies to substantive tests and not tests of compliance.

In spite of all good evidence, the auditor must still perform adequate tests. No matter how good the internal control system, there is no automatic protection against failure to comply with its regulations. No matter how apparently good the supervision nor how high the quality of the personnel involved, there is no guarantee against error, either accidental or deliberate. Only a test or series of tests can objectively develop the facts concerning the adequacy of the execution of the record keeping.

Nevertheless, it will be seen later that the auditor's other appraisals do have an impact upon making the decisions which result in sample size determination.

A test to establish that the internal control system is effectively in operation is often referred to as a *test of compliance* with internal controls, or more loosely as a *test of transactions.*

SAMPLE PRECISION

As noted before, the first required decision relates to the necessary sample precision. How close is it necessary for the auditor to estimate the population parameter? In other words, if the test objective is to determine the *rate* of existence of error in some type of records, how closely or how exactly does this value have to be known to accomplish the test objectives?

As an illustration, is it sufficient to know that the error rate is somewhere between 4 and 8% (sample precision of ±2%), or must it be known that it is between 5.5 and 6.5% (sample precision of ±5%)? Obviously, a test that results in the conclusion that the error rate is somewhere between 1 and 15% will, in most instances, be of no value to the auditor when he has fixed upon an error rate of 10% as intolerable. The spread of possibilities includes both the good and bad.

The acceptable sampling precision must then be sufficiently small to distinguish the bad from the good, except perhaps in the marginal cases, where further testing will be required, when no resolution is provided by the test results.

This situation obviously indicates that no automatic rule is, or could be, available to provide the auditor with an indication of a required sampling precision. The auditor must carefully consider the objectives of his tests and the question of a tolerable level of error rate.

Obviously, it is not desired to tolerate any errors, but humans are fallible. If the errors provide no evidence of deliberate fraud, management must be content to live with some low rate of errors, unless they are willing to spend very large sums of money to eliminate them. Further, no matter how much is spent in time and money, in any really large-scale operation, the complete elimination of error can only be a target and not an accomplishment.

Thus, the auditor, while professionally required to reject the occurrence of any errors as unacceptable, nevertheless must be prepared to recognize that the existence of such errors (if they provide no evidence of fraud) at a very low level is the best that may be achieved.

The auditor generally has some idea as to a level of error rate which would be considered intolerable. This level will vary with the character and importance of a given type of error.

It must be recognized that some errors are virtually certain to occur in any extensive set of records. The auditor then expects to encounter some errors in his tests and examinations. It is only when the rate of errors is excessive that he will be concerned.

It is not likely that the auditor has a very precise figure in mind when he undertakes the test. He has only a general idea which may indicate various levels of tolerable error rates.

While any errors will be of concern, if the errors are of a minor nature, do not involve large sums of money, do not provide evidence of extensive evasions of the internal control system, and are inadvertent, he will not be concerned severely with an error rate which might well be considered catastrophic if they involved large sums of money, were deliberate, or indicated evasion of internal controls.

Actually evidence produced by statistical sampling tests indicates relatively high error rates in some areas. For instance, error rates in inventory balances in perpetual inventory systems ranging from 15 to 25% have been encountered in commercial and governmental installations.

On the other hand, in some situations an error rate of as low as 1% might be considered intolerable because of their character or importance.

In using estimation sampling, however, the auditor is not required to fix on a particular specific value for his tolerable error rate (say 2.3%), but may establish only generally the area within which the tolerable error rate may fall. This general level of errors may be referred to as the *maximum tolerable error rate (MTER)*.[3] Perhaps it may be described best as an area or zone rather than a specific value. Thus no auditor would be prepared to state that, while an error rate of 4.7% or more indicates a situation requiring further action, an error rate of 4.6% indicates a satisfactory condition.

The maximum tolerable error rate may be construed as a level of errors which, if it were known to exist, would require some action on the part of the auditor, since it indicates a breakdown in the internal control system or some other situation requiring that suitable steps be taken. His sampling precision must then be sufficient to enable him to distinguish the tolerable from the intolerable situation in all but the marginal instances. Of course, if the sample reliability is not sufficiently confined, all cases but the very extreme will become marginal, and the test will be useless.

On the other hand, if an attempt is made to reduce the sampling error to an unnecessarily low value, the size of the sample will be sharply increased, and the

[3]Sometimes referred to as the *maximum allowable occurrence rate.*

cost of the audit may become prohibitive. Judgment must be exercised to establish a required sample precision which will not create unnecessary test costs by oversampling nor result in sample sizes such that the broad sampling variability permissible results in indecision in most tests and therefore in their extension, again with high costs.

Obviously, a sampling precision requirement of $\pm.01\%$, or say confidence limits which may be 2.99 to 3.01%, in an audit test represents carrying a good thing too far and at considerable cost. On the other hand, knowledge that the test indicates an error rate of somewhere between 2 and 16% will be of little value. The auditor might well be satisfied to know that the error rate is between 1 and 3%, with a resulting much smaller sample size requirement.

Of course, if in fact the situation is very bad (for instance, an error rate in the vicinity of 25%), the auditor does not require that the actual rate of error be established very precisely. It is sufficient to know that the rate is very high, or between 20 and 30%. Similarly, if the situation is very good (say 1% of error), he does not have to establish the value very precisely either. But here it must be established with sufficient precision to demonstrate that the situation is, in fact, good.

Nevertheless, in marginal situations, close sample precision may be required to separate the good from the bad. Of course, it may be objected that it is not known in advance whether the situation is marginal. In answer to this contention, it is to be noted that it is common practice for auditors, when in doubt, to extend their tests. A statistically designed test may be extended, too, and without difficulty, if initial or partial sample results indicate a marginal situation.

In estimation sampling of variables, a similar situation arises. For instance, it may be desired to estimate the total dollar value of a group of records or of an inventory. The same question must be answered here but in different terms; i.e., how closely is it necessary to estimate the unknown dollar value? Again, the answer is that it must be estimated with sufficient precision to establish that the departure of the value shown on the record from the estimation of the true value is not sufficiently great as to be intolerable.

In general it may be stated that to be useful, the projection from a sample result should have an innocuous sampling error, or in other words, a sampling error sufficiently small that it will not interfere with the test objective. Since such limitations of sampling errors can be purchased only with adequate sample sizes and since sample size here represents audit time, care must be exercised not to provide any greater degree of sample precision than is actually required for the test objective.

THE CONFIDENCE LEVEL

However, even after the sampling precision has been fixed, a second decision must be reached. No absolute guarantee can be provided that the value obtained from the test sample will in fact depart from the true value (population parameter) by no more than the amount of the sample precision. The achievement of this sample precision can be expressed only in terms of probability (confidence level).

The auditor is then confronted with the need for an additional decision as to the probability that the sampling variability will indeed be confined to the promised range. This probability must be sufficiently high to be reasonable. While in most sampling work, levels of probability of 95 or 99% or even higher are used, the actual establishment of an acceptable probability level (confidence level) is the responsibility of the sampler.

While a departure greater than the promised sample reliability may be encountered because a lower level of probability is used (say 95%), this does not mean that there is any appreciable probability of a *much* greater departure, provided the selected confidence level is reasonably high. For instance, a sample size of 350 drawn from a field of 4,000 records where the actual but unknown rate in the population is 10% gives a sampling reliability of ±3% at the 95% confidence level. However, it can be calculated that there is a 99% probability that the estimate will fall not farther away than a little less than ±4% from the true value, and a 99.9% probability that it will be within ±5%. Thus, when a reasonably high probability is used for a confidence level in the first place, even if the improbable does occur and an unusual sample develops with more than the anticipated departure from the true value, the departure will most likely be confined to one not too much greater than that anticipated.

It should be emphasized here, to prevent any misunderstanding, that in these discussions when a sampling precision is expressed as say ±2%, this is meant in absolute terms. For instance, if the true population value is 8%, this would indicate that a sample value would be expected to be within the range of 6 to 10% (8% ± 2%) and *not* 8% ± (2% of 8%) or 8% ± .16%. All tables in this volume refer to precision in this absolute rather than a relative sense.

As will be explained later, the actual sample precision achieved at a given confidence level is a function of the unknown characteristics of the field or universe being sampled. Since these characteristics are unknown (or else sampling would be unnecessary), certain assumptions must be made which automatically result in rendering the determination of required sample size an *approximation.*

The actual sampling precision *achieved* can be established only after the sample is at hand. This sample precision can be better or worse than that anticipated. However, if the proper approach is used, it will be as good as, or better than, that desired except in the most unusual samples, as will be seen later. Nevertheless, it is essential, after the sample has been secured and the sample result computed, that the result be appraised to determine its actual sample precision. The method of accomplishing this end will be discussed in later chapters.

The sample size required to achieve the test objective then becomes a function of *both* the required sampling precision and the desired confidence level. This point will be discussed more fully later. However, it can be stated that it is desirable to establish the confidence level first and *not* to change that decision later, after the required sample size is known.

A 95% confidence level can be interpreted to mean that if the same test sampling were performed repeatedly from the same population, 5 times in 100 or 1 in 20 tests would result in a greater deviation than anticipated of the sample value from the result which would be obtained by a complete examination of all sampling units. However, as discussed previously, the deviation which might result should *not* be expected to be of indefinite magnitude. Most likely it will be not too much greater in magnitude than anticipated.

To emphasize this point, another example may be taken. Assume that a sample of 200 is drawn from a field of 15,000 sampling units where the actual but unknown rate of error is 5%. The expected sampling precision at the 95% confidence level is ±3%. However, there are 99 chances in 100 (confidence level) that the sampling precision will be slightly less than ±4%.

The auditor must decide the risk he is willing to run that his sampling variability will be somewhat greater than he wishes it to be. This risk decision results in the selection of a confidence level.

As will be seen later, the higher the confidence level (lower the risk), the larger the sample that will be required. This is another way of saying that to reduce the risk of being wrong, the sample size must be larger. Since no absolute guarantee of adherence to the promised sampling reliability is possible, the auditor must weigh the risk in the light of the situation confronting him.

Unfortunately, there is no fixed and simple rule available to establish the proper confidence level. The auditor must consider the possible impact of a possible greater deviation from the true value than he desires. Of course, this risk can be reduced to any low level desired, but the penalty is a large sample size. On the other hand, a small sample size will result from the acceptance of a greater risk, but the penalty is the possibility of a greater sampling error than that desired.

The auditor must pay for the protection he desires. However, there are limits. No risk at all requires a 100% sample at great cost. An excessive risk renders the result meaningless. For instance, if a 50% confidence level were accepted, there would be a 50-50 chance that the sampling error would be greater than that hoped for and that the sampling variability to be anticipated at the 99% confidence level would be 3.7 times as great for the same size sample (when the field size is very large).

Several considerations may enter into making the decision as to the confidence level. If the desired sample reliability is "tight" or closer than that absolutely necessary, a greater risk (in terms of a lower confidence level) may be accepted. Conversely, if the sampling precision is established loosely, the auditor cannot afford a considerable risk.

Here, too, the auditor's other findings may enter the picture. If, from other examination and tests performed as part of the same audit, he has a high degree of confidence that all is well but nevertheless wishes to test, he may be willing to run a greater risk.

The final decision as to an acceptable confidence level rests with the auditor, and the auditor alone. However, this decision is not to be reached casually or arbitrarily.

The requirement for the exercise of the auditor's judgment in this manner may lead some to feel that the scientific approach has been obviated. However, it may be observed that when this decision is reached, the probability that a sample will fall within the specified range from the true value is fixed and applies to all samplers and all situations. It is defensible objectively, and the only possible question that might be raised is whether the auditor took too large a risk, if found to be wrong, or on the other hand, whether he was too careful and ran up unnecessary audit costs.

After these general comments on the question of establishing the required confidence level and sampling precision, consideration may be given to the actual determination of sample size. This technique is discussed in the next section of this chapter, first for attributes sampling and then for variables sampling.

ATTRIBUTES SAMPLING—SAMPLE SIZE

Concepts

In Chapter 4, it was shown that if a sample of a given size is drawn from a field or population of sampling units which includes some specified proportion of a certain characteristic, then the probability that the sample will contain any specified proportion of this characteristic can be calculated.

For instance, it was indicated that if a sample of 2 balls is drawn from a very large number of balls, 50% of which are black, the probability that no (.0%) black balls will be contained in the sample is 25% (or ¼). Similarly, the probability that both (100%) of the balls in the sample would be black is 25% (or ¼). For a drawing of a sample of 3 balls, the probability that none would be black was 12.5% (or ⅛), while for a sample of 10 balls the probability of no black balls in the sample is .0977% of (1/1,024).

It became apparent that certain sample results (such as zero black balls in a sample of 10 when drawn from the above population) were most improbable. Conversely, it was possible to establish the most probable sample results and a range of sample results which would include the bulk of the possible samples. Since it is quite unlikely that any sample drawn from such a population would fall outside of that range, it could be said with a specified degree of confidence (probability) that a sample drawn at random would fall within that range or not further away from the population proportion than one-half that range of sample results.

Thus, it could be said that there was a given probability, which was calculable, that any sample result for a random sample drawn from a field containing a given proportion of a certain characteristic would deviate from the population proportion by not more than a certain amount for a specified sample size.

Recall that the possible distribution of sample results (sampling distribution of a proportion) was the binomial distribution. Remember that the binomial distribution approached the normal distribution as the sample size was increased, so that for appreciable sample sizes the normal curve was a good approximation of the binomial.

While the sampling distribution of a proportion is properly described as a binomial distribution for a very large field, the computation of the terms of this distribution which would be required to establish the confidence limits would be extremely arduous. However, since the normal distribution is an approximation of the binomial, the values for the confidence limit are established by assuming that the sampling distribution is normal. The resulting confidence limits are often referred to as the *normal approximation limits* as contrasted with the exact binomial limits.

Since the proportion of the observations contained within any given distance from the arithmetic mean (in terms of the standard deviation, see Table 4-3) is known for normal distributions and since the standard deviation of the binomial distribution (in per cent) is known to be[4]

$$\sigma_{\%} = \sqrt{\frac{p(1-p)}{n}}$$

the probability that a sample proportion would occur within any given distance from the population proportion can be determined.

Thus, the sampling precision of a proportion, when the population size is very large, can be stated as

$$\text{Sampling precision of a proportion} = \pm t\sqrt{\frac{p(1-p)}{n}}$$

where t = number of standard deviations which could include a proportion of the sample results equivalent to confidence level when measured on both sides of population proportion (see Table 4-3)

p = proportion in population

n = sample size

For a sample of 200 observations, randomly obtained from a universe containing a very great number of such units, where 40% actually fall in a specified category, it may be said that there is a 99% probability (confidence level) that the sample reliability (maximum expected departure of the proportion in the sample from the population proportion 40%) is

$$\text{Sample precision} = \pm 2.58\sqrt{\frac{.40(.60)}{200}}$$

$$= \pm .089 \text{ or } \pm 8.9\%$$

It is evident that as n (the sample size) is increased, the sampling variability is reduced. Then, at a given confidence level (which supplies the t factor), it is possible by varying the sample size to fix the sampling precision at any desired value or to ensure with the specified confidence level that the sample proportion will not depart from the population proportion by more than the specified sample precision.

[4] See p. 66, Chap. 4.

By the inverse solution of the above formula,[5] when a desired sample precision is indicated and a confidence level is specified, the value of n necessary to meet these requirements is established. For instance, assume that a sample is to be drawn from a very large population in which 40 per cent of its sampling units have some specified characteristic. It is desired to obtain a sample which will have a sample precision of ±7% at a 99% confidence level. Substituting in the above formula,

$$\pm .07 = 2.58 \sqrt{\frac{(.40)(.60)}{n}}$$

$$n = 326$$

It is interesting that because of the square root (radical) in the above calculation, the reduction in sampling variability is *not* in direct proportion to the increase in sample size. For instance, doubling the sample size does *not* halve the sampling variability. As an illustration, in the above example cited for the sample size of 200 from a very large population containing 40% of the sampling units with a specified characteristic, at the 99% confidence level the precision was found to be ±8.9%. If, in the same situation, the sample size is increased to 400, at the same confidence level, the sample precision becomes ±6.3%.

It is observed that in the example given, it was assumed that the field or population was very large. If the sample constitutes an appreciable portion of the field (more than 1% as a rule of thumb), the formula to be used is

$$SE_{\%} = \pm t \sqrt{\frac{p(1-p)}{n}} \sqrt{1 - \frac{n}{N}}$$

and although it is still possible to find n by inverse solution,[6] it is somewhat more arduous.

It is also noted that the above sampling precision for a given sample size and con-

---

[5] The inverse form of this formula is

$$n = \frac{p(1-p)}{(SE/t)^2}$$

where SE = desired sample precision
p = per cent of occurrence in field
t = confidence level factor (see p. 56)
n = sample size

[6] The inverse form of this formula is

$$n = \frac{p(1-p)}{(SE/t)^2 + p(1-p)/N}$$

where SE = *desired* sample precision
N = field size
p = per cent of occurrence in population
t = confidence level factor (see p. 56)

fidence level is dependent on the value of p or the proportion of the characteristic in the population. Of course, this proportion in the population is ordinarily not known, or the sampling would not be required. However, certain principles discussed in Chapter 4 will permit the solution of this dilemma. It will be noted that in the above calculations, the sample variability for a given sample size reaches a maximum when $p = .50$ (see page 69, Chapter 4).

Thus, one possible solution would be to solve the above formula, using $p = .50$. This would always result in a conservative statement of sample reliability. Conversely, the solution of the formula to determine the sample size required to achieve a specified sample precision would always give the largest sample necessary to achieve the objective. If p is actually some value other than .50 (or 50%), the sample size would then result in a better precision than that specified. The sample would be unnecessarily large and wasteful whenever p was not .50, since it would be more than enough to achieve the desired precision.

To approach the problem properly, an assumption to establish the value of p is necessary for a more efficient estimate of the required sample size and a reduction in the magnitude of any oversampling that might result.

However, the impact of the assumption must be examined. When confronted by a need to estimate the sample size required to provide a specified sample precision at a stated confidence level, the auditor will estimate the highest proportion he considers probable that he will encounter in the population in a bad situation. This selected rate of occurrence should be higher than the rate actually anticipated but should not be beyond the range of possibility in a reasonably bad situation.

Thus, for instance, if an auditor wishes to test for errors in a set of records by means of a sample, he can be reasonably certain that the actual rate of error is less than 50%. It may be that for these records a rate of error of 10% would be unexpectedly high, but possible, and would indicate a bad situation. He would then use this maximum value (.10 or 10%) for p and solve the formula for n. Actually, tables have been prepared to eliminate the need for such calculations and are included as an appendix to this book.

In another situation with a different type of error or violation, a rate of 2% might be considered excessive. In this case p may be made equal to 2%. In other words, if p is made equivalent to some rate of occurrence which is considered the maximum likely to be encountered, a conservative estimate of sample size will result which may be slightly larger than necessary but will most likely not be underestimated. This level of occurrence, used for this purpose, will be referred to as the *maximum expected rate of occurrence*. It is to be emphasized that this is *not* the expected rate of occurrence anticipated by the auditor as likely to be the actual rate in the field.

Tables for attribute sample size

While the sample size required by the auditor can be determined by the inverse solution of the formula given above (page 85) for a desired sample precision and confidence level, this solution may be awkward and time-consuming. To avoid this computation, tables have been developed which provide the solution directly and thus give estimates of the sample size required to achieve a given sample precision at a given confidence level for fields of various sizes. A set of such tables is contained in Appendix D.[7]

In the light of the previous discussion, it is desirable to use a table based on the maximum expected rate of occurrence appropriate to the test at hand. Thus, these tables are divided into sections according to the maximum rate of occurrence to be expected in the field to be sampled. Each section is headed, "Expected Rate of Occurrence Not over ______%." Tables are provided to cover maximum expected rates of not over 2, 5, 7.5, 10, 15, 20, and 30%, and for 50%. Each table provides sample sizes for three confidence levels, 90, 95, and 99%, and for various field sizes.

As an illustration, assume that an auditor wishes to perform a test to establish the rate of error that might exist in certain types of entries. He wishes to have a sampling precision of ±2% at a 95% confidence level. He believes that the rate of error of this type even in a relatively bad situation will not exceed 5%. There are 10,500 such entries or sampling units. He turns to the table and he finds the section of the table headed "Expected Rate of Occurrence Not over 5%" and locates the division of the table for the 95% confidence level (page 335). On that page he finds the column headed reliability ±2% and the row for the appropriate field size (10,500). At the intersection of this column and row, the necessary sample size is given (437).

It will be noted that, in the formula

$$\text{Sampling error} = t\sqrt{\frac{p(1-p)}{n}}$$

if the sample precision is specified and the confidence level is indicated, the size of the sample required is determined by the product

$$p(1-p)$$

An examination of Table 5-1 discloses that the product $p(1-p)$ is the same for

TABLE 5-1

When p equals	$(1-p)$ equals	And $p(1-p)$ equals
.10	.90	.09
.20	.80	.16
.30	.70	.21
.40	.60	.24
.50	.50	.25
.60	.40	.24
.70	.30	.21
.80	.20	.16
.90	.10	.09

[7] The method of computation of these tables is explained in Technical Appendix VI.

$p = .10$ and for $p = .90$, and thus the sample sizes for these two p values will be the same. Similarly, the product $p(1 - p)$ will be the same for $p = .20$ and $p = .80$ or for any two values of p where their sum is 1.00. Therefore, the same sample size will result for two such complementary values of p whether the table is entered with p or $1 - p$ as the expected maximum rate of occurrence. Thus *either* p or $1 - p$ may be used to find the proper table.

Thus, for instance, if the expected rate of occurrence, say of some event such as late shipments, to be estimated from a sample is anticipated to *exceed* 50%, no table in this book will be found with a suitable heading. However, instead of p a value of $1 - p$ may be used. If the rate is estimated to be not *less* than 60%, the table "Expected Rate of Occurrence Not over 40%" may be used. Note that in Table 5-1, the product $p\ (1 - p)$ moves equally in *opposite* directions from the product for $p = .50$. For this reason, above a 50% rate of occurrence, the rates must be interpreted on the basis of a "not *less* than" value while when below 50% on the basis of a "not *more* than" rate. The table in Appendix D may be read as indicated in the secondary heading. For instance, for the table headed "Expected Rate of Occurrence Not over 15%," the secondary heading is "Expected Rate of Occurrence Not Less than 85%."

However, what if the auditor was wrong in his assumption and if the actual rate of occurrence in the field is either much less or much more than the maximum expected rate used in entering the table? The implications of such a situation may be seen by resorting to principles previously described.

It was noted that the closer p (or the actual field rate of occurrence) is to 50%, the larger the sample size necessary to achieve the desired sample precision at the specified confidence level. Thus, if the actual rate (below 50%) is higher than that chosen as the maximum expected, the sample precision will be less than anticipated. Conversely, if the actual p of the universe sampled is less than that anticipated, the auditor will gain in sampling precision.

Actually the table "Expected Rate of Occurrence Not over 15%" was computed on the basis of the assumption that the proportion in the population, p, actually is 15%. Likewise, each of the other sections of the tables was constructed on the assumption that the p value indicated as the maximum expected rate of occurrence was the actual proportion in the population.

As an illustration of the impact of the improper selection of a maximum expected proportion, assume that the auditor wished to achieve a sample reliability of ±3% with a confidence level of 95% and a field size of 10,000. He believes that the error rate in the field will not exceed 10% at the worst. Appendix D (page 337) indicates the proper sample size to be 370.

Assume now that the actual but unknown rate of occurrence in the population is higher than that anticipated, say 15%. The table in Appendix D based on a 15% value for p indicates (by reading the table backwards) that a sample of this size for a 95% confidence level will have a sample precision near ±4% (actually ±3.7%) instead of the desired ±3%.

Thus, when the actual rate of occurrence is higher than that anticipated, the resulting sampling error will be greater than that expected. However, in such a case, even with the increased sampling error, it will be apparent to the auditor that the rate of occurrence in the field is far greater than that anticipated. In addition, later sections of this book show that it is necessary to reappraise the sampling precision findings *after* the sample result is at hand.

On the other hand, if the actual population rate of occurrence is lower, or only 5%, the table in Appendix D (page 356) indicates a sample precision of between ±2 and ±3% (actually 2.1%). The sample precision here instead of being ±3% as anticipated is ±2.1%. A gain in sample precision results.

While it is possible that the occurrence rate may depart widely from the anticipated rate, it is to be observed that a final evaluation of the sampling error after the sample results are obtained will protect the sampler.

Nevertheless, if economy of sampling effort is to be achieved, a wise choice of a maximum expected rate is essential. Failure in this respect may mean the use of too large a sample with an unnecessarily small sampling error achieved at great cost or the discovery after sampling that the sample was too small to provide an adequate sample precision for the purpose.

In the event that the auditor has no idea whatsoever of what to expect as the maximum rate of occurrence or does not care to make an estimate, he may use the table headed "Rate of Occurrence 50%." In this case he will be supplied with the most conservative possible sample size estimate and will in no case find he has a poorer sample precision than desired, although his sample may be unnecessarily large.

STEPS IN DETERMINING SAMPLE SIZE—ATTRIBUTES

The steps necessary to determine the sample size for sampling attributes may be summarized as follows:

1. Establish the required sample precision, i.e., ±1%, ±2%, etc.
2. Establish the desired confidence level, i.e., 90, 95, or 99%.
3. Estimate the maximum rate of occurrence anticipated in a bad situation (maximum expected rate of occurrence).
4. Determine the approximate field size.
5. Refer to the sample size table (Appendix D).
   a. Select the table for the maximum expected rate of occurrence.
      (1) If the maximum expected rate exceeds 50%, enter the table with $1 - p$.
      (2) If it is not possible to estimate the maximum rate of occurrence, use the table for the expected rate of occurrence 50%.
   b. Select the section of the table for the desired confidence level.
   c. Find the row for the field size.
   d. Find the column for the desired sample reliability.
   e. The sample size is at the intersection of the column and row.

GENERAL SAMPLE SIZE CONSIDERATIONS—ATTRIBUTES SAMPLING

It is remembered that no matter which table is used, the result is an *estimated* sample size for the purpose, and it will be necessary to reappraise the sample precision when the sample result is achieved so that at the end the auditor will know the actual sample precision.

The reason for presenting tables based on *p* values as high as 30 or 40% may be questioned by the reader, since it is doubtful that error rates would run that high. However, it is to be remembered that attributes sampling is not confined to establishing error frequency but may cover any characteristic of the sampling units. The proportion of receivables overdue beyond a certain number of days or other similar data may well fall within this range of the given values for *p*.

It is to be noted that making a simple linear interpolation from the tables in Appendix D to obtain sample sizes for sample reliabilities between those given in the tables (or field sizes between those given in the tables) will *not* result in the correct values. It is always safe, however, to use the next *lower* desired sample precision or the next *higher* field size, since this will never understate the required size.

An examination of the sample size tables included with this chapter can result in a number of enlightening conclusions and a better understanding of sample precision for attributes.

There exists a popular impression that if some fixed per cent (say 5 or 10%) of the field is included in a test, the same degree of reliability will always be attained. In fact, in the explanation of the audit scope, it is not uncommon to find mention of the proportion of the field included in the test. A brief examination of the sample size tables will quickly explode this myth. For instance, in the table headed "Expected Rate of Occurrence Not over 5%—Confidence Level 95%" (Appendix D, Table 2B, page 334), the sample size required for a sample precision of ±2% for a field size of 5,000 is 418, or 8.4% of the field. For a field size of 10,000 (or twice as large) from the same table, the sample size is 436, or 4.4% of the field, while for field size 100,000 the required sample size is 454, or .5% of the field, to obtain the same sample precision at this confidence level.

Thus, where the sample size was 418 for a field of 5,000, for a field 20 times as large (100,000), the sample size increased only to 454. It is apparent that it is the absolute size of the sample that is of primary consideration and *not* its relative size.

Actually, whenever the sample size is less than about 1 per cent of the field size, the field size is almost entirely irrelevant. Thus the sample size requirement of 454 for a field size of 100,000 under the above conditions becomes 456 for a field (population) of 500,000.

The tables provide no sample sizes for populations over 500,000. However, in view of the above discussion, the sample sizes given for field size 500,000 may be used for all larger field sizes with negligible error.

General considerations

It is to be noted that the table for appraisal of sample precision for attributes samples (Appendix F) can be used inversely to establish sample size requirements. Such an approach has certain merits but other disadvantages. The possible use of these tables for that purpose is discussed in Chapter 6 after the description of the tables, where the pros and cons for such possible use of these tables are indicated, as well as the manner in which they may be used.

VARIABLES SAMPLING—SAMPLE SIZE

Concepts

As previously indicated, there are situations in which the auditor will desire the answer in terms of "how much" rather than "how many." This may arise where a test objective is designed to disclose such facts as the total dollar value of the errors made, the total dollar value of an inventory group of accounts or items such as disallowances, or the average number of days required to effectuate shipments at a warehouse, etc.

The purpose of such variables estimation sampling (sometimes referred to as *dollar-value sampling*) may be to:

1. Establish the reasonableness of account balances recorded on financial statements or otherwise claimed or the dollar-value impact of certain types of errors, or
2. Establish unknown values, such as the value of an inventory where no physical inventory is taken, for use in financial statements or other purposes, the dollar value of reserves, such as reserves for bad debts, or
3. Establish the amounts of money due in intercompany settlements, such as in the sale of airline tickets.

In such instances, the problem becomes one of variables sampling with the answer to be given in dollars, days, tons, or other variables units. In order to accomplish this end, it is necessary to estimate the *average* value and perhaps through it the total value. It will be necessary to estimate this average (or total) with some given degree of precision with a desired degree of confidence (confidence level).

The desired degree of precision can be thought of either as being within some number of dollars (or other variables unit) of the true value, or in terms of some percentage of this value. In the latter case, it is advisable to convert this percentage precision to absolute terms (dollars, etc.).

Caution must be exercised not to confuse such a percentage with that encountered in attributes sampling. A statement that it is desired to estimate a total dollar value with an accuracy of ±5% *of its actual value* relates to an estimate within so many dollars. On the other hand, in attributes sampling the estimate is to be made of the rate of occurrence or frequency of certain events, namely, a count, not a dollar value or measurement.

For example, to estimate the total dollar value of an inventory of 10,000 items where it is believed that the total value of the inventory is $4,000,000, it is desired to have a sample reliability which will place the sample within ±2% of the true inventory value or, in absolute terms, within ±$80,000 or 2% of $4,000,000 (at some specified confidence level). The average (usually audited) value of the 10,000 items is to be estimated by sampling and then projected by multiplying by 10,000 to obtain the total value.[8] If the total value is to be estimated with a sampling precision of ±$80,000, the average will have to be estimated with a sampling precision of ±$8.00 or $80,000 divided by 10,000 (at an appropriate confidence level).

In Chapter 4 it was shown that the arithmetic means of all possible samples (sampling distribution of the mean) drawn from a given population will tend toward the normal form, with the standard deviation of such a distribution equal to[9]

$$\sigma_{\bar{X}} = \frac{\sigma}{\sqrt{n}}$$

where $\sigma_{\bar{X}}$ = standard deviation of sampling distribution of means, or standard error of the mean

σ = standard deviation of universe from which the samples were drawn

n = sample size (number of sampling units in sample)

The sampling precision of a mean can then be established at any selected confidence level by multiplying this standard error of the mean by a factor selected from Table 4-3, representing the number of standard deviations required to include the desired percentage of the sampling distribution (the confidence level).

However, it is seen that the solution of the formula for the standard error of the mean requires knowledge of the value of the standard deviation of the values in the field (universe), which of course is unknown.

As has been seen in Chapter 4, the size of a sample required to achieve the desired degree of sampling reliability at a selected confidence level is a function of the amount of variability of the values of the observations comprising the universe. This is measured by the standard deviation.

Thus, it becomes necessary to *estimate* the value of the unknown standard deviation of the population in order to *estimate* the sample size required to achieve the desired sample reliability. In other words, it is not possible to establish the required

[8] There are other more efficient sampling methods of accomplishing this end, through such techniques as ratio estimate sampling (see Chaps. 10 and 11).

To distinguish the method described above from these other methods, it will be referred to as a *direct projection.*

[9] For the finite population case this becomes

$$\sigma_{\bar{X}} = \frac{\sigma}{\sqrt{n}}\sqrt{1 - \frac{n}{N}}$$

sample size for a variable estimate without some knowledge of the population variability. This knowledge can best be achieved through an estimate based on an advance or preliminary sample or through data from past samplings of the same or a similar field.

While a sample result from a previous audit can be used as a guide in this area, it is a somewhat dubious procedure since the universe may have changed radically since the last audit.[10] On the other hand, since only an *estimate* of the required sample size is needed and the final sample result will be appraised later for the actual sample precision attained, it may be possible to use previous audit results for this purpose if desired. The penalty resulting from a change in the character of the field will be an under or oversampling which will be discovered subsequently when the sample result is appraised. However, this procedure can become awkward, especially in situations in which it is no longer possible to extend the sample.

A better method is to make use of an advance sample from the field. In other words, a relatively small sample will be taken, and after the variability of the field has been estimated from it, the sample will be extended to the extent necessary according to findings of the preliminary sample.

To establish the variability of the population values in order to resolve the formula for computing sample reliability, it will be necessary to calculate the standard deviation of the initial sample.

A method of computing the standard deviation was detailed in Chapter 4. However, the method outlined is tedious and time-consuming for any appreciable number of observations (any more than 10). While more efficient methods of establishing the value of the standard deviation from larger groups of data can be used, they are complex and require some study and training.

To avoid this situation, a simpler method of *estimating* the standard deviation for a group of data can be used. It is not quite as accurate as the direct method, but this loss of accuracy is more than offset by its simplicity.[11] The method is explained below.

Assume that it is desired to establish the sample size necessary, at some confidence level, in order to estimate an average with a specified sampling precision.

An estimate of the population standard deviation to accomplish this end must be obtained. For this purpose, an advance *random* sample is secured. About 50 sampling units should suffice.

The values for the selected sampling units are recorded in the *same order as their numbers occurred in the table of random numbers* or in the order of occurrence if a systematic sample is used. *This is important.* If, for convenience in drawing,

[10] It is to be noted that it is generally the audited value population for which such a determination must be established.

[11] It must be emphasized that this method provides an approximation of the standard deviation of the population based on the assumption that the values in the population are distributed in the form of a normal distribution. Since many populations of accounting data are violently nonnormal, care must be exercised in the use of this method.

the random numbers have been arranged in their numerical sequence, the values must be put back in their original random sequence.

The items are then arranged in groups of six, seven, or eight items, whichever is more convenient in making full use of the observations attained.[12] For each group the range, or the difference between the highest value and lowest value in that group, is obtained. The overall average group range is then calculated. The resulting average range is divided by a factor[13] given in Table 5-2, depending on the group size used in the process.

The result of this computation is an estimate of the population standard deviation which may now be used to establish the required sample size. Ordinarily this would be accomplished by the inverse solution of the formula given above for sample size determination. However, Appendix E provides tables which make possible the determination of sample sizes without the necessity for solution of the formula.

TABLE 5-2. ***Factors for Estimating the Standard Deviation from the Average Range***

$$\text{Estimated } \sigma = \frac{\text{average range}}{d_2} = \frac{\overline{R}}{d_2}$$

Group size	*d_2 factor*
6	2.534
7	2.704
8	2.847

Tables for variables sample size

Appendix E provides a series of tables which give the sample sizes required to achieve given sample precision for a variety of field sizes and confidence levels of 90, 95, 99, and 99.9%, where the desired sample precision is expressed as a ratio to the standard deviation of the population.[14]

For instance, assume that it is desired to estimate the total dollar value of a field of 5,000 values with a 95% confidence level and a sample precision of the total value of ±$50,000 or for the average ±$10.00 (or $50,000 divided by the field size of 5,000). Assume further that the standard deviation, estimated from an advance

[12] It is evident that the best sample size for this purpose will then be a multiple of six, seven, or eight.

[13] This is called the d_2 factor. Such factors are available for other group sizes, but these group sizes are efficient statistically and convenient. This technique for estimating the standard deviation is widely used in statistical quality-control work. A more complete explanation of the method with its mathematical background may be found in: F. E. Grubbs and C. L. Weaver, "The Best Unbiased Estimate of the Population Standard Deviation Based on Group Ranges," *Journal of the American Statistical Association*, vol. 42, 1947, pp. 224–241.

[14] Technical Appendix V provides a description of the method of computation of these tables.

sample or by other methods, is found to be $50.00. The desired sampling precision is then 20% of the estimated standard deviation (or $10.00 divided by $50.00).

By resorting to the table on pages 378–379 (Appendix E), the field size section for 5,000 is located, and the column for the 95% confidence is chosen. Since the desired sampling error is 20% of the estimated population standard deviation, the row for .20 in the column headed "Ratio of Sampling Error to Sandard Deviation" is located. The estimated sample size for these conditions may now be found at the intersection of that row and the 95% confidence level column. The sample size is found to be 94.

A more detailed example of the use of these tables is shown below. In this case, it is desired to estimate the total value of an inventory (or group of account balances) for the purpose of determining the reasonableness of a total value recorded on the books.

The total value shown on the records is $1,105,862.37 for 5,000 items. It is desired to estimate the value from a sample projection which will provide an accuracy (sample precision) of the total value of ±$50,000 at the 95% confidence level. An advance or preliminary sample of 48 items is drawn by resorting to probability sampling methods (random numbers), and the sample values so obtained are tabulated in Table 5-3 in their random sequence in groups of six sampling units. For each group of six values, both the high and the low value are established (indicated by *H* and *L* in Table 5-3). Great care should be exercised here, since it is easy to overlook a high or low value if this is done hastily, and understatements of the group range and of the standard deviation might result.

The difference between the high and low value of each group (group range) is then established. These eight group ranges are averaged to provide an average range ($182.07 in this instance), which is then divided by the d_2 factor (2.534 for group size 6) to provide an estimate[15] of the standard deviation ($71.85).

Since the desired sample precision is $50,000.00 and there are 5,000 items, the sample precision for the average will be $50,000.00 divided by 5,000, or $10.00.

The sample average precision desired is then compared with the estimated standard deviation and is found to be 13.9% of that standard deviation ($10.00 divided by $71.85). This is expressed as a ratio to the standard deviation of .14.

By referring to page 378 (Appendix E), selecting the section of the table relating to field size 5,000, and by using the confidence level column for 95% and a ratio of .14, it may be seen that the appropriate sample size is 189. Since 48 items were drawn in the preliminary sample, it is necessary to extend the sample to include an additional 141 values. It is important to remember that the preliminary sample is used as part of the final sample.

As in the case of attributes, it is to be remembered that this is a sample size estimate based on a relatively small sample and that it will be necessary to appraise the

[15]When computed by formula (see p. 53), the standard deviation is equal to $71.01. The distribution from which this sample was drawn was moderately skewed.

TABLE 5-3

Item number	Amount	Item number	Amount	Item number	Amount	Item number	Amount
5747	$316.10	4680	$283.64	6270	$299.79	7788	$229.76*L*
2639	220.45	4669	317.00	4207	183.17*L*	4739	248.64
2539	404.44*H*	6219	303.57	1925	347.24	2306	289.41
6477	78.97*L*		261.80*L*	2195	354.00	5881	276.82
4341	390.11	7945	269.93	9558	391.84*H*	3607	232.71
7790	261.36	9354	381.87*H*	2342	294.98	9052	324.09*H*
1015	218.07	1426	414.97*H*	8185	287.10	1215	305.00
2533	278.45	7115	258.79	6463	258.54	8501	327.62*H*
8894	436.24*H*	7389	357.02	8816	222.86*L*	1361	252.40
6847	292.89	7943	259.67	9726	308.07*H*	1197	312.80
5604	251.55	2982	216.52	6746	258.05	6962	274.13
3054	159.59*L*	1200	153.79*L*	1588	229.75	6237	242.67*L*

Group Ranges

	$325.47		$120.07		$208.67		$ 94.33
	276.65		261.18		85.21		84.95

$$\text{Average range} = \bar{R} = \frac{\$1456.53}{8} = \$182.07$$

$$d_2 \text{ factor for group size } 6 = 2.534$$

$$\text{Estimated } \sigma = \frac{\text{average range } (\bar{R})}{d_2}$$

$$= \frac{\$182.07}{2.534} = \$71.85$$

sample results after the sampling is completed to establish more firmly the actual reliability achieved.

At this point a word of caution is to be inserted. As detailed in Chapter 4, the sampling distribution of the average will be a normal distribution when the distribution of the values in the field is also normal. In other cases, when sampling from nonnormally distributed data, the sampling distribution of the mean will tend toward normality as the sample size is increased.

However, if the values in the field are very badly skewed, as often occurs in accounting data when the bulk of the values fall in one range but a few very high values occur, the sampling distribution will also be skewed, and the sample reliability estimates will not be accurate.

In such an instance, to avoid this difficulty, the auditor should resort to a method which he usually follows anyway, namely, the use of stratification.

Whether or not he uses statistical methods, it is usual for an auditor, when confronted by such a situation, to test separately the unusually high values by checking either all or a high proportion of these items for reasons of materiality. This method of dealing with high-value items will eliminate the difficulty described above.

The methods for stratified sample precision and size determination will be discussed in detail in a later chapter.

STEPS IN DETERMINING SAMPLE SIZES—ESTIMATION SAMPLING—VARIABLES

The steps to be followed in determining the appropriate sample size in estimating variables, such as total dollars, average days for shipments, etc., may be summarized as follows:

1. Determine the desired sample precision in terms of the average value.
2. Determine the desired confidence level.
3. Obtain a preliminary random sample of about 50 items.
4. Arrange these values in subgroups of six or seven items *in original random sequence.*
5. Obtain the range for each subgroup and the average for all subgroups.
6. Divide the average range ($\overline{R}$) by the appropriate d_2 factor (see page 94) to obtain an estimated standard deviation.
7. Divide the desired precision of the average by the estimated standard deviation to obtain a ratio.
8. Find the appropriate field size section in the tables of Appendix E. Locate the row for the rates calculated in step 7 and the column for the desired confidence level. The sample size is at the intersection of this column and row.

GENERAL SAMPLE SIZE CONSIDERATIONS—VARIABLES

The tables in Appendix E relating to sample size requirements for variables sampling provide some interesting facts about the relation between sample sizes and sample precision.

Once again, it will be observed that a given percentage of the field as a sample does not provide equal protection.

An examination of these tables indicates that the sample size required for a sample precision of ±.10 times the standard deviation (±$10.00, if the standard deviation equals $100.00) at the 99% confidence level for a field size of 2,000 is 500, whereas for a field size of 5,000 it is only 588. Thus with a field size 2½ times as great, the sample size rose only 18%.

SAMPLE SIZE ESTIMATION FOR MULTIPURPOSE TESTS

It is not uncommon that an audit test sample is used for several purposes simultaneously. Thus, a test of transactions may be used to establish the frequency of occurrence for each of several types of errors or failures, as well as the dollar value of these errors or other dollar values.

If such multipurpose tests are performed using a single sample for the purpose, the problem of the required sample size becomes complex. It is evident, from the discussion in this chapter, that the sample size estimate is dependent on the maximum expected error rate, which may vary widely for different kinds of errors, and certainly the sample size for the variables (dollar-value) estimate may bear little relation to that required for the attributes estimate.

The effect of this situation is to result in varying sample size requirements within the same test. This problem can be dealt with in several ways.

Assume the following situation. An auditor is seeking to establish the frequency of occurrence of three different kinds of errors in a population. The sample size requirements for the estimate of the frequency of each type of error are as shown below:

Error type	*Sample size*
A	250
B	175
C	125

From the viewpoint of the simplest and least elaborate approach, the auditor might use sample size 250 (the largest sample size) for all of the errors and thus examine all 250 selected records for all three types of errors. This will result in oversampling for some types of errors, but because of the simplicity of approach it may nevertheless not result in an appreciable increase in the audit time expenditure.

However, the audit time expenditure required to establish the occurrence of some types of errors for an individual sampling unit may be considerable, while the sample size necessary for that type of error may be less than for other types of errors. In such a situation, it is quite proper to terminate the examination for certain types of errors while continuing to check for others, *provided the sampling units are examined in their original random order of selection.*

Thus, in the example given above, if the documents are audited *in the sequence of their original random drawing*, examination for error type C may be terminated after the audit of the first 125 sampling units, while the audit for error types A and B continues. After the examination of the 175th sampling unit, the audit would continue for error type A.

It is to be noted, however, that if systematic sampling has been used for the selection of the sample, it is not proper to terminate the audit examination of individual records at an early stage. If the examination of a sample drawn by systematic methods is terminated prior to the end of the sample, the results of that sample can be projected to represent *only that portion* of the file of documents covered. Thus, if the examination of the systematic sample is terminated halfway through the sample, the results are projectable only to the first half of the file. There is no reason to assume that the two halves of the file are alike in the frequency of occurrence of these errors, and thus a result projectable to the first half of the file is not of necessity indicative of the condition of the entire file.

OTHER SAMPLING METHODS—ESTIMATION SAMPLING

As previously explained, various other sampling methods discussed in this chapter beyond the unrestricted random sampling technique may be used to increase sample efficiency or to lower cost. These methods include stratified sampling, cluster sampling, and ratio and difference estimates.

The problem of sample size determination when these methods are used will be discussed in detail in later chapters.

SIX

Appraisal of Sample Results

(Attributes)

THE NEED FOR POST-SAMPLING APPRAISAL

In Chapter 5 methods were developed to estimate the sample size required to achieve a desired sample precision at a selected confidence level for estimation sampling of attributes. Tables were provided for this purpose.

However, it was noted in that discussion that in order to achieve such an estimate, it is necessary to make an assumption as to the rate of occurrence in the field. To the extent that the rate assumed as existent in the field is incorrectly estimated, the actual sample precision attained by the sample will depart from the expected sample precision. Thus, it is always necessary to reevaluate *after* the sampling is completed to determine the sample precision actually achieved.

It may well be, because of the effect of the admonition given in Chapter 5, that the maximum expected rate used for sample size estimation is well *above* the expected rate and thus that the actual reliability attained by using a sample of the indicated size is actually appreciably better than that anticipated. On the other hand, the unexpected may take place and the actual rate of occurrence may far exceed the anticipated, with the result that the sample size used will provide a much poorer reliability than that desired.

To provide protection against either of these two events, it is essential that the sample result be appraised *after* the sampling is completed to establish its true sampling precision.

Further, as will be explained below, the method used to *estimate* the required sample size to achieve a given sample precision is approximate owing to the nature of the computation. More exact results will now be achieved on the basis of the information available from the sample.

PRINCIPLES OF SAMPLE APPRAISAL

In Chapter 4, the principles involved in establishing sample precision for attributes were explored. It will be remembered that the basis for such an evaluation was the sampling distribution, or the distribution of all possible sample results, when samples of a specified size were used.

An example of this principle was given in Chapter 4 (page 64), where all possible outcomes for tosses of 10 coins (or drawings of 10 balls when the population contained 50% black balls) were given as shown in Table 6-1. This is shown graphically in Figure 6-1.

TABLE 6–1. *Outcome of Tosses of 10 Coins (or Drawings of 10 Balls from Universe Containing 50 Per Cent Black Balls)*

Number of heads (or black balls)	*Probability*
0	0.0977%
1	0.977
2	4.395
3	11.719
4	20.508
5	24.609
6	20.508
7	11.719
8	4.395
9	0.977
10	0.0977

The resultant sampling distribution is symmetrical and close to normal, and it was shown that as the number of coins tossed (or balls drawn) increased, the resulting distribution approached the normal curve. This fact made it possible to assume that the distribution actually was normal and to use the percentages of observations included within a given number of standard deviations as indicated in Table 4-3 as a reasonable approximation, computing the standard deviation from

$$\sigma_{\%} = \sqrt{\frac{p(1-p)}{n}}$$

However, in the example given, p was assumed to be 50%. If p departs from 50%, another form of distribution arises. For instance, assume that 10 balls are drawn from a large population of balls containing only 20% black balls. The probabilities for this case are shown in Table 6-2.

The data in Table 6-2 are shown graphically in Figure 6-2. It is seen that this

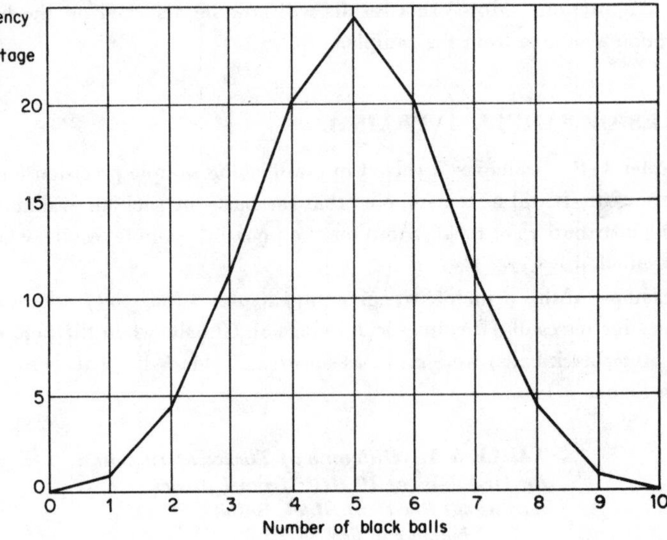

FIGURE 6–1

distribution is no longer symmetrical. It is skewed and cannot be considered a normal distribution. The method of the use of the standard deviation described above cannot be used here to approximate the sample precision without serious error, since the distribution is no longer normal.

While it is true that, if the number of balls drawn (sample size) is greatly increased, the approximation to the normal distribution will be approached, this is not true for smaller sample sizes, particularly when p departs appreciably from 50%. A more

TABLE 6–2. ***Outcome of Drawings of 10 Balls from Population Containing 20 Per Cent Black Balls***

Number of black balls	*Probability*
0	10.74%
1	26.84
2	30.20
3	20.13
4	8.81
5	2.64
6	0.55
7	0.08
8	0.01
9	*
10	*

* Less than 0.01%

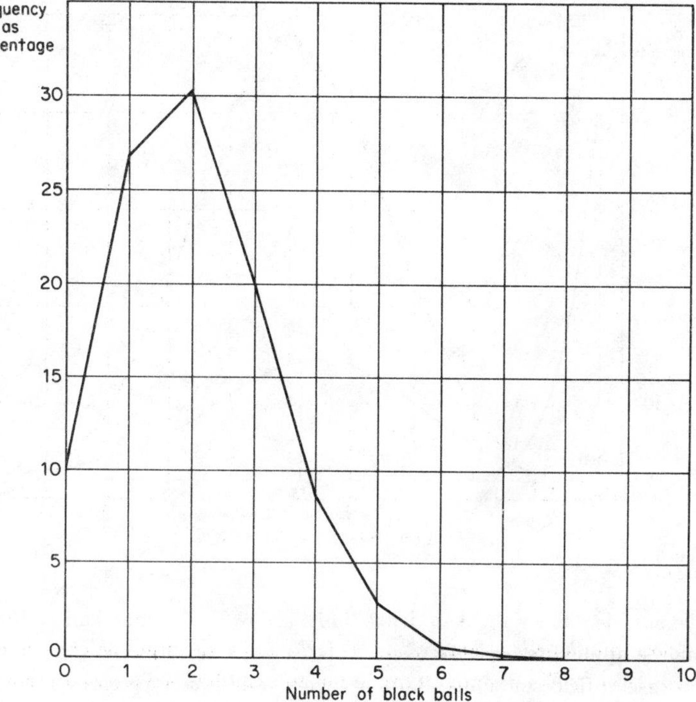

FIGURE 6-2

exact method is needed—the computation of the detailed binomial probabilities described above. Since this is too complex for computation by most auditors, tables are provided to eliminate the need for this calculation in Appendix F. These tables provide the exact binomial sampling precision by stating the upper and lower confidence limits when the sample contains a given percentage of the attribute (at a given confidence level).

The values in these tables were secured by calculating the percentage of occurrence in the field that would be required to provide the specified probability that a sample containing the indicated per cent of occurrence would be encountered.

The percentage in the sample is referred to as the *point estimate* of the population error rate.

For instance, if a sample of 100 containing 3% of errors is drawn from a very large field, a twofold calculation would be necessary. Assuming that a 95% confidence level is desired, the highest percentage in the field should be calculated so that there would be a 2½% probability of obtaining a sample containing 3% of errors or less. The 2½% probability is used since a 95% confidence level requires that there be a probability of 95% that the field error rate be within the confidence limits and 5%

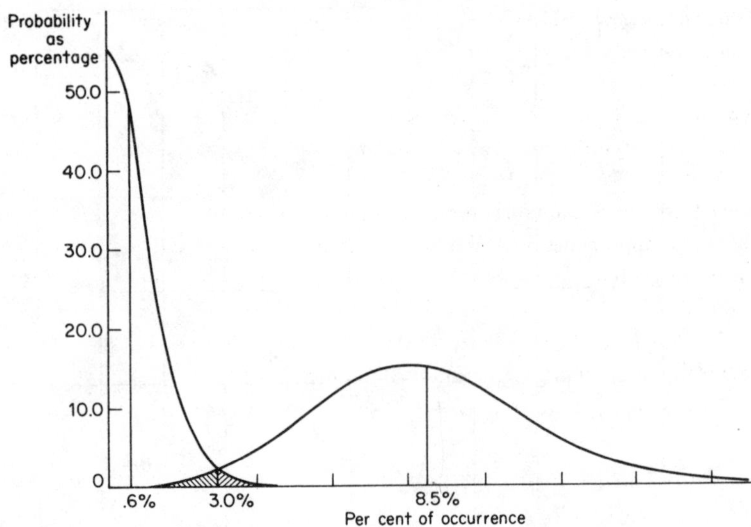

FIGURE 6–3

that it be outside. Since the confidence limits are two-sided, one-half of the 5% or 2½ would be applied to each side.

In this case, a field containing 8.5% of errors would have precisely a 2½% probability of giving rise to a sample of 100 containing 3% or less of errors. If the error rate in the field were higher, the probability of a 3% or less sample error rate would be less than 2½%.

Conversely, on the other end of the distribution the *lowest* error rate that could cause a sample with an error rate of 3% or more with a probability of 2½% is .6%. Any field with a lower error rate than .6% would have less than a 2½% probability of producing a sample with an error rate of 3% or greater. Thus, there are 95 chances in 100 that the field generating the sample containing a 3% error rate has a field error rate of between 0.6 and 8.5%. This calculation is shown graphically in Figure 6-3.

When this approach is used, no assumption as to the rate of occurrence in the field is involved, but the sample appraisal is based in its entirety upon the actual sample findings.

It is noted that these confidence limits are *not* equidistant from the sample 3%, with the lower limit (.6%) being closer to the sample value (3%) than the upper limit (8.5%). This condition arises from the previously described skewness of the sampling distribution.

Yet according to the method used in the sample-size determination tables of Chapter 4, the sampling reliability would be ±3.3%. Actually the confidence *interval* (difference between upper and lower limits) of 6.6% by this former method is less than that obtained by the new method (8.5 − .6 = 7.9). It will be seen that the new, more precise method indicates a greater deviation on the upper side than on the lower. This is important since under the previous, less exact method, the highest expected rate in the field based on 3% in the sample of 100 would be 6.3% or (3% + 3.3%), while the more precise method indicates a maximum probable rate in the field of 8.5%.

An examination of the tables indicates that as the sample size is increased, or as the value of p approaches 50%, the asymmetry noted above tends to diminish and to vanish entirely when p is equal to 50%. Then the results of the previous approximate method and the new, more exact method will tend to coincide.

The auditor does not need to make the exact calculations for the sample evaluations, since he may find the answers in the tables.

THE TABLES (SAMPLE PRECISION FOR RELATIVE FREQUENCIES)

The tables in Appendix F make it possible to evaluate the precision of the projection of a rate of occurrence found in a probability (random) sample as a statement of the rate of occurrence in the field.

These tables provide the confidence limits for a sample proportion at three specified confidence (probability) levels, 90, 95, and 99%, for a selected group of sample and field sizes when the *sample* contains certain specified rates of occurrence. These confidence limits indicate the range of values which have the probability indicated of containing the true field rate of occurrence based on the sample finding. The rates of occurrence in the sample for which tables are provided range from 1 to 20% by intervals of 1% and from 20 to 50% by intervals of 5%. While this does not cover every possible sample result, methods are described below for use of the tables when specific values for a given situation are not included.

The use of the tables may be illustrated by an example when the exact values are contained in the table. For instance, assume that a random sample of 200 items is drawn from a field of 10,000 and is found to contain 2% of errors. It is desired to establish the confidence limits at a 99% confidence level or, in other words, to state the limits within which there is a 99% certainty that the actual rate in the field will be included. Refer to page 394 of Appendix F for a table applying to the situation where the sample is found to contain 2% of errors or other occurrences. The table provides confidence limits at the 99% confidence level. The appropriate column for the sample size (in this case 200) and the row for the field size (10,000) are located, and at their intersection the confidence limits of 0.4 and 6.1% are found. This indicates that there are 99 chances in 100 that this sample was drawn from a field containing between 0.4 and 6.1% of errors.

Of course, it is entirely possible that the sample will disclose *none* of the events being investigated, such as errors. It is to be emphasized that this does not of necessity signify that there are no instances of errors (or other type of occurrence) in the field. As will be seen, it is quite possible to obtain a perfect sample from a field containing a relatively high rate of error. To cover this situation, a special table is provided on page 469 of Appendix F. Since, for such a sample, it is always possible that the field contains no error, the lower confidence limit is always zero and is not given. In addition, since this is a different situation, the upper limit is computed somewhat differently. To obtain the values in this table, a calculation was performed to find the rate of error that the field must contain to give rise to a sample containing *no* errors with a probability of 100% minus the confidence level. For instance, for the 95% confidence level, it would be the field rate of error which would provide exactly a 5% (or 100% − 95%) probability of generating a sample with zero errors and for the 99% confidence level, a 1% probability that such a sample would be drawn. Thus, in the first case, the probability is 95 chances in 100 that the field contained not more than the stated value, and in the second case, 99%.

Thus, the interpretation of this section of the table is somewhat different from that of the rest of the table. The value given is the highest field rate of occurrence that would be expected to give rise to a perfect sample with the probability (one minus the confidence level) indicated.

For example, a sample of 50 items is drawn from a field of 10,000 and no errors are found. The table (page 469) indicates a value of 8.8% at the 99% confidence level. This may be interpreted to mean that since there was only one chance in 100 that a field of 10,000 containing 8.8% of error would generate a sample of 50 containing no errors, there are 99 chances in 100 that the field from which this sample was drawn did not contain *more* than 8.8%—a very high figure, considering that the sample was perfect. However, the sample was quite small. A sample of 200 from the same field containing no errors could be interpreted to mean that there are 99 chances in 100 that the field did not contain errors in excess of 2.3%.

A word of caution must be given here to emphasize that this indication did *not* mean that the field actually contained as much as 2.3% of errors (or 8.8% in the previous example). In fact, this would be quite unlikely. The value given in the table is a *maximum* probable value. It is most likely that the field contained somewhat less than the value given in the table.

On the other hand, it is quite obvious from the values given in this table that the occurrence of a sample without error is *not* to be taken as evidence of a perfect field but that it merely fixes the highest expected rate of error in the field.

The dangers arising from a naive acceptance of a perfect sample as evidence of a perfect field are especially serious when the sample size is small. To emphasize this point, it may be seen that a sample of 30 from a field of 500 in which no errors are found merely indicates that there are 99 chances in 100 that the error rate in the field is less than 13.8% and 95 chances in 100 that the rate in the field is less than 9.2% (see tables).

VALUES NOT COVERED BY TABLES

It is obvious that not every sample size, field size, and per cent of occurrence could be included in the tables in Appendix F, or they would be of indefinite size. However, in this set as much coverage as was possible was given. Nevertheless, it will never be possible, even with a greatly expanded set of tables, to cover all possible situations. Therefore, it is necessary to know how to deal with situations where the tables do not provide the exact field size, sample size, or rate of occurrence in the sample required.

Missing field sizes

It will be noted from an examination of the table that differences in field sizes have little effect on the confidence limits unless the sample size constitutes a large proportion of the field size. This is illustrated in Table 6-3 by values taken from the table for rate of occurrence in the sample of 4%.

From these figures, it may be concluded that unless the sample constitutes an appreciable portion of the field (more than 10% as a rule of thumb), exact knowledge of the field size is not very important, and little harm will be done if the value is not in the table, provided that the next *higher* field size available in the table is used. This is the most conservative approach.

Thus, in any instance in which the tables do not provide the exact field size, the next available higher field size may be used with assurance that this will result in only a small overstatement of the confidence interval.

TABLE 6-3

When field size is	95% confidence limits for			
	Sample size 50		Sample size 200	
	Lower	Upper	Lower	Upper
500	.7%	13.2%	2.3%	6.9%
1,000	.6	13.5	2.0	7.3
5,000	.5	13.7	1.8	7.7
100,000 and over	.5	13.7	1.7	7.7

In the area where the sample size is a larger proportion of the field size, a greater number of field sizes are given to limit this overstatement.

Missing percentages in sample

Rates of occurrences in the sample are given in 1% intervals to 20%, and in 5% intervals thereafter to 50%. Confidence intervals for missing percentages can be readily approximated.

The method used is the adjustment of the confidence limits for the next *higher* percentage as a conservative estimate.

For instance, assume that a sample of 200 is drawn from a field of 2,000 and the sample discloses a 23.5% occurrence of some type of event. The tables provide confidence limits for samples containing 20 and 25% but not 23.5%. For this purpose the confidence limits will be taken from the 25% table and adjusted, since that is the next *higher* percentage given in the tables beyond 23.5%.

At the 99% confidence level, the confidence limits are 17.9% and 33.2%. To adjust for the percentage found in the sample, it is necessary only to *subtract* from both confidence limits the difference between the sample per cent and the *table* per cent (25.0% − 23.5%) or 1.5%. Subtracting 1.5% from 17.9 and 33.2% gives new confidence limits of 16.4 and 31.7%.[1]

Limits obtained in this manner are conservative, since the confidence interval resulting is slightly overstated.

In some investigations where the auditor is dealing with an occurrence other than errors, the rate of occurrence in the field may exceed 50%. While the tables are given only up to a 50% occurrence in the sample, the same tables can be used for percentages over 50% by a simple adjustment.

The table for the complement of the percentage involved is used. For instance, for 85%, the table for 15% (or 100% − 85%) may be used with an adjustment. The tables to be used (with appropriate adjustment for various percentages in the sample over 50%) are shown in Table 6-4.

The adjustment consists of merely subtracting the values in the table from 100%. Thus, for instance, if a sample of 400 from a field of 25,000 is drawn and discloses a rate of occurrence of 80%, the table for 20% would be used. This table gives, at the 95% confidence level, confidence limits of 16.2 and 24.2%. Subtracting each of these from 100% gives 83.8 and 75.8%, which are the new confidence limits.

One precautionary note. To determine limits where sample percentages of occurrence are not given in the table because they are in excess of 50%, the table for the next *lower* percentage would be used for occurrences over 50% and the difference between the sample per cent and the table per cent would be *added* in such cases.

Missing sample sizes

If the sample size used is not one of those given in the table, two possible approaches are available.

[1] In some rare instances such a subtraction may cause the resulting lower limit to be less than that shown in the table for the next lower per cent. In such an event, the value in the table for the next lower per cent should be used.

TABLE 6-4

When per cent in sample is	*Use adjusted value from table for*
99%	1%
98	2
97	3
96	4
95	5
94	6
93	7
92	8
91	9
90	10
89	11
88	12
87	13
86	14
85	15
84	16
83	17
82	18
81	19
80	20
75	25
70	30
65	35
60	40
55	45

One method would be to use the next lower available sample size, but this would be equivalent to throwing away part of the sample insofar as the sample reliability determination is concerned.

On the other hand, while a simple linear interpolation in the table will not give exact results, it will not be far wrong and will be a conservative estimate, since it overstates the confidence interval, if all calculations proceed from the lower sample size.

As an example, assume that a sample of 175 is drawn from a field of 2,000 disclosing 12% of errors and that the confidence limits at the 99% confidence level are desired. The 12% table does not contain sample size 175, but it does contain columns for 160 and 180, giving confidence limits as follows:

Sample size	Lower limit	Upper limit
160	6.6%	19.7%
180	6.8%	19.2%

Since the difference in sample size from the table value of 160 (with the lesser value for the confidence limit) is 15 and the total difference between the given values 160 and 180 is 20, 75% (15/20) of the difference between the confidence limits may be taken and added to the smaller of the two values to determine the lower limit.

Thus, in this instance, the calculation proceeds as follows:

Lower limit

160	6.6%
180	6.8
	.2

Difference	.2
75% of difference	.15
New lower limit	6.75% or 6.8%

Upper limit

160	19.7%
180	19.2
	.5

Difference	.5
25% of difference	.125
Plus smaller value	19.2
New upper limit	19.325% or 19.3%

For the upper limit, working from the smaller of the two values, namely, 19.2%, it is seen that the difference between 180 and 175 is 5, and thus 25% (5/20) of the difference in the upper confidence limits is added to the smaller value to determine the upper confidence limits.

ONE-SIDED CONFIDENCE LIMITS

The sample appraisal method outlined above provides *two-sided* limits, namely, a statement that there is a certain probability that the actual rate of occurrence in the field is between *two* stated values (confidence limits). Thus, in the example previously cited when a sample of 200 out of a field of 10,000 disclosed 2% of occurrences, the table indicated that there were 99 chances in 100 that if the entire field were examined, a rate between .4 and 6.1% would be found.

However, the auditor's objective may be different. Instead of establishing two limits within which there is a specified probability that the field error rate occurs, he may wish to establish only a single value (one-sided confidence limit) below which, or conversely above which, there is a certain probability that the value obtainable from a 100% test would be found.

For instance, he may desire merely to demonstrate that there is a high probability that the rate of occurrence is *less* than some indicated value. On the other hand, his objective may be to show that there is a high probability that the rate of occurrence is really more than some stated value. Either of these objectives can be accomplished with the proper use of the tables already described.

It will be recalled that the two-sided confidence limits, as illustrated in Figure 4-3, are based on the highest and lowest value of the rate of occurrence in the field that would give rise to a probability of 1.00 minus the confidence level, divided by 2. Thus, for the 99% confidence level there was a separate determination of the lowest field rate of occurrence which would give rise to a .5%, or (1.00−.99)/2, probability of producing a sample containing the specified rate of occurrence or more and the highest rate of field occurrence which would produce a sample with the specified error rate or less. Thus, there was a 99% probability of occurrence *between* these two limits.

For a one-sided confidence limit, the approach is the same but in one direction only. For instance, in the above example (200 out of 10,000 with 2% in the sample), it is noted that the upper limit is 6.1%, which means that there is only a .5% probability that a sample of 200 would have produced 2% or less of occurrences if the field contained 6.1% of occurrences.

Since there is only a .5 chance in 100 that the field containing 6.1% of occurrences could have produced a sample containing 2% or less of occurrences, there is a 99.5% probability that the rate of occurrence of the field which produced this sample was not more than 6.1%.

Thus, the same tables may be used, provided that only one limit, the high or the low, is selected and that the confidence limit is recomputed to be

$$1.00 - \frac{1.00 - CL}{2}$$

where CL = two-sided confidence limit for table. Where appropriate, all of the tables in the various appendixes are labeled with an indication of the two-sided and one-sided confidence levels appropriate to that page of the table. In the few cases where they are not, only a two-sided confidence level is specified. This, however, may be converted by reference to the formula above.

The use of one-sided confidence limits may be illustrated as follows. An audit test based on a sample of 300 out of a field of 100,000 disclosed an error rate of 4%. Using Appendix F, it is seen that for the 95% *(two-sided)* confidence level, the upper confidence limit is 6.8%. Thus, it may be said that there are 97.5 chances in 100 (*one-sided* confidence level) that the error rate in the field *is less than* 6.8%.

Another sample of 200 from a field of 10,000 disclosed 8% of errors. Page 412 of Appendix F indicates a lower limit (at a two-sided confidence level of 99%) of 4.0%. Here, it may be said that there are 99.5 chances in 100 (one-sided confidence level) that the actual rate of error in the field is in excess of 4%.

INTERIM APPRAISALS

It is possible to evaluate the reliability of a sample result at any point during its compilation, *provided that the items have been taken for audit in their random number sequence.* This is a most important possibility, because it means that an audit test, so developed, can be terminated at the earliest possible time with possible appreciable savings. If the items are taken in their original random number sequence, at any point during the audit test the auditor can consult the tables for appraisal of sample reliability for attributes estimation sampling, and if the results provide him with the desired information, he may terminate the test.

It will be recalled that, in determining the appropriate sample size, the rate of occurrence used to calculate the sample size was an overestimate (when the rate is less than 50%, or an underestimate when it is more) in order to provide a conservative estimate of the required sample size. Thus, the highest anticipated rate of occurrence was used.

However, in many audits the situation is good, and the rate of error is quite low. In such a case, the sample size indicated as required is much too large and will result in oversampling together with unnecessary costs. If the auditor stops after auditing a reasonable number of the selected sampling units (assuming they are audited in their random sequence), calculates the percentage of error, and evaluates the sample precision of that percentage at that point, he may be able to achieve considerable savings by an early termination of the test.

To illustrate the application of this technique, assume that an auditor is to conduct a test to determine the rate of occurrence of a certain type of error. He feels that if the rate of occurrence does not exceed 5%, the condition of the records may be considered satisfactory. He believes that the error rate will not exceed 10% in any case. In order to ensure avoiding an indeterminate result, he feels that a sampling precision of ±3% will be necessary and chooses a 95% confidence level. The field size is 24,000.

The sample size dictated for a maximum rate of occurrence of 10% with a sample reliability of ±3% at the 95% confidence level is shown in Table 2C of Appendix D as 378.

Assume further that after the first 200 items are audited in their random sequence, he finds that his rate of occurrence in the sample is only 1%. Consulting the appropriate table in Appendix F for rate of occurrence in the sample of 1%, he finds that the confidence interval is from 0.1% to 3.6% at the 95% confidence level. Since he had desired a sample with a sample precision of ±3% and has a confidence interval much better than the desired precision, he may terminate his test at this point and draw his conclusions at this stage.

It is observed that a decision made on the basis of the smaller sample, provided the confidence interval is sufficiently small to make this decision possible, is just as valid as a decision based on the larger sample. The limitation of the smaller sample is that usually the confidence interval is too wide to make any decision feasible. However, a conclusion that a sample result is within certain limits at a given confidence level is valid in terms of that confidence level regardless of the sample size.

If the rate of error runs very high and the confidence limits from the interim sample appraisal indicate that the error rate will exceed the acceptable level, the auditor at that point must decide what to do, as though the test had been completed. He may then take appropriate action, such as extending the test to pin down the error rate more precisely or preparing an audit finding to the appropriate authority or, if the situation is sufficiently serious, refusing to certify or issue a qualified certification. He *may not,* however, elect to continue sampling, since he cannot then evaluate the results of the expanded sample using the methods described in this chapter. Certainly he cannot continue sampling to a large sample size in the hope that a larger sample will indicate a lower rate.

However, if a definite conclusion cannot be reached from the interim interval estimate, while sampling can continue, it is no longer possible to obtain a valid interval estimate from Appendix F of this book. A conditional probability situation has been created which negates the use of these tables.

There is a method of sampling called *two-step sampling* which establishes in *advance* of the actual sampling a small first sample and an additional sample to be used if certain conditions are encountered in the first or initial sample, such as finding more than a specified number of errors. A special method enables the determination of the true confidence limits when this approach is used.[2] It is to be cautioned that these confidence limits are different from those in Appendix F for the same total sample size.

This method may save considerable audit time when it is anticipated that there are few or no errors in the population and the anticipation actually turns out to be correct.

The method of interim appraisal is possible *only* if the items are audited in their random sequence. If, for the sake of convenience in locating the items in the file, the random numbers selected were placed in numerical sequence and audited in that sequence, a random sample does not exist at an interim point.

ANOTHER APPROACH TO SAMPLE SIZE ESTIMATION

The tables for appraisal of sample results for attributes (Appendix F) can be used to establish sample sizes by using them inversely. Thus, instead of resorting to the Appendix D tables, the auditor may establish his confidence level, desired sampling tolerance (precision), and maximum expected error and refer to the appropriate table of Appendix F. The maximum expected error rate may then be used as equivalent to the rate of occurrence in the sample in determining which of the pages of Appendix F to use.

Some use the F tables inversely by considering only one limit, usually the upper limit. For instance, the AICPA lesson in their Individual Study Series[3] provides a table for sample size determination which is based on such an approach.

[2]Herbert Arkin, *Sampling Methods for the Auditor, An Advanced Treatment,* McGraw-Hill Book Co., New York, 1982, pp. 26–34.

[3]*Sampling for Attributes, An Auditor's Approach to Statistical Sampling,* American Institute of Certified Public Accountants, New York, 1967.

The approach suggested in the AICPA lesson is that the rate of occurrence to be used is an estimate of the actual rate of occurrence. The tables provided in the AICPA lesson assume an infinite population.

This one-sided approach requires that the upper limit of the confidence interval be equated to the *maximum tolerable error rate* (MTER). Thus, if Appendix F is used inversely and the auditor decides that the MTER is 9% with a maximum expected rate of occurrence of 5% and a 95% confidence level, when the population is 10,000, reference would be made to Table F5 of Appendix F, since this is the table for rate of occurrence in a sample of 5% which is now equated to the maximum expected error rate. The page for the two-sided 90% confidence level would be used, since this is a one-sided 95% confidence interval estimate.

Using the column for field size of 10,000, it will be noted that an upper limit of 9% occurs on the line for sample size 150. Thus, the required sample size is 150.

However, the use of such an approach creates new problems. It is based on the assumption that the auditor is concerned only with the upper confidence interval and that his test objective will be accomplished if it can be determined that the upper confidence limit is *not more* than the maximum tolerable error rate (MTER). Such a condition will indeed be established *if* the rate of occurrence actually determined for the sample on completion of the audit test does not exceed the error rate (maximum error rate) estimated by the auditor in advance and used for entry in the table. In this situation, there is assurance that the actual rate in the population is less than the maximum tolerable error rate.

However, if the auditor has poorly estimated the maximum expected rate (or expected rate) of occurrence, or if an unexpected situation develops with the result that the *sample* contains more errors than expected, there is no provision for a determination as to whether the situation is in fact bad (too high an error rate in the population) or merely indeterminate because a large enough sample was not used. *Thus, the method presupposes that all audit tests will always disclose a good situation.*

This dilemma cannot be resolved by merely extending the sample, since the sampling technique then resolves itself into a form of double or multiple sampling plan (see page 155), where the calculations for the confidence limits cannot be accomplished by resorting to either the tables in this book or those in the AICPA lessons. The resulting calculations are sufficiently complex to indicate the need for a computer in each situation. Further, because of the innumerable possible combinations of first and second (and perhaps third) sample increments, complete tables for this purpose are not practical.

Lack of knowledge of a lower limit makes it impossible to establish that the actual rate of occurrence is in fact higher than the maximum tolerable error rate. To establish this fact it would have to be determined that the lower confidence limit *exceeded* the MTER.

A further difficulty with this type of approach was encountered in previous discussions (see page 79) where it was noted that, in a test of compliance with internal control, the concept of the maximum tolerable error rate does not provide a precise percentage to be tested, but rather a general level or area of errors which would be considered to be sufficiently serious to provide an indication of failure in the internal control system. Few auditors would be prepared to state that a rate of occurrence of deviation or errors of not more than 5.0% indicates compliance while 5.1% does not, even if these figures were obtained from a 100% audit of all the records.

If a *precise* value for the maximum tolerable error rate (MTER) cannot be established, neither can the sample size by this method.

Of course, this approach does seem more reasonable in concept because of the fact that the Appendix D-type tables are based on the assumption that the sampling distributions for attributes are normal, while it is now recognized that often they are skewed and with asymmetrical limits. If these tables are used on a *two*-sided confidence interval basis, the Appendix F tables are appropriate for sample size determination, although somewhat difficult to apply.

The use of the Appendix F tables on a two-sided basis presents problems. It will be remembered that the confidence limits encountered in the audit situation are likely to be asymmetrical with a smaller interval below the point estimate than above it.

A possible approach, which permits sample size determination for two-sided confidence interval estimates, consists of establishing the sample size by considering the sampling error on the upper side only, since this is the larger of the two intervals. This sampling error is the difference between the percentage found in the sample and the upper confidence limit. Thus, the sampling error (precision) on the upper side (between the per cent in the sample and the upper confidence limit, $-SE_{\%U}$) is greater than the sampling error on the lower side (between the per cent in the sample and the lower limit, $-SE_{\%L}$). Conservatively, the sample size estimate can be established by using only $SE_{\%U}$ for the desired sample precision, with the assurance that the sampling error on the lower side will be somewhat less.

When the sample size is small (for a given p), the disparity between the upper and lower precisions may be considerable. However, as the sample size is increased, the difference between the two precisions diminishes.

It is to be cautioned that if this method is applied, a rate of occurrence somewhat higher than that anticipated should be used in place of *rate of occurrence in the sample* in entering the tables.

If, after the sample is audited, the actual rate of occurrence in the sample exceeds the rate of occurrence used, the sampling error on the higher side will be larger than that desired. On the other hand, if the rate of occurrence in the sample is less than that used, the sampling error will be less.

Of course, after the audit test is completed, the actual sample precision can be established by reference to Appendix F.

SEVEN

Appraisal of Sample Results

(Variables)

THE NEED FOR POST-SAMPLING APPRAISAL

In Chapter 5 methods were developed to estimate the sample size required to provide a sample precision at a selected confidence level for an average or total (variables sampling). In other words, it was possible to determine a sample size which would be sufficient to ensure with a specified probability (confidence level) that the arithmetic mean (or a total) derived from a random sample would depart by not more than some specified amount from the value which might have been obtained if all the values in the field had been used to compute the average (or total).

It will be recalled that this method for the determination of sample size required that a preliminary sample be obtained from which it was possible to estimate the standard deviation of the values in the field. This estimate of the standard deviation was the determining factor in estimating the sample size, since the size of the sample required to achieve a given degree of precision was a function of the variability of the values contained in the field.

In Chapter 5, too, it was suggested that this initial, or preliminary, random sample include about 50 observations, a relatively small sample size. An uncertainty exists in the estimate of the standard deviation and, therefore, in the size of the sample actually required to achieve the desired sample estimation results.

After the sampling has been completed, a larger sample is available for the estimation of the standard deviation, thus providing the possibility of a more accurate estimate. On the basis of this larger sample, it is now possible to state with a greater degree of accuracy the sampling precision actually achieved.

ESTIMATING VARIABILITY

The group range method for determining the standard deviation outlined in Chapter 5 may be applied to the entire sample now that the sampling has been completed. However, it is to be recognized that the group range method provides only an approximate estimate of the population standard deviation. The preferable method is to calculate the standard deviation directly, using the formula on page 55 or in Technical Appendix I. This calculation can be greatly facilitated by using a pocket electronic calculator with statistical features including a standard deviation key. There are a number of calculators available that have this feature. In addition, there are a number of time-sharing computer programs which will perform this calculation. The advent of personal micro computers has provided another method for the computation. However, the average range method may be sufficient when a high degree of accuracy is not required.

The average range method consists of arranging all the items in the completed sample in groups of six, seven, or eight as a first step, *retaining the original random sequence in which the random number or systematic sample was attained.*

Let us reemphasize that the retention of these items in their original random sequence is essential. If, for convenience, the random numbers were arranged in numerical sequence to facilitate the location of the sample items in a file, the values must be restored to their original random sequence *before* this grouping is achieved.

As before (see Chapter 5), the range of the values in each group of six or seven items will then be obtained. These ranges will then be averaged for all groups and divided by the appropriate d_2 factor (see page 94, Chapter 5) to obtain a better estimate of the standard deviation.

Actually, a better estimate of the standard deviation than that yielded by the average range method is obtained by computing the standard deviation directly by the method outlined in Chapter 4 (page 55) or the method described in Technical Appendix I. However, these methods are arduous when any considerable amount of data are involved, and if the sample size on which the standard deviation is based exceeds 100, there will not be too much difference in the results obtained, with certain exceptions to be noted later.[1] Thus, for samples of reasonable size, the average range method will be sufficiently accurate for internal use. On the other hand, if the results of a test are to be presented as legal evidence, it would be well to use the more exact method in spite of the more arduous calculation required.

Once the standard deviation has been estimated from the entire sample used, it is possible to obtain a final determination of the reliability of the projection of the sample average to obtain the average or total of the field.

[1] In general, the average range method should not be used when estimating the total value of errors or other differences, since it will tend to underestimate the standard deviation of the population.

THE TABLES

Tables are provided in Appendix G which make it possible to determine the actual sampling precision achieved for an average based on this better estimate of the standard deviation.

These tables include a number of selected field sizes, sample sizes, and confidence levels and provide a ratio which when multiplied by the standard deviation gives the sample precision for the average at the specified confidence level.

In addition, a means is provided for determining sample precisions for sample sizes and field sizes not specified in the basic tables. This method will be discussed in detail later.

The use of the tables may be demonstrated by means of an example. To carry through the method completely, the example will start with the initial determination of sample size as demonstrated in Chapter 5 and then proceed to the additional drawings of sampling units to complete the required sample size and finally to the appraisal of sample results.

Assume that it is desired to estimate the *total value* of a certain type of expense voucher. It is known that there are 2,000 of these vouchers.

As before, the method will be to work through the average value and its reliability and to convert to a total value by multiplying the results by the field size N.

In this instance the objective is to estimate the total value of these vouchers to within ±$11,000.00 at the 95% confidence level. Since there are 2,000 of these vouchers, the average value will have to be determined to within

$$\pm \frac{\$11{,}000.00}{2{,}000} \text{ or } \pm \$5.50$$

A preliminary sample of 48 items is secured for the purpose of establishing the sample size required to achieve a sample precision of ±$5.50 at the 95% confidence level. The random sample drawings for the preliminary sample of 48 are shown in Table 7-1.

The average range $\bar{R}$ for all eight groups is $66.83. By dividing by the appropriate d_2 factor (for group size 6), the estimate of the standard deviation becomes:

$$\sigma = \frac{\text{average range}}{d_2} = \frac{\$66.83}{2.534} = \$26.37$$

Since the required sampling precision is ±$5.50 at the 95% confidence level, the ratio of the precision required to the standard deviation becomes:

$$\text{Ratio to } \sigma = \frac{\$5.50}{\$26.37} = .209$$

Appendix E on page 377 for field size 2,000 and for the 95% confidence level indicates that a sample size of 84 would be required to achieve a sample reliability equivalent to a ratio of .21 between the sampling error and the standard deviation.

TABLE 7-1

Voucher number	Amount	Voucher number	Amount	Voucher number	Amount	Voucher number	Amount
3018	$121.32*L*	7995	$132.27	7266	$157.48	6070	$170.40
2926	190.60*H*	2000	167.75*H*	6115	168.55	3973	140.50
1269	178.93	6445	160.68	3133	194.45*H*	6971	174.18
8759	189.58	5258	150.40	0411	122.70*L*	0182	188.03*H*
3377	121.72	9460	88.47*L*	4661	185.50	5136	182.60
6692	133.75	6338	117.92	4017	190.85	3981	89.47*L*
7393	185.48	8630	140.42	2855	109.42*L*	9992	163.45
0660	175.28	7241	154.30	1368	149.25	6052	141.07
6739	149.97	5470	141.72	4488	155.00	5579	193.43*H*
9441	198.45*H*	6465	128.25*L*	8966	151.03	0694	181.25
3681	172.40	5100	131.80	2285	149.05	6822	165.45
8749	146.32*L*	3230	161.63*H*	6991	168.70*H*	6627	122.42*L*
Group Ranges							
	$69.28		$79.28		$71.75		$98.56
	52.13		33.38		59.28		71.01

This sample of 84 may now be attained, but since 48 items have already been selected, only 36 additional items need be drawn.

The sample vouchers selected at random for the *additional* 36 items are listed in Table 7-2.

The previous ranges for the preliminary sample may now be included with the above to provide the average range for all 14 groups of six items each. This new average range is $66.49. Dividing the average range by the d_2 factor provides an improved estimate of the standard deviation.

$$\sigma = \frac{\text{average range}}{d_2} = \frac{\$66.49}{2.534} = \$26.24$$

When computed by the formula[2]

$$\sigma = \sqrt{\frac{\sum(X - \bar{X})^2}{n}}$$

[2]Another version of this formula generally used for electronic calculators or for programming computers is described in Technical Appendix I.

TABLE 7-2

Voucher number	Amount	Voucher number	Amount	Voucher number	Amount
5309	$180.00	3288	$162.25	5462	$114.10*L*
1316	155.77*L*	0356	170.15	3772	204.98*H*
3670	160.45	4965	152.68	6258	132.20
7365	202.98*H*	2747	194.50*H*	2260	165.78
6896	160.30	8887	123.87*L*	0189	157.35
1773	162.95	7347	132.87	6729	117.87
6545	160.48	2541	103.67*L*	2449	145.30
6106	142.55	2036	126.37	4097	139.55
6630	168.83*H*	3449	142.50	6154	149.60
9485	113.67*L*	8877	129.92	3610	96.17*L*
3286	127.90	5112	167.90*H*	4089	147.42
3867	133.07	4038	158.48	2137	164.30*H*

Group Ranges

	$47.21		$70.63		$90.88
	55.16		64.23		68.13

the standard deviation is found to be $26.55 rather than the estimate of $26.24 as obtained by the average range method.

The average of all 84 items is now obtained and found to be $152.5282. The sampling error of this average (point estimate) may now be established by referring to the G tables. For the field size of 2,000 and the 95% confidence level, the table indicates for sample size 80 that the sampling error as a multiple of the standard deviation is ±.2147.

The value for sample size 84 is not given, but a method will be explained later to cover missing sample values. In the meanwhile the value for sample size 80 rather than 84 will be used as a conservative estimate.

The factor obtained from these tables means that the sample precision (sampling error) of the *average* is ±.2147 times the standard deviation (at the 95% confidence level) or

$$\text{Sample precision for average} = \pm.2147(\$26.24) = \$5.6337$$

Thus, it is now found that the sampling precision achieved for the average is somewhat poorer than the ±$5.50 which was desired.[3] Multiplying this sample preci-

[3]This arises out of the fact that sample size 80 ratio rather than 84 was used in the calculation. On the basis of sample size 84 the sampling error becomes ±$5.49 (see later computation).

sion for the average by the field size of 2,000 indicates a sampling precision at the 95% confidence level for the *total* value of ±$11,267.40. The overall sample average of all 84 items was noted to be $152.5282. It may now be said that there are 95 chances in 100 that the average value of all these vouchers is between $152.5282 ±$5.6337 or between $146.8945 and $158.1619.

Multiplying each of these limits by the field size of 2,000 places the confidence limits for the *total* value of all 2,000 vouchers between $293,789.00 and $316,323.-80. When the standard deviation calculated by the formula method is used, the confidence limits become $293,655.80 to $316,457.00.

VALUES NOT COVERED BY TABLES

It is not possible to prepare tables which will cover any and every situation, for they would be too large. Thus, it may happen that either the specific field size or the specific sample size used is not included in the table. To provide coverages for such a situation, a special method making use of two tables has been developed.

As explained on page 72 of Chapter 4, the sample precision of an average may be determined from the following formula when the field size is very large as compared to the sample size or when it is infinite.

$$\text{Sample precision of average} = \pm t\frac{\sigma}{\sqrt{n}}$$

where t = a factor determined by the confidence level based on Table 4-3 (For the 95% level the factor is 1.96; for 99% it is 2.58.)

σ = standard deviation

n = sample size

A table has been developed (Appendix H) for sample sizes from 40 to 300 (by 1) and for certain values beyond this, which provides the solution of this formula for the confidence levels given in the other tables, on the basis of a standard deviation assumed to be equal to 1. Multiplying the value in this table by the standard deviation of the sample at hand will provide a statement of the actual sample precision at the selected confidence level for an infinite field size.

This table covers appraisal of sample precision of averages for all very large (in effect, infinite) fields. The coverage with reference to the number of items in the sample here will provide for most cases likely to be encountered by the auditor.

However, it was observed in Chapter 4 (see page 74) that when the sample constitutes any appreciable proportion of the field, a further correction is necessary, making use of the "finite correction factor." This factor is used as a multiplier of the value in the infinite field size table to provide for any field size.

The table of finite correction factors is given in Appendix I. To obtain the finite correction value, the proportion of the field included in the sample is calculated by dividing the sample size n by the field size N. The table then gives the finite correction directly.

For a specific problem not covered by the table, the method may be outlined as follows:

1. Determine the standard deviation of the sample values, using the average range and d_2 factor or by formula as before.
2. In the table for infinite field size (Appendix H), select the column for the desired confidence level and the row for the sample size. Read off the ratio indicated.
3. In the finite correction factor table (Appendix I), find the line appropriate to the percentage of the field included in sample of n/N. Read off the finite correction factor.
4. Obtain the product of the three values determined in steps 1, 2, and 3, or

$$\text{Standard deviation} \times \text{ratio} \times \text{finite factor}$$

The result will be the sample precision.

The method may be illustrated using the problem previously worked out in this chapter. It was noted that the sample size of 84 was not included in the tables for field size 2,000. Sample size 80 was used as an approximation. The exact value may now be computed.

Step 1. The standard deviation was determined by the method of the average range (page 119) and found to be \$26.24 (by formula, \$26.55).

Step 2. In the table for infinite field size the ratio for sample size 84 at the 95% confidence level is .2139.

Step 3. The percentage of the field included in the sample is found by dividing the sample size by the field size.

$$\frac{84}{2{,}000} = 4.2\%$$

The table of finite correction factors gives a value of .9788 for 4.2%.

Step 4. The sampling precision of the average of this sample is then the product of these three values.

$$\text{Standard deviation} \times \text{ratio} \times \text{finite factor} = \$26.24 \times .2139 \times .9788 = \pm\$5.49$$

This figure of ±\$5.49 compares to the previous approximation based on sample size 80 of ±\$5.63.

ONE-SIDED CONFIDENCE LIMITS

The projection of the average or total value based on the average obtained from the sample is called a ***point estimate.*** The statement of the confidence limits is referred to as an ***interval estimate.*** The difference or spread between these two limits is called the ***confidence interval.*** The ***sample precision*** is the difference between the point estimate and the confidence limits or, for variables sampling, one-half of the confidence interval.

As for attributes estimation (see Chapter 6), the projection in terms of the confidence limits provides two-sided confidence limits, or, in other words, a statement that there is a specified probability that the value, which would have been obtained if all the items in the field had been used, would have been not less than the lower confidence limit nor more than the upper.

Thus, in the example given above, a sample of 84 out of a field of 2,000 gave a point estimate of $305,056.40 and an interval estimate of between $294,076.40 and $316,036.40.

Once again, the auditor's interest may not be to establish the fact that the true value is between the two stated limits, but rather that it is not less than some given value or, as another possible objective, not more than some specified value.

Figure 4-8 shows the general form of the sampling distribution for averages. This diagram illustrates that 95% of all the possible arithmetic means obtainable from this field would be included within a range of

$$1.96\frac{\sigma}{\sqrt{n}} \quad \text{(for infinite field sizes)}$$

about the value which would have been obtained if all the items in the field had been included in the computation.

However, the true value is unknown. Therefore, it can only be concluded that 95 chances in 100, the sample value is no further from the true value than $1.96\sigma/\sqrt{n}$. For example, assume that a random sample of 100 items is drawn from a very large field and that the sample discloses a mean of $200.00 and a standard deviation of $80.00. On this basis it would be expected that the sampling distribution would be such that of 95 chances in 100 any given sample value would be no further from the true mean than

$$1.96\,\frac{\$80.00}{\sqrt{100}} = 1.96\,(\$8.00) = \$15.68$$

This is shown graphically in Figure 7-1.

This situation may be looked at from a different viewpoint, although the same answer will result. The question may be asked as to the highest value of the average that could exist in a field (with this same standard deviation) and give rise to a sample with a mean equal to or less than that observed and a probability equal to 1 minus the confidence level divided by 2, or in this case

$$\frac{1 - .95}{2} = .025 \text{ or } 2.5\%$$

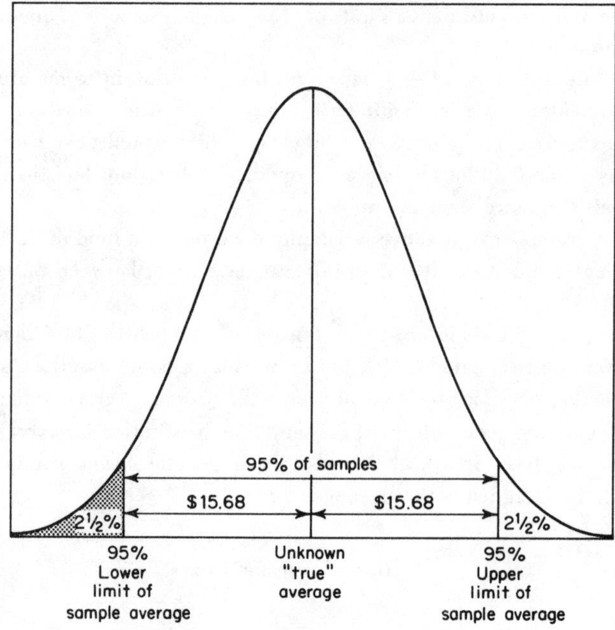

FIGURE 7-1

Thus, the highest value of the average of the field that might exist and still have a probability of 2½% of producing a sample average as low as or lower than the one observed is the observed value plus $1.96\sigma_{\bar{X}}$ (see Figure 7-2). Any higher value of the average in the field would have less than a 2½% probability of producing a sample with the observed average. Thus, it may be said that there is a 97.5% probability (100%−2½%) that the actual field average will be not more than the sample average plus $1.96\sigma_{\bar{X}}$. It will be noted that this value is equivalent to the *upper* confidence limit for the 95% confidence level, but the probability associated with it is 97.5% instead of 95%.

A similar line of reasoning can be used to establish a one-sided lower limit. In other words, the upper and lower confidence limits may be used *separately* as one-sided confidence limits but with a change in the confidence level. The relations between one-sided and two-sided confidence level interpolations are shown in Table 7-3.

TABLE 7-3

When the two-sided confidence level is	*Then the one-sided confidence level is*
.90	.950
.95	.975
.99	.995
.995	.9975

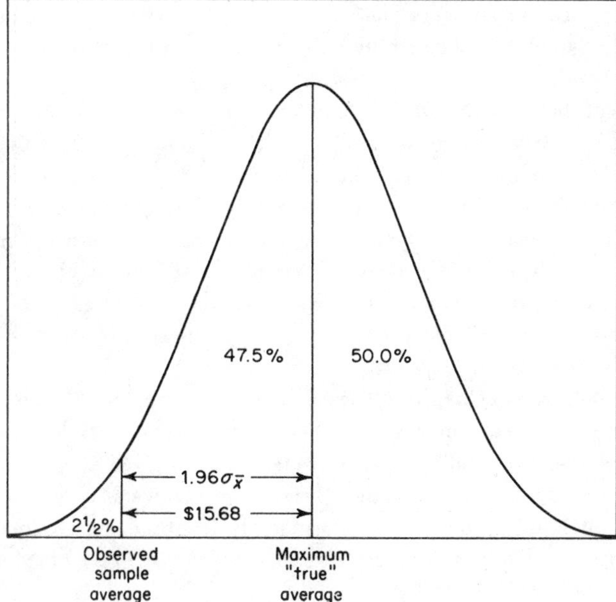

FIGURE 7–2

The one-sided confidence level concept can be used in a variety of situations in auditing. For instance, it can be used to establish that the total dollar value of the errors determined by an audit does *not exceed* some amount (at a specific confidence level). In another situation, a one-sided confidence limit can be used to demonstrate that the total dollar value of an inventory is *not less than* some amount (at a given confidence level).

GENERAL CONSIDERATIONS

In previous discussions, it was noted that precise knowledge of the field size was not required in order to ascertain the reliability of an average value or percentage of occurrence obtained from a sample unless the sample included a larger percentage of the field. Since such a circumstance is uncommon, a reasonable approximation of the size of the field generally would suffice for establishing the reliability of an average or percentage obtained from a sample.

For instance, if a sample of 300 observations is drawn from a field of 10,000, the precision of the sample average is ±.1114 times the standard deviation, while from a field of 20,000 it is .1123 times the standard deviation. A very small difference indeed!

However, it is to be noted that the auditor's object often will be to estimate a *total* rather than an average value. The mechanism for establishing an estimate of a total value together with its confidence interval is to secure the average and its confidence limits from the sample and then multiply these values by the number of items *in the field, N.*

To the extent that the field size is incompletely or inaccurately known, this multiplication will introduce an error or bias *in addition to and apart from* the sampling variability. Thus, decidedly incorrect knowledge of the field size may result in severe errors in estimating totals far beyond the magnitude of the sampling errors, rendering the results of limited value. Of course, it may not be practical to attempt to ascertain the field size precisely, but in such cases it is essential that it be established with some reasonable assurance that no major error exists in such an estimate.

Certain methods are available when a precise population size cannot be established. These are discussed below.

Once again, as noted in Chapter 4, special precautions must be taken in estimating an average or total from a sample when the field is badly skewed. In such a situation, it will be remembered, the bulk of the values fall within a given range, but relatively few values are greatly different from the others. For instance, in a group of accounts receivable the bulk of the account balances may be less than some value, say $500 or $1,000, with a few items of very great value included, say in the range of $50,000 to $100,000 or more.

In such an instance, the method of separating and testing separately these very high-value accounts is appropriate. This is called ***stratified sampling.*** The very high-value balances may be examined on a 100% basis or may be sampled, but they are dealt with as separate fields and the results then combined.

The methods to be used to obtain an idea of the overall reliability of an estimate of an average or total secured from a stratified sample will be discussed in a later chapter, as will other sampling methods of a more sophisticated nature.

It is important that a note of caution be sounded at this point relative to a problem unique to the application of sampling techniques in auditing. This problem arises when estimating a total, as in the validation of an account balance.

For instance, assume that it is desired to establish the reasonableness of the stated book record value of an inventory by taking an independent probability sample of inventory items which are to be counted, priced, extended, and projected. This is to be done in lieu of the less adequate method of inventory "observation" as generally practiced. As a result of such a test, a valid interval estimate of the total value of the inventory can be achieved with a specified confidence level.

However, there may be two different kinds of errors in the original establishment of the inventory book record value. There may be errors arising from the process of fixing the total values of each inventory item, resulting from inaccurate counting, pricing, and extending. On the other hand, there may be errors in accumulating the total value of all inventory items, arising not only from possible errors in footing but from the possibility of other cumulating errors.

In any case, a cumulating error if of material magnitude will cause a disparity between the result of the sample projection and the book record value which will be discovered provided the confidence interval is sufficiently small.

However, it must be emphasized that the effects of errors in calculating the values of individual items included in the book record inventory value (such as counting, pricing, or extending) will be reflected *only if some of these errors affecting the individual items are included in the sample.*

Since such errors may be rare, if the sample is not of sufficient magnitude to include some of these errors, the projection of the sample will merely establish the validity of the cumulation process. Of course, stratification involving 100 per cent examination of all inventory items which have values of sufficient magnitude to include a material error will be of great help, at least insofar as errors of overstatement are concerned. On the other hand, if there are, say, 20 stock items which are not in themselves material in amount but include errors, each amounting to one-tenth of a material error, out of a possible 5,000 inventory items, an error twice the amount of a material error could exist in the book record value without being detected, unless the sample size was sufficient to provide a high probability that at least some of these errors are included *in the sample.*

The concepts of discovery sampling discussed in the next chapter will be helpful in establishing the sample sizes which give adequate assurance of such protection.

It is emphasized that all of the methods discussed thus far for all types of sampling (estimation, discovery, and acceptance) have been based on the assumption of an unrestricted random sample obtained by drawing individual observations one at a time from the whole field without distinction.

Special sampling techniques which obtain samples by other than unrestricted random sampling will be discussed in detail later.

ESTIMATING TOTAL VALUES WHEN POPULATION SIZE IS UNKNOWN

The mechanism of establishing the point estimate of a total value is to establish the average value of the sampling units included in the sample and multiply that average by the population size (N). The interval estimate may then be established by multiplying the sampling error of the average by N to secure the sampling error of the total.

However, there are situations in which the population size (total number of sampling units in the population) is not known precisely or is not known at all.

If an imprecise population size (N) is used, the point estimate of the total value, and thus the interval estimate of the total value, will be incorrect. This error is unrelated to sampling variations and this is *not* allowed for in the calculation of the interval estimate. Of course, if the error in knowledge of the population size is negligible, the point estimate and the interval estimate of the total will, in turn, be in error by a negligible amount.[4]

However, even if the population size is not known at all, or if it is known only very

[4]This error in the knowledge of the population size will have little effect on the interval estimate of an *average* value and none on the point estimate of an average.

approximately, there are methods which nevertheless may be used to provide valid point estimates or interval estimates of total values.

The lack of precise knowledge of population size can be offset by creating a "pseudo" population by adding empty or blank sampling units.

When this technique is used, the population size is deliberately overestimated.[5] When random numbers are drawn for selecting the sampling units, some may select units in the range beyond the actual number in the population.

For instance, in a situation where page and line number sample selection techniques are used and there are numerous pages with less than all lines occupied or with an unknown total number of lines, the population size cannot be established unless all lines are counted. However, this would not be practical if the population is large. In this situation, the approach would be to assume that not more than some maximum number of items appears on the page. This maximum must be equal to or, more conservatively, more than the actual number of lines on *any* page.

When the sample is selected, some of the selected units may be on lines which have no entry or value. If these items are selected, their value is considered to be *equal to zero.* The population size is then the total number of pages times the theoretical maximum number of lines per page used. This value of N may be used for multiplying the average sample value to obtain the point estimate of the total.

Another situation in which this kind of problem may arise exists when sampling from listings such as payrolls, where each sampling unit may consist of a varying number of lines of entry so that if the sampling units (say employees) are not numbered consecutively, the determination of the population size (N) for large populations may present a serious problem.

It is to be noted that this technique has the disadvantage that the inclusion of the zero values obtained for the empty sampling unit may increase the variability of the population and thus result in a higher standard deviation, both for the sample and for the population. This, in turn, will result in a higher sampling error than would have resulted had the technique not been used.

However, there are some instances where the population size is completely unknown and the use of empty sampling units is not practical.

For instance, it was desired to obtain the total value of the amounts indicated on a set of documents numbered in the hundreds of thousands which were stored in hundreds of dead file boxes. The population size was known to be between 200,000 and 500,000.

It was possible to select the sample without knowledge of the population size by choosing random numbers for file box numbers and another set of random numbers for item numbers in the box. The sampling units to be included were then found by locating the box specified by the first random number and counting down to a specified document.

[5]It is essential that this deliberate overestimate be of sufficient magnitude to make certain that it is greater than the true population value.

The average value of the documents in the sample can be established from the sample. However, a population size was necessary. This was accomplished by taking a random sample of the boxes in which these documents were stored. The *average* number of documents in the sampled boxes was multiplied by the total number of boxes. This point estimate of the population size (N) was then multiplied by the average value of the documents in the other sample to provide a point estimate of the total value.

However, since *both* the average value (X) and the population size (N) were determined from samples, there are two sampling errors, one for the average value and one for the population size. These two sampling errors may be combined as shown below:[6]

$$SE^2_{\text{Total}} = N'^2 SE_{\bar{X}}^2 + \bar{X}^2 SE_{N'}^2$$

where SE_{Total} = sampling error of total
$SE_{\bar{X}}$ = sampling error of average value
SE_N = sampling error of estimate of N
$\bar{X}$ = average value of sample items
N' = point estimate of population size from the other sample

The method may be illustrated by the following example. Assume that there are 653 boxes containing these documents. A sample of 500 documents is selected and provides an average value ($\bar{X}$) of $10.00 with a standard deviation of $2.00. A separate sample of 80 boxes are counted and it is found that there is an average of 610 documents per box and a standard deviation of these counts equal to 50. Thus the estimate of the population size (N') is calculated as follows:

$$N' = \bar{N} n_B = 610(653) = 398{,}330$$

where N' = point estimate of total number of documents
$\bar{N}$ = average number of documents in boxes sampled
n_B = number of boxes sampled

The point estimate of the total value of all documents in the population is

$$\text{Total} = N'\bar{X} = 398{,}330\ (\$10.00) = \$3{,}983{,}300.00$$

The sampling error of the average value can be calculated as described in the first part of this chapter as follows:

A. From Appendix H

n = 500
Confidence level = 95%
Factor (sampling error as multiple of standard deviation) = .0877

[6]The method described may be used only when two independent samples are used to estimate the average and population size.

B. Finite Population Correction (f.p.c.) Factor

$N = 398{,}330$
$n = 500$

$$\text{f.p.c.} = \sqrt{1 - \frac{500}{398{,}330}} = .9984$$

C. Sampling Error of Average ($\overline{X}$)
Sampling error average = factor × f.p.c. × standard deviation

$$SE_{\overline{X}} = (.0877) \times (\$2.00) \times (.9984) = \$.1752$$

The sampling error of population size estimate (N') is computed as follows:

A. From Appendix H

$n_B = 80$
Confidence level = 95%
Factor (sampling error as multiple of standard deviation) = .2191

B. Finite Population Correction Factor (Appendix I)

$$N_B = 653$$
$$n_B = 80$$
$$\frac{n_B}{N_B} = \frac{80}{653} = 12.3\%$$

$$\text{f.p.c.} = .9370$$

C. Sampling Error of Average (N')

$$SE_{\overline{N'}} = (.2191) \times (.9370) \times (50) = 10.26$$

D. Sampling Error of Population Size (N')

$$SE_{\overline{N'}} = 10.26$$
$$SE_{N'} = (10.26)\,653 = 6{,}667$$

E. Sampling Error of Total Value

$$SE_{\overline{X}} = \$.1752$$
$$SE_{N'} = 6{,}667$$
$$\overline{X} = \$10.00$$
$$N' = 398{,}330$$

$$SE^2_{\text{Total}} = N'^2 SE_{\overline{X}}^2 + \overline{X}^2 SE_{N'}^2$$
$$SE^2_{\text{Total}} = (398{,}330)^2 (\$.1752)^2 + (\$10.00)^2 (6{,}667)^2$$
$$SE_{\text{Total}} = \$96{,}515.17$$

The interval estimate of the total value is then

$$\$3{,}983{,}300 \pm \$96{,}515 = \$3{,}886{,}785 \text{ to } \$4{,}079{,}815$$

It is interesting to note that, in this instance, the lack of knowledge increased the sampling error from ±\$69,915.00 to \$96,515.00 or about 38% above the sampling error with known population size.

EIGHT

Discovery Sampling

THE PLACE OF DISCOVERY SAMPLING IN AUDITING

As defined in *Codification of Statements on Auditing Standards,*[1] the auditing process calls for a study of and evaluation of the existing internal control system as a basis for the determination of the extent of testing, followed by the examination of evidential matter in support of the opinion. The standards state that "sufficient competent evidential matter is to be obtained through inspection, observation, inquiries, and confirmations to afford a reasonable basis for an opinion regarding the financial statements under examination."[2] However, it is evident that the examination of evidential matter is concerned with the validity of the conclusions drawn from the study of the internal control system as well as with the desire to create a reasonable basis for an opinion regarding the financial statements under examination.

Evidence of numerous clerical errors, failure to comply with the internal control system in numerous instances, frequent violations of accepted accounting principles, or evidence of manipulation or fraud will render the previously drawn conclusions as to the effectiveness of the prescribed system of little value in assessing the financial statements.

The *Codification of Statements on Auditing Standards* states that "the auditor's examination, based on the principle of selective testing of the data being examined,

[1]*Codification of Statements on Auditing Standards,* American Institute of Certified Public Accountants, Commerce Clearing House, Chicago, 1982, Sec. 320.
[2]*Ibid.,* p. 93.

is subject to the inherent risk that material errors or irregularities, if they exist, will not be detected."[3] Irregularities are defined as deliberate manipulations or misrepresentations.

This situation arises, according to that publication, because "the auditor's objective in making an examination of financial statements . . . is to form an opinion on whether the statements present fairly financial position, results of operations and changes in financial position. . . ."[4] It is noted that because of this objective and cost limitations, the examination is limited and therefore subject to the above risks. Hence, "in view of these and other limitations . . . the subsequent discovery that errors or irregularities existed during the period . . . does not, in itself, indicate inadequate performance. . . ."[5]

The point is made that the auditor's function is to establish that "financial statements taken as a whole are not materially misstated as a result of errors or irregularities."[6]

Nevertheless, few auditors would claim complete indifference as to the possible existence of irregularities, such as fraud, in the records being examined, even if the amount of these irregularities is less than that required to create a material error in the financial statements. In addition, there may be times when, by the terms of a special engagement or for a particular reason, the auditor considers himself especially responsible for making some effort to disclose deliberate manipulations of the accounts, particularly if they are committed with any degree of frequency.

The auditor is concerned, therefore, with detection of three types of disparities: (1) inadvertent clerical or arithmetic errors; (2) violations of the internal control system; (3) evidence of manipulation or fraud. The objective of the independent auditor in performing his test usually is to determine either the frequency with which errors or violations of internal control procedures exist or to evaluate the dollar-value impact of disparities upon the stated balances.

Usually some form of estimation sampling provides indication as to the possible extent of error which might exist in the record keeping as well as the impact of these errors on the end result.

However, it is entirely possible that he may have an additional or different objective in mind when he performs his test. Insofar as serious individual disparities, such as material errors, flagrant evasions of critical phases of the internal control system, or instances of fraud or manipulation are concerned, his interest may well be not in determining how often such instances occur or their dollar-value impact but rather to find at least a single example of such a violation if it occurs. His interest is channeled along these paths because he has decided in advance that, upon discovery, other procedures would be devised to determine the complete extent of

[3]*Ibid.*, p. 108.
[4]*Ibid.*, p. 104.
[5]*Ibid.*
[6]*Ibid.*, p. 108.

the occurrence and the characteristics of the system that allowed the unsatisfactory incident to take place. The discovery of the type of transaction that went wrong becomes the important thing.

The commercial independent auditor has a somewhat indefinite attitude toward his responsibility in relation to detecting fraud. Bulletin no. 30 of the AICP[7] states that "the responsibility of the independent auditor for failure to detect fraud (which responsibility differs as to clients and others) arises only where such failure clearly results from non-compliance with generally accepted auditing standards." The internal auditor is not in so comfortable a position with relation to protection from fraud or irregularity against his organization. This is also true of the government auditor.

Thus, the internal auditor by means of his tests must attempt to seek evidence of flagrant violations of the system, massive errors or defalcations, and in doing so he must assure himself that, if such situations do exist, he will have a reasonable probability that he will disclose evidence to this effect in his test.

The type of evidence required here, as noted before, need be only one example of such a serious deviation or irregularity. If found in the test, this one instance is sufficient to precipitate vigorous action on the part of the auditor, such as a broader test or even a detailed examination. Here the objective is different. It is not desired to find out how many instances of such irregularities exist nor the dollar values involved. It is merely to provide a reasonable probability of bringing *at least one* example of such an irregularity to light in the sample or test.

The question to be answered here is how big a sample will be required to give reasonable probability of disclosure. At this point, it should be recognized that there is no way of guaranteeing or even achieving a reasonable probability of finding the "needle-in-the-haystack" type of case when a test or sample is used. For example, if there is one instance of fraud in a million records, no sample short of virtual complete examination can give any reasonable assurance that the case will be found. There is some doubt, owing to the sheer mass of the records to be examined, that even a 100% check would disclose such a unique instance.

Thus, at best, an auditor can hope to find examples of such irregularities in a large field *only* if they occur with some minimum frequency or represent a *pattern* of irregularities. While an auditor would be seriously concerned with even a single case of fraud, his practical inability to examine all the items in a large field makes it necessary that he be content to seek to find more frequent occurrences or patterns of irregularities.

Actually, a similar situation applies in even relatively small fields. For instance, if an auditor is confronted with a field of 1,000 documents and finds it impractical to examine all of them, perhaps because of the time required for examining each

[7]*Responsibilities and Functions of the Independent Auditor in the Examination of Financial Statements*, Bulletin no. 30, Statements on Auditing Procedure, American Institute of Certified Public Accountants, New York, September 1960.

document, a sample of even 400 will provide him with only a 40% probability of finding an example of the irregularity in his test, if there is only one in the field.

If the auditor will accept this premise, it is possible through the use of the theory of probability to determine the sample size which would be required to provide any desired degree of assurance that the sample will include *at least one* specimen of the type of event sought, provided it occurs in the field with *some minimum frequency* or rate. Of course, a probability (random sample) will be required. This type of approach to the test has been given the name *discovery*[8] or *exploratory*[9] sampling.

While such sample size determination is possible by resorting to prepared tables of the type included in Appendix J, the proper use of these tables can best be achieved if the principles upon which they were compiled are understood. For this reason, a brief explanation follows as to how the theory of probability is used in arriving at the sample sizes given in the table.

PRINCIPLES OF DISCOVERY SAMPLING

If a sample of specified size is drawn from a universe containing a given proportion of some events, it is possible to compute the probability that the sample will contain none of these events, one of these events, two of these events, etc. Of course, such calculations are possible only if a probability (random) sample is used so that the laws of probability are operative.

In the simplest case, the sample is drawn from a very large universe (say in the millions). This situation will be used to illustrate the basic principles. In Chapter 4, it was shown that if a specified number of balls are drawn from a very large container of thoroughly mixed balls containing 50% black and 50% white balls, it would be possible to calculate the probability that the sample would contain no black balls, 1 black ball, 2 black balls, etc. (see page 61). This situation can be compared to an auditor's search for a given event occurring in a very large field when 50% of the sampling units (or records) represent the type of event sought. The black balls can be used to represent the specified type of event sought. A question may be raised about the probability that his sample will contain various numbers of black balls.

Chapter 4 demonstrated the calculation of the probabilities for drawings of 2 balls, 3 balls, and 10 balls in such a situation. The results of these computations are summarized in Table 8-1 together with some additional probabilities for other sample sizes.

Just as this computation has been performed for various numbers of balls drawn (sample sized) from 2 to 10, it can be computed for larger sample sizes.

[8]H. Arkin, "Statistical Sampling in Auditing," *The New York Certified Public Accountant*, July 1957, pp. 467–469.

[9]L. N. Teitelbaum and M. A. Schwartz, "Practical Improvements in Audit Testing," *Journal of the Institute of Internal Auditors*, September 1958, pp. 10–11.

TABLE 8–1. ***Outcome of Drawings of Various Numbers of Balls from Large Population Containing 50 Per Cent Black Balls***

Sample size	0 black balls	1 black balls	2 black balls	3 black balls	4 black balls	5 black balls	6 black balls	7 black balls	8 black balls	9 black balls	10 black balls
2	25.00%	50.00%	25.00%								
3	12.50	37.50	37.50	12.50%							
4	6.25	25.00	37.50	25.00	6.25%						
5	3.13	15.62	31.25	31.25	15.62	3.13%					
6	1.56	9.38	23.44	31.25	23.44	9.38	1.56%				
7	0.78	5.47	16.41	27.34	27.34	16.41	5.47	0.78%			
8	0.39	3.13	10.94	21.87	27.34	21.87	10.94	3.13	0.39%		
9	0.20	1.76	7.03	16.40	24.61	24.61	16.40	7.03	1.76	0.20%	
10	0.10	0.98	4.39	11.72	20.51	24.61	20.51	11.72	4.39	0.98	0.10%

The probability for *at least one* black ball in the sample can be obtained by adding the probabilities for 1 black ball, 2 black balls, etc., for each sample size or more simply by subtracting the probability of *zero* black balls from 100% (see Table 8-2).

Thus, based on Table 8-2, if an auditor draws 10 records (number of balls) from a large number of records (balls) containing 50% of a given type, the probability that at least one (or more) containing that type of event (black ball) will be included in the sample will be 99.90%.

Of course, the auditor need not worry about finding an example of such an instance if the event is so prevalent that it includes 50% of the records. However, by resorting to appropriate mathematical calculations,[10] the same computations can be performed when other proportions exist in the population. The result of the calculation is shown in Table 8-3 for sample size 10 from populations with various proportions of these events.

It is seen in Table 8-3, that if a large population contains only 1% of the type of event, the probability of finding at least one of these events in the sample of 10 is

[10]The formula for the calculation of the probability of at least one occurrence becomes:

$$Pr = 1 - \frac{C_o^d C_n^{N-d}}{C_n^N}$$

where N = field size

n = sample size

d = number of events in field

Pr = probability of at least one event in sample

$$C_n^N = \frac{N!}{n!(N-n)!}$$

$$C_a^b = \frac{b!}{a!(b-a)!} \text{ generally}$$

TABLE 8–2

Sample size	Probability of zero black balls	Probability of one black ball or more
2	25.00%	75.00%
3	12.50	87.50
4	6.25	93.75
5	3.13	96.87
6	1.56	98.44
7	0.78	99.22
8	0.39	99.61
9	0.20	99.80
10	0.10	99.90

TABLE 8-3. *Probabilities of* at Least One *Occurrence in Sample of 10 Balls Drawn from Large Populations Containing Various Proportions of Black Balls*

Per cent in population	Probability of zero black balls	Probability of at least one black ball or more
1%	90.44%	9.56%
5	59.87	40.13
10	34.87	65.13
15	19.69	80.31
20	10.74	89.26
25	5.63	94.37
30	2.82	97.18
35	1.35	98.65
40	0.60	99.40
45	0.25	99.75
50	0.10	99.90

less than 1 in 10 (actually 9.56%). Thus, if an auditor seeking evidence of some type of event (say duplicate payment) which actually occurs as often as 1 in every 100 records takes a sample of size 10 for his test, his probability of including any of these instances in his sample is very small.

Of course, this deficiency in the test can be overcome by taking a larger sample. The problem here relates to how large a sample is required to raise his probability of including *at least one* such event in the sample of a reasonable level. This can be calculated. The problem is complicated mathematically when the field or population is not very large. However, the probabilities may be calculated here as well.[11] To avoid the need for intricate mathematical calculations, tables have been prepared which provide the values required for auditor's decision.

TABLES FOR DISCOVERY SAMPLING

A set of tables is included in Appendix J which provides the auditor with the information which will enable him to develop a discovery sampling plan in a given situation. More extended sets of tables for discovery (exploratory) sampling have been published by the office of the Auditor General of the United States Air Force.[12] However, the tables given here will provide the basis for all but very rare situations.

[11]See footnote 10 for the formula for the calculation of the probability of at least one occurrence.

[12]*Tables of Probabilities for Use in Exploratory Sampling,* Auditor General, Department of the Air Force. This set of tables is based on the *number* of events in the population rather than the *proportion* of events in the field. This results in a much larger table.

These tables indicate for various field and sample sizes the probability that *at least one* example of the event sought will be included in the sample when it occurs in the field at a specified rate.

The use of these tables is best demonstrated by means of an illustration. Assume that an auditor is concerned with the probability that a certain type of evasion of internal control procedures is occurring. He has a field of 10,000 documents which might be examined to determine whether there are such violations, but an effort of this magnitude is beyond his ability in time and cost.

He realizes that if he takes a sample as the basis for his examination, he cannot have certainty that he will find either every violation or, for that matter, any examples if the number of instances of these violations are few in number. However, if any examples are encountered, he will extend his investigation.

Because of time and other practical limitations, he must use a partial examination or sample test, but nevertheless he wants reasonable assurance of encountering an example of such a violation if it exists. On the other hand, he recognizes that if there are only one or two violations among the 10,000 records, no reasonable sample size will provide a useful assurance or probability that he will find one of them in a sample.

While he would like to find such a violation, even if only one or two occur, he must satisfy himself with obtaining such assurance if a greater number of instances or a pattern occurs. He is willing to decide that if as many as .5% (or 50 out of 10,000) of the records contain violations, he must have high assurance that he will find such an example in his test.

The auditor will have to decide on the risk he is willing to run of not finding an example if it occurs in this field at the rate of .5% and thus his sample size will be fixed. For example, he may decide that since he cannot eliminate all risk, he would be satisfied with a 95% probability of finding at least one example, if it occurs in the field at the selected rate.

Turning to the table in Appendix J headed "Probability Level 95%," and locating the row for field size 10,000 and the column for 0.5%, the auditor will note that a sample size of 582 will be required to meet his needs.

It is to be noted that if the incidence actually is .5% in the field, this will be the *largest* sample size required to ensure finding at least one example. However, it is not known whether the example will turn up as the first, last, or some intermediate sampling unit selected. Of course, if an example is found before the entire 582 are selected, the auditor may terminate his sampling at this point and take whatever action is appropriate. In other words, it is quite possible that the entire sample size will be required to accomplish this purpose, or it may require the selection of some part, perhaps only a small part, of the sample items before the example is found.

In interpreting the method, it should be emphasized that the selection of the plan on the basis of .5% in the field does not preclude finding examples when the actual occurrence rate is less than .5%. For instance, if the rate of occurrence is as low as only .3% instead of .5%, the probability of finding at least one example with sample size 582 is 83.4%, or quite a high level. In fact, if the actual incidence is only .1%, there is still almost a 50% chance (45.1% to be exact) of locating an example.

Conversely, if the actual rate of incidence in the field is higher than that selected, the probability of including at least one example in the sample is increased. For instance, the sample size 600 selected on the basis of .5% in the field will actually yield an almost certain probability of disclosing at least one example in the sample (99.8%) if the actuul rate is 1.0%.

GENERAL CONSIDERATIONS

It is to be noted that a sample drawn for discovery sampling can also be interpreted to give an indication as to the level of error rate. For instance, if a discovery sample is completed *without disclosing an example* of the type sought, this may be interpreted to mean that there is a high probability that the error rate is *less* than that used for sample size selection.

Thus, for sample size 582 for a field of 10,000, selected as above, to give a 95% probability of disclosing at best one example in the sample, if the field contains .5% *and none are found*, the result may be interpreted to mean that there is a 95% probability that the rate is *less* than .5%. Similarly, it was shown that sample size 582 gives an 83.5% probability of disclosure if the rate is .3%. Thus, if none are found, there is an 83.5% probability that the rate is less than .3%.

Since they comprise a probability sample, the data obtained from the sample used for discovery sampling can be interpreted as other forms of sampling plans.

Actually, the discovery sampling plan itself has been used as an acceptance sampling plan (with a zero acceptance number) for rejection or acceptance, but it is important to note that this was not the original *intent of the plan.* The interpretation of this approach will be discussed later. The purpose of discovery sampling is disclosure, not acceptance or rejection.

DISCOVERY SAMPLING AND ESTIMATION SAMPLING

Discovery sampling can be used in conjunction with estimation sampling to provide an estimate of the rate of occurrence in the field. If the application of discovery sampling discloses an event of the type sought, the auditor can easily convert to the use of the estimation sampling approach to estimate how many such events exist. On the occurrence of the first such error, the auditor can determine how large a sample he will have to take to provide an estimate of the rate of occurrence by using the principles outlined in Chapter 5.

Since his initial sample up to this point has been chosen by random (probability sampling) methods, he may use the data already included in the test and merely extend his sample size to provide the sample reliability and confidence level desired. He will, of course, reappraise his sample result when he obtains it.

NINE

Acceptance Sampling

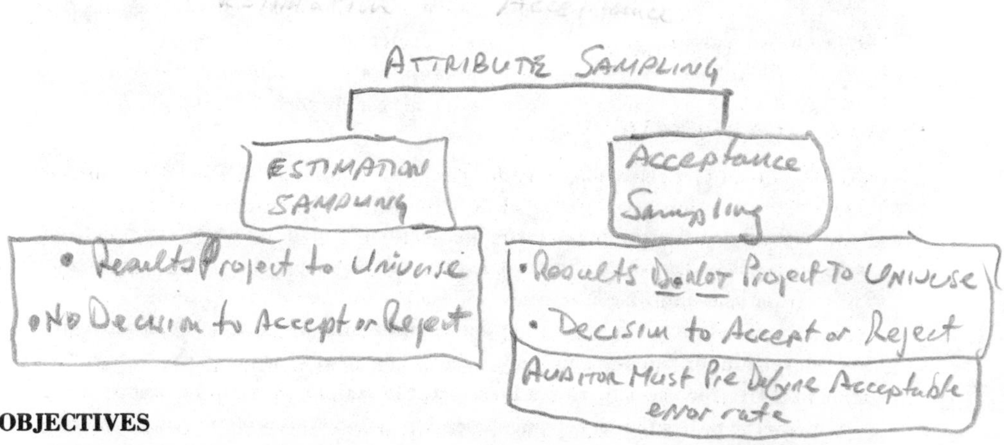

OBJECTIVES

Another possible approach to sampling is by using acceptance sampling methods. Acceptance sampling consists of the selection of a sample of a given size from a given field (by random methods) and rejection of the field if the sample contains more than a certain minimum number of disparities. If less than the minimum number of errors is found in the sample, the field is "accepted."

Acceptance sampling deals only with the rate of occurrence of events such as errors, disparities, etc., and therefore is a form of *attributes* sampling. It does *not* deal with dollar values or other variables and thus cannot provide any indication of the dollar impact of these errors such as can be obtained from variables estimation sampling.

As an attributes sampling procedure dealing only with the frequency of occurrence of events such as errors, the acceptance sampling approach is generally restricted to tests of transactions, as in testing compliance with internal controls.

The outcome of the application of acceptance sampling is an automatic decision to "accept" or "reject." The method does not in itself provide any estimate of the extent of error in the field nor its amount but merely classifies the field as "good" or "bad." On the other hand, estimation sampling provides an estimate of the frequency or amount of error in the field but does not include an automatic classification of the field as either good or bad. When estimation sampling is used, the auditor must consider his sample estimate and, in light of other findings, appraise the significance of the indicated error rate or amount.

Remember that, to the auditor, a rejection of the field by acceptance sampling, or a decision that the conclusions of estimation sampling indicate a bad situation, will result in either an extension of the test, the use of other audit procedures, or a reported *finding.*

The acceptance sampling plan consists of a statement of the field size N, sample size n, and the acceptance number c. These values are chosen to provide a high probability of rejection of fields containing more than a certain percentage of error as well as to provide certain other forms of protection.

It is evident that the selection of an appropriate plan requires a decision by the auditor, in advance of the sampling, as to the maximum tolerable rate of errors.

ADVANTAGES AND LIMITATIONS

The simplicity of the acceptance sampling method, which has been borrowed from industrial quality control techniques, has considerable appeal in that it is only necessary to sample and to count errors, and an automatic decision results. This is especially desirable when the actual accomplishment of the test is delegated to a lower-level auditor (such as a junior), since the necessary judgment can be exercised prior to the test by the superior, who selects the sampling plan to be used.

A further appeal is that acceptance sampling methods are widely used by industry and government in quality control inspections of lots of procured materials and are generally accepted by all. In fact, the similarity of the situation in the acceptance or rejection of lots of material and the objective of the audit test in apparently "accepting" or "rejecting" entries or documents based on the number of errors in the sample has been quite appealing to some. This resulted in early attempts to apply the acceptance sampling methods of industry and government to the auditor's problem.

However, there are marked differences in the situations confronting the industrial sampler and the auditor. Usually the industrial sampler applies his acceptance sampling to a stream of lots which arrive over a period of time. The auditor usually performs his test once for each audit.

The industrial acceptance sampler has as his prime objective the rejection of bad lots of purchased materials. He is particularly interested in the rejection of very bad lots. He will not be too concerned about accepting moderately bad lots or even a few very bad ones. He expects to, and can afford to, reject a few good lots because of sampling variations. These risks are recognized and computed in quality control acceptance sampling. He will generally be satisfied if he *averages* out to a desirable quality level for a number of lots. The auditor, sampling but once in each audit, cannot have the same attitude.

It is evident that in using acceptance sampling techniques and in selecting an appropriate sampling plan, a decision must be made *before* sampling as to the rate of errors which calls for rejection. This rate must be established as a specific percentage value, and a practical plan must be selected that will reject virtually all fields with more than that rate of error and accept most with less than that error.

On the other hand, the concept of the ***maximum tolerable error rate*** (MTER) previously discussed did not contemplate a specific percentage but rather a general level or zone. It would be difficult, if not impossible, for the auditor to develop an exact rate of occurrence beyond which there is clear indication of failure of the internal controls and below which satisfactory operation of the internal control system would be indicated.

If industrial sampling indicates a bad lot, the possible courses of actions are

1. Return the lot to the vendor
2. Screen the lot by 100 per cent inspection
3. Use it anyway

By contrast, the auditor's objective in his sampling test is to evaluate the quality of the accounting work done, to appraise the effectiveness of the operation of the internal control system, to discover the frequency of occurrence of material errors, and to seek possible evidence of fraud. His is not the task of acceptance and rejection of defects at a specific percentage point with small concern about moderately bad situations. If his appraisal indicates trouble, his action is to enlarge his investigation and to analyze the nature and impact of the defects and their cause; his is not merely a "send it back" or "do it over" attitude. He may, if he deems the internal control operation to be unsatisfactory, place less reliance on internal controls and resort to other audit procedures or tests.

This difference, both in aims and in actions subsequent to sampling, requires a somewhat different approach to the auditor's sampling problem. Existing quality control acceptance sampling methods cannot be adopted bodily simply because they are readily available. The methods must be appraised in the light of the new objectives, and although the same basic principles are used, those means which will best serve the auditor's needs must be considered.

Another basic difference between the two situations is in the nature of the defects. The purchaser of physical materials has a set of specifications and tolerances such as thickness, length, strength, and other physical properties. He knows that if a micrometer is applied to each item of the sample, he will be able to determine whether or not the item is within the specified tolerances for thickness. In other words, he knows in advance just what he is looking for and is prepared to deal with defects if they occur.

The auditor, on the other hand, is exploring an unknown area of defects. He will not know their nature until he finds them, at which time he will evaluate their importance. He does not have a set of specifications and tolerances similar to that of the purchaser of materials. He must find and appraise. This difference renders of limited value to the auditor the straightforward use of acceptance sampling tables to reject lots with more than a certain percentage of defectives.

Any of the acceptance sampling plans involve a certain amount of risk. For instance, the sampler might fail to reject lots containing more than the tolerable rate of error or reject lots that include less than the maximum error rate.

While it is possible to limit these dangers, sample size limitations always result in some risk, the nature of which must be fully understood and will be studied later. However, the auditor cannot afford any but a negligible risk of rejecting a good field and of failing to reject a bad one.

The industrial sampler can place a specific dollar cost on the occurrence of a defective and can compute, in terms of dollars and cents, the alternative costs of various levels of defectives; therefore he can establish a level of defectives above which it is economically desirable that rejection take place and below which it will not pay to reject since the alternative costs will be lower. The auditor is not in so fortunate a position, and he is generally unable to establish a specific rate of errors above which rejection *must* be accomplished and below which acceptance is necessary. He usually examines the errors in terms of numbers (and perhaps dollar value), types, and in relation to his other findings before he will accept or reject. It is likely that the auditor will have a general (although not precise) idea of a level of errors which would be intolerable.

It is true that in some instances a fairly high occurrence of errors can be permitted, as in a multitude of small transactions, if only their dollar-value impact is considered, but the auditor would not be unconcerned about such evidence of sloppy bookkeeping.

Nevertheless, it must be recognized that as long as humans are involved, or for that matter even when machines are used, errors will be found. It cannot be presumed that any mass clerical operation is, or can be, perfect. A minimum error rate must be conceded, but the actual *precise* determination by the auditor of a tolerable level of error is another matter.

Next, the auditor must decide the risk he is willing to run of failing to reject a field which actually contains as much as the maximum permissible proportion of errors. Existing industrial quality control acceptance sampling tables such as the well-known *Dodge-Romig* tables[1] automatically fix this risk at 10 per cent. If these tables are used, the auditor will fail to reject a field containing a proportion just beyond that maximum permissible proportion of error in one out of every 10 tests. Of course, if the field contains much more than this allowed error, the probability that it will pass the test will be much smaller, but will nevertheless exist. This would indicate that these tables are not precisely appropriate for the auditor.

In this type of approach, there is another risk, although not usually specified by the table, that a field containing *fewer* than the maximum permissible proportion of errors will nevertheless be rejected. For instance, a field containing just *under* the maximum tolerable proportion of errors may have almost a 90% probability of rejection.

Thus the application of acceptance sampling to the auditors' tests must be considered of limited value. On the other hand, it must not be considered that this approach is never useful in accounting or auditing. Yet this technique, possibly because of a lack of adequate understanding of the background, is used directly or indirectly by some auditors.

[1]H. F. Dodge and H. G. Romig, *Sampling Inspection Tables* (revised), John Wiley & Sons, Inc., New York, 1959.

However, the most important application of acceptance sampling in accounting is for the *control* of error *during* the clerical operations. Thus, it is possible to apply an acceptance sampling plan to the output of an individual in a clerical operation (a coder, a clerk, or a card-punch operator) and to make a decision whether a 100% verification of that worker's output for the period sampled is necessary. These and other applications will be discussed in a later section.

STATISTICAL PRINCIPLES

The probability that a given field submitted to an acceptance sampling plan (say lot size $N = 7{,}000$, sample size $n = 190$, and acceptance number $c = 3$) will be accepted is a function of the actual rate of error (or other event) in the field. It is thus seen that the specifications for an acceptance sampling plan include a statement of a field size N, a sample size n, and an acceptance number c.

The acceptance number is the maximum number of errors or other events which are allowed in the sample for the field to be considered satisfactory. Thus an acceptance number of 3 means that the field will be acceptable if the sample contains zero, one, two, *or* three errors.

The probability of each such occurrence can be determined by computing the probability that a sample drawn from this lot, containing a specific rate of error, will include a number of errors not in excess of the acceptance number.

This calculation is similar to that for finding a specified number of heads in tosses of 100 coins (such as zero, one, two, or three) as outlined in Chapter 4. However, here the probability for any one event is no longer one-half, as for heads in tosses of coins, and might be any value.

This computation can be performed on the supposition that the field might contain any incidence of error. For instance, for the above plan ($N = 7{,}000$, $n = 190$, $c = 3$), it can be assumed that a field or lot containing 5 per cent of errors has been submitted to the plan. The probability of acceptance of this field when this sampling plan is used may then be determined.

The field will be accepted if the sample contains zero, one, two, or three errors. The probability that the sample will contain each of these numbers of errors is shown in Table 9-1.[2]

[2] Since unlike the tosses of coins, the problem relates to a finite size field or lot, the method of computation will be different from that outlined in Chap 4. For the mathematically minded, the formula is

$$\frac{C_r^E \, C_{(n-r)}^{(N-E)}}{C_n^N}$$

where E = number of errors in field
N = field size
n = sample size
r = number of errors in sample

and generally $C_b^a = \dfrac{a!}{b!(a-b)!}$

TABLE 9-1. *Probability Sample Will Contain Various Numbers of Errors for Sampling Plan (N = 7,000; n = 90; c = 3) When Field Contains 5 Per Cent Errors*

Number of errors in sample	*Probability*
0	.01%
1	.05
2	.27
3	.91
0, 1, 2, or 3	1.24%

As shown in Table 9-1, the probability of zero, one, two, *or* three errors in the sample, or that the lot will be accepted, is then the sum of the probabilities that the sample will contain *either* zero, one, two, or three errors. Thus the probability that a field containing 5% of errors will be accepted when submitted to this sampling plan is only 1.24%.

Now assume that some other rate of error exists in the lot, say 2%. The results in Table 9-2 are obtained on the basis of this supposition.

TABLE 9-2. *Probability Sample Will Contain Various Numbers of Errors for Sampling Plan (N = 7,000; n = 190; c = 3) When Field Contains 2 Per Cent Errors*

Number of errors in sample	*Probability*
0	2.04%
1	8.14
2	16.03
3	20.78
0, 1, 2, or 3	46.99%

The probability that a sample from a field containing 2% of errors will call for the acceptance of this field when it is submitted to the acceptance sampling plan $N =$ 7,000, $n = 190$, and $c = 3$ is 46.99%. The same calculation can be accomplished for all possible rates of error in the lot from zero to 100%. If the results of these calculations are plotted, the graph in Figure 9-1 is obtained.

This graph shows the relation between all possible rates of error in the field submitted to the plan and the probability of acceptance. For instance, Figure 9-1 indictates that when the field contains error rates of less than 2%, the probability of acceptance is high, while when the error rate exceeds 3%, it is low.

SELECTION OF A PLAN

1. *Rejection of bad fields*

Each possible acceptance sampling plan generates a curve of the type shown in Figure 9-1. This curve, known as the operating characteristic *(OC)* curve, indicates

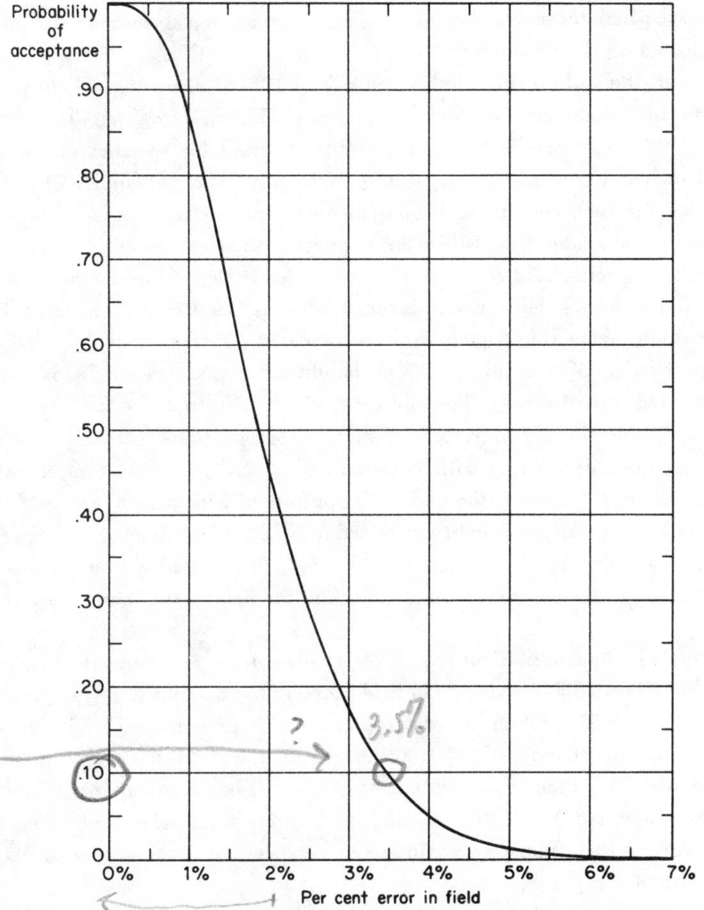

FIGURE 9-1 ***Operating characteristic curve for acceptance sampling plan (single sampling).***

how the plan performs with reference to the probability of acceptance for fields containing various rates of error.

The curve indicates that at any level of error (except perfection or 100% error) there is some probability of acceptance and some probability of rejection, no matter how small. However, if the probability of acceptance is quite small, the field in all probability will be rejected. The sampler must select a level of risk which he will consider "quite small" which is to apply to the probability of acceptance of a field with some specified rate of errors.

In industrial quality control, this level of risk is usually fixed at 9 out of 10 chances of *rejection* (10% probability of acceptance) for some undesirable level of defects. The graph in Figure 9-1 indicates that the error rate which gives rise to a probability of acceptance of 10% for this plan is 3.5%. This is called the *lot tolerance per cent defective (LTPD)*. The *LTPD* thus is the error rate corresponding to a specified low probability of acceptance for a given acceptance sampling plan (as indicated on the *OC* curve).

However, the auditor may find that a risk of 10% of accepting a field which has some specified bad error rate may be too great. The risk level (similar to the confidence level) must be selected by the auditor to meet his specific purposes in the light of the conditions that confront him. Of course, the probability of acceptance will be less for fields containing more than the specified error rate (*LTPD*).

Tables are available that will make it possible to select an acceptance sampling plan with a specific *LTPD*. Such a set of tables is Dodge and Romig's *Sampling Inspection Tables.*[3] However, this set of tables is based on a (consumer's) risk of 10%, which means that a plan with an indicated *LTPD* (say of 3%) will have a 90% probability of rejection (10% probability of acceptance) of fields containing the indicated rate of error. The auditor may not wish to incur this risk (10%).

A set of tables in Appendix K is more flexible as a basis for such selection of a sampling plan in accordance with a desired risk, since the auditor himself can select his own risk level. Thus if the auditor is confronted with a field size of 1,000 and wishes to have a 95% probability of rejection of a field containing 3% of error, he can select a sampling plan which will give him the desired characteristics. This will result in a greater probability of rejection for fields containing *more* than 3% errors.

The table in Appendix K on page 494 is used since it applies to field size 1,000. The column headed 3% error rate in field is entered and scanned to find plans which provide about a 5% probability of acceptance (95% probability of rejection). The column shows that the plan $N = 1{,}000$, $n = 100$, and $c = 0$ has a probability of acceptance of 4.0%. Plan $N = 1{,}000$, $n = 150$, $c = 1$ has a probability of acceptance of 4.6%, while plan $N = 1{,}000$, $n = 200$, $c = 2$ has a probability of acceptance of 4.2%. Any of these plans approximately meets the risk requirement of about 5% probability of acceptance.

At first glance the obvious selection would be the plan with the smallest sample size ($n = 100$, $c = 0$), since this would result in the lowest sampling cost. However, all that has been required thus far is that there be a low probability of accepting fields containing 3% errors and an even lower one for fields containing higher error rates. Nothing has been indicated as to how the plan responds to good fields. Is there any appreciable probability that good fields will be rejected?

2. *Acceptance of good fields*

The auditor must assure himself that the selected sampling plan will provide a very small probability that good fields are rejected. He must exercise special care to avoid, or to minimize, the possibility of the rejection of a field which in fact contains less than the objectionable error rate.

For the sampling plan, $N = 7{,}000$, $n = 190$, $c = 3$, for which the *OC* curve is

[3]*Op. cit.*

shown graphically in Figure 9-1, the *LTPD* (with a 10% risk) was found to be 3.5%. This means that fields containing precisely 3.5% of errors when submitted to the test have a 90% probability of rejection (10% probability of acceptance). If the rate in the field is as high as 4% of errors, then the probability of *rejection* as seen from the graph rises to 95% (5% for probability of acceptance).

But what about rates of error lower than 3.5%? Will fields containing *lower* rates of error be accepted? From Figure 9-1, it is seen that fields with a rate of error of 3.0% have an 82.5% probability of rejection (17.5% probability of acceptance), while a field with an error rate of 2% will be rejected more than half the time (55% probability of rejection). It is not until the error rate falls below 1% that the probability of rejection falls below 10%. Thus, there is a considerable probability of rejection at low error rates, although the objective was to discard only fields with more than 3.5% of error.

This plan thus does not meet the needs of the auditor if he wishes to limit the probability of rejection of good fields. Another plan must be selected which must specifically provide that certain low-error-rate fields will almost certainly be accepted. It is not possible to design a sampling plan which will reject *all* fields with an error rate above some fixed value and accept *all* fields with an error rate less than that value unless a 100% test is used. However, it can be specified that there be a low probability for the acceptance of fields containing more than the indicated error rate, and a high probability for fields containing error rates less than some other specified rate. For instance, a plan with an *LTPD* of 3.5% (based on a 10% risk) will have a probability of acceptance of fields containing 3.5% of errors of only one in 10, and less for fields containing a lower error rate.

It may now be stated that the plan must provide a high probability of acceptance, if the error rate is as small as some lower value, say 1% of errors. For example, the probability of acceptance of fields containing 1% of errors can be set at 95%. Such a specification is called the *acceptable quality level (AQL)*. The plan mentioned above for which the *OC* curve is given ($N = 7{,}000$, $n = 190$, $c = 3$) will not meet the *AQL* specification of 1% although it has the proper *LTPD* (3.5%). The plan $N = 7{,}000$, $n = 263$, $c = 5$, however, not only has the required *LTPD* of 3.5% but also the required *AQL* of 1%, since the probability of acceptance when the field contains 1% of errors is about 95%.

Thus, it is possible, by resorting to suitable tables, to find a plan which will provide both the desired *LTPD and* the desired *AQL*. However, note that as these two values come closer together, the sample size requirement will increase sharply.

For instance, for a plan requiring an *LTPD* of 5% and an *AQL* of 1%, the sample size will be appreciably smaller than for a plan with an *LTPD* of 5% and *AQL* of 3%. When the two values (*LTPD* and *AQL*) are identical, a 100% sample is required.

In other words, narrowing the range in which the probability of both acceptance and rejection for a given rate of errors in the field is appreciable or making the plan more discriminative in the area between *LTPD* and *AQL* increases the cost of the protection owing to the necessity for an increased sample size.

USE OF THE TABLES

As seen above, the basis for the selection of an acceptance sampling plan consists of establishing a high rate of error, which will result in rejection of the field most of the time *(LTPD)*, and a low rate of error, for which the field will be accepted most of the time *(AGQ)*.

Actually, the best method is to examine the probability of acceptance (or rejection) at all levels of error and to select a plan on the basis of its overall performance characteristics. However, this is quite difficult to accomplish, since most tables do not provide the necessary data.

The acceptance-sampling-plan tables appended to this volume provide an indication of the probability of acceptance for a wide range of error rates for selected sampling plans (field sizes *N*, sample sizes *n*, and acceptance numbers *c*). While these tables are of necessity limited in their coverage of field sizes and sampling plans, they provide a basis for the selection of a plan for many situations.

For example, to test a field containing 1,000 sampling units (records) for errors of a certain type, the sampling plan should be selected so that there will be a high probability of rejection (say about 90%) if the field contains as much or more than 4% errors but a very high probability of acceptance (95% or better) if the error rate is as low as or lower than 1%. In the zone between 1 and 4% of errors there will be an area of appreciable probability of either acceptance or rejection.

By scanning the table for field size 1,000 in the column marked 4% error rate for plans with a low probability of acceptance, Table 9-3 shows that the following plans all have a probability of acceptance for a field with 4% errors in the vicinity of 10% (90% probability of rejection).

TABLE 9–3

Field size, *N*	Sample size, *n*	Acceptance number, *c*	Probability of acceptance at 4%
1,000	50	0	12.3%
1,000	100	1	7.6
1,000	150	3	12.5

However, all these plans do not equally meet the requirement of a very high probability of acceptance at 1% of errors in the field. By scanning the table for these three plans by moving horizontally across the row until the required 95% (approximately) is found, the column heading indicates the per cent of errors in the field which will have that probability of acceptance.

The results are shown in Table 9-4 for the above three plans.

Only the last plan meets, even approximately, the requirement that the *LTPD* be 4% (at about a 10% probability of acceptance) and that the *AQL* (at about 95% probability of acceptance) be 1%.

TABLE 9-4

Field size, N	Sample size, n	Acceptance number, c	Probability of acceptance	Per cent of errors
1,000	50	0	95.0%	0.1
1,000	100	1	94.8	0.4
1,000	150	3	95.1	1.0

The question may now be raised as to the probabilities of acceptance for fields containing *between* 1 and 4% of errors. Reading horizontally across the line for this plan ($N = 1{,}000$, $n = 150$, and $c = 3$) in the table for values between 1 and 4%, the results shown in Table 9-5 are obtained. Thus, it is apparent that the probability of *rejection* is high for fields containing error rates of 2 to 3.9%, even though these rates are below the desired rejection rate of 4% of errors in the field.

It is this dubious zone that limits the use of the acceptance sampling approach in the audit test. However, as will be explained later, the method *does* have important

TABLE 9-5. *Probabilities of Acceptance for Plan ($N = 1{,}000$; $n = 150$; $c = 3$) When Field Contains between 1 and 4 Per Cent Errors*

Per cent of errors in field	*Probability of acceptance*
1.5	82.4%
2.0	64.8
2.5	46.9
3.0	31.8

and valuable applications in the control and elimination of errors when it is employed on a continuing basis. Some illustrations of this usage, which becomes an addition to the internal control system, are explained in a later section of this chapter. Further, acceptance sampling techniques are effective when combined with estimation sampling methods (see later in chapter).

Because of the abbreviated nature of the attached tables, the sampler may not find a table for the particular field size in which he is interested. In such an event he can use the next larger field size. This will produce a conservative statement, since the actual probability of acceptance will be lower at the levels of *LTPD* and *AQL* than that given in the table for the next higher field size. For instance, assume that the auditor wants to examine a field size of 800. The tables provide for field sizes of 500 and 1,000. Using the sampling plan $n = 150$, $c = 3$ for both of these field sizes, he finds the probabilities of acceptance indicated for fields containing 1% and 4% of errors as shown in Table 9-6.

The plan for field size 800 will yield probabilities between those in Table 9-6. The value of probability of acceptance for 1% of errors in a field size 800 (sample

TABLE 9-6

Per cent error in field	Probability of acceptance for plan (n = 150; c = 3) when field size is	
	N = 500	N = 1,000
1	97.0%	95.1%
4	10.2	12.5

size 150) is 95.5% as compared with 95.1% for field size 1,000. For fields with 4% of error for field size 800 the probability of acceptance is 12.0% as compared with 12.5% for field size 1,000.

In both cases, a conservative probability of acceptance results from the use of field size 1,000 rather than 800. This means that a good field must have a lower rate of error to have the same probability of acceptance, while a bad field has a higher probability of rejection when field size 1,000 is used rather than 800. This is the most conservative approach.

AVERAGE ERROR RATES

When applied as a continuing system for controlling errors (see section on Applications, below), the acceptance sampling system can be used to *limit* the long-run or average error rate to some predetermined level, provided that *rejected* fields are 100% inspected, and errors corrected. Fields which pass the acceptance sampling test are *not* further checked but are accepted as they are.

The principle of this method may be illustrated by the plan for which the *OC* curve is given on page 147. Assuming that the fields that are rejected are in fact 100% inspected and all errors are eliminated while accepted lots are not further inspected, it is possible to determine how the remaining error rate will average if fields containing any specified error rate are submitted to the test by means of a simple calculation.

Table 9-7 may be prepared by reading the values off the *OC* curve in Figure 9-1.

For each point on the curve, as for each of the above values, a computation can be performed to indicate the average long-run outcome of the acceptance sampling plan. For instance, by using the above values and assuming that the field submitted to the test actually contains 1% of errors, the following calculations can be performed from Table 9-7.

1. 87.8% of all fields will be accepted in the long run if the field has a 1% error rate.

2. 12.2% of all fields will be rejected in the long run (100.0% − 87.8%).

3. Fields rejected will be 100% inspected to eliminate all errors, thus resulting in an error rate after inspection of 0.0%.

TABLE 9-7. ***Probability of Acceptance for Acceptance Sampling Plan ($N = 7{,}000$; $n = 190$; $c = 3$)***

Rate of error in field	Probability of acceptance	Probability of rejection
0.0%	100.0%	0.0%
0.5	98.0	2.0
1.0	87.8	12.2
1.5	66.5	33.5
2.0	45.0	55.0
3.0	17.5	82.5
4.0	5.0	95.0
5.0	1.3	98.7

4. Fields accepted will not be further inspected and will contain the same error rate before and after the test (in this instance 1%).

5. The average error rate can be obtained (using a weighted average) as shown in Table 9-8.

The result of this calculation is called the *average outgoing quality* (*AOQ*). This value indicates the long-run average of the errors remaining in the field after the sampling plan has been applied and after the rejected fields have been 100% examined and corrected if all the fields submitted to the test contain the error rate from which the *AOQ* value was computed.

This same calculation can be performed for all points on the *OC* curve. For the values in Table 9-8, the results are shown in Table 9-9.

The average rate of error rate after inspection (*AOQ*) rises as the error rate in the field increases and then, after reaching a maximum, declines. A more detailed calculation for many more points on the *OC* curve is plotted in Figure 9-2 in the form of an *AOQ* curve. The highest point on this curve (1.0%) is the limit, or maximum average error rate after inspection, when this sampling plan is used, *no matter what the error rate is in the fields submitted to the test,* provided that the rejected fields

TABLE 9-8

	Proportion of fields	Error rate after inspection	Product
Accepted	.878	.01	.00878
Rejected	.122	.00	.00000
Total	1.000		.00878

$$\text{Weighted average error rate after inspection} = \frac{.00878}{1.000} = .878\%$$

TABLE 9–9. *Average Outgoing Quality for Acceptance Sampling Plan (N = 7,000; n = 190; c = 3)*

When rate of error in field is	*Average rate of errors (AOQ) after inspection* is*
0.0%	0.0 %
0.5	0.490
1.0	0.878
1.5	0.998
2.0	0.900
3.0	0.525
4.0	0.200
5.0	0.065

* Assuming that a 100% inspection of the rejected field is made.

are 100% inspected. This maximum is called the *average outgoing quality limit* (*AOQL*). This value may be interpreted to be the highest remaining rate of error in the field after the application of the stated acceptance sampling plan, *regardless* of the actual rate of occurrence in the field.

Each acceptance sampling plan has a specific *AOQL* which may be calculated. The previously mentioned Dodge-Romig tables contain plans which provide a specified *AOQL*. Remember that the *AOQL* concept has no meaning unless rejected fields are 100% examined.

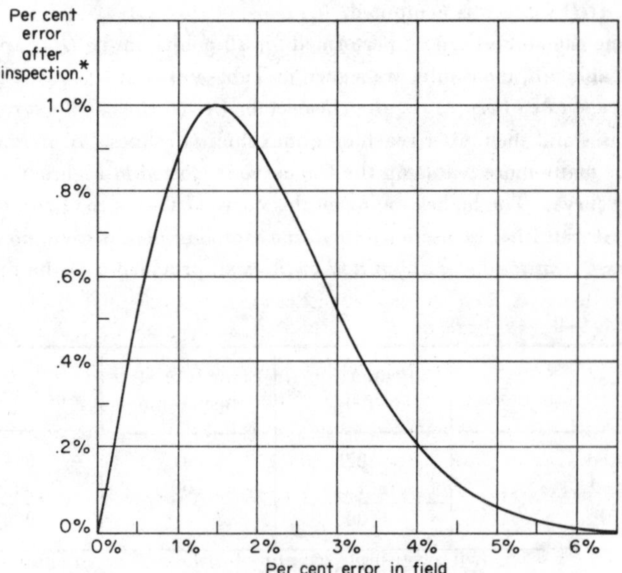

FIGURE 9–2 *AOQ curve for single sampling plan.*

MULTIPLE SAMPLING PLANS

The type of acceptance sampling plans outlined above are known as single sampling plans. In these plans, a single sample is drawn, and a decision is reached about accepting or rejecting.

Other plans are also based on the drawing of more than one sample or, to be exact, on the drawing of a sample in parts. The object of these plans in industrial applications is to save inspection or, in other words, to reduce the average amount of sampling necessary to reach a decision.

In the simplest form, double sampling is used. The principle is that only a small sample is necessary to reject very bad fields or accept very good ones.

In a typical double sampling plan, the specifications include the field size *N*, the sample size for both the first (n_1) and the second samples (n_2), and both an acceptance *and* a rejection number. For instance, a double sampling plan may be specified as field size 2,000, sample sizes $n_1 = 70$ and $n_2 = 50$, acceptance number 1, and rejection number 3. In applying this plan, a sample of 70 is drawn. If it contains one error or less (acceptance number), the field is accepted. If it contains three or more, it is rejected. If it contains two, a further sample of 50 is selected, and acceptance or rejection is then based on the rejection number 3 only, so that if less than three are found in the entire sample ($n_1 + n_2$), the field is accepted; if three or more, it is rejected.

For fields that are very good or very bad, acceptance or rejection will be established with the first sample of 70, while only for fields in the marginal area will the additional sample be necessary. However, in auditing tests the saving in sampling may be an illusion since in the event of rejection, an extension of the test will probably be desired.

Multiple sampling provides a similar approach, where, instead of taking two samples, several are obtained (usually of equal size). For each sample, a decision is reached to accept, reject, or take an additional sample up to some limit.

Sequential sampling carries this plan to the ultimate where, starting with a sample of a small size, additional individual units (sample increment size one) are taken, each time either accepting, rejecting, or drawing another unit.[4]

The complexities of record keeping in such a plan, the nonavailability of appropriate tables for the auditor's use, and the fact that for rejected fields as well as for marginal ones the test must be extended, together with the previously mentioned disadvantages of using acceptance sampling in auditing, limit the practical value of these multiple sampling plans for the auditor.

Only when the field is very good is early termination of sampling possible. Another

[4]More complete discussion of multiple sampling for those interested can be read in:
E. L. Grant and R. S. Leavenworth, *Statistical Quality Control,* 4th ed., McGraw-Hill Book Co., New York, 1972.
Dudley J. Cowden, *Statistical Methods in Quality Control,* Prentice-Hall, Englewood Cliffs, N.J., 1957.

approach, discussed later, accomplishes this same result without these complex multiple or sequential sampling plans.

OTHER TABLES

In addition to the tables appended to this chapter there are two other widely used acceptance sampling tables:

1. H. F. Dodge and N. G. Romig, *Sampling Inspection Tables (revised)*, John Wiley & Sons, Inc., New York, 1959.
2. Military Standard 105D—Sampling Procedures and Tables for Inspection by Attributes, Department of Defense, Washington, D.C., April 29, 1963.

The Dodge-Romig tables contain sampling plans which are indexed according to *LTPD* in one section and *AOQL* in another, so that it is possible to find a plan for a specific *LTPD* or *AOQL*. The tables provide plans of the single and double sampling types. The risk associated with the *LTPD* in these tables is 10%.

The tables known as Military Standard 105A (later 105C and now 105D) have plans indexed according to *AQL*, or acceptable quality level, only and provide single, double, and multiple plans. The probability of acceptance associated with its *AQL* values is a high value between 80 and 99%. The latest revision (Military Standard 105D) also contains a table of *LQ* values. These *LQ* values are equivalent to the *LTPD* previously discussed in this book. The risk level associated with the *LQ* value is 10%. However, these values are given only for the plans included on the basis of *AQL*, and thus plans are not provided for all desirable levels of *LTPD*.

Because of these limitations, especially the inappropriate risks for audit purposes, these tables will be found to be of limited value to the auditor. However, both tables contain graphs of the operating characteristic curves of the plans given, and on the basis of these curves, it is possible for the auditor to select an appropriate plan. Nevertheless, the average auditor may find such an effort too involved to be worthwhile.

APPLICATIONS

In addition to the possible application of acceptance sampling to the audit test, there are others which may be applied to accounting problems.

The acceptance sampling method provides an excellent technique for controlling clerical errors in a continuing operation. These errors may be of any type, including errors in punching in IBM installations, arithmetic errors in documents such as payrolls, coding errors, errors in posting, etc. This method is especially useful when it is performed continuously by several persons.

When this method is applied, an acceptance sampling plan with the required characteristics is selected and the sample is chosen from the output of each worker for a given period (say one day). If the sampled output is rejected, the output of that worker is 100% checked, and all errors are corrected. If accepted on the basis of the sample, nothing else will be done.

In such a situation not only can a plan be selected to reject bad work, but it can also provide a given *AOQL* which will restrict the average per cent of errors in the work in the long run to not more than some predetermined level.

Such a method has been found to be more effective than a complete 100% check, since this massive effort usually results in neglecting to find numerous errors. In some instances with IBM installations, this approach has replaced the usual 100% machine verification.

Another promising application is in the control of accuracy in perpetual inventory balances. Both the Ordnance and the Signal Corps services of the United States Army are using acceptance sampling for this purpose at their depots.

It was found early that maintaining accurate perpetual inventory records at the vast depots of the Army was not an easily solved problem. An attempt to overcome these difficulties by requiring annual physical inventories accomplished little, since these enormous physical inventories required many personnel, some of whom were not competent. As was later established, many of the errors in the perpetual inventory balances arose from mistakes in the physical inventories taken.

An experimental attempt was then made to overcome this difficulty by statistical sampling rather than a 100% physical inventory. Independent tests by both Ordnance and Signal Corps have demonstrated the method to be so effective in the reduction of errors in balances that 100% inventorying has been discontinued in the depots of these technical services except for certain classified, critical, and sensitive items.

The technique is applied by obtaining samples of relatively small groups of items at each depot. The sample items are carefully inventoried by specially trained teams, and during a year all groups of items are sampled. If the number of errors in the balances for the sample items is such that rejection is called for, the items in the group from which the sample was drawn are 100% inventoried. If not, no further checking is accomplished.

The sampling is conducted on a continuing cyclical basis and replaces the 100% shutdown inventory. The results of the initial application of this method have already given indication of a very large improvement in inventory accuracy.

The application of this method has been encountered in numerous other areas, including control of errors in the preparation of invoices in a department store, punched-card preparation in the Census Bureau and elsewhere, pricing of long-distance telephone calls, and other similar situations.

TEN

Stratified Sampling

THE REASONS FOR SPECIAL SAMPLING PLANS

In all discussions up to this point, the techniques described apply to only one type of sampling plan, the unrestricted random sample. It will be recalled that this type of sampling operation provides for the drawing of the sampling elements or units from the entire field or population, one at a time, without special treatment for any portion of the field. Among other effects of this approach was that each sampling unit in the population was provided with an equal probability of being included in the sample.

While the use of simple, unrestricted random sampling methods may provide the tool for the bulk of the tests performed by the auditor, under certain circumstances others may be used generally either to increase sampling efficiency or to reduce the costs of drawing the sample.

As will be disclosed in detail later, it is possible to increase the sample efficiency of unrestricted random sampling, under certain circumstances, by using several possible sampling plans to reduce the sampling error, even though the same size of sample is used. By a wise choice of a sampling plan, it may also be possible to accomplish the same sample precision as achieved with an unrestricted random sample, but with a smaller sample size.

When these special plans are used, special techniques are needed to determine the resultant sampling precision or to compute the required sample size. A variety of such special sampling plans are discussed below, together with the techniques necessary to establish the sample precision and to determine the sample size.

STRATIFIED RANDOM SAMPLING

Stratified random sampling consists of dividing the field (population) into segments (strata) and random sampling independently within each stratum. The results of the several samplings for the different strata may then be combined into an overall estimate for the entire field.

There are several possible reasons for stratified sampling techniques.

1. To gain sampling efficiency or, in other words, to obtain a lower sampling error with the same sample size as compared with unrestricted random sampling
2. To offset the effect of extreme values (skewed distributions)
3. To give special attention to certain categories within the field
4. To combine the results of the audit test where separate and independent samples are drawn by different auditors for different parts or offices of the same organization.

As will be shown later, it is generally possible to achieve greater sample reliability with a given size of sample when stratified sampling techniques are used instead of unrestricted random sampling. However, these gains are not automatic, for it is possible to have a stratified random sampling situation in which the sample precision is no better than that obtained by unrestricted random sampling.

The various conditions which lead to an advantage or disadvantage from the use of stratified random sampling methods will be discussed in detail later.

In Chapter 7, during the discussion of appraisal of variables samples, it was noted that it was essential to separate extreme or unusual values from the rest of the data in order to avoid errors in stating sample reliability. This separation of high-value items from others, with a 100% test or heavier sampling of these items, is a method long used by auditors which finds full support in statistical theory. It is not to be construed, however, that such a technique must be used in every sampling situation where a variables estimate (average or total) is to be made. Only when relatively *few* items of high value constitute a *large* proportion of the total value is this technique necessary.

However, one of the most frequent reasons for resorting to stratified sampling arises from the necessity of partitioning the audit test among several auditors. When the records to be sampled are widely distributed at various locations, or when the field to be sampled is too large for a single auditor to undertake, the work is divided among several auditors with each drawing independent probability samples of different segments of the field.

If each of the participating auditors draws his own probability sample from different parts of the population, the result is a stratified sample. The population has been divided into segments (strata) for this purpose and the sample projection must be evaluated as a stratified sample. Of course, stratification arising from such administrative requirements can be avoided by centrally selecting the sampling units to be audited from the entire population regardless of location or type. This method would result in the creation of an unrestricted random sample of the entire population.

The auditors then would be supplied with the sampling unit numbers. Each auditor would then audit the specified sampling units centrally selected for inclusion from his segment of the population.

Finally, a test may be made of certain segments of the field separately for reasons unrelated to the statistical aspects of sampling. For instance, in testing an inventory, it may be desired to give special attention and more complete testing to sensitive, pilferable, or security items. This approach automatically results in a stratified random sample if all categories are sampled randomly and separately when an overall estimate is required.

Whenever a population is divided into segments (strata), *for any reason,* and an independent sample is drawn from each stratum but the results are combined to obtain an overall projection for the entire population, a stratified sample results.

If the field is divided into segments according to the dollar values of the sampling units, *dollar-value* strata are obtained. If the population is divided according to location, type of transaction, or on any other qualitative basis, *natural strata* are created. In the audit situation, gains in sample efficiency generally arise from the proper use of dollar-value or other forms of measurement strata. Nevertheless, as previously observed, there may be good reasons for the use of natural strata even though they may not produce gains in sample efficiency.

SAMPLING EFFICIENCY—STRATIFIED SAMPLES

In the discussion of variables sampling, it was noted that the sample precision for a given size sample was dependent upon the range of the values in the field from which the sample was drawn. This variability was measured by, and is reflected in, the standard deviation.

In dealing with a field with a wide variability of values it may be possible to divide up the field into several sections, each with a smaller standard deviation than the entire field, by grouping values of similar magnitude together or by arranging them so that all but one small group has a low standard deviation. If separate sampling is then performed in each of these segments of similar magnitudes, the sampling precision of the estimate for each segment may be better than that obtained from a simple overall sample, and the combined estimate so obtained may have a lower sampling variability than that of the unrestricted random sample.

If one small group has a higher standard deviation than all the other data, the effect of that group can be reduced by sampling all or a large part of that category. This may be illustrated by a hypothetical example. Assume that a field contains values such as:

$ 100.00
10.00
50.00
1,000.00
100.00

1,000.00
10.00
50.00
. . . . . .

Note that this field is comprised of a constant repetition of four values ($100.00, $10.00, $50.00, and $1,000.00). It is apparent that if the field is divided into four strata (one containing all the $100.00 values, one containing all the $10.00 values, one with all the $50.00 values, and one with all the $1,000.00 values), then each stratum would have no variability at all, and a single unit from each stratum together with the knowledge of the number of items in each stratum would give a perfect estimate with no sampling error. Yet if unrestricted random sampling is used, a fairly large sample would be required to establish the average value with a high degree of sample precision. The more homogeneous the values within each stratum, the more efficient the sampling.

While such a situation will not be encountered in practical situations, the same general principles of segregating similar (although not exactly the same) values into separate strata may be used to increase the sample precision.

For instance, in an audit of inventory values, the data in Table 10-1 might arise if inventory items are segregated into value groups (strata).

The standard deviation of all the 10,570 values before separating them into strata was $278.79. It will be noted that only the high-value group comprising a few items has a standard deviation larger than the overall standard deviation. Since this high-value stratum is a small group, it can be tested in its entirety so that there will be no sampling error at all for this stratum, and the effect of its unusually high standard deviation on the sampling error is completely eliminated. Thus, a sample from each of the remaining categories can now provide a high degree of precision, since the

TABLE 10–1

Value group (strata)	Number of items in strata, N	Standard deviation of values in each stratum	Average values for strata, $\bar{X}$
Over $1,000.00	70	$1,247.00	$3,010.75
$200.00 to $1,000.00	500	105.50	580.60
Under $200.00	10,000	29.50	89.78

sample for each stratum is confronted with a lower standard deviation than that of an unrestricted sample.

This point will be explained in further detail by means of illustrations later, but it is important to repeat at this point that this improvement in sample precision over the unrestricted random sample does not of necessity automatically accrue merely because stratified sampling is used. It arises from the strategic assignment of the sample units to the strata.

The sample precision of a value computed from a stratified sample may be better or the same as that for a given sample size as compared with that computed from an unrestricted random sample, depending on the manner in which the sample sizes are allocated to the strata.

Whenever the sample size is assigned to the strata on a proportional basis, the sample precision will be as good as or better than that of an unrestricted random sample. *Proportional allocation* means that the sample size is assigned to the strata according to the ratio that the stratum size bears to the entire field.

However, it must be observed promptly that other methods of sample allocation may result in much greater gains in sample precision than are obtained with proportional allocation. These methods will be discussed later. In the audit situation, proportional allocation will usually *not* result in the most efficient sample design for a stratified sample.

Nevertheless, regardless of the method of allocation used, the resulting sample is valid and may be projected and the sampling error calculated by the appropriate method. The method of allocation affects only efficiency, *not* validity.

Gains in sampling efficiency usually will result only if the groupings, or strata, are created on the basis of the characteristics to be measured. For instance, in the inventory problem, if the data were stratified by some type of stock number grouping and if these groups are unrelated to value, there would be little or no effect on sampling precision as a result of the grouping.

To be able to explore the effects of various allocations of the sample to the various strata, it is necessary to understand the method of appraising sample precision for stratified samples. Remember that the appraisal of the sampling precision of values computed from a sample takes place *after* the sample results are at hand.

In the following sections, the method of appraising sample results for values obtained from stratified samples will be explored first for variables sampling, then for attributes sampling, after which sample allocation in stratified sampling will be discussed further.

SAMPLE APPRAISAL—STRATIFIED SAMPLING—VARIABLES

Assume that it is desired to estimate the total value of an inventory in order to establish the reasonableness of the book value. Arbitrarily it is decided that a sample of 350 inventory items is to be tested and evaluated. The reason for the selection of this sample size is irrelevant at this point. The method for determining the sample size will be discussed later.

As previously, the estimate of the *total* value will be achieved by estimating the average value and multiplying by the total number of items in the inventory.

It is found that there are a few high-value items which constitute a large propor-

TABLE 10-2

Value group (strata)	Number in strata (N_i)	Standard deviation within strata from sample (σ_i)
Over $1,000.00	70	$1,247.00
$200.00 to $1,000.00	500	105.50
Under $200.00	10,000	29.50

tion of the total value. This may be seen from the data in Table 10-2, where the items have been segregated into value groups (strata).

As might be expected the standard deviation of the values in the highest-value stratum is greatest, with appreciably smaller standard deviations in the other groups.

Because of the importance of the high-value items (over $1,000.00), with 70 items comprising 15% of the total value, it was decided to do a 100% test of these items. A statistical reason for this approach was the expected high variability (standard deviation) of the high-value items. However, it should be noted that, apart from considerations of statistical efficiency, auditors frequently examine all of the values higher than some specified value on the grounds of materiality. The remaining sampling units of the 350 sample size were distributed equally into two remaining groups as shown in Table 10-3. Note that this is *not* the most effective distribution, as will be demonstrated later.

The results obtained from the sample are shown in Table 10-4. The standard deviations of the sample were computed from the individual values as described in previous chapters. This computation is not shown here.

The overall average value may now be obtained by taking a *weighted* average of the strata averages. In this computation, the sample average value for each stratum is multiplied by the number of items in the population of each stratum (*not the sample numbers*). The products are added for all strata, and the resultant total is divided

TABLE 10-3

Value group (strata)	Number of items in strata (N_i)	Assigned sample size (n_i)
Over $1,000.00	70	70
$200.00 to $1,000.00	500	140
Under $200.00	10,000	140
Total	10,570	350

TABLE 10-4

Value group (strata)	Number of items in strata, N_i	Sample size, n_i	Sample average, $\bar{X}_i$	Sample standard deviation, σ_i
Over $1,000.00	70	70	$3,010.75	$1,247.00
$200.00 to $1,000.00	500	140	580.60	105.50
Under $200.00	10,000	140	89.78	29.50
Total............	10,570	350		

by the number of items in all strata. In formula form this becomes

$$\bar{X} = \frac{\Sigma(N_i\bar{X}_i)}{N}$$

where $\bar{X}$ = overall average estimate

Σ = sum, or total, of

N_i = number of items (sampling units) in each statum, i.e., N_1, N_2, N_3, etc.,

where N_1 = number of items in field in first stratum, etc.

N_2 = number of items in field in second stratum, etc.

Note: This does *not* refer to number of items in sample from each stratum.[1]

$\bar{X}_i$ = the average sample value for *reach* stratum, i.e., $\bar{X}_1$, $\bar{X}_2$, $\bar{X}_3$, etc., where

$\bar{X}_1$ = average of sample values from first stratum

$\bar{X}_2$ = average of sample values from second stratum, etc.

N = total number of items in the field (population)

Note: This value will equal $N_1 + N_2 + N_3 + \ldots + N_n$.

The calculation of the overall average may now proceed as shown in Table 10-5. It is to be noted that the total of the last column ($1,398,852.50) is the estimate of the total inventory value and is equal to the total number of items times the average value, or $N\bar{X}$. Observe that the sample sizes did *not* enter this computation.

Now that the estimate of the overall average has been established, its sampling precision may be determined. To do this, first the sample precision of the estimated average of each stratum is determined separately by the methods previously described for variables samples.

The tables in Appendix G or H are used to find the sampling error for each stratum in terms of a multiple of the standard deviation. As in previous discussions of appraisal of variables samples, the sampling error is then multiplied by the value of the standard deviation to obtain the estimate of sample precision required.

As an initial step, the standard deviation is obtained separately from the sample data for each stratum. The average range method, previously described, may be used for this purpose, provided that there are at least 48 observations in each stratum.

[1] The small letter (lowercase) *n* is used to represent *sample* numbers.

TABLE 10-5

Value group (strata)	Number of items in strata, N_i	Sample average for strata, $\bar{X}_i$	$N_i\bar{X}_1$
(1)	(2)	(3)	(2 × 3)
1. Over $1,000.00	70	$3,010.75	$210,752.50
2. $200.00 to $1,000.00	500	580.60	290,300.00
3. Under $200.00	10,000	89.78	897,800.00
Total...........	10,570		$1,398,852.50

$$\text{Average} = \frac{\$1{,}398{,}852.50}{10{,}570} = \$132.34$$

If not, for those strata with less than this number, the standard deviation must be computed directly by a method such as the computation outlined in Chapter 4 and Technical Appendix I.[2]

The value for the ratio of the sampling error to the standard deviation is now obtained from the tables in Appendix G or H, by using the field size and the sample size for that stratum and the desired confidence level.

Based on a 95% confidence level, the method is illustrated in Table 10-6.[3] Since the entire stratum was included in the sample (100% test) for stratum 1, its

[2] It is to be emphasized, however, that since the average range method provides only an approximation, it is more desirable to use the formula method where practicable, and especially if the results may be used as legal evidence.

[3] The method of appraisal described is based on the assumptions that the same confidence level and, therefore, the same t value are used for all strata and that no stratum contains fewer than 30 sampling units.

TABLE 10-6

Value group (strata)	Number of items in strata, N_i	Sample size for each stratum, n_i	Strata standard deviation, σ_i	Sampling error as ratio to standard deviation*	Sampling error of stratum average, 95% confidence level†
1. Over $1,000.00	70	70	$1,247.00	0	±0
2. $200.00 to $1,000.00	500	140	105.50	0.1406	±$14.83
3. Under $200.00	10,000	140	29.50	0.1645	±$ 4.85

* These figures are taken from the table in Appendix G.

† The values in this column are the product of those on the same line in the two previous columns.

sampling error is zero, and the ratio is entered as zero. For stratum 2 with field size 500 and sample size 140, the sampling error ratio is obtained from the table on page 470 of Appendix G, where for the 95% confidence level, the indicated sampling error ratio is .1406. Multiplying this ratio by the standard deviation for that stratum gives the sampling error for the strata average.

In a similar manner, for stratum 3 the sampling error ratio is found on page 473 of Appendix G to be .1645 for a field size of 10,000, a sample size of 140, and a 95% confidence level. This ratio is multiplied by the standard deviation computed from this stratum to obtain the sampling error of the stratum average.

However, the sampling error of the overall average is desired. The sampling errors for the averages for each stratum may be combined to obtain the overall sampling error by obtaining a *weighted* average of the *square* of the sampling errors for each stratum, using the *square* of the strata *field* size as weights. The square root of the result is the sampling error of the overall average.

In formula form this is[4]

$$(SE_{\bar{x}})^2 = \frac{\Sigma[N_i^{\,2}\,(SE_{\bar{x}_i})^2]}{N^2}$$

where $SE_{\bar{x}}$ = sampling error of overall average
= square root of $(SE_x)^2$
Σ = sum, or total, of
N_i = field size for *each* stratum
$SE_{\bar{x}_i}$ = sampling error separately obtained for each stratum
N = total field size

The detailed calculation is shown in Table 10-7.

The value ±\$4.64 is the sampling precision of the overall average inventory value (95% confidence level). To obtain the sampling precision of the total inventory value, it is merely necessary to multiply this value (±\$4.64) by the total field size (10,570), with a result of ±\$49,044.80 (at the 95% confidence level).

It would be interesting at this point to compare the sampling precision attained through the use of stratified sampling with that which would have been obtained through unrestricted random sampling.

For an unrestricted random sample of the same size (350) drawn from the same population (10,570) with an equivalent overall standard deviation (\$278.79), the sampling precision at the 95% confidence level may be computed as outlined in Chapter 7. Since this field size is not given in the tables, the second method, using the infinite field size and finite correction factor, is used.

[4]This formula may also be written as

$$(SE_{\bar{x}^2}) = \Sigma(W_i^2 SE_{\bar{x}^2})$$

where $W_i = N_i/N$ or per cent of total population (number) in specified stratum.

TABLE 10-7

Value group (strata)	Number of items in strata (N_i)	Sampling error of stratum average $(SE_{\bar{x}i})$	N_i^2	$(SE_{\bar{x}i})^2$	Product $N_i^2(SE_{\bar{x}i})^2$
(1)	(2)	(3)	(4)	(5)	(6)
1. Over $1,000.00	70	0	4,900	0	0
2. $200.00 to $1,000.00	500	$14.83	250,000	$219.93	$ 54,982,500.00
3. Under $200.00	10,000	4.85	100,000,000	23.52	2,352,000,000.00
Total............	10,570				$2,406,982,500.00

$$N = 10{,}570$$
$$N^2 = 111{,}724{,}900$$
$$(SE)^2 = \frac{2{,}406{,}982{,}500.00}{111{,}724{,}900.00} = 21.54$$

$$\text{Sampling error of overall average} = \sqrt{SE^2} = \sqrt{21.54} = \pm\$4.64$$

Note: See previous table for computation of the value in column 3.
Column 4 contains the square of the figure on the same line in column 2.
Column 5 contains the square of the figure on the same line in column 3.
Column 6 contains the product of the values in columns 4 and 5 on the same line.

For sample size 350, at the 95% confidence level, and for the infinite field size, the ratio of the sampling error to the standard deviation is given as .1048 on page 480 of Appendix H.

The sample (350 items) is 3.3% of the field size (350/10,570). By using the value from the table on page 481 of Appendix I, a finite correction value of .9834 is obtained. Multiplying the product of these two values by the standard deviation

$$.1048 \times .9834 \times \$278.79$$

gives a sample precision for the average of ±$28.73.

Thus it is clear that the stratified sampling approach, although it did not use the best allocation of the sample items to the strata, nevertheless resulted in a considerable reduction in the sampling error of the overall average value from the ±$28.73 of the unrestricted random sample to ±$4.64 for the stratified random sample.

Thus, it is evident that the sampling error of the average (and therefore of the total) has been cut to about one-sixth of the level for unrestricted random sampling. To achieve the sampling precision attained by the stratified sample (±$4.64 for the average or ±$49,044.80 for the total), the sample size requirement for the unrestricted random sample would have been 5,996, or about 17 times as large!

The sample precision for the total cited above was obtained by multiplying the sampling error for the average (±$4.64) by the field size (10,570) to obtain the overall sampling error of the total.

The sampling error for the total can be obtained directly without the need for an extra step from[5]

$$SE_T^2 = \sum (N_i^2 SE_{\bar{x}_i}^2)$$

or

$$SE_T = \sqrt{\sum (N_i^2 SE_{\bar{x}_i}^2)}$$

where SE_T = sampling error of total
N_i = number in field in each stratum
$SE_{\bar{x}_i}$ = sampling error of the *average* for each stratum

For the above,

$$SE_T = \sqrt{\sum (N_i^2 SE_{\bar{x}_i}^2)}$$

From Table 10-7,

$$SE_T = \sqrt{2{,}406{,}982{,}500.00}$$

$$SE_T = \pm\$49{,}061.01$$

with the difference ($49,061.01 compared to $49,044.80) due to rounding.

A further reduction of the sampling error can be achieved by a different allocation of the sample sizes to the strata which will be discussed later.

ALLOCATION OF SAMPLE ITEMS TO STRATA—VARIABLES SAMPLING—ARBITRARY SAMPLE SIZE

In the discussion above it was noted that the distribution of the total sample size among the strata was not the best. Another assignment of sample sizes to each stratum would have resulted in a smaller sampling error.

The best, or optimum, allocation of sample sizes for variables to the strata would result if the assignment to each stratum was made in accordance with the following proportions:[6]

$$\text{Proportion of sample in strata} = \frac{N_i \sigma_i}{\sum (N_i \sigma_i)}$$

[5]This derives from the fact that $SE_T = NSE_x$ and

$$SE_T^2 = N^2 SE_{\bar{x}}^2 \quad \text{but} \quad SE_{\bar{x}}^2 = \frac{\Sigma(N_i^2 SE_{\bar{x}i}^2)}{N^2}$$

and therefore

$$SE_T^2 = N^2 \left[\frac{\Sigma(N_i^2 SE_{\bar{x}i}^2)}{N^2}\right]$$

$$SE_T^2 = \Sigma(N_i^2 SE_{\bar{x}i}^2)$$

[6]It is to be noted that the assumption is made that the cost of finding and auditing sampling units is the same regardless of the strata in which they occur.

where N_i = number in field in each stratum
σ_i = standard deviation of values within each stratum

The standard deviation can be estimated by an advance sample in each stratum, by using the average range method or past similar data such as last year's inventory, when available. A rough approximation of the standard deviation can be obtained by using one-fifth of the difference between the highest and lowest value in any stratum if such information is available from present or past data. Alternatively, preliminary samples of about 50 items from each strata may provide this information (see page 94).

Of course, since the standard deviation is estimated, the result may be only a rough approximation to the best allocation. The calculation of the optimum allocation for the above problem of estimating the total value of an inventory is shown in Table 10-8.

The proportion of the sample to be assigned to stratum 1 then becomes

$$\frac{\$\,87{,}290.00}{\$435{,}040.00} = 20.1\%$$

Since the sample size to be used was decided to be 350, the sample size becomes 20% of 350 or 70.

For stratum 2 the calculation is

$$\frac{\$\,52{,}750.00}{\$435{,}040.00} = 12.1\%$$

and the sample size for stratum 2 is 12.1% of 350 or 42. For stratum 3,

$$\frac{\$295{,}000.00}{\$435{,}040.00} = 67.8\%$$

and the sample size for stratum 3 becomes 67.8% of 350 or 238.

When the sampling error of the overall average is computed on this basis, it is found to be ±$3.79, as compared with the sampling error of ±$4.64 when the sample allocation previously applied is used, and ±$28.73 for an unrestricted random sample, or a further reduction of about 18% in the sampling error.

TABLE 10-8

Value group (strata)	Number of items in strata, N_i	Standard deviation of values in strata, σ_i	$N_i\sigma_i$
1. Over $1,000.00	70	$1,247.00	$ 87,290.00
2. $200.00 to $1,000.00	500	105.50	52,750.00
3. Under $200.00	10,000	29.50	295,000.00
Total..........			$435,040.00

Again a comparison can be made with the unrestricted sampling technique. The sample size required to achieve this sample precision for the average, if unrestricted random sampling had been used, would have been 7,007, as contrasted with the 350 actually used.[7]

OTHER ALLOCATION METHODS

It must be emphasized that, in the audit situation, the population being sampled is the population of audited values. However, the population characteristics are not actually known unless a 100 per cent audit is conducted. If stratified sampling is used, the population sizes (N_i) for each stratum must be known with precision if accurate estimates are to be secured. Usually the strata are comprised of dollar-value groupings. Since the population sizes of the various strata for the *audited* values are not known, the strata dollar-value groupings and population sizes must be based on the *book record* values. In turn, the choice of strata boundaries are also based on the book record values.

To the extent that there is a close correlation between the audited and book record values, the sampling efficiency will be achieved. To the extent that the values differ, the sampling efficiency will be less than expected.

However, it must be recognized that regardless of the allocation method used, the sample projection will be valid even though one method is less *efficient* than another. It is merely that one allocation method or disparities between audited and book record values will produce larger sampling errors than another situation.

Of course, if the strata used are not dollar-value groupings (say location, type of item, etc.), the sampling precision achieved will not be affected by disparities between the audited and book record values.

Since most stratified sampling plans for audit purposes are based on dollar-value strata, it follows that since the book record values must be used to create strata and to provide stratum population values, the sample design must be imperfect to some degree.

In addition, allocation methods for variables sampling require an estimate of the strata standard deviations of the audited values, which can be obtained only from preliminary samples. When for any reason the standard deviation values are not available at the time of allocation, the optimum allocation method previously described cannot be used.

PROPORTIONAL ALLOCATION (STRATUM POPULATION SIZES)

One method of allocation commonly used, particularly in other fields of application, is *proportional allocation* based on strata population sizes. This method allo-

[7]These comparisons assume that the standard deviations indicated for the strata are population standard deviations.

cates the overall sample size to each stratum based on the proportion of the total population contained in that stratum. Thus:

$$n_i = n\left(\frac{N_i}{N}\right)$$

where N = total number of sampling units in population
n = total number of sampling units in sample
N_i = number of sampling units in specified stratum
n_i = assigned sample size for specified stratum

This type of allocation method is used to attempt to achieve a lower sampling error than might be achieved on the basis of an arbitrary allocation. In addition, there are some who feel that this type of allocation will provide a better cross section of the population.[8]

However, it will be remembered that the optimum allocation is dependent on the relationship:

$$n_i = \frac{N_i\sigma_i}{\Sigma(N_i\sigma_i)}$$

The optimum allocation for a given stratum is then dependent on the product of the stratum population size (N_i) and the stratum standard deviation (σ_i) and not on the population size alone.

It is to be noted that for dollar-value strata, there is an inverse relationship between deviation values for accounting data. This inverse relationship is the natural outcome of the fact that most distributions of accounting data are severely right skewed. This typical relationship may be seen in the example given in Table 10-9.

This inverse relationship is the natural outcome of the fact that most distributions of accounting data are right-skewed distributions.[9]

TABLE 10-9

Strata	Number of sampling units, N_i	Standard deviation, σ_i
A. Over $2,000.00	60	$1,106.00
B. $100.00 to $2,000.00	500	103.50
C. Under $100.00	6,000	45.00
Total	6,560	

[8]This method is not to be confused with the *quota* sampling technique where, although the sample for each stratum is selected in proportion to the populations in each stratum (category), the selection of individual sampling units is on a nonramdom basis.

[9]See Chap. 4.

Thus, for accounting data, it may be anticipated that allocating on stratum population size alone is not likely to produce an efficient sampling plan.

For the data of Table 10-9, the proportional allocation based on strata population sizes is shown below:

Strata	Number of sampling units, N_i	Per cent of total	Number in sample
A. Over $2,000.00	60	0.92%	3
B. $100.00 to $2,000.00	500	7.62	27
C. Under $100.00	6,000	91.46	320
Total	6,560	100.00%	350

This allocation obviously compares very unfavorably to the optimum allocation for the same data, as shown below:

Strata	Number in sample	
	Proportional allocation	Optimum allocation
A. Over $2,000.00	3	60
B. $100.00 to $2,000.00	27	47
C. Under $100.00	320	243
Total	350	350

Using the standard deviation values given in Table 10-9, it is possible to compute the resulting sampling errors for the estimate of a total dollar value for the two allocations.[10] The sampling error for the above proportional allocation would have been ±$164,360.00 as compared with a sampling error of only ±$36,300.00 for the optimum allocation sample.

While the advantage of the optimum allocation approach will vary with the values of the strata standard deviation situations in various populations, it is clear that for most accounting data, the proportional allocation method based on strata population sizes will produce very poor results in most cases.

[10]This computation was performed by using the indicated strata standard deviations as though they were population standard deviations and did not vary from sample to sample. In the actual situation the estimates of the population standard deviations in the samples would vary.

PROPORTIONAL ALLOCATION (STRATUM DOLLAR TOTALS)

Another possible strategy is to allocate the sample among the strata in accordance with the total dollar values contained within each stratum as compared with the total dollar value of the entire population. Again, it must be pointed out that such an allocation would have to be based on the *book record* values rather than the values of the targeted population in the audited values.

To the extent that the total dollar values of each stratum are correlated with the standard deviations of those strata, this strategy of allocation will be successful. Since for accounting data the bulk of the total dollar values frequently occur in the high-unit-values strata, some gain in sample precision is likely to be achieved. These high-unit-values strata will have larger standard deviations for the book record values and most likely for the audited values as well.

An example of a proportional allocation according to stratum total dollar values is shown below:

Strata	Number of sampling units, N_i	Dollar value	Per cent of total dollar value	Allocated number in sample, n_i
A. Over $2,000.00	60	$210,720.00	23.13%	85
B. $100.00 to $2,000.00	500	392,500.00	44.95%	157
C. Under $100.00	6,000	270,000.00	30.92%	108
Total	6,560	$873.220.00	100.00%	350

In this instance, the number of sampling units allocated to stratum A exceeds the number in the population for that stratum. The action to be taken is to allocate to the sample for that stratum the total number in that stratum and then to allocate the remaining 290 sampling units proportionately to the rest of the strata according to the total dollar values.

Strata	Number of sampling units, N_i	Dollar value	Per cent of total dollar value	Allocated number in sample, n_i
B. $100.00 to $2,000.00	500	$392,500.00	59.2%	172
C. Under $100.00	6,000	270,000.00	40.8%	118
Total	6,500	$662,500.00	100.0%	290

The final allocation would then be

Strata	Sample size
A. Over $2,000.00	60
B. $100.00 to $2,000.00	172
C. Under $100.00	118
Total	350

While a precise comparison between the results of this method of allocation with that of the prior optimum allocation method is difficult, since a new variable, the dollar value of each stratum, has been introduced, it is apparent that the results are much closer than the prior method. The sampling error of the total for this allocation is ±$48,500.00 as compared with ±$36,000.00 for the optimum allocation sample.

In actual situations, of course, the disparity will vary with the actual distribution of the dollar values among the strata. However, as pointed out previously, because of the nature of the distribution of accounting values, it can be expected that a relatively efficient, but not optimum, result can be obtained by this method.

SAMPLE SIZE DETERMINATION—STRATIFIED SAMPLES—VARIABLES

In the previous illustrations, the overall sample sizes used were considered to be established arbitrarily. In the discussion of optimum allocation, consideration was given to the best possible distribution of the sample among the strata, but in each instance an arbitrarily determined sample size was used.

The question of the proper overall sample size to be used to achieve a desired sampling precision for an average or a total must be faced. Given a desired sample precision and a specified confidence level, it is possible to determine the required sample size for each stratum based on optimum allocation by using the following formulas.[11]

For the 95% confidence level:

$$\text{Number of sample items for each stratum} = \frac{N_i\sigma_i\Sigma(N_i\sigma_i)}{N^2(.51SE_{\bar{x}})^2 + \Sigma(N_i\sigma_i^2)}$$

[11]The numerical values in the formulas were determined as follows:

1. For the 95% confidence level, .51 = 1/1.96, where the 1.96 is based on Table 4-3, p. 56.
2. For the 99% confidence level, .3876 = 1/2.58, where the 2.58 is based on Table 4-3, p. 56.
3. For other confidence levels, the reciprocal of the value t from Table 4-3 may be used.

For the 99% confidence level:

$$\text{Number of sample items for each stratum} = \frac{N_i\sigma_i\Sigma(N_i\sigma_i)}{N^2(.3876SE_{\bar{x}})^2 + \Sigma(N_i\sigma_i^2)}$$

To solve these formulas some knowledge of the standard deviation of each stratum is required. This can be estimated from a preliminary sample.

Assume that it is desired to estimate the total value of a bill of materials and establish its reasonableness by auditing a sample of items to determine the correctness of each value in the sample and by projecting the audited results.

It is desired to estimate the total value of a bill of materials containing 1,600 items with a precision of ±\$7,500.00 at the 95% confidence level. The average value will have to be determined with a precision of ±\$4.69 (or \$7,500.00/1,600).

The necessary data together with the required computations are shown in Table 10-10.

Substituting in the 95% confidence level formula,

$$n_i = \frac{N_i\sigma_i\Sigma(N_i\sigma_i)}{N^2\ (.51SE_{\bar{x}})^2 + \Sigma\ (N_i\sigma_i{}^2)}$$

For stratum 1 this becomes

$$\begin{aligned} n_1 &= \frac{38{,}000(78{,}000)}{(1600)^2[(.51)(4.69)]^2 + 15{,}640{,}000} \\ &= \frac{2{,}964{,}000{,}000}{2{,}560{,}000(2.3919)^2 + 15{,}640{,}000} \\ &= \frac{2{,}964{,}000{,}000}{2{,}560{,}000(5.7212) + 15{,}640{,}000} \\ &= \frac{2{,}964{,}000{,}000}{14{,}646{,}272 + 15{,}640{,}000} \\ &= \frac{2{,}964{,}000{,}000}{30{,}286{,}272} \\ &= 98 \end{aligned}$$

TABLE 10-10

Value group (strata)	Number of items in strata, N_i	Standard deviation of strata, σ_i	$N_i\sigma_i$	$N_i(\sigma_i)^2$
1. Over \$500.00	100	\$380.00	38,000	14,440,000
2. \$100.00 to \$500.00	500	40.00	20,000	800,000
3. Under \$100.00	1,000	20.00	20,000	400,000
Total	1,600		78,000	15,640,000

For stratum 2,

$$n_2 = \frac{20{,}000(78{,}000)}{(1600)^2[(.51)(4.69)]^2 + 15{,}640{,}000}$$
$$= 52$$

For stratum 3,

$$n_3 = \frac{20{,}000(78{,}000)}{(1600)^2[(.51)(4.69)]^2 + 15{,}640{,}000}$$
$$= 52$$

The sampling plan is shown in Table 10-11.

If the standard deviations used are good estimates of the strata standard deviations, the sample will total 204 and will yield an average with a 95% confidence level precision of ±\$4.69 and a precision of the estimated total of ±\$7,500.00.

It is possible that the sample size allocated to a given stratum may exceed the number of sampling units in the field in that stratum. For instance, in the above calculation, if the standard deviation for stratum 1 had been \$500.00 instead of \$380.00, the sample size for that stratum would be 110, which exceeds the total number of sampling units available in that stratum. In such an instance, all available sampling units in the stratum would be included in its sample. In other words, the stratum would be sampled 100%. As a result there would be a zero sampling error for that strata.

The number required for the other stratum can now be computed by dropping the first stratum out of the calculation completely, since it contributes nothing to the sampling error, and by redetermining the sample size for the remaining strata by the method outlined above.

STRATIFIED SAMPLING—ATTRIBUTES

It is apparent from the previous discussion that the gain in sampling efficiency which arose from variables stratified sampling came from the ability to allocate sampling units to strata which exhibit the greatest variability (standard deviation). This ad-

TABLE 10-11

Value group (strata)	Sample size for each stratum, n_i	Number of items in strata, N_i
Over \$500.00	100*	100
\$100.00 to \$500.00	52	500
Under \$100.00	52	1,000

*Actually, in this case 100 would be used in place of the estimated 98.

vantage accrues because the sampling error of an average (or total) is dependent on the standard deviation of the field from which it is drawn. This may be seen from the fundamental formula for computing the sampling error of an average.

$$SE_{\%} = t\frac{\sigma}{\sqrt{n}} \sqrt{1 - \frac{n}{N}}$$

In attributes sampling, however, the sample reliability for a given sample size is dependent upon the rate of occurrence in the field p. This may be seen from the formula for the sampling error of an attributes sample:

$$SE_{\%} = t\sqrt{\frac{p(1-p)}{n}} \sqrt{1 - \frac{n}{N}}$$

In the above formula, as p approaches .50 (or 50%), the sampling error approaches its maximum. This means that if the method of stratified sampling is used, a gain in efficiency will result when the sample is allocated to concentrate the sampling units in those strata with percentages of occurrence which are closer to 50%.

However, the rate of occurrence in the various strata will not be known in advance in the typical auditing situation. Of course a small preliminary sample could be drawn to establish the rate of error in each strata, but this involves two difficulties. The first is that a small attributes sample, because of its large sampling error, provides little information about the precise level of the rate of occurrence. The second is that little information is generally available on how to form these strata.

As a result, stratified sampling methods applied to attributes sampling usually result in little gain. Nevertheless, stratified sampling for attributes may be required for a test of transactions because the population may be divided into segments and sampled independently by different auditors in situations in which the records are kept in widely scattered offices or otherwise require separate auditors for different portions of the population because of the size of the populations.

However, there may be some occasions when a stratification might also be desired for other reasons. For instance, in an inventory test to establish the accuracy of the balances as indicated on perpetual inventory records, special attention to items especially likely to be pilferable might be desired, so that a larger sample might be taken in this area.

When the population is stratified by other than the dollar values of the sampling units (or some other variable), the strata are referred to as *natural strata*. Thus, there may be a stratification by location, type of transaction, stock item grouping, etc.

However, as previously noted, the precision of a stratified sample will generally be as good as or better than an unrestricted random sample. Thus, the methods for unrestricted random samples may be used in such instances with the knowledge that the sampling error resulting may be an overstatement.

The method of establishing the exact (binomial) confidence limits as outlined in

Chapter 6 cannot be used for stratified samples for attributes. However, approximate confidence limits can be fixed.

The formula for the sampling error of a percentage (normal approximate) can be used to establish the sample precision for each stratum.

$$SE_{\%} = t\sqrt{\frac{p(1-p)}{n}}\sqrt{1-\frac{n}{N}}$$

Once the sampling error of each stratum is established, all can be combined into an estimate of the overall precision of the estimate by using the same method described for variables earlier in this chapter. The formula converts to

$$SE_{\%}{}^2 = \frac{\sum(N_i{}^2 SE_{\%i}{}^2)}{N^2}$$

where N_i = population size for each stratum
$SE_{\%_i}$ = sampling error of percentage for each stratum
N = population size

The point estimate of the overall percentage can be accomplished by using the weighted averages of the percentages (point estimate) of each stratum in a manner similar to that previously described for combining averages

$$p = \frac{\sum(N_i p_i)}{N}$$

where N_i = population size for each stratum
p_i = percentage in sample (point estimate) for each stratum
N = population size

As an example, assume that four auditors are sent to four different offices of a national company at widely dispersed locations where these offices contain all of the records of some type to be audited. Each auditor is instructed to draw an independent sample of 100 documents (say invoices) and to audit to establish the frequency of occurrence of errors. The objective, however, is to establish the frequency of occurrence of such errors for the company as a whole. The results of the audit are shown below:

Location (strata)	Number of items in strata, N_i	Assigned sample size, n_i	Sample error rate, p_i
A	10,000	100	3.0%
B	12,000	100	5.0
C	8,000	100	6.0
D	6,000	100	2.0

The weighted average of these percentages is computed for the point estimate of the percentage at all four locations as follows:

Location (strata)	Number of items in strata, N_i	Sample error rates, p_i	$N_i p_i$
A	10,000	.03	300
B	12,000	.05	600
C	8,000	.06	480
D	6,000	.02	120
	36,000		1500

$$p = \frac{\Sigma(N_i p_i)}{N} = \frac{1{,}500}{36{,}000} = .0412 = 4.2\%$$

The sample precision may now be established by computing the sample precision for each stratum as a first step, where the sampling error is computed from:

$$SE_{\%i} = t\sqrt{\frac{p_i q_i}{n_i}}\sqrt{1 - \frac{n_i}{N_i}}$$

Location (strata)	Number of items in strata, N_i	Sample error rate, p_i	Sample size, n_i	Sampling error, $SE_{\%}$ (95% confidence level)
A	10,000	.03	100	.0333
B	12,000	.05	100	.0425
C	8,000	.06	100	.0462
D	6,000	.02	100	.0272

For instance, for location A (95% confidence level),

$$SE_{\%i} = 1.96\sqrt{\frac{(.03)(.97)}{100}}\sqrt{1 - \frac{100}{10{,}000}} = .0333$$

or 3.3%

The sample precision for the overall estimate for the entire company may be computed by combining these sample precisions for the individual locations.

$$SE_{\%}{}^2 = \frac{\Sigma(N_i{}^2 SE_{\%i}{}^2)}{N^2}$$

Location (strata)	Number of items in strata, N_i	Sampling* error of stratum, per cent $SE_{\%i}$	N_i^2	$SE^2_{\%i}$	Product $N_i(SE_{\%i}^2)$
A	10,000	.0333	100,000,000	.00111	111,000
B	12,000	.0425	144,000,000	.00181	260,640
C	8,000	.0462	64,000,000	.00213	136,320
D	6,000	.0272	36,000,000	.00074	26,640
	36,000				534,600

*From the table above.

$$N = 36{,}000 \qquad N^2 = 1{,}296{,}000{,}000$$

$$SE_{\%}{}^2 = \frac{\sum (N_i^2 SE_{\%i}{}^2)}{N^2} = \frac{534{,}600}{1{,}296{,}000{,}000} = .0004125$$

$$SE_{\%} = .020 \text{ or } 2.0\%$$

The confidence interval is obtained by adding and subtracting this sampling error (2.0%) from the point estimate of 4.2%. The 95% confidence interval is thus 2.2% to 6.2%

GENERAL CONSIDERATIONS

The primary purpose of stratified sampling is to provide an overall estimate, and only secondarily, if at all, is it designed to provide useful estimates for the individual strata used. Generally, if an efficient sample design is used, the number of sampling units within each stratum will be insufficient to draw useful conclusions about each stratum with a sufficiently tight sampling precision, while the sample precision will be adequate for the overall estimate. If the population is split into segments (say offices) only for the purpose of drawing a separate conclusion for each, the result is *not* a stratified sample.

While the stratified sampling approach, especially for variables estimates, can be very efficient, there are limitations upon its use. Stratified sampling cannot be used effectively for audit purposes (at least for variables estimates) unless the number of sampling units in the population in each stratum is known precisely. Any inaccuracy in such knowledge will distort both the calculation of the point estimate and the sampling error. Since this disparity is not a sampling error, it is not included in the statement of sample precision, and the interval estimate can be very wrong.

This problem can usually be resolved simply where computerized (EDP) or punched-card (ADP) accounting systems are being used. In other cases, the auditor may be confined to a less efficient, two-strata sample design, where one consists of all high-value items. These high-value sampling units are usually readily identifiable.

Another possibility, when high-value items are numerous, is to use three strata, where the top stratum contains all items of an amount equal to a material error, which are sampled 100%, while the other two strata contain the remaining high-value items as one stratum and the lower-value items as another and both are sampled on less than a 100% basis.

Further, it is necessary that a practical method for the selection of sampling units be available so that the number of sampling units required for each stratum can be obtained without too great a cost in time and effort. The use of nonproportional samples, the kind most efficient in auditing, may create a problem in this respect.

In sampling for audit tests involving dollar values, although the usual purpose is to project the true value (equivalent to audited value) of the population, the stratification must be accomplished on the basis of the unaudited values. To attempt to do otherwise would require a 100% audit of the entire population, a most expensive method and one which would make the test sample unnecessary.

To the extent that the true (audited) values of the population, as reflected in the sample, depart from the unaudited values, the stratified sampling techniques become less efficient.

As a result of these disparities between the unaudited values used for stratification and the audited value, a sampling unit in the sample may have an audited value which would place it outside of the stratum to which it was originally assigned. For instance, a sampling unit may have been assigned to a stratum of values of less than $100.00 because the unaudited value was $47.98, while it is discovered that the true or audited value was $147.98, which is in the next stratum. Nevertheless, the sampling unit, regardless of its audited value, would be retained in the sample in its originally assigned (unaudited) value group.

It must be remembered that there may be other sampling units in the population, but not in the sample, with similar misassignments in either direction, which are represented in the sample by sampling units such as these.

It is to be noted that the sample size determination techniques, such as optimum allocation methods, may result in small sample sizes for some strata. It is suggested that it is unwise to include less than 30 sampling units in the sample for any stratum unless the sample constitutes all of the items in that stratum (100% sample). This minimum sample size requirement of any stratum (other than those sampled 100%) is necessary to avoid the problems arising from using the "small sample t" value. If small samples are used for any stratum, the methods available for computing the sample precision become complex and approximate.

ELEVEN

Cluster Sampling

THE REASON FOR CLUSTER SAMPLING

The method of stratified sampling described in the previous chapter is used primarily to achieve an increase in sampling efficiency, that is, to reduce the sampling error for a given size sample or, conversely, to reduce the sample size necessary to achieve a given sample precision.

Other reasons may develop which dictate the use of other forms of samples. For instance, in the previously described sampling methods, it is necessary in creating the sample to draw *individual* sampling units (records, entries, etc.) one at a time at random from among the sampling units comprising the field. Under certain circumstances this requirement may be arduous and expensive. A method of sampling which does not require the drawing of individual sampling units but in groups or clusters would be preferable under such circumstances.

In certain situations, the actual location and selection of the individual sampling units called for by the random numbers chosen may be very time-consuming. It is even possible that, in some cases, the time involved in locating and selecting the individual sampling units may be as great as, or greater than, the time involved in the audit examination of the sampling units when located.

In addition, the selection of these documents may require the prior preparation of a long list of random numbers with considerable clerical work involved in the elimination of duplicates, arrangement in order, etc. In such cases, the time consumed in the examination itself may be small compared to that involved in the preparation for selection and in the actual location of the sampling units.

THE CLUSTER SAMPLE

Under such conditions, a technique which provides for the selection of more than one sampling unit at a time is recommended. For instance, instead of drawing 500 random numbers and selecting one sampling unit at each point indicated, it may be desirable to select say 100 random numbers, and to pick five sampling units at each point, or perhaps 50 random numbers with 10 sampling units used at each random point.[1] This method would appreciably reduce the time involved both in the preparation for and in the selection of the sampling units since fewer points in the file would have to be located.

However, as will be seen in later discussions, the savings from this method, known as *cluster sampling*, may be offset in whole, or in part, by a loss in sample precision which may require a larger sample size than that needed by other methods. In fact, the loss in sample reliability may be so great as to require a large increase in sample size, which may cause a net loss rather than a saving when this method is used.

Whether the use of the cluster sampling method will result in a lower or a higher cost than that obtained by other methods of selection will depend on the circumstances. As will be explained below, it is unfortunately true that the net effect of using this method frequently cannot be determined readily in advance of the actual drawing of the sample in the audit situation. However, an understanding of the principles involved will aid in recognizing the probable outcome insofar as its effect on sampling precision is concerned.

The impact of this method upon sample precision may be illustrated by a hypothetical example, which, although it is unrealistic from an audit viewpoint, is designed as a demonstration of the principles, rather than as an application of them.

Assume that it is desired to estimate the total amount of a military payroll at a given location where the individual pay records are arranged alphabetically *within grade or rank* and that a very large number of military personnel are involved. To simplify the example, suppose that all personnel have been stationed at the installation for the same period of time, that they all have the same time in grade, that they all have the same deductions, and that all within a certain grade receive about the same pay.

For purposes of illustration, assume that 15 clusters of 10 pay records each are to be drawn from the file at 15 random points selected by means of random number tables.

In such a case the pay records within each cluster will probably result in almost identical amounts, since it is most likely that they will be for the same grade or rank. In other words, any one pay record would have served the same purpose as any other within a given cluster. Thus, a sample of one at each sampling point

[1] For purposes of this volume, a cluster sample consists of a number of groups of *contiguous* sampling units selected at random. Subsampling of clusters is *not* considered here.

would have served the same purpose as the sample of 10 in deriving information about the pay rates, and hence the nine additional sampling units within each cluster are completely wasted. Therefore, since nine-tenths of the sampling units are wasted, the sampling efficiency of the method is only a fraction as good as that of an equivalent unrestricted random sample of individual sampling units.

While a situation similar to that just described, where all persons in the same grade or rank receive identical pay, is unlikely to be encountered, it is apparent that the amounts of pay within different grades on any payroll will tend to be similar or at least show smaller differences than between grades. Thus, through a similar line of reasoning, while a sample of one will no longer suffice for each cluster, since there will be some variation in amounts within the cluster, the number of sampling units required to establish the cluster average with a high reliability will remain small. It will be wasteful to use large clusters.

An example at the other extreme would be encountered when a similar sample is to be obtained from a file where the filing arrangement is completely at random with respect to the amount of pay. In such a case, any cluster, no matter where it is drawn, will contain a random cross section of the entire file. Under these circumstances, one cluster is as good as any other, and a single cluster of a given size will have the same sample reliability as an unrestricted random sample of single units drawn from many points in the file. It is necessary to add here that such a situation would arise only if the file is truly randomly arranged, a most unlikely circumstance.

It would seem, then, that the sampling efficiency of the cluster method will depend upon the amount of variability to be encountered within each cluster, as contrasted with that between the clusters.

Books dealing with advanced statistical sampling theory also observe that under certain conditions a cluster sample may be *more* efficient than a sample of equivalent size drawn as individual units. However, this requires that the variability within the clusters be greater than that between. It is extremely unlikely that such a situation would be encountered in the type of sampling accomplished by auditors, and therefore it may be assumed that in auditing work this will not happen.

Without prior knowledge of the field or without a preliminary sample, it will not be possible to evaluate the relative sampling reliability of cluster sampling versus individual unit sampling. Even when such data are available, the computations required are extensive. Nevertheless, a general idea can be obtained if some knowledge of the probable extent of the variability within the clusters, as contrasted to that between the cluster averages, is available. In addition, it is observed that the basic consideration in choosing either of the two methods is the question of cost.

It may be said that, in most auditing situations, there will be a definite loss in sample reliability when cluster sampling is used. However, in situations such as those described earlier in this chapter, where the cost of location of the individual sampling units together with the costs of preparation for random sampling is high compared with the cost of examining the sampling units, clusters may be more economical, even though it is necessary to use a larger number of sampling units to offset the poorer sampling reliability of the cluster method. This will be especially true when the values within the clusters are not too much alike.

Some examples of situations which might merit the use of cluster sampling techniques may be cited.

In an audit of invoices, it was found that all invoices were paid at the home office of a corporation, although the corporate divisions are physically separate. Further, payments of invoices for several divisions to the same vendor were combined, and one check issued. Invoices after payment were filed by the vendor without regard to month or corporate division. Supporting documents were attached to each invoice. The voucher register did not identify those invoices applicable to each division. Thus, an audit with respect to divisions or even an overall audit would present serious problems in sampling individual units. Sampling clusters would be much simpler.

In a contractor's plant, purchase orders for commercial business and government business were intermingled. However, government purchase orders were issued in numerical blocks of 25. The total number of purchase orders was 20,000. If a random number sampling of government purchase orders was used, a very large task would arise in the preparation of the random number list, since there are numerous small blocks of such orders, and a very large portion of the random numbers would not apply. It is possible that cluster sampling might be more effective in such a case.

In another case, an auditor was called upon to verify a large listing of documents that were several years old. The documents were no longer in use and had been removed from the files, bound in 25,000 batches of 10 each, and stored in a warehouse. A considerable reduction in the time required for locating the sampling units would result if clusters of 10 were used.

In addition, any situation where a large sample is used requiring withdrawal of numerous records from a wide variety of points in a file in active use, together with a resulting delay in returning these units to their widely dispersed positions in the file, might seriously interfere with the normal use of the file. Here the use of clusters would enable a faster selection and return of the items to the file, since each cluster can be handled as a block. Further, a concentration of missing documents is easier to deal with than widely scattered individual missing documents insofar as normal file operations are concerned.

An evaluation of the results of a cluster sample to determine the sampling error of the projection obtained therefrom will establish its actual reliability. The methods for such appraisal of cluster sample results will be discussed later.

DRAWING A CLUSTER SAMPLE

A cluster sample may be obtained by using either random number or systematic sampling techniques.

When random number sampling methods are used, the document or entry specified by each drawn random number is located and that sampling unit plus a sufficient number of the sampling units that follow it to comprise a cluster of the desired size is selected.

When systematic sampling is used, a similar technique may be applied with a sufficient number of items drawn after that specified by the sampling interval to comprise the cluster of the desired size. It is recommended that a cluster sample *include at least* 20 *clusters.*

APPRAISING THE DETERMINATION– A CLUSTER SAMPLE–VARIABLES

As for samples obtained by drawing individual sampling units, the sampling reliability of a projection of an average or total from the results of the sample can be computed.

To establish the sampling error of a cluster sample, when the average value of the clusters is used to estimate the average of the field from which these clusters were drawn or to estimate the total value of the field by multiplying the average value per sample unit by the number of the items in the field, the first step consists of computing the average value of each cluster. It is necessary[2] that all the clusters contain the same number of sampling units. The overall average can then be established by averaging the cluster averages.

The sampling error of these estimates may now be calculated by treating each cluster average as though it were one observation and using the methods outlined in Chapter 7 for appraising the reliability of an average (variable sampling). Thus, if 20 clusters of 10 items each were used, this would yield 20 averages. These values would then be treated as though they had been generated as a sample of 20 individual observations. A specific example of such a calculation is illustrated below.

Assume that it is desired to estimate the total value of a certain group of 5,000 vouchers. This is to be accomplished by estimating the average value per voucher by means of a sample and then multiplying the resulting average by the field size (5,000). Cluster sampling is to be used, and it is decided to draw a sample of 20 clusters of five vouchers each. A total of 20 random numbers is secured from a random number table by the methods previously discussed.

The voucher bearing each of the selected random numbers is located, and it and the next four vouchers are drawn from the file. The results of the drawing are shown in Table 11-1.

The average value from each cluster is then obtained as shown in Table 11-2.

The overall average of the cluster averages ($118.93) then represents the sample

[2]If the methods outlined in this chapter are to be used. The method of appraising values computed from variable-sized clusters is much more complex. See Chap. 14.

TABLE 11-1

Cluster number	Random number	Amount	Cluster number	Random number	Amount
1	0346	$ 65.02	8	2291	$ 99.83
		93.54			190.10
		125.10			201.00
		112.20			183.10
		91.72			217.50
2	1216	173.20	9	0508	191.30
		184.70			27.43
		47.53			88.09
		83.80			96.80
		91.62			37.99
3	1436	198.30	10	1258	66.60
		226.70			178.10
		136.00			253.70
		283.70			152.70
		81.95			82.08
4	0456	155.20	11	1420	101.80
		162.50			48.35
		88.38			90.40
		113.30			137.30
		97.46			97.06
5	2014	178.00	12	3468	67.00
		314.70			67.53
		53.67			91.49
		36.18			209.20
		116.90			89.57
6	3568	89.93	13	0199	93.43
		261.00			116.70
		64.23			109.30
		87.62			168.40
		226.50			66.01
7	3236	29.38	14	0163	42.38
		107.20			14.99
		77.30			99.83
		83.04			115.70
		180.40			80.17

TABLE 11-1 *(Continued)*

Cluster number	Random number	Amount	Cluster number	Random number	Amount
15	0137	$ 56.47	18	2411	$156.20
		92.54			73.67
		135.60			94.92
		40.83			109.80
		72.41			106.10
16	4645	54.62	19	2550	80.10
		69.05			93.50
		119.20			56.67
		85.35			224.90
		98.51			97.85
17	3684	90.07	20	4851	64.66
		212.70			163.50
		69.11			131.90
		198.10			229.00
		242.90			79.70

average (per voucher). Multiplying by 5,000 (the number of vouchers in the field) yields an estimate of the total value of all the vouchers as follows:

$$\$118.93 \times 5{,}000 = \$594{,}650.00$$

The methods of Chapter 7 are then applied to compute the sample precision by using the cluster averages as though each comprised an individual observation.

The first step is to establish the standard deviation of the sample values (cluster averages). If less than 48 clusters have been used, as in this example, it is *not* appropriate to use the average range method to determine the standard deviation, but

TABLE 11-2

Cluster number	Average amount	Cluster number	Average amount	Cluster number	Average amount
1	$ 97.92	8	$178.31	15	$ 79.57
2	116.17	9	88.32	16	85.35
3	185.33	10	146.64	17	162.58
4	123.37	11	94.98	18	108.14
5	139.89	12	104.96	19	110.60
6	145.86	13	110.77	20	133.75
7	95.46	14	70.61		

the value of the standard deviation must be computed *directly* by the method outlined on page 53, Chapter 4.

The direct computation method (see Chapter 4) is used as illustrated in Table 11-3.[3]

Now that the standard deviation is available, the methods of Chapter 7 may be used. It will be remembered that the sampling error was computed by multiplying the value of the standard deviation by a factor (or factors) selected on the basis of the confidence level, the field size, and the sample size desired.

When less that 40 clusters are used, it is necessary that the factors be computed on a slightly different basis to take into consideration the theory of small samples. A set of tables of such factors is included at the end of this chapter. As in the case where the precise field size and sample size were not covered by the tables (see Chapter 7), two tables are given, one for the basic factor, and the other for the finite correction factor.[4]

These tables indicate that for the sample size of 20 clusters and a selected confidence level of, say 99%, the basic factor is .6561 (see Appendix L). The finite correction factor is obtained by calculating first the percentage that the number of *clusters in the sample* is of the *number of clusters in the field*, or

$$\text{Number of clusters in sample} = 20$$

Number of clusters in field,

$$\frac{5{,}000}{5} = 1{,}000$$

Per cent of total clusters in sample,

$$\frac{20}{1{,}000} = 2.0\%$$

Appendix I (page 481) indicates a finite correction factor of .9899 when the sample comprises 2.0% of the field. The previously computed standard deviation is then multiplied by the basic factor and the finite correction factor to obtain the *sample precision of the average*, or

$$\$31.61 \times .6561 \times .9899 = \pm\$20.53$$

If the above sampling error for the average is then multiplied by the field size, *the sample precision of the total* is established.

$$\$20.53 \times 5{,}000 = \pm\$102{,}650.00$$

[3] The method outlined in Technical Appendix I may be used for this purpose.

[4] See Technical Appendix III for an explanation of the method of arriving at these values.

TABLE 11-3

Cluster number	Cluster average	Difference between each cluster average and overall average	Square of each difference
1	$ 97.92	−21.01	441.4201
2	116.17	− 2.76	7.6176
3	185.33	66.40	4,408.9600
4	123.37	4.44	19.7136
5	139.89	20.96	439.3216
6	145.86	26.93	725.2249
7	95.46	−23.47	550.8409
8	178.31	59.38	3,525.9844
9	88.32	−30.61	936.9721
10	146.64	27.71	767.8441
11	94.98	−23.95	573.6025
12	104.96	−13.97	195.1609
13	110.77	− 8.16	66.5856
14	70.61	−48.32	2,334.8224
15	79.57	−39.36	1,549.2096
16	85.35	−33.58	1,127.6164
17	162.58	43.65	1,905.3225
18	108.14	−10.79	116.4241
19	110.60	− 8.33	69.3889
20	133.75	14.82	219.6324
Overall average..	$118.93		19,981.6646

$$\sigma = \sqrt{\frac{19981.6646}{20}} = \sqrt{999.0832}$$
$$= \$31.61$$

SAMPLE SIZE DETERMINATION—CLUSTER SAMPLES—VARIABLES

While in principle the methods of Chapter 5 can be used to determine the *number of clusters* necessary to achieve a given sample precision at a given confidence level, remembering that each cluster is handled as though it was a single sampling unit, certain difficulties are encountered in practice.

The method for determining sample size in Chapter 5 required a preliminary sample from which the standard deviation could be estimated. The use of the average range method required a preliminary sample of about 50 sampling units. However, it is unlikely, in many audit tests, that more than this number of *clusters* will be required in the final sample. Thus, the idea of a preliminary sample of this size is not practical.

Of course, it would be possible to take a preliminary sample of fewer clusters and to use the long method of computing the standard deviation. However, such a small sample, if it is to be a small part of the final sample, is unlikely to give a satisfactory estimate of the standard deviation.

It was previously noted that, in most audit situations, the cluster sample will be less efficient than the unrestricted random sample. Thus, it would be possible to estimate the sample size required if unrestricted random sampling was used (Chapter 5) and single sampling units were selected.

If this sample size is divided by the desired cluster size, an estimate of the number of clusters required results, with the realization that this sample may provide a somewhat poorer sample reliability than desired.

After the sample is completed, the precision of the cluster sample can be determined by the method just described. If the precision so ascertained is not adequate, the sample can be extended by securing additional random clusters as required.

APPRAISING THE PRECISION OF CLUSTER SAMPLES—ATTRIBUTES

Cluster sampling methods may be used for attributes estimation sampling. As described above, this technique involves drawing the samples as groups of contiguous sampling units. Here the purpose is to estimate a rate of occurrence (such as an error rate) from a sample.

In order to appraise the sampling precision of the results, it is necessary that the percentage of error be established separately for each cluster. Once these data are established, the calculation of the sampling precision proceeds as though the problem related to a *variables* sample.

To illustrate the method, assume that 21 clusters of 20 items each are selected from a field of 4,000 sampling units and that each sampling unit is checked for error or other occurrence in which the sampler has an interest. In general it is desirable that there be not less than 20 clusters. Assume that the results in Table 11-4 were obtained.

The average percentage of error in the sample is then 10%. To obtain the sample precision, *percentages are treated as though they were variables measurements,* and the method previously described for variables is used. Hence the first step is to compute the standard deviation of the percentages, again using the direct method since there are less than 48 clusters. The computation of the standard deviation is shown in Table 11-5.

If a 95% confidence level is used, the basic precision factor can be found in the table in Appendix L (page 504) and is .4673. The finite correction factor is obtained as follows:

$$\text{Number of clusters in sample} = 21$$

TABLE 11-4

Cluster number	Cluster size	Number of errors in cluster	Per cent error in cluster
1	20	3	15
2	20	2	10
3	20	2	10
4	20	0	0
5	20	4	20
6	20	2	10
7	20	1	5
8	20	3	15
9	20	1	5
10	20	1	5
11	20	3	15
12	20	5	25
13	20	2	10
14	20	0	0
15	20	1	5
16	20	4	20
17	20	0	0
18	20	2	10
19	20	3	15
20	20	2	10
21	20	1	5
Overall average...			10

Number of clusters in field,

$$\frac{4{,}000}{20} = 200$$

Percentage of clusters in sample,

$$\frac{21}{200} = 10.5\%$$

From the finite correction factor table (page 481), the finite correction factor is found to be .9460.

The sample precision may then be computed as follows:

$$6.73\% \times .4673 \times .9460 = 2.98\%$$

Since the sample estimate was 10%, *the confidence limits at the 95% confidence level* become

$$10\% \pm 2.98\% \quad \text{or} \quad 7.02 \text{ to } 12.98\%$$

TABLE 11-5

Cluster number	Per cent error in cluster	Difference between each cluster percentage and overall percentage	Square of each difference
1	15	5	25
2	10	0	0
3	10	0	0
4	0	−10	100
5	20	10	100
6	10	0	0
7	5	− 5	25
8	15	5	25
9	5	− 5	25
10	5	− 5	25
11	15	5	25
12	25	15	225
13	10	0	0
14	0	−10	100
15	5	− 5	25
16	20	10	100
17	0	−10	100
18	10	0	0
19	15	5	25
20	10	0	0
21	5	− 5	25
Total			950

$$\sigma = \sqrt{\frac{950}{21}} = \sqrt{45.238} = 6.73\%$$

SAMPLE SIZE DETERMINATION—CLUSTER SAMPLES—ATTRIBUTES

In the previous section, it was noted that sample precision for attributes cluster samples is computed by treating the percentages for each cluster like a variables measurement.

Advance determination of sample size requirements would then require the use of variables methods involving a preliminary sample to estimate the standard deviation of the *cluster* results. Once again this is not a very practical approach for the reasons given under the discussion of variables cluster sample size determination.

Therefore, a similar solution to that suggested for variables cluster sample size determination would be appropriate here. The sample size required for an unrestricted random sample of single sampling units would be determined by the methods of Chapter 5, and attributes methods would be used. This sample size would be divided by the size of the cluster desired to determine the number of clusters to be taken.

After the sample is at hand, it should be appraised for its sampling precision, and if this is not adequate, additional random clusters should be taken.

GENERAL COMMENT ON CLUSTER SAMPLING

In the examples and discussion above, cluster sampling was covered as a form of unrestricted random sampling. However, cluster sampling can be used in conjunction with stratified random sampling or with the forms of sampling discussed later.

When cluster sampling is used with stratified sampling, the field is divided into strata, and the clusters are drawn separately from each stratum. The methods of stratified sampling variables sample appraisal can then be applied to the sample results dealing with the average or percentage of each cluster as though it represented the observation on a single sampling unit. Beyond this, the methods described in Chapter 10 can be applied without change.

TWELVE

Difference and Ratio Estimates

THE REASON FOR DIFFERENCE AND RATIO ESTIMATES

Various efficient sampling methods are available which will provide a smaller sampling error for samples of a given size or require a smaller size sample to provide a given sample precision than when less sophisticated sampling techniques are used. An example of such methods which provide a greater sampling efficiency has been discussed previously, namely, stratified sampling. However, there are other plans available which, under certain conditions, will provide even more dramatic reductions in sampling errors.

Among these improved methods are the methods of *difference* or *ratio estimates*, which may be used for certain types of tests. These methods are confined to *variables estimation sampling* for audit test purposes. Further, they cannot be applied to all tests but require the existence of certain circumstances.

Assume that it is desired to estimate the total value of an inventory, group of vouchers, bill of materials, etc., from an audited sample where corrections have been made by the auditor on the value of some of the items examined as part of the sample. The objective is to estimate the total value that would have been obtained if all the items comprising the field had been examined and corrected where necessary. Such a situation might arise where it is desired to establish the reasonableness of the total.

The method proposed in the previous discussions was to project the average corrected (audited) value of the sample by multiplying by the number of sampling units in the field.

The sampling precision of the average is then established as outlined in Chapter

7. To accomplish this, the standard deviation of the sample values is computed and multiplied by an appropriate factor to provide the sampling precision of the average. This is then multiplied by the number of sampling units in the field to provide the sample precision of the *total.*

Note that this sample precision is largely determined by the magnitude of the standard deviation. When the sample values differ greatly in value from item to item, as in an inventory, the confidence interval covers a wide range as a result of the poor sample precision. This can be offset only by resorting to a large sample size.

To overcome this difficulty, a new approach is required. This is to sample either the differences or ratios between the book and audited values and to project this difference or ratio rather than the values themselves. These methods are described in detail below.

An estimate of a total value based on the projection of the average (usually audited) value of a sample can be accomplished, even though individual item values or, for that matter, a total book value are not available. For instance, a sample of a suitable number of items in stock can be taken, counted, and priced, and if the total number of these items in the field is known, the total value of the entire inventory can be estimated by multiplying the average value of the sample items by the total number of items in stock.

However, only when the item-by-item records used to establish the original or unaudited total book value are available, together with a total unaudited book value based on these item evaluations, and only then, can the more efficient difference or ratio estimate methods be used.

DIFFERENCE ESTIMATES

The increased efficiency of a difference estimate is achieved through a reduction in the standard deviation of the items to be sampled. This is accomplished by a new approach when both audited and unaudited values are available on an item-by-item basis.

The difference method is applied by determining the correct or audited value for each sample value and obtaining the average difference between the audited value and the recorded book or record value for each item from the sample. This average difference is then multiplied by the number of items in the field to obtain the total correction and is added to (or subtracted from) the book value to obtain a corrected total value.

An illustration of this computation is shown below for a hypothetical sample of 100 observations, perhaps from a group of vouchers or other documents. Assume that there are 10,000 of these vouchers and that their total value shown on the records is $1,281,587.21. The object is to establish the reasonableness of the total book value. In Table 12-1 the record value for each document is shown in one column, while the corrected, or audited, value is shown in another. The differences as well as the average difference for all items are shown in a third column.

TABLE 12-1

Voucher number	Record value	Audited value	Difference	Voucher number	Record value	Audited value	Difference
2895	12.42	12.42	0	7686	241.49	241.49	0
4183	64.82	64.82	0	7373	81.88	81.88	0
4733	220.22	220.22	0	3008	86.21	86.21	0
9023	293.58	293.58	0	4706	176.12	176.12	0
5647	27.17	27.17	0	1215	106.67	106.67	0
7490	72.84	72.84	0	3412	239.68	257.96	+18.28
1787	154.21	154.21	0	1224	149.12	149.12	0
8832	98.68	98.68	0	3371	76.41	76.41	0
4948	151.81	170.09	+18.28	3991	202.93	202.93	0
6975	86.27	86.27	0	4094	99.80	99.80	0
5126	175.53	175.53	0	2767	76.41	76.41	0
6611	59.64	42.02	−17.62	9078	122.78	122.78	0
3815	181.91	177.87	−4.04	3912	68.32	124.02	+55.70
6434	258.82	258.82	0	5933	32.91	32.91	0
3518	111.28	111.28	0	2738	145.22	145.22	0
6718	215.98	215.98	0	0094	42.28	42.28	0
8024	129.67	139.41	+9.74	4431	204.67	204.67	0
0184	78.06	78.06	0	9608	39.61	39.61	0
8284	41.97	41.97	0	8921	159.71	195.21	+35.50
2973	215.60	215.60	0	2876	143.97	143.97	0
5268	85.68	85.68	0	6450	65.55	65.55	0
1863	62.28	62.28	0	9152	86.40	79.20	−7.20
9596	81.09	81.09	0	3158	176.36	176.36	0
1911	98.71	145.01	+46.30	9315	127.89	127.89	0
6260	101.99	101.99	0	3851	257.02	257.02	0
9282	255.02	291.88	+36.86	8620	188.07	188.07	0
8738	92.81	92.81	0	0139	70.37	70.37	0
3706	86.14	86.14	0	3119	127.07	127.07	0
5168	129.95	129.95	0	8717	162.48	162.48	0
0645	65.65	65.65	0	3832	70.30	63.84	−6.46
5445	61.52	61.52	0	8621	51.92	51.92	0
6552	142.31	142.31	0	9471	129.79	129.79	0
8194	103.85	118.45	+14.60	4809	60.93	60.93	0
2513	145.90	145.90	0	1685	332.99	332.99	0
9645	80.20	80.20	0	2820	49.91	67.47	+17.56
0624	141.86	141.86	0	3456	89.84	89.84	0
1640	89.70	89.70	0	0856	225.13	246.33	+21.20
2063	102.31	102.31	0	2996	62.18	62.18	0
7922	338.36	338.36	0	8031	101.25	101.25	0
3926	154.50	173.36	+18.86	1053	178.25	178.25	0
0332	70.37	98.49	+28.12	3252	182.24	182.24	0
3019	140.62	140.62	0	9694	99.44	99.44	0
7498	198.58	198.58	0	9890	244.27	244.27	0
8381	122.53	137.95	+15.42	7810	69.44	69.44	0
6788	111.96	134.76	+22.80	9512	76.70	62.04	−14.66
5169	117.21	132.71	+15.50	1957	67.36	67.36	0
4210	87.26	87.26	0	9141	47.13	47.13	0
5834	33.97	33.97	0	1725	146.03	146.03	0
4579	94.23	94.23	0	3831	171.67	171.67	0
3073	244.46	244.46	0	3740	188.99	188.99	0
				Averages	126.9466	130.1940	+3.2474

If previously described methods are used, the average of the audited values would be projected by multiplying it by the field size. However, the sampling precision of the projection is dependent on the variability of the items sampled.[1]

The audited values in Table 12-1 indicate a wide variability (range from $12.42 to $338.36) and thus a high standard deviation ($70.56). On the other hand, the variability of the differences is much less (range from −$17.62 to +$55.70) than that of the original values, with a resulting lower standard deviation ($8.36). The lower standard deviation is generally the result of the fact that even in a relatively poor accounting situation, the majority of the values are correctly stated. Therefore, most of the differences will be zero, resulting in a high degree of uniformity, which will be reflected in a low standard deviation. Thus, the sampling error of the *average difference* between the audited values and the book values will be much less than that of the *average audited value*, and the projection of the average difference is thus more reliable.

The average difference may now be used to project the total value as shown in the computation below.

The average difference between the book and the audited values *for the sample* has been established at +$3.2474. Multiplying this by the number of items in the field (10,000) yields an estimated difference of +$32,474.00 for the entire field. Adding this to the known book value total gives an estimate of a corrected total value as follows:

Book total value	$1,281,587.21
Difference	32,474.00
Corrected total value	$1,314,061.21

It is necessary to determine the sampling precision of this estimate. To accomplish this the standard deviation of the *differences* is determined.

Experience with accounting data has indicated that the group range (d_2) method will, under certain circumstances, badly underestimate the standard deviation *of the differences.* Therefore, it is recommended that the basic formula be used.[2]

[1] See Chap. 4. The sampling precision is computed from the formula

$$SE = t\frac{\sigma}{\sqrt{n}}\sqrt{1-\frac{n}{N}}$$

It will be seen that high values of the standard deviation result in large sampling errors.

[2] The short formula (see Technical Appendix I) may be used for this computation,

$$\sigma = \sqrt{\frac{\Sigma(X^2)}{n} - \left(\frac{\Sigma X}{n}\right)^2}$$

where X is equal to the different between the audited and unaudited values for each item. Since the solution of this formula requires only the sum of the squares of the differences $|\Sigma(X^2)|$ and the sum of differences (ΣX), and since most of the differences are zero, the computation can be performed easily by merely squaring the nonzero differences and summing these nonzero differences. These values may be inserted in the above formula. It is important to note that the divisor (n) is the number of items in the sample and *not* the number with nonzero differences.

The computation is shown below.

The standard deviation is

$$\sigma = \sqrt{\frac{\sum(X - \bar{X})^2}{n}} = \sqrt{\frac{11{,}324.02}{100}} = \sqrt{113.24}$$

$$\sigma = 10.6414$$

The precision of the average difference can now be fixed by using the factor given on page 473 of Appendix G for field size 10,000, sample size 100, and a 95% confidence level. The factor is .1950. The computation is as follows:

$$\$10.6414 \times .1950 = \pm 2.0751$$

If the precision of the average difference is 2.0751, the reliability of the total difference for the entire 10,000 items will be $20,751.00. Thus, the confidence interval for the estimated difference will be

+ $32,474.00		+$32,474.00
− 20,751.00	to	+ 20,751.00
+$11,723.00		+$53,225.00

The confidence interval for the estimate of the total value is then

$1,281,587.21		$1,281,587.21
11,723.00	to	53,225.00
$1,293,310.21		$1,334,812.21

Thus, the sampling precision of the total value is also $20,751.00, or the same as that for the total difference.

It is interesting to compare the precision of the sample, obtained by the difference method, with that which would have been obtained if a direct projection of the audited sample value, without using the difference method, had been made.

The average audited value of the 100 sample values is $130.1940. Since there are 10,000 items in the field, this gives a projection of the corrected total value as $1,301,940.

To fix the sampling precision of this estimate, the standard deviation of the audited values in the sample is determined. It is $70.56 for these audited values. The precision factor from the table is 0.1950 at the 95% confidence level (Appendix G). The sampling precision of the average is then

$$\$70.56 \times \pm .1950 = \pm \$13.7592$$

The computation of the standard deviation may also be facilitated by the use of a pocket electronic calculator. A number of these calculators are now available with special standard deviation keys which solve the above formula directly.

TABLE 12-2

Random Number	Difference Book vs. Audited Values	$X - \overline{X}$	$(X - \overline{X})^2$	Random Number	Difference Book vs. Audited Values	$X - \overline{X}$	$(X - \overline{X})^2$
2895	0	− 3.25	10.56	1640	0	− 3.25	10.56
4183	0	− 3.25	10.56	2063	0	− 3.25	10.56
4733	0	− 3.25	10.56	7922	0	− 3.25	10.56
9023	0	− 3.25	10.56	3926	+18.86	15.61	243.67
5647	0	− 3.25	10.56	0332	+28.12	24.87	618.52
7490	0	− 3.25	10.56	3019	0	− 3.25	10.56
1787	0	− 3.25	10.56	7498	0	− 3.25	10.56
8832	0	− 3.25	10.56	8381	+15.42	+12.17	148.11
4948	+18.28	15.03	225.90	6788	+22.80	+19.55	382.20
6975	0	− 3.25	10.56	5169	+15.50	+12.25	150.06
5126	0	− 3.25	10.56	4210	0	− 3.25	10.56
6611	−17.62	−20.87	435.56	5834	0	− 3.25	10.56
3815	− 4.04	− 7.29	53.14	4579	0	− 3.25	10.56
6434	0	− 3.25	10.56	3073	0	− 3.25	10.56
7686	0	− 3.25	10.56	2738	0	− 3.25	10.56
7373	0	− 3.25	10.56	0094	0	− 3.25	10.56
3008	0	− 3.25	10.56	4431	0	− 3.25	10.56
4706	0	− 3.25	10.56	9608	0	− 3.25	10.56
1215	0	− 3.25	10.56	8921	+35.50	+32.25	1040.06
3412	+18.28	15.03	225.90	2876	0	− 3.25	10.56
1224	0	− 3.25	10.56	6450	0	− 3.25	10.56
3371	0	− 3.25	10.56	9152	− 7.20	−10.45	109.20
3991	0	− 3.25	10.56	3158	0	− 3.25	10.56
4094	0	− 3.25	10.56	9315	0	− 3.25	10.56
2767	0	− 3.25	10.56	38.51	0	− 3.25	10.56
9078	0	− 3.25	10.56	8620	0	− 3.25	10.56
3912	+55.70	52.45	2751.00	0139	0	− 3.25	10.56
5933	0	− 3.25	10.56	3119	0	− 3.25	10.56
3518	0	− 3.25	10.56	8717	0	− 3.25	10.56
6718	0	− 3.25	10.56	3832	− 6.46	− 9.71	94.28
8024	+ 9.74	6.49	42.12	8620	0	− 3.25	10.56
0184	0	− 3.25	10.56	9471	0	− 3.25	10.56
8284	0	− 3.25	10.56	4809	0	− 3.25	10.56
2973	0	− 3.25	10.56	1685	0	− 3.25	10.56
5268	0	− 3.25	10.56	2820	+17.56	14.31	204.78
1863	0	− 3.25	10.56	3456	0	− 3.25	10.56
9596	0	− 3.25	10.56	0856	+21.20	17.95	322.20
1911	+46.30	43.05	1853.30	2996	0	− 3.25	10.56
6260	0	− 3.25	10.56	8031	0	− 3.25	10.56
9282	+36.86	33.61	1129.63	1053	0	− 3.25	10.56
8738	0	− 3.25	10.56	3252	0	− 3.25	10.56
3706	0	− 3.25	10.56	9694	0	− 3.25	10.56
5168	0	− 3.25	10.56	9890	0	− 3.25	10.56
0645	0	− 3.25	10.56	7810	0	− 3.25	10.56

TABLE 12-2 *(Continued)*

Random Number	Difference Book vs. Audited Values	$X - X$	$(X - X)^2$	Random Number	Difference Book vs. Audited Values	$X - X$	$(X - X)^2$
5445	0	− 3.25	10.56	9512	−14.66	−17.91	320.77
6552	0	− 3.25	10.56	1957	0	− 3.25	10.56
8194	+14.60	11.35	128.82	9141	0	− 3.25	10.56
2513	0	− 3.25	10.56	1725	0	− 3.25	10.56
9645	0	− 3.25	10.56	3831	0	− 3.25	10.56
0624	0	− 3.25	10.56	3740	0	− 3.25	10.56

For the total, the sampling precision then becomes

$$\$13.7592 \times 10{,}000 = \pm\ \$137{,}592.00$$

Thus, it is seen that the sampling error of the estimate of the total by the direct method (±$137,592.00) is many times as great as that of the difference estimate (±$20,751.00).

RATIO ESTIMATES

An alternative approach to the same problem is accomplished by the use of *ratio estimate* sampling plans. The difference estimate method is based on the difference between the audited and book values. The ratio estimate method is based on the ratio of the audited to the book values. Either of the two methods may result in better sampling efficiency, depending on certain conditions which will be discussed later. When they can be applied, both plans usually result in sharp reductions in the sampling error.

To illustrate the ratio estimate technique, assume that it is desired to estimate the total dollar value for an inventory for which there is a stated book value and for which the detailed perpetual inventory records, or results of a physical inventory on which the book value is based, are available. The object is to confirm the reasonableness of the dollar value of the inventory. The books show the inventory to be valued at $1,274,616.34, and there are 10,000 inventory items. A random sample of 100 items is selected by random number methods, and the items are counted, priced, and extended. The results are shown in Table 12-3.

The ratio between the book value of the sample items and the audited value is then computed.

$$\text{Ratio} = \frac{\text{audited value}}{\text{book value}} \quad \frac{\$12{,}336.74}{\$12{,}634.95} = .9764$$

TABLE 12-3

Item number	Book value	Audited value	Item number	Book value	Audited value
7483	117.07	117.07	1176	32.42	32.42
5939	95.61	95.61	1781	340.80	340.80
2685	213.20	213.20	3825	99.54	99.54
7674	214.10	214.10	0032	53.40	53.40
2961	161.27	161.27	8140	93.80	86.99
5690	74.06	74.06	5059	106.50	83.96
5888	289.99	246.91	7536	160.68	160.68
9226	260.01	260.01	1585	122.34	122.34
4578	93.14	72.62	6908	64.13	64.13
4423	198.09	165.48	2081	178.62	178.62
4607	81.42	81.42	7765	60.50	53.18
8069	327.32	327.32	7168	92.61	92.61
0261	94.79	94.79	9362	118.29	118.29
0092	30.17	30.17	7666	92.34	92.34
8741	93.83	89.65	7271	293.86	293.86
9546	148.65	148.65	3837	44.10	44.10
8534	250.89	250.89	5527	178.41	161.13
4943	113.79	113.79	0291	51.85	51.85
3890	125.47	125.47	9008	158.80	158.80
9899	98.25	98.25	4541	94.23	94.23
2733	45.06	45.06	3495	23.80	23.80
8497	110.89	110.89	0014	120.79	120.79
5388	83.30	75.15	4506	137.66	137.66
8228	59.74	59.74	8141	79.94	70.57
5502	116.66	116.66	5152	141.93	141.93
9736	45.72	45.72	2399	206.03	206.03
1117	136.35	136.35	8079	91.39	74.27
6509	87.30	76.88	9962	123.85	96.30
7114	57.76	57.76	8777	129.83	129.83
2778	138.40	138.40	3100	70.40	70.40
5114	92.61	92.61	2902	81.45	69.22
8774	106.49	106.49	1832	189.87	189.87
3822	178.66	178.66	5885	98.91	98.91
1094	155.76	148.43	8586	87.33	87.33
1395	80.10	80.10	1205	140.28	138.76
4624	130.97	130.97	2196	199.04	199.04
5402	75.38	75.38	9748	309.66	309.66
2302	109.06	93.97	3156	93.30	93.30
6347	61.59	61.59	0613	184.20	184.20
9276	85.15	85.15	3353	141.65	141.65
8746	174.46	174.46	2460	84.29	84.29
3320	71.95	71.95	7395	58.59	58.59
1389	52.38	52.38	0077	116.41	116.41
0406	372.92	340.25	2580	130.37	135.52
8797	114.50	114.50	8107	185.95	185.95
9702	270.97	270.97	4608	99.37	91.80
5202	47.60	47.60	4704	38.22	38.22
8408	198.83	198.83	3362	154.04	154.04
3273	46.01	46.01	6491	91.02	91.02
8981	130.96	130.96	1385	69.51	69.51
			Total...	$12,634.95	$12,336.74

A point estimate of the overall inventory value for the entire field can now be established by multiplying the inventory *book* value by this ratio.

$$\$1{,}274{,}616.34 \times .9764 = \$1{,}244{,}535.39$$

Now it is necessary to establish the sampling precision of this estimate.

The first step is, as before, to compute a standard deviation. However, in this method the computation proceeds in an unusual way. It is necessary to use the direct method (Chapter 4), but instead of using the difference between each value and the average of them all, the difference between the audited value and the ratio times the book value for each item is secured.

$$\text{Difference} = \text{audited value} - (\text{ratio} \times \text{book value})$$

The standard deviation is then based on the squares of these differences.

$$\sigma = \sqrt{\frac{\Sigma(\text{audited value} - \text{ratio} \times \text{book value})^2}{n}}$$

The actual tabulation of these values for the above illustration is shown in Table 12-4. The standard deviation is then obtained from

$$\sigma' = \sqrt{\frac{5{,}913.9974}{100}} = 7.69025$$

By applying the sampling precision factor for variables samples with field size 10,000, sample size 100, and confidence level 95% (see Chapter 7), of .1950, the sampling precision of the average is

$$\$7.69025 \times .1950 = \pm\$1{,}4996$$

Since there are 10,000 items in the field, the sampling precision of the total is

$$\pm\$1.4996 \times 10{,}000 = \pm\$14{,}996.00$$

The confidence interval for the total estimate then becomes

$$\$1{,}244{,}535.39 \pm\$14{,}996.00$$

or $$\$1{,}229{,}539.39 \quad \text{to} \quad \$1{,}259{,}531.39$$

where the value $1,244, 535.39 is the projected value previously obtained above by multiplying the book value by the ratio.

It is interesting to note here that if a direct projection of the sample average of the audited value had been made, its sampling reliability, as computed by the usual methods for an unrestricted random estimation sample, would have been ±$137,202.00 instead of the ±$14.996.00 obtained by the ratio estimate method.

Another method of calculating the standard deviation in a ratio estimate, a method that is much easier when a pocket electronic calculator is available, makes

TABLE 12-4

Item number	Book value	Audited value	Ratio* times book value	Difference between audited value and ratio times book value	Square of differences
7483	117.07	117.07	114.31	2.76	7.6176
5939	95.61	95.61	93.35	2.26	5.1076
2685	213.20	213.20	208.17	5.03	25.3009
7674	214.10	214.10	209.05	5.05	25.5025
2961	161.27	161.27	157.46	3.81	14.5161
5690	74.06	74.06	72.31	1.75	3.0625
5888	289.99	246.91	283.15	−36.24	1,313.3376
9226	260.01	260.01	253.87	6.14	37.6996
4578	93.14	72.62	90.94	−18.32	335.6224
4423	198.09	165.48	193.41	−27.93	780.0849
4607	81.42	81.42	79.50	1.92	3.6864
8069	327.32	327.32	319.59	7.73	59.7529
0261	94.79	94.79	92.55	2.24	4.8841
0092	30.17	30.17	29.46	0.71	0.5041
8741	93.83	89.65	91.62	− 1.97	3.8809
9546	148.65	148.65	145.14	3.51	12.3201
8534	250.89	250.89	244.97	5.92	35.0464
4943	113.79	113.79	111.10	2.69	7.2361
3890	125.47	125.47	122.51	2.96	8.7616
9899	98.25	98.25	95.93	2.32	5.3824
2733	45.06	45.06	44.00	1.06	1.1236
8497	110.89	110.89	108.27	2.62	6.8644
5388	83.30	75.15	81.33	− 6.18	38.1924
8228	59.74	59.74	58.33	1.41	1.9881
5502	116.66	116.66	113.91	2.75	7.5625
1176	32.42	32.42	31.65	0.77	0.5929
1781	340.80	340.80	332.76	8.04	64.6416
3825	99.54	99.54	97.19	2.35	5.5225
0032	53.40	53.40	52.14	1.26	1.5876
8140	93.80	86.99	91.59	− 4.60	21.1600
5059	106.50	83.96	103.99	−20.03	401.2009
7536	160.68	160.68	156.89	3.79	14.3641
1585	122.34	122.34	119.45	2.89	8.3521
6908	64.13	64.13	62.62	1.51	2.2801
2081	178.62	178.62	174.40	4.22	17.8084

* Ratio is the previously computed value of .9764.

TABLE 12–4. ***(Continued)***

Item number	Book value	Audited value	Ratio* times book value	Difference between audited value and ratio times book value	Square of differences
7765	60.50	53.18	59.07	− 5.89	34.6921
7168	92.61	92.61	90.42	2.19	4.7961
9362	118.29	118.29	115.50	2.79	7.7841
7666	92.34	92.34	90.16	2.18	4.7524
7271	293.86	293.86	286.92	6.94	48.1636
3837	44.10	44.10	43.06	1.04	1.0816
5527	178.41	161.13	174.20	−13.07	170.8249
0291	51.85	51.85	50.63	1.22	1.4844
9008	158.80	158.80	155.05	3.75	14.0625
4541	94.23	94.23	92.01	2.22	4.9284
3495	23.80	23.80	23.24	0.56	0.3136
0014	120.79	120.79	117.94	2.85	8.1225
4506	137.66	137.66	134.41	3.25	10.5625
8141	79.94	70.57	78.05	− 7.48	55.9504
5152	141.93	141.93	138.58	3.35	11.2225
9736	45.72	45.72	44.64	1.08	1.1664
1117	136.35	136.35	133.13	3.22	10.3684
6509	87.30	76.88	85.24	− 8.36	68.8896
7114	57.76	57.76	56.40	1.36	1.8496
2778	138.40	138.40	135.13	3.27	10.6929
5114	92.61	92.61	90.42	2.19	4.7961
8774	106.49	106.49	103.98	2.51	6.3001
3822	178.66	178.66	174.44	4.22	17.8084
1094	155.76	148.43	152.08	− 3.65	13.3225
1395	80.10	80.10	78.21	1.89	3.5721
4624	130.97	130.97	127.88	3.09	9.5481
5402	75.38	75.38	73.60	1.78	3.1684
2302	109.06	93.97	106.49	−12.52	156.7504
6347	61.59	61.59	60.14	1.45	2.1025
9276	85.15	85.15	83.14	2.01	4.0401
8746	174.46	174.46	170.34	4.12	16.9744
3320	71.95	71.95	70.25	1.70	2.8900
1389	52.38	52.38	51.14	1.24	1.5376
0406	372.92	340.25	364.12	−23.87	569.7769
8797	114.50	114.50	111.80	2.70	7.2900

TABLE 12-4. ***(Continued)***

Item number	Book value	Audited value	Ratio* times book value	Difference between audited value and ratio times book value	Square of differences
9702	270.97	270.97	264.57	6.40	40.9600
5202	47.60	47.60	46.48	1.12	1.2544
8408	198.83	198.83	194.14	4.69	21.9961
3273	46.01	46.01	44.92	1.09	1.1881
8981	130.96	130.96	127.87	3.09	9.5481
2399	206.03	206.03	201.17	4.86	23.6196
8079	91.39	74.27	89.23	−14.96	223.8016
9962	123.85	96.30	120.93	−24.63	606.6369
8777	129.83	129.83	126.77	3.06	9.3636
3100	70.40	70.40	68.74	1.66	2.7556
2902	81.45	69.22	79.53	−10.31	106.2961
1832	189.87	189.87	185.39	4.48	20.0704
5885	98.91	98.91	96.58	2.33	5.4289
8586	87.33	87.33	85.27	2.06	4.2436
1205	140.28	138.76	136.97	1.79	3.2041
2196	199.04	199.04	194.34	4.70	22.0900
9748	309.66	309.66	302.35	7.31	53.4361
3156	93.30	93.30	91.10	2.20	4.8400
0613	184.20	184.20	179.85	4.35	18.9225
3353	141.65	141.65	138.31	3.34	11.1556
2460	84.29	84.29	82.30	1.99	3.9601
7395	58.59	58.59	57.21	1.38	1.9044
0077	116.41	116.41	113.66	2.75	7.5625
2580	130.37	135.52	127.29	8.23	67.7329
8107	185.95	185.95	181.56	4.39	19.2721
4608	99.37	91.80	97.02	− 5.22	27.2484
4704	38.22	38.22	37.32	0.90	0.8100
3362	154.04	154.04	150.40	3.64	13.2496
6491	91.02	91.02	88.87	2.15	4.6225
1385	69.51	69.51	67.87	1.64	2.6896
Total....					5,913.9974

$$\sigma' = \sqrt{\frac{5913.9974}{100}} = \sqrt{59.1400} = 7.69025$$

use of the formula[3]

$$\sigma' = \sqrt{\frac{\Sigma Y^2 + r^2\Sigma X^2 - 2r\Sigma(XY)}{n}}$$

where X = book value
Y = audited value
r = ratio of audited to book record value, $\Sigma Y/\Sigma X$
n = sample size

To accomplish this calculation, it is only necessary to accumulate the sums of the X and Y values and the sums of their squares and cross products in the memory registers of the calculator.

For the data of Table 12-4, the necessary totals are

$$n = 100$$
$$\Sigma X = 12{,}634.93$$
$$\Sigma(X^2) = 2{,}112{,}629.38$$
$$\Sigma(XY) = 2{,}061{,}236.03$$
$$\Sigma Y = 12{,}336.03$$
$$\Sigma(Y^2) = 2{,}017{,}006.45$$
$$r = \frac{12{,}336.03}{12{,}634.93} = .9764$$
$$\sigma' = \frac{2{,}017{,}006.45 + (.9764)^2(2{,}112{,}629.38) - 2(.9764)(2{,}061{,}236.03)}{100}$$

and the standard deviation equals[4]

$$\sigma' = 7.6906$$

It must be noted that ratio estimates are biased (in the statistical sense). Thus the average of all ratio estimates in the sampling distribution is not equal to the value for the entire population. There is no method of precisely calculating the amount of this bias, but it is known to be inversely proportional to the sample size. For reasonable-size samples (say 100 or more), the statistical bias is generally ignored. However, as a result, the ratio estimate is more of an approximation than that for a difference estimate. Thus, the difference estimate approach is to be preferred unless a large gain in precision, as contrasted with the difference estimate, will result.

[3]When the ratio estimate calculations are programmed on a computer, this is the formula used to calculate the standard deviation.

[4]The small difference in the values calculated by the two methods arises from the rounding when using the prior method. This method is more accurate.

GENERAL COMMENTS ON DIFFERENCE AND RATIO ESTIMATES

The sampler can choose to use either the difference or the ratio estimate method when the appropriate conditions for these methods exist. These conditions require previously established record values for each item and a total book value for all items in the field.

The difference method will generally provide better sample reliability when the amounts of the errors or their differences are not related to the amount of the book value of each item, whereas the ratio estimate method will be better when the errors are related in their magnitude to the values of the individual items. In other words, if there is a tendency for large errors to occur for large book value items (when they do occur), and vice versa, the ratio estimate method will be better.

Because of the fact that in most audit situations most of the values are correct with a resulting zero difference (or ratio of 1), it is to be expected that even though such errors as do occur may be related in size to the magnitude of the value on which they occur, *overall* there is a poor relationship. As a result it might be expected that there would be little or no difference in the sampling precision attained by the two methods.

As noted previously, the ratio estimate is not an unbiased estimate, and since both theory and practice indicate there is little expectation of much difference in the sample precision, the difference estimate method is generally to be preferred in the audit situation, especially considering the more complex computations required for the ratio estimate.

However, there may be some situations when the ratio estimate method may produce greater precision. An example would be in an estimate to be used to establish a reserve for bad debts: this is accomplished by sampling receivables to determine the amounts due beyond some fixed periods. In some, but not all, cases, the ratio estimate may produce a much tighter sample precision than a difference estimate.

It is not to be expected, in every instance, that the difference or ratio estimate methods will reduce the sampling error to the great extent found in the two illustrations given above. However, for most accounting data, when conditions make these methods feasible, greatly improved sample reliability will result. This improvement can be translated into smaller sample sizes to accomplish the same purpose with resulting savings in time and money.

A word of caution: If error or differences between the book values and audited values are very rare, the sample must be of sufficient size to include at least a few of these errors. If, because of an inadequate sample size, no errors are included in the sample, the standard deviation will become zero, and the obviously impossible result that there is no sampling error will be obtained. In other words, care must be exercised to avoid using very small sample sizes with these methods, preferably one of not less than 100, unless errors are frequent.

Difference or ratio techniques can be used in combination with stratified sampling methods. However, it is unlikely, owing to the nature of the situation, that any important gain will result from such a combination because of the difficulty in allocating sample size properly.

To gain appreciably through the use of stratified sampling, it is essential that similar values be contained within each stratum. In difference estimates, this would mean that differences (between audited and book values) of a similar magnitude would have to be contained within the same stratum, whereas in the ratio estimate method, ratios of a similar magnitude would be grouped in the same strata.

Since the nature of the departure between the book and audited value is unknown until the audit test is completed and since stratifying by the magnitude of the book value may not result in such groupings, it would be difficult if not impossible to achieve a useful stratification.

On the other hand, it is true that if a few items comprise a large portion of the total, the separation of these items into a stratum which is either 100 per cent audited or heavily sampled will have the effect of eliminating, or greatly reducing, the sampling error for that large portion of the total and may provide a marked improvement when the departure of the differences or ratios in this stratum is similar to that in other strata or shows a greater within-stratum variability.

It should be noted that since both the difference and ratio estimate methods are dependent on projecting errors in individual items, neither of these methods provides protection against errors in compilation. Thus, for instance, in ascertaining the reasonableness of a value established by a physical inventory, the impact of errors in counting and extending to obtain the dollar values for individual stock items will be projected. However, if there are compilation errors, such as footing errors and errors arising from including the same value twice, their effect will not be projected.

It will be remembered that the ratio and difference estimate methods both base the point estimate upon the *book record value.* If the book record value is incorrect because of errors of compilation (footing errors, etc.), this error will not be found when these methods are used.

However, the direct projection method will disclose both types of errors. Thus, the increased efficiency of the ratio and difference estimate techniques is obtained at the cost of less protection. It is advised that, if a ratio or difference estimate is used, other procedures be provided to protect against compilation errors. This can be accomplished by refooting the entire population or by using a direct projection of the unaudited values.

THIRTEEN

Multistage Sampling

THE REASON FOR MULTISTAGE SAMPLING

Circumstances may dictate the advisability of a different approach to a sampling plan. Suppose, for instance, that it is desired to establish the total value of an inventory which is dispersed in groups over a wide area such as might occur in a chain store with many widely distributed units or in an organization with numerous small warehouses. If the method of unrestricted random sampling is used here, the sample might require the inventorying of items at every locality. An enormous amount of time might be required in traveling as well as in the completion of the sampling.

It might be desired under such circumstances to take a random sample of the locations and a random sample of items within the location. This process is known as ***multistage sampling.***

Such a plan is called a ***two-stage*** sampling plan, since there is sampling at two levels, both among the primary units (stores or warehouses) and among the elementary or secondary units (the items within the stores). While sampling plans can be developed with further levels of sampling, these plans are generally not appropriate for auditing or accounting purposes.

LIMITATIONS

The use of multistage sampling, however, is restricted by the implicit assumption that while the inventory values (or other variables) may differ from location to location (among primary units), the ***situation*** is relatively homogeneous with respect to the localities.

If there are some entirely unique locations (primary sampling units), there is some danger that the random sample may omit these locations. For instance, if a chain consists of several hundred small stores but also includes one or two stores of a magnitude and type entirely different from the others, the sampling of primary units might miss these units. Since the value of these inventories might be equal in value to that of a considerable number of the other stores, failure to include them might lead to a biased sample projection.

This difficulty can be overcome by combining multistage sampling with stratified sampling. In such a situation, the unique types of stores could be segregated into separate strata, and multistage samples drawn from each strata.

The use of this method for accounting purposes might best be restricted to situations in which such homogeneity can be expected. For instance, it might be desired to test the extent of error in terms of dollars in processing credit adjustments initiated by stores in a chain, including the failure to process individual adjustments. Such a test would have to begin at the stores to sample the initiated adjustments at their source.

Ordinarily, when an unrestricted random sampling plan is undertaken, it is necessary to sample the adjustments at every store, requiring that they all must be visited. However, a multistage sample requires visits only to a limited number of stores.

Homogeneity with respect to the stores can certainly be assumed in this example, since the processing at the central office, which would be homogeneous with respect to all stores, is being tested. Thus, multistage sampling consists of a random selection of *groups* of sampling units (primary units) and a random subsampling of the individual sampling units comprising these groups (secondary units).

SAMPLE PRECISION

The discussion of multistage sampling in this book is confined to the special case where two-stage sampling is used.

It is apparent that the random sampling of groups of sampling units is akin to the cluster sampling process described in Chapter 11; but in this instance, instead of using the entire group, a sample is taken from each group.

In a multistage sample of this type (two-stage), the sampling error of an average or a total consists in a combination of the sampling error created by sampling *within* the selected groups and in that created by the sampling of the groups (primary sampling units) themselves.

The projection of an average value from a two-stage sample of the type described above can be accomplished by obtaining the average value *per item* and multiplying it by the number of items in the entire field, including those in secondary units not in the sample.

The average value of the items can be secured from the sample by using a weighted average.

$$\text{Average value} = \frac{\Sigma(N_p\bar{X}_p)}{\Sigma N_p}$$

where N_p = number of secondary items in each primary unit sampled
$\bar{X}_p$ = average value per item in sample of secondary items in a primary unit

The total value is obtained by multiplying by the total number of secondary units in all primary units, regardless of whether they were included in the sample.

$$\text{Total value} = N\left[\frac{\Sigma(N_p\bar{X}_p)}{\Sigma N_p}\right]$$

where N = total number of secondary units in entire field

The sampling error of the average is then achieved as follows:[1]

$$SE_{\bar{x}}^2 = SE_{pri}^2 + \frac{m}{M}\overline{SE}_{sec}^2$$

where $SE_{\bar{X}}$ = overall sampling error estimate of average
SE_{pri} = sampling error of averages of primary sampling units
$\overline{SE}^2_{sec}$ = *average* square of sampling error of averages of secondary sampling units within each primary unit
m = number of primary sampling units in sample
M = number of primary sampling units in field

The sampling error of the primary sampling units (in the above example, stores) may be obtained by the methods described for establishing the sampling precision for cluster samples described in Chapter 11. This value is then squared and entered in the above formula.

The average sampling error of the secondary sampling units within each primary unit may be obtained by resorting to the methods for evaluating the sampling error and the unrestricted random sample described in Chapter 7. In this case the sampling error *within* each primary sampling unit is established separately and averaged for all primary sampling units. This value is then squared and inserted in the above formula. The solution of this formula is the square of sampling reliability of the overall *average* value per item in the inventory. The square of this value may now be obtained.

Multiplying this sampling error by the total number of sampling units (or items) will provide the sample precision of the total.

[1] Based on formulas given by Cochran and by Yates (see Technical Appendix IV).

AN ILLUSTRATION

For instance, assume that in the sampling of a government inventory of spare parts scattered at many locations or installations, the object is to estimate the total inventory value. Assume also that 15 of 200 installations were selected at random and that a sample of 50 items at each location were selected at random with results shown in Table 13-1.

The first step is the projection of the sample averages for each primary sampling unit to obtain an estimate of the total value. As noted previously, this is accomplished by multiplying the average value per item obtained from the sample of secondary items for each secondary unit (location) by the total number of items in the entire field, including those secondary units not covered by the sample.

The average value per item for the sampled primary units is obtained as shown in Table 13-2.

It was established that at all 200 locations, of which these 15 were only a sample, there was a total of 450,000 secondary sampling units (line items). The estimate of the total value of the entire inventory would then be the previous average per item times this number of items, or

$$\$198.8239 \times 450{,}000 = \$89{,}470{,}755.00$$

TABLE 13–1

Location	Number of items stocked at location	Number of items sampled	Average value of items in primary unit	Standard* deviation of values in sample
a	3,000	50	$209.68	$66.88
b	2,500	50	202.43	50.22
c	3,000	50	203.06	55.01
d	2,700	50	184.51	46.42
e	1,500	50	190.20	54.67
f	2,000	50	192.59	44.29
g	3,000	50	201.37	57.29
h	2,500	50	195.06	58.38
i	2,000	50	196.35	50.13
j	1,800	50	192.19	52.01
k	2,700	50	196.57	55.92
l	1,700	50	209.39	54.20
m	1,600	50	212.80	56.87
n	2,000	50	209.58	56.27
o	1,800	50	183.64	48.36
Total.....		750		

* This column was calculated from sample values by the methods outlined in Chap. 4 or Chap. 5.

TABLE 13-2

Location (primary unit)	Average value per item of primary unit from sample (1)	Number of secondary items in primary unit (2)	(1 × 2)
a	$209.68	3,000	$629,040.00
b	202.43	2,500	506,075.00
c	203.06	3,000	609,180.00
d	184.51	2,700	498,177.00
e	190.20	1,500	285,300.00
f	192.59	2,000	385,180.00
g	201.37	3,000	604,110.00
h	195.06	2,500	487,650.00
i	196.35	2,000	392,700.00
j	192.19	1,800	345,942.00
k	196.57	2,700	530,739.00
l	209.39	1,700	355,963.00
m	212.80	1,600	340,480.00
n	209.58	2,000	419,160.00
o	183.64	1,800	330,552.00
Total........		33,800	$6,720,248.00

$$\text{Average} = \frac{\$6{,}720{,}248.00}{33{,}800} = \$198.8239$$

The sampling precision of this estimate may be established by the method previously outlined.

The calculation of the values for the formula

$$SE_{\bar{x}}^{2} = SE_{pri}^{2} + \frac{m}{M}\,\overline{SE}_{sec}^{\,2}$$

may now proceed one part at a time. For the first part (SE_{pri}^2) the method indicated was the cluster sampling approach. This requires the computation of the standard deviation of the average value per primary unit as shown in Table 13-3.

By resorting to the cluster sampling table (Appendix L) and the 90% confidence level, the precision factor obtained is .4704 for the 15 primary units. The finite population correction factor for 15 primary units out of 200 is obtained from Appendix I, where

$$\frac{15}{200} = 7.5\%$$

The factor is .9618. The product of these three factors, the standard deviation, the sample precision factor, and the finite correction factor provides the sampling

TABLE 13-3

Location	Average value per item in primary unit	Deviation from overall averages, $198.63	Deviation squared
a	$209.68	+11.05	122.1025
b	202.43	+ 3.80	14.4400
c	203.06	+ 4.43	19.6249
d	184.51	−14.12	199.3744
e	190.20	− 8.43	71.0649
f	192.59	− 6.04	36.4816
g	201.37	+ 2.74	7.5076
h	195.06	− 3.57	12.7449
i	196.35	− 2.28	5.1984
j	192.19	− 6.44	41.4736
k	196.57	− 2.06	4.2436
l	209.39	+10.76	115.7776
m	212.80	+14.17	200.7889
n	209.58	+10.95	119.9025
o	183.64	−14.99	224.7001
$\bar{X}$	$198.6280		

$$\sigma = \sqrt{\frac{\Sigma(X - \bar{X})^2}{n}} = \sqrt{\frac{1195.43}{15}} = \sqrt{79.70} = \$8.93$$

error of the *primary* units, or

$$SE_{pri} = \$8.93 \times .4704 \times .9618 = \pm\$4.20$$

and $$SE^2_{pri} = 17.64$$

The second portion of the formula ($\overline{SE^2}_{sec}$) can now be obtained by using the methods of Chapter 7 separately for each primary unit and then averaging the results. Since the field sizes are not covered by the tables, the second method, involving a separate precision factor (Appendix H) and a separate finite population correction factor (Appendix I), is used. The calculations are shown in Table 13-4.

The complete formula will now read

$$SE_{\bar{x}}^2 = SE^2_{pri} + \frac{m}{M}\overline{SE}^2_{sec}$$

$$= 17.64 + \frac{15}{200}(154.41)$$

$$= 29.22$$

$$SE_{\bar{x}} = \$5.40556$$

Multiplying by the number of secondary sampling units in the population (450,000) gives a precision of the total of ±$2,432,475.00. While this sampling error is a

TABLE 13–4

Location primary unit	No. of items stocked	No. of items in samples	Precision* factor at 90% confidence level	Proportion of population in sample	Finite† population correction factor	Sample standard deviation	Product of precision factor, finite correction factors of standard deviation	Square of sampling error
a	3,000	50	.2326	1.7%	.9915	$66.88	$15.42	237.7764
b	2,500	50	.2326	2.0	.9899	50.22	11.56	133.6336
c	3,000	50	.2326	1.7	.9915	55.01	12.69	161.0361
d	2,700	50	.2326	1.9	.9905	46.42	10.69	114.2761
e	1,500	50	.2326	3.3	.9834	54.67	12.51	156.5001
f	2,000	50	.2326	2.5	.9874	44.29	10.17	103.4289
g	3,000	50	.2326	1.7	.9915	57.29	13.21	174.5041
h	2,500	50	.2326	2.0	.9899	58.38	13.44	180.6336
i	2,000	50	.2326	2.5	.9874	50.13	11.51	132.4801
j	1,800	50	.2326	2.8	.9859	52.01	11.93	142.3249
k	2,700	50	.2326	1.9	.9905	55.92	12.88	165.8944
l	1,700	50	.2326	2.9	.9854	54.20	12.42	154.2564
m	1,600	50	.2326	3.1	.9844	56.87	13.02	169.5204
n	2,000	50	.2326	2.5	.9874	56.27	12.92	166.9264
o	1,800	50	.2326	2.8	.9859	48.36	11.09	122.9881
Total....	33,800	750			Average square of the sampling errors.....			154.4120

Average of squares of secondary sampling error = 154.41

* From Appendix H (infinite field size).
† From Appendix I.

large sum of money, it is only 3% of the estimated value. The confidence limits at the 90% confidence level can be fixed as

$$\$89{,}470{,}755.00 \pm \$2{,}432{,}475.00$$

or from $87,038,280.00 to $91,903,230.00

GENERAL

The above method of calculating the sampling precision of a multistage sample is quite complex. Further, it does not provide for a procedure for attributes estimation in multistage sampling, although it is possible to use this same approach.

It is suggested the replicated sampling, outlined in the next chapter, may provide an easier method of solution and a means of computing sample precision when multistage sampling is used in combination with other methods. For instance, when multistage sampling is used in conjunction with stratified sampling or cluster sampling, the complexity of the problem is greatly reduced.

FOURTEEN

Other Sampling Plans

POST STRATIFICATION (STRATIFICATION AFTER SAMPLE SELECTION)

While it is always desirable to use a stratified sampling plan when applying estimation sampling to variables in the audit situation, there are circumstances in which it is not feasible to do so before actually drawing the sample. The reason may be the difficulty of obtaining separate unrestricted (simple) random samples independently from each stratum. Unless separate lists of the sampling units in each stratum are available, there may be practical difficulties in attempting to select the items to be included in the sample.

Generally, it is feasible to separate the very high-value items into a 100 percent stratum, but to gain efficiency additional strata may be required. It is the sampling of these other strata which causes difficulties when there is a large population.

In addition, there are occasions in which the auditor may not have used a stratified sampling approach and recognizes its desirability only after the sample has been drawn and the sampling units audited. This recognition may arise from the information obtained in the audit of the sample.

In such instances, the technique of *post stratification* may be used. In this method, the unrestricted (simple) random sample already drawn is used by assigning the sampling units to their appropriate strata based on their *book record* values, or, for natural strata, their characteristic relative to the stratification method. The results are then analyzed as a post-stratified sample.

However, such a stratification after sampling can be accomplished only if the strata population sizes are known and the sample is of sufficient size to obtain a number of sample values for all strata.

While technically any sample size in excess of two or more for a given stratum may be used, it is not wise to have less than 30 sampling units in any non-100% stratum. Of course, if there are too few sampling units in any stratum, additional sampling units may be drawn, but they must be obtained as a continuation of the original unrestricted random sample, with the additional units assigned to whatever stratum in which they fall.

The result of such an approach is to provide a stratified sample with a sample allocation to the strata roughly approximating a *proportional allocation (based on stratum population size)*. See pages 170–174 for the discussion of the implications of such an allocation. In those pages, it is noted that, *in the audit situation,* a proportional allocation is inefficient compared with optimum allocation methods for a variables sample.

Further, since the number of sampling units falling within each stratum is a random variable, there is an additional sampling error as compared with a sample with a deliberate prior proportional allocation. Hence, this method is less efficient than such an allocation.

As a result of these deficiencies and the fact that in the audit situation for a variables sample the efficiency of a proportionally allocated sample is generally very poor, the use of post-stratication techniques for audit purposes is likely to be very limited. However, in situations where the standard deviations of the various strata are not too greatly different *while* the strata population sizes vary greatly, such an approach may be useful. Further, the method may be of value when *natural* strata (location, type of trasactions, etc.) rather than dollar-value strata are being used.

The point estimate of the arithmetic mean of a post-stratified sample can be computed from

$$\overline{X} = \frac{\Sigma(N_i \overline{X}_i)}{N}$$

where $\overline{X}_i$ = mean of given stratum

N_i = number of sampling units in population in given stratum

The sampling error of that estimate can be determined from[1]

$$\sigma_{\bar{x}}^2 = \left[\frac{\Sigma(N_i\sigma_i^2)}{Nn} + \frac{\Sigma(1 - N_i/N)\sigma_i^2}{n^2}\right]\left(1 - \frac{n}{N}\right)$$

where σ_i = standard deviation of values within a specified stratum

n = number of sampling units in entire sample

[1]Based on a formula given by M. H. Hansen, W. N. Hurwitz, and W. G. Madow, *Sample Survey Methods and Theory,* John Wiley & Sons, Inc., New York, 1953. See Technical Appendix VIII.

TABLE 14-1

Office	Number of records in strata, N_i	Sample size for each stratum, n_i	Sample strata average, X_i	Sample standard deviation, σ_i
A	2,000	115	$220.00	110.00
B	1,000	60	190.00	150.00
C	3,000	125	100.00	130.00
Total	6,000	300		

and the sampling error of the average ($SE_{\overline{X}}$) is

$$SE_{\overline{X}} = t(\sigma_{\overline{X}})$$

The sampling error of the total may be obtained by multiplying the sampling error of the average by the population size.

As an illustration, assume that an auditor has selected a sample of 300 sampling units in order to project a total audited value based on an unrestricted random sample. Though the records to be audited are at three different offices, a simple random sample of the entire population of records was obtained to provide an overall estimate.

However, after completion of the examination of the selected records and establishment of the audited values for each sampling unit in the sample, the auditor concludes that a better sample precision could be obtained if the sample is treated as a stratified sample. He decides to use post stratification.

The strata are to be by office (a natural strata situation). The 300 sampling units which were drawn for the unrestricted random sample are sorted by office and assigned to their appropriate strata. The result is shown in Table 14-1.

The point estimate of the average is obtained as shown below:

Office	N_i	$\overline{X}_i$	$N\overline{X}_i$
A	2,000	220	440,000
B	1,000	190	190,000
C	3,000	100	300,000
	6,000		930,000

$$\overline{X} = \frac{930,000}{6,000} = 155.00$$

The point estimate of the total is then

$$\text{Total} = N\bar{X} = 6{,}000(155.00) = \$930{,}000.00$$

The values required for the solution of the equation for the sampling error are as follows:

Office	N_i	n_i	σ_i^2	$N_i\sigma_{i2}$	$1 - \frac{N_i}{N}$	$\left(1 - \frac{N_i}{N}\right)(\sigma_i^2)$
A	2,000	115	12,100	24,200,000	.66667	8,066.707
B	1,000	60	22,500	22,500,000	.83333	18,749.925
C	3,000	125	16,900	50,700,000	.50000	8,450.000
	6,000	300		97,400,000		35,266.632

Then

$$\begin{aligned}\sigma_{\bar{X}}^2 &= \left[\frac{97{,}400{,}000}{(300)(6{,}000)} + \frac{35{,}266.632}{(300)^2}\right] 1 - \frac{300}{6{,}000}\\ &= (54.111 + .39185)(.95)\\ &= 51.778\\ \sigma_{\bar{X}} &= 7.1957\end{aligned}$$

The sampling error of the average at the 95% confidence level is

$$SE_{\bar{X}} = (1.96)(7.1957) = 14.1036$$

The sampling error of the *total* is

$$SE_T = (6{,}000)(14.1036) = \$84{,}621.60$$

Had the sample of 300 been evaluated as an unrestricted (simple) random sample rather than using post stratification, the sampling error would have been \$91,789.00 instead of the sampling error of \$84,621.60.

It should be remembered, however, that, as mentioned previously, a gain in efficiency will not always be obtained by the use of post-stratification methods. In this case, the gain arises because of the large relative differences in strata population sizes as contrasted with the much smaller relative differences in the standard deviations differences.

RATIO ESTIMATE OF A RATIO

In Chapter 12, the *ratio estimate* as a method of estimating a total (or average) was discussed. However, there are certain conditions in which the accountant will find that the ratio itself is the value of interest. An example of such a situation relates to the LIFO (last-in, first-out) method of evaluating an inventory. The determination of a LIFO index from a sample may be necessary. This index expresses the ratio of the values of the inventory at current prices to the value of the same inventory at base-period prices.

When there are a great number of items in the inventory, computing this ratio on a 100 per cent basis for all stock items may be too costly or time-consuming to be practical. In such a case, resort must be made to establishing the ratio from a sample. Here the value of interest is the ratio itself. However, the sample projection of the ratio is subject to a sampling error, and unless the sampling error is determined, little reliance can be placed on the point estimate. The sampling error should be sufficiently small so as not to create the possibility of a material error.

The method detailed in Chapter 12 may be used with little modification. However, in this situation the values may not be the audited and book record values. Because of this, resort will be made to a more general set of symbols. The value in the numerator of the ratio will be referred to as the Y variable and that in the denominator as the X variable. Thus, in the LIFO index, the numerator is the inventory value at current prices, while the divisor is the value of the same inventory at base-period prices.

$$\text{LIFO index} = \frac{\text{inventory at current prices}}{\text{inventory at base-period prices}}$$

or, more generally,

$$r = \frac{\Sigma Y}{\Sigma X}$$

The method of computing the sampling error detailed in Chapter 12 produces the sampling error of the average Y value in dollars. To obtain the sampling error of the ratio, it is necessary to divide the sampling error of $\overline{Y}$ by $\overline{X}$, or

$$SE_r = \frac{SE_{\overline{Y}}}{\overline{X}}$$

The sampling error of $\overline{Y}$ may be computed as before for a ratio estimate.

$$SE_{\bar{y}} = t\frac{\sigma'}{\sqrt{n}}\sqrt{1 - \frac{n}{N}}$$

where

$$\sigma' = \sqrt{\frac{\Sigma(Y - rX)^2}{n}} \qquad \text{(Formula A)}$$

or, alternatively,

$$\sigma' = \sqrt{\frac{\Sigma(Y^2) + r^2\Sigma(X^2) - 2r(\Sigma XY)}{n}} \qquad \text{(Formula B)}$$

To obtain SE_r, the above sampling error is divided by $\bar{X}$, providing the formula

$$SE_r = \frac{t(\sigma'/\sqrt{n})\sqrt{1 - n/N}}{\bar{X}}$$

These determinations may be illustrated by an example. While the method applies to any ratio computed from a sample, the example relates to the computation of a LIFO index. The data relevant to the problem are included in Table 14-2. It is important to emphasize, however, that this example has been greatly simplified for purposes of demonstration. The sample used in the example is much too small for such a purpose. A very much larger sample would be needed to avoid the possibility of an error which would be material.

Table 14-2 contains values for a number of sample stock items, with the values of these items in the quantities as of the current period, but priced at both current and base-year prices. The ratio (LIFO index) point estimate is obtained by totaling the dollar amounts at the base-year prices and dividing that total by the total dollar value at the current-year prices.

The ratio (in this case the LIFO index) is then

$$r = \frac{\Sigma Y}{\Sigma X} = \frac{\$166{,}167.50}{\$157{,}237.00} = 1.0568$$

Thus, the *point estimate* of the ratio is 1.0568. It is then necessary to compute the sampling error of this *ratio* to demonstrate that the sampling error could not generate a material error. Our example is based on a very small sample for illustration purposes, but in practice the projection of a LIFO index with a nonmaterial sampling error would require a sample in the hundreds and perhaps even more. For such large samples the use of Formula B (above) is the preferable method, especially if an electronic calculator is available. It is merely necessary to obtain the sums of the values and their squares and the sums of their cross products to resolve that formula. When this calculation is programmed for a computer, this method is appropriate.

For the data in Table 14-1, the required values are

$$\begin{aligned} N &= 1{,}000 \quad \text{(population size)} \\ n &= 20 \quad \text{(sample size)} \\ \Sigma X &= \$157{,}237.00 \\ \Sigma Y &= \$166{,}167.50 \\ \Sigma(X^2) &= 3{,}931{,}785{,}510.00 \\ \Sigma(Y^2) &= 4{,}389{,}459{,}000.00 \\ \Sigma(XY) &= 4{,}151{,}456{,}800.00 \end{aligned}$$

TABLE 14-2

Stock number	Inventory value At base-year prices (X)	At current-year prices (Y)
#2771	$214.00	$236.00
7616	500.00	550.00
7597	1,500.00	1,560.00
0950	1,428.00	1,784.00
7296	820.00	1,140.00
5347	600.00	720.00
5366	6,000.00	6,300.00
1493	3,200.00	3,520.00
4814	1,400.00	1,680.00
5024	6,000.00	6,500.00
3367	125.00	127.50
3627	47,000.00	51,000.00
8414	3,750.00	4,000.00
3651	22,000.00	22,000.00
2421	7,500.00	7,650.00
4936	5,000.00	6,000.00
3313	29,200.00	29,600.00
0670	10,000.00	10,500.00
0540	1,000.00	1,250.00
7918	10,000.00	10,050.00
Total	$157,237.00	$166,167.50

Then σ' can be computed by inserting the above values in Formula B as follows:

$$\sigma' = \sqrt{\frac{4{,}389{,}459{,}000 + (1.0568)^2(3{,}931{,}785{,}510) - 2(1.0568)(4{,}151{,}456{,}800)}{20}}$$

$$= 550.5$$

The sample precision factor for sample size 20 at the 95% confidence level can be obtained from Appendix L and is equal to .4795. Since the sample size (20) divided by the population size (1,000) is 2 per cent, the finite population correction factor (Appendix I) is .9899.

The sampling error of the *average* is then

$$SE_{\bar{X}} = (550.5)(.4795)(.9899) = 261.2987$$

To obtain the sampling error of the *ratio*, the sampling error of the average is divided by the average X value (or $157{,}237/20 = 7{,}861.85$).

$$SE_r = \frac{261.2987}{7{,}861.85} = .03324$$

The interval estimate of r is

$$1.0568 \pm .03324$$

or

$$1.0236 \quad \text{to} \quad 1.0900$$

In this example, the sampling error is obviously too large for the purpose (LIFO index). This arises because a sample of 20 is not adequate. A much larger sample is required.

SAMPLING WITH UNEQUAL SIZE CLUSTERS

Cluster sampling was discussed in Chapter 11. However, the method for obtaining the point estimate and sampling error described in that chapter were confined to the situation in which all clusters had the same number of sampling units. When the number of units in the clusters vary, the method is no longer applicable.

While it is often possible to control the number of sampling units in each cluster, there are situations in which it is not practical to attempt to do so. For instance, in an audit the sampling unit may be the invoice, but the invoices may be attached to check copies to which they apply. The most feasible method of sampling such a file is to select random checks and audit all the invoices attached to them.

A different method must be applied to the sample results than that described in Chapter 11. The application of a ratio estimate similar to that described in the previous section must be used, a ratio estimate of a ratio.

As noted previously, a ratio is merely one value divided by another. An arithmetic mean may be looked upon as a ratio. It is the ratio of the total value of the items to the number of items included, or

$$\bar{X} = \frac{\Sigma Y}{n}$$

or, when the items are clustered,

$$\bar{Y} = \frac{\Sigma Y}{\Sigma m_i}$$

where m_i is the number of sampling units in each cluster.

Thus, the arithmetic mean can be treated as a ratio between the total value of all the sampling units and the total number of sampling units in the clusters. The methods described for dealing with a ratio estimate of a ratio may be applied.

The point estimate of the arithmetic average is obtained merely by adding the values of all sampling units in the sample in all clusters and dividing by the total number of sampling units in all clusters.

The sampling error can be calculated as for a ratio estimate of a ratio, considering the totals of the clusters as the Y variable and the number of units in each cluster as the X variable. Once again the formula is

$$SE_r = \frac{t(\sigma'/\sqrt{n})\sqrt{1 - n/N}}{\overline{X}}$$

or, in this situation

$$SE_r = \frac{t(\sigma'/\sqrt{m})\ \sqrt{1 - m/M}}{\overline{m}_i}$$

where $\overline{m}_i = \frac{\Sigma m_i}{c}$

m = number of clusters in sample
M = number of clusters in population

Assume a file of 2,000 checks with the invoices pertaining to each check attached to it. The sampling unit is to be the invoice. A random sample of 20 checks is selected, resulting in 20 clusters of invoices of varying size. The results are shown in Table 14-3. It is known that there are 8,100 invoices in the file.

Since there are few clusters and the value of σ' is obtained from the cluster totals, the Formula A method (see page 222) may be used.

$$\sigma' = \sqrt{\frac{\Sigma(Y - rX)^2}{m}}$$

It is to be remembered that for purposes of computing the sampling error, the clusters become sampling units and hence the division is by m (the number of clusters) rather than n (the number of original sampling units—invoices in this example).

The point estimate of the arithmetic mean is

$$r = \overline{Y} = \frac{\Sigma Y}{n} = \frac{\Sigma Y}{\Sigma m_i} = \frac{\$14{,}401.48}{83} = \$173.51$$

This is the average (arithmetic mean) amount per *invoice.*

The point estimate of the total is

$$N\overline{Y} = 8{,}100(\$173.51) = \$1{,}405{,}431.00$$

where N is the total number of *invoices* in the file.

The sampling error can be computed by first solving for the value of σ'.

$$\sigma' = \sqrt{\frac{\Sigma(Y - rX)^2}{m}}$$

$$\sigma' = \frac{373{,}249.39}{20} = 136.61$$

TABLE 14-3

Cluster number	X Number in cluster (m_i)	Y cluster totals*	rX	$Y - rX$	$(Y - rX)^2$
#3580	7	$1,103.71	1,214.57	−110.86	12,289.9400
4683	1	200.78	173.51	27.27	743.6529
4889	2	374.96	347.02	27.94	780.6436
2786	2	463.59	347.02	116.57	13,588.5650
9880	9	1,237.56	1,561.59	−324.03	104,995.4400
7471	4	722.17	694.04	28.08	788.4864
9245	1	114.47	173.51	−59.04	3,485.7216
3770	3	424.45	520.53	−96.28	9,269.8384
6406	8	1,182.01	1,388.08	−206.07	42,464.8450
7475	2	400.10	347.02	53.08	2,817.4864
3937	2	374.30	347.02	27.28	744.1984
4199	5	894.08	867.55	26.53	703.8409
7226	6	1,076.79	1,041.06	135.73	1,276.6329
5815	6	1,146.91	1,041.06	105.85	11,204.2230
1853	1	149.82	173.51	−23.69	561.2161
2958	3	301.35	520.53	−219.18	48,039.8720
3821	9	1,864.39	1,561.59	302.80	91,687.8400
7591	1	261.22	173.51	87.71	7,693.0441
5445	8	1,482.19	1,388.08	94.11	8,856.6920
4209	3	626.63	520.53	106.10	11,257.2100
Total	83	$14,401.48			373,249.3900

*The cluster totals in this example are the totals of the *audited* values. The same method may be used for projection of errors or disallowances by using the totals of these amounts in each cluster. Where there are no errors in a cluster, the total error would be zero.

Then, from Appendix L for sample size 20, the precision factor is .4795 at the 95% confidence level. Since 20 out of 2,000 clusters were sampled (or 1%), the finite population factor (Appendix I) is .9950.

The sampling error of the average cluster total ($\overline{Y}_t$) is

$$SE_{y_t} = (136.61)(.4795)(.9950) = 65.177$$

and

$$SE_r = SE_{\bar{y}} = \frac{SE_{\bar{y}_t}}{m} = \frac{65.177}{4.15} = 15.705$$

where $\overline{m} = \dfrac{83}{20} = 4.15$

The sampling error of the total audited invoice values is

$$N(SE_r) = 8{,}100(15.705) = \$127{,}210.50$$

The confidence interval can now be established. The lower limit is \$1,405,431.00 − \$127,210.50, or \$1,278,220.50. The upper limit is \$1,405,431.00 + \$127,210.50, or \$1,532,641.50.

It is to be noted that the point estimate and sampling error of the *average* can be determined with only a knowledge of the number of clusters in the population, but the calculation of the same values for the *total* requires knowledge of the number of sampling units (in this case, invoices) in the population.

If the number of sampling units in the population is not known, the methods for unknown population size in Chapter 7 (pages 127–131) may be used but will result in a poorer sample precision.

THE REPLICATED SAMPLE

Replicated sampling is not a new sampling *method* but rather a device for simplifying the calculation of sample precision for any type of sampling operation.

Prior discussions have indicated that the computation of sampling reliabilities of averages and proportions can be quite complex in some instances. Further, where the several methods of sampling are combined as, for example, when a stratified multistage cluster sampling operation is performed, great difficulty may be encountered in calculating the sampling error. However, in these complex sampling situations, the sampling precision can be computed without much difficulty if the method of replicated sampling is used.

Replicated sampling requires, instead of drawing one overall random sample of size n, that k random subsamples of size n/k be obtained.[2] Thus, if a sample of 200 items is to be used, instead of a single sample of the 200 items, perhaps 20 samples of 10 items each are drawn. These samples can be obtained by assigning the random numbers used for the selection to each of the subsampling groups in turn. Thus the first random number will be assigned to subsample #1, the second to subsample #2, etc., until a sufficient number have been apportioned to all groups that comprise the sample.

Another kind of replicated sampling can be achieved by using k systematic samples, each with its own random start. The average of each of the subsamples (or proportions) is then used as the basis for computing the sampling precision.

It will be seen that the differences which exist among the results (averages or proportions) obtained from the several subsamples must be due to sampling fluctuations alone, since each subgroup is a separate random sample. In effect an empirical sampling distribution has been created.

[2]For a complete discussion of replicated sampling see W. E. Deming, *Sample Design in Business Research*, John Wiley & Sons, Inc., New York, 1960.

The precision of the overall average of the several subsamples can thus be obtained by the formula for the sample precision of a *variables* estimate as given previously in Chapter 4.

$$\text{Sampling precision of an average} = t\frac{\sigma}{\sqrt{n}}\sqrt{1 - \frac{n}{N}}$$

Which now can be rewritten to prevent confusion in symbols as

$$\text{Sample precision of a replicated sample average (of values or proportions)} = t\frac{\sigma}{\sqrt{m}}\sqrt{1 - \frac{m}{M}}$$

where t = factor determined by confidence level chosen
σ = standard deviation of the several subsample results (averages or proportions)
m = number of subsamples used
M = total possible number of subsamples or N/n_i, where N = field size and n = number of items in each subsample.

Since the number of subsamples is usually small, the methods and tables described for use in cluster sampling are appropriate here. Thus, the tables may be used instead of calculation to solve the above formula to obtain the sample precision. However, it *will* be necessary to compute the standard deviation of the results obtained from each of several subsamples (averages or proportions) by the method outlined in Chapter 4.

While technically it is possible to use any number of subsamples, other than one, it is desirable to use at least ten. Further, the number of individual items in each subsample should not be too few.

To illustrate the above process, assume, in a simple situation, that it is desired to estimate the total amount of a certain type of voucher and that a sample of these vouchers has been obtained. However, in obtaining this sample, the random numbers were assigned to 20 different subsamples at random, with the results as shown in Table 14-4. In this case, the field size was 5,000 vouchers, and 20 subsamples of 15 items each were obtained.

The projection of the average value *per voucher* from the overall sample average to secure the total value of the vouchers is accomplished by multiplying it by the total number of vouchers in the field.

$$\$102.059 \times 5{,}000 = \$510{,}295.00$$

The sample precision of this projection may now be computed. The first step is to calculate the standard deviation (see Table 14-5) of these sample averages by the method outlined in Chapter 4.

The sample precision is computed using this standard deviation. By using the tables for cluster sampling (Appendix L), the sample precision factor for a sample of size 20, since 20 subsamples were involved, is .4795 at the 95% confidence level.

Since 20 out of a possible 333 groups of 15 items were used, the finite population correction factor of 6.0%, located in Appendix I, is .9695.

TABLE 14-4

Subsample	Sample* average value	Sample size
1	$ 96.56	15
2	98.10	15
3	104.71	15
4	103.12	15
5	91.88	15
6	98.21	15
7	105.81	15
8	93.09	15
9	107.25	15
10	102.56	15
11	102.85	15
12	106.34	15
13	100.62	15
14	116.49	15
15	108.06	15
16	110.17	15
17	99.52	15
18	108.93	15
19	93.14	15
20	93.77	15
Average....	$102.059	

* Of the 15 items in each subsample.

The product of these three values, the standard deviation, the sample precision factor, and the finite population correction factor, is now obtained and represents the sampling error of the *average* of the entire sample of 300 (20 groups of 15 each).

$$\$6.43 \times .4795 \times .9695 = \pm\$2.9891$$

Multiplying by the field size provides the sample precision for the total dollar-value estimate.

$$\pm\$2.9891 \times 5{,}000 = \pm\$14{,}945.50$$

The confidence interval (95% confidence level) then becomes

$$\$510{,}295.00 \pm \$14{,}945.50$$

The replicated method of establishing sample precision can be used in conjunction with any form of estimation sampling, such as unrestricted random sampling, stratified sampling, etc., or any combination thereof, and for both variables and attributes. Frequently, it provides the simplest approach to sample reliability calculations, but it does require additional effort in separating the overall sample into subsamples and especially in keeping track of each item selected to ensure its recording in the proper subsample.

TABLE 14-5

Subsample	Subsample averages	Deviation of subsample averages from overall sample average, $(X - \bar{X})$	Square of deviation, $(X - \bar{X})^2$
1	$ 96.56	−$ 5.50	30.2500
2	98.10	− 3.96	15.6816
3	104.71	+ 2.65	7.0225
4	103.12	+ 1.06	1.1236
5	91.88	− 10.18	103.6324
6	98.21	− 3.85	14.8225
7	105.81	+ 3.75	14.0625
8	93.09	− 8.97	80.4609
9	107.25	+ 5.19	26.9361
10	102.56	+ 0.50	.2500
11	102.85	+ 0.79	.6241
12	106.34	+ 4.28	18.3184
13	100.62	− 1.44	2.0736
14	116.49	+ 14.43	208.2249
15	108.06	+ 6.00	36.0000
16	110.17	+ 8.11	65.7721
17	99.52	− 2.54	6.4516
18	108.93	+ 6.87	47.1969
19	93.14	− 8.92	79.5664
20	93.77	− 8.29	68.7241
Average......	$102.06		
Total........			827.1942

$$\sigma = \sqrt{\frac{827.1942}{20}} = \sqrt{41.36}$$
$$= \$6.43$$

COMBINATIONS OF SAMPLING PLANS

In order to achieve the objectives of an audit test based on a sample with maximum efficiency, it may be necessary to use more than one of the sampling plans previously described, in combination. Any of these sampling plans can be combined in any sequence. Thus, it may be desirable to use stratified sampling with cluster sampling within the strata, or multistage sampling with ratio estimates within the primary units.

For instance, an audit sample of the payments in a government training compensation plan was based on a multistage sample of several segments of the population combined into a stratified sample to achieve an overall estimate. The objective of the test was to establish the total amount of payments to individuals in the program who were actually ineligible to receive such payments. The records were maintained at about 1,000 different locations, but groups of these locations were under the administration of several different agencies.

Because of the numerous locations, it was necessary to resort to multistage sampling within each administrative segment. The results of these samples provided the basis for a conclusion in the audit report of each administrative area. These samples were then combined into an overall audit report conclusion by the use of stratified sampling, where each administrative area became a stratum.

The method is straightforward in that the sampling errors arising from the multistage sample for each administrative group were used as the strata sampling errors, which were then combined using the stratified sampling formula to obtain the overall sampling error.

In another audit test, the sequence was reversed, with a multistage sample on the top level and a sample stratified by dollar value at each primary sampling unit. In the first case described above, resort was made to stratified sampling out of necessity, but in the second case it was used to gain efficiency.

It will be noted that in combinations of sampling plans such as those above, each sampling plan constitutes a separate level; the sampling error is computed in the usual fashion for that plan and is then used at the next higher level.

The most frequently used combination of sampling plans in audit tests is the stratified difference estimate. When the intent is to project the total dollar value of errors or disallowances and a stratified sampling plan is used, this combination of sampling plans results. However, resort may be made to the difference estimate approach even when the intent is to project the total dollar amount of the audited value because of the greater efficiency of the difference method.

In comparing the results obtained from the *stratified difference estimate* with those obtained from the *stratified direct projection* of audited values, it will be noted that the point estimates of either the average or the total will be the same. However, as explained in Chapter 12, since the efficiencies of the plans differ, the sampling errors of the two methods will not be the same. As a result, the confidence interval estimate of the two methods will not be the same.

If in doubt as to the best combination of sampling plans, it is appropriate to compute the sampling error of the projection using both methods and then select the result with the lower sampling error. However, under *no* circumstance is it permissible to select the plan merely on the grounds that it produces a result more desired by the sampler. The choice is limited to the magnitude of the sampling error.

All of the sampling plans and all combinations of the sampling plans described in this volume are in accordance with generally accepted statistical principles. The choice of the combination of sampling plans in a given audit situation is then dependent only on the purpose of the test and the efficiency of the plans.

APPENDIXES

APPENDIX A
RANDOM NUMBERS

A

	(01)	(02)	(03)	(04)	(05)	(06)	(07)	(08)	(09)	(10)
(0001)	9492	4562	4180	5525	7255	1297	9296	1283	6011	0350
(0002)	1557	0392	8989	6898	1072	6013	0020	8582	5059	9324
(0003)	0714	5947	2420	6210	3824	2743	4217	3707	5894	0040
(0004)	0558	8266	4990	8954	7455	6309	9543	1148	0835	0808
(0005)	1458	8725	3750	3138	2499	6017	7744	0485	3010	9606
(0006)	5169	6981	4319	3369	9424	4117	7632	5457	0608	4741
(0007)	0328	5213	1017	5248	8622	6454	8120	4585	3295	0840
(0008)	2462	2055	9782	4213	3452	9940	8859	1000	6260	2851
(0009)	8408	8697	3982	8228	7668	8139	3736	4889	7283	7706
(0010)	1818	5041	9706	4646	3992	4110	4091	7619	1053	4020
(0011)	1771	8614	8593	0930	2095	5005	6387	4002	7498	0066
(0012)	7050	1437	6847	4679	9059	4139	6602	6817	9972	5360
(0013)	5875	2094	0495	3213	5694	5513	3547	9035	7588	5994
(0014)	2473	2087	4618	1507	4471	9542	7565	2371	3981	0812
(0015)	1976	1639	4956	9011	8221	4840	4513	5263	8837	5868
(0016)	4006	4029	7270	8027	7476	7690	6362	1251	9277	5833
(0017)	2149	8162	0667	0825	7353	4645	3273	1181	8526	1176
(0018)	1669	7011	6548	5851	8278	9006	8176	1268	7113	4548
(0019)	7436	5041	4087	1647	7205	3977	4257	9008	3067	7206
(0020)	2178	3632	5745	2228	1780	6043	9296	4469	8108	5005
(0021)	1964	3043	3134	8923	1019	8560	5871	7971	2233	7960
(0022)	5859	7120	9682	0173	2413	8490	6162	1220	3710	5270
(0023)	2352	1929	5985	3303	9590	6974	5811	4264	0248	4295
(0024)	9267	0156	9112	2783	2026	0493	9544	8065	4916	3835
(0025)	4787	0119	1261	5197	0156	2385	9957	0990	6681	2323
(0026)	5550	0699	8080	1152	6002	2532	3075	2777	8671	4068
(0027)	7281	9442	4941	1041	0569	4354	8000	3158	9142	5498
(0028)	1322	7212	3286	2886	9739	5012	0360	5800	9745	8640
(0029)	5176	2259	2774	3641	3553	2475	1974	4578	3388	6656
(0030)	2292	1664	1237	2518	0081	8788	8170	5519	0467	4646
(0031)	6935	8265	3393	4268	4429	1443	4670	4177	7872	9298
(0032)	8538	5393	8093	7835	0484	2550	0827	3112	1065	0246
(0033)	4351	0691	0592	2256	4881	4776	4992	2919	3046	3246
(0034)	6337	8219	9134	9611	8961	4277	6288	2818	1603	4084
(0035)	2257	1980	5269	9615	8628	4715	6366	1542	7267	8917
(0036)	8319	9526	0819	0238	7504	1499	8507	9767	1345	7509
(0037)	1717	8853	2651	9327	7244	0428	6583	2862	1452	8061
(0038)	6519	9348	1026	4190	4210	6231	0732	7000	9553	6125
(0039)	1728	2608	6422	6711	1348	6163	4289	6621	0736	4771
(0040)	5788	5724	5388	5218	8929	3299	0945	6760	8258	5305
(0041)	7495	0547	0226	1188	1270	0689	5048	7689	9477	2210
(0042)	1519	1689	9573	7207	4188	1155	1366	1517	1943	2399
(0043)	0493	2858	2812	7122	4852	7317	6895	3666	5095	7681
(0044)	7235	8838	6680	7231	3713	9231	8510	6206	8596	3657
(0045)	2240	8303	9164	9119	3531	8567	9007	6877	5646	6305

Arkin, Herbert, Table of 120,000 Random Decimal Digits, Bernard M. Baruch College, 1963.

Random Numbers (Continued)

	(01)	(02)	(03)	(04)	(05)	(06)	(07)	(08)	(09)	(10)
(0046)	4539	6934	7314	9138	9071	7599	2762	9489	0800	6898
(0047)	6428	7624	7347	4177	9707	8847	4126	3270	8129	2446
(0048)	0707	2166	0762	3306	9799	1157	2166	7164	5023	1596
(0049)	0630	3833	5571	1457	2408	2978	9564	3414	5744	0618
(0050)	9870	4299	6423	6188	6362	1751	4872	0554	9954	3081
(0051)	9685	8520	6757	2659	5673	8523	2946	7749	2423	6695
(0052)	3860	4176	4318	7592	2774	4185	5805	0115	2999	1506
(0053)	8607	5680	0736	4242	0378	8863	8128	9386	5696	1016
(0054)	7912	5960	0812	2198	9343	1053	3463	9982	4779	9984
(0055)	6296	6078	4008	4121	0015	7592	2614	6325	8406	9076
(0056)	5479	5863	1245	4687	7746	0852	0058	3541	5392	0327
(0057)	3740	5968	8481	7308	2022	7322	9933	6969	9585	2357
(0058)	8524	4978	2958	2144	0526	2525	0985	1125	4178	4196
(0059)	8828	4883	8285	3774	7167	8484	5357	9543	0039	2875
(0060)	7756	5930	2313	4698	7270	3631	9377	8245	1421	7281
(0061)	0930	7668	3903	1619	2069	0851	1784	2010	8101	3319
(0062)	5602	0968	1261	1043	6543	2464	4916	8068	5119	6259
(0063)	5436	5923	1780	5282	8887	1866	2025	1153	6650	8894
(0064)	9506	1315	2689	4151	3113	0942	6696	6387	1199	6215
(0065)	2642	2633	9329	7731	3397	1088	3060	5455	5190	9115
(0066)	6391	7373	0080	0473	2805	0262	0586	3635	0279	1517
(0067)	0286	2779	1941	5215	4739	8685	3267	2703	0235	6703
(0068)	1486	4670	2705	0534	6266	8488	9256	0074	3141	2132
(0069)	7053	2280	4882	0259	3234	3542	8133	6124	5002	1135
(0070)	0657	2943	3145	4293	6777	8015	4814	7581	5304	8967
(0071)	7573	3251	5325	3223	1094	7806	7877	4848	6058	4267
(0072)	4211	2592	3955	1584	9515	6412	4771	5040	3411	7757
(0073)	7724	0442	9604	9317	2643	2484	9413	7580	6403	3337
(0074)	2721	0887	3318	7409	0267	9633	8664	2579	0166	6237
(0075)	3672	3948	7223	0032	9214	4281	6105	7308	5557	2270
(0076)	9210	4507	5163	9504	6244	3647	3347	7843	3105	2262
(0077)	8577	0413	1196	9801	6686	7777	9192	0307	8331	4190
(0078)	5109	2474	6546	6164	4213	7141	6502	9030	5152	8142
(0079)	3983	6229	4737	6058	5028	9052	7233	1926	5319	5668
(0080)	5983	9482	2211	0430	2900	8135	1502	3343	9838	6355
(0081)	8256	8329	9936	5944	0064	9737	7245	9857	4067	5125
(0082)	1655	6024	8617	9097	7105	4217	6816	0668	7095	4315
(0083)	7575	0304	5094	4424	9428	0368	4092	9059	0594	6627
(0084)	4209	8418	3790	2331	3586	1092	0121	6190	4100	8502
(0085)	0335	9932	5971	3361	0412	1561	3537	7885	1034	6415
(0086)	4797	9017	3290	7541	3484	8133	4365	9159	2412	8583
(0087)	6925	3766	8963	9955	5537	6630	6184	2918	3426	4957
(0088)	9831	1106	4360	7662	7012	3732	8154	7516	8022	4702
(0089)	9335	6205	9238	1105	3253	1135	7390	7228	4261	2218
(0090)	1404	5166	8964	4631	8126	3649	6534	3783	7432	8450
(0091)	7512	1813	7765	9402	3325	3420	7663	6999	6263	9187
(0092)	1862	2407	7511	9628	3434	2974	1856	4809	3677	2110
(0093)	6107	4728	8577	4409	4488	5739	9894	4058	5622	6048
(0094)	9477	0224	6193	4002	9865	6468	1944	4337	3270	1891
(0095)	5565	1437	4899	3250	6592	6904	2172	2280	8692	2276

	(01)	(02)	(03)	(04)	(05)	(06)	(07)	(08)	(09)	(10)
(0096)	7151	5953	6566	8961	7726	5831	4193	6523	3750	1412
(0097)	4187	4573	3192	7128	5029	6569	1942	2369	8287	9756
(0098)	8748	2766	3110	4674	2484	2614	9455	0809	4219	8389
(0099)	0567	6206	0839	0579	6737	8570	3107	2116	4237	1903
(0100)	3328	5823	3335	4364	8911	1887	5811	1961	1735	3027
(0101)	8801	6585	2558	7356	1701	6430	6871	1419	7624	0513
(0102)	0317	6887	1104	7576	1901	9604	3907	0083	3395	4216
(0103)	5048	6687	5504	4273	1133	6544	4671	5347	4200	6026
(0104)	0995	8386	8933	4293	9577	2120	2410	0521	5763	1942
(0105)	3240	3645	1961	1496	3193	8259	8491	0414	9010	9438
(0106)	4658	1248	9667	2871	7378	1640	5825	5357	2050	1909
(0107)	4477	6091	8369	7133	0081	7208	1475	2728	5342	6966
(0108)	0400	3299	9139	5179	5400	4090	3116	9359	7430	1842
(0109)	9477	1188	1146	9247	4119	5225	3871	9051	8112	6060
(0110)	4499	5137	0650	0034	6048	3662	5931	2826	5716	2178
(0111)	9829	5866	3403	9321	4708	5284	5170	0436	8397	6632
(0112)	0579	1102	7518	6177	1405	5576	0346	1254	7104	5194
(0113)	9715	7720	4017	5601	8392	8902	3156	0625	9642	0864
(0114)	4853	0109	0308	7940	7209	0198	1813	4343	4236	8946
(0115)	7460	6866	4015	6510	4631	1818	3302	1959	7917	3228
(0116)	4337	8028	6281	3751	0953	0686	6680	3692	1457	4886
(0117)	4286	8028	0498	8199	2666	7193	9352	5464	5147	0770
(0118)	6178	1510	3498	5461	5934	8084	5077	6837	7992	3515
(0119)	5062	1105	8616	8320	8632	9704	8916	5163	2553	3104
(0120)	3820	3864	9627	8428	6835	4113	0881	3926	0240	7652
(0121)	0368	6983	0506	6514	2128	8810	2274	1662	4258	2066
(0122)	6441	2999	6791	6379	6769	8948	4811	3896	3902	1146
(0123)	2709	7061	7723	3923	4786	1184	8797	4199	5818	6612
(0124)	2861	2998	1210	6759	2936	0618	7199	9012	4989	3402
(0125)	8911	3514	9962	7989	8305	7879	4089	0491	7884	5071
(0126)	9192	0104	9212	8308	0100	0894	3990	8278	1472	3584
(0127)	1377	0898	1001	0175	0240	9504	6882	9044	3436	0955
(0128)	9970	8383	7218	7488	0413	3411	7062	5836	5527	8204
(0129)	4211	5354	7437	3709	1856	9678	0815	5073	0071	9103
(0130)	2192	7415	2306	4293	4950	6195	1508	0764	8668	3886
(0131)	8192	7192	5060	4594	9339	4470	3396	2002	5958	5455
(0132)	7894	9936	7010	2787	6397	8973	7274	7204	1478	0071
(0133)	8447	8298	9805	9467	1533	4834	0423	1161	7979	2053
(0134)	6112	1157	3822	3226	0856	6555	2117	4783	9229	0984
(0135)	4849	1203	1921	7152	2339	5914	9871	2457	3517	4836
(0136)	0725	0659	9814	1875	5956	3195	6635	7228	2909	9838
(0137)	1205	4059	5064	7073	4108	6047	7111	1299	3184	0923
(0138)	4222	1165	9332	1070	3444	1565	5823	7333	0486	3343
(0139)	9243	9553	5440	4970	5980	6768	2181	9375	9114	0594
(0140)	0428	0201	4791	6554	7782	4656	6338	1636	4888	8586
(0141)	7086	0198	9522	6072	7184	9682	5553	0059	6040	7542
(0142)	2506	9864	1398	0371	3219	8448	6429	7130	4130	4397
(0143)	9936	9122	5086	0182	1056	0953	5118	0656	5406	5835
(0144)	4773	5836	9834	7593	0910	3656	0478	2095	1980	6920
(0145)	5727	8727	2964	0373	9037	1584	2964	7033	4178	9261

Random Numbers (Continued)

	(01)	(02)	(03)	(04)	(05)	(06)	(07)	(08)	(09)	(10)
(0146)	7814	6176	2221	0384	5416	2417	7628	8304	5082	7341
(0147)	0987	0474	4367	8285	1257	9178	1192	0851	0345	0891
(0148)	3499	6887	9615	2561	3123	6242	4838	3174	2105	7426
(0149)	2473	8915	7161	6731	7376	2933	7679	8622	2032	5433
(0150)	3468	7145	1342	2213	4125	5687	2330	1875	2002	4037
(0151)	7233	2686	1404	4853	5566	2461	9513	5665	0927	2143
(0152)	1887	4148	9798	8373	3495	6268	2599	8801	8962	8414
(0153)	5544	3876	4339	2219	1265	0523	9516	0955	2401	9379
(0154)	0179	5842	3729	3340	3249	2555	6903	1714	4091	1841
(0155)	7391	8523	8474	5597	3337	8515	1297	1040	4808	3566
(0156)	2303	3701	2695	7803	7690	5659	0894	7850	1144	2813
(0157)	4886	7455	1559	8948	5166	3736	4106	9205	3367	2635
(0158)	3065	7779	5286	2678	8827	3919	0139	1791	2825	3178
(0159)	2119	9270	0345	1743	7043	5979	1356	8093	6764	9576
(0160)	9038	7103	5347	6188	0168	0566	3044	4337	7771	3171
(0161)	1511	9414	4255	9629	4538	4147	8834	0602	0997	2753
(0162)	9240	1242	2842	8514	9167	6925	0498	9344	3812	2618
(0163)	2077	7100	2633	7441	4074	7211	1504	6025	1855	6846
(0164)	2623	8877	9352	3313	2701	4491	8996	9236	3342	4783
(0165)	7298	7206	4573	4197	3542	5103	2352	2470	4330	5440
(0166)	5986	7900	1350	8900	8740	6066	2760	6208	8724	9192
(0167)	8521	6098	8329	7385	5198	6184	1432	5094	7769	0326
(0168)	0798	6809	6905	6806	2705	3231	0120	1302	8933	4488
(0169)	3141	6850	8030	5323	9749	0909	5950	0068	2849	9438
(0170)	8471	1915	3468	4163	4382	2172	9230	5776	2578	6770
(0171)	9486	0189	6969	6910	9760	3828	8592	8482	2675	5438
(0172)	9625	6330	9712	0437	7578	3931	9778	2846	8068	8348
(0173)	2843	1538	1339	5537	4642	1290	7388	5352	1535	7534
(0174)	7207	8684	7667	9248	3969	9533	2888	3179	3681	8631
(0175)	7162	6501	7660	3762	9156	1808	6011	1878	8194	8795
(0176)	2829	1977	9385	6780	1715	1989	4421	0486	5621	3474
(0177)	7002	8011	1309	4396	5335	9388	4001	7068	9213	3612
(0178)	1872	6182	1733	5603	5374	2340	0952	9639	7597	6102
(0179)	7604	3507	6564	9944	2771	4170	0159	6957	7726	8709
(0180)	3114	5262	8477	6312	9289	7221	3621	3049	0420	7323
(0181)	3248	9183	7908	2584	5714	1932	6895	2854	1196	5114
(0182)	0818	2328	7663	2854	5211	6057	7980	4293	1877	3725
(0183)	5581	1914	9551	2393	7088	4766	1703	2045	1834	3729
(0184)	9586	0039	3814	9863	9075	1951	7798	3016	6358	8459
(0185)	9373	3087	1692	9179	4946	3682	1401	9262	7781	1486
(0186)	7595	0010	0500	3598	6734	2144	4396	7137	5116	4832
(0187)	4387	6818	8454	2952	1738	2333	6626	0602	4948	6271
(0188)	0071	9889	3130	1189	6195	4194	2927	5323	2815	6540
(0189)	0209	9279	8681	7286	3993	8869	2827	2467	7810	5015
(0190)	1860	0708	3473	3136	8193	7865	1330	5149	6126	3433
(0191)	7039	4857	1568	6146	0136	1458	5408	0186	4900	4135
(0192)	0051	8780	8434	3489	6870	0017	7026	6209	5339	3740
(0193)	9199	5107	5319	7826	9188	1620	5997	1379	0262	0067
(0194)	1331	8686	5553	9538	2345	8770	4621	8969	0470	1089
(0195)	4991	2775	2602	6812	5987	2476	8858	5079	6398	2333

	(01)	(02)	(03)	(04)	(05)	(06)	(07)	(08)	(09)	(10)
(0196)	7894	9036	3802	5360	9525	0026	5271	4061	8901	5134
(0197)	0367	0459	6885	6767	8992	2637	0407	7181	4493	7525
(0198)	1408	8217	3286	0843	6976	5282	4347	5196	9440	7838
(0199)	9892	3873	7464	6244	1348	4221	8441	8762	2234	0288
(0200)	0843	4715	0516	2507	9710	6557	8226	9865	0475	6125
(0201)	4317	6451	8605	2549	7492	6720	7460	1905	0418	1284
(0202)	5530	3447	7416	7557	4534	3960	0223	4469	0778	0610
(0203)	7983	5869	5018	0543	9507	6039	5741	9207	6965	3147
(0204)	3271	7782	7306	3215	4826	8187	3827	7218	1630	0317
(0205)	4164	8625	4956	0781	4050	7424	1867	2025	3901	0765
(0206)	0110	5155	4946	4587	6062	4345	4522	4335	1719	3560
(0207)	2444	1561	8565	6518	6111	4194	2849	0602	7625	1796
(0208)	6658	8002	6355	1662	2493	2644	9159	2570	5009	9709
(0209)	5474	7239	6277	5019	7489	9067	7297	3203	5025	2811
(0210)	7336	0429	5302	1899	9291	0052	6772	2261	9045	7192
(0211)	1247	3330	3378	8408	4505	3913	2505	0671	3738	1445
(0212)	1986	9530	7869	4125	6582	9784	5212	6987	0028	1721
(0213)	7057	8850	4084	1892	6765	5342	6247	6926	1949	9305
(0214)	7350	2370	1839	4275	7759	0935	0126	4098	0143	1645
(0215)	0453	4183	1591	5891	3868	3726	9210	8093	2026	9249
(0216)	7318	4416	1916	3698	9728	4307	5407	5884	3745	6907
(0217)	0686	3050	3805	6361	7043	4785	8868	2828	1830	9717
(0218)	9469	5899	6564	9075	9417	5696	8907	4959	6676	2565
(0219)	3175	4344	1997	0343	0416	5054	4149	2179	8496	8614
(0220)	4340	5957	6553	5984	0974	5346	0405	6379	8687	1005
(0221)	4820	0671	3410	5692	5523	2684	8012	3817	5194	1397
(0222)	4914	4139	5711	1389	8275	1560	0062	5474	9653	3740
(0223)	1990	9996	3662	0417	4014	5427	6998	4878	4424	1736
(0224)	7340	0014	7836	0518	7746	3140	9540	9775	0772	5633
(0225)	2116	2449	8466	2485	6014	4060	7297	0363	0055	9836
(0226)	7282	7113	4972	9758	4366	9975	9236	0651	7717	9700
(0227)	8478	8951	9171	2902	3756	7531	3180	9331	6643	0620
(0228)	6416	9187	4269	3750	7789	5635	1825	1037	7371	4377
(0229)	2956	3447	1910	4774	2984	3253	1404	1915	9148	4593
(0230)	0782	5598	8039	4084	3765	4567	3893	8557	1720	3988
(0231)	1013	3504	7955	6412	2045	1081	0072	1609	5314	9617
(0232)	1994	2044	5445	3473	5112	1076	3456	0140	0668	6973
(0233)	8948	6375	8778	6517	6977	7927	1344	3256	0716	4852
(0234)	5546	7835	6694	2345	8252	3629	8441	0717	8569	1943
(0235)	4157	1335	6430	3140	7419	9480	4495	9465	1727	7971
(0236)	8169	5303	6643	9466	9297	5156	0674	1028	5520	0123
(0237)	7260	6947	0775	7190	4693	8956	9195	0803	6411	8471
(0238)	8246	5409	1006	7899	7051	1050	5368	3544	5218	5992
(0239)	3999	8377	7034	3456	8695	6411	3630	9603	6365	2612
(0240)	5315	3344	8055	8868	8930	5349	0842	3088	1256	3489
(0241)	7901	6411	7875	8382	4711	9970	6104	6270	7095	0483
(0242)	4591	8819	2349	6092	1192	3391	0114	7691	6476	8490
(0243)	2256	0936	7359	1890	9267	2880	4577	9106	3704	3653
(0244)	2480	4663	6887	6225	7910	8344	3143	7922	9271	9332
(0245)	1102	8540	9670	5871	5420	8659	4653	7754	0582	7760

Random Numbers (Continued)

	(01)	(02)	(03)	(04)	(05)	(06)	(07)	(08)	(09)	(10)
(0246)	2185	9765	5796	9095	0469	1954	1453	4517	7679	8707
(0247)	1637	7939	2831	0385	1060	2944	9453	4558	9150	0394
(0248)	9895	8140	6582	5946	4249	2651	4661	8171	5106	0527
(0249)	7741	5415	2579	5262	2526	2341	5010	7836	1427	9912
(0250)	8303	3420	1586	9915	3367	9256	3806	8003	2960	1217
(0251)	0963	9273	9817	1437	9172	9761	5158	9266	0950	6443
(0252)	0479	5914	0920	4946	9688	4669	8162	5558	5027	6734
(0253)	7274	7967	2223	7235	5745	3476	8096	7899	1506	7972
(0254)	7625	0524	3695	3469	0763	1494	1980	7885	4880	9662
(0255)	3599	4031	6719	5952	5191	6833	4323	4006	5852	9884
(0256)	8176	3578	8876	7310	2934	7113	6000	6364	9110	8079
(0257)	3124	5553	7426	3795	4338	8717	0749	5330	4201	2425
(0258)	4457	5784	5589	1308	7169	9350	7405	6199	3254	7208
(0259)	4264	6373	4013	0731	1910	9249	9982	0076	2793	7300
(0260)	7954	4065	6672	3353	6338	1653	7213	2859	0590	3811
(0261)	4744	1304	4988	2767	8451	5171	8951	0325	7462	2189
(0262)	7476	2438	2444	6400	5341	3950	4730	1298	7878	6661
(0263)	7505	7435	6334	8789	8973	0123	1402	3887	8548	3772
(0264)	4045	8470	0455	2836	6866	9440	1266	2492	3378	9362
(0265)	1193	2030	1690	9574	7596	2492	1778	8589	9181	1212
(0266)	8311	5496	7264	9367	2284	0977	0050	5703	1314	3572
(0267)	3297	8671	7176	3213	8252	6834	3599	5367	6784	2950
(0268)	4738	5246	7348	1998	7806	4763	9704	3388	2412	9429
(0269)	0355	2015	4630	9559	8820	3548	5635	9041	7496	7858
(0270)	1832	0203	8597	6055	9376	3010	2289	8942	7018	8852
(0271)	7137	3264	0054	6439	5057	8565	7177	8166	9411	4591
(0272)	9278	9266	8761	0563	0883	3418	6075	4584	4751	4261
(0273)	6571	1035	0382	0636	5875	3767	9626	6992	7138	5503
(0274)	5331	1068	8468	4455	3839	6017	1600	2122	8614	7070
(0275)	9028	7390	4581	6599	1791	9202	2689	6792	9227	7671
(0276)	2108	5279	5974	0487	8928	5920	5366	1248	0451	5030
(0277)	0974	8407	8844	7344	7591	0474	8078	7568	1276	6804
(0278)	2087	1508	2614	3695	0024	0598	3878	3514	2264	9022
(0279)	7759	2089	1807	0351	3327	3558	0865	2145	1058	0082
(0280)	0191	0829	3684	9169	6744	2372	4385	9181	8292	9714
(0281)	7567	6449	3991	3155	3291	1591	0966	3151	8675	6339
(0282)	3906	0874	7073	4683	1405	6732	8175	6863	0085	5723
(0283)	9344	0717	2278	6868	1779	9791	1328	4060	2766	1048
(0284)	1514	9384	3289	6463	0375	7438	1090	7668	2103	3218
(0285)	2834	2047	8938	5835	5578	0502	5477	3782	2820	9953
(0286)	8219	5431	7556	0330	9684	8966	5883	3152	2961	2117
(0287)	1566	4587	5433	0006	8313	2862	7617	3805	7887	6172
(0288)	6690	2828	0538	5396	0992	1988	3649	5479	8820	4039
(0289)	0029	4981	3899	1485	2273	8388	8495	6983	1716	1372
(0290)	3774	1600	0206	6362	6360	9450	5818	1837	9317	9078
(0291)	8441	1644	9728	4212	4438	0099	6192	7770	3420	5747
(0292)	9792	4278	5448	8457	6363	7568	4392	0288	0830	7434
(0293)	7811	7294	8036	5983	1403	1056	2241	5439	5605	7093
(0294)	9426	9965	0788	8172	6599	7322	5474	3027	9974	0401
(0295)	4295	6544	2179	5117	2206	5143	2949	0972	3991	5546

	(01)	(02)	(03)	(04)	(05)	(06)	(07)	(08)	(09)	(10)
(0296)	2694	7935	3229	3249	6048	4119	8942	6310	4553	3433
(0297)	4550	7968	8394	9401	9572	5316	8576	9562	8653	5072
(0298)	0818	7288	2140	9992	8116	5106	0843	3873	1608	9960
(0299)	2724	7014	6048	6866	2356	1684	8307	7385	5112	5301
(0300)	9895	6162	3125	2485	6776	3682	3438	4323	2620	7047
(0301)	3614	5521	1607	4848	9335	6581	6454	7329	6596	5499
(0302)	7839	4225	0741	4383	7537	1210	0523	0673	9604	5123
(0303)	8419	4136	0237	3079	8687	1111	2129	7313	4916	9796
(0304)	3157	8106	4371	7594	5648	4802	9790	4884	6908	4828
(0305)	7123	4071	0015	4687	5321	9996	4778	0547	4122	7350
(0306)	8910	0766	6284	9568	2358	8461	1360	2848	0692	0390
(0307)	9031	9845	5905	9508	1491	7044	1434	0738	5100	3394
(0308)	8805	4978	5468	8805	4073	3924	4283	3450	3389	2503
(0309)	0418	5921	8995	3107	7079	3802	6212	4857	6208	4662
(0310)	6208	2377	4269	1536	1578	2456	4389	9059	3678	0486
(0311)	3380	5742	4371	7530	0167	5037	7900	6750	2688	5098
(0312)	3068	9047	0080	9115	1236	9465	9337	6071	6215	6859
(0313)	9902	0424	8750	7946	6767	0125	7936	2894	9619	5365
(0314)	2782	7091	4297	0456	9087	5861	8050	2858	2544	6581
(0315)	1054	5715	1488	1023	6543	7547	8735	6682	6771	9975
(0316)	9357	0963	2347	8784	4058	8270	3216	3996	5380	2264
(0317)	9387	6783	4143	4175	1818	2616	1652	9984	1285	3266
(0318)	8680	5391	4026	4152	3990	6590	3819	4485	3946	9010
(0319)	4040	0079	5784	2413	0923	2750	1843	2851	6973	0658
(0320)	3065	5721	3876	1374	8845	4461	9002	7218	3405	4469
(0321)	0779	7881	5427	1711	4452	1115	2406	1829	9620	2296
(0322)	2011	9110	9284	6889	6412	9535	7338	0026	7538	8986
(0323)	7580	1996	6998	0517	9851	9464	5811	6069	8829	0028
(0324)	1806	2119	0361	7732	6848	0359	7076	9420	0707	3290
(0325)	6171	2990	4852	1838	9978	5479	3803	0464	5850	3514
(0326)	1982	0477	6677	9360	1491	2112	1241	6864	5365	9390
(0327)	2684	6104	3748	4789	0305	2018	6917	4843	9722	4934
(0328)	3810	6911	4116	8841	8624	2636	2928	4737	1919	3758
(0329)	2163	5289	0731	4202	6643	7850	3510	1937	8279	9543
(0330)	4313	7985	4569	5853	1717	9307	2713	4160	2656	4004
(0331)	9209	7598	4087	5938	0434	1668	6601	4951	8060	8460
(0332)	1288	7562	5700	6630	7987	5247	2909	7549	7156	9643
(0333)	3667	0172	9273	1653	3552	9276	3921	1962	3847	9259
(0334)	5032	8676	0825	0555	6776	8272	3410	9030	2159	0079
(0335)	9183	8481	1429	4120	6446	9147	7155	1611	6281	3028
(0336)	2039	9846	2767	3915	2559	9098	3909	2822	1174	6818
(0337)	5947	9941	7887	3817	7153	9050	6024	6459	2402	3867
(0338)	2819	4719	3024	7801	4963	3532	8108	7323	9046	8440
(0339)	3435	3774	4039	6663	6752	1022	4238	2059	5247	2382
(0340)	3143	2563	9950	4181	6816	0049	6460	5717	7101	6535
(0341)	7970	0702	3994	1301	8589	7145	7326	2348	6801	8661
(0342)	0264	4258	2758	3846	9278	1982	9609	9129	3265	1490
(0343)	6715	3749	5884	5781	8320	9157	6739	6952	9890	0161
(0344)	8233	0114	9421	2032	5822	7441	1643	0425	5683	9624
(0345)	1669	0488	7662	3661	0073	1692	7469	7778	4014	5447

Appendix A
Random Numbers (Continued)

	(01)	(02)	(03)	(04)	(05)	(06)	(07)	(08)	(09)	(10)
(0346)	5148	0089	8776	0472	8125	1725	1190	0327	8652	5194
(0347)	6883	2948	2653	6902	3598	9093	3844	5347	7267	0559
(0348)	5355	0725	7969	5781	9942	6562	3322	6694	5135	1292
(0349)	5766	6270	9094	0325	0045	1427	3696	2875	2951	8233
(0350)	0869	7140	6506	9918	5101	9321	1589	4546	9977	7212
(0351)	6625	6319	7455	8612	6893	0829	0010	6368	4609	4679
(0352)	6433	9452	6221	6176	3294	7792	0172	6926	6590	1615
(0353)	7983	8648	8280	5109	6315	4106	4272	6756	7554	6700
(0354)	9096	7335	6062	5228	0671	2258	4871	2746	0512	8143
(0355)	4430	2657	7768	4058	7986	9831	5370	7582	1418	9311
(0356)	5856	5119	6855	6987	6613	1991	6428	0093	5105	6454
(0357)	3791	8784	6712	8691	4966	6292	6199	6527	7943	1589
(0358)	4084	3584	5648	9924	4383	4002	0698	1140	3637	8358
(0359)	8065	2757	8210	0691	0225	2369	7826	5509	0174	6555
(0360)	0172	6487	9085	5081	1911	3171	8718	9753	8607	8550
(0361)	8184	5230	9078	0553	1881	7414	3445	2463	3103	5995
(0362)	2045	0256	0668	0585	3514	4206	9632	4116	8670	0560
(0363)	5352	5713	1871	9385	6403	7132	0611	6965	6460	6764
(0364)	5758	7693	8908	5582	9972	1027	8323	2356	3825	8851
(0365)	6072	2865	9800	5605	9448	6893	8133	5786	1671	1638
(0366)	6872	9360	7813	2644	2273	1372	4665	5808	1605	6855
(0367)	2162	1920	3439	8415	2447	7930	4540	0043	9814	5103
(0368)	9500	7232	5473	9176	0973	9971	0365	6053	4260	0529
(0369)	0045	1396	0548	2903	6448	9844	8501	0098	0477	0422
(0370)	9833	0497	8186	0499	5759	4890	7707	8798	9649	6681
(0371)	5519	8938	8430	6531	8358	3750	5925	6106	9566	0108
(0372)	2006	3833	2103	6372	5542	9059	7661	7313	7130	0614
(0373)	7113	5750	8018	6634	5102	2243	9042	4311	7709	4335
(0374)	2542	4802	4442	0706	2759	3589	4736	2314	4983	6857
(0375)	9553	2095	1058	0402	1401	9698	5388	4371	7512	3719
(0376)	0878	5527	7923	2893	0684	5360	4217	7444	0042	2720
(0377)	8921	0961	4274	8203	3792	5007	3494	7765	1371	6372
(0378)	8136	3826	0755	3304	5070	8523	8346	3570	2464	9973
(0379)	1118	4609	4468	0537	1516	4598	0152	6174	3181	8347
(0380)	2749	5069	5984	1290	6204	8213	8794	7205	1456	9824
(0381)	2960	7175	2896	6932	6772	6668	0424	4259	9110	0386
(0382)	4696	5291	0161	6400	2674	0534	0005	8267	2406	3525
(0383)	0065	9374	0531	2026	2111	3517	5400	8038	2164	6785
(0384)	2336	3085	4510	7901	8821	1871	7685	5794	5437	8135
(0385)	3516	6643	6175	6063	5499	7798	5035	6864	7306	9706
(0386)	5330	7480	3712	5275	5269	2324	7430	7019	4508	8496
(0387)	3182	4427	4343	0770	0749	4878	6349	0614	3278	8511
(0388)	7339	3142	0650	2631	2603	0704	5135	4776	3954	7520
(0389)	3984	1909	7441	3308	6974	8832	8411	5267	3614	1140
(0390)	4482	0531	0621	0388	3912	5233	4803	7234	1206	5179
(0391)	9968	3140	6896	9655	8878	7537	3069	0270	1940	0039
(0392)	8766	2257	2088	3467	1361	8641	7664	0831	9663	4190
(0393)	8957	4770	6651	3547	7317	1568	1541	5524	8414	6745
(0394)	7126	0057	4466	5286	9137	9502	9578	4488	6250	2703
(0395)	8004	9713	0194	6398	9997	6680	7498	0671	0030	9330

	(01)	(02)	(03)	(04)	(05)	(06)	(07)	(08)	(09)	(10)
(0396)	2283	3023	7317	1213	5668	0890	2426	3083	4287	1920
(0397)	0082	2860	4082	4271	0950	8299	0774	2125	6484	7742
(0398)	4077	2144	7363	2742	3418	9581	1215	2968	4577	6954
(0399)	4374	9330	3924	8677	1707	8575	1908	4554	9310	7210
(0400)	1486	3004	0257	1501	3099	0813	1771	8368	6994	8482
(0401)	0531	4968	5961	1760	0778	1945	5802	8843	0826	6523
(0402)	0903	8902	1919	0772	0612	0307	2820	7873	0655	7993
(0403)	6772	8095	6866	9291	4376	6993	5992	9904	3544	5472
(0404)	3752	7658	4575	2923	2012	1377	7484	2007	0034	7237
(0405)	5752	5178	4371	8423	6956	4022	3002	5054	2499	7845
(0406)	0953	8593	8387	1975	1951	4535	9969	7822	4368	0700
(0407)	6797	3091	6390	2708	3170	0163	4609	8527	2569	9217
(0408)	6359	7934	7809	4557	4238	9948	4516	0789	9198	6247
(0409)	8091	6221	7381	7302	1639	4286	2271	7476	1465	8859
(0410)	2602	1089	5216	5273	1987	2508	9721	1886	2066	8290
(0411)	7798	0860	6898	4448	2462	0687	0330	5836	7915	5237
(0412)	1937	0429	9951	7104	0021	4710	0192	2603	9953	7792
(0413)	2986	4019	8924	7257	4175	5817	1477	4860	1284	5134
(0414)	4502	8966	4340	9569	3284	2501	3468	4042	3676	4675
(0415)	4860	5699	9086	5169	3010	0069	5990	5683	7154	8098
(0416)	5950	7883	7919	3010	3209	7055	1709	7380	3598	2900
(0417)	4896	0045	4054	2288	8156	2584	3362	1067	9260	0029
(0418)	6004	2712	7506	3879	3707	4113	1219	8233	5887	0144
(0419)	9152	8781	2166	4217	1365	8047	1834	8661	5806	8265
(0420)	7080	8696	9916	1349	3516	8381	4696	9594	4105	8892
(0421)	1405	1683	6129	7666	7817	7406	3894	0492	2390	3603
(0422)	8811	2919	5026	5328	2856	3221	2194	2911	4964	9226
(0423)	3644	6235	4906	2236	7286	2667	8623	9000	5965	0911
(0424)	6413	6301	4099	3340	5543	9097	8887	9582	4202	4411
(0425)	5572	7316	9737	0044	9297	4427	7669	7337	1912	9201
(0426)	9850	7438	7773	4096	0123	2041	2481	7356	5935	8243
(0427)	2575	2655	0986	1250	5128	0612	0206	6173	8707	1941
(0428)	3696	6374	3872	9350	7396	3533	7826	0543	6701	3560
(0429)	0190	8758	5088	9642	4894	1644	0588	8693	6568	9016
(0430)	4598	9862	7128	6170	1305	3587	2695	4458	3353	3235
(0431)	6795	8625	7452	7935	1847	8448	7006	1693	3299	5189
(0432)	8460	7502	9762	5343	3165	1128	4958	7941	4312	6920
(0433)	0246	4043	6866	6674	1729	6272	7944	3440	6964	2855
(0434)	5789	0792	5087	5597	6103	2476	9692	6142	9270	9199
(0435)	2937	5654	6623	3574	9225	4693	5314	5071	0191	2720
(0436)	4391	5794	7866	2396	7134	9434	2895	6365	4088	9487
(0437)	4321	5244	9283	0997	0692	8746	1903	1116	7489	3934
(0438)	5278	0610	5612	4311	2016	4738	8238	8276	4939	3390
(0439)	6525	0566	3825	5075	2498	7666	5397	1507	4459	8460
(0440)	1834	4936	9447	4593	1033	2861	0975	6498	0640	3980
(0441)	6974	9198	7894	6497	5905	7614	6887	8279	7126	9861
(0442)	7010	5796	5287	6386	1360	8068	7049	8917	3764	1693
(0443)	1254	6729	2769	5643	4884	6828	6185	5248	4126	9258
(0444)	6536	2599	5357	2296	9290	7784	1803	0310	0156	6545
(0445)	8350	3312	3794	5980	5576	1909	5631	1103	2233	1631

Appendix A
Random Numbers (Continued)

	(01)	(02)	(03)	(04)	(05)	(06)	(07)	(08)	(09)	(10)
(0446)	2602	1797	8107	9417	0123	2344	9532	5143	6490	5173
(0447)	5978	0565	1450	4770	5591	3789	2587	3714	6593	6101
(0448)	5510	6521	5866	0916	5326	7949	4473	0058	3775	6370
(0449)	3181	4086	6353	7623	8083	0278	1962	1623	5096	6653
(0450)	4842	1198	2499	5801	7003	9342	7113	7167	6420	1598
(0451)	5412	7173	6390	3803	7711	4341	1108	3275	2477	6604
(0452)	8003	9448	8282	3745	8135	4180	9838	7001	6632	0905
(0453)	3681	2828	4638	5477	7413	0974	5541	0854	8405	8562
(0454)	7905	8759	7424	9474	1381	8721	8082	4721	3507	4524
(0455)	6797	1794	8150	4783	5626	1982	0495	7767	2253	2087
(0456)	9119	3809	9004	2468	8764	3210	2066	8629	7827	7542
(0457)	3354	1569	5222	7332	7331	4628	7664	5173	2392	3834
(0458)	7982	3856	2024	6870	0293	2584	8307	1483	3200	7935
(0459)	6054	3870	4060	4104	1300	9988	7517	9005	4562	4405
(0460)	7378	8431	6857	0254	3716	7853	7122	1343	5118	6636
(0461)	9150	9340	9058	5896	1767	7274	7087	9897	3803	6923
(0462)	1132	2865	1799	8813	2129	1827	1805	5815	5165	2998
(0463)	0054	7167	1234	2215	3034	6873	8393	5440	8721	7104
(0464)	2241	5746	3648	8008	2074	8509	4526	6301	1469	3147
(0465)	3156	8003	1656	3756	3500	5425	8957	2903	3524	3191
(0466)	1121	8427	2352	4904	6217	7101	4839	8621	2248	7176
(0467)	7971	3323	7622	3475	4245	8315	0073	8443	6493	6923
(0468)	8198	7468	9882	1536	3215	2505	0309	4730	4563	1011
(0469)	9584	9385	9048	6331	9870	5870	4846	5588	6746	0325
(0470)	6756	7839	3725	7190	4773	7383	6598	0368	6534	3731
(0471)	1445	2547	3607	5212	4597	2494	1627	0671	7214	2866
(0472)	2892	1741	9232	8276	7132	0320	3456	0380	4020	0792
(0473)	2089	8164	3853	3947	3754	5740	8295	4461	3599	6343
(0474)	1797	6083	0669	8081	0551	8577	2485	6716	0453	0751
(0475)	7561	9574	8662	0771	4225	5632	0496	6131	0662	1243
(0476)	6276	1340	9318	8586	2973	7067	8759	4806	5275	4257
(0477)	3342	3093	0877	4411	9996	4449	4100	5462	4558	4432
(0478)	4686	9731	3311	3887	1924	7022	3778	1798	2975	2406
(0479)	7572	4242	7921	1449	6194	7908	4976	0325	9967	4574
(0480)	2344	9460	0106	9393	5647	5585	0171	1965	1417	4920
(0481)	2878	7607	3914	3096	0445	7714	8068	5554	6757	0381
(0482)	4861	9242	6338	9672	9467	6382	3245	6796	8282	9745
(0483)	9356	0367	4308	3667	0183	7709	6466	8129	1310	6467
(0484)	9327	0832	4308	3136	5174	8854	9580	0882	6346	7262
(0485)	1784	3672	6032	0101	7794	5181	2880	5258	3582	8441
(0486)	9268	6854	8308	5340	6339	4705	6278	6914	6847	3655
(0487)	7173	8346	1099	9676	2364	8570	0545	9078	2133	3709
(0488)	9546	6616	9447	9604	8913	7364	3791	8174	0907	5383
(0489)	4988	1419	1691	4523	4356	3318	3908	8122	2701	0580
(0490)	6472	0528	9763	8380	1218	4594	8797	9226	5162	8083
(0491)	8448	3187	7582	7898	1700	2686	9251	9855	8490	2454
(0492)	0777	3231	2035	0471	5607	5021	1225	7142	6861	7103
(0493)	9396	4905	3561	8196	4748	4883	4087	9229	8515	8784
(0494)	8592	4075	4942	7311	6008	4236	3638	5280	6895	3556
(0495)	2782	2802	9492	6697	6409	1826	0654	8613	2653	3796

	(01)	(02)	(03)	(04)	(05)	(06)	(07)	(08)	(09)	(10)
(0496)	7557	0444	3747	0130	0596	5047	7700	6930	8119	3135
(0497)	7097	5429	8112	1781	2248	8034	8420	4803	6227	0452
(0498)	2976	8560	6392	7729	0640	9951	3838	5175	7405	0936
(0499)	4892	3503	0868	7935	9607	9778	7310	2038	4557	1063
(0500)	3544	0849	5295	1994	9436	7132	6387	2557	7097	8021
(0501)	6042	0031	1122	9157	3745	5046	7016	2525	9045	8087
(0502)	7268	0799	0453	8195	6927	6113	7328	3292	2102	1921
(0503)	1337	3717	2818	2693	4071	9384	0712	6999	3300	7702
(0504)	3998	3111	1319	3000	4518	7854	7973	9316	4033	0545
(0505)	4548	9078	9751	0881	6626	7248	4864	0804	1486	0778
(0506)	9501	5746	5226	9485	6671	9458	2255	3052	2701	2267
(0507)	6153	2154	2231	3820	2865	4409	3775	8742	0488	6224
(0508)	5466	1201	5945	2124	9204	0740	5607	1099	5102	5814
(0509)	9000	3157	4845	3366	1194	4443	7244	8353	5349	6091
(0510)	5708	6724	1762	0567	5775	4757	8585	5245	1229	8873
(0511)	4472	9870	7429	3939	1100	5710	3690	1220	9838	4740
(0512)	1690	5471	8219	5707	5455	5438	4821	4182	1205	8967
(0513)	8177	6238	6923	1465	7877	7249	8107	0013	8411	5428
(0514)	4806	0996	8100	5877	8283	0532	6422	8113	5985	1209
(0515)	9547	9173	4632	4934	8806	8921	0930	9850	3761	5656
(0516)	9042	7638	8603	2931	1983	2556	9261	4702	6949	9986
(0517)	2798	1337	3748	2686	7004	2078	1762	7876	0742	4566
(0518)	9790	9843	5565	3097	3162	6382	0048	1165	8275	9782
(0519)	9438	0936	6070	2369	9733	0274	6158	6173	4247	6074
(0520)	9252	7635	7436	8218	8265	0629	0908	3951	9160	3448
(0521)	4215	1143	6761	8604	7049	3018	1360	7109	4874	9095
(0522)	4045	7795	1547	0299	9057	3834	2685	0931	4269	3383
(0523)	6192	6009	9033	6357	3432	6582	7486	5699	4856	4157
(0524)	5410	7619	4992	0625	5222	4753	1515	9138	3474	4639
(0525)	0199	5009	7008	5041	2498	3794	1765	6361	1036	5284
(0526)	3528	0633	3206	4795	0996	0702	1690	5757	5883	2575
(0527)	4184	9683	8595	1099	1435	7609	1352	4036	5364	8305
(0528)	5801	2777	8172	6193	1705	4055	2589	7609	9410	5407
(0529)	3863	0198	4840	6738	9559	1022	4311	2952	3886	6990
(0530)	2738	9779	4694	1211	4263	4226	8142	2516	7992	0734
(0531)	9056	5955	5402	6737	6945	6269	5745	6833	0446	0300
(0532)	3829	6966	9742	6610	6323	5774	2215	8061	7447	3682
(0533)	4970	8189	0526	1409	8112	2386	4408	3744	1837	6126
(0534)	3700	9442	4858	8338	7434	5163	2177	1252	7776	0867
(0535)	8124	0719	4414	5045	9335	4699	5210	0654	0921	0351
(0536)	3215	4138	3362	4273	6958	5157	8644	6956	7808	1909
(0537)	7038	5498	4131	6775	2501	3567	6520	9257	8965	9083
(0538)	3798	6405	9568	6422	0388	4825	7273	9342	7564	7435
(0539)	9682	6474	7107	9513	4104	7019	0992	1189	3963	5552
(0540)	3399	8016	0018	3218	8201	5409	0799	2457	6042	0089
(0541)	8353	8425	8121	3688	1164	4330	5809	4344	5171	4134
(0542)	3491	4865	2162	7088	3843	6012	2463	3970	3914	3558
(0543)	9211	5810	7314	6748	8418	2463	7694	1886	3470	2979
(0544)	6086	6595	6171	1852	2931	6211	1038	5233	2220	5297
(0545)	1558	9283	8438	2375	9222	9660	4985	9109	7403	4060

Appendix A
Random Numbers (Continued)

	(01)	(02)	(03)	(04)	(05)	(06)	(07)	(08)	(09)	(10)
(0546)	6865	6937	7089	4307	5602	9988	0831	3705	3016	7393
(0547)	8386	7503	8664	6542	9696	9630	7650	3920	5919	3994
(0548)	9065	7768	8036	4458	8822	8618	4239	5869	2570	6678
(0549)	5112	1243	9982	0526	8952	3885	1740	1597	8696	2927
(0550)	4445	7988	8929	9249	3178	5803	1338	9695	0604	9126
(0551)	8762	6040	4674	4625	6437	3464	0754	6748	5045	5958
(0552)	7699	2996	7835	7709	9730	7210	5752	1673	4484	7719
(0553)	8232	9933	7735	8088	2975	7360	2192	8272	1735	2247
(0554)	8680	7394	3084	7323	2028	0202	0454	6420	5923	1889
(0555)	3982	2003	2340	9052	9671	2345	2021	2205	7175	7614
(0556)	1175	5194	3697	7462	1309	1724	3256	2679	1498	4018
(0557)	2415	3747	4532	7842	8069	5539	5143	8081	9629	7106
(0558)	2849	2700	6524	2128	9596	0635	1439	9994	1147	3046
(0559)	5070	1885	0234	0863	1960	4055	0719	3034	0972	6580
(0560)	6266	7158	5851	9514	5741	2359	5878	3678	0677	3655
(0561)	0408	1822	4454	3256	5606	1078	7257	2816	4596	0011
(0562)	7427	1555	2702	9458	8331	1145	7173	1448	2868	6235
(0563)	2406	5141	3498	6849	1987	4770	8684	9219	5791	9072
(0564)	0155	8612	8066	5180	9164	2946	9086	6635	2259	1110
(0565)	4292	9578	5923	2873	5040	3751	2189	5878	1515	3208
(0566)	3362	5017	3140	2821	8266	9435	2838	0241	2786	1439
(0567)	2401	2063	4397	6497	8420	0322	2438	7749	0077	7097
(0568)	8372	2448	6613	7825	3140	4084	9335	7572	5464	9490
(0569)	8543	4805	1963	6351	3980	7706	4185	4070	6678	3171
(0570)	4872	4010	7752	7554	9277	3983	3514	1766	6251	4473
(0571)	8240	1178	5332	9792	0751	2308	8365	6524	2047	3624
(0572)	4725	8142	6024	6103	2662	2083	3297	1636	9687	2674
(0573)	6623	5891	9252	9083	1531	2873	6040	8998	3711	6898
(0574)	4517	1476	7984	5247	4243	7069	5194	4346	5654	0548
(0575)	5880	5247	0489	2343	7456	7584	5908	9270	6078	1223
(0576)	4925	7608	6965	1906	7153	5735	8693	3948	3993	3130
(0577)	5198	3308	6923	5084	7463	3115	9474	2084	5903	2959
(0578)	1648	9764	6438	6885	8169	1252	2006	4929	1249	4742
(0579)	5376	5104	5381	5411	9055	5240	6274	3916	9993	9931
(0580)	6802	2224	7863	1735	6164	7774	0555	1281	2271	8363
(0581)	7278	4289	7299	0339	3431	7436	5884	1776	3441	4714
(0582)	4822	8027	0412	3328	7371	5213	2627	6546	8548	5796
(0583)	2717	1801	7237	2605	1262	6302	1037	0183	6529	8442
(0584)	9792	1005	2973	1598	9591	8747	5282	8808	2440	9045
(0585)	2304	7896	5011	6394	8970	6293	9832	4667	5018	2116
(0586)	2382	6659	2125	0932	6787	3144	2016	1185	9901	7197
(0587)	1908	0030	1583	1310	7415	0622	3169	9876	5073	9612
(0588)	9456	8764	2429	0572	7474	3528	2315	8274	6317	4915
(0589)	2976	6725	9917	5249	4320	8643	5151	5692	6539	8277
(0590)	8124	0244	9926	4054	1536	2218	3465	2364	3104	4097
(0591)	2210	6820	9321	2658	8663	4055	0209	9013	7461	9876
(0592)	1063	5243	1765	8042	2142	9114	4141	1329	8913	4752
(0593)	0525	5842	7594	8958	7642	9755	7105	5130	4782	6326
(0594)	5957	2103	8609	0148	9762	1953	6252	3454	3347	2232
(0595)	5513	8729	7886	5763	7826	1000	5212	4429	8528	6233

	(01)	(02)	(03)	(04)	(05)	(06)	(07)	(08)	(09)	(10)
(0596)	5290	4452	1109	3560	2341	5425	9881	7830	8857	3538
(0597)	2456	4918	4376	9772	1595	9605	2481	2790	4482	8567
(0598)	8747	5089	5979	1552	1010	5010	6578	9468	7914	1662
(0599)	9937	4025	3790	7513	0774	2563	3411	6108	1327	3427
(0600)	1847	5480	6974	0629	0837	6271	1735	2277	3560	1152
(0601)	8475	7352	3471	0274	9089	8764	6198	0828	4228	0866
(0602)	3310	2025	5125	2938	7569	6095	3960	0733	2252	1577
(0603)	1759	6632	1526	5382	6200	9534	5652	2255	3672	9840
(0604)	0397	0613	3655	1372	8359	2988	7975	1082	7216	4655
(0605)	4117	4159	9881	4754	3784	6041	0446	0043	3477	8119
(0606)	0079	3468	8422	9437	7589	6824	8226	5711	9127	5479
(0607)	8197	3902	9158	0614	6216	9881	0621	0559	0535	4391
(0608)	8815	2986	2557	1741	9296	4742	6580	1339	1596	0334
(0609)	9538	1012	8693	0982	2414	2131	3693	3031	4688	3659
(0610)	9815	5040	2873	9499	0531	6127	5709	3688	7521	5234
(0611)	1160	7550	2939	3381	0974	2480	1555	5317	1858	0006
(0612)	0072	1506	8885	3730	7068	4014	8806	3998	8146	5018
(0613)	5738	0008	2295	8538	6325	9244	1524	8354	2865	2703
(0614)	2543	6003	3129	6854	6766	8919	0082	7141	7696	8452
(0615)	0525	8541	9523	6703	3349	0853	8483	3581	4762	7755
(0616)	0391	3208	2866	8528	6515	1153	6078	2067	9862	8035
(0617)	7724	0404	8519	6749	3981	7985	0230	2291	4485	5595
(0618)	0382	6987	7368	8180	9271	6002	6926	8574	2794	4416
(0619)	2451	3431	0219	8018	3848	0665	0922	1322	3448	1559
(0620)	3122	8642	0078	9153	2191	5328	9525	7620	7340	5351
(0621)	3917	5875	6016	7364	0231	5364	4599	2884	6775	3526
(0622)	8458	7362	0202	3406	1383	8461	0823	5965	8988	3023
(0623)	3367	3572	4629	9636	8462	5985	4960	9868	8539	8404
(0624)	7304	7954	3166	2512	6764	2353	8081	1048	7228	7558
(0625)	3028	0812	7161	6768	1943	6943	5217	3181	7950	8740
(0626)	5659	1611	5849	8119	0627	1251	9059	9820	4459	4289
(0627)	5179	1059	7502	6622	2107	0418	1211	5591	1192	4036
(0628)	5499	3597	6883	2850	0044	8492	5389	8749	0299	8059
(0629)	5558	4151	7739	6019	8044	5079	5475	1571	0852	3468
(0630)	7634	2672	2121	3134	0987	2402	0483	1998	4212	9280
(0631)	1011	5255	8585	9871	9314	7152	9252	1343	0060	3786
(0632)	2158	4498	9569	0531	7569	9327	1764	4836	8693	3927
(0633)	3841	5880	2707	6099	4374	3986	2417	9862	5950	8393
(0634)	8089	3188	9711	4189	1604	5214	9589	6186	7094	5609
(0635)	8159	8594	5348	7040	4190	5291	8775	6727	3619	9468
(0636)	2082	1699	4984	4090	4884	6657	0041	7319	6656	9439
(0637)	7025	9315	2555	7561	7800	7825	5472	7237	0420	6038
(0638)	4673	2699	3854	0924	5624	7782	6924	1196	2231	6330
(0639)	6108	3694	4303	0956	8897	7423	4463	0962	1204	6493
(0640)	8963	3515	0926	9708	8249	4292	1062	4191	6247	8930
(0641)	3710	3030	1001	4051	7276	5045	0682	6524	8965	1490
(0642)	2879	7811	2297	4312	1504	9971	2134	5692	3894	2245
(0643)	5582	2818	5307	4083	5303	9032	6130	0434	1735	8016
(0644)	3426	8191	5388	6146	6433	9728	9395	8569	6319	5909
(0645)	8551	3791	5876	0575	6729	7192	1346	2697	4019	8782

Appendix A
Random Numbers (Continued)

	(01)	(02)	(03)	(04)	(05)	(06)	(07)	(08)	(09)	(10)
(0646)	6534	0640	1886	3406	1181	0640	9943	7034	6930	2357
(0647)	9132	9809	4791	3554	6835	8780	1424	0765	0257	2167
(0648)	6053	9159	9546	3359	7024	8433	2949	8966	4220	0417
(0649)	1447	1398	6862	6042	2359	6920	5690	3481	1396	9523
(0650)	1980	1066	8969	5535	5180	8988	1097	0714	1191	1241
(0651)	8139	8129	1816	9610	0404	0050	2252	1294	7397	1583
(0652)	8589	2962	3121	8156	5775	5066	9344	0955	1688	0549
(0653)	4689	9186	5669	9683	1550	9624	9059	9390	4748	9075
(0654)	5036	4160	3447	7156	9980	7950	6298	9891	3787	3708
(0655)	7065	2166	7773	2417	0537	0686	1799	8190	0488	6048
(0656)	6723	3077	8472	7817	2676	9319	2649	6932	8464	9545
(0657)	7044	9240	1447	1801	8484	3864	4667	5717	0402	8088
(0658)	4731	4877	2389	1569	2464	8630	5046	9293	9455	3149
(0659)	0177	4036	2795	3794	5361	1665	0928	4522	5115	2074
(0660)	0504	6231	9475	2874	0840	6470	4812	2245	0052	8473
(0661)	7792	8976	3281	3857	6905	4431	2170	3967	5038	3788
(0662)	7649	6683	7183	3622	1600	9879	8130	3842	5384	5300
(0663)	2994	2204	9859	0643	2664	8676	1711	8892	8060	1974
(0664)	2524	3617	4192	9436	3528	5222	3021	7361	0396	3560
(0665)	7366	6184	0538	9030	3608	9924	8743	6390	0693	6503
(0666)	6981	5886	8488	9838	9537	8479	2438	2833	1343	6492
(0667)	6943	1201	7963	6832	0518	3277	0723	2684	4160	6246
(0668)	4985	9648	4400	1933	0487	8677	8459	2370	4906	5774
(0669)	1391	5225	1358	8277	0183	2156	1124	2628	8134	9989
(0670)	0918	5060	9770	5703	6666	5634	0210	6035	6378	8073
(0671)	3374	7573	0552	0504	0503	9521	9479	4494	5280	4698
(0672)	9719	4726	8113	6981	3319	8897	6255	7543	6580	0231
(0673)	0557	4097	0361	6854	0706	9392	7418	4827	3944	3124
(0674)	7639	5980	0979	0014	3239	8936	9181	3927	2187	2698
(0675)	1234	4297	1680	0273	5470	7599	0792	2025	4813	0114
(0676)	8415	7467	8055	9800	4123	1719	5462	9294	5327	8239
(0677)	6793	1937	2880	9505	9459	5928	7710	0236	3338	5412
(0678)	5623	9177	6991	2509	5904	0170	6474	6861	1242	7831
(0679)	5509	8769	8265	4621	5507	9019	5759	4546	4171	2164
(0680)	2467	2255	5200	1213	6591	6731	3986	6462	6933	6158
(0681)	6307	3208	1827	1981	4413	8837	6785	5273	7732	7021
(0682)	1032	6210	7413	8069	2031	4015	0603	0757	0707	1496
(0683)	2737	1992	7837	1363	7859	1759	6195	1300	8374	0679
(0684)	3700	7527	6328	2813	0106	8583	5311	1360	0402	0838
(0685)	7441	0054	7486	1744	2732	8451	0041	5269	7174	4909
(0686)	6987	7236	1617	2231	6389	8989	1185	7577	2928	1207
(0687)	7974	2335	0139	1800	1805	1007	8763	7265	3919	8035
(0688)	2691	5274	2138	0057	8628	2166	4687	2075	4320	2574
(0689)	6441	0920	2727	2908	9661	4895	9724	6632	9602	3804
(0690)	3406	5457	0003	0488	2666	3525	4840	5218	6114	6479
(0691)	9504	3183	7165	6889	1694	2093	7096	0549	9926	3805
(0692)	1509	7852	3468	8376	0982	6637	7680	3331	9293	5469
(0693)	9099	0661	2828	0125	4952	4941	2468	9833	9589	4995
(0694)	3761	3181	9101	0531	2544	2371	3978	3511	5689	3833
(0695)	6856	5262	0676	6098	8926	1670	3812	2981	0722	9462

	(01)	(02)	(03)	(04)	(05)	(06)	(07)	(08)	(09)	(10)
(0696)	4171	5748	6808	1811	4359	6087	1138	6702	8936	5446
(0697)	0638	8296	6775	7427	0557	8048	7108	2599	7864	3116
(0698)	7164	3334	9492	8816	8758	5761	5872	9730	0117	8813
(0699)	2727	0632	7649	9218	1808	4890	5098	8393	5465	6965
(0700)	4982	7135	0666	3372	3817	4135	1769	6059	0409	2444
(0701)	5611	1844	4965	3094	2866	9969	3683	5041	8586	6642
(0702)	2241	8476	1709	1137	7573	6879	9307	1425	5374	1775
(0703)	1440	9840	6362	0648	2207	2709	2534	6157	8272	9227
(0704)	0003	7833	3120	6855	4591	3609	6104	1353	4052	4567
(0705)	6893	6254	7283	7639	0679	7541	0774	2804	8233	4481
(0706)	3094	1454	3435	9232	6025	4422	1670	1807	4418	0674
(0707)	5759	0034	6902	7795	0576	1639	9564	4689	4225	5049
(0708)	9992	8446	8965	3765	1532	7194	3502	9246	2393	1315
(0709)	5778	7200	0282	3940	0932	8552	9815	3682	6578	3535
(0710)	1732	5934	8611	8284	6209	6717	4035	1073	5276	3180
(0711)	1208	7020	1152	6095	1362	8538	2947	0617	4204	7649
(0712)	6393	5503	4796	6935	0326	1184	9838	5463	9334	6839
(0713)	1936	5889	8893	0455	4391	7842	3327	5687	3260	8944
(0714)	9664	5342	0174	5504	2306	8883	3926	4083	0824	0596
(0715)	3966	0039	3035	3585	3858	9012	8179	4987	3502	7164
(0716)	0502	9928	1955	1383	3718	2173	3298	1538	7767	1508
(0717)	9307	9303	6814	4938	5091	8172	6723	8802	6833	2854
(0718)	2024	1266	5528	8515	8469	5064	3613	2321	6533	2091
(0719)	9092	0388	6266	1850	2946	4776	6124	8344	0963	0770
(0720)	5779	2904	1183	3777	3298	7407	2154	0330	6723	1392
(0721)	4522	9969	9882	5068	6576	4765	7625	8380	8397	6725
(0722)	0563	9867	7788	5798	7323	0478	1081	2376	2487	6707
(0723)	9590	4700	6386	1026	5315	6299	9914	2858	7661	4583
(0724)	2582	8643	3668	9425	3540	0091	3144	4163	8728	7328
(0725)	8538	9255	1185	8067	6897	4535	4159	9674	8168	5693
(0726)	6554	9028	1314	2506	9984	2218	7192	7846	3982	6812
(0727)	6354	6818	8235	5065	6935	7701	5464	6319	2883	2284
(0728)	5954	4193	4032	6150	7531	9443	3421	1850	8230	1568
(0729)	5684	4899	8442	6737	7681	5827	7149	0267	4031	4085
(0730)	0220	8590	3882	0787	1661	6724	5662	8533	1082	5019
(0731)	1705	7107	3815	9046	0724	4932	8482	6318	8217	6912
(0732)	6998	4801	7898	0796	2042	5985	1373	2710	0711	9433
(0733)	1724	9286	0934	5815	9075	9045	0792	6729	7451	3195
(0734)	6071	9278	7907	7553	2046	4509	5427	3933	2033	4813
(0735)	1766	3707	3910	4111	2277	0489	6078	8376	2384	2734
(0736)	3784	4613	2169	3158	4443	5264	2467	8751	2391	3218
(0737)	3348	1716	0277	0555	7702	1046	6693	1632	6966	1987
(0738)	9314	3414	4267	7293	3743	6996	7858	7966	1831	8262
(0739)	6117	8729	1433	9475	1667	0631	7174	6092	4200	7699
(0740)	6878	3232	4613	9294	8430	6681	0337	0766	1629	3623
(0741)	3928	1654	0008	4764	5062	9364	0634	1397	8793	7104
(0742)	2566	5741	4481	5665	3823	2826	5450	8082	5437	7804
(0743)	2890	5658	1222	5732	1135	8192	0508	1830	4558	7723
(0744)	8265	1045	4027	7383	0196	8017	8276	8643	7697	5856
(0745)	6443	7789	4756	1419	9209	2038	1752	3176	4238	4724

Appendix A
Random Numbers (Continued)

	(01)	(02)	(03)	(04)	(05)	(06)	(07)	(08)	(09)	(10)
(0746)	7281	0910	4995	7982	8468	5783	7183	4379	3749	9371
(0747)	2190	7939	5538	4529	2178	6548	6755	1939	3654	4986
(0748)	1893	8822	3088	5028	8481	3659	8475	0984	0762	5513
(0749)	1117	7494	6114	4217	0073	9846	6646	8821	6171	4526
(0750)	8916	1513	4030	5336	7272	4701	6181	6513	3929	4532
(0751)	6769	0543	6710	1740	7089	1605	0899	0941	3749	5562
(0752)	9414	8874	5684	4424	8595	6680	4868	8345	6415	6526
(0753)	6014	9587	3390	9091	5157	4277	8863	6976	3401	1038
(0754)	7712	0453	5056	7502	2141	9951	7818	1565	7396	4169
(0755)	0609	9057	5360	3360	0734	1784	7928	8831	5497	6612
(0756)	3605	8858	7026	7081	6958	9417	0658	4766	9322	0493
(0757)	9475	5486	5700	3485	0771	0735	0988	0269	0566	6089
(0758)	8144	0281	2834	7705	4467	1841	1297	6019	3243	1630
(0759)	4541	1380	3885	3335	3522	8085	3421	0024	3861	2982
(0760)	3835	2958	1654	8160	0923	5955	7896	3984	4560	5040
(0761)	8692	2767	9775	9640	4431	6359	2537	0009	0285	3757
(0762)	9929	5383	3934	9388	5462	9264	6830	7115	5315	7792
(0763)	9329	0420	1724	8831	7490	2117	4260	7175	9202	6574
(0764)	9145	4433	8801	7684	2831	9620	9653	0327	2932	8643
(0765)	9750	8529	2033	8209	6060	0468	4289	4106	4646	2045
(0766)	8943	8822	4633	2101	7498	1429	3095	3660	4055	4380
(0767)	4191	1083	2856	0157	8128	7200	1461	4949	3559	9059
(0768)	0879	2735	8183	3449	0107	2480	0868	9168	6236	8643
(0769)	8465	9939	9894	6374	7900	3575	7442	1427	4849	8701
(0770)	0672	2165	2377	4254	3246	3098	1783	0781	2067	1119
(0771)	0177	4934	2660	0969	4543	4248	1452	2258	4753	9626
(0772)	2747	1895	7884	0264	5513	1861	3682	8770	5019	3160
(0773)	9373	1006	1156	5301	5749	4160	7624	6564	5213	4804
(0774)	0502	4854	9608	8976	2798	1436	5510	2205	5444	2762
(0775)	9678	3070	0045	5958	2649	8355	4070	2294	2717	6486
(0776)	1972	2927	6493	3247	7575	0875	4142	1645	8584	8074
(0777)	6661	3723	6121	3420	5236	9929	2678	0831	9236	9538
(0778)	7772	7547	8137	8438	3883	6784	0493	1814	2206	4820
(0779)	9724	0755	5453	7547	0697	2908	6216	2452	2846	3399
(0780)	4746	1754	5856	5062	5885	8279	3451	5560	1726	0059
(0781)	1378	9955	9376	4931	5788	7316	4087	6150	5244	2450
(0782)	2308	0913	6725	6888	7411	5235	4397	7968	6623	6558
(0783)	7417	2786	4802	6852	4190	6308	0993	3882	3317	8488
(0784)	1765	7964	7718	2163	0045	8101	3559	2992	0061	7616
(0785)	1391	3764	2138	3658	3413	5954	8527	5996	6938	6673
(0786)	2507	6860	4392	1272	2700	4447	2675	3264	2879	3880
(0787)	3017	3418	3182	6066	7506	5370	5286	0701	3383	2192
(0788)	3204	9788	8326	7956	6284	2513	1508	3562	8560	4742
(0789)	9233	2020	2763	5122	6985	0239	0112	9512	4271	3923
(0790)	9745	7502	1562	7205	5093	4552	8847	9147	7182	3369
(0791)	3538	8951	1692	5928	6217	7265	6584	7111	2429	3112
(0792)	3959	6409	8332	7467	2328	4901	1159	1889	2299	2449
(0793)	7072	2108	1512	3437	8804	9389	9058	5769	4055	7838
(0794)	3621	3922	8942	8055	8894	5213	6728	9501	6314	3637
(0795)	4827	9336	1850	9038	1114	1566	9689	9370	9285	2698

	(01)	(02)	(03)	(04)	(05)	(06)	(07)	(08)	(09)	(10)
(0796)	8644	9867	4366	3095	5570	2477	2043	9804	2764	9260
(0797)	0643	5873	6914	9935	2789	9041	4930	3041	7002	2910
(0798)	7827	1591	3634	4528	0053	3104	3036	9366	3795	6359
(0799)	5756	7772	4649	8500	8411	4974	3392	0734	3714	6227
(0800)	5196	5083	4940	1418	6029	2631	9510	6955	8917	1111
(0801)	3116	1400	5277	8522	2155	6305	8549	8693	5699	9795
(0802)	3137	5970	9837	0026	7407	8780	8063	7477	7329	3495
(0803)	4217	0434	6702	8747	8524	3093	5107	3734	6608	2124
(0804)	0295	7860	1202	7786	8865	3137	3779	8132	0880	4350
(0805)	9299	4686	1880	7537	9438	2071	9576	8590	0983	9663
(0806)	8888	3589	3813	9911	6808	7730	5361	6022	4617	9723
(0807)	1299	3551	5447	9755	4777	1545	5109	6274	9595	6374
(0808)	2380	2854	7563	7040	7324	3512	0747	0099	1276	6490
(0809)	6815	1785	9059	7875	0439	5494	8792	1799	1622	7361
(0810)	3053	2650	7918	6947	3666	3087	4794	8370	4007	5401
(0811)	7257	1315	1105	2874	3074	1833	1738	1365	4286	8386
(0812)	2957	4380	4779	2441	1325	6259	5898	8752	7128	5525
(0813)	5955	0701	0293	6332	7297	1250	5095	5638	5364	2864
(0814)	0190	9213	9307	4453	8318	6934	9277	9636	8068	8426
(0815)	0586	3247	0180	6782	9098	1187	5589	7132	8274	6896
(0816)	1142	6778	3882	4992	0609	9008	2623	1647	7739	2197
(0817)	4549	9224	9583	6316	8879	4913	6421	9186	8918	4245
(0818)	0469	2882	4560	5123	1599	3294	5277	8499	1948	8513
(0819)	1600	0716	3679	4540	6905	0401	5311	2678	2137	9894
(0820)	7519	6867	8359	6636	7603	9126	4313	0724	1195	0162
(0821)	2859	2601	5332	5435	6703	6507	7500	0565	4098	2848
(0822)	4716	9195	0826	9017	1733	2031	0505	6993	5393	2843
(0823)	2313	7496	4246	0255	0927	3130	9764	9965	6047	5607
(0824)	4605	9784	6546	7678	7295	9611	8505	4811	6035	3349
(0825)	8961	1939	8390	1286	2757	0918	6222	9735	3709	2941
(0826)	3925	1915	0612	3367	9544	4905	8853	7399	4043	7354
(0827)	2720	0049	8888	3627	2009	8354	1424	4569	4600	7043
(0828)	9290	9394	2931	8414	2523	0429	9186	3512	8424	9058
(0829)	9991	9094	2421	3651	2947	6690	3936	2836	4942	8911
(0830)	0752	1913	4936	7317	4295	4784	2938	1191	5741	6791
(0831)	0935	2689	3313	9946	2771	4568	4618	3805	2953	7157
(0832)	3259	9945	0670	5434	7616	4247	8844	8336	7541	5893
(0833)	1636	8664	0540	7733	7597	5507	2458	7683	3091	7280
(0834)	0762	2946	7918	1284	0950	1467	3271	4981	6718	1418
(0835)	7084	6247	1959	7163	7296	6455	8518	4910	2177	6372
(0836)	0338	1173	1765	2251	5347	0160	9223	4214	2148	8161
(0837)	9610	1555	7467	2940	5366	6729	7038	0121	4676	8043
(0838)	4172	2269	5296	9347	1493	1348	8642	6586	2664	6357
(0839)	2380	8904	1583	0158	4814	5027	5098	8295	3762	6517
(0840)	8783	4842	0708	1580	5024	6335	9719	8175	0504	8364
(0841)	7948	2813	6930	3545	6834	1132	6308	0099	0532	8813
(0842)	0926	5724	1272	3947	3555	5866	7630	6282	4574	9746
(0843)	0915	9383	6128	8217	2364	7584	4033	4780	0258	2885
(0844)	3860	5962	0074	7075	3611	9242	2792	2182	0840	1003
(0845)	4717	2819	7127	4705	2172	1784	3984	0652	0041	1200

Appendix A
Random Numbers (Continued)

	(01)	(02)	(03)	(04)	(05)	(06)	(07)	(08)	(09)	(10)
(0846)	3187	4239	4166	6408	6419	6239	4886	8671	0654	8419
(0847)	1359	3470	5508	8446	1448	3746	8485	0233	0453	2712
(0848)	1425	6071	9579	4267	9726	4367	6895	5237	1883	1445
(0849)	5224	4262	8868	7404	6159	1366	8041	5768	0087	4259
(0850)	4891	5131	9307	6346	1528	5664	9311	5415	3721	1851
(0851)	3908	7725	4274	0385	4474	2343	7704	1929	1991	6477
(0852)	4148	1197	4376	1532	5786	5306	8790	3247	2226	7075
(0853)	5613	2568	2612	4334	8382	1697	4366	0404	5273	4472
(0854)	0229	9353	3798	2934	4885	5325	0360	9409	9372	3733
(0855)	6847	9865	8575	5570	2109	9834	3077	9266	0835	7110
(0856)	6098	9397	2716	7588	5664	9997	0069	2602	9010	3817
(0857)	4121	4488	9168	4438	4846	1271	3124	8489	5607	8864
(0858)	0415	3179	7505	0361	5085	6453	0361	7698	6963	9726
(0859)	8332	2074	1243	6094	5130	1071	2830	2810	5623	6072
(0860)	7154	4203	1326	7292	0924	7507	4767	6846	2251	9238
(0861)	0060	7468	1009	1448	1922	2908	2341	6706	9158	3362
(0862)	5020	6791	7375	1683	9306	2466	9192	2887	1683	4949
(0863)	3498	9584	8911	7420	5721	1521	6067	7844	0697	0692
(0864)	8487	0109	2315	8769	5936	4964	9564	3365	0719	8956
(0865)	8380	2296	3911	7384	0196	2056	4791	3403	4685	8104
(0866)	9532	2837	8051	0212	8723	2181	6996	1973	8910	6280
(0867)	9402	3168	9065	2104	4477	1279	1431	8720	1453	4517
(0868)	7517	9422	9288	4161	5760	1921	7707	9932	4023	4471
(0869)	1135	2329	1528	3998	7640	9051	6283	6701	6367	7157
(0870)	7957	8522	8944	1593	7010	7061	2464	0954	5498	1978
(0871)	9327	6203	1880	0256	9741	9659	5112	8196	4337	9276
(0872)	2310	5621	1505	1610	0960	2922	1941	0674	5712	5277
(0873)	7180	9065	8017	1542	7806	4254	9028	6069	6339	1820
(0874)	9662	9661	6524	1405	8136	2354	7031	7429	4126	2449
(0875)	2787	1110	4864	7455	9510	3940	9936	1030	1908	5917
(0876)	5521	6851	2278	1399	4197	9288	2847	7042	1199	6200
(0877)	6187	4716	1858	2525	1259	5367	5626	9135	9302	0377
(0878)	9813	7761	8394	3657	3119	6611	3999	0393	3573	6020
(0879)	9201	6680	2151	6306	4909	6514	5638	0966	4105	8298
(0880)	4236	3038	2471	1860	2101	3173	7411	0517	1969	1954
(0881)	7278	1168	2435	1323	8517	4830	4567	7779	8776	8780
(0882)	9457	9199	8395	6779	7344	9078	3116	1489	0519	2707
(0883)	0579	0483	9233	9773	0263	6683	5029	1703	0206	0855
(0884)	9260	3414	8135	2834	4311	0947	4148	3558	0726	3541
(0885)	5412	5958	3973	5545	8003	8220	2967	2507	8467	2934
(0886)	3581	1610	5795	8866	7126	2784	5640	4309	9634	1852
(0887)	8436	2893	8257	0777	4540	6009	5477	1334	3534	6580
(0888)	9640	2527	3691	8136	4592	7541	6396	7739	9477	5192
(0889)	7586	6815	3515	1886	2264	3426	6367	1191	3598	9381
(0890)	3060	1874	0397	8338	6069	4762	4917	4169	4050	8970
(0891)	3382	6204	0522	3293	9465	8134	4615	5019	7880	9931
(0892)	4744	4147	4574	3527	8031	3703	9791	2450	2506	1464
(0893)	0942	2028	2411	8015	8464	5548	1249	2350	5545	9075
(0894)	3702	0894	2571	7338	8411	1417	7891	6654	5180	5057
(0895)	2885	1537	6255	0894	4233	6107	4106	5087	8805	1926

	(01)	(02)	(03)	(04)	(05)	(06)	(07)	(08)	(09)	(10)
(0896)	3576	6949	2484	2551	9675	8900	3174	7995	7461	1236
(0897)	9662	6259	2696	8137	9479	2601	1907	2981	2396	0007
(0898)	1869	3433	1447	0945	0577	2452	5442	7141	4180	9753
(0899)	1374	0475	1034	3132	4952	2729	1958	4333	9060	0321
(0900)	0766	8975	0608	4026	5839	8318	0650	9464	2706	6525
(0901)	2100	7326	7018	9958	9445	2643	9421	9157	4185	1032
(0902)	6807	6792	5816	4349	3092	7956	3394	3058	0645	8111
(0903)	7234	1494	9442	4269	4978	8125	6341	6765	1635	5961
(0904)	8776	0850	5546	7913	8524	6617	1285	1985	8018	5080
(0905)	5177	3641	0195	6622	2408	0312	4961	6502	8367	9283
(0906)	2402	3998	5325	7027	0220	9941	4140	3928	5612	1411
(0907)	6060	4630	8633	0222	8301	4723	7557	0725	9077	4985
(0908)	4291	3518	8346	8914	0354	1545	6221	0681	1126	4889
(0909)	5592	9667	2719	0648	3855	6811	1348	5231	5018	7240
(0910)	2206	7188	2454	8878	0097	0502	8531	1664	9198	5898
(0911)	8579	6161	8772	8794	1013	7690	3133	7367	3560	0811
(0912)	6339	8758	3452	1874	9922	3415	5967	1249	6401	3693
(0913)	1257	3342	0578	0421	7136	0986	1779	3030	5529	0456
(0914)	3364	5830	6880	9511	8283	1373	4703	3970	8559	3616
(0915)	4205	8860	2834	5777	8087	0858	3563	4480	8567	3092
(0916)	9836	4178	6117	3532	4786	2595	1104	8810	4898	8722
(0917)	9027	1980	7938	1043	3316	7052	3053	7698	3688	9244
(0918)	8197	4627	2600	7308	2581	1697	6551	2078	6064	4583
(0919)	0000	3976	3912	5342	9810	8641	5803	4944	5978	7550
(0920)	9621	4713	8841	9875	3234	5235	4926	0943	2688	8284
(0921)	6769	9007	8506	2608	7019	1505	3674	5388	6541	8016
(0922)	8213	9055	2613	0032	0996	3930	7931	7295	1276	3014
(0923)	3988	0159	0608	6186	6682	1464	4326	9993	2359	8382
(0924)	9452	4120	5002	6801	2003	7341	6796	1589	4672	2199
(0925)	2381	0993	6767	6008	1107	2032	1751	7440	8815	8768
(0926)	7524	5485	6068	4254	2047	7742	2245	1759	4640	5881
(0927)	4606	4843	1984	5230	1255	6114	2318	5946	6766	5590
(0928)	1848	5140	1087	1506	0634	3004	3640	2911	2764	3557
(0929)	3936	9811	2454	3704	4403	0774	5404	0055	0420	6970
(0930)	6476	3957	5010	3716	4116	4246	6806	8430	5740	6938
(0931)	5281	0159	5006	0973	7525	7844	8395	4393	3050	9421
(0932)	8797	7672	0003	0216	7986	1179	0479	4632	7066	3436
(0933)	3428	8087	1303	7174	9212	6988	3913	5341	6468	5038
(0934)	6508	3295	6353	5977	8630	8486	6703	7846	6209	2368
(0935)	5281	0147	1511	3823	5925	6631	4546	3278	1040	6250
(0936)	2092	4579	2416	8650	7171	9144	8815	9567	4323	4400
(0937)	0837	1924	8488	5961	4880	7635	9185	5772	5522	8768
(0938)	2692	9746	2683	2433	3701	0385	1898	9057	3887	3651
(0939)	2498	1796	9704	9252	8598	5785	0079	0973	9757	0219
(0940)	5191	8288	5151	6474	7942	2545	3535	6372	6998	9471
(0941)	7784	1486	2190	3590	5284	9276	7741	2987	5485	7021
(0942)	8643	8979	4173	0605	5006	1828	5150	4595	1732	3991
(0943)	6702	6683	2110	1017	6506	6960	3530	9214	3174	6651
(0944)	8842	0882	0413	7626	7581	1198	3411	0669	1596	9053
(0945)	1181	4773	1291	2165	9961	9974	4646	7845	5514	9147

Appendix A
Random Numbers (Continued)

	(01)	(02)	(03)	(04)	(05)	(06)	(07)	(08)	(09)	(10)
(0946)	6175	6752	5911	0616	2288	9490	1870	7893	5805	9646
(0947)	7089	7457	1975	7832	6045	5171	2515	8175	5161	8416
(0948)	3578	3430	8952	2195	6192	4579	8932	1701	0391	2763
(0949)	5713	7775	3952	1465	1286	7283	6609	8156	8086	1183
(0950)	6459	9951	1753	7498	3749	6813	3538	8005	3414	5435
(0951)	6139	7434	5599	5505	2102	7682	1286	3310	0565	0334
(0952)	7474	5267	3866	8649	8627	7352	7351	5256	6336	2236
(0953)	5966	4197	6904	6805	3141	8759	2373	1990	3573	3233
(0954)	6103	5744	3420	7920	5496	1987	7518	9868	5013	4646
(0955)	4419	0211	2427	3619	5788	3109	9676	3253	3779	9372
(0956)	6852	0499	6425	7158	9236	2629	1532	4931	1421	0857
(0957)	7466	0818	4912	2345	5768	4679	7649	0650	6631	7136
(0958)	3374	1183	7893	7158	3423	7007	1673	3750	4731	6810
(0959)	6969	0549	5498	8611	4107	5090	5259	5562	0411	9146
(0960)	9563	5082	8709	5541	3084	7411	5474	7134	8403	9290
(0961)	1285	7372	5300	8148	6579	2746	9931	8769	7927	6983
(0962)	8191	8654	8174	0184	4040	9767	1422	9940	8601	1699
(0963)	2325	6875	7200	3629	5954	8916	3368	9306	9443	6263
(0964)	6506	0242	6167	3730	0076	4664	6429	1242	0924	9825
(0965)	8857	8392	3415	1481	8163	2389	1981	9805	2116	9082
(0966)	3616	0100	4060	5199	9565	8405	5163	5539	2429	6207
(0967)	4362	4360	9416	2916	6550	8004	9289	2890	0022	9313
(0968)	8931	5756	4918	4696	6610	2090	4056	6476	8968	9738
(0969)	6173	1506	9108	4737	7826	1662	6574	4411	8847	1488
(0970)	3829	6480	4295	4146	9751	6942	1004	3424	4442	4083
(0971)	9931	5941	7958	8663	8610	7132	8324	0803	6611	9014
(0972)	2642	3552	2306	6364	3038	2760	9561	8498	3428	3362
(0973)	4273	3537	0607	3179	2689	9566	8793	4522	9702	7553
(0974)	5844	9966	5278	8376	2003	8016	8657	7745	9839	9465
(0975)	9128	0372	1093	2126	0403	5516	6257	0305	0414	3850
(0976)	6420	7590	4611	8426	0091	9089	4580	3581	7927	5047
(0977)	2828	6616	3557	5857	3605	7502	9691	0471	0384	1735
(0973)	0077	3175	7409	4289	0947	2580	4679	9201	3675	1205
(0979)	9008	5320	6743	0018	8816	3486	3799	1721	5736	8857
(0980)	8662	6213	8331	1274	3146	4338	5313	2234	2123	6129
(0981)	7919	4186	6876	9219	0906	7561	0172	2113	7563	1431
(0982)	5317	3771	3924	2605	2744	3392	3806	4732	4647	7111
(0983)	813/	1338	2489	8719	8187	6150	4979	0656	2865	8039
(0984)	5379	9078	1477	9409	1300	4823	1573	3339	2263	9721
(0985)	1625	6028	4571	8623	3733	4170	8499	6929	9511	7228
(0986)	3912	8891	1539	6050	2731	8109	1978	5070	0048	1607
(0987)	0493	1419	7088	2381	1503	1962	0277	8794	2421	3674
(0988)	6879	4002	2154	0100	3226	8934	3495	8476	6846	8499
(0989)	2371	8646	3729	6962	6761	2821	0476	6715	0340	7879
(0990)	7631	4064	5632	5938	3035	9938	7295	2728	6287	5855
(0991)	3817	8756	5483	0260	4261	2484	7767	8860	2393	2113
(0992)	3099	2722	1173	6905	0432	6262	1365	7353	0953	9048
(0993)	8414	8599	9223	8546	6816	3294	3099	3524	2939	8820
(0994)	0678	2259	0751	1523	3748	8831	3167	9020	3476	1149
(0995)	3654	2435	7973	9592	2217	8272	1919	5524	3239	4759

	(01)	(02)	(03)	(04)	(05)	(06)	(07)	(08)	(09)	(10)
(0996)	8916	6660	4518	8027	6525	8778	4967	8065	5392	8828
(0997)	8007	5569	4804	9190	3833	3791	5380	5135	3335	7930
(0998)	6729	8544	5686	7975	5458	9391	4099	9628	4774	9336
(0999)	5526	2610	3108	4631	8367	8688	4020	0241	7263	1199
(1000)	3965	6792	5548	2015	6253	5481	7713	5676	0614	0945
(1001)	6298	9080	0817	3385	4615	2152	9548	8808	0625	6622
(1002)	9928	8727	9740	9117	9476	9090	7641	5288	9120	8665
(1003)	0397	3560	5072	1189	9492	0400	4325	2152	8754	8071
(1004)	9311	8654	1898	0131	5061	4212	3470	5980	1519	1179
(1005)	4758	9230	5374	0188	2969	3180	9323	4745	9775	1331
(1006)	7512	0043	5092	9177	1860	3677	4151	8705	2635	7960
(1007)	2748	4062	2544	9106	5540	6298	4071	1925	1413	9034
(1008)	3577	3003	2259	8262	2545	1887	3451	3104	8751	6624
(1009)	3064	8749	3702	4763	7709	4810	4134	8618	3431	2247
(1010)	8669	5741	9872	0400	7751	8792	5222	1001	2758	3346
(1011)	4436	4910	4001	8123	9930	0956	5191	5313	4593	8167
(1012)	9093	5498	6399	3938	5836	9880	8812	1788	1097	8511
(1013)	7441	0292	6687	7705	5546	9752	5317	2828	8332	5660
(1014)	2612	5953	3044	3086	9952	9610	4392	4971	1149	0436
(1015)	0037	6782	3614	0705	3264	8306	0918	5928	1837	5541
(1016)	2388	3242	0438	0877	8071	6615	8845	9425	9707	2709
(1017)	5039	4691	1071	4995	6792	0410	8178	0391	0910	7918
(1018)	1314	6690	1070	6634	2462	3822	4095	8373	0929	4047
(1019)	1457	6784	4526	9707	0077	6508	1121	7536	7698	4185
(1020)	2103	2573	4812	1416	0804	7846	7468	6875	8857	6925
(1021)	9427	7746	9571	3215	5175	8864	8545	6096	6064	5257
(1022)	2848	8233	8049	8292	7185	9232	7999	2812	5500	3331
(1023)	7280	9709	9913	7575	4713	0944	6730	1798	8183	5546
(1024)	4205	9020	9855	7801	9286	2139	1099	9841	7765	2490
(1025)	0690	5140	9659	5598	8158	3650	1893	7391	5996	4337
(1026)	4384	8848	3274	9901	4556	8919	1260	4119	5213	5592
(1027)	5926	7845	2515	1275	8162	4707	1017	9049	5457	9800
(1028)	4878	9360	5214	1184	6398	6153	8811	9116	5085	5061
(1029)	1535	1050	5852	8298	9842	4866	2604	4474	9686	3323
(1030)	3083	5707	0565	0330	2319	4725	1122	3715	0357	6293
(1031)	6094	9390	5022	1428	7535	9567	9765	9749	2440	0262
(1032)	2948	4476	3213	2795	5845	0900	7333	1495	2636	0649
(1033)	2887	0653	3070	8721	9610	9963	5798	0926	6933	9701
(1034)	4619	4401	4076	2642	5227	2219	0330	2059	9472	7867
(1035)	2447	8595	1840	6617	9321	8080	0025	7335	4461	5226
(1036)	1195	0421	2542	4442	6613	5192	2443	4266	1272	9666
(1037)	5379	7354	4999	8987	3202	9842	3877	0450	1287	3863
(1038)	8405	1797	2008	9259	0070	6545	4147	5689	1573	6046
(1039)	3717	1254	2609	1664	8697	9506	1356	7124	6407	0462
(1040)	4838	7616	6032	7532	6722	7724	5180	8229	0632	5100
(1041)	8901	2812	1375	2706	7379	6664	5958	3549	7398	4661
(1042)	8524	5770	0178	0444	6067	0391	7413	1635	9162	3688
(1043)	7403	3885	0978	6629	3165	9034	3502	4911	8341	9019
(1044)	0720	0365	4598	5055	0603	3294	7190	5608	1727	2402
(1045)	3052	5114	8015	6061	7839	6774	7527	9219	7406	7621

Appendix A
Random Numbers (Continued)

	(01)	(02)	(03)	(04)	(05)	(06)	(07)	(08)	(09)	(10)
(1046)	6604	0998	2870	3620	1116	9379	9705	4450	4190	8979
(1047)	4320	7996	5082	4524	7503	5056	4148	6534	7837	8910
(1048)	5562	1865	5915	4707	3974	0338	3133	9373	1518	9787
(1049)	1348	0430	6576	7639	0680	2533	3689	8513	4991	4286
(1050)	3757	3937	4405	5679	9745	7271	4862	3004	9485	7509
(1051)	5693	2153	5938	7934	5940	4843	7157	2198	1044	1321
(1052)	7186	2318	8587	1573	5576	6918	0449	4913	0681	3064
(1053)	3917	5044	5786	8371	1165	8775	1300	8085	1842	1461
(1054)	3463	4800	4790	8911	3270	5399	2385	5777	3865	2722
(1055)	7239	4219	0889	3773	4615	1081	5317	8778	5848	7846
(1056)	1650	2670	2552	5729	7782	4960	7037	4277	7213	5571
(1057)	4020	4312	4748	8005	6840	8807	1783	3813	8703	3073
(1058)	9833	6341	9503	1243	9380	2817	2755	9943	3479	1423
(1059)	6170	1067	6022	0524	2790	3771	2724	6157	8194	8766
(1060)	2348	4928	1370	2096	3262	0188	4461	5062	1767	1432
(1061)	4802	9180	3495	0578	8960	0459	9693	8205	9599	3775
(1062)	7419	2660	3658	6741	6702	5953	1515	1437	3420	2708
(1063)	4725	8598	8323	4810	8286	5287	3183	4978	2050	0150
(1064)	9081	3785	4525	9318	7047	7410	2544	2860	7618	1719
(1065)	5922	9535	1465	4186	6696	2342	2514	0832	9953	9270
(1066)	2147	9138	0665	2087	2617	7462	8793	7629	7471	0673
(1067)	9480	5595	9918	1514	1995	8497	1119	5364	7544	9807
(1068)	7819	6332	1195	0954	0943	7099	2855	3259	7751	6621
(1069)	8162	9746	3559	8286	4285	4122	1967	7167	2891	1926
(1070)	2354	8617	1659	2849	8407	7133	5227	3966	5386	1434
(1071)	5637	5655	3449	5971	0870	4505	2271	7473	8684	8845
(1072)	4673	7262	7583	4410	3010	6697	6995	8571	2007	1293
(1073)	2233	8495	6293	3658	2957	8334	5596	2312	8025	1597
(1074)	7406	5941	6638	0219	7959	4708	3401	5042	4786	2652
(1075)	4107	4742	5406	2913	4322	4520	0271	5008	6958	9965
(1076)	1148	7441	7378	4721	9454	1846	4809	9027	8659	0722
(1077)	8091	1526	2283	3454	4861	8758	4520	9719	4826	5974
(1078)	9652	4862	1765	1098	4897	1330	2558	5876	9997	9951
(1079)	8490	4221	2208	5302	6985	6898	3151	5353	0486	4773
(1080)	1629	1124	7891	9667	4010	4255	3777	8725	8715	2451
(1081)	6414	9125	6632	0762	7086	1824	8819	4761	8871	1554
(1082)	8066	1189	9482	6951	2949	4739	0089	3068	9951	6695
(1083)	5476	1324	9676	2553	4412	5533	1687	8801	2507	7480
(1084)	7112	5950	0354	7714	5969	7999	4451	0196	4318	0048
(1085)	4725	9971	1695	6533	0870	6879	1673	2288	3209	3757
(1086)	7742	5929	1185	4112	8461	1600	3955	6209	4969	2431
(1087)	9083	7123	3923	4878	0120	9542	5174	9078	2030	2760
(1088)	6907	2000	8132	1728	8108	8356	1800	8620	3929	5123
(1089)	9427	2168	9017	8452	0286	1809	3188	8547	4363	4444
(1090)	4671	0931	1749	3245	4982	7790	4441	4165	8156	9309
(1091)	2374	8754	9120	5074	5126	3763	2273	7203	0605	8107
(1092)	1270	1001	6385	0062	8266	5602	4374	4763	8719	4272
(1093)	7814	3283	5762	8660	4735	4188	5809	9143	5716	3375
(1094)	3287	0030	5441	8424	2462	6389	3816	7045	1597	7673
(1095)	1782	9669	5084	1892	0722	8005	5738	8036	9397	0855

A

	(01)	(02)	(03)	(04)	(05)	(06)	(07)	(08)	(09)	(10)
(1096)	0136	7696	7145	4645	9540	4656	9305	3789	7969	6844
(1097)	1046	5995	0048	7537	0636	5269	3449	1766	3784	2508
(1098)	8551	9412	9924	0815	1688	8249	9641	6234	8920	6212
(1099)	2860	2652	6287	6001	6985	3448	7113	2168	1040	2384
(1100)	3008	6796	2967	7178	5682	2084	8379	4223	2826	1112
(1101)	2146	6023	1609	7252	5376	8007	5887	7190	7155	6140
(1102)	9063	5186	7137	8421	6120	2471	0698	9049	5805	2443
(1103)	2976	5576	1700	9242	6105	0734	3492	5900	7875	6756
(1104)	0059	6742	1564	6457	8246	6393	1704	0621	2272	3331
(1105)	3122	0759	4205	3082	7490	8516	3306	7565	7394	3871
(1106)	2964	8729	9645	6407	8850	7231	4440	0985	2322	4160
(1107)	0400	5876	3827	5613	9292	5894	9404	0031	0387	2961
(1108)	1694	2121	8428	5146	5639	2928	3838	5645	2188	4273
(1109)	2466	9064	5202	6429	2698	9509	2384	4484	7221	9942
(1110)	1340	6417	4590	6281	0902	0291	1966	7264	1234	4954
(1111)	7714	5834	1586	8493	2727	7428	1942	4079	1050	3609
(1112)	8426	2600	9038	2803	3266	7995	2052	8079	4552	7728
(1113)	3429	4534	4825	8122	2641	4271	4560	5412	8234	5545
(1114)	9456	6490	8590	7171	7702	5956	6799	9018	2591	0034
(1115)	6206	6073	0527	2819	7301	1814	9243	8653	8594	7906
(1116)	7930	5671	0663	1306	7642	5920	1925	3713	6293	5591
(1117)	2020	5100	7899	6561	8843	4576	0673	2494	9082	2353
(1118)	8123	8340	3396	2719	9280	1912	1903	3779	9529	8196
(1119)	5244	5152	6939	1252	1815	9671	1227	6758	9942	5420
(1120)	7945	3770	9188	0521	3840	2296	4926	3637	0785	2475
(1121)	3472	4586	4887	3926	6695	9575	5912	8344	1842	5489
(1122)	8462	3133	4069	2858	8869	4528	8488	9966	4809	1330
(1123)	4234	1054	8850	9160	3570	2175	3851	5849	0184	6780
(1124)	8975	9633	7257	8855	6518	8632	5189	2958	1739	7303
(1125)	4209	1434	1479	0413	7367	0743	2355	3225	7341	4071
(1126)	1919	8974	1219	8989	5904	7534	8117	1251	1579	9282
(1127)	9936	8379	0450	0921	0624	6677	6592	3864	2689	2118
(1128)	1607	0316	3218	5841	2217	7541	7149	1495	9247	8582
(1129)	2593	8948	3306	8088	7313	7099	5306	8437	5600	6900
(1130)	4974	2241	5701	4643	2254	3261	1634	7127	6066	1532
(1131)	9882	9035	8896	6824	5023	5681	8429	4428	7172	1928
(1132)	1310	9651	0807	5106	7334	1606	5030	7232	1498	8759
(1133)	9890	4551	7622	8247	1567	6473	1512	4561	7977	5143
(1134)	4839	4810	9442	9235	7696	2225	4837	0084	8570	8442
(1135)	0222	0532	9933	8581	8999	4718	0137	4317	0476	3888
(1136)	3043	8368	0375	3356	1773	7073	4031	9779	1653	7328
(1137)	0816	5889	1464	3697	4558	2627	0890	0262	2970	0310
(1138)	5245	3927	7584	2625	1218	4991	8552	2796	0351	1248
(1139)	3650	4843	4521	5292	5904	9236	6205	6001	9312	1640
(1140)	3714	3978	0107	2757	0363	2002	6856	7214	6595	3782
(1141)	9999	3883	8482	4192	8045	3185	4589	9873	9376	8562
(1142)	1829	2914	2858	4096	2343	5651	1691	8881	7984	2432
(1143)	2219	4548	3441	2108	2574	9190	7852	5413	6904	2588
(1144)	3712	9396	1860	5997	2602	5561	6404	8895	0647	9151
(1145)	4156	0426	5478	0367	3264	9015	5656	0046	2351	6093

Appendix A
Random Numbers (Continued)

	(01)	(02)	(03)	(04)	(05)	(06)	(07)	(08)	(09)	(10)
(1146)	3060	3673	6294	3222	8810	0450	9568	1085	9719	5979
(1147)	7190	8803	9280	8941	7517	5241	6873	5616	2942	7189
(1148)	7297	4287	1311	4530	6807	6769	9489	7723	5617	3509
(1149)	1282	6442	1575	6381	8272	7991	7657	2255	7146	4863
(1150)	5645	1857	3799	4246	1815	1650	9494	1474	4832	8897
(1151)	9253	3155	6176	2600	9266	1227	7226	2275	9649	4815
(1152)	3547	0801	4063	8574	7087	5595	7480	5180	6446	4092
(1153)	5206	3205	2582	8106	4587	3692	6193	7903	3403	5383
(1154)	3593	8391	6283	9937	9299	5445	9755	1418	2504	0183
(1155)	3467	8544	6381	1647	5800	9402	7216	3533	8803	8058
(1156)	5539	7034	4503	5288	7305	6278	2202	3351	7375	9635
(1157)	2332	5236	3219	4764	7693	4379	6049	7683	3043	7044
(1158)	3401	7991	7726	7669	6011	7617	5993	4971	9327	2068
(1159)	4006	4828	1846	1056	3851	8729	9313	4472	6484	9433
(1160)	7648	9917	4148	7523	5468	2821	4603	2407	7907	4819
(1161)	9780	6802	0204	6182	3721	6910	7570	1905	6385	1070
(1162)	3052	3298	4275	2833	7971	2017	6374	2596	8154	6820
(1163)	2663	2055	2416	3289	1048	2048	7973	9491	9484	1588
(1164)	5182	7322	6740	9146	8209	7396	5181	0710	7288	4268
(1165)	9934	6617	5550	4842	4859	4053	3441	4524	2411	7051
(1166)	7235	9042	8250	7905	0904	5495	7233	3766	5565	2284
(1167)	0395	3862	5074	0831	8896	1334	1817	3628	0180	8244
(1168)	2529	6482	1181	4828	6265	5608	0756	0399	9283	5592
(1169)	6935	0275	6445	5347	2492	5881	1207	6501	4217	7176
(1170)	1634	6310	9915	0702	1883	3827	1212	2288	4288	4172
(1171)	9508	9590	4808	4345	6612	0475	4637	1891	2773	4042
(1172)	1831	6838	5478	6495	4766	9808	1821	6305	0141	9652
(1173)	8992	8589	1789	1108	7225	3422	6566	7632	0615	1621
(1174)	6923	6755	2966	9059	6448	5013	4220	9280	9667	6948
(1175)	2997	9950	2591	8103	8299	9762	7439	4957	2421	8664
(1176)	8987	8140	1766	7609	4409	3320	1490	6651	8536	9968
(1177)	9065	0279	2100	1168	6736	6202	0048	7366	4337	5429
(1178)	4815	4092	8563	9749	3369	2710	4394	4510	6398	9841
(1179)	7041	7485	3172	2849	3862	5931	2410	1825	3465	4009
(1180)	1140	0628	1285	5159	7033	1208	5920	2213	8529	9995
(1181)	6447	7575	8673	5876	4803	6833	1517	6403	2740	1731
(1182)	2394	4621	3044	9240	8037	2125	5321	3562	1891	8643
(1183)	7619	6909	3956	8585	5257	1063	2930	3241	9239	1354
(1184)	2189	9735	5469	7594	4849	7588	0180	5850	3715	8143
(1185)	9960	9602	7450	3254	7330	6833	4786	9059	4899	5570
(1186)	4519	0768	1918	8881	5860	9757	9013	7579	8104	7948
(1187)	0050	1163	1991	5696	5171	8314	7403	8927	6039	2595
(1188)	1826	4313	0841	4366	9680	3337	4613	7012	7626	4183
(1189)	4374	2505	3358	6943	6978	5800	8787	8169	4539	4802
(1190)	8985	3388	9911	2834	1772	7550	7026	2501	4010	0226
(1191)	1497	7197	9253	2068	9570	2697	8914	4882	5417	9605
(1192)	9216	2297	3938	0536	1012	8676	7086	4890	9828	5059
(1193)	2052	0866	6222	3327	7898	4369	3020	8839	7899	2199
(1194)	7476	6387	1678	2599	3926	7759	6746	8508	0850	6727
(1195)	7261	7839	9937	0691	6230	2065	7889	4234	0626	5029

	(01)	(02)	(03)	(04)	(05)	(06)	(07)	(08)	(09)	(10)
(1196)	7330	4106	4506	9518	3260	7302	7240	4573	0363	4550
(1197)	3134	7143	2198	2452	3867	5014	7662	7911	9477	4754
(1198)	5343	1161	0933	8196	5729	4679	3614	6756	7813	2236
(1199)	5897	3395	2127	7463	8201	3508	4916	5038	0595	8466
(1200)	5710	4289	5392	9949	0497	3680	2578	4080	9142	3485
(1201)	8703	7538	3193	0367	8593	2491	0599	5845	3753	1855
(1202)	9493	0485	7062	4162	8261	7314	0795	1409	8634	7192
(1203)	3314	5959	7163	9690	5378	8762	5317	2816	7533	3659
(1204)	5065	5143	0078	6189	3947	1808	8700	1883	1732	8790
(1205)	7143	2177	0048	3662	9194	6806	6494	7008	1520	1344
(1206)	7233	5228	4494	8294	6761	6920	8040	1123	8431	2372
(1207)	7471	1343	9461	5205	1821	8322	3269	9706	2294	0555
(1208)	7474	0048	6384	6339	4715	7988	5025	2492	3437	8358
(1209)	5715	1426	8104	1191	4312	5525	2450	7387	6937	9082
(1210)	9859	7876	6072	8398	7358	6042	6438	2346	1101	8249
(1211)	7789	2984	5550	3346	2254	1253	9147	5427	9734	0751
(1212)	2111	3490	1840	0260	9754	5391	1669	9988	8013	7590
(1213)	0104	4678	5774	9870	2658	7318	9608	8394	8502	4444
(1214)	0958	8465	8878	2099	7294	7346	9974	8263	6626	3885
(1215)	8005	2971	4485	3481	5946	0383	3979	8241	0547	9038
(1216)	4410	0460	4268	5645	1055	1424	9103	9743	8109	6403
(1217)	7446	8061	9342	5015	5121	7761	0499	3301	9763	4201
(1218)	8392	8202	0172	0864	4418	8172	2890	0074	1087	6874
(1219)	9748	1829	7840	4908	7890	7113	4892	8844	4938	3733
(1220)	1996	3075	3002	8167	8936	6654	4098	2972	7873	4119
(1221)	0272	8983	9599	6760	8752	2091	5641	5598	2201	2845
(1222)	2733	0879	0556	1927	1505	4566	7470	9329	4676	6464
(1223)	1709	6532	1577	5098	2130	3233	4202	0957	2168	8414
(1224)	8284	9164	7994	7735	2423	3292	9609	5610	5586	6752
(1225)	1257	6953	5323	3893	2966	2839	6106	3907	6697	2586
(1226)	1005	2426	9231	0198	3314	5060	9106	4083	3516	0893
(1227)	3266	2898	5979	0996	9377	1488	2496	0357	2921	4440
(1228)	2332	0681	7697	4958	0953	3753	0248	6521	6741	2228
(1229)	5448	1814	8257	2176	4032	1227	5852	7455	4017	1719
(1230)	9331	6848	7052	0071	2471	8829	5976	8169	0917	0716
(1231)	9497	5049	3571	0686	4991	3539	7204	2356	1264	5807
(1232)	3289	7787	8036	6973	0638	9393	5884	1252	4782	1451
(1233)	1880	7606	6380	9942	2012	8845	8551	4789	4730	4739
(1234)	7938	1513	1396	1679	2517	7501	4951	6808	5774	4696
(1235)	9020	6658	5101	6057	8629	9700	6196	4264	7236	3644
(1236)	9776	6957	2690	3111	3189	9923	5334	0052	5045	4052
(1237)	0608	6689	7584	2604	8809	7773	3402	5103	4811	7875
(1238)	4144	9094	1903	2110	7697	7742	3820	3434	5754	2988
(1239)	7640	6373	9705	8252	8092	8576	8680	4287	9146	6986
(1240)	7209	9375	0767	9417	1134	7495	4390	9297	6173	3108
(1241)	2541	7478	6661	1641	6966	7995	0341	0263	8145	7113
(1242)	9199	9188	8036	0832	9499	6028	1187	7535	2362	9184
(1243)	1931	4927	8710	6320	2600	5670	3739	8036	7437	1481
(1244)	4780	3818	1120	3399	0684	8579	7676	7950	8830	1430
(1245)	7569	2083	9258	4808	1128	1000	5780	5589	6523	7562

Random Numbers (Continued)

	(01)	(02)	(03)	(04)	(05)	(06)	(07)	(08)	(09)	(10)
(1246)	8708	2907	4421	3023	0288	2100	4248	3949	0977	5341
(1247)	9200	6070	7354	0375	7848	3298	9109	2237	0524	0798
(1248)	7784	7486	7824	6157	0716	5059	9423	8137	0242	2664
(1249)	5464	8489	1283	5164	7398	6691	4293	7945	1085	5373
(1250)	8208	7105	1799	1069	3848	2853	4288	3057	1478	4948
(1251)	4912	4429	6293	3071	2641	7038	0527	2174	4951	4295
(1252)	3136	4348	5129	6696	8603	8987	6452	0399	0408	1533
(1253)	9116	2600	7249	0350	1379	4936	5870	5211	0353	2265
(1254)	1139	5077	9334	1608	9191	0575	8492	4809	9745	9380
(1255)	2350	9075	0636	4925	6239	7518	9952	0832	5339	6524
(1256)	5846	2779	7723	1568	5228	7303	2658	9427	7993	2102
(1257)	5870	1193	6657	9277	8604	7045	7876	9212	1622	4206
(1258)	0350	5032	1120	9649	5079	7659	1490	2916	1820	8980
(1259)	3037	7925	1858	9633	6856	0547	1980	7900	7642	5048
(1260)	9787	4332	7212	4908	9123	1996	0232	9953	5247	4874
(1261)	3251	4217	4117	0432	7389	9226	4723	0168	0672	3278
(1262)	5306	1831	8945	9665	3343	2507	1246	0835	5565	3879
(1263)	3972	0200	0152	5121	2442	5553	1632	7356	4264	5779
(1264)	1298	8389	4643	6635	9532	5800	6729	7242	3484	5293
(1265)	9794	7327	5073	2724	9683	1508	2586	4883	1461	2875
(1266)	9322	0610	1019	4869	2599	1367	3441	2927	3235	1751
(1267)	3341	4716	8845	3923	2054	7784	1719	4965	7106	0248
(1268)	0244	6252	2617	6837	9822	0950	5718	2876	7906	7339
(1269)	4644	0244	2661	6773	3496	8694	0367	5319	0754	3481
(1270)	8167	7107	8755	4122	9839	0995	0633	2652	1134	0694
(1271)	0518	1863	0754	4085	8720	4194	6146	8238	6653	3293
(1272)	5749	1803	2394	7607	2985	7043	9802	0844	4011	8431
(1273)	1072	8182	5485	6917	7267	7242	7789	5801	7298	1636
(1274)	9466	9137	2175	6692	7881	2910	5310	6026	9436	0318
(1275)	3934	8763	8272	7439	6207	0130	2816	2105	6179	6516
(1276)	5878	9126	1493	7375	7227	3632	9723	1559	0326	5906
(1277)	2888	8817	2375	1626	4565	9678	8732	6016	9686	0536
(1278)	8310	6721	7102	8209	1231	2431	8986	6288	3348	4674
(1279)	4930	6324	8870	7977	0771	7523	4954	4086	1011	6420
(1280)	6729	4829	9909	9308	4781	7401	0319	9012	4364	5380
(1281)	9462	5089	0549	0042	2020	2376	7121	9160	4466	7392
(1282)	1561	1278	1488	1054	8476	4209	0167	1524	3073	9038
(1283)	5732	6671	9548	3931	9373	9519	6041	9175	9863	5107
(1284)	5697	5933	9495	7322	0462	2972	0407	3669	0352	7349
(1285)	6793	3598	1933	7529	2378	5382	1105	1437	1911	1459
(1286)	0863	7127	4145	8467	8375	8764	6861	1496	9541	8209
(1287)	3809	4307	3995	0512	7711	2621	6234	6416	6429	1381
(1288)	1615	4580	9746	1092	2787	2545	9687	9858	9417	4458
(1289)	0091	2740	1400	6563	2554	3730	8113	3577	2086	7032
(1290)	0533	1218	1332	2274	9745	8001	5386	4541	7979	3823
(1291)	5463	7511	5406	9925	2567	4181	5246	7915	4432	4408
(1292)	7747	9466	6153	5264	4561	9627	3419	7289	0587	5592
(1293)	3300	2667	9829	1606	1827	4115	4523	4388	1056	3660
(1294)	7251	4231	3166	3895	9853	8448	7910	5856	3650	3489
(1295)	9572	4563	1577	4840	4276	2804	7402	3981	9707	1438

	(01)	(02)	(03)	(04)	(05)	(06)	(07)	(08)	(09)	(10)
(1296)	4305	5773	3713	2859	6648	2802	7355	2525	1982	9318
(1297)	5841	9996	0092	4738	0703	0874	9799	8442	4149	7382
(1298)	2928	9351	9874	3248	4124	9853	0532	9857	0564	9691
(1299)	5458	6295	5021	9033	9280	5515	1970	0281	1263	1979
(1300)	9211	3869	8757	0262	7382	9625	4855	5746	1694	7887
(1301)	5166	0217	2299	1501	6577	9450	4056	0586	8663	0453
(1302)	9363	3255	5424	8484	8650	0233	0059	3558	0222	5395
(1303)	3239	6649	4633	4471	2661	1941	2046	2816	5793	7493
(1304)	4948	2421	0477	1762	0131	1515	8032	9223	7064	9160
(1305)	6026	8028	7494	8172	4189	9100	8294	1542	5031	2471
(1306)	3080	0955	3755	8332	7886	3862	8718	2456	3252	6008
(1307)	9003	0938	8154	7602	9880	5589	4255	5219	0945	2168
(1308)	7987	0651	4767	3626	6464	2643	2856	5609	8374	4324
(1309)	9550	0288	6232	8493	8205	6181	3869	7382	7608	1144
(1310)	4742	7140	1381	6234	7407	4660	5701	8740	7815	3941
(1311)	4136	3630	4252	4686	0504	1420	4450	5896	4336	5324
(1312)	9826	2698	6682	7506	2661	9090	4225	7320	9250	0167
(1313)	1210	5643	8127	4946	0951	8527	5919	1641	3894	8626
(1314)	8044	7168	3825	5558	6438	3275	9703	1610	9955	9371
(1315)	7975	9383	5691	8017	9708	4490	2791	3513	8326	9949
(1316)	1532	6639	6370	3469	9493	1256	7098	1851	6834	0851
(1317)	0562	1380	4827	5846	1957	0129	7713	4242	5087	5829
(1318)	1469	2306	7437	7886	4504	5626	8576	3593	4142	2401
(1319)	5886	3616	7772	9163	2530	7279	4506	5655	0968	9322
(1320)	7196	4942	6387	1053	3581	4144	2752	3496	0528	8978
(1321)	8720	6232	0373	4796	7471	3226	4431	2820	2146	5065
(1322)	5714	2083	0072	3974	2538	9090	8661	1681	5175	5908
(1323)	6425	8172	2847	9816	9508	1613	5896	3967	1790	6814
(1324)	8635	4787	9291	9123	1177	1321	3376	1765	3810	7531
(1325)	8560	0488	2909	3469	9992	0955	0485	2817	2153	0203
(1326)	6102	1012	5090	5431	9990	0107	3441	7177	1742	0582
(1327)	5312	9623	8644	0203	7149	6869	9849	2888	4244	9287
(1328)	3115	6905	7946	2188	1315	7661	4918	2814	7821	8085
(1329)	2018	3917	8020	5023	5285	6011	5145	9528	6839	2970
(1330)	9251	6378	3445	7748	5442	7811	1271	7201	4517	3836
(1331)	7298	1824	6001	4912	9310	3680	5160	3539	1310	2383
(1332)	1374	8832	9719	8848	5827	0006	0519	5980	6876	3233
(1333)	9129	2733	4690	0004	4150	7294	9898	3887	0700	3716
(1334)	8790	4449	9062	1140	7411	8626	6182	1369	8454	7357
(1335)	5393	7135	1672	0442	6041	8762	3023	2455	1750	2031
(1336)	5153	2448	0393	1147	8018	2405	1258	3521	5736	2617
(1337)	2008	4734	2474	9091	3139	0537	1800	2141	8656	6755
(1338)	3416	0552	8551	3277	9086	9688	4392	7450	9499	4611
(1339)	6988	3447	3182	7409	5416	0167	4948	0167	6442	4900
(1340)	4519	3280	0410	9087	8994	2031	6608	0970	0620	7184
(1341)	6211	9996	2240	1924	9865	9691	8207	9586	2224	5519
(1342)	1760	0173	9081	9389	7611	8181	5832	2269	8281	5846
(1343)	7069	3103	5826	8137	3476	8595	5877	1850	8590	4114
(1344)	5288	2182	1467	0045	7262	9493	5977	1002	3895	4018
(1345)	3793	8009	3030	2032	6458	9249	5559	3558	5892	8393

Appendix A
Random Numbers (Continued)

	(01)	(02)	(03)	(04)	(05)	(06)	(07)	(08)	(09)	(10)
(1346)	7494	2683	0297	9002	9954	0414	0701	4761	6703	4607
(1347)	6330	3957	6463	8835	9746	1291	5373	5985	3343	5702
(1348)	4080	8924	7992	6256	1779	1305	0070	8927	2079	7464
(1349)	4645	4609	6218	2805	4631	4582	2961	7108	0787	0894
(1350)	0244	2394	0127	0642	8351	8739	6279	4848	9318	3361
(1351)	2504	5947	1780	3036	3295	5255	4567	0359	6112	2039
(1352)	4899	7282	8059	5055	5501	3069	5927	8710	0351	5545
(1353)	0615	4983	2249	1154	2473	2434	9580	4109	1838	8651
(1354)	5811	8703	3268	8103	8121	8926	7262	4651	8360	1425
(1355)	0817	1418	7811	7417	9824	0426	0240	9438	3227	4945
(1356)	0254	5922	4544	4444	9925	5361	9328	0648	0011	8994
(1357)	8628	8653	6825	1095	9044	0647	3209	9992	9336	2473
(1358)	4577	8362	8537	3019	7782	6538	7262	5253	1025	0942
(1359)	0874	9725	6886	0721	1530	9902	3303	0908	7804	3970
(1360)	6066	1099	3636	5943	4297	6624	5352	6574	5067	3953
(1361)	1168	0229	3770	0691	0885	7917	8761	5701	7851	9421
(1362)	9070	7706	9801	0966	7217	1806	4907	8817	5517	4810
(1363)	5717	2873	0125	1855	1349	1802	0213	4589	9675	7841
(1364)	8022	6673	4355	4180	5393	1032	4725	9680	5039	3091
(1365)	4969	0447	0445	6984	2002	7771	0665	3379	9812	7267
(1366)	7247	8407	8394	1968	4744	3674	3140	2449	4197	3862
(1367)	8260	1006	7080	6723	7605	3714	2540	9996	6822	4241
(1368)	5463	6155	6829	1634	9136	2085	5504	5060	8685	2906
(1369)	6172	3818	8662	2058	7790	9393	9495	1341	0688	2451
(1370)	9353	1084	5824	6533	4162	2047	7610	9030	7240	3321
(1371)	4060	9598	8753	9523	9927	7727	2517	5237	0910	5340
(1372)	7345	0326	0230	7026	6665	5223	5233	3028	2570	4429
(1373)	6180	2832	6496	2234	8242	3448	3659	4183	6031	1545
(1374)	3541	4967	2290	0423	1685	0643	7767	2917	3334	3998
(1375)	3204	3067	8612	8703	8246	6411	9222	3076	3428	6741
(1376)	1239	7301	2280	4906	7268	9083	9759	7818	3881	5150
(1377)	5465	8105	2879	8799	9562	2828	3647	1859	7758	2506
(1378)	5127	7167	6218	8188	5325	2662	7148	3138	8623	9634
(1379)	2338	3203	4517	8545	8769	3032	2449	4479	5461	7270
(1380)	6619	5541	0291	3831	6095	5159	3933	1976	1709	0650
(1381)	0221	8806	1393	4511	7865	3046	1510	5080	3826	2634
(1382)	7306	6052	4707	2468	7816	7256	1839	6238	2180	4673
(1383)	4616	5445	6656	0328	5959	4228	0643	9583	9550	6047
(1384)	0685	7189	3320	1095	5475	2352	2324	9080	7397	1555
(1385)	1276	2746	0523	4902	4726	4681	6271	1789	0116	0364
(1386)	3338	1104	6525	3583	9939	9277	4653	1907	0030	1373
(1387)	2045	2875	4346	7075	6015	0728	3267	2148	4140	3146
(1388)	3213	9717	5136	2560	0670	5044	9589	9304	0419	4708
(1389)	0581	7511	3801	4710	1685	6444	0230	9478	7340	2285
(1390)	7945	2255	4499	6847	9631	4164	1792	7907	3225	7665
(1391)	8534	7604	4566	6080	4407	0202	2454	3438	2122	9795
(1392)	7036	4035	7639	3855	1233	4609	3899	4288	9545	6469
(1393)	0511	4291	1034	8313	4344	5194	0876	1714	1140	5344
(1394)	1213	0533	4578	8655	0434	9348	3771	9715	1251	5693
(1395)	6277	7002	2344	3056	8943	9451	6306	6287	8050	1040

	(01)	(02)	(03)	(04)	(05)	(06)	(07)	(08)	(09)	(10)
(1396)	8310	4260	7722	2623	7628	5454	7343	3851	2582	1180
(1397)	9580	5799	2322	6382	1103	2698	3905	6407	5696	2780
(1398)	7341	7574	1160	8631	4951	3488	2896	2856	3300	0645
(1399)	2506	4807	0658	4248	6969	8891	1249	3053	5611	6100
(1400)	1353	4666	7733	4125	2022	6148	2701	9452	6394	1612
(1401)	1173	9580	1715	0322	0484	3029	9367	2111	5527	5924
(1402)	3295	1435	2139	0342	9520	2071	9816	5698	5968	9630
(1403)	1020	5411	1398	3623	4532	3882	7018	3059	5952	9049
(1404)	7632	9501	3557	0167	3709	4448	0638	5456	2667	6075
(1405)	7443	5364	2321	1056	5247	4723	1153	8750	9991	7529
(1406)	5756	6268	5242	5034	7538	2110	1647	6273	3421	9420
(1407)	2050	3173	2368	0534	5408	7620	7684	5077	0457	7858
(1408)	9617	6350	5190	4690	7215	2558	9022	1460	2335	4234
(1409)	1114	5188	0023	7125	7329	2754	2166	2074	3512	5058
(1410)	1125	5012	2146	4941	6648	7297	2071	7195	4499	5311
(1411)	4909	3390	2945	6412	0870	2151	2633	3236	9869	9975
(1412)	9690	2851	0367	9618	0448	4763	3221	2986	8713	2096
(1413)	1956	3662	2059	4947	1194	8335	4393	4818	8927	7523
(1414)	1741	9822	2395	6825	1115	4171	4141	3902	7051	3129
(1415)	7543	7897	2671	0618	8394	0414	3009	2380	5086	2935
(1416)	8131	6109	2396	0683	1528	1988	0481	0336	1390	6003
(1417)	0654	8357	9496	1194	0081	8037	4115	2996	5268	9137
(1418)	5031	2602	2170	3652	4846	1656	1135	1014	8513	7161
(1419)	4698	2626	8295	3982	7102	0729	0179	1682	9834	5119
(1420)	0675	6892	5021	4973	6212	6761	8535	2595	1549	3307
(1421)	7084	3578	6741	9682	9007	6683	6948	4888	4040	7569
(1422)	6240	5161	1932	2507	7969	6327	8898	0240	3193	3765
(1423)	2568	7914	1202	0600	1825	2876	3715	3913	5791	2407
(1424)	8570	2159	9398	5186	5576	0451	1565	2863	9332	8191
(1425)	8578	1305	9622	9101	7931	5104	2929	2411	3036	0442
(1426)	4124	4217	5093	5614	3882	0575	1331	2528	3097	2708
(1427)	9835	0226	6038	5131	8301	4917	7030	9435	8882	4785
(1428)	4130	2535	5580	5255	3758	1200	0916	5375	7321	9446
(1429)	5803	8604	4487	9952	0500	8166	2005	5402	1302	0386
(1430)	2783	6581	3412	1123	8880	7760	1037	8943	0394	8778
(1431)	7809	9823	1232	9519	3078	3402	3330	8570	4983	9244
(1432)	1249	6271	7859	9374	5724	1435	7535	3848	3212	9330
(1433)	6602	7011	0855	2085	5018	2208	7892	3836	7951	9633
(1434)	8552	3105	6897	8324	8627	2881	3731	4530	3131	6398
(1435)	8626	2380	1971	1214	0463	0956	2109	8168	9065	3526
(1436)	3800	5876	3449	2764	2915	1055	9252	9855	5532	5020
(1437)	4055	4435	9632	4719	2560	4301	5056	3220	6139	1272
(1438)	5136	7567	0065	1619	8477	7053	9742	7209	4559	5017
(1439)	0696	5931	7169	0397	0406	2138	8539	0522	2294	6823
(1440)	3225	9111	0965	9394	8361	3775	0947	6661	1685	9829
(1441)	3207	1762	0229	0877	8546	1731	3817	4818	1630	2984
(1442)	0705	3930	2648	1782	8314	3009	3425	3404	3729	7334
(1443)	5249	3526	7480	2023	7817	4376	8999	8106	7591	0185
(1444)	2844	7849	8808	9712	8425	8489	6272	1144	5584	2201
(1445)	2177	1919	3953	6965	0873	1515	4358	7435	4209	0684

Random Numbers (Continued)

	(01)	(02)	(03)	(04)	(05)	(06)	(07)	(08)	(09)	(10)
(1446)	7998	3677	0254	7986	2496	3849	7248	3355	7541	3260
(1447)	3859	0091	6543	4125	7692	4507	2590	3773	4828	9606
(1448)	3696	5809	6449	1768	3394	3701	3416	1784	9075	1357
(1449)	8046	2798	8064	9621	7327	8010	3017	0398	0018	6278
(1450)	0788	3169	5874	5897	9882	9172	0309	3052	0871	9034
(1451)	0620	5510	5469	2099	6855	4419	8195	5413	7838	5076
(1452)	2107	5279	6799	3874	9131	5235	8105	2288	2093	5441
(1453)	7943	1235	2113	6639	2242	3273	1166	8368	4560	4172
(1454)	6009	6417	0881	5540	8586	2737	3364	2402	3940	8568
(1455)	7129	4531	0911	7659	5603	9967	5752	8847	5484	6853
(1456)	4328	0499	1546	7632	5653	5623	8611	0237	1158	6932
(1457)	9830	4810	4230	3487	3220	6885	4230	2129	7407	0796
(1458)	7210	2190	7681	6768	1259	0639	3541	6037	0451	2812
(1459)	3780	7675	8991	6984	1954	3111	7296	7401	2662	6628
(1460)	0338	4271	4497	8588	0073	9387	0944	4743	5214	2012
(1461)	8086	2051	2472	2391	0174	0072	9790	5687	6412	6953
(1462)	3892	3625	3080	4202	3589	1147	7833	6336	7041	7678
(1463)	1814	9527	9220	1237	8618	9526	5230	4552	0265	0310
(1464)	1907	5322	5265	8933	8185	8593	7519	1846	4611	8922
(1465)	1531	0590	5464	8796	6922	6485	4146	2407	6056	4363
(1466)	6664	2800	6099	7183	8977	4856	4177	8340	0799	2639
(1467)	8415	8271	5276	6617	9215	5414	3893	5120	6276	7645
(1468)	4843	7055	8166	9235	8147	9173	0333	9297	9495	1503
(1469)	6561	4892	1583	5574	0275	7231	7622	3244	9369	8074
(1470)	0976	6077	9997	6048	4031	2342	8478	1173	6843	0949
(1471)	8804	8760	7965	7038	7871	1326	5823	5439	4073	9418
(1472)	8360	4276	8778	6967	5849	5444	1075	4275	0473	6524
(1473)	9854	3814	7698	8171	4793	8721	2829	2546	6655	3846
(1474)	5316	9317	9515	9015	3909	8312	8693	1892	8623	6344
(1475)	2333	9817	9267	3167	1728	6208	3763	2745	5664	4206
(1476)	9215	7201	4736	3050	1231	7374	9429	9650	4475	3730
(1477)	4710	5848	5578	5038	3626	5829	3757	2326	8167	1588
(1478)	9120	0599	2354	6676	7805	3660	6585	0995	3159	5085
(1479)	0038	8012	4681	1515	1675	3669	9515	6341	2698	2484
(1480)	1434	1053	5895	4156	7209	7344	2318	5703	9764	9378
(1481)	2455	0635	0813	7525	9715	0709	4911	3636	5377	0443
(1482)	2582	1730	8079	2310	1544	4372	4472	8113	8815	1732
(1483)	9012	3186	4889	1985	7472	5163	5579	0795	8408	0246
(1484)	5847	8490	1536	3800	5681	8380	6381	3350	8650	8376
(1485)	4755	6364	9211	4175	8740	1254	4323	7566	9919	6642
(1486)	7573	7383	5385	9578	3610	1789	1805	4523	5063	7796
(1487)	2563	2616	0822	8764	4821	7059	3860	8537	5499	6799
(1488)	8066	6718	4862	9368	5821	7286	6885	4286	3168	9728
(1489)	9942	9132	8633	0955	1045	1721	7585	4835	1180	0372
(1490)	8199	1996	4043	7950	9708	7710	9505	1511	9212	3031
(1491)	8233	2398	1265	0675	3073	8346	1508	6324	3346	1712
(1492)	1629	6817	4909	2279	9336	9961	3611	3043	5319	4668
(1493)	9022	6792	7935	3891	0903	2015	3870	0897	5311	5335
(1494)	7829	5057	5794	3802	3269	8369	1781	9500	1202	4613
(1495)	0165	6918	3965	4846	3416	7641	4086	8172	0017	6735

A

	(01)	(02)	(03)	(04)	(05)	(06)	(07)	(08)	(09)	(10)
(1496)	9604	4564	6380	3159	3691	0797	2132	8017	9730	3349
(1497)	6598	0800	6690	6148	2915	3627	0368	1019	7519	5076
(1498)	7505	0916	5728	3706	3590	9962	2915	7981	6593	0865
(1499)	8846	7040	5003	5364	6765	2780	4258	2247	9319	5412
(1500)	4254	1761	1314	2717	1587	4831	4270	0227	0302	0963
(1501)	9052	6428	1174	0638	2782	8072	1475	4452	5703	6451
(1502)	1396	4119	6274	7309	7388	5866	2510	7384	9610	0191
(1503)	8398	5748	4984	3821	4531	9442	4903	8418	5442	3890
(1504)	9528	6553	5718	1864	4142	0409	3485	6829	6320	3562
(1505)	8450	4200	4066	4297	5048	2768	9723	1701	6047	9979
(1506)	0529	3105	0132	6071	0776	4620	0649	0715	5478	8558
(1507)	4101	5356	9334	9617	1207	4980	4617	1882	2447	0575
(1508)	4669	9080	2646	7499	9236	6031	9318	6910	6258	0632
(1509)	1225	9008	4116	3928	2914	2590	4883	2461	7749	5504
(1510)	7978	6064	7019	4492	9224	4269	7235	5164	8697	4123
(1511)	5277	9974	7685	8759	0589	0147	1114	5233	7398	4167
(1512)	3217	6027	7403	9924	0039	7177	8508	4918	8251	8538
(1513)	9648	0141	8478	4497	0763	0732	1574	6928	1727	5043
(1514)	5345	7580	3916	1995	3123	2657	7952	6403	5873	4119
(1515)	4502	0486	3002	3084	2072	1925	8915	3138	0616	3485
(1516)	3004	8124	3000	3693	7803	4576	0844	0343	9660	5814
(1517)	9046	2456	7897	6498	4454	6530	9049	8841	1237	9025
(1518)	8678	2668	1408	8856	4922	8914	8484	9375	7737	9065
(1519)	6448	2843	8553	2660	9001	4471	5346	0396	1266	2405
(1520)	2861	1009	5194	6060	5990	6408	9863	1490	8430	3432
(1521)	6723	2132	3215	6078	1512	5322	6136	1908	0426	1063
(1522)	6397	5296	2015	2616	3302	9869	6445	0509	2871	7536
(1523)	9291	1250	7572	1725	0638	8759	1678	1759	6540	6065
(1524)	8142	0363	3291	8712	5178	7562	7129	3060	4524	7739
(1525)	6440	5954	2148	5155	7841	7981	6023	4429	5113	1697
(1526)	2398	3224	8505	5584	1632	8066	5971	7480	0138	9665
(1527)	7580	2311	9370	6322	1644	1597	8250	1520	1756	0720
(1528)	5007	7089	1375	5235	4355	8247	6326	9828	7244	6850
(1529)	4120	0187	3897	2737	7190	5746	7865	1765	7860	3206
(1530)	7243	3816	4006	6841	8037	5302	5621	0962	5762	4531
(1531)	3087	3088	5172	1425	2862	6301	0161	3954	6153	7429
(1532)	4627	7520	4480	5088	5185	1705	1976	0239	4712	5164
(1533)	2627	3349	2369	6135	4021	1720	6342	3091	6443	4447
(1534)	8846	5897	9856	5528	5298	6665	5041	8280	3333	4781
(1535)	8415	9156	5422	1557	6053	3342	6338	3293	8419	6744
(1536)	6219	7702	9995	3318	0034	0635	9401	3544	4721	1606
(1537)	3447	4706	7018	5929	6725	5940	2438	7676	3424	2775
(1538)	6570	9338	3657	2780	5253	0101	9614	8050	6949	2075
(1539)	4706	5489	2895	9144	8490	3748	1486	1098	1525	9374
(1540)	9761	0063	5941	1305	2276	3385	8117	8239	6022	8094
(1541)	6238	8327	7126	5817	5745	3395	5617	4037	9250	2904
(1542)	0521	7322	4132	1225	3350	0339	2517	1412	2927	5738
(1543)	1142	2641	6092	4958	3957	6173	0999	7019	3456	7814
(1544)	1737	0220	0984	3967	7795	6741	2963	9459	3308	5438
(1545)	8775	3610	5819	6172	4160	4979	1497	9122	6573	6514

Appendix A
Random Numbers (Continued)

	(01)	(02)	(03)	(04)	(05)	(06)	(07)	(08)	(09)	(10)
(1546)	3514	4869	0244	3384	6426	1045	2773	3669	7754	3623
(1547)	5436	3798	2572	0541	7811	1407	0422	3144	8077	7208
(1548)	9737	1912	2926	1984	2687	7093	6880	5121	8209	7632
(1549)	3807	1884	3202	7632	1434	4929	7861	0170	9861	7251
(1550)	3818	7951	9125	3615	0105	7344	9427	9672	0908	0551
(1551)	2756	1774	0083	5253	1870	4933	6897	1760	8905	1879
(1552)	5480	6340	4328	8840	9853	2138	5732	8136	1036	8893
(1553)	7321	6417	6441	5542	4536	5277	7193	6688	9772	7439
(1554)	7977	6034	0656	7426	4415	5063	8794	3336	6759	9277
(1555)	0570	9121	5398	9754	0583	4135	4586	1201	7465	4224
(1556)	3077	2795	4331	5825	5717	7920	3216	1671	5075	7835
(1557)	4171	3226	7389	7683	5722	9977	4507	8850	5256	3213
(1558)	0531	4538	7540	3873	6981	0463	4572	4576	5531	9425
(1559)	1179	7727	1740	3778	1677	6052	8356	1855	2842	4906
(1560)	2190	1870	5468	8464	5087	8868	0243	2670	4773	8073
(1561)	7055	3046	3478	5022	7859	4661	9063	2649	4449	8143
(1562)	2187	7296	9733	5655	4325	8987	3202	3076	8024	7785
(1563)	6386	0064	8493	6998	2368	0702	0077	1563	9003	4946
(1564)	5831	5204	1812	9309	6922	6210	7162	8428	3803	6706
(1565)	0729	5363	2627	8016	4025	6119	5062	1889	1675	0116
(1566)	8901	8648	8964	8831	4199	1990	5674	4331	3437	5043
(1567)	8472	0594	7260	6123	6630	0962	2583	9386	5530	3605
(1568)	9345	8496	5557	9741	5651	4977	6358	4572	3576	5857
(1569)	6420	7435	4173	3921	6783	4134	4485	9137	3482	5431
(1570)	0358	1637	6493	7999	8881	0516	6082	5411	5590	4751
(1571)	8962	1250	1837	0729	5008	3953	8559	5738	6950	7079
(1572)	1522	0924	1035	3906	2470	5580	1987	4644	0542	1462
(1573)	0304	4956	5862	0968	6328	9963	0390	2418	1034	0680
(1574)	5721	4856	5124	8446	4492	3490	8040	2077	5810	1556
(1575)	2959	8387	9997	3128	2967	0841	4729	7479	1727	0573
(1576)	6331	4186	0340	0554	6612	6576	8914	1022	4622	9792
(1577)	5686	7036	4563	5407	1788	2839	0929	1075	5786	5203
(1578)	2376	1057	2131	9905	5922	7442	7951	3249	4853	4669
(1579)	9106	4393	5141	5684	1600	7274	2612	0333	6400	9727
(1580)	3859	9774	3560	0897	9756	4601	6537	3978	2873	8506
(1581)	6675	1140	8871	8346	2928	9342	5025	8823	4686	6376
(1582)	7420	5461	9831	2763	0928	1720	3681	4262	8370	8799
(1583)	2074	4387	2093	4224	4204	4590	1590	7780	7431	3259
(1584)	2810	2567	5355	0477	1741	2584	3553	8284	0740	7164
(1585)	8269	9954	1931	1916	6704	8191	6023	8515	0685	6996
(1586)	6267	3640	3580	7849	7028	8349	1668	5109	9578	1528
(1587)	1406	9629	1751	2012	3074	4343	3615	6565	8329	5392
(1588)	3990	1000	5015	7663	8934	3429	7799	4520	6399	9141
(1589)	7267	9424	3537	5131	8806	0651	1833	6323	5184	2134
(1590)	3880	7981	7752	2659	7634	8595	6566	6703	5461	8433
(1591)	5175	9939	2913	1593	9546	4148	0508	7562	3178	0849
(1592)	2999	2688	5731	7120	7963	9231	5259	6734	0448	4637
(1593)	9352	7993	9044	4390	6488	5890	5198	6901	3003	4210
(1594)	8966	7290	4169	0184	0896	3251	8752	9447	2667	1783
(1595)	6557	0955	2578	1165	1902	6154	8836	5530	4415	3627

	(01)	(02)	(03)	(04)	(05)	(06)	(07)	(08)	(09)	(10)
(1596)	3210	3651	5398	9543	2055	1444	9753	6626	8822	2074
(1597)	6482	2233	3463	6593	3632	0259	6039	0982	4032	8423
(1598)	1342	1937	3230	0444	3537	6010	2241	0978	2036	9646
(1599)	9155	3299	2999	6786	4869	3910	4435	3499	6603	1973
(1600)	4223	5346	9275	5558	1530	5555	2322	5609	3681	8397
(1601)	0781	5726	3907	7534	7375	8017	1476	8214	7297	8367
(1602)	3029	3279	5363	4385	3962	0397	7792	3276	6722	4205
(1603)	3650	1151	0772	1466	1742	7196	4314	0168	9315	9165
(1604)	7251	4929	8789	1025	6310	7222	6843	0855	2553	9865
(1605)	2259	1089	1108	4837	4601	3185	0794	6093	6591	8578
(1606)	7273	5101	0285	3288	9896	4359	2110	1254	7382	0885
(1607)	9400	2051	8859	0271	4896	0717	9065	9014	1299	6575
(1608)	3993	2730	3658	4492	2387	1658	4980	4482	1767	7708
(1609)	6445	9643	6102	6155	4419	7665	3105	3772	1594	4887
(1610)	0439	5123	7755	1644	9088	2455	3886	2327	0323	9814
(1611)	9432	5673	9244	8089	4342	0740	4991	4802	4471	7748
(1612)	5505	5523	1985	1133	0827	3938	5813	1714	5366	9015
(1613)	2332	3956	4154	7475	3747	3386	8926	7516	9990	0383
(1614)	3475	7330	5018	8379	1736	0836	5751	8268	2852	0375
(1615)	5163	7315	6747	6943	0785	3508	3352	3441	4571	9185
(1616)	4542	1557	4431	5188	8049	8090	5787	4276	5566	1428
(1617)	8790	1449	5250	1869	8980	5839	1249	6758	0052	9235
(1618)	0448	9768	5368	4385	5137	4851	5080	4140	4735	6574
(1619)	3234	2330	4945	0993	8726	8087	0526	9671	9732	6558
(1620)	1616	6550	3053	5506	1538	2641	7578	0955	4785	7539
(1621)	6123	1040	5406	8538	4521	0369	0044	8482	9291	3595
(1622)	3519	3539	2602	4306	5172	6717	2922	6532	6380	8762
(1623)	7537	8644	2487	4938	2020	5068	5423	5712	8527	1647
(1624)	7150	5033	6795	8032	2825	4500	9225	1070	8291	2408
(1625)	9939	7009	4924	2702	2486	3332	9192	4069	4011	9905
(1626)	1714	6715	1994	8467	4767	1845	9016	7942	9394	1386
(1627)	7490	6697	6344	3760	6787	4315	5871	4765	5998	0033
(1628)	1726	6471	9908	4322	2394	5361	9614	0119	3388	8376
(1629)	3878	4429	9700	8260	6652	9397	8562	8376	4834	5231
(1630)	8758	6440	4165	4742	8617	5540	3349	1595	2751	6818
(1631)	7841	5742	7752	6585	3851	4994	9858	7706	5057	3363
(1632)	9118	9702	2386	1065	1402	7591	1598	4994	0448	4047
(1633)	2336	2132	4528	3303	9864	0053	8378	6741	5899	8678
(1634)	1404	4907	9134	1779	2238	4345	8138	0886	8385	7936
(1635)	2333	8872	7958	6243	5413	2109	5598	4730	0030	0386
(1636)	7261	6460	3164	5649	5302	8899	3391	9297	9985	3539
(1637)	6202	4889	1354	7056	1140	7857	3034	9558	3289	3411
(1638)	7885	7739	5268	6766	8437	4140	4647	6174	6405	1748
(1639)	1796	4422	7482	0618	1557	2559	1511	4420	4933	5357
(1640)	4399	7616	8570	9075	4229	9719	5121	4161	9817	1428
(1641)	1970	3823	4811	2959	1743	4262	2077	6785	5972	6069
(1642)	2580	8955	0831	5863	5051	2245	0975	9024	8495	5845
(1643)	5858	9571	7757	0466	7455	8037	5847	1538	3344	6783
(1644)	9396	1143	1038	0899	5740	0362	5226	5364	8266	9610
(1645)	4042	6745	9114	6419	0532	6671	1569	9031	8815	0515

Appendix A
Random Numbers (Continued)

	(01)	(02)	(03)	(04)	(05)	(06)	(07)	(08)	(09)	(10)
(1646)	9728	7444	5907	9224	5108	3482	4858	9749	3030	4557
(1647)	9325	8358	3546	2021	0176	3372	8549	9571	2258	9533
(1648)	3381	0863	2894	4879	6094	4605	2062	5193	2788	8301
(1649)	7018	0768	7722	4851	2650	8831	9949	0684	6654	7408
(1650)	3210	0422	0684	3946	2961	0147	9698	7182	3784	0517
(1651)	3790	7829	7523	0202	3488	5242	4351	4905	8286	0149
(1652)	3428	1608	5899	8416	8789	5335	8055	9475	0942	3586
(1653)	4825	8311	3113	7388	1812	7352	8172	1945	5638	0569
(1654)	3297	4263	9854	0481	1443	9027	3100	0469	0153	8565
(1655)	9758	7440	2739	3350	7707	8099	3200	5003	9398	8846
(1656)	1973	2273	6381	3069	0449	6240	6334	5186	6984	0951
(1657)	3681	4069	9157	4301	0962	8686	1863	9729	2436	4313
(1658)	9001	9491	8207	9027	3597	1921	8765	0931	0514	3629
(1659)	1061	4247	0772	5645	2805	8019	3512	0399	5194	2078
(1660)	7092	5326	4915	3167	4990	9173	3816	5297	4735	4013
(1661)	3054	3194	2513	5308	2135	9227	8059	1034	1482	1701
(1662)	7978	4876	8945	0374	7737	3159	0357	8272	6768	9160
(1663)	0754	6336	8289	5400	3017	8241	3139	4870	9045	1621
(1664)	4567	1568	5151	7824	8268	9477	0545	2611	6762	4608
(1665)	7914	3779	9116	3742	1459	2802	7277	1431	8152	4303
(1666)	4699	1918	4618	0538	5247	3429	1514	5189	6211	4565
(1667)	1341	4848	6496	2140	7640	6970	3138	8793	7457	1198
(1668)	5761	2663	9860	4951	0736	3852	0178	7786	9156	0887
(1669)	8820	4429	6033	3506	5007	6981	7522	6863	5572	4087
(1670)	2552	3315	0855	3869	5329	5950	6352	8513	9164	8835
(1671)	1446	6284	7370	9822	6920	9799	4050	2182	2445	6416
(1672)	7581	6481	7203	9225	7846	7638	5940	8971	2483	6708
(1673)	8617	4929	6504	9411	0299	1954	5204	9102	6696	2649
(1674)	3611	7353	4079	1907	7231	4819	0540	9208	3070	8126
(1675)	8666	0894	1642	6869	5765	7663	8616	0448	3611	0974
(1676)	0590	7094	8180	6076	0702	0805	3411	1637	8008	6686
(1677)	1033	0185	8575	0254	7820	3312	3765	7655	9578	2413
(1678)	2735	2926	1943	5268	0465	1262	9223	7589	9880	0642
(1679)	3569	4873	6280	2578	0849	3064	4003	9844	3016	6122
(1680)	4130	5191	5973	5614	6833	7580	1688	6850	8277	2993
(1681)	8604	0241	1734	5988	9022	3850	8568	1170	8131	6864
(1682)	0306	0673	6977	2778	7102	1392	7454	7248	4000	6263
(1683)	3639	5276	5568	2246	6710	6491	3157	9726	1211	3208
(1684)	2685	8206	6398	1542	1166	1016	7098	1818	6446	2580
(1685)	2333	3235	5956	5925	6183	6390	7574	9465	7949	1870
(1686)	9825	4081	1165	2989	0419	8659	3380	8151	2934	6470
(1687)	2853	9837	0242	2228	8324	2466	8844	3375	9442	5145
(1688)	1810	7197	3108	4726	6596	3934	6150	3686	3097	7879
(1689)	6435	6284	6936	6638	7213	7541	2387	9992	3296	3810
(1690)	1153	5243	4651	9792	7346	3287	0007	4250	0136	9463
(1691)	8513	1666	9420	3906	5124	8044	2889	5699	3673	6426
(1692)	4737	6456	6178	6155	0939	1531	2011	3622	8258	8030
(1693)	1632	1949	5476	6497	5516	1697	3045	8768	4295	1197
(1694)	6683	1339	9602	7850	8550	0878	6097	6753	4343	2501
(1695)	5548	0384	6399	5451	1370	9070	7694	3681	2225	4223

	(01)	(02)	(03)	(04)	(05)	(06)	(07)	(08)	(09)	(10)
(1696)	3639	8928	3672	1500	8855	4782	2119	3757	5297	0183
(1697)	5804	4494	0747	0914	1878	5278	3432	0105	5903	9506
(1698)	3507	2735	7489	3017	6358	3445	5910	6371	7825	8041
(1699)	2575	7869	9065	5565	8568	0078	1386	3061	2222	2669
(1700)	2776	6843	1933	7989	0394	0046	1240	3779	1361	6995
(1701)	7746	2032	7542	0598	3520	9310	7892	3402	3154	7261
(1702)	1013	8924	1967	8620	4241	3343	3086	5646	8066	3296
(1703)	9478	0789	2138	7341	3096	5113	3718	8632	9477	8907
(1704)	5173	5131	2559	0426	2919	0798	9807	4367	2948	4425
(1705)	8377	2043	7962	6285	5344	4296	0266	8125	4225	9310
(1706)	6809	3118	1767	2142	2821	5539	7878	0363	5373	4956
(1707)	9675	7758	3756	6976	8262	8846	9177	5141	0087	5497
(1708)	9898	2495	8749	8832	8942	6444	0386	4642	8137	5603
(1709)	9721	6848	2074	3094	4023	0624	3981	3086	1624	6218
(1710)	3650	2510	8144	1236	1571	5857	0858	4734	9914	8599
(1711)	7465	8507	2264	7609	8230	0364	2625	0011	8320	6794
(1712)	8137	2118	4972	2168	5660	0056	8414	4319	0073	0123
(1713)	7913	8804	3000	4401	8217	6294	7333	3004	7945	8457
(1714)	6519	6812	8320	0866	8084	8651	3799	6396	5431	7408
(1715)	1452	4628	7332	6329	6168	8166	1639	3613	7093	3811
(1716)	5430	0011	4909	3043	2989	9482	1326	1515	7524	1326
(1717)	7075	4266	2842	4551	0026	0268	5573	9772	0251	7151
(1718)	9264	3392	1929	1464	2140	9818	3066	7632	5122	2067
(1719)	3539	9678	1507	1244	5481	5237	9646	7779	6206	6280
(1720)	1774	6304	7375	1808	8649	3262	1476	3277	1907	9272
(1721)	1529	0384	3558	1342	2058	6354	4547	7274	5270	7498
(1722)	7007	6069	3630	7473	7685	2272	3846	0850	4148	1203
(1723)	2837	9007	9404	8117	7802	0529	5691	8495	6574	8129
(1724)	7662	2236	7654	5914	5431	9654	4165	8498	8076	0243
(1725)	6933	8275	1591	6106	3042	6436	4267	1050	2152	5266
(1726)	9737	9114	3510	7962	2595	6606	5302	9381	4204	9788
(1727)	1766	6195	5510	2788	1589	4475	5882	8656	5175	4124
(1728)	1393	2881	5394	8343	0285	1562	0431	8112	5005	5427
(1729)	8972	4750	8985	3466	4192	9341	0065	3817	6554	3337
(1730)	1056	4225	3501	7636	8987	7816	3827	3354	4588	0546
(1731)	1786	6694	3302	9655	7874	4169	0372	8595	0810	3294
(1732)	0856	1977	0685	0940	3044	5274	7804	1230	5148	5804
(1733)	7232	7418	6377	5284	4393	0244	7987	5357	1963	6944
(1734)	1129	8040	2262	6400	5651	8038	4027	3400	3267	0303
(1735)	7253	4120	2025	2592	2949	5158	0430	9497	4216	8929
(1736)	6805	8798	0524	5630	8202	9095	3772	7871	3513	1904
(1737)	3621	1452	3737	8539	4197	1730	8301	2834	9011	2805
(1738)	3795	6590	0719	5066	7841	7825	6659	2878	1264	6998
(1739)	3150	4157	6389	7372	0033	9254	4354	5860	3355	0018
(1740)	3180	2605	4950	8455	2973	0034	7808	8828	1858	9100
(1741)	5891	5609	7498	7626	6596	1613	6050	6266	9752	2274
(1742)	0370	5099	1893	1074	2726	7451	1097	9708	4119	8371
(1743)	0826	8209	0642	6440	8606	2181	3598	5665	5617	7466
(1744)	9608	4566	0289	5890	6254	3760	0629	3575	4675	6721
(1745)	6100	8525	3323	3758	3587	3162	7829	5839	4883	6429

Appendix A
Random Numbers (Continued)

	(01)	(02)	(03)	(04)	(05)	(06)	(07)	(08)	(09)	(10)
(1746)	7093	7046	8001	4645	9587	9906	6733	7328	0388	6599
(1747)	0460	5279	8595	3508	5091	7508	6145	1551	2337	1646
(1748)	2634	8024	8118	3133	4712	1098	5704	2003	5473	5198
(1749)	7721	2735	2901	8209	6165	8204	3099	9881	9259	9709
(1750)	0321	1282	2097	7257	7355	6189	3524	8828	4952	2863
(1751)	8163	6439	3764	3725	0705	4214	4514	3965	7625	7406
(1752)	4281	5505	4135	3056	8181	2703	9658	0403	2768	6682
(1753)	5308	2842	5353	5348	7037	3453	8923	1141	7144	6192
(1754)	8116	5876	0016	4336	7588	5561	9942	2422	6067	0614
(1755)	4281	4619	8247	7421	9449	5347	0374	7908	2359	6309
(1756)	6638	7508	0197	6925	6611	7585	8487	1919	3163	7007
(1757)	6917	0122	0032	8393	3627	9755	1263	3789	1635	9842
(1758)	6555	4984	9489	5974	9915	4551	1655	3773	0176	2741
(1759)	8525	9938	6127	9215	9247	5041	9763	7661	0864	6090
(1760)	4009	4061	4086	7204	6033	7180	6262	1782	1633	1412
(1761)	7204	6174	8026	1689	9812	9152	2725	0688	8629	5398
(1762)	5856	6137	8110	4655	7067	7729	1238	4294	6368	5614
(1763)	8797	8999	4740	9563	7661	0748	2896	7884	2595	0426
(1764)	2758	6135	4042	2045	9456	8000	1493	7679	9568	1394
(1765)	8452	0427	2763	8313	4715	5278	7883	2595	7841	0445
(1766)	7291	5822	4816	5556	8116	6217	0105	5096	4627	8279
(1767)	6947	3852	3115	1583	7682	8916	3272	6182	6095	9911
(1768)	8178	2109	3648	3994	9733	4866	8568	3544	1199	7166
(1769)	7645	8534	3098	8672	3244	5782	6682	1010	4049	2721
(1770)	5534	6437	5145	8585	0616	4064	3943	6001	8037	8262
(1771)	9478	3628	5520	3488	1200	6355	7638	1768	7281	5814
(1772)	7703	8771	3862	2746	3868	5025	8801	8239	4122	9011
(1773)	9115	5557	5826	5649	8215	0723	8700	3294	9038	7498
(1774)	2390	5064	5872	5596	9155	5799	9509	9170	9893	3062
(1775)	7902	3026	5268	6465	8551	7479	0757	5474	7966	0796
(1776)	5336	6150	2527	5776	8323	9429	4862	0130	3259	8286
(1777)	5298	8400	9408	3677	8938	2888	1091	9954	5776	0122
(1778)	0878	0241	0285	2487	2841	2246	4631	8519	0256	8679
(1779)	9700	8093	5073	2847	8149	6658	8991	7333	1187	6336
(1780)	0787	6457	8284	7889	6731	1342	3490	9947	9332	9932
(1781)	4149	8879	6698	9872	7784	8121	1705	8143	2478	1555
(1782)	8028	2691	5179	8544	6291	9197	6429	7637	6178	8227
(1783)	5267	2113	0415	2476	9188	2813	7930	4819	6436	3418
(1784)	5659	3542	9716	7884	7405	1831	5094	5707	4083	4039
(1785)	1204	9291	9432	1797	1863	2008	5776	3943	2304	4075
(1786)	3449	4399	8154	6499	5071	1453	5451	5836	1558	2788
(1787)	9493	5235	8219	5705	6670	9621	1938	0941	2151	2477
(1788)	7687	8961	9011	3904	3310	6985	7620	6026	5224	4984
(1789)	7957	7314	5153	0897	0540	3754	0609	7958	1717	6658
(1790)	7917	3824	8509	0610	0276	7484	3129	2864	8034	9227
(1791)	5416	0823	7747	0489	1186	0998	6470	7581	0491	8425
(1792)	3464	6495	6228	5899	9674	7778	2314	1987	6896	4316
(1793)	9664	6745	7758	3761	0324	6609	8338	2780	5382	7851
(1794)	5445	4650	4521	1852	5531	9876	5398	0315	0518	9447
(1795)	3148	0803	7759	7447	3728	4106	8923	7963	1158	3006

A

	(01)	(02)	(03)	(04)	(05)	(06)	(07)	(08)	(09)	(10)
(1796)	6434	4389	9295	3249	5010	5098	8475	3266	3147	7418
(1797)	9472	1529	1443	5376	7049	1141	1410	2829	4227	8969
(1798)	8901	6025	7085	4891	5475	3818	4796	4009	4356	6290
(1799)	4794	1561	6085	1774	0258	8899	3595	5521	7389	7293
(1800)	8824	7045	6128	0008	2820	3904	5430	2636	6198	8707
(1801)	9873	0452	5986	4418	9489	3095	4545	1178	1382	4609
(1802)	9294	8497	0403	6770	3377	9253	9813	7339	4264	8901
(1803)	8097	0986	6726	1091	0037	2701	1611	4755	0032	9128
(1804)	9345	6993	1245	1034	1325	2014	8778	7904	3107	7790
(1805)	5389	0081	3895	2518	5888	7521	6674	7132	5877	3143
(1806)	9948	3239	1161	6348	9170	7139	3520	3421	5183	1740
(1807)	6643	6448	6424	2518	2769	5326	5510	5397	0397	2474
(1808)	6728	7760	7649	1784	3473	1101	3357	7793	7503	5612
(1809)	7190	3179	7118	7435	5786	4767	0815	9330	3969	5561
(1810)	3717	5582	1247	7937	8956	9245	9750	3282	6030	6709
(1811)	0652	4035	5194	4128	6666	3938	2496	7575	9477	1093
(1812)	1895	5808	8672	1724	1351	1901	5332	5980	3008	5268
(1813)	4145	6994	6864	3494	6444	2846	3498	7997	1961	1659
(1814)	9067	3783	1942	2157	0025	2476	7666	9299	0865	4410
(1815)	6093	8708	6832	0507	4808	7868	6824	2891	9227	6196
(1816)	7644	8739	4291	3072	5637	1348	5535	3124	8163	2889
(1817)	0579	8198	4880	4755	6289	9123	1776	3352	7455	5220
(1818)	3580	4467	7035	2789	6716	9187	4140	5652	1058	7536
(1819)	3201	7431	5487	0776	5289	7847	3296	0894	1460	0192
(1820)	4449	7934	8248	6087	0555	3874	2479	2078	5859	7363
(1821)	6270	1603	1066	2874	4413	9120	8077	1859	8776	2616
(1822)	4553	0904	0472	0800	3338	0557	8144	1153	8262	5383
(1823)	4768	4587	0085	5896	4037	6844	6937	9987	6117	8617
(1824)	7920	0778	6740	9356	5893	6308	2051	0991	4601	2390
(1825)	5500	0105	4530	7979	3277	9117	9358	8870	6548	8357
(1826)	2815	4670	3971	1739	8695	7433	6697	6248	5947	0366
(1827)	3132	1787	6462	5666	6389	4973	3100	8035	8738	2623
(1828)	8557	5708	6082	5356	7663	5237	1092	8345	6855	4675
(1829)	8399	9440	2710	4603	1205	0637	2996	5845	5739	0683
(1830)	5214	2186	1377	2537	6685	5409	6648	5113	3861	0164
(1831)	6627	1945	8041	6571	0010	2841	8684	0322	7697	5701
(1832)	7892	7698	6088	5247	2092	0530	1189	8853	0455	4099
(1833)	3272	7349	2589	9849	3837	2069	1568	1109	4899	2212
(1834)	3222	8183	9253	6565	7390	4357	4531	7899	4025	7937
(1835)	5652	9528	1007	4005	0878	5484	8296	3643	1482	1900
(1836)	9084	8735	3695	2882	7519	4258	2888	2842	6398	7371
(1837)	4150	0118	2754	5696	0767	4222	6545	3004	8010	4949
(1838)	2204	4421	6041	2795	8337	2559	0953	2911	0346	6762
(1839)	9185	6513	2496	9920	8069	5085	9604	0291	7455	0790
(1840)	4319	7672	7632	9703	4870	9070	7223	9543	2487	6818
(1841)	4735	3510	9424	1281	1251	4885	5578	1308	4275	9604
(1842)	2632	5122	5621	5642	2493	9210	6772	8810	4068	0927
(1843)	9941	7794	1038	5533	7832	2849	5921	8830	3418	1637
(1844)	6545	8043	9993	5175	9766	9261	1276	6811	0237	0659
(1845)	2642	7283	1302	9907	9762	6221	1997	8811	4935	7026

Appendix A
Random Numbers (Continued)

	(01)	(02)	(03)	(04)	(05)	(06)	(07)	(08)	(09)	(10)
(1846)	6267	6854	5278	3156	0964	2493	2356	2584	6083	7867
(1847)	1444	4018	4683	4486	5811	6483	9058	6515	9655	2161
(1848)	4199	2170	0379	4629	4443	2265	0581	4932	5904	9293
(1849)	4635	5356	6397	3551	3862	9170	4300	2238	5199	0387
(1850)	7268	3864	4062	3215	6237	4371	4479	8381	2673	3585
(1851)	2814	0306	0234	9577	7468	7295	9739	3318	5400	0917
(1852)	7927	7974	7389	2958	8787	0471	0979	3462	7854	1195
(1853)	9503	8048	2534	6301	5740	8251	2380	5906	0820	0392
(1854)	4658	4601	4609	8312	9526	6779	1354	5076	9698	7492
(1855)	0072	9359	2131	7698	4767	1777	0467	6497	9799	8411
(1856)	1575	5024	2335	0251	4153	0029	7613	7793	0375	9843
(1857)	1093	5152	1588	6585	9354	8417	1583	9247	0258	2464
(1858)	5087	0696	7918	7409	3277	3196	7926	8559	0473	1797
(1859)	1076	2683	1292	6948	5122	3824	3945	4542	9013	0757
(1860)	7060	7827	6590	3585	4947	5064	9844	7561	9470	4249
(1861)	7081	5584	5082	7223	0000	3320	9479	2110	5143	7854
(1862)	0125	9912	8453	3301	9825	9395	1855	4600	7981	6433
(1863)	9736	2134	4100	1252	5591	1289	2198	0335	9950	4680
(1864)	8357	9551	4327	5455	3151	5815	3015	4373	4698	8995
(1865)	4080	9431	6325	4636	5967	6753	9955	5443	3582	4746
(1866)	1695	5930	7393	2589	2286	1934	5631	0561	3541	6824
(1867)	7429	2039	0345	2850	9072	2912	6527	4487	2345	1981
(1868)	2477	0772	3877	3544	1155	3066	3017	0347	0514	4408
(1869)	4019	1611	6937	6835	1825	3179	2643	2220	7813	2876
(1870)	6247	7668	4199	7583	7432	4182	3343	1750	5694	6126
(1871)	5563	5869	8381	2431	1715	5780	4064	0034	1999	7467
(1872)	6128	5299	7811	7579	4829	5083	0797	3536	4983	1855
(1873)	2340	3732	2964	3283	7496	7923	2473	6468	7906	7041
(1874)	8162	0427	8808	9541	3696	4139	8015	3909	2133	2484
(1875)	9228	2137	0512	5866	1604	3804	2211	6066	2556	0807
(1876)	7521	3150	3468	5882	5475	5938	3659	2996	1733	4960
(1877)	0001	8037	8651	5632	4889	5124	9565	4923	6606	4061
(1878)	7331	4037	5552	4272	8756	5899	3375	5345	5524	2469
(1879)	3695	6996	5194	9262	5684	7950	8495	9863	7084	1079
(1880)	7379	4213	2072	4460	6162	4019	0774	4547	2124	8306
(1881)	5287	9612	1173	5895	3674	6409	7544	2546	7427	7389
(1882)	2087	8338	7761	3572	1206	8989	6081	5153	2276	0146
(1883)	0562	4804	6871	6647	5085	2204	5876	3608	2955	0721
(1884)	9751	4856	5285	1161	5364	9518	6410	2454	3388	6288
(1885)	0944	8057	6609	9171	4930	9558	7228	6181	3200	7656
(1886)	0971	7942	5587	2652	4329	5627	0519	9655	0141	3739
(1887)	0742	5206	8916	4206	0515	8391	4416	4354	5929	3384
(1888)	4247	2147	6139	4073	3111	4604	7677	4722	2652	5337
(1889)	0944	0346	3329	1068	9342	8702	7169	3070	2924	3353
(1890)	6512	7420	5463	9329	4799	9754	0276	4299	0684	2916
(1891)	5041	1138	8501	0916	6424	8528	9397	4308	7810	3681
(1892)	9586	6677	1224	6857	5665	8873	8563	7304	8225	4711
(1893)	4397	0788	7976	3000	8172	6158	1677	0439	7254	7413
(1894)	1794	8504	6487	6480	2147	9901	4044	3570	6065	8544
(1895)	0149	1191	5733	5057	4355	4823	5858	8421	4108	4062

A

	(01)	(02)	(03)	(04)	(05)	(06)	(07)	(08)	(09)	(10)
(1896)	4090	7578	1996	5008	6150	2879	8102	5345	2576	2406
(1897)	5096	7151	0849	8130	6983	4380	6302	3220	9537	0627
(1898)	4969	1922	6188	0724	0319	5405	8492	4522	1981	7464
(1899)	6985	5617	9976	8697	0977	4262	8106	4563	0517	1420
(1900)	8177	7382	2063	2731	1567	7228	1782	8204	1815	5744
(1901)	8254	5325	0488	7560	6755	5907	6519	6951	8115	2052
(1902)	4583	5563	9496	8480	9945	3904	7729	2602	2900	2889
(1903)	7914	2971	4636	8972	3058	4752	5366	8077	6217	5681
(1904)	4733	3894	9875	1163	0970	8621	9039	2309	5470	8297
(1905)	0077	5029	7638	9698	8917	8146	7091	2147	2716	2694
(1906)	5643	6036	6932	2876	0864	6694	9089	8826	0803	5825
(1907)	8208	5772	2617	7483	9751	6970	1078	9077	5403	3322
(1908)	4990	1840	2021	9141	9035	3818	9331	9408	5205	3028
(1909)	8833	0075	7778	2289	9493	2146	3493	7188	4598	6395
(1910)	9454	2255	4175	7229	4345	0717	7399	0806	2831	4417
(1911)	0946	5268	1520	5296	9082	8148	4911	8359	5880	2803
(1912)	0213	6021	6804	0252	6286	9176	8118	0654	3993	9352
(1913)	9315	5396	1318	5140	0731	7958	5080	0716	9251	7412
(1914)	3867	9832	1310	3463	2615	9914	9336	6943	5421	9746
(1915)	1606	2312	7909	2607	9348	2711	2901	9044	3081	1889
(1916)	1517	0912	4507	7324	5663	5361	0579	8166	6268	4397
(1917)	6039	8163	7451	7156	5908	4878	9674	5687	1677	5817
(1918)	0771	2756	1170	7461	2885	0094	3258	4358	6501	3534
(1919)	6114	4204	4844	2660	7160	5290	1023	5574	3898	2361
(1920)	1461	7090	8652	9583	2014	6161	9304	1763	9573	9946
(1921)	4518	5425	3191	1477	9958	7075	0649	4768	2779	4813
(1922)	2270	1243	7411	9453	8378	2519	0725	9201	4667	9492
(1923)	0128	1122	2114	2456	8836	2188	9123	4050	2971	4184
(1924)	8116	2858	1368	5269	4732	9009	9724	9582	9002	9927
(1925)	5964	2895	9707	9160	7434	6121	0033	8256	5138	0862
(1926)	2794	9164	2187	8528	8565	9086	9160	4494	4401	9465
(1927)	5493	4807	2684	7248	7154	4171	9433	1264	3805	6524
(1928)	3492	2658	2087	8773	4805	6860	0204	3272	0602	5365
(1929)	7096	4969	6661	4657	3779	5384	6862	3765	9180	9340
(1930)	0983	8701	9395	2703	9086	8042	5686	4184	8036	8294
(1931)	0432	0147	6145	2889	3100	6965	8361	3348	8849	9371
(1932)	6535	2684	1078	4187	1225	0512	8812	2375	1233	0414
(1933)	5017	8323	4295	0007	0256	7609	3665	8242	0384	5124
(1934)	3252	5041	9126	8557	2643	9733	2529	3244	5549	4949
(1935)	2347	6896	8091	8711	2887	4733	0882	3166	8097	0670
(1936)	8287	2460	6432	4248	1884	0828	7676	5366	2454	7148
(1937)	5465	2875	1872	6327	2426	5472	1540	9582	1464	1637
(1938)	4805	6158	9639	2986	5179	0518	5360	9394	7037	9672
(1939)	9432	2302	5735	4810	2460	3859	1576	5084	5097	6747
(1940)	7848	1683	6784	1201	3307	0299	6309	5172	7613	5612
(1941)	7575	1953	0002	8487	0508	7832	8679	7364	7898	8954
(1942)	3785	6673	0100	2814	3960	0661	8031	4918	8114	2123
(1943)	5879	2299	4320	2931	0164	5604	1342	3985	6981	2547
(1944)	7406	1527	9912	8887	2914	3097	7717	0960	9573	0466
(1945)	4738	9040	7449	9560	4791	5349	3516	5608	4153	2005

	(01)	(02)	(03)	(04)	(05)	(06)	(07)	(08)	(09)	(10)
(1946)	5041	1073	4150	7928	5005	5672	7330	7818	6703	2449
(1947)	3735	6854	4808	0328	0958	9342	1447	8896	5418	2866
(1948)	2124	8517	9532	4104	3480	2331	0358	7120	0231	8008
(1949)	8670	3439	2747	6785	0286	6864	8798	1650	4102	5141
(1950)	8127	0029	6794	8248	6775	4170	6318	8801	9923	3000
(1951)	9412	0479	4846	1371	0581	1664	1122	8002	4225	2501
(1952)	3093	4415	2053	8206	6010	2495	3530	2168	5916	6299
(1953)	3007	7020	9723	2119	2861	3721	8225	5841	0124	7226
(1954)	9477	2357	0145	0505	6760	3635	8241	8973	3864	0373
(1955)	8923	6579	7875	0905	3718	9447	0302	9632	7274	3415
(1956)	2852	9010	6954	5021	0542	3716	1126	2860	1986	1668
(1957)	8285	8147	9413	9468	0221	2539	0346	2163	9051	6755
(1958)	1134	6751	6730	3924	5614	0179	3810	1359	0885	3243
(1959)	0752	9314	8206	0765	9447	4072	9370	9330	8351	6903
(1960)	2498	2351	1138	7849	0262	9586	3288	4142	1539	9768
(1961)	4772	8844	5757	6192	8012	9544	4026	3533	6088	4888
(1962)	0994	7245	3885	3382	5253	0540	3371	6159	0831	9939
(1963)	0814	5177	3539	1879	6787	4664	0716	2408	5511	2957
(1964)	9680	7299	2197	2933	1913	6065	7020	5853	5205	2455
(1965)	5577	6487	4534	8313	3850	6254	6642	4169	3619	3805
(1966)	2457	2132	5730	5388	4006	7591	5531	6849	9622	9781
(1967)	1772	5681	4664	0202	8921	4672	8530	2502	8241	0209
(1968)	2659	1755	5402	8881	1312	5115	3537	6801	4030	6185
(1969)	5429	5789	0098	4923	8009	4356	8931	6141	6613	2443
(1970)	0487	2511	6904	2047	7625	1509	9072	2937	9136	9743
(1971)	5123	0197	5012	0946	4377	5382	6104	3250	1239	7011
(1972)	6551	2297	4662	0939	1719	0211	5349	1608	4414	8245
(1973)	4866	4660	6564	0906	7029	0861	9224	0388	6624	1356
(1974)	9399	9720	8629	3671	5071	4211	6620	5310	9515	9834
(1975)	5771	8967	7096	2380	5353	7045	6525	7975	4511	9024
(1976)	6627	7462	6385	2312	7009	4317	8783	8337	6165	5038
(1977)	9032	5907	2428	3526	0997	0809	8893	5108	2658	2805
(1978)	9312	2486	4988	2438	5655	9369	2159	5673	0090	6727
(1979)	1654	5551	6457	0199	8107	2240	7819	0414	4007	7681
(1980)	9169	7880	0543	2303	2601	3724	9152	3486	9925	0608
(1981)	2483	4709	6257	9719	6698	8442	7298	8327	6706	4546
(1982)	1137	0645	2696	6125	6291	8282	1007	6335	0072	7447
(1983)	2343	4673	0549	7204	8418	7153	5975	1250	0185	5777
(1984)	3025	7450	4081	1672	8406	8875	4268	9690	3401	2364
(1985)	8247	9521	4400	1474	2721	5309	8128	3043	2509	1671
(1986)	7315	4821	4074	3677	4300	3912	5342	6734	5595	2045
(1987)	6960	9142	2970	7386	4068	6310	3701	6859	4667	1775
(1988)	9730	8462	0694	5276	4700	6548	0896	2971	8644	7635
(1989)	0139	7469	8321	1234	3806	1091	7663	3619	1257	8029
(1990)	4028	7594	5276	9291	5892	5997	7211	6918	4077	0958
(1991)	0153	6062	1701	9226	9755	8664	2188	5660	8202	2722
(1992)	2827	3291	8767	1245	3931	7579	3612	0199	5761	8575
(1993)	2748	5258	1936	2791	2477	5192	0623	4648	2608	4538
(1994)	7013	5272	4698	3932	7090	5487	4022	6223	4520	5198
(1995)	7479	8087	0277	2716	3587	9441	3956	1052	4914	0036

	(01)	(02)	(03)	(04)	(05)	(06)	(07)	(08)	(09)	(10)
(1996)	3970	7135	5875	6720	7324	8521	1416	7072	8517	6592
(1997)	5397	8500	1382	7872	6306	7497	8410	9988	3956	8959
(1998)	7642	9131	8826	8093	3454	9903	5578	9776	4861	9613
(1999)	8573	8456	9716	7323	9933	4240	9516	7025	2334	2050
(2000)	3301	8940	9317	0504	7585	2354	8894	3236	3516	4683
(2001)	8371	9638	7226	3948	5895	9726	0962	9407	3537	3980
(2002)	9674	1288	4449	6721	7376	4014	2595	3282	1514	5078
(2003)	1036	8561	9563	8882	1665	9733	1631	9124	9014	6671
(2004)	8778	6394	6587	4081	8147	1287	3670	7216	8808	8702
(2005)	7117	7763	0663	4221	7576	3389	0296	1375	2927	2157
(2006)	4947	3526	8164	9492	4304	2241	3681	0552	3217	2754
(2007)	1248	7864	4638	6229	6785	6266	2147	4926	9801	7003
(2008)	7615	8305	6448	5024	9641	2454	3976	9103	6268	7924
(2009)	4452	9652	9445	3282	6992	1259	3533	3943	4162	8440
(2010)	0368	7061	9059	0350	1090	1194	5785	1037	3089	5520
(2011)	1119	5612	5272	0851	8934	8690	0990	3785	5493	8503
(2012)	8514	4371	6737	8678	3228	0946	9707	1927	8572	5858
(2013)	7052	5946	8423	0670	2982	3339	7849	1147	9485	8310
(2014)	1260	2728	8727	1032	8520	1997	1508	4052	0841	7196
(2015)	2276	8236	4799	0387	9288	9225	0726	6154	2970	2561
(2016)	2886	1264	8431	2465	2633	7445	6105	7349	8463	2136
(2017)	3316	8636	9639	1108	5286	7952	4945	2951	8927	5194
(2018)	6344	7786	6093	8402	3837	6417	5177	2537	9766	6222
(2019)	1779	8323	3897	4586	2160	6378	4729	4903	1034	8892
(2020)	7587	6741	6393	6948	0354	3505	6345	4842	7973	8876
(2021)	5468	3873	8236	9294	0578	2162	3762	1135	3788	7275
(2022)	2725	8335	0634	7507	5223	0223	4248	7947	2602	6112
(2023)	6405	0288	4866	6892	5444	6248	8784	5849	6665	9607
(2024)	0945	3746	4109	7033	3311	0027	1476	6616	6035	5681
(2025)	6145	7179	0867	2679	2527	2277	5244	7867	1700	0747
(2026)	7120	8015	8365	2277	8140	6465	6324	2181	4528	3826
(2027)	3841	6527	1443	5913	7130	5975	7252	5923	4729	0319
(2028)	5585	5827	7085	7034	9804	4220	5246	0484	4893	5669
(2029)	2628	6471	4236	9912	3901	4500	9990	3472	2599	0641
(2030)	5197	8017	4893	9279	1163	8989	1187	9095	1685	0156
(2031)	4159	1921	6862	7400	1203	5875	2574	8838	7465	1381
(2032)	9421	0667	3736	4659	4007	0485	0577	0055	6313	2197
(2033)	8136	7248	4537	1558	4785	9943	3882	0959	1114	1581
(2034)	9645	1530	7424	6878	3746	0549	6401	3607	8812	0470
(2035)	9154	7184	3437	8972	1597	0701	3173	7218	5867	0934
(2036)	6086	8957	8256	3495	3210	3359	3842	2527	8002	5941
(2037)	5415	7752	0074	4192	9251	2019	0910	1641	0629	5604
(2038)	4504	6388	3865	7824	7429	6934	2841	0575	2212	9201
(2039)	7653	5310	6806	6830	1930	1697	8092	0244	0835	5666
(2040)	5340	4186	7010	2396	2359	8958	0215	8209	6122	9315
(2041)	9726	4890	6941	0506	3652	5341	0983	8786	5325	0647
(2042)	4304	8135	3903	5907	4496	7542	7396	9061	1141	1230
(2043)	0168	0043	9405	9584	0677	9111	2029	5650	6378	9427
(2044)	9951	7204	9900	9443	5778	3001	9884	0297	7924	9833
(2045)	4884	5994	7176	6666	2415	2068	9824	4566	3754	3509

Random Numbers (Continued)

	(01)	(02)	(03)	(04)	(05)	(06)	(07)	(08)	(09)	(10)
(2046)	3012	4827	1132	1438	7315	5994	6691	7368	7295	0934
(2047)	9239	9852	9088	7341	1449	1808	0577	4116	1941	4086
(2048)	3160	9373	5558	5568	0082	5974	0232	1272	0050	9998
(2049)	1569	4873	4862	0094	4964	9291	6905	0484	9932	6517
(2050)	5015	7682	8299	8170	0868	4326	0117	0785	9892	3985
(2051)	0954	8308	0227	8575	2541	9332	1721	5731	2245	2469
(2052)	2612	3635	4170	7697	7124	9320	9536	0485	5765	0040
(2053)	7123	7210	2065	7637	6794	7765	5923	9676	0409	9488
(2054)	7299	6734	3556	1192	7274	8082	5472	4625	6574	7557
(2055)	8475	2182	9735	3958	1701	2013	9026	5386	9101	1987
(2056)	1852	3821	5237	9693	6975	0600	1562	5057	1492	2172
(2057)	3279	2121	2374	8840	1282	1678	1280	9301	8498	7717
(2058)	3153	8266	1291	3663	6574	1355	4298	6544	9479	6263
(2059)	2558	8201	2605	4730	2538	9545	2943	4945	5975	0177
(2060)	5416	3400	9735	0863	3973	1947	0293	4374	4958	2013
(2061)	7294	7558	7153	8556	2058	3647	8727	8230	1739	5636
(2062)	9619	2041	1722	7876	7594	7619	2143	8331	6115	7199
(2063)	4838	1041	5981	2132	1972	3122	0838	3422	0610	2677
(2064)	8344	4753	2050	2498	4125	7203	2914	6683	1890	6555
(2065)	8531	3926	4061	9519	7911	9433	3137	4918	1483	8678
(2066)	7870	5916	1380	3554	0517	6240	6745	9093	5811	6371
(2067)	1260	0241	3234	1445	1487	9995	2587	0687	5381	1470
(2068)	1820	4543	3468	7714	9676	9523	0266	1355	9561	4026
(2069)	6531	8572	9719	7355	5463	3848	5650	6609	7352	6979
(2070)	6632	3164	7484	1140	5185	6971	8745	9176	8966	4392
(2071)	2905	1237	8412	8563	4202	9170	8462	7700	6793	9398
(2072)	5582	0050	8566	8729	4052	9213	2840	3584	9811	4078
(2073)	3072	7457	6891	1277	9659	0574	8332	6818	1498	0690
(2074)	0947	0024	7144	7613	7046	7066	0404	1651	0794	3466
(2075)	6187	4354	8212	0637	2603	5966	6246	1742	0217	7584
(2076)	4086	8184	4463	3005	9527	3717	4309	2151	1686	2066
(2077)	7235	1573	0102	6812	6006	2246	3330	1254	4104	8465
(2078)	9601	5265	8945	9413	8832	8304	7700	6394	9751	8168
(2079)	8577	5448	9598	5961	4102	2482	7934	6261	4727	5305
(2080)	0541	6915	3318	1184	2779	2028	4934	1136	7657	8480
(2081)	2074	5343	6594	7413	8925	4020	5771	9543	9670	2655
(2082)	2562	9807	8537	6607	4391	8005	4551	7671	3379	5038
(2083)	6532	5804	2605	8075	2739	8074	9277	2313	1896	4086
(2084)	0607	1448	0043	3792	4232	9175	8140	9367	2704	2499
(2085)	8265	2013	2779	3790	7859	6479	5903	0948	8497	8976
(2086)	3232	1929	9055	1587	6246	9749	2452	4414	4761	5901
(2087)	9520	8415	7041	7394	1433	8575	8537	3901	7818	4193
(2088)	3528	1052	8933	0431	6507	2858	8341	8725	9460	7938
(2089)	4137	6717	6414	6892	9812	3797	3914	2143	5276	9380
(2090)	6994	6262	6828	9203	2300	5390	9608	4943	5406	7663
(2091)	4061	6579	6156	5018	8325	4823	9243	8037	5304	2124
(2092)	9840	2909	0945	0563	9300	0404	5158	2670	5681	8422
(2093)	0307	1365	1375	7836	7170	3294	9984	5458	1275	4750
(2094)	4150	6042	4784	5834	9484	0162	1987	2535	6535	7434
(2095)	5876	5006	1035	1711	2737	1181	1499	1014	8608	5398

	(01)	(02)	(03)	(04)	(05)	(06)	(07)	(08)	(09)	(10)
(2096)	0807	5303	8379	4816	1209	5063	0062	0947	2713	8720
(2097)	3821	8983	1856	6260	3113	5630	3031	4147	0036	8888
(2098)	5774	3333	0428	0969	5474	1551	6611	5079	9256	6825
(2099)	0113	6506	4449	6566	3643	7351	7271	6542	0228	9435
(2100)	3639	3432	7962	2325	4240	6918	2644	7225	5967	4769
(2101)	6483	4870	4465	7256	4541	9023	6135	9163	7505	2100
(2102)	1144	8039	4297	1483	0661	7090	0404	9019	1139	1316
(2103)	1874	4866	0038	1726	5527	5648	2558	6054	9746	2713
(2104)	3621	9598	0998	7920	5211	6033	3562	5373	7113	6007
(2105)	6277	3043	0565	0753	1151	1025	2255	8210	4843	0338
(2106)	8099	9128	1929	0410	2754	8580	7667	9321	2299	1132
(2107)	2850	4335	9390	8278	4315	0802	5420	0726	2350	2046
(2108)	5852	5102	2250	1232	7516	0600	4688	6407	7204	2543
(2109)	2227	8490	4777	6143	9900	3226	0210	2708	2364	0168
(2110)	3712	0520	7617	2833	0870	6183	9387	1304	1397	5083
(2111)	1970	8297	2310	4737	9122	6851	4323	4102	9765	2951
(2112)	7637	0202	4254	0282	8826	8070	6738	1166	4378	6890
(2113)	9126	1221	9940	2132	8661	4487	5074	5093	1347	3458
(2114)	9471	2909	3080	1587	6694	3635	1675	1447	6321	8708
(2115)	9834	8074	1023	9795	6932	8975	5171	1302	0430	1308
(2116)	9343	6028	5873	3928	7069	3867	2289	6352	4033	7080
(2117)	2039.	0262	8998	8067	4682	9001	8874	1103	4416	0276
(2118)	5171	5488	8325	0389	7136	9502	6796	3099	0460	6322
(2119)	1827	7885	2712	9422	2723	8121	1727	5819	4289	8831
(2120)	6350	0482	1392	0352	6172	7932	4256	6196	2685	8405
(2121)	9463	7739	7949	4230	4611	3264	7605	3682	7566	4429
(2122)	3931	0966	5039	9227	2730	6341	1970	5864	8299	2717
(2123)	5656	8174	5376	6446	0554	4751	8432	1258	9195	7328
(2124)	5901	3277	7681	9985	1358	8474	9310	6920	0433	6997
(2125)	9534	5171	6268	2698	3804	4786	1619	8967	0483	1146
(2126)	0807	6894	0647	7165	1875	9594	4204	3604	4397	5671
(2127)	0100	6155	0517	6841	7475	2698	3517	9844	7045	3218
(2128)	0384	0437	9678	0024	4441	4360	9257	8750	5649	7811
(2129)	3103	8124	0160	4465	9196	5025	2303	8569	1377	1966
(2130)	3896	4111	2476	9461	7455	0120	8626	9178	4437	3568
(2131)	1727	5594	8813	4284	2573	8034	4495	3437	8271	1318
(2132)	4909	1314	8044	5505	8424	3937	3296	3626	7248	9401
(2133)	0025	2334	1541	1401	4191	4442	0374	6890	9699	9219
(2134)	5067	1083	2708	5780	1953	2696	4779	0677	7886	1911
(2135)	8339	3141	0083	3888	7143	2484	5607	3197	6970	7641
(2136)	9413	6075	7899	5135	9676	0953	2049	2725	7422	0394
(2137)	0273	4684	5578	6709	0118	4309	7467	0919	3970	6736
(2138)	1536	5881	9226	8543	1152	1151	6125	5401	7356	8695
(2139)	4412	6101	1274	3406	5255	9303	0165	2660	2585	5688
(2140)	2296	8697	2150	7988	3044	4446	3767	7232	4564	6998
(2141)	1512	9792	2667	9156	2514	9464	9387	3832	1103	2545
(2142)	2272	8074	2522	6587	7933	0587	5045	3504	1947	1456
(2143)	9385	5733	7410	3717	5488	3254	7061	3214	2304	1318
(2144)	1347	3907	0749	8913	7339	1084	6386	2045	4644	7450
(2145)	8538	0095	6483	5495	2534	4837	8914	3037	3733	5211

Appendix A
Random Numbers (Continued)

	(01)	(02)	(03)	(04)	(05)	(06)	(07)	(08)	(09)	(10)
(2146)	9966	0031	9625	2336	7076	0244	4288	1895	4470	0071
(2147)	1407	2040	2905	7123	7340	3684	6316	6562	4211	1210
(2148)	0468	0091	9341	0106	9711	1144	5449	4372	5706	1394
(2149)	7324	9764	0857	9660	7597	5657	9959	1195	0263	1989
(2150)	9951	4041	6657	0419	1082	8343	6226	5791	0078	4453
(2151)	2780	8620	8515	3947	5553	8623	0692	9286	2941	7702
(2152)	7399	5201	1686	7767	5073	6850	8846	4111	9942	1521
(2153)	1383	9346	3669	2634	2155	4351	8502	0004	8193	4531
(2154)	7819	8778	3174	6106	4953	9523	3410	8004	6955	7620
(2155)	0777	9539	3138	9877	5968	1989	7780	4070	3611	4451
(2156)	1298	8420	1893	1968	8031	7435	7671	4842	9779	5756
(2157)	5165	3005	9296	0625	7356	8206	5982	5083	0324	6088
(2158)	4999	8625	8757	2935	8573	5479	2672	0408	3307	9564
(2159)	1704	5249	7563	9849	8688	8094	6156	2501	7708	7961
(2160)	7742	0069	3308	4144	1448	9142	7378	0649	1873	6472
(2161)	6977	7804	1907	1479	2037	0956	7850	1069	4731	3176
(2162)	2019	9514	3236	3757	1821	8131	6098	4278	2286	3782
(2163)	3572	4173	1618	4188	5982	5713	0138	5521	4965	9164
(2164)	2245	5758	2474	0101	9077	4349	5646	7985	3668	9215
(2165)	8542	1476	1942	0369	2170	0481	9816	4276	7534	6230
(2166)	5471	0256	8753	9215	5905	8791	8311	0593	6403	3138
(2167)	6415	0525	5671	6070	7729	6599	8949	3585	6534	6355
(2168)	8340	8307	9095	7244	5846	3625	1736	6804	4387	9183
(2169)	1441	4092	6916	1905	8164	4745	4350	2085	0324	0727
(2170)	8038	9610	3960	7778	0337	5565	6221	6676	6319	4040
(2171)	8818	5796	4974	3589	8499	8462	7536	6996	2270	1751
(2172)	4790	9830	5766	6698	3245	2597	1932	1356	5623	1867
(2173)	1447	8636	3831	4703	9820	8161	7269	4589	9320	0165
(2174)	2613	7809	5232	8703	8565	0688	3993	0536	7146	3457
(2175)	3282	4552	6789	9708	4138	1285	4068	5739	5720	6729
(2176)	1335	5407	7177	8110	9948	8703	3723	5058	6423	7648
(2177)	3563	9396	8266	4813	9445	1732	3283	9128	7512	5543
(2178)	4172	2992	6510	2074	3306	2926	4968	6800	8938	1621
(2179)	4309	4913	5818	2925	5749	4167	0501	7649	4775	7259
(2180)	7606	3040	3279	6545	1090	4522	0859	1312	4062	8463
(2181)	9221	4181	7626	7736	0259	2224	5552	8356	1901	2188
(2182)	8725	2869	0892	0644	2847	2310	9383	7291	8179	5173
(2183)	0614	3563	8757	4697	4886	5911	9015	0830	2363	8578
(2184)	0007	4616	1386	7605	9987	6366	0182	6489	1626	9838
(2185)	2586	5447	6666	0946	7491	5894	4952	4778	3241	3244
(2186)	5915	4642	0544	4304	1624	7086	3620	0682	5470	7488
(2187)	4461	5139	0452	4366	2038	5303	2477	8414	5375	2473
(2188)	6751	4283	8247	7849	7182	5796	9971	1479	9787	7883
(2189)	3200	2785	0673	9188	7909	1963	6063	6827	1802	5421
(2190)	5078	7618	3052	1847	0033	5060	2156	1073	2928	5819
(2191)	8058	1095	1491	1852	8954	5822	8605	7294	9609	6242
(2192)	8084	0356	4394	9463	3263	8527	5750	4919	9026	8907
(2193)	1667	8810	8615	1621	1218	8492	6904	5360	6754	1802
(2194)	0606	9044	3383	7028	2955	4505	2717	0816	6531	7128
(2195)	2977	6032	0121	7613	5830	8773	4367	5013	6358	4525

	(01)	(02)	(03)	(04)	(05)	(06)	(07)	(08)	(09)	(10)
(2196)	1285	8187	8710	4030	0584	7618	8956	1376	0110	0785
(2197)	5499	6165	7906	7413	3272	3878	8078	9117	5790	5913
(2198)	6840	8434	8165	9325	0234	6998	4087	6999	4648	2583
(2199)	0160	8967	9316	3847	5685	8698	9569	8103	3661	9387
(2200)	1557	0117	9507	6394	7914	4507	9532	1350	7234	9035
(2201)	7378	2867	5128	4126	0749	8489	0076	2041	3603	5649
(2202)	7699	4071	8136	4098	2311	3466	3670	8647	8435	9964
(2203)	7404	5550	4574	0035	8322	0006	7931	5561	7311	8370
(2204)	6971	5164	9672	7304	1600	2396	6346	3822	8085	1201
(2205)	0402	5753	5454	1922	0774	3179	1988	1550	8649	3810
(2206)	2335	0325	2268	2635	3083	9867	0368	3708	6466	8631
(2207)	7497	3561	1230	7892	0988	2732	7899	6526	2172	9838
(2208)	6219	7935	2022	7225	3768	8500	8978	6822	5986	4604
(2209)	7502	7552	7212	4093	7748	4587	9258	5360	8975	3773
(2210)	1857	7892	0572	3351	5841	4583	3849	1239	6458	1233
(2211)	5760	0593	3734	1431	6888	3643	7791	1968	6943	8786
(2212)	1788	7866	2643	3461	5459	1655	7172	5984	8098	8740
(2213)	4506	9398	6563	2281	7095	7525	9182	1124	8528	7983
(2214)	7063	8625	9533	3956	2229	5430	8674	6133	2956	8385
(2215)	5235	5036	0585	3128	1726	5416	0698	9739	7702	2294
(2216)	6286	9884	2552	1371	7885	4468	3892	6696	1683	3175
(2217)	2065	6890	3811	9527	4597	5862	1637	4120	3628	0196
(2218)	7360	9948	8859	1240	2063	4420	6402	9825	4659	5129
(2219)	8024	4582	6678	0098	3027	4251	2186	3033	3785	2800
(2220)	5502	6726	8750	5549	2285	8037	9466	1708	0970	7004
(2221)	3690	2183	6419	7997	6146	5869	4103	1108	7996	7072
(2222)	2965	1047	6026	4399	9139	0410	9489	6606	0296	1297
(2223)	4664	1198	3954	1445	2893	5816	9590	2373	7654	2567
(2224)	1816	6130	3007	0596	6131	4369	6452	0738	2856	7422
(2225)	2775	6215	5428	8875	3258	5684	3132	6115	1347	2122
(2226)	9289	3559	2738	2219	2436	0180	7189	6314	5931	7679
(2227)	2415	7885	9931	4109	1482	5273	9011	6818	3575	9856
(2228)	2601	9846	7023	8142	8869	5280	0330	3485	3254	5314
(2229)	9972	1930	8132	4477	1491	0339	6024	1810	4347	7559
(2230)	4810	6743	5323	2783	4787	4888	2613	7622	8049	4211
(2231)	2103	3791	8958	7433	5050	8183	7248	0537	2814	3958
(2232)	3586	2308	4223	2959	4501	3074	8877	4794	2009	1179
(2233)	1079	7651	8873	3126	9279	2207	5561	3403	8441	0974
(2234)	2912	2728	0698	5115	0833	3856	9002	1366	2365	6028
(2235)	1037	9600	7989	2003	5611	2022	8335	5288	1971	7219
(2236)	8151	7960	0719	8474	4631	4833	7333	9256	9687	7370
(2237)	4656	2278	0689	7505	2592	9848	8988	6296	7607	4684
(2238)	7398	6856	5586	9863	3879	9326	8463	9991	6260	8061
(2239)	0476	4499	2244	5104	2660	0250	1742	7122	1996	3667
(2240)	5597	5290	7558	8390	2428	4164	9158	3451	2424	4226
(2241)	4087	0998	0038	5965	3664	9069	2966	2295	0392	9136
(2242)	1353	4146	3036	3268	0868	3804	4775	9955	1310	9115
(2243)	0970	0476	4488	0329	6663	3509	3594	6766	2172	0564
(2244)	1455	5964	0126	7337	3047	5355	8113	8850	5908	7637
(2245)	5529	4611	8341	5347	1255	7690	7969	2669	2688	0020

Random Numbers (Continued)

	(01)	(02)	(03)	(04)	(05)	(06)	(07)	(08)	(09)	(10)
(2246)	1592	6997	3352	6780	1835	7580	8112	5164	3906	1188
(2247)	2639	4421	8766	2537	2010	5628	2643	8427	9577	7603
(2248)	9129	8877	3585	1405	3214	2896	8654	9070	3207	5958
(2249)	9236	1305	0770	5221	9499	3580	6894	9206	3393	6721
(2250)	9763	4164	4230	6352	8196	3542	8592	5068	9076	0488
(2251)	5606	1739	6349	1060	4728	0934	7716	2483	0303	9911
(2252)	3089	3948	2869	3770	2893	7746	5754	7399	4282	8356
(2253)	5528	7376	1807	0646	4963	3502	8053	9424	1995	4131
(2254)	1922	7166	6678	9013	7761	3307	2821	8455	4730	6942
(2255)	4378	2832	5803	0607	0120	3475	1622	3296	4493	5063
(2256)	1049	9948	6258	5145	6069	5556	4290	1279	5994	6508
(2257)	5655	6479	3664	3950	8324	8020	6815	5445	5927	6130
(2258)	7487	6602	9657	7916	1082	4165	7537	7225	8071	2289
(2259)	8816	8430	6457	2983	1383	5880	3953	8173	1779	5375
(2260)	6506	9693	2856	9956	1133	5342	3198	3326	1879	1423
(2261)	6422	0050	4044	2159	5773	4796	6042	6626	6017	2249
(2262)	8918	7982	2610	9349	4085	2988	8585	9120	8711	2496
(2263)	8026	4327	2282	0642	9034	9614	9858	4182	0900	2369
(2264)	9695	5974	0926	2464	4025	9888	5739	5535	2564	5348
(2265)	7167	8741	5938	4474	9583	8386	2370	7604	8189	1251
(2266)	4155	1811	6604	9022	2746	1691	0212	5128	2596	5867
(2267)	4903	6439	6752	8554	3892	1506	8399	9911	9627	8682
(2268)	0873	7566	8415	1679	0711	7790	3727	3771	8240	6194
(2269)	7426	2184	9267	9188	7543	9951	5174	0881	5403	4038
(2270)	9305	7754	5624	7477	5075	7257	0602	0496	0423	7772
(2271)	1584	6521	4159	7835	2320	3260	7711	1037	9615	8686
(2272)	9992	0107	5489	3289	6456	4133	4538	8092	0603	8924
(2273)	0938	1739	1955	0553	5179	6962	5522	6513	4407	0515
(2274)	2067	3379	6882	4593	8587	4882	7603	0668	0078	5080
(2275)	5700	2179	5234	4380	4074	4519	2258	2784	3221	5596
(2276)	8511	9647	2179	7625	8540	5954	5415	5480	3228	2765
(2277)	0382	8761	0423	4275	1380	7246	8430	7680	2989	1321
(2278)	1245	2678	7382	8387	7990	5381	4251	1322	8272	4539
(2279)	6119	6583	1108	5095	4219	6419	2652	7579	7072	2072
(2280)	6240	4969	8039	3460	9647	9055	6849	2776	9191	8055
(2281)	7280	6428	0231	5915	8107	7777	2138	2798	9636	9419
(2282)	0108	5345	1242	3550	5136	1192	0930	5201	2577	4455
(2283)	9794	3414	8755	7980	8305	9069	7229	1685	4877	4072
(2284)	0319	6529	2870	6104	6358	3116	1064	7463	2536	3220
(2285)	2015	1272	2321	4730	9465	9686	9743	9549	8510	3094
(2286)	7139	7260	6589	7506	4138	5208	3406	5020	7771	4317
(2287)	9114	4711	4896	5628	0221	7520	4527	9545	3619	7311
(2288)	5474	7513	4928	9361	5668	5234	1383	8634	3515	3419
(2289)	4204	7458	5320	5295	9276	2804	5289	2866	2143	5243
(2290)	0416	4733	5910	1700	4781	7023	9799	8951	1200	4384
(2291)	1922	5606	6402	7926	5467	5265	0583	7554	3068	1301
(2292)	3801	8386	4147	0774	5747	3503	2007	9675	7544	0351
(2293)	0107	4428	1875	1307	7041	6280	4833	2145	9023	6316
(2294)	9126	6400	2147	6754	1223	3437	7349	1055	2936	2291
(2295)	2311	0142	7899	1013	0713	9707	8989	4038	4457	9971

	(01)	(02)	(03)	(04)	(05)	(06)	(07)	(08)	(09)	(10)
(2296)	1079	3603	4772	9244	7708	0409	7716	8283	5165	0385
(2297)	1114	0293	6625	8287	5934	4772	6912	9696	1497	3125
(2298)	7022	8907	4517	5353	1758	5034	0317	0783	3066	4670
(2299)	3063	9547	1033	1901	2376	4215	7017	4973	4666	6210
(2300)	6091	0714	4356	9394	5677	5915	6991	4609	8366	9043
(2301)	8685	4583	9221	0351	8753	5841	4513	4624	5382	0141
(2302)	1734	0993	1065	2799	3858	8740	1418	2818	3471	4756
(2303)	6096	2386	8004	8985	5983	7608	0514	4599	8066	0771
(2304)	4038	4492	7613	7974	0427	5819	3129	1237	2168	7232
(2305)	7118	8953	3545	6258	7197	4675	6282	7909	7496	7560
(2306)	7283	1981	1563	3405	7079	9910	2273	1647	6330	2572
(2307)	4048	7942	1137	2476	4926	9167	3760	5606	0831	5833
(2308)	0892	7279	9458	4064	4032	7458	4075	4094	9423	9899
(2309)	3680	9089	9780	1285	3160	9047	3712	0945	0717	0578
(2310)	3174	0035	3561	9154	6012	3874	0902	3381	6763	0893
(2311)	0874	1262	3002	0169	1850	1183	3946	7005	4606	8008
(2312)	8480	3119	6678	9830	7062	5935	0813	6747	1844	3148
(2313)	5859	4553	5858	8420	2183	5050	8149	5776	7428	7258
(2314)	2452	6519	1203	0746	3280	9630	7018	1135	8433	1060
(2315)	9451	7805	7063	2824	0765	5132	3015	5099	0838	1605
(2316)	6958	0738	6160	0986	1471	0004	2846	6174	2950	4184
(2317)	2230	5986	9639	8494	5205	1256	5210	3450	5006	5715
(2318)	8602	2482	5251	3688	4486	7630	2189	7892	3150	1528
(2319)	6091	2989	0823	0381	8418	1865	5138	5143	0912	2237
(2320)	4439	3363	8703	2313	6725	7616	2184	0527	2636	3093
(2321)	8013	5116	0818	4372	9288	4812	9924	7801	5474	1451
(2322)	6062	4840	7759	4539	5110	8288	9866	5095	6020	6513
(2323)	8660	2013	8210	0299	4342	6973	5186	8530	6142	8641
(2324)	7415	0677	8420	8517	6707	6331	9915	3277	8706	4389
(2325)	5832	0896	0953	8973	3151	1867	2208	3289	4216	4093
(2326)	0503	8142	1071	4411	1702	0012	8863	0094	1967	4218
(2327)	8851	9784	1666	7944	9171	5907	7258	9898	2122	2918
(2328)	8305	8057	5949	6601	6152	3476	3093	0001	1193	5273
(2329)	9958	3332	4399	5122	7546	0161	8332	4973	4493	6335
(2330)	1822	5163	4372	0051	2585	1701	0009	1333	4052	2381
(2331)	6185	7158	0612	1127	3616	5777	5702	4187	4781	0388
(2332)	7134	0693	9414	9571	6922	2496	8854	8622	5665	1278
(2333)	8413	5960	9170	5818	4304	3338	6656	0629	2692	5612
(2334)	1623	0082	8724	4182	5101	7782	9834	2405	2172	9517
(2335)	6234	1023	8218	9709	3109	1842	3241	5103	8548	4115
(2336)	7639	6025	9802	7838	5016	4605	6534	8558	1350	5392
(2337)	5224	3437	7980	3323	6147	8658	6536	9647	6108	3896
(2338)	0724	7774	7425	7673	7484	1099	1062	3347	9198	4459
(2339)	7834	3046	9165	7472	5623	8413	4806	9806	3231	6343
(2340)	3223	7649	9742	0329	1328	4335	9191	3860	9076	1502
(2341)	9818	9454	2030	6282	0993	6326	5905	1262	9133	1202
(2342)	8424	0243	9827	3846	0037	7536	6362	4878	4768	3752
(2343)	3652	9680	5247	1421	1887	4783	0496	4688	7396	6163
(2344)	3185	5193	4997	7045	6360	6413	2600	7092	5450	6351
(2345)	8578	7614	4511	7933	6127	0659	7797	4580	2742	1486

Appendix A
Random Numbers (Continued)

	(01)	(02)	(03)	(04)	(05)	(06)	(07)	(08)	(09)	(10)
(2346)	3769	3985	6521	6133	9568	5754	7243	7930	3605	2612
(2347)	9387	7511	9045	0123	6437	6412	1910	9590	1698	9906
(2348)	3745	4272	4057	2310	3799	0914	7857	0206	6200	1755
(2349)	3138	2975	5370	1750	2615	2011	4703	0851	8147	9513
(2350)	2271	0898	5146	8871	8236	5240	2952	6199	5603	2589
(2351)	7642	3386	8163	6509	9539	0622	4670	3536	7585	1354
(2352)	4963	9436	3281	0846	8263	7855	3880	8334	4144	3405
(2353)	6639	9926	4676	9615	0872	9355	1122	6133	3668	7314
(2354)	6883	8957	1648	5930	8272	4544	4992	1272	6154	4113
(2355)	8923	0809	6873	6130	6206	4614	3305	7913	5168	9337
(2356)	1892	1087	4769	7229	3603	2839	7935	4658	7828	4868
(2357)	9007	4917	1402	8398	5404	0096	9529	1142	3696	9900
(2358)	8345	1991	0032	3616	7507	7367	0780	3642	5666	7917
(2359)	5362	7367	1327	9150	2149	9820	1146	1833	1778	3674
(2360)	6189	6866	6722	5493	6190	6561	8301	3283	9146	9994
(2361)	0062	3527	3206	6487	1776	6343	1617	5322	5988	4442
(2362)	1846	3805	1277	5849	2775	9348	4284	2095	5278	6724
(2363)	2095	0877	1707	7123	5115	7560	4065	0839	7633	2876
(2364)	9317	1867	0706	2850	3317	7289	2946	4742	6302	9461
(2365)	9533	5184	2818	7955	2421	5713	3278	7208	9320	7470
(2366)	0037	1411	8581	5016	0575	6432	7132	5607	3384	4887
(2367)	4532	5572	9776	0562	2171	1767	5275	8462	4713	2588
(2368)	1403	7899	6649	6489	5125	3675	2158	3553	2489	4202
(2369)	3516	6875	9914	4151	7050	2033	7851	5264	0947	4922
(2370)	0598	2935	0982	9516	9067	1438	4104	8330	7544	8661
(2371)	4473	9797	9406	2194	0585	2100	4795	3478	6325	2857
(2372)	4656	7628	4372	4277	1081	7168	1631	3770	5531	6283
(2373)	6846	7868	8663	6411	9258	5814	3827	0275	1057	9530
(2374)	5615	5722	3112	1641	7811	3993	8186	3054	6303	8544
(2375)	7461	3165	2859	3455	9819	9769	4208	2271	7143	7242
(2376)	4206	7103	4534	7350	2858	0544	5375	1801	8436	3809
(2377)	7646	4142	5196	9869	3847	2521	6354	0740	9413	9780
(2378)	1699	8293	7537	0028	2196	6348	5124	7764	4364	6634
(2379)	5305	6348	2874	0723	9060	4052	4928	9823	8056	1894
(2380)	6218	2199	3093	2778	2078	5852	9262	1751	0035	2748
(2381)	6188	8483	9173	5854	6803	3530	1032	7479	7591	7863
(2382)	6394	8521	8558	1346	3310	1722	4495	0620	7950	4353
(2383)	6082	2362	4948	9470	1749	4604	1442	0306	5293	4506
(2384)	5526	6209	2995	1114	1819	8260	4786	0865	6603	1444
(2385)	4487	9559	2328	3916	2602	0718	7711	7795	8861	5008
(2386)	7334	3100	6294	5236	3690	0581	0560	1733	5373	1492
(2387)	8312	1149	9420	1878	7159	6296	9801	8585	8411	9405
(2388)	3476	4711	6254	1713	3557	0851	0118	3079	8381	1726
(2389)	0333	3942	9997	5574	7903	5233	9484	2668	2295	4168
(2390)	7595	7315	6210	3695	3447	8675	5388	7086	4740	6874
(2391)	3883	0531	2954	5070	1712	6787	7196	1434	6191	6502
(2392)	5725	9638	9901	1465	0775	4942	9603	2957	3787	5499
(2393)	8544	2609	0381	7737	0342	6143	9806	3128	5826	4966
(2394)	1265	9347	3744	5610	0662	1923	5685	7236	0327	6065
(2395)	1960	1520	0752	3348	3862	7907	1379	7007	2996	9144

	(01)	(02)	(03)	(04)	(05)	(06)	(07)	(08)	(09)	(10)
(2396)	9003	1264	6522	0398	0552	9833	6052	3246	2707	4280
(2397)	8971	3404	4345	0141	9747	0731	4368	9495	9141	3546
(2398)	2298	9624	3043	0954	7216	4756	6817	3184	3346	9549
(2399)	2214	3432	0940	4792	2835	1787	9274	6050	6214	5837
(2400)	9201	0989	0642	9100	0913	3783	5330	2473	6500	3186
(2401)	3627	0916	7920	3007	7598	9434	3712	7175	9099	1895
(2402)	9063	0076	6142	7709	0957	8569	0760	4536	7436	4071
(2403)	5179	7232	7538	7772	4772	9206	3697	5198	4104	6944
(2404)	5625	2440	3990	0784	3316	8626	0323	7748	4364	8269
(2405)	3296	4052	9157	6346	9206	5841	7311	0919	8528	8972
(2406)	0767	6493	7663	8701	7126	6103	6936	4835	7305	9782
(2407)	3859	7030	1489	5268	6212	5399	5740	6431	1973	6384
(2408)	4183	0779	0073	8708	8752	8307	6705	3240	9662	6783
(2409)	2219	5695	3911	3810	4172	7300	6891	1611	5900	1760
(2410)	4588	5012	9532	7020	9249	0007	6384	6338	4430	2289
(2411)	8263	4439	2413	6367	3919	6348	4231	2805	8405	5842
(2412)	6905	4595	9415	2810	2171	7308	2490	2959	9610	6285
(2413)	1517	2419	6362	3684	2098	1995	8514	6745	3452	0148
(2414)	1733	0150	0280	6703	5335	1509	2947	9197	2004	6948
(2415)	5345	3382	6808	0561	7439	9372	7188	5000	5442	2116
(2416)	9462	0632	6332	3752	7310	6815	7717	2108	4822	9971
(2417)	6907	5341	9753	6945	5395	7090	8208	6833	6099	2467
(2418)	3950	0936	1341	5056	6033	3206	6809	8120	4430	3364
(2419)	4298	9143	8073	3854	5297	3679	8533	9376	4598	9588
(2420)	5645	3036	0045	3513	9901	1588	7922	0702	8508	8049
(2421)	9602	7814	9520	6536	8917	3996	8600	5451	1583	6996
(2422)	9119	7334	1753	3307	5672	4151	8363	1688	9667	4834
(2423)	2199	4023	1968	9782	1872	8155	1462	7279	8101	6014
(2424)	8055	9303	9108	5355	9939	7845	8974	4097	6405	0778
(2425)	7271	2211	9948	3842	8952	4509	5503	9622	6538	4593
(2426)	7355	6148	2597	5689	2188	7878	6309	6784	8903	0078
(2427)	2357	6997	7392	8203	1667	2698	6355	6031	7169	2469
(2428)	9140	3238	1631	3785	9017	6981	5616	8747	1041	9349
(2429)	4194	4010	1703	9822	3484	6644	4582	8344	7409	9767
(2430)	5928	8853	8880	6417	4023	2958	8165	5333	0262	5634
(2431)	8593	9287	0383	3518	7376	5626	6350	7478	4834	7714
(2432)	1726	9015	0852	9871	7422	8152	1708	2164	3278	5234
(2433)	3829	0625	6275	4308	1901	9787	1060	4282	8470	2991
(2434)	0794	7400	5087	2170	9153	6401	0943	3468	6868	1054
(2435)	6295	8136	6347	2943	1644	8768	4168	5197	9435	4410
(2436)	5287	1408	9412	1551	6212	0394	3324	1567	9895	0155
(2437)	5906	9091	2469	6509	5767	7351	5674	3127	0853	4153
(2438)	7796	9994	9844	5971	2055	2521	4872	5163	9333	4732
(2439)	2559	1410	1825	9980	8364	0074	0063	2478	8471	2183
(2440)	5901	3929	8105	4971	0766	1126	3540	2092	0182	9742
(2441)	8220	7844	0002	2963	9759	3925	9148	8521	5920	9464
(2442)	0247	9047	5163	5684	1171	6749	6131	6432	6637	2068
(2443)	9650	2159	4507	6890	8180	6590	8817	7264	7778	0652
(2444)	9316	3330	5790	0067	2205	0114	3175	2439	5459	8740
(2445)	2147	5784	0742	3659	5780	9436	2929	8752	3999	2317

Appendix A
Random Numbers (Continued)

	(01)	(02)	(03)	(04)	(05)	(06)	(07)	(08)	(09)	(10)
(2446)	6194	8365	8174	8771	3864	0521	1308	1567	9217	8967
(2447)	7830	8871	2041	1123	0950	0958	9991	2269	6901	3478
(2448)	5331	3593	9572	5908	5937	6320	9230	0754	0718	6176
(2449)	0910	3130	9178	4233	6218	9470	2270	4915	3532	5908
(2450)	4771	6160	1359	0634	3776	7320	3509	4723	4191	2733
(2451)	5073	2451	6159	6684	7808	8422	2856	5484	4678	2290
(2452)	4857	0883	9290	1812	5672	3456	8301	2073	9660	6710
(2453)	2117	4753	7011	7748	8545	2766	2854	1897	7043	8399
(2454)	6089	3504	1105	0493	4553	0973	7349	3033	2049	5573
(2455)	2233	1196	0680	4452	2173	2764	8076	7535	9223	2415
(2456)	7071	5812	9403	4943	4695	9296	0590	4668	9970	6496
(2457)	8171	4432	0872	2355	1528	5035	8299	4807	7029	1084
(2458)	8551	8877	9938	5619	2196	8858	7586	0739	2014	2062
(2459)	8615	6380	4303	1864	4115	9234	9600	5561	7637	4038
(2460)	8498	2440	5759	1184	6496	2389	7936	1491	5186	7438
(2461)	2583	8584	9481	1914	4584	3236	4405	3511	9404	9699
(2462)	6028	8926	7676	1331	8873	8637	7693	7855	7929	2404
(2463)	7658	0149	6930	3551	2512	5151	5642	0236	5305	6558
(2464)	9620	8046	6244	9592	6124	6332	0522	7567	3555	0916
(2465)	8770	1434	6224	1337	4979	8325	4488	9455	3884	3751
(2466)	6095	3004	8840	7420	0170	8362	1208	9306	1159	7714
(2467)	2707	6557	5103	8941	5412	4251	7420	2537	5602	8972
(2468)	9216	6060	4192	2396	6625	5504	9579	7166	5530	0970
(2469)	7538	7919	8031	5280	9981	3642	7755	0205	5252	8368
(2470)	9687	3559	7437	6759	6888	9121	0972	6344	4178	4862
(2471)	7817	7006	5041	7094	3711	3048	8732	7648	8708	2994
(2472)	4724	0049	4938	1516	4320	8846	3251	5795	0781	9438
(2473)	1551	7769	3525	4772	8201	0413	3756	2799	7798	4384
(2474)	0274	9641	8123	8804	9991	3576	0360	4639	4469	2145
(2475)	0359	2400	2331	7580	6657	6967	8499	4424	3144	5595
(2476)	0482	3623	9522	2167	9845	8981	6866	0735	5562	9164
(2477)	4892	5194	1086	5131	0356	1539	7211	5031	6716	8387
(2478)	3765	8586	1876	7257	2042	5663	1072	6665	5760	5750
(2479)	1946	3646	7223	8623	2703	2679	6353	2517	9815	2822
(2480)	1040	0561	9182	6425	9742	5808	4138	7387	3102	5356
(2481)	6498	6937	9793	3267	4002	7985	0000	1946	9086	2577
(2482)	2015	6956	3002	2323	5601	7186	7156	8212	3191	9576
(2483)	6693	0668	6747	0016	0396	2683	4337	4473	7560	8885
(2484)	3408	0525	2401	1611	4991	1908	7666	6171	7535	2683
(2485)	1908	1498	8904	0311	7737	0703	5980	2419	0127	4424
(2486)	9938	7660	9111	0485	4923	6913	7506	6677	7591	0880
(2487)	1586	2185	4713	4566	3173	7865	0362	3357	4760	7630
(2488)	1621	7805	4274	0175	2194	1799	7569	4466	0766	0537
(2489)	2542	7702	0467	7343	5355	2184	3889	4153	4649	1715
(2490)	6415	6842	3064	7850	3661	7853	7357	3526	7964	1623
(2491)	6469	6462	2162	9267	1490	8056	0096	3751	8562	4076
(2492)	3672	6170	0000	9181	4682	0567	0273	1076	1180	9846
(2493)	4203	7457	0867	4736	2394	4531	5389	5285	3763	6596
(2494)	3767	6582	7015	2199	4083	9615	0926	8870	0762	3598
(2495)	2167	3512	9495	1163	3373	4868	4033	5260	0629	2514

	(01)	(02)	(03)	(04)	(05)	(06)	(07)	(08)	(09)	(10)
(2496)	4678	5395	8166	2960	1741	8752	9234	4151	3635	4268
(2497)	6058	1574	6887	1808	3908	5079	1289	9368	2354	4064
(2498)	8228	9299	9597	1161	9968	9889	8358	6945	9327	8396
(2499)	4115	3428	1406	1729	0894	4803	3955	9240	0549	9551
(2500)	0497	0379	7830	4209	8632	8222	9313	0199	7159	8294
(2501)	8128	7551	3752	7087	7930	9371	3335	6646	6178	1692
(2502)	9369	8918	4134	0235	8595	1332	8719	1140	7608	3865
(2503)	5582	7366	4621	6636	1569	8327	8611	5259	1325	5356
(2504)	0753	7289	1033	8914	6151	8846	7176	0508	9622	5814
(2505)	0950	8741	2649	0003	4118	0285	1935	8666	4151	7538
(2506)	9613	1342	4857	6371	1653	9002	2361	7619	1973	6596
(2507)	5624	3280	3023	0603	3933	9606	3043	3150	5152	0531
(2508)	9729	2419	0751	3299	0125	3135	7590	4038	2076	0301
(2509)	3331	1817	5629	6746	4424	5048	3498	3243	3458	7965
(2510)	9979	6105	9600	7710	5544	4488	6832	7800	3523	3991
(2511)	9097	2365	7757	8737	3001	9071	2079	3792	8994	5983
(2512)	9906	1111	7832	1317	4113	2259	9663	3168	6805	6083
(2513)	9978	6156	6371	4334	1209	9367	1624	4912	4052	6993
(2514)	6594	4224	6642	0122	0869	4328	1750	7501	9796	4910
(2515)	0692	3041	2305	5877	0580	7494	5163	8031	6669	7197
(2516)	6849	2622	7400	8090	4178	6607	5481	8658	0023	7889
(2517)	0342	0787	5156	3056	0446	2787	4892	0487	9391	7283
(2518)	6956	2195	4710	9280	2064	1224	0841	6694	9458	8255
(2519)	1577	4967	1009	0901	1018	1744	1908	3096	9059	5155
(2520)	5034	2501	6909	2465	6071	6317	8201	4869	3852	5554
(2521)	8550	8723	7425	5318	4957	0857	9001	2218	9303	1155
(2522)	7423	3140	2504	3267	1971	7099	8664	1022	0077	6285
(2523)	5261	6805	7836	1898	4615	3045	9572	6401	6630	7733
(2524)	0158	8051	3359	9816	1070	5962	2169	2342	4950	5047
(2525)	1537	4778	5221	4528	6861	7026	2935	9130	3026	1871
(2526)	2428	7806	9597	0573	2506	5776	6658	6238	8099	1962
(2527)	3066	6692	4546	6895	1631	1168	9462	1257	5427	2821
(2528)	4436	7752	1184	0578	8586	0359	3383	3396	0123	7925
(2529)	4294	2705	0781	1226	7225	1493	2564	4285	3919	6500
(2530)	3919	3524	9270	6531	5122	6070	2692	8454	1506	7893
(2531)	6261	6579	0236	2071	4582	1978	3439	7884	1496	7330
(2532)	9607	9244	3212	0370	2878	2227	7908	0433	0625	2738
(2533)	0399	5763	1153	3384	5870	8916	9785	5059	3082	8266
(2534)	4226	7330	8354	4464	8509	3963	7727	9605	7743	2879
(2535)	3695	9993	9033	5255	6806	2033	3680	6953	9331	4607
(2536)	3026	2943	4128	1789	4525	8425	4815	3376	3938	8759
(2537)	7590	2621	7471	9040	9454	8159	6598	7432	4408	3598
(2538)	6349	2684	9183	1869	4420	0140	0214	9585	9778	2091
(2539)	3576	4951	1864	2778	7547	0549	8049	8752	3039	9642
(2540)	6936	5756	7262	8427	4193	3614	4226	5390	5845	4678
(2541)	8762	9819	0122	8568	5793	2005	3422	0347	2237	6790
(2542)	9494	1494	1220	8683	4696	3511	6458	8054	3681	9688
(2543)	1987	2101	4060	2202	6272	4223	2375	9286	1529	1609
(2544)	3029	6402	5485	9084	0283	1981	8600	6783	9728	5610
(2545)	7629	4650	1365	0331	9527	7621	1292	5450	2358	1392

Appendix A
Random Numbers (Continued)

	(01)	(02)	(03)	(04)	(05)	(06)	(07)	(08)	(09)	(10)
(2546)	1149	6918	6728	6521	9618	1349	1080	9741	4594	9791
(2547)	1319	0310	4437	0466	5864	3486	3902	1751	2625	0489
(2548)	3166	2278	3859	7617	4043	9358	4729	7051	4359	3063
(2549)	5724	1239	1036	7142	3852	7187	3152	1339	3762	1995
(2550)	1161	3528	8019	2222	3051	1592	3355	0029	0372	3813
(2551)	1117	2554	8803	2182	1210	5537	1970	4018	2871	2561
(2552)	1775	7970	3216	8848	0596	7248	9401	6379	5847	2214
(2553)	3000	8479	6004	6232	4580	5181	3557	9267	5395	3685
(2554)	4252	1920	5570	8230	8569	3511	0028	8682	7267	0955
(2555)	1851	9263	1212	5468	8710	1382	0221	1270	0733	2592
(2556)	8444	8081	1271	9802	7375	3389	1950	4667	1007	1812
(2557)	4464	8938	7689	5793	9167	9441	0519	3982	9382	0663
(2558)	4139	2086	8505	5799	8948	6184	1604	4436	0241	0508
(2559)	9740	9037	3710	1507	2207	0293	0322	2176	6800	6319
(2560)	9929	8038	9028	7864	4952	7215	3614	5844	1562	0968
(2561)	2194	7153	3298	8977	6398	6510	3513	1299	7065	6440
(2562)	5891	7921	4705	5970	8444	2537	8281	9916	5824	0701
(2563)	3088	2455	4982	9184	8180	5225	5650	5278	6226	3543
(2564)	2175	0596	1783	1699	1442	5365	4942	9124	1130	5328
(2565)	5641	7785	0316	5571	6803	2198	7471	4467	8607	1025
(2566)	6988	6862	6402	9707	5129	3331	5793	1991	7267	1759
(2567)	9858	8053	2095	3717	0516	1765	4725	2796	7344	2110
(2568)	2246	5710	4245	5714	1524	5176	2864	7995	0093	3227
(2569)	2354	7038	9509	2395	9511	9955	2827	2893	7828	6093
(2570)	7762	6437	4556	2061	3439	1447	6771	6204	0349	4377
(2571)	4951	0271	0568	5569	4568	9957	4990	1554	9511	3880
(2572)	9899	8174	2283	4972	7387	9871	3636	2834	6053	6325
(2573)	7109	7751	2718	9682	7787	7938	2872	9474	1515	4172
(2574)	1992	1306	9016	0024	5391	7748	3573	0738	7738	3175
(2575)	4025	4994	6327	0211	1066	4614	7116	5573	7723	7095
(2576)	1144	5122	7794	1081	2411	4927	0942	2928	8029	6098
(2577)	7559	5459	8832	4396	6551	2407	2251	9099	8673	2219
(2578)	9279	3730	8060	7554	3869	1200	7598	8352	4008	2415
(2579)	5063	0218	7775	4448	3908	1980	5307	4065	2001	0265
(2580)	2982	7173	9676	0957	8176	7156	7457	9563	6743	5069
(2581)	7727	1700	3649	6996	5492	9397	7876	0534	9542	1975
(2582)	9032	7758	9705	4182	1496	1913	4976	1778	1434	6351
(2583)	4052	4438	6092	1051	7780	7306	2974	3179	8644	7462
(2584)	5723	0560	5937	0550	4184	5257	7910	3653	0082	9285
(2585)	1584	1404	6056	1473	1598	5979	0686	4244	2681	1255
(2586)	3861	5425	1492	8842	1243	2313	1116	2796	7274	2347
(2587)	9170	3236	5301	3719	1565	3438	4610	3508	0088	1790
(2588)	7713	8323	1248	1889	8332	6096	8595	5418	7283	1842
(2589)	9258	0980	7422	2450	6382	9550	6040	9643	5236	4220
(2590)	5650	0755	2650	7931	7508	0972	7461	4736	0317	7621
(2591)	3600	2805	3097	4948	8809	3991	0384	4858	6681	5086
(2592)	4969	8198	6928	4865	0472	1701	9523	0653	0000	4661
(2593)	4430	2124	3553	4087	3152	2079	9580	0815	2214	9307
(2594)	8989	2712	7100	8848	6082	4111	4756	7965	4833	1530
(2595)	8117	0953	6855	2517	5370	9964	0141	8302	1029	6032

	(01)	(02)	(03)	(04)	(05)	(06)	(07)	(08)	(09)	(10)
(2596)	3857	8371	8697	7766	2580	9756	6787	8664	4235	9769
(2597)	0410	5019	5290	9011	6011	6333	9830	8999	8952	0802
(2598)	4004	0504	1050	9080	9555	5845	4482	4107	0764	6257
(2599)	1319	0270	3822	8615	0038	5129	2796	4667	1063	4297
(2600)	0319	2881	5821	8283	7965	7492	2308	3414	5374	5530
(2601)	2933	6535	3733	9386	6486	0855	1001	7748	3284	8429
(2602)	5651	0907	5170	4647	3019	0085	3786	0149	0628	4869
(2603)	6836	7533	4990	1418	3183	5184	8178	7946	9562	7536
(2604)	5719	0217	6187	2634	5622	9774	1262	5590	1019	0425
(2605)	8825	6725	2234	5137	9541	9543	4661	5463	0128	9646
(2606)	8863	5862	6951	1740	8421	9833	6437	9156	3372	0888
(2607)	0107	6115	8345	8890	0238	8722	8667	2316	7051	0965
(2608)	1639	5231	1271	7793	1162	9003	0183	1938	5399	0179
(2609)	9821	1959	5605	3058	2570	8320	4840	8997	1657	2742
(2610)	6832	5605	8390	9681	9180	0693	8975	2334	5437	6706
(2611)	1293	2057	2567	5763	3956	6244	3761	9072	5523	6700
(2612)	3050	5922	7522	5131	9288	9878	6931	4701	8091	4434
(2613)	4706	4683	3732	3298	9580	7851	0351	9495	3708	0508
(2614)	4080	9879	7255	6521	1826	1612	6860	1616	5965	1523
(2615)	6153	3227	4026	7641	0290	5112	1590	1116	9619	0076
(2616)	6416	1773	8262	8363	4720	9633	1756	4402	2879	5865
(2617)	7182	5229	7165	4073	1760	4391	9731	2929	8614	0597
(2618)	4901	4746	8371	9838	2734	8148	3912	0602	2386	0133
(2619)	8616	2652	0073	5334	5248	1362	2267	6639	8217	3946
(2620)	3027	0197	2840	8980	0515	4798	0752	9203	5306	8716
(2621)	9449	0466	2568	2698	4545	1525	0027	7475	7999	5400
(2622)	9288	0204	0980	9923	4000	5423	0178	7439	5049	5170
(2623)	9288	1792	6073	6208	6051	4660	4044	5750	8240	4951
(2624)	2793	0952	2191	0489	8839	0176	2164	8819	1169	9165
(2625)	1183	0648	8541	5665	4418	4590	9367	6194	8581	4380
(2626)	7576	1513	7666	7217	7599	1963	1074	2677	6126	6872
(2627)	0225	1957	4772	4531	9609	6217	6970	6353	1616	3020
(2628)	7044	5923	3672	7307	5461	7187	2196	5060	9805	7852
(2629)	8108	4227	2105	4611	2906	5747	6343	6728	7092	1544
(2630)	3531	3751	0192	3683	0789	4363	0270	1937	8168	9950
(2631)	7330	6960	4313	5773	4812	2695	1266	4032	3067	2690
(2632)	2671	1015	4924	9851	7948	2403	6238	1675	7792	1974
(2633)	7313	0527	9456	9413	6941	3570	4117	8947	6825	2198
(2634)	9346	6756	8053	6580	8699	1851	0605	1976	1858	5252
(2635)	6283	9145	0778	7043	1204	2527	0923	1159	0845	5244
(2636)	7627	1881	0022	1968	0466	1252	2726	4867	1569	8320
(2637)	4703	3863	3760	2508	6877	0045	9392	6415	7566	4954
(2638)	0030	6544	3741	3034	5791	5451	0705	6109	9522	4137
(2639)	3629	8213	2701	2767	8029	7945	1399	6533	0406	4237
(2640)	7370	8412	9932	3437	0383	6125	6228	1291	0934	5630
(2641)	3071	0377	3650	8769	2995	6170	8441	6386	1583	9052
(2642)	8785	7483	4948	8817	1952	5921	2636	9215	2916	7234
(2643)	6356	5944	9096	3292	9537	4006	6717	1325	1674	9300
(2644)	4823	2611	7131	9813	6003	1235	7244	9909	2744	1297
(2645)	9864	5231	3372	7969	4418	2223	2459	0973	2164	7209

Appendix A
Random Numbers (Continued)

	(01)	(02)	(03)	(04)	(05)	(06)	(07)	(08)	(09)	(10)
(2646)	3868	7218	7642	7785	7673	4751	9852	0813	3969	7094
(2647)	7372	6311	1833	9307	8544	2937	2195	6403	5186	9498
(2648)	2483	1263	9162	6973	4711	9530	8527	7360	8944	7118
(2649)	1437	1682	3913	4247	8962	2826	2325	7126	8175	9968
(2650)	9792	6316	4546	8563	0756	5176	8788	9069	5093	4865
(2651)	4523	8690	7387	4605	9689	7213	1846	5321	4506	6688
(2652)	0815	3911	3939	7656	9110	3809	5108	4152	6203	5322
(2653)	7165	7226	8213	2497	8151	4865	7007	6712	7038	6077
(2654)	7068	4933	1119	0237	0434	9929	5584	2617	8601	0956
(2655)	2723	3813	8113	5899	6301	0856	4815	1053	3211	4984
(2656)	6372	0683	2567	1911	2818	8491	7501	6003	2502	9016
(2657)	2990	6198	1407	0440	6336	5519	7200	5372	7828	0766
(2658)	2536	3243	9835	6757	6214	7571	6529	6683	8375	2770
(2659)	5744	2710	0013	7338	4875	6383	4738	7700	6030	9120
(2660)	5589	0798	0060	7818	7497	4603	9074	4795	1498	2328
(2661)	9222	1369	4493	1565	4472	0567	6856	0740	6999	5524
(2662)	3504	4058	3930	7563	8521	4344	2035	6713	4741	6636
(2663)	6016	3634	7455	4767	9041	9650	0436	5741	4403	3713
(2664)	0675	0162	1145	0409	3797	1554	2922	1843	0106	3287
(2665)	7431	7646	2629	7689	4289	1433	1524	4796	0511	0724
(2666)	6718	6007	2985	2059	2959	6977	0906	4605	5110	0331
(2667)	9539	4567	5551	3343	6402	0497	0428	7866	2396	7840
(2668)	3379	1859	7110	1262	2918	7438	5789	5173	8409	9946
(2669)	7270	8011	3554	5845	9140	8475	0878	6294	2720	0415
(2670)	0339	8575	5893	0263	0531	4384	8638	1482	3731	2733
(2671)	6979	7611	9968	4280	6411	5011	4063	4755	5994	7531
(2672)	0842	6663	7691	2139	1266	7714	0659	8485	8543	5466
(2673)	1090	9683	1070	0520	9272	0687	7065	2557	5144	1277
(2674)	8881	0449	9887	9543	9356	8200	3817	3498	0066	3241
(2675)	4981	0798	8483	5368	6033	8203	5206	1394	2965	3751
(2676)	0481	2830	9131	7109	8705	1776	4860	0070	1839	1671
(2677)	8421	9550	9831	5493	5541	2890	8274	5163	0286	2725
(2678)	8551	1021	9761	1112	0470	5956	8862	8372	4445	3914
(2679)	4297	5199	9612	9357	6059	1851	0628	9418	8913	5514
(2680)	0828	8938	3682	7551	0426	4077	7732	4326	0148	9633
(2681)	2510	2121	1462	0590	7839	9038	7603	6584	7515	3205
(2682)	5476	9054	1120	3543	7357	2666	7493	1813	5550	7041
(2683)	5564	1836	5073	1257	9179	2146	7084	2391	8413	1848
(2684)	6935	1084	9389	5303	4623	9747	8279	9347	0484	2311
(2685)	6586	5247	5006	2102	7411	7947	3456	8265	6383	2730
(2686)	8353	4182	1587	5594	8149	2167	0058	6594	8637	1043
(2687)	6398	6522	9118	4182	4783	7878	1764	9213	0308	8630
(2688)	0830	6872	8690	2859	9724	6370	9485	7155	9606	3188
(2689)	5558	0032	6051	7980	6355	2273	1386	6418	0680	4376
(2690)	5084	4428	6234	7174	9254	7379	3496	3594	8184	5517
(2691)	5887	0115	7452	8100	9818	0950	1931	0632	5408	8396
(2692)	1419	5544	4219	0744	9950	6958	1842	8994	7577	4557
(2693)	9560	6964	7597	5961	5837	1613	9038	5463	5068	9920
(2694)	1660	9604	7711	7000	7963	9015	9586	2027	5456	2175
(2695)	8099	3337	0346	4029	6830	4550	9394	3117	1165	6026

	(01)	(02)	(03)	(04)	(05)	(06)	(07)	(08)	(09)	(10)
(2696)	2530	7134	1969	4283	9447	1189	5517	0040	7847	0136
(2697)	8511	9411	6715	1078	1841	7347	0004	4439	0195	0106
(2698)	0421	4706	8878	5588	4021	1837	5057	9246	6896	3271
(2699)	9993	7471	1158	8233	5244	4323	4132	5102	7314	7626
(2700)	4671	3020	3725	2038	4994	3401	9130	6967	5811	2329
(2701)	8126	6409	5905	1694	9483	8201	7736	1936	1119	4910
(2702)	8978	0080	3967	2188	7258	7071	5331	8751	4492	9817
(2703)	2474	3895	5984	7980	8574	2473	1195	5535	7855	0942
(2704)	8888	2462	3540	8468	0131	0043	3119	2654	5210	2774
(2705)	5334	4235	6251	4004	8561	1240	1967	1955	3737	7638
(2706)	5335	0624	6243	0343	6036	2421	2832	8141	3825	1691
(2707)	8055	2222	2705	3095	2132	5796	9713	5511	2688	1049
(2708)	1419	7874	8289	0217	8046	4175	9436	3081	2043	5955
(2709)	6237	7249	4281	4020	7425	3067	8196	0850	7848	2652
(2710)	4498	5736	1732	6557	2105	1793	1962	3277	3951	9485
(2711)	1098	6375	8441	4237	0866	4739	8640	1425	0657	1609
(2712)	0295	1655	3530	7798	0497	5765	9284	3251	4520	7876
(2713)	7710	9257	5108	4870	1556	7592	0495	4294	2980	1796
(2714)	7996	4922	2323	0634	9104	2331	3103	0883	5265	7961
(2715)	7506	1941	8406	8073	7708	9944	6329	1829	0684	7072
(2716)	6537	5229	4888	3701	0504	6389	2172	6199	1924	3091
(2717)	8151	0006	5034	0729	7098	2714	4760	6193	8143	3522
(2718)	3320	4284	9541	8947	6109	3469	5744	5357	1580	8570
(2719)	8581	8326	9416	0328	6899	4773	8756	6591	1123	2074
(2720)	9571	3509	5656	9959	3077	5589	5026	2463	5268	7745
(2721)	4260	0961	8665	8855	8054	9657	0760	6682	5715	1957
(2722)	0651	2862	6666	6759	0555	9975	7714	2466	9791	2930
(2723)	9654	5164	7313	2744	7441	1701	2060	4484	4891	7550
(2724)	6703	4739	3639	9894	0757	2887	8798	6507	3863	6917
(2725)	0449	0417	9799	8790	3211	4410	2051	6457	0198	2293
(2726)	8905	9218	5657	0782	6894	2058	7940	9587	7591	9669
(2727)	4977	5039	7081	7328	6508	7647	6888	6027	0331	4527
(2728)	7957	3348	4263	6420	9818	0187	8750	4431	4085	8944
(2729)	2864	5452	6754	8792	3512	7343	6171	9949	5778	2147
(2730)	5599	1973	6565	3188	6149	3138	9392	1906	4023	0856
(2731)	9666	7634	3634	1381	8877	5070	9177	4943	4124	7754
(2732)	0788	2228	0638	0327	3757	1771	3881	8117	6467	8320
(2733)	7001	4140	9242	2267	4314	8991	3621	0554	9922	2778
(2734)	4943	6370	5061	8553	4281	6746	0917	9666	3011	9659
(2735)	4624	7623	3322	0319	7088	8886	0749	5268	0201	3369
(2736)	3283	9414	9626	0325	0961	9196	8926	5889	9547	8707
(2737)	5507	0691	5985	0998	1396	4878	9485	8871	4033	6055
(2738)	8132	9995	8361	1070	0019	9535	1912	4249	7694	1554
(2739)	6090	3789	9179	5244	1013	3354	4806	6851	5949	6382
(2740)	1278	2397	2256	3337	4037	5768	3255	2453	0020	1353
(2741)	3862	6243	5514	2855	4923	4201	4884	2830	9434	9454
(2742)	3951	8534	4419	8601	9974	9484	2424	9705	0463	5344
(2743)	2674	3356	1187	0389	1799	4340	3365	2334	6650	0048
(2744)	5414	3846	2377	3842	7697	2306	7345	4131	6051	3389
(2745)	8459	2749	8689	4702	6062	7466	3358	8658	8356	8547

Random Numbers (Continued)

	(01)	(02)	(03)	(04)	(05)	(06)	(07)	(08)	(09)	(10)
(2746)	6085	7285	0831	2463	2938	0916	7880	8994	5664	0706
(2747)	7607	6455	1984	7758	1482	3728	7391	8201	1105	9831
(2748)	5760	8340	9458	3053	7975	2789	2060	1907	1453	7498
(2749)	8429	5236	4469	4135	3053	0409	2996	5825	6323	3259
(2750)	2522	8593	3356	4177	4876	0866	5267	7009	3523	4534
(2751)	1958	2162	5473	2719	4412	3907	4080	0089	1367	9184
(2752)	7977	2922	8746	0603	0860	6662	9554	8270	3071	0268
(2753)	6128	7415	5006	9142	7993	8693	5012	7913	5087	5023
(2754)	4775	9626	4366	7360	9138	2994	7780	5969	9005	2623
(2755)	6581	5456	5792	4657	0033	5434	8478	2615	3253	5017
(2756)	3838	1531	9732	0303	8545	7704	3871	8025	0021	7251
(2757)	8630	9964	6297	7105	4347	5531	9954	4195	1126	8483
(2758)	7332	8192	6193	0274	8258	1332	7912	1778	4333	4489
(2759)	7503	2322	2851	3369	2475	9859	0085	5685	7860	1034
(2760)	8935	0489	9354	0322	8012	1723	0183	8994	3193	6297
(2761)	1485	4984	2702	1293	8663	2028	9698	8572	8681	3495
(2762)	7799	8732	6849	7018	4909	6821	2807	8009	2182	8121
(2763)	5012	2651	9351	3176	8059	3931	8568	8183	5926	4436
(2764)	9238	2422	8506	1010	7944	1107	4151	9247	0838	9178
(2765)	4391	8946	4755	2391	0120	8614	8088	7974	7996	4482
(2766)	1377	4272	4385	0538	8488	8614	0796	5037	4156	9595
(2767)	5990	8079	6171	5532	0501	0398	6828	8026	7452	4313
(2768)	3501	2927	7902	0298	4249	1983	6991	4646	3946	0335
(2769)	5875	0990	2890	7624	7292	9620	2924	6774	8552	7846
(2770)	5145	8144	4341	8656	1217	4457	3549	5989	1509	1521
(2771)	6876	0399	8346	1332	8861	1349	8771	4338	6985	3027
(2772)	3812	4604	5501	8415	7343	1378	9503	4634	6798	9261
(2773)	2262	0099	9275	6307	8688	7596	3870	7899	4148	9448
(2774)	2274	8762	7851	9605	7462	5609	3605	6434	4438	1394
(2775)	8120	0839	1918	5333	6483	2901	5928	3059	3877	7704
(2776)	7065	0323	0714	8722	3414	1744	5678	3773	3160	6511
(2777)	6091	1605	4130	0748	4357	0600	5977	9081	2961	2625
(2778)	8374	7255	6918	4633	4799	0665	5093	3708	0587	0908
(2779)	8629	0236	3976	7282	9985	2162	7740	9035	6635	2689
(2780)	0217	9686	2132	3686	5697	4615	8437	1911	7506	2967
(2781)	5382	1489	9527	3113	0048	3852	7681	0225	7444	9490
(2782)	8818	4510	6780	6658	3967	5361	3534	6376	9235	9752
(2783)	1337	0984	8281	9512	2566	1146	1750	2193	1383	7157
(2784)	3622	4379	2588	7836	7815	5102	5398	5270	1859	2738
(2785)	2903	5921	3368	5487	6615	8590	2340	9754	3174	2527
(2786)	2967	2324	4182	3796	0885	4652	1162	4328	4138	8737
(2787)	5444	9353	8863	0653	8975	5120	5829	4947	4053	3108
(2788)	8780	3079	0655	3358	0990	6317	0086	1447	1304	9592
(2789)	2367	3762	1935	8854	0165	9324	3795	3742	4704	7468
(2790)	5382	4975	2072	3055	8134	3702	7254	3051	5875	7940
(2791)	0865	0504	0673	7081	6467	0732	4552	2186	7534	3445
(2792)	8608	6230	1947	5647	0463	6513	1376	1677	9914	7162
(2793)	2942	3667	7316	2053	7351	8150	0888	2141	0763	2014
(2794)	3702	8743	7988	5360	1742	9242	6621	1991	4468	7714
(2795)	1596	1930	1965	9366	5589	5616	5263	4773	0503	5854

	(01)	(02)	(03)	(04)	(05)	(06)	(07)	(08)	(09)	(10)
(2796)	2802	6412	2819	2733	6567	4365	6900	4734	9405	0547
(2797)	2221	6075	9506	3382	3403	2211	3631	7689	9181	8592
(2798)	8448	1951	3226	3354	9297	0715	7343	1193	0274	0717
(2799)	6232	6423	5924	0878	4773	5803	6072	1897	4925	0198
(2800)	8292	7790	2384	1412	1282	2376	7992	1583	5188	6045
(2801)	2677	0673	4346	8831	3690	0142	0375	2227	5877	1067
(2802)	6919	3499	8681	5733	1861	5813	1962	8511	1471	0596
(2803)	9117	4359	0378	6533	3764	7563	7754	1078	7348	0090
(2804)	8700	1443	7718	2219	9542	6800	9534	5973	2325	1766
(2805)	1675	6090	3743	1602	4437	5913	0271	4679	8414	9504
(2806)	1025	5967	0650	3547	5362	9492	2163	6495	1770	2224
(2807)	8968	9184	9136	9644	8639	5294	7515	2932	6606	8847
(2808)	5579	6243	6489	2330	7250	2004	8892	2120	9361	8298
(2809)	2356	6044	4391	6433	7461	8864	2241	8432	2966	7047
(2810)	4612	2512	8575	3983	8071	5940	0121	3947	1584	3375
(2811)	5139	5784	9754	7185	7939	8022	1070	7260	0566	8748
(2812)	3594	8680	5513	5098	6399	8881	6339	2324	1847	7537
(2813)	0523	5066	9313	0028	6869	9770	5551	6490	5897	3053
(2814)	3320	6972	1967	4222	3988	1151	8228	9764	9341	6790
(2815)	2996	2754	2488	0015	7970	2624	6185	5002	9307	5873
(2816)	2344	7931	8315	3559	7287	1643	7873	9617	2796	2833
(2817)	1939	8978	7727	1675	6718	7415	0311	3567	4652	8593
(2818)	5123	8282	0962	5202	7773	3189	3597	7125	9536	4715
(2819)	0489	9726	9714	1644	6538	6952	1171	5449	0947	3500
(2820)	3057	8537	5461	8115	7422	2945	5980	4401	6789	2226
(2821)	3276	0258	2468	7463	0842	0497	8097	4505	1373	6029
(2822)	8620	3522	8696	1893	4000	2812	4395	0385	5561	1418
(2823)	2236	7551	5755	0287	5305	4124	6422	6986	3823	7306
(2824)	0147	4477	6176	1357	1123	2253	6485	4997	8709	8671
(2825)	8082	7799	7939	1665	0461	0430	7656	8767	0342	9291
(2826)	9301	0210	3674	3013	6533	5796	0682	4226	8345	7881
(2827)	3185	6950	0925	1344	6375	2497	7523	3659	9874	7151
(2828)	6011	3468	7032	3847	3021	3498	1450	0592	2661	8820
(2829)	1824	6131	2455	8578	7781	4159	5028	6172	4112	6760
(2830)	9063	1838	2382	6250	1245	8652	0321	0664	9935	4722
(2831)	2544	7675	9838	1014	5763	6614	7894	1647	9250	9936
(2832)	7822	8396	7888	5946	2600	9609	5872	7258	5478	6016
(2833)	5349	3470	4637	9250	3732	7957	7108	3176	4779	0184
(2834)	6220	9114	8865	6005	8304	9899	3243	3227	4458	1928
(2835)	8421	0676	8915	0903	0948	8258	1151	1924	8864	9259
(2836)	5366	6849	1203	9536	0539	1196	3226	2586	7202	5509
(2837)	2756	3492	9275	2241	4860	8179	9509	5948	0571	9910
(2838)	5914	0627	6963	6880	7538	8001	0494	8425	9379	3080
(2839)	3022	8500	6442	6509	9261	4723	9941	7432	1532	2932
(2840)	5539	2073	7895	6364	1624	5739	1219	4271	3180	0171
(2841)	7691	7803	7184	3825	3238	1901	1427	6396	0709	5530
(2842)	3071	2447	2529	1357	1431	8846	9895	2365	0152	7531
(2843)	5979	1703	7697	8650	2747	3908	5814	9197	9060	8351
(2844)	7485	3462	2219	6401	2904	6696	4933	5537	4223	0580
(2845)	0220	6971	7947	0439	8196	8454	6068	3971	6566	1514

Random Numbers (Continued)

	(01)	(02)	(03)	(04)	(05)	(06)	(07)	(08)	(09)	(10)
(2846)	7632	4368	0833	9899	7558	2391	6771	3067	8439	1956
(2847)	9410	0080	9911	6688	0379	4770	5789	3363	5210	1053
(2848)	9242	8529	4049	6877	9511	9563	6086	5666	5651	2538
(2849)	2672	2375	3530	6458	2752	5645	5508	7316	0505	8941
(2850)	4355	1808	4899	0650	1242	6689	1684	4798	3571	8463
(2851)	9199	4257	0003	2548	1378	3624	6606	3004	9606	4592
(2852)	5128	5085	9534	4651	4302	3346	7875	7698	0679	7339
(2853)	8739	1121	0826	9397	9143	0017	7238	1104	2215	4756
(2854)	4109	9980	7086	6649	2855	4276	2470	4985	8948	5057
(2855)	5087	1088	3948	0937	6572	7036	3708	4843	0078	8522
(2856)	2975	3794	3400	9273	0249	0250	1017	1627	1904	1298
(2857)	3351	1999	9188	0881	5560	6107	5692	5272	7319	4331
(2858)	6420	4917	7640	5173	7062	9172	4988	4421	4896	9850
(2859)	2705	1212	8882	9482	8990	7828	0468	0362	4289	6104
(2860)	2875	5161	7065	8492	4430	5672	3213	7747	5560	1267
(2861)	0562	1956	2390	2771	0274	1874	6495	7311	3810	4203
(2862)	7879	5204	8302	6042	3457	0062	6116	7682	9626	2101
(2863)	2606	2916	3974	4993	5929	7014	3533	5536	0525	2913
(2864)	7955	9627	5203	9227	2301	4050	5883	5946	1711	4579
(2865)	5551	8533	2614	3123	0682	0500	8707	1062	5227	0122
(2866)	6136	2467	0060	4450	6339	7667	7637	2230	1442	7550
(2867)	7482	6377	8911	3106	3350	5847	5628	1629	8250	0952
(2868)	3371	3019	7363	2807	8763	5989	7282	7062	0334	5903
(2869)	6812	1140	2816	8585	3513	0495	6221	7166	4549	1755
(2870)	3700	0504	1286	2965	1379	4000	9647	2097	1775	2515
(2871)	5788	9574	9365	9509	3786	5766	3087	4622	3217	6264
(2872)	5468	9068	0608	0292	3317	3935	6603	1123	3620	3843
(2873)	9384	9885	0071	4377	7672	4455	4440	2843	3308	0963
(2874)	6165	0396	5853	1759	7891	7432	2848	4428	1038	7888
(2875)	9929	7778	4239	5156	5094	4910	0417	4924	7853	6399
(2876)	7801	9462	1909	5441	6844	7842	6137	3554	0688	0865
(2877)	7591	8002	8225	6325	1408	7547	1512	0317	1160	6171
(2878)	6511	8483	8009	6517	5341	1407	3661	1916	6552	7217
(2879)	8511	9807	4140	2264	3980	7410	7387	0174	0648	2842
(2880)	9027	9914	3331	0501	9191	2131	3361	4345	1802	6909
(2881)	4054	7247	1767	0393	5927	2342	8518	7389	6329	5104
(2882)	0186	9089	1880	5528	5058	3802	3853	2804	0495	9326
(2883)	7073	7487	0038	2272	9240	5585	7667	7611	8013	4210
(2884)	9106	7524	6943	9499	1524	6807	3696	5524	7613	0427
(2885)	8210	6251	2414	0940	5646	7386	7970	0145	9183	7150
(2886)	8491	0578	7691	1213	7783	8771	5643	2302	5624	6642
(2887)	1998	6047	2829	4824	2615	1974	7582	6395	7121	7148
(2888)	0673	7852	9306	2735	6506	1477	0817	8070	9698	5123
(2889)	8766	9867	6067	0330	4692	2266	5482	0679	5847	8561
(2890)	5950	1211	0685	9709	9917	5362	8737	1113	6296	9417
(2891)	1820	3375	9682	9463	1683	6896	4217	8259	9446	2753
(2892)	7238	4557	1449	5077	6871	3275	1354	6469	9762	1626
(2893)	0233	8485	0416	8135	3189	1480	9456	1196	0710	3609
(2894)	2496	6493	4474	3201	3435	5890	6320	1817	9678	3384
(2895)	1985	6685	4421	7153	8320	5043	2798	5363	8183	7208

	(01)	(02)	(03)	(04)	(05)	(06)	(07)	(08)	(09)	(10)
(2896)	1997	7180	5348	7996	4828	3351	5493	5313	7583	7393
(2897)	3291	3769	8530	2272	5934	9197	0770	2546	8095	5198
(2898)	0571	3680	4408	7294	6051	5440	6159	6046	6022	6783
(2899)	9436	1648	9919	0204	3021	3574	1415	4027	2171	1464
(2900)	7288	2326	7209	7563	9020	1283	4523	3479	5293	8135
(2901)	5097	5257	6804	8890	6035	7193	4935	2000	6974	9837
(2902)	7062	0878	7498	3103	7397	3558	3384	9197	2446	8690
(2903)	2283	2704	1192	8745	3919	6186	3298	6908	2641	8834
(2904)	6923	9496	3886	4332	0175	8456	8802	8081	4311	1535
(2905)	1702	7352	5054	9636	2887	0846	3025	9842	0552	1299
(2906)	5811	7740	0646	2134	6386	7436	8181	8406	9220	5991
(2907)	0615	8536	3623	9905	6202	8187	6533	2347	2205	1475
(2908)	1134	0086	3187	8942	9322	3434	2144	5698	4950	4679
(2909)	4305	6714	8918	3416	2166	0590	9626	1248	8383	2225
(2910)	6726	0550	1523	4141	8402	7898	0166	5674	0715	6032
(2911)	3634	0762	6765	6456	4655	9610	6065	6135	0876	2239
(2912)	5580	0301	5030	5762	9354	1143	9135	0010	1233	0323
(2913)	6129	3708	2337	3174	5767	7137	9270	7883	7492	5407
(2914)	0954	7137	5402	1723	0596	1694	6023	4810	9636	5924
(2915)	1213	2672	9502	3090	0247	6370	6167	5141	9493	8891
(2916)	7296	5562	7483	5473	0284	5777	9201	5920	8571	6316
(2917)	9332	1425	8937	0891	3323	0947	7953	1638	7725	2767
(2918)	7876	1561	6810	3632	3971	4283	9808	2684	4032	7289
(2919)	5342	5267	0302	0591	6222	1416	5206	2902	8276	9545
(2920)	8843	8479	2126	8455	3933	0607	8465	1922	1638	7840
(2921)	8892	9320	8277	2734	5397	7802	2268	6788	1371	1746
(2922)	2354	5931	1260	3607	9714	9244	0834	8142	5712	5454
(2923)	3701	8240	5691	2897	0116	1873	6968	2496	8822	1767
(2924)	6547	0707	4186	1714	8224	6732	2917	2520	5316	0032
(2925)	1154	9012	4481	3298	1743	8098	7240	3740	4972	8645
(2926)	7186	7519	3885	9317	6223	0749	4404	8564	9783	3370
(2927)	3208	9576	0989	7637	4308	3468	3963	7787	8954	2889
(2928)	1545	3224	1889	8776	9729	4002	6388	5881	8969	6939
(2929)	8629	4239	4887	4494	4623	7593	0985	4259	1717	1429
(2930)	6193	2345	2464	5902	5675	1150	8186	8127	8373	4755
(2931)	8690	2454	4914	5072	0806	9430	8317	6443	3833	5596
(2932)	9137	9840	9872	8699	1818	2802	4019	0271	2061	6194
(2933)	3527	5962	5682	9427	4437	4580	4241	5244	1561	7758
(2934)	0821	8270	2324	4660	1749	2397	6719	7962	0549	3976
(2935)	4270	8124	1751	0464	4074	3724	9359	7183	9614	5123
(2936)	9073	2128	4143	8072	6079	2832	0051	7038	8831	2738
(2937)	1551	8778	9317	9229	0866	2459	1390	1529	9414	7424
(2938)	1004	2543	6788	5726	6550	4005	8897	9621	6503	6781
(2939)	6307	5174	0732	8307	3165	1659	7632	7470	4360	5785
(2940)	1721	5707	3203	0915	2478	2492	8813	4513	1302	9630
(2941)	8789	8880	2426	7471	5634	7593	0015	4944	7439	9780
(2942)	7437	8735	8992	2074	1507	7919	2954	0457	4686	1222
(2943)	7811	0239	5068	8744	4009	7627	8644	1266	1861	1433
(2944)	1609	0854	8116	3520	9512	2928	6127	7286	2397	1787
(2945)	0877	3133	1081	9164	9939	4643	0726	6304	6530	9606

Appendix A
Random Numbers (Continued)

	(01)	(02)	(03)	(04)	(05)	(06)	(07)	(08)	(09)	(10)
(2946)	5753	1584	7938	8028	7004	3716	7959	5201	4308	6712
(2947)	9592	1733	5313	7289	8140	7470	0488	8601	6802	5230
(2948)	0224	9054	7807	8929	1490	1680	4244	3705	6178	4313
(2949)	4193	2056	7476	8513	8267	0306	1554	2832	9585	0657
(2950)	3086	0062	4006	1024	6278	8250	5038	7589	6271	4708
(2951)	9518	3425	6155	1462	9882	5375	3548	3588	2294	0900
(2952)	1698	8961	4917	2134	5873	8076	9273	7167	2846	7891
(2953)	2578	2809	1582	8001	1550	1478	4753	6020	2035	7550
(2954)	3674	8312	4907	5514	6942	3224	5097	2265	1355	7904
(2955)	6970	3307	0296	4039	1622	0335	1979	3337	3533	5325
(2956)	8093	3498	3260	5125	1907	7655	0077	3321	7123	9817
(2957)	3156	4418	8915	8639	0218	8665	4036	6052	9328	9135
(2958)	4029	7011	4717	3802	9343	4518	9880	8506	0159	9451
(2959)	6544	1332	1848	4513	6279	6027	2805	5741	0260	5630
(2960)	4932	0477	9095	5147	0626	4368	9531	5133	8300	3190
(2961)	3943	7825	6037	9615	2878	0215	9973	2493	4547	4828
(2962)	4783	8611	0918	5295	7014	2919	4277	8018	6226	6580
(2963)	0830	0805	9476	5064	4051	5769	2139	1727	2919	3447
(2964)	7492	3365	2204	3007	5725	7466	8085	8987	5926	1974
(2965)	5996	9546	1314	0821	3863	3299	4294	3379	1229	7179
(2966)	6272	8641	5839	9361	3384	3163	8423	6163	1587	6978
(2967)	3633	4926	2185	6766	4506	7799	9843	9345	8216	2568
(2968)	1939	5139	0163	2176	1481	6062	3078	3107	3954	1606
(2969)	2883	9306	1031	8303	6928	9563	0020	9400	3570	7806
(2970)	3295	5271	2685	7720	1345	8770	3159	9078	9694	9428
(2971)	2343	6407	5769	2548	3581	4063	4666	3447	4606	4433
(2972)	7115	0714	2806	8476	2649	3546	1768	0929	5906	0101
(2973)	3551	4407	3135	6815	7139	6577	7582	9772	2900	1836
(2974)	3692	9422	8494	8990	0697	9485	0322	3277	4088	5167
(2975)	4240	4230	1034	8968	0831	5483	4481	8601	1990	9683
(2976)	0932	6439	1669	1115	4318	4979	6401	3093	5549	2763
(2977)	3505	1719	6232	8293	4622	4644	2523	1353	1914	4318
(2978)	8096	0927	9745	3493	4599	8070	9295	0402	7494	7415
(2979)	6609	7240	0606	0535	6725	3046	9096	9717	2178	2126
(2980)	2210	5793	4697	3767	6957	4348	7302	8524	6293	1900
(2981)	6112	1886	4993	8239	6296	8189	4227	7219	5804	2716
(2982)	9298	0599	3141	1714	9624	4185	6700	6343	0948	5549
(2983)	7001	2001	4715	4470	6425	9305	7204	0700	4466	8430
(2984)	6779	5493	2778	7890	5152	2404	8037	3088	3541	4252
(2985)	3093	9142	4713	5298	2713	8577	3405	6446	7533	2717
(2986)	4829	3094	2457	0446	2381	6080	0894	5648	5277	4332
(2987)	5791	5701	3376	5810	8167	3677	7657	7985	5856	6864
(2988)	7598	0435	3307	1980	0409	1497	8463	8463	8579	8873
(2989)	6104	6646	2581	8268	4437	9623	3341	5397	5770	6986
(2990)	2975	8974	7274	7257	1436	2748	0514	9512	1193	2235
(2991)	1128	2239	2850	3354	7689	4089	3820	7852	0287	3609
(2992)	0226	1521	4533	9618	3981	7318	9132	6416	2472	0513
(2993)	7782	6065	2516	1002	9491	6065	9402	4594	3560	5006
(2994)	8039	3150	8526	3771	6257	5615	2540	2896	5489	5896
(2995)	0488	7033	3273	8194	0238	7461	9478	4752	8097	6209

A

	(01)	(02)	(03)	(04)	(05)	(06)	(07)	(08)	(09)	(10)
(2996)	4739	0529	8771	1594	0662	6968	2276	7361	0837	5807
(2997)	0410	0599	1890	9227	3850	1295	8480	7567	7242	5470
(2998)	1757	7651	5154	2646	0360	9406	9233	0179	2826	3610
(2999)	4625	1060	5026	0286	7529	1914	4524	2748	6432	6728
(3000)	2095	5559	6659	9557	4806	5437	4208	4680	5093	5463

APPENDIX B
RANDOM LETTERS OF THE ALPHABET

JHLKI LOWDS	RKDBJ QEQZT	NPOHN XPSIB	ECNFQ QNZKP	ZZATA SMIHB
HZYGJ FXWVM	LPEOT EBXBH	VZGUH BXQLD	TORUC ZMRAY	EIJIJ PGTXM
JLZQY TSUDL	KWRWN VGEWT	EOQIY KPBNT	FYLTK WIIHS	UUGJF JLUSX
PTCCP BFGFO	PLXRT KQACG	FWRMS NGJMT	WXVKI RSJPX	MXPVD MLEJU
EMGKD GKLGQ	LJTIF XDIAZ	GTDGH WEWQH	QLQZL EMIUF	IFDOB MRGHO
CDFDE INHPZ	CQHAT RRSFS	HZDOQ XCSKV	KTOYD NEGJU	GPHSA GKYFR
PDIDJ GNGNR	EMDPF FLTED	XBOIR RYVQP	UHNNO TPTET	SXWWF OGZAY
FKMKQ JAKKA	DOARL EGNGV	TNOZY RKMSV	PIOSC VSNBJ	RNPTR RTSWH
RFSTJ CDKVG	SOKQH MJYFS	FUOLL ENMXC	KZPGJ WOKKR	UMFJC OXSQH
WMVWB PPWYV	QYHXX NXUAM	UXMLA GXFEE	GBAFI ZQIUK	NZOUY NQGUY
EUKIF PJQUW	GPJIL NLHBY	KRJYV SHRZK	DVQIP IFTHP	HTKEE MSCXN
UEMIW EFBOE	KLZGU QYKBW	GKHIF ZIRWU	QPSPH ZLVGT	GTFYX DAPGJ
CNNMZ EYONS	HRIME IIZST	NAMCF CFWUN	BRWGR JWSLZ	YDLZA RHCPX
LUFOH GKSSC	GUDLW HJEZM	EDJQU UNVSY	OTBEA AGLMD	ZGQBH QNQIO
ZHYUF AZLLW	MIPAY BBFDI	DWOSF GXGHM	QYIGI VWBRP	AGOBV FLBGX
JFWXP NAZHJ	MBLYW SSYNM	KWUCR BZAFN	VQPMM YVDOP	HASDI PJOIQ
NSKIR ZURKF	HCIKP QRWIX	SLJHA ZOWIK	MYREJ QSDVR	MLGZK YTUXX
ANUJQ OBMYN	ZPWLN KYXLG	XFCOA XTVXN	UCGTY THTOW	ASEVA GMCPT
PCNFV XRXOG	WPUIE ONHTJ	TMPKE CNJMR	DELBL HZCYL	WUKBO DMDFT
TJNCA KVSPM	NLCWR DGPVT	HBQBI NOUBN	WSDRR UHVMH	KROPD UBTSO
SPMZE GTUKE	SZCRT HMRCM	QCYNH LTLTN	BNLAR WHVVU	JOXAS TGKHW
ZNSMW UYXPQ	PIREQ COHRF	GZWUP OEJQH	KPKGX XSQUM	DKTZD OOJVM
NOKNU VRRSU	SVDYK LVFCK	YIIFN DOYLF	BQKHV PEZQT	ODTDA MAXON
PWGQS JGYKN	ESYUQ NIUGH	FFVHY SYSUU	BKTQF ZJZDI	OFAIF DLTDF
QEMKY TXACZ	HFLPY GOEBJ	VDARG ATVAO	YKVMB YLJIV	SPLDB OUTVI
NYWMA EZMUC	SJDPH ZHGGK	JPFHE JBMDC	KRNTG GOKYR	NILEL GPHQC
WZTPL QZIJF	XHOCI CKHLI	HGSZE QUHPE	BMGSQ KDLPM	QARMN ERDNU
GKMSB PDZMD	BZXUV WCSRH	QUWXL OLPXD	HBXKA XKAWC	YFWHQ URQNX
GRSEP YBDSF	RXFWR THVEQ	HICTC SWECR	ULQRB RXHIK	JWRBJ CBPHC
QQVNE MDOIZ	BMKUC JRUHS	MKFXI RIVIK	MNBDT AZRGA	YLUPO PPWZV
JJTYR EKZFW	ICYCK JWEEE	LOPAT IELAA	FPJBP SQLGG	MDIBK WTMDD
OEIAF EPFSG	MICRH KEIRP	MNMIV PJYWD	AMJOZ SIDOH	PFWCC QXBEW
SXGQW NJPAI	FEBLY ZDCRP	OFHFO JNEHO	RFOVB ZVSCB	YSYSA TTWZS
AKWSV LERLS	PXLKF LEFYR	SEIEC XWWBB	LVSCF XFDGU	QIKND WOEXB
MDHUJ REQUF	XLTNH JQKNI	CLZNS YCUTI	JJKYB YWHGT	REQTP APEIA
VGUBI SEQRJ	DPTBU LBROM	WLOPX NQTGF	XKZCA QTYFP	GJMEM ZXCIX
ZZSGM TUIXY	UHDMF LPLZB	MUHZQ HNRGA	EWMRE JQIND	TUKCD GZOBR
UBTJR SAMVN	DVVUE FWUQW	YBANK KRDZA	IQTUQ OOJAP	KZANP PEHES
YGVRW PYVIP	UNSZSAXBEZ	ZANRI VKISZ	ITCBE EMAPZ	OWQFG BUPBX
KXVXC QEUIZ	SYQBU TZELC	QQRBD FZNPY	DQJAV WFROI	PQGPD VVNCC
UGEVV RPMQR	AJYTO JNCSD	APEWO IFATY	CEZVN YBYPZ	YLRVI VHUBJ
IJMXN ATKWW	PBYCL NLUAD	KBGMK DGAAO	ZPVHQ PPTEZ	UMUNR RJREU
IHQGK QLLXH	UIBPD IIMNU	ZVWIP SWPSP	JGTCK RPXYK	QWRRJ HCMSB
RVUMR INKPN	CCXJN ERXIQ	XPHHN DOLVR	GIUWB GHFPY	FHSUW FUULB
AUZJO DRLCD	DPIUP KWWCU	QUFUW SFKTH	MPNND EHQTQ	YMNVR DKJIC
HWJQU EEBLW	CZOCY ANQKA	MIXLR EWVYU	CZBHD BWLNC	XJMYT PPCDV
BGTFC NOSXX	MPEJF PTKKE	DXQTO ZGCNN	MPTGE WQDYE	MJMOD ZJXMW
QRCEO KJBIF	ADDJT VDIST	ITNEZ CBDDC	DNHKN YDYLW	XONGS AJDVI
AFWMK KEZBO	CVPXU JFWAX	UQMLL DVAPV	DBEJG DUEIS	SPNSY KYBVV
RDDJI MDOFM	UWXHD USQNY	CZBJL RHAKH	OCVGL UVHMI	UWFOA KUYZH

B

DUIRB ZBNVB EYAIR JKPIA GKYKV RBFZP UKNNL CNJLJ LXQDY ZENYU
ISNYF YRRMJ MDDFG HIQDG XTHFW ZWXBW QHPPY AKDAQ MOUAF KOJRK
IEBSI RGTVD SSLIM VIFTC CMRRC UVJCX TFGEX IKGXQ NFWHZ VQGIU
EDJDW MYEZD UUNUY HAOQN LXZHB VPAEN YRDCF LZIUT RMQAT VIVVI
LGCOT JINUD TMEWM MWDCI MJUVS DTISC QTEDW JLOAJ ECVIZ JHMRI

RAXEO QWPQG GVGWY ZIRRC GRYEO CGXZH EIKDL JULAL FJPRV FWXRW
MBIEZ KXBWE NJPUA DMAFI WBQQG WVRHR JRSTV VBNWG WCCPX SBEZZ
XGDWK BZWVV KQOJS ZXEPJ FYRVX YTTAJ SBFHR AWEBD VXTBH YHRWL
VGXXO TDEGT KSNOR VCUDV RQECS SDCVO FXYPD OUALW TNGLG HXMSI
ICFSJ KMAMV UJDBR BQXEI WJQSJ BGTHV VEURE ILAHY YXJGM RUDSK

IYQNO DDBYS PPJFH OTAYX QCFSL PODJS UEHIP AKFMC QCFBY WSTKS
LERPU HXNEG ZJEUZ WMEHT TMWYB GQDOL BPCOH AGSVG YTYXT GCCPZ
IUMOE LGCDG PHAMN CLPCV EWFUP MCKPP YGZBC YDLFI HBDEE PXKCA
RFEYM PVSPJ SSODM PTCGT CVAIT RIPAS XJGND TRSDN ENQJK QKDEG
VNGIH ZWESU PLZGM WIRSX ABMJU VNRND CIXJJ PZBSI WKONM LBGTM

JEMIB EFVLF PDNAR KXMBW PEFPN OOQUG ZDOZY HUXVJ MIXXO BEVTW
QIPXQ VZQYW YTYUN JDIQX JJDNK WWZRM AZIPL HKBUK ZPELK LBZPZ
DUIXQ WYGFJ GPURC ESDUD EWHNA KITOH CEVQG MOKEM BGZJW SPTWQ
TRHIA OHDUL BPQNU MVXOS TIRHV JJTTP PNYRI WAKPG GFKXX JDQFJ
JZMKH AAQSG JRREJ CYLCM IAZKL ZMZOG DQOEH GPANB UXWYA POLQK

CZEQT PUNSZ JDLPK OCBIO TULVR YSMDQ TFANZ VPZAV TLXDA DGJWO
RCCOL UUUUF ZROPJ QMJVF XUQKN GJVPX DQVPC JRGAU KWSQQ RJXDK
WHKLV PRHLW YFDZO VYLTI AKQZG GCGVR ETBHG CXXDO LXXZE MJPBX
KDSWK VETGP CAVOK ESQRU ZJVWR ISGAW NSTOB VAPFK HWENO QBODE
GMDJF HUFGI ADQRI SPVYY ZHKHH CJQSX TCTGG LADJN EUXWO CLEYW

JAKAT KPQCG TSGVY YBVXM DVIOQ CTAPF XPGEO DQCFL SQMEF NKAZM
JGKRF URYEF WJPSA UJJSS ERIFA RCWGK BQCHY KYEYF EWHOP NRWMJ
OAGIW RZRBH LWEKC VIAQA KJKWV ALJBG KDWPJ SGGHO IUHUY FNGSB
MBXSA RSEAA ODRMT SOPYP WUMIQ WIZFQ MYRJP SYJXN PBDVQ DUDYV
XUJYZ FOXOV IWZXT AFFUL PKVIR YOMCG RXSSX TZLPI VDWXZ MHYEH

LHOZY BYFZM FIEMY VDFTD LRKEZ VVIFX XPGRT KTHRQ HTGYZ HXGVH
PQSKH HABOA LQLPX KZCLH RQEIO MXETY GUKIL JOTUB HCNCR WDCFO
EUXQR JVYUX ITEZP GTJRF GPDJX NTQCX FXMBZ IGOYE KRKNV ZFGYU
BMHEV OISZN MWJJW SHTCV WXPQA ZGJTB IVODT WMVSP SWLWZ RPRDO
LNCWL QTWRS EISDV VIVKA AJJMR BDEPU MUYCG LLTWD ENUPS TGYWA

OGQST TYVPV SJPCS TUWMF WAXCQ PPALW YWVYB HAOWR TCMID KHELT
UAKQO YREGZ LXVLY NZIDX EXPHV YKKEE FIRLX DALRU ATMLK XQQGN
DSTJJ YSLNV TUAJF KOFOT TNHIC VTMVP SYZAT ENYXG KDAQK DGNWC
ULITJ XBCZY XXRLY SKYAZ MBOZF GRFWD MSLLG TJXVQ DRIKO MTVIW
CSVKV FUPGM KXPLO JGTYX IYTQW WUNRN MSFTP ORJBT ODSCO NBXRK

TOJSW OTNVY PKUHG AKBYK MSVMH TMXGD VNMHV MPZUA ZGQCC AWUEL
PCFDE YOUKO BOXCW APKQJ JIWUW NTJZT OGQOW RXXTJ PXDJV NGIFS
EBEQA PGNHI YEYUU PPTXE ZUFJP JXJHY KTOUK RYXGY XMHOC GLISV
LYZIS VGMZT JALUN XABYU GJITU NMQFP DRIKI DQUQC ZWHYE ZGVDG
UKBCR IACLU EVZUU HMQCG TGKVE WDWDB MJDHY YDDCL BHQNL UNHIO

KSBBM WINMF QUAHO FPLIA PHDNU ICHIR VANQA RKXDY YQWFN IKWCS
OVVTZ GWYQG TKMBY IFEAR GCHQD VJXZP CUPDN IIGRV JCMIL TBVEU
ACZVW XIKZP MDIYQ TTWTR NONSP RCZYJ MQZYF RZRIS SIKSM QJPNV
BQODA RSKYM OSTXC BBQPB GGQUV ETUWZ IYNRU YNBDV JPYJV XYNWM
XCDTC OQOSV XISJZ MXMEC ACUAK STTYK TWVPM ASESN BTPTJ GZJXL

APPENDIX C
RANDOM MONTHS

MAR SEP MAR AUG SEP	MAR DEC AUG MAY JAN	APR JAN APR MAY FEB	JUN JUL MAY MAR APR
MAY OCT SEP SEP JUN	APR MAY MAY OCT APR	JUL JUL DEC DEC FEB	APR MAY SEP AUG NOV
DEC FEB DEC SEP DEC	FEB JUN MAY SEP DEC	SEP MAY MAY JUL NOV	APR JUN JUN MAR MAY
NOV JUL MAY NOV DEC	FEB DEC AUG JUN APR	DEC AUG MAY DEC MAR	SEP NOV APR MAR MAY
DEC FEB JUN JUL MAY	OCT NOV JAN NOV NOV	JUN JUN AUG JUL DEC	NOV NOV APR SEP NOV
FEB MAR JAN NOV NOV	APR JAN JUN JAN OCT	FEB NOV MAY MAR JUL	NOV AUG DEC NOV DEC
DEC DEC FEB MAR MAY	JUN MAY FEB FEB FEB	FEB JAN SEP MAY OCT	NOV JUL MAY JAN JAN
NOV JAN NOV DEC JAN	JUN JUL OCT JUL JUN	NOV JUL JUL SEP APR	DEC MAY MAR DEC OCT
AUG SEP APR SEP SEP	OCT DEC SEP AUG NOV	FEB DEC JUL JUN APR	DEC JAN SEP SEP JUN
AUG OCT OCT AUG OCT	JAN JUL MAR JUL MAR	FEB OCT DEC FEB JUL	JUL JUL MAY OCT DEC
NOV JUL MAR APR OCT	JAN APR JUN JUN JUN	AUG SEP AUG FEB APR	NOV AUG JUL MAY FEB
JUN APR FEB SEP MAR	APR MAY SEP MAY SEP	JUL FEB MAR OCT APR	JAN AUG DEC OCT JUL
MAR DEC NOV FEB MAR	AUG APR AUG FEB JUL	JAN MAY JUL FEB AUG	AUG DEC SEP NOV JUL
JUN NOV JAN SEP NOV	SEP JUL JUL MAR OCT	JUN SEP JAN APR NOV	APR MAY AUG MAR NOV
FEB MAY AUG OCT JUL	FEB JAN JAN NOV APR	MAY OCT AUG MAR SEP	OCT MAR AUG JUN APR
MAR NOV FEB MAR JUL	DEC FEB JAN JAN JUN	JUN JAN APR JUL JUN	JUN APR SEP JUL MAY
NOV DEC AUG AUG SEP	OCT AUG FEB OCT MAR	AUG JUN SEP JAN NOV	JAN JUL MAR SEP MAY
AUG JAN MAY JUN FEB	OCT AUG AUG MAR FEB	FEB MAR MAY JAN FEB	JUL FEB JUN APR JUN
JAN MAR AUG OCT OCT	JUN AUG NOV APR AUG	MAY MAY APR JAN JUL	AUG JAN JUL FEB AUG
MAY FEB SEP AUG MAY	APR SEP MAR NOV JUN	JAN SEP NOV JUL MAR	JUL JUN OCT FEB APR

```
JAN OCT JAN JAN DEC   FEB AUG DEC JUL OCT   FEB MAR DEC AUG NOV   OCT DEC MAY JUN AUG
NOV AUG SEP MAY AUG   MAR APR OCT APR OCT   SEP OCT AUG DEC NOV   OCT AUG JUL AUG FEB
APR AUG NOV SEP JUN   FEB JUL NOV MAR SEP   APR DEC JAN MAR MAR   OCT JAN JUL NOV MAR
FEB APR DEC AUG DEC   JUL FEB AUG OCT DEC   DEC AUG JAN MAR AUG   OCT MAR JAN SEP MAY
AUG JAN DEC MAY APR   JUL APR FEB AUG MAR   JUN FEB MAR APR NOV   JUN OCT SEP MAY OCT

JUN FEB DEC JUL DEC   DEC JUL FEB NOV OCT   APR MAY APR SEP OCT   JAN AUG JUN FEB FEB
JAN NOV SEP MAY APR   SEP NOV NOV AUG SEP   AUG SEP APR JUN AUG   MAR NOV JAN AUG OCT
OCT JAN APR AUG APR   OCT MAR APR APR MAR   NOV MAR OCT JUL FEB   NOV APR APR JUL FEB
NOV MAY JUN APR OCT   JUN APR MAR APR JAN   MAY JAN NOV SEP SEP   SEP MAY FEB MAR JUL
FEB MAY JAN AUG AUG   MAR MAY MAY SEP DEC   JUN FEB MAY SEP DEC   OCT DEC MAY JAN APR

MAR JUL OCT DEC DEC   NOV NOV AUG OCT NOV   AUG MAR APR APR SEP   FEB JAN JAN JUL AUG
JAN AUG MAR JUL MAR   MAY AUG JUN MAY OCT   AUG NOV OCT NOV JUL   NOV MAY AUG NOV MAY
FEB DEC JUN DEC NOV   AUG AUG JAN SEP MAY   JAN OCT JAN SEP OCT   JUL OCT JAN MAR MAR
MAY JUL FEB NOV MAY   APR FEB MAY JAN APR   MAY SEP FEB FEB OCT   DEC APR JAN JUN SEP
FEB JUL SEP NOV JAN   AUG JAN OCT DEC AUG   SEP AUG JAN JUN JUL   NOV DEC APR DEC JUL

NOV SEP APR MAR MAY   APR JUN AUG APR AUG   SEP OCT JAN APR NOV   OCT MAR AUG MAR NOV
NOV MAY MAY JUN JAN   JUN APR SEP FEB APR   OCT MAY JAN JUN OCT   OCT DEC AUG SEP MAR
OCT OCT JAN FEB MAY   AUG MAY JUL APR JUL   NOV JAN FEB MAR OCT   JUN MAR MAR JUN MAR
FEB DEC JUL JUN APR   FEB JUN APR SEP AUG   JUL NOV NOV JAN MAR   JAN AUG JUN JUN DEC
JUL APR DEC MAR FEB   JUL MAR MAY AUG JUN   JUL MAR JUN APR JUL   AUG NOV DEC MAY JUN

SEP JUL JAN FEB NOV   AUG NOV APR NOV AUG   JAN JUN JUN NOV OCT   JUN APR AUG FEB JUN
SEP SEP APR SEP JUL   JAN FEB MAR MAY JUN   FEB JUN DEC JAN NOV   DEC MAR JAN JUL AUG
JUN MAR JAN MAR NOV   MAY AUG SEP JUN MAY   FEB SEP MAR JUN DEC   JUL JUN NOV FEB JAN
MAY NOV JAN SEP MAR   NOV APR NOV APR AUG   MAR JAN SEP JUL JUN   SEP JAN FEB APR MAR
NOV JUL OCT DEC AUG   NOV FEB NOV MAR APR   APR NOV JAN SEP AUG   APR SEP SEP MAY DEC
```

C

Appendix C
Random Months (Continued)

DEC SEP JUL NOV MAR   SEP AUG AUG APR JUN   MAY JUL SEP AUG MAY   MAR APR JUL MAY JAN
JUL SEP NOV MAR JAN   DEC AUG JAN AUG DEC   NOV JUN APR APR JUL   JUN NOV MAY OCT FEB
JUN APR DEC JUN DEC   JUL JUL FEB OCT APR   APR APR DEC AUG AUG   JAN JUL JUN JUN NOV
MAR OCT OCT OCT AUG   AUG NOV OCT APR MAY   JAN OCT APR SEP DEC   JUL SEP JUN OCT NOV
MAY SEP JAN APR MAR   MAR OCT AUG FEB OCT   MAY DEC APR FEB JUL   MAR AUG MAR NOV JAN

MAR JAN JUL JAN AUG   FEB NOV SEP JUL JUL   FEB OCT MAR SEP AUG   MAY JAN MAR MAY OCT
MAY JUN MAY AUG FEB   JUN DEC NOV MAR JUL   SEP FEB DEC JUL JUL   OCT OCT AUG AUG SEP
SEP JAN FEB JAN OCT   MAR SEP AUG OCT JUN   JUL NOV SEP FEB FEB   JUL FEB JAN NOV SEP
AUG NOV FEB JAN MAY   MAR OCT MAY JUL MAR   OCT SEP MAR NOV FEB   SEP OCT SEP APR SEP
DEC JUL DEC FEB MAR   JAN MAY JUN FEB APR   MAY DEC AUG APR OCT   JAN NOV FEB OCT DEC

FEB MAR SEP JUL JUN   DEC OCT MAY JUL OCT   OCT MAR JUN DEC APR   NOV SEP MAR NOV NOV
JAN NOV JUL OCT FEB   JUN AUG OCT OCT FEB   AUG JUL DEC APR OCT   JUL APR DEC MAR NOV
FEB AUG SEP JUL APR   DEC FEB AUG JUN MAR   OCT NOV DEC AUG JUN   JUL FEB OCT APR MAR
AUG APR MAR DEC MAR   JUN APR MAY SEP JUL   FEB APR OCT JUL APR   MAR SEP NOV SEP NOV
JUN MAR MAY JAN MAY   JAN JAN NOV AUG JUN   APR APR OCT DEC OCT   NOV MAR FEB NOV MAY

JUN APR MAY JUN AUG   FEB OCT FEB APR APR   JAN APR APR JAN JAN   NOV AUG SEP OCT APR
NOV JUL DEC JAN MAY   NOV MAR OCT NOV FEB   FEB MAY JUN OCT AUG   MAR MAY SEP MAY APR
MAR OCT JAN APR AUG   SEP NOV JUL MAR OCT   SEP JUN SEP MAY DEC   AUG FEB APR DEC SEP
AUG SEP DEC JAN JUN   JUN AUG JUL JUL MAR   OCT DEC OCT JAN NOV   MAY AUG MAR DEC APR
FEB OCT DEC JAN JUL   OCT MAR JAN JUL JUL   APR MAR NOV DEC NOV   DEC AUG NOV SEP NOV

JAN APR OCT DEC APR   MAY APR JUL JUN MAR   MAR JUL FEB JAN NOV   NOV NOV SEP JUL AUG
NOV AUG DEC DEC DEC   SEP AUG SEP JAN AUG   JAN JAN NOV MAR NOV   JUL APR APR SEP APR
OCT JUL MAR JUL DEC   JAN MAR MAY OCT AUG   DEC JAN MAY MAY AUG   SEP FEB MAR AUG MAY
JAN OCT JUN JUL SEP   SEP JUL JUN JUL APR   NOV NOV AUG FEB APR   MAY MAY MAR DEC MAY
DEC AUG AUG MAY MAY   AUG JUL AUG JAN FEB   JAN SEP APR OCT JUL   MAY MAR JAN OCT JUN

OCT JAN FEB MAR NOV   SEP JAN APR JAN DEC   MAY MAR NOV MAR FEB   AUG JAN DEC JUL APR
MAR OCT SEP APR OCT   DEC FEB APR NOV MAR   FEB APR APR AUG APR   MAR MAR JUL MAR OCT
MAR APR JAN NOV FEB   FEB FEB AUG MAY JUN   JUN JUN SEP APR FEB   AUG FEB JUN MAR SEP
NOV FEB SEP JUN AUG   AUG MAY APR APR JUL   JUN AUG OCT FEB MAR   FEB NOV MAY NOV AUG
NOV FEB JAN JUN DEC   FEB DEC FEB DEC AUG   AUG MAR MAR JAN JAN   AUG FEB OCT DEC DEC

OCT NOV NOV FEB JUN   JUL JUN MAY MAR MAY   MAY MAR FEB APR OCT   DEC JUN MAR MAY DEC
SEP JUL NOV SEP JUL   NOV MAY MAY JAN NOV   NOV MAY AUG NOV SEP   JUL FEB JUN FEB MAR
MAY AUG MAR DEC JUL   FEB SEP MAR APR AUG   SEP NOV SEP JAN JUL   MAY SEP MAR JUN FEB
FEB OCT JUN FEB MAR   APR DEC FEB JUL APR   OCT AUG NOV JUN JUN   FEB NOV DEC SEP JAN
SEP FEB OCT FEB JAN   DEC SEP JUL APR OCT   FEB MAY MAR APR JAN   NOV APR SEP MAR JUN

APR JUL MAR MAY AUG   MAR NOV DEC MAR JUN   MAR APR DEC OCT JAN   JAN APR APR JUL JAN
NOV NOV NOV SEP DEC   NOV MAY MAR JUN OCT   FEB FEB AUG AUG SEP   SEP JUL FEB FEB JUL
APR JAN DEC OCT APR   APR MAY OCT JUN JUL   MAR AUG OCT MAR JUL   JUL NOV JUN JAN NOV
FEB APR NOV MAR DEC   AUG DEC FEB JUN AUG   APR OCT AUG SEP OCT   SEP OCT OCT DEC OCT
FEB AUG MAR JUN OCT   JUN JAN JUN JUL AUG   OCT MAR NOV FEB FEB   FEB AUG NOV OCT APR

MAY AUG NOV SEP FEB   SEP OCT APR FEB JUL   JUN MAR NOV SEP OCT   JUL MAY APR JUN FEB
NOV MAR MAR FEB FEB   JUN JUN APR DEC FEB   MAR DEC FEB JAN NOV   MAR MAR JAN MAR NOV
AUG DEC MAR AUG JUL   FEB MAR FEB FEB APR   JAN JUN JUL DEC OCT   MAR MAR JUL OCT FEB
AUG JUN NOV DEC JUL   NOV NOV MAR JAN OCT   FEB AUG MAY SEP MAR   MAR JUN FEB DEC MAR
FEB APR JAN JUN JUL   DEC JUN DEC MAR DEC   FEB NOV DEC APR AUG   JAN MAY DEC JUN OCT

APR JAN DEC MAR APR   APR FEB JAN MAY JAN   JUN FEB JAN SEP JUL   JUN OCT MAR JAN MAR
JUL MAR OCT MAY NOV   JAN JAN AUG JAN APR   JUL JAN JAN JAN JAN   NOV JAN FEB DEC JAN
JUN DEC MAR JAN JAN   JUN APR FEB MAR APR   MAY SEP APR NOV MAR   JUN MAY MAY JUL JUL
NOV JUN NOV JUN FEB   APR OCT JAN FEB DEC   MAR DEC JAN JAN MAR   FEB JUL APR AUG DEC
APR JAN AUG DEC DEC   MAR MAR OCT MAR MAR   APR SEP FEB JUL SEP   FEB SEP APR APR MAY

C

Appendix C
Random Months (Continued)

JUL JUN DEC JUN APR	JAN FEB DEC MAR JAN	FEB MAR JAN NOV MAY	JUN FEB AUG MAR SEP
OCT MAY JUN MAR JUL	MAY JUN MAR JUL JUN	SEP JUN JAN DEC SEP	MAR MAR APR JUN NOV
AUG JUL JAN AUG FEB	OCT SEP JUN JUL MAY	JUN NOV JUL JUL DEC	MAR SEP OCT SEP NOV
MAR APR NOV FEB JUN	MAR JUN AUG JUN APR	NOV APR SEP AUG FEB	JAN JUN MAY APR MAY
NOV MAY AUG NOV JUN	FEB OCT APR MAR NOV	NOV FEB DEC JUN APR	JUL FEB FEB JAN JUL
JUL MAY AUG NOV MAR	SEP MAR APR JUL FEB	APR JUN OCT FEB DEC	OCT FEB MAY AUG MAY
JAN MAR JUN FEB MAR	JAN FEB APR AUG JUL	DEC FEB FEB JUN OCT	SEP DEC AUG JUL FEB
MAY MAY FEB OCT APR	OCT MAR AUG SEP DEC	SEP AUG JUL NOV SEP	JUL JUL JUN FEB APR
SEP SEP NOV OCT OCT	NOV APR FEB SEP MAR	FEB JUN JUL FEB SEP	MAY JUN AUG FEB DEC
DEC SEP JUN SEP SEP	NOV OCT AUG MAY SEP	MAY DEC SEP MAR JUN	MAR MAR MAY SEP DEC
APR AUG OCT FEB JUN	FEB AUG JAN JUN OCT	MAR NOV AUG APR SEP	JUN MAY JAN JUL FEB
AUG JAN JAN JAN APR	AUG NOV MAY NOV NOV	FEB OCT MAR JAN JUL	DEC FEB AUG JAN NOV
APR MAY APR JUL AUG	JUL JAN SEP NOV SEP	NOV MAY MAR JUL MAR	JUL MAR MAY SEP JAN
FEB FEB OCT NOV DEC	JAN MAY MAY JUL AUG	MAR JUL JUL JAN DEC	NOV JAN APR JUL SEP
JAN FEB SEP JAN FEB	MAY OCT NOV NOV AUG	SEP MAR NOV SEP OCT	JUL NOV FEB JAN JUN
JUL JAN FEB MAY SEP	JUN MAR SEP AUG DEC	JAN MAY APR AUG MAY	MAY MAY OCT MAR SEP
AUG JUN DEC FEB SEP	APR FEB MAY FEB DEC	AUG FEB JUL JUN JUN	NOV MAR SEP FEB NOV
JUN DEC JUN MAR JUL	MAY OCT MAR SEP MAR	JUL APR DEC APR DEC	DEC DEC JUN SEP JUL
DEC JUL APR AUG JUL	AUG JUN DEC DEC JUL	MAR MAR JAN DEC DEC	MAR JAN JUL NOV MAY
OCT JAN NOV FEB JAN	DEC AUG MAR OCT OCT	APR JUL AUG AUG JUL	JUN MAY MAR JUN AUG
JUL NOV MAR SEP SEP	JUL APR NOV DEC FEB	APR NOV NOV MAR SEP	MAR JUN MAR NOV JUL
JAN MAR SEP APR JAN	JAN SEP MAY AUG MAR	SEP AUG DEC JUL NOV	MAY AUG NOV DEC SEP
MAY DEC JUN MAY SEP	AUG DEC JUN MAR MAY	SEP OCT SEP SEP SEP	JAN MAY OCT AUG JUL
MAR MAR SEP FEB MAY	FEB OCT DEC OCT JUL	MAR APR DEC NOV JUN	OCT MAY OCT OCT SEP
AUG SEP MAR APR NOV	OCT MAY NOV JUL JAN	DEC JAN AUG JAN FEB	JUL MAR JUL OCT NOV

C

MAY MAY FEB MAY JUN   JUN MAY MAR DEC JUL   DEC MAR AUG MAY JUL   JUN FEB JAN OCT SEP
OCT JUL FEB JAN JUL   FEB MAY SEP AUG JUN   DEC APR APR JUL OCT   JAN JUN NOV MAY MAY
APR JUN FEB JUL OCT   MAR AUG SEP JUL DEC   JUL JUL JUN SEP APR   FEB JAN OCT APR JUN
APR JUN SEP NOV MAY   APR AUG AUG JAN JAN   MAY APR FEB DEC AUG   JUN JUN DEC FEB JAN
DEC OCT JUN NOV JAN   JUL SEP APR APR JAN   OCT MAY MAY JUL DEC   JUN DEC MAR APR JUL

MAY APR JUL AUG JAN   JUL JAN DEC MAR NOV   APR OCT FEB JUN JUN   FEB DEC JAN MAR JAN
JAN JAN JAN JUL AUG   JUN AUG JUN OCT AUG   APR JUL OCT APR AUG   MAR JUL MAR SEP OCT
NOV JUL DEC AUG JAN   AUG AUG FEB JAN OCT   FEB JAN JAN DEC DEC   JAN JUL SEP DEC NOV
SEP FEB JAN JUL MAY   JUL JUL AUG JAN JUL   AUG NOV MAR MAY FEB   FEB AUG OCT DEC MAY
SEP MAY OCT MAY OCT   AUG AUG JAN NOV APR   MAY DEC MAR NOV AUG   FEB AUG NOV DEC MAY

OCT AUG MAR JAN APR   JUN JUL JUN JUL NOV   APR MAR JUL AUG AUG   SEP JUN FEB JUN JAN
AUG FEB DEC OCT MAR   MAY FEB MAY APR MAR   SEP MAY MAY SEP NOV   SEP FEB FEB DEC DEC
SEP SEP NOV SEP MAY   MAY JUL AUG APR AUG   MAR MAY AUG MAR AUG   AUG MAY NOV NOV JAN
MAR NOV APR NOV APR   MAR OCT JUL SEP MAY   JAN SEP SEP FEB JAN   JUL MAY OCT DEC OCT
OCT MAR JUN MAR JUN   JUN OCT JAN APR JAN   MAR DEC JUN JUL JUN   OCT OCT DEC NOV MAY

MAY NOV MAY JAN AUG   AUG OCT NOV NOV SEP   JUL DEC SEP NOV JAN   JUL APR OCT JUN JUL
AUG JUN JUL SEP AUG   MAR AUG DEC JAN MAR   SEP AUG SEP MAR JUN   AUG DEC MAY NOV MAR
JUN MAR JAN FEB MAR   JUL FEB JUN JAN JUL   APR APR SEP MAR MAR   FEB SEP MAY JAN MAR
NOV JUN NOV JAN JUN   JUN MAR OCT NOV SEP   JAN JAN JUL OCT MAY   JAN FEB APR DEC JAN
MAR DEC AUG MAR DEC   MAR APR JAN MAY JUL   JAN APR AUG MAY NOV   FEB JAN FEB AUG MAY

MAY FEB OCT MAY MAY   MAY NOV JUN SEP NOV   AUG MAY OCT OCT APR   NOV JUN JUN JUN OCT
DEC FEB JUL MAR AUG   DEC FEB FEB JUN AUG   AUG NOV MAY APR SEP   FEB MAY APR MAY DEC
JAN FEB APR JUN JUL   FEB OCT AUG DEC DEC   MAY OCT APR DEC OCT   AUG MAR OCT MAY JAN
OCT NOV JUN APR SEP   DEC MAR JAN SEP DEC   OCT MAR JUL APR JUN   APR MAY NOV APR MAR
MAY OCT AUG APR FEB   JAN AUG JUL OCT JUL   JUL FEB SEP OCT MAY   SEP AUG SEP JAN MAR

Appendix C
Random Months (Continued)

```
AUG JAN FEB JAN JAN   DEC DEC JUL AUG FEB   APR JUL NOV AUG FEB   MAY JUL JUN NOV JUL
OCT JAN NOV AUG OCT   JUL OCT JUN NOV AUG   APR JAN DEC SEP JUN   JUL APR SEP MAY NOV
DEC NOV JUL APR JUN   JAN MAR JAN JUL OCT   JAN JAN MAY SEP FEB   MAY APR JUL SEP JAN
FEB APR NOV NOV JAN   JUN JUN OCT NOV JUL   NOV JUN JAN JUL MAR   MAY SEP AUG JUL APR
DEC NOV APR NOV DEC   JAN JAN JUL MAY MAY   DEC FEB SEP MAR NOV   JUL JUN JUL APR MAR

JUN MAY JUL APR NOV   DEC JUN JUL AUG NOV   MAY OCT OCT JUL MAR   JUL OCT FEB APR JAN
JAN APR JAN FEB MAR   FEB AUG AUG APR DEC   SEP NOV APR JAN JUN   MAY FEB MAR AUG JUN
APR JUL FEB NOV MAY   SEP JUN JUN MAR MAR   SEP SEP OCT FEB DEC   FEB SEP MAY OCT MAY
FEB OCT MAY OCT APR   JUN FEB MAR JUL MAR   JAN APR AUG JUN SEP   MAY JAN SEP JAN JAN
FEB APR JAN JUN SEP   SEP JAN JAN NOV FEB   JAN JUL OCT JUL MAR   DEC AUG MAR JUL NOV

SEP MAR FEB OCT MAY   NOV APR OCT JUL APR   OCT DEC SEP JUL AUG   AUG SEP JUL FEB APR
APR JUL DEC APR FEB   SEP MAR OCT OCT OCT   APR SEP JAN FEB FEB   NOV MAY APR JUN APR
JUL OCT FEB APR AUG   SEP MAR MAR NOV MAY   MAY SEP AUG MAR MAR   MAY JUL JAN FEB JUL
MAR AUG NOV MAR FEB   FEB DEC MAY JUL JUL   JUL FEB DEC JAN JUL   MAY AUG JUN OCT NOV
APR JUL SEP FEB FEB   JAN JUL MAR JUN MAY   JUN NOV OCT FEB MAR   FEB APR DEC JUL APR

JAN OCT JAN AUG JUN   JUN AUG APR JUL OCT   DEC NOV AUG MAY JAN   OCT JUL DEC MAY SEP
MAR OCT FEB AUG APR   OCT APR FEB JUN JAN   AUG MAR FEB JUN JUL   DEC JUL FEB SEP DEC
JAN MAY NOV AUG APR   JUN JUN JUN NOV JUL   MAR JUN FEB JAN APR   APR SEP JUL NOV JAN
JUN JUL FEB NOV DEC   SEP FEB OCT JUN NOV   FEB JUN APR FEB JUN   APR JAN FEB MAY MAY
MAY OCT DEC DEC DEC   DEC AUG JUN JAN MAR   NOV APR SEP JAN AUG   FEB FEB OCT SEP FEB

JAN JUN OCT OCT APR   JUN NOV APR AUG AUG   FEB FEB JUN JAN SEP   NOV MAY MAR DEC JUN
JUN OCT SEP JUL JAN   JAN AUG FEB OCT JUN   AUG NOV DEC SEP OCT   DEC FEB OCT FEB NOV
NOV NOV NOV JUL JUL   APR JUN SEP JUN SEP   NOV JUN AUG APR SEP   AUG OCT DEC MAR MAR
JAN JUL APR JUL MAR   MAR MAY OCT APR AUG   JUN MAR DEC MAY FEB   MAY DEC JUL MAY DEC
OCT MAR MAR NOV JAN   SEP MAR APR JUL DEC   JUL JAN JAN JUN SEP   APR MAR JUN DEC MAR
```

SEP JUN JAN FEB AUG	JUL OCT AUG JUL OCT	APR SEP JAN OCT MAY	MAR JUL AUG JUN JUN
JUL DEC AUG DEC DEC	SEP NOV FEB DEC MAR	SEP OCT SEP MAY JUN	JUN DEC MAR SEP MAY
FEB AUG NOV FEB JUN	JAN MAR FEB FEB DEC	SEP DEC OCT MAY APR	NOV APR JUL JAN JAN
JAN MAR MAY JAN AUG	AUG SEP JAN JUN SEP	MAY JAN APR AUG APR	NOV MAR JUL SEP JAN
NOV SEP NOV DEC JUN	JAN DEC OCT OCT APR	DEC JUN NOV OCT SEP	AUG OCT JUL MAY MAR
AUG APR AUG MAY JAN	MAR SEP MAY JUN AUG	APR AUG DEC OCT NOV	AUG OCT FEB DEC AUG
FEB SEP NOV MAR OCT	DEC AUG MAR NOV MAR	MAY JAN OCT MAY NOV	MAR APR SEP APR OCT
JUL AUG NOV MAY MAR	AUG SEP MAY JAN AUG	JUN NOV APR AUG DEC	FEB JUN JUL DEC APR
AUG FEB JUN NOV SEP	DEC MAY JUL MAY JAN	MAY OCT NOV MAR MAR	MAR OCT AUG SEP DEC
NOV JAN AUG NOV FEB	JUN MAR JUL MAY OCT	SEP DEC JUN DEC JUN	AUG NOV JUL AUG AUG
APR JAN APR JUL OCT	DEC JAN JAN FEB AUG	JUN JUN JUL NOV JAN	SEP NOV OCT DEC JUN
JAN DEC JAN MAR APR	AUG AUG OCT SEP MAY	MAY JAN DEC NOV JUL	OCT MAR FEB OCT JUN
SEP OCT NOV DEC MAY	AUG SEP SEP AUG AUG	DEC DEC OCT MAR SEP	FEB MAY JUN SEP APR
FEB JUL JUL APR JAN	MAY JUN FEB MAY DEC	JUN MAY APR JAN MAY	JUN MAY APR SEP FEB
FEB MAY NOV FEB FEB	SEP MAY JUN FEB JAN	MAY SEP SEP OCT MAR	JAN AUG MAY SEP MAR
JUN JUN FEB APR JUN	JUL NOV OCT SEP APR	NOV JUN JUN MAY OCT	FEB OCT FEB JUN NOV
FEB AUG SEP FEB MAR	AUG FEB JAN JUL MAY	FEB NOV MAR JUN JUL	FEB MAY MAY MAR JUN
APR MAY AUG NOV JUL	MAR MAR OCT APR NOV	FEB JUN MAY JAN JUL	MAR JUL MAR FEB JAN
APR JUL AUG AUG APR	AUG JUL JUN OCT APR	MAR OCT JAN JUL FEB	JUL DEC OCT NOV DEC
APR MAR JUN DEC AUG	DEC APR APR DEC FEB	MAR APR JUN JAN JUL	MAY APR OCT APR MAR
JUN AUG APR FEB JAN	SEP MAY DEC FEB SEP	JAN JUN OCT FEB JUN	APR FEB AUG NOV JUN
MAR NOV AUG JAN SEP	JUL JUN JUN APR NOV	MAR MAY FEB MAR MAR	JAN OCT DEC NOV MAY
SEP MAR AUG JUL JUN	DEC AUG FEB MAY MAR	AUG JAN OCT SEP AUG	OCT MAR JAN OCT OCT
OCT JUL DEC NOV JUN	MAR JUL OCT JUL JAN	JAN JUL FEB AUG JAN	SEP JUL FEB JUN DEC
MAY AUG MAR SEP AUG	DEC APR AUG OCT FEB	JUN FEB FEB AUG OCT	JUL MAY OCT MAR SEP

C

Appendix C
Random Months (Continued)

MAR MAY SEP OCT OCT   JUL FEB SEP SEP JUN   APR JUL JAN JUN SEP   JAN NOV FEB JUN NOV
JUL SEP MAR OCT SEP   AUG NOV NOV APR JUN   OCT OCT SEP AUG SEP   NOV NOV APR JUN MAY
MAY JUN MAY DEC AUG   APR JUN SEP MAR APR   SEP AUG OCT AUG FEB   DEC AUG AUG AUG MAR
SEP OCT OCT DEC FEB   MAY APR MAY MAR FEB   NOV JAN DEC DEC DEC   JAN JAN MAY OCT SEP
APR OCT JUL MAR SEP   APR JUN NOV APR JUN   JAN MAY FEB FEB FEB   JUN MAY MAR JAN NOV

MAY JUN DEC AUG MAY   FEB MAR JUN APR AUG   AUG DEC MAR JAN MAR   APR APR MAR DEC AUG
JUN NOV MAR FEB FEB   DEC JUN MAY AUG JAN   OCT OCT JUL MAY MAY   AUG AUG OCT MAY APR
MAR NOV SEP SEP JUL   JUN AUG MAY FEB SEP   DEC APR JUN AUG MAY   JUN DEC MAR JUN DEC
DEC MAY JUL JUL MAY   APR JAN SEP NOV AUG   FEB DEC SEP APR DEC   DEC APR JUL NOV MAR
MAR MAY DEC JAN AUG   DEC JUL MAY APR JAN   JUN FEB AUG OCT DEC   MAR JUL MAY MAY AUG

MAY MAR JUL OCT APR   OCT MAY FEB AUG AUG   JUN JAN APR NOV NOV   OCT DEC FEB JUN JAN
NOV NOV FEB DEC MAR   NOV JUL MAR JUL NOV   MAY JAN SEP JAN AUG   MAR JUL AUG MAY AUG
JUN MAY JAN FEB MAR   OCT FEB JUL OCT AUG   DEC APR MAY MAR DEC   DEC DEC MAR JUN DEC
FEB JAN OCT JUN JUN   AUG JAN JUL OCT DEC   MAR MAR APR SEP JAN   MAY MAY JUL DEC DEC
JUL SEP MAY MAR APR   NOV AUG NOV JUN MAY   AUG DEC JUL APR AUG   DEC AUG DEC FEB DEC

JUN MAR SEP AUG JAN   MAR AUG MAR NOV NOV   NOV DEC SEP APR NOV   MAR OCT JUL DEC NOV
OCT OCT AUG SEP DEC   JUN MAR NOV AUG MAY   AUG FEB SEP NOV MAR   APR APR MAR OCT DEC
JUN DEC OCT NOV NOV   APR DEC MAR JUL JAN   MAY FEB APR AUG JAN   DEC DEC MAY FEB DEC
OCT JAN JAN JUL SEP   SEP FEB AUG SEP MAR   MAR MAR DEC AUG AUG   FEB SEP JUN MAR APR
DEC FEB MAY AUG DEC   NOV AUG JAN NOV SEP   MAY APR AUG MAY MAY   MAR OCT JAN AUG MAR

SEP JUL JUL JAN JUL   AUG APR DEC APR DEC   JUL AUG JAN FEB NOV   JUL DEC MAR AUG AUG
MAR OCT JAN MAY AUG   JUL OCT JUN FEB JUN   OCT JAN MAY AUG DEC   DEC SEP JUN APR MAR
JUN MAR FEB NOV FEB   JUL OCT JAN MAR DEC   APR JUL DEC FEB SEP   JUL SEP FEB FEB AUG
SEP FEB MAY MAY MAR   SEP OCT JUN SEP MAY   MAR APR MAR FEB FEB   DEC AUG JUN AUG SEP
JUN NOV SEP MAR MAR   MAY MAR FEB OCT AUG   MAR DEC JUL AUG MAY   JUL AUG OCT MAY NOV

AUG MAR NOV APR JAN   SEP NOV MAY JAN DEC   JUL MAY DEC MAY APR   FEB APR AUG JUL DEC
SEP MAR JAN DEC NOV   FEB FEB JAN AUG JUL   NOV MAY JAN MAR FEB   NOV NOV JAN MAY AUG
OCT MAY MAR APR MAY   DEC MAY MAY APR JUN   AUG DEC JAN JAN SEP   JAN FEB SEP JUL AUG
JAN JAN JUN DEC APR   JAN FEB SEP JAN FEB   NOV SEP OCT JUL JUN   FEB OCT APR AUG OCT
JAN DEC NOV JUN DEC   JUN MAR AUG JUL MAY   SEP FEB JUN APR SEP   JUL FEB JAN NOV JUL

AUG DEC JUL APR SEP   JAN JUL SEP APR JUN   JUL DEC MAR SEP JAN   MAY JUN AUG JUN AUG
DEC MAY DEC SEP MAR   JUL JAN AUG FEB NOV   JUL NOV JUL DEC DEC   JAN DEC JAN SEP NOV
JUN JAN NOV JUL JAN   OCT APR JUL DEC FEB   AUG JUN AUG JUL MAR   MAY NOV JUL MAY DEC
APR OCT MAR AUG AUG   FEB JUL FEB JUL NOV   SEP MAY JUL OCT MAR   OCT APR MAY NOV MAY
APR SEP OCT MAR DEC   AUG OCT APR NOV MAY   FEB OCT JAN MAR JUN   APR DEC MAY MAY AUG

JUN OCT FEB DEC OCT   DEC JUN OCT AUG FEB   MAR JUL DEC MAY SEP   OCT JUL AUG MAY MAR
FEB MAY FEB NOV JUN   OCT FEB FEB FEB JUN   DEC NOV SEP NOV MAY   SEP SEP AUG NOV JUN
AUG MAR JAN DEC SEP   MAR AUG FEB DEC SEP   FEB DEC OCT DEC APR   DEC JUL SEP OCT APR
MAY DEC NOV DEC NOV   SEP DEC AUG APR JAN   APR JAN JUN SEP JUN   MAR AUG SEP OCT OCT
APR DEC MAY MAR AUG   MAR NOV JUL NOV DEC   JUN MAY DEC AUG AUG   JUN NOV JUL SEP APR

NOV DEC JUL APR JUN   JAN FEB JAN OCT OCT   FEB MAY SEP OCT OCT   JUN MAY APR NOV JUN
NOV DEC MAY JUL JUL   MAY JAN APR JAN MAR   SEP JAN FEB MAR JUL   AUG MAY DEC MAR JAN
JUL JUL APR SEP NOV   JUN MAR JUN MAY MAR   OCT APR AUG NOV APR   JUL NOV MAY AUG MAR
DEC AUG SEP JUN JAN   FEB SEP DEC NOV OCT   AUG MAY AUG JUN OCT   SEP JAN NOV JUN JAN
AUG JUN APR OCT JAN   APR SEP JAN SEP DEC   MAR JAN JAN AUG JUL   OCT APR MAY OCT AUG

APR SEP NOV AUG DEC   SEP NOV OCT OCT DEC   AUG FEB MAY APR SEP   NOV JAN DEC NOV MAR
NOV JUL NOV SEP JUL   AUG JUL JUN APR APR   MAR SEP AUG OCT JAN   JUN JAN MAY JUN JAN
JAN DEC SEP AUG JUL   FEB MAR OCT OCT MAY   MAY OCT APR AUG JUL   MAR NOV NOV DEC JAN
FEB DEC APR AUG NOV   DEC SEP FEB JUN AUG   JAN DEC FEB DEC MAR   SEP MAY MAR FEB MAY
JUL FEB FEB JUL MAR   DEC AUG FEB DEC DEC   JUN OCT MAY FEB FEB   SEP JUL JUL MAY JUN

Appendix C
Random Months (Continued)

MAY OCT SEP FEB NOV	JAN DEC MAR MAY MAR	MAR DEC OCT FEB NOV	APR MAY SEP NOV SEP
MAY AUG NOV MAR SEP	MAR SEP APR SEP APR	JAN OCT NOV JUN DEC	SEP AUG JUN NOV MAY
DEC JAN JAN MAR DEC	JUL JUN FEB DEC NOV	JUL JUL FEB JAN JUN	DEC FEB SEP APR FEB
SEP DEC JAN DEC MAR	MAR DEC AUG AUG SEP	AUG MAR OCT APR DEC	JAN MAR MAY JUL JUL
NOV AUG OCT APR JAN	FEB JUN AUG JAN FEB	DEC JUN DEC NOV JAN	NOV MAR NOV JUL JUN

APPENDIX D
ESTIMATING SAMPLE SIZE–ATTRIBUTES

D

	Table
Attributes	
(1) Tables for 90% Confidence Level	
Rate of Occurrence Not over:	
2%	D-1A
5%	D-1B
10%	D-1C
15%	D-1D
20%	D-1E
30%	D-1F
40%	D-1G
50%	D-1H
(2) Tables for 95% Confidence Level	
Rate of Occurrence Not over:	
2%	D-2A
5%	D-2B
10%	D-2C
15%	D-2D
20%	D-2E
30%	D-2F
40%	D-2G
50%	D-2H
(3) Tables for 99% Confidence Level	
Rate of Occurrence Not over:	
2%	D-3A
5%	D-3B
10%	D-3C
15%	D-3D
20%	D-3E
30%	D-3F
40%	D-3G
50%	D-3H

TABLE D-1A Sample Sizes for Sampling Attributes for Random Samples Only—Expected Rate of Occurrence Not over 2% or Expected Rate of Occurrence Not Less than 98%. Confidence Level 90% (Two-sided).

Population Size	Sample Size for Precision of: ±.5%	±.75%	±1%	±1.25%	±1.5%	±2%
200					109	80
250					122	87
300				160	133	92
350				173	141	97
400				184	149	100
450				194	155	103
500			258	203	161	105
550			271	210	166	107
600			282	217	170	109
650			293	223	173	111
700			302	229	177	112
750			311	234	180	113
800			319	239	183	114
850			327	243	185	115
900		461	334	247	187	116
950		474	341	251	189	117
1,000		486	347	254	191	118
1,050		497	353	257	193	118
1,100		508	358	260	195	119
1,150		519	363	263	196	119
1,200		529	368	265	198	120
1,250		538	373	267	199	120
1,300		547	377	270	200	121
1,350		556	381	272	201	121
1,400		564	385	274	202	122
1,450		572	389	276	203	122
1,500		579	392	277	204	122
1,550		587	396	279	205	123
1,600		594	399	281	206	123
1,650		601	402	282	207	123
1,700		607	405	283	208	124
1,750		613	408	285	208	124
1,800		619	410	286	209	124
1,850		625	413	287	210	124
1,900		631	415	288	210	124
1,950		636	417	290	211	125
2,000		641	420	291	211	125
2,100	1055	651	424	293	212	125
2,200	1081	661	428	295	213	126
2,300	1104	669	431	296	214	126
2,400	1127	677	435	298	215	126
2,500	1148	685	438	299	216	126
2,600	1169	692	441	301	217	127
2,700	1189	699	444	302	217	127
2,800	1207	706	446	303	218	127
2,900	1226	712	449	304	219	127
3,000	1243	718	451	305	219	127
3,100	1260	723	453	306	220	128
3,200	1276	729	455	307	220	128
3,300	1292	734	457	308	221	128
3,400	1307	739	459	309	221	128

Population Size	Sample Size for Precision of: ±.5%	±.75%	±1%	±1.25%	±1.5%	±2%
3,500	1321	743	461	310	221	128
3,600	1335	748	463	311	222	128
3,700	1349	752	464	311	222	129
3,800	1362	756	466	312	222	129
3,900	1375	760	467	313	223	129
4,000	1387	764	469	313	223	129
4,100	1399	767	470	314	223	129
4,200	1410	771	471	315	224	129
4,300	1421	774	473	315	224	129
4,400	1432	777	474	316	224	129
4,500	1442	780	475	316	224	129
4,600	1452	783	476	317	225	129
4,700	1462	786	477	317	225	129
4,800	1472	789	478	318	225	130
4,900	1481	791	479	318	225	130
5,000	1490	794	480	318	226	130
5,500	1531	805	484	320	227	130
6,000	1568	815	488	322	227	130
6,500	1600	824	491	323	228	130
7,000	1629	831	494	324	229	131
7,500	1654	838	496	325	229	131
8,000	1684	846	498	326	230	131
8,500	1698	849	500	327	230	131
9,000	1717	854	501	328	230	131
9,500	1735	858	503	328	231	131
10,000	1751	862	504	329	231	131
10,500	1765	866	505	329	231	131
11,000	1779	869	506	330	231	132
11,500	1792	872	507	330	231	132
12,000	1803	875	508	331	232	132
12,500	1814	877	509	331	232	132
13,000	1824	880	510	331	232	132
13,500	1834	882	511	332	232	132
14,000	1843	884	512	332	232	132
14,500	1851	886	512	332	232	132
15,000	1859	888	513	332	233	132
15,500	1867	889	513	333	233	132
16,500	1880	892	514	333	233	132
17,500	1893	895	515	333	233	132
18,500	1904	898	516	334	233	132
19,500	1914	900	517	334	233	132
20,000	1919	901	517	334	233	132
22,000	1935	905	518	335	234	132
24,000	1950	908	519	335	234	132
25,000	1956	909	520	335	234	132
26,000	1962	910	520	336	234	132
28,000	1973	913	521	336	234	132
30,000	1982	915	522	336	234	133
31,000	1986	916	522	336	234	133
34,000	1997	918	523	337	235	133
38,000	2010	921	524	337	235	133
40,000	2015	922	524	337	235	133
42,000	2020	923	524	337	235	133
47,000	2030	925	525	338	235	133
50,000	2036	926	525	338	235	133
55,000	2043	928	526	338	235	133
65,000	2055	930	527	338	235	133

TABLE D-1A Sample Sizes for Sampling Attributes for Random Samples Only—Expected Rate of Occurrence Not over 2% or Expected Rate of Occurrence Not Less than 98%. Confidence Level 90% (Two-sided) (Continued).

Population Size	Sample Size for Precision of:					
	±.5%	±.75%	±1%	±1.25%	±1.5%	±2%
75,000	2064	932	527	338	235	133
80,000	2067	932	527	339	236	133
100,000	2078	935	528	339	236	133
135,000	2089	937	529	339	236	133
150,000	2092	938	529	339	236	133
200,000	2100	939	529	339	236	133
300,000	2107	940	530	340	236	133
350,000	2109	941	530	340	236	133
450,000	2112	941	530	340	236	133
500,000	2113	942	530	340	236	133

TABLE D-1B Samples Sizes for Sampling Attributes for Random Samples Only—Expected Rate of Occurrence Not over 5% or Expected Rate of Occurrence Not Less than 95%. Confidence Level 90% (Two-sided).

Population Size	Sample Size for Precision of:						
	±.5%	±1%	±1.5%	±2%	±2.5%	±3%	±4%
150						74	53
200					102	84	58
250					113	91	61
300				156	123	97	64
350				168	130	102	66
400				179	136	106	67
450				188	142	109	69
500				196	146	112	70
550				203	150	114	71
600				210	154	116	71
650			305	216	157	118	72
700			315	221	160	119	73
750			325	225	162	120	73
800			334	230	164	122	74
850			342	234	166	123	74
900			350	237	168	124	74
950			357	241	170	125	75
1,000			364	244	171	125	75
1,050			370	247	172	126	75
1,100			377	249	172	127	75
1,200		621	388	254	176	128	76
1,300		647	397	257	178	129	76
1,400		671	406	262	180	130	76
1,500		693	414	265	181	131	77
1,600		713	421	268	183	132	77
1,700		732	428	271	184	132	77
1,800		750	434	273	185	133	77
1,900		767	440	275	186	133	78
2,000		783	445	277	187	134	78
2,100		798	450	279	188	134	78
2,200		812	454	281	189	135	78
2,300		825	458	282	189	135	78
2,400		838	462	284	190	135	78

D

Population Size	±.5%	±1%	±1.5%	±2%	±2.5%	±3%	±4%
2,500		849	466	285	191	136	78
2,700		871	472	288	192	136	79
2,900		891	478	290	193	137	79
3,100		909	483	292	193	137	79
3,300		926	487	293	194	137	79
3,500		941	492	295	195	138	79
3,700		954	495	296	195	138	79
3,900		967	499	297	196	138	79
4,050		976	501	298	196	138	79
4,100		979	502	298	196	139	79
4,400		995	506	300	197	139	79
4,700		1010	510	301	198	139	79
5,000	2535	1023	513	302	198	139	80
5,500	2658	1042	518	304	199	140	80
6,000	2769	1059	522	306	199	140	80
6,500	2871	1074	526	307	200	140	80
7,000	2965	1086	529	308	200	140	80
7,500	3051	1098	531	309	201	141	80
8,000	3130	1107	534	310	201	141	80
8,500	3204	1117	536	310	201	141	80
9,000	3272	1126	538	311	202	141	80
10,000	3396	1139	541	312	202	141	80
10,500	3452	1146	542	312	202	141	80
11,500	3553	1157	545	313	203	142	80
13,000	3685	1170	548	314	203	142	80
14,500	3796	1181	550	315	203	142	80
15,000	3830	1184	551	315	203	142	80
16,500	3920	1193	553	316	204	142	80
19,000	4047	1204	555	316	204	142	80
20,000	4091	1208	556	317	204	142	81
22,000	4168	1215	557	317	204	142	81
26,000	4293	1225	559	318	205	143	81
30,000	4390	1233	561	318	205	143	81
32,000	4430	1236	562	319	205	143	81
40,000	4556	1246	564	319	205	143	81
41,000	4569	1247	564	319	205	143	81
50,000	4663	1254	565	320	205	143	81
60,000	4736	1259	566	320	205	143	81
100,000	4891	1270	569	321	206	143	81
150,000	4972	1275	570	321	206	143	81
200,000	5013	1278	570	321	206	143	81
250,000	5038	1279	570	321	206	143	81
300,000	5055	1280	571	321	206	143	81
500,000	5090	128[illegible]	571	322	206	143	81

TABLE D-1C Sample Sizes for Sampling Attributes for Random Samples Only—Expected Rate of Occurrence Not over 10% or Expected Rate of Occurrence Not Less than 90%. Confidence Level 90% (Two-sided).

Population Size	Sample Size for Precision of: ±.5%	±1%	±1.5%	±2%	±2.5%	±3%	±4%
250							95
300						143	101
350						153	108
400					198	162	111
450					209	169	114

TABLE D-1C Sample Sizes for Sampling Attributes for Random Samples Only—Expected Rate of Occurrence Not over 10% or Expected Rate of Occurrence Not Less than 90%. Confidence Level 90% (Two-sided) (Continued).

Population Size	Sample Size for Precision of: ±.5%	±1%	±1.5%	±2%	±2.5%	±3%	±4%
500					219	176	117
550					229	182	120
600					237	187	122
650					244	192	124
700				326	251	196	126
750				337	257	199	127
800				346	263	203	128
850				355	268	206	130
900				364	272	209	131
950				372	277	211	132
1,000				379	281	213	133
1,050				386	285	216	133
1,100			546	392	288	218	134
1,150			558	399	292	220	135
1,200			570	404	295	221	136
1,250			581	410	298	223	136
1,300			591	415	300	224	137
1,350			601	420	303	226	137
1,400			611	425	306	227	138
1,450			620	429	308	229	138
1,500			629	434	310	230	139
1,550			638	438	312	231	139
1,600			646	442	314	232	139
1,650			654	445	316	233	140
1,700			662	449	318	234	140
1,750			669	452	319	235	141
1,800			676	455	321	236	141
1,850			683	459	322	237	141
1,900			690	462	324	237	141
1,950			697	464	325	238	142
2,000			703	467	327	239	142
2,100			715	473	329	240	142
2,200			726	477	332	241	143
2,300			737	482	334	243	143
2,400			746	486	336	244	144
2,500		1234	756	490	337	245	144
2,600		1258	765	494	339	246	144
2,700		1281	773	497	341	246	145
2,800		1303	781	501	343	247	145
2,900		1324	789	504	344	248	145
3,000		1345	796	507	345	249	145
3,100		1364	803	509	347	249	146
3,200		1383	809	512	348	250	146
3,300		1402	816	515	349	251	146
3,400		1419	822	517	350	251	146
3,500		1437	827	519	351	252	146
3,600		1453	833	521	352	252	147
3,700		1469	838	523	353	253	147
3,800		1485	843	525	354	253	147
3,900		1500	848	527	355	254	147

Population Size	Sample Size for Precision of: ±.5%	±1%	±1.5%	±2%	±2.5%	±3%	±4%
4,000		1514	852	529	356	254	147
4,100		1528	857	531	356	254	147
4,200		1542	861	532	357	255	147
4,300		1555	865	534	358	255	148
4,500		1581	873	537	359	256	148
4,700		1605	880	540	360	256	148
4,900		1627	887	542	361	257	148
5,000		1638	890	543	362	257	148
5,500		1688	905	549	364	258	149
6,000		1733	917	553	366	259	149
6,500		1772	928	557	368	260	149
7,000		1807	938	561	370	261	149
7,500		1839	946	564	371	262	150
8,000		1868	954	566	372	262	150
8,500		1894	961	569	373	263	150
9,000		1917	967	571	374	263	150
9,500		1939	972	573	375	264	150
10,000	4935	1959	977	574	376	264	150
10,500	5054	1977	982	576	376	264	151
11,000	5167	1994	986	577	377	265	151
11,500	5275	2010	990	579	377	265	151
12,000	5377	2025	993	580	378	265	151
12,500	5475	2039	997	581	378	265	151
13,000	5569	2052	1000	582	379	266	151
13,500	5659	2064	1003	583	379	266	151
14,000	5745	2075	1005	584	380	266	151
15,000	5907	2096	1010	586	380	266	151
16,000	6056	2114	1014	587	381	267	151
17,000	6193	2131	1018	588	381	267	151
18,000	6321	2146	1022	589	382	267	151
19,000	6440	2159	1025	590	382	267	152
20,000	6551	2172	1027	591	383	267	152
21,000	6655	2183	1030	592	383	268	152
22,000	6752	2193	1032	593	383	268	152
23,000	6844	2203	1034	594	384	268	152
24,000	6930	2212	1036	594	384	268	152
26,000	7087	2227	1040	595	384	268	152
28,000	7228	2241	1043	596	385	269	152
30,000	7354	2253	1045	597	385	269	152
32,000	7469	2264	1047	598	385	269	152
35,000	7621	2277	1050	599	386	269	152
38,000	7754	2289	1053	600	386	269	152
40,000	7834	2296	1055	600	386	269	152
42,000	7908	2302	1056	601	387	269	152
45,000	8009	2311	1057	601	387	269	152
50,000	8154	2323	1060	602	387	270	152
55,000	8276	2333	1062	603	387	270	152
65,000	8472	2348	1065	604	388	270	152
75,000	8622	2359	1068	604	388	270	152
90,000	8791	2372	1070	605	388	270	152
100,000	8877	2378	1071	606	389	270	152
110,000	8950	2383	1072	606	389	270	153
140,000	9108	2394	1075	607	389	271	153
150,000	9148	2397	1075	607	389	271	153
200,000	9290	2407	1077	608	389	271	153
275,000	9409	2415	1079	608	390	271	153
350,000	9478	2419	1080	608	390	271	153
500,000	9556	2424	1081	609	390	271	153

D

TABLE D-1D Sample Sizes for Sampling Attributes for Random Samples Only—Expected Rate of Occurrence Not over 15% or Expected Rate of Occurrence Not Less than 85%. Confidence Level 90% (Two-sided).

Population Size	Sample Size for Precision of: ±1%	±1.5%	±2%	±2.5%	±3%	±3.5%	±4%
200							104
250						133	116
300						146	126
350					183	157	134
400					196	166	141
450					208	174	146
500					217	181	151
550				276	226	187	155
600				288	234	192	159
650				299	242	197	162
700				309	248	201	165
750				318	254	205	168
800				327	260	209	170
850			429	335	265	212	173
900			441	343	269	215	174
950			453	350	274	218	176
1,000			464	356	278	220	178
1,050			474	362	281	223	179
1,100			484	368	285	225	181
1,150			493	373	288	227	182
1,200			502	379	291	229	183
1,250			511	383	294	230	184
1,300			519	388	297	232	185
1,350			527	392	299	234	186
1,400			534	396	301	235	187
1,450			541	400	304	236	188
1,500		759	548	404	306	238	189
1,550		771	555	408	308	239	190
1,600		783	561	411	310	240	191
1,650		795	567	414	312	241	191
1,700		807	573	417	313	242	192
1,750		818	578	420	315	243	192
1,800		829	584	423	317	244	193
1,850		839	589	426	318	245	194
1,900		849	594	428	319	246	194
1,950		859	599	431	321	247	195
2,000		868	603	433	322	247	195
2,100		887	612	438	325	249	196
2,200		904	620	442	327	250	197
2,300		921	628	446	329	251	198
2,400		936	635	449	331	253	198
2,500		951	642	453	333	254	199
2,600		965	648	456	335	255	200
2,700		978	654	459	336	256	200
2,800		991	660	462	338	256	201
2,900		1004	665	464	339	257	201
3,000		1015	670	467	340	258	202
3,100		1026	675	469	342	259	202
3,200		1037	680	471	343	259	203
3,300		1047	684	473	344	260	203
3,400	1713	1057	689	475	345	261	203

Population Size	Sample Size for Precision of: ±1%	±1.5%	±2%	±2.5%	±3%	±3.5%	±4%
3,500	1738	1067	693	477	346	261	204
3,600	1762	1076	696	479	347	262	204
3,700	1786	1085	700	481	348	262	204
3,800	1809	1093	703	483	349	263	205
3,900	1831	1101	707	484	350	263	205
4,000	1853	1109	710	486	350	264	205
4,100	1874	1117	713	487	351	264	205
4,200	1895	1124	716	488	352	264	206
4,300	1915	1131	719	490	352	265	206
4,400	1934	1138	722	491	353	265	206
4,500	1953	1144	724	492	354	266	206
4,600	1972	1151	727	493	354	266	206
4,700	1990	1157	729	495	355	266	207
4,800	2008	1163	732	496	356	267	207
4,900	2025	1168	734	497	356	267	207
5,000	2042	1174	736	498	357	267	207
5,500	2121	1200	746	502	359	268	208
6,000	2191	1222	755	506	361	270	209
6,500	2254	1241	762	509	363	270	209
7,000	2312	1258	768	512	365	271	210
7,500	2364	1274	774	515	365	272	210
8,000	2411	1287	779	517	366	273	210
8,500	2455	1300	784	519	367	273	211
9,000	2495	1311	788	521	368	274	211
9,500	2531	1321	791	522	369	274	211
10,000	2566	1330	795	524	370	274	212
10,500	2597	1339	798	525	370	275	212
11,000	2627	1346	800	526	371	275	212
11,500	2654	1354	803	527	371	275	212
12,000	2680	1360	805	528	372	276	212
12,500	2704	1366	807	529	372	276	212
13,000	2727	1372	809	530	373	276	213
13,500	2748	1378	811	531	373	276	213
14,000	2769	1383	813	532	374	277	213
14,500	2788	1387	814	532	374	277	213
15,000	2805	1392	816	533	374	277	213
15,500	2823	1395	818	534	375	277	213
16,000	2839	1400	819	534	375	277	213
16,500	2854	1404	820	535	375	277	213
17,000	2869	1407	821	535	375	278	213
17,500	2882	1410	822	536	376	278	214
18,000	2896	1413	824	536	376	278	214
18,500	2908	1417	825	537	376	278	214
19,000	2920	1419	826	537	376	278	214
19,500	2932	1422	827	537	376	278	214
20,000	2943	1425	827	538	377	278	214
21,000	2964	1430	829	538	377	278	214
22,000	2983	1434	831	539	377	279	214
23,000	3001	1438	832	540	378	279	214
24,000	3017	1442	833	540	378	279	214
25,000	3032	1445	834	541	378	279	214
26,000	3046	1449	835	541	378	279	214
27,000	3060	1451	836	541	378	279	214
28,000	3072	1454	837	542	379	279	214
29,000	3084	1457	838	542	379	279	215
30,000	3095	1459	839	543	379	280	215
32,000	3115	1464	840	543	379	280	215
34,000	3133	1468	842	544	380	280	215
36,000	3149	1471	843	544	380	280	215
38,000	3163	1474	844	545	380	280	215

TABLE D-1D Sample Sizes for Sampling Attributes for Random Samples Only—Expected Rate of Occurrence Not over 15% or Expected Rate of Occurrence Not Less than 85%. Confidence Level 90% (Two-sided) (Continued).

Population Size	Sample Size for Precision of:						
	±1%	±1.5%	±2%	±2.5%	±3%	±3.5%	±4%
40,000	3177	1477	845	545	380	280	215
42,000	3189	1480	846	545	380	280	215
44,000	3200	1482	846	546	381	280	215
46,000	3210	1484	847	546	381	280	215
48,000	3219	1486	848	546	381	281	215
50,000	3228	1488	848	547	381	281	215
55,000	3247	1492	850	547	381	281	215
60,000	3263	1496	851	547	381	281	215
65,000	3277	1499	852	548	382	281	215
70,000	3289	1501	853	548	382	281	215
75,000	3299	1503	853	548	382	281	216
85,000	3316	1507	854	549	382	281	216
95,000	3330	1510	855	549	382	281	216
100,000	3336	1511	856	549	382	281	216
105,000	3344	1512	856	550	382	281	216
120,000	3354	1515	857	550	383	281	216
135,000	3365	1517	858	550	383	282	216
150,000	3373	1518	858	551	383	282	216
175,000	3384	1521	859	551	383	282	216
200,000	3392	1522	859	551	383	282	216
215,000	3396	1523	860	551	383	282	216
250,000	3404	1525	860	551	383	282	216
300,000	3411	1526	861	551	383	282	216
350,000	3417	1527	861	552	383	282	216
450,000	3424	1529	861	552	384	282	216
500,000	3427	1529	862	552	384	282	216

TABLE D-1E Sample Sizes for Sampling Attributes for Random Samples Only—Expected Rate of Occurrence Not over 20% or Expected Rate of Occurrence Not Less than 80%. Confidence Level 90% (Two-sided).

Population Size	Sample Size for Precision of:						
	±1%	±1.5%	±2%	±2.5%	±3%	±4%	±5%
200							92
250							103
300						143	110
350						153	116
400						162	121
450						169	126
500					245	176	129
550					257	182	132
600					267	187	135
650					278	192	137
700				349	286	196	139
750				358	294	199	141

Population Size	Sample Size for Precision of: ±1%	±1.5%	±2%	±2.5%	±3%	±4%	±5%
800				372	301	203	143
850				382	308	206	144
900				392	314	209	146
950				401	320	211	147
1,000				410	325	213	148
1,050				418	330	216	149
1,100			546	426	335	218	150
1,150			558	433	340	220	151
1,200			570	440	344	221	152
1,250			581	446	348	223	153
1,300			591	452	352	224	153
1,350			601	458	355	226	154
1,400			611	464	359	227	155
1,450			620	469	362	229	155
1,500			629	474	365	230	156
1,550			638	479	368	231	156
1,600			646	484	370	232	157
1,650			654	488	373	233	157
1,700			662	493	375	234	158
1,750			669	497	378	235	158
1,800			676	501	380	236	158
1,900			690	508	384	237	159
1,950		969	697	512	386	238	160
2,000		981	703	515	388	239	160
2,100		1005	715	521	392	240	160
2,200		1027	726	527	395	241	161
2,300		1048	737	533	398	243	162
2,400		1070	746	538	401	244	162
2,500		1088	756	543	404	245	162
2,600		1106	765	548	406	246	163
2,700		1124	773	552	409	246	163
2,800		1141	781	556	411	247	164
2,900		1157	789	560	413	248	164
3,000		1173	796	563	415	249	164
3,100		1188	803	567	417	249	165
3,200		1202	809	570	419	250	165
3,300		1216	816	573	420	251	165
3,400		1229	822	576	422	251	165
3,500		1242	827	579	423	252	166
3,600		1254	833	581	425	252	166
3,700		1266	838	584	426	253	166
3,800		1278	843	586	428	253	166
3,900		1289	848	589	429	254	166
4,000		1300	852	591	430	254	166
4,100		1310	857	593	431	254	167
4,200		1320	861	595	432	255	167
4,300		1330	865	597	433	255	167
4,400	2183	1339	869	599	434	255	167
4,500	2207	1348	873	601	435	256	167
4,600	2231	1357	877	603	436	256	167
4,700	2254	1366	880	604	437	256	168
4,800	2277	1375	884	606	438	257	168
4,900	2299	1382	887	607	439	257	168
5,000	2321	1390	890	609	439	257	168
5,500	2423	1426	905	616	443	258	168
6,000	2515	1458	917	622	446	259	169
6,500	2599	1485	928	627	448	260	169
7,000	2676	1510	938	631	451	261	170
7,500	2745	1532	946	635	453	262	170

D

TABLE D-1E Sample Sizes for Sampling Attributes for Random Samples Only—Expected Rate of Occurrence Not over 20% or Expected Rate of Occurrence Not Less than 80%. Confidence Level 90% (Two-sided) (Continued).

Population Size	Sample Size for Precision of: ±1%	±1.5%	±2%	±2.5%	±3%	±4%	±5%
8,000	2810	1552	954	638	454	262	170
8,500	2869	1570	961	641	456	263	170
9,000	2924	1585	967	644	457	263	170
9,500	2975	1601	972	646	458	264	171
10,000	3022	1614	977	648	459	264	171
10,500	3066	1627	982	650	460	264	171
11,000	3107	1638	986	652	461	265	171
11,500	3146	1649	990	654	462	265	171
12,000	3182	1659	993	655	463	265	171
12,500	3216	1668	997	657	464	265	171
13,000	3248	1677	1000	658	464	266	171
13,500	3279	1685	1003	659	465	266	171
14,000	3307	1692	1005	660	466	266	172
14,500	3335	1699	1008	662	466	266	172
15,000	3360	1706	1010	663	467	266	172
15,500	3385	1712	1012	664	467	266	172
16,000	3408	1718	1014	664	468	267	172
16,500	3430	1724	1016	665	468	267	172
17,000	3451	1729	1018	666	468	267	172
17,500	3471	1734	1020	667	469	267	172
18,000	3491	1739	1022	668	469	267	172
18,500	3509	1743	1023	668	469	267	172
19,000	3527	1748	1025	669	470	267	172
19,500	3543	1752	1026	669	470	267	172
20,000	3560	1756	1027	670	470	267	172
21,000	3590	1763	1030	671	471	268	172
22,000	3618	1770	1032	672	471	268	172
23,000	3644	1776	1034	672	472	268	172
24,000	3668	1782	1036	674	472	268	172
25,000	3691	1787	1038	675	472	268	172
26,000	3712	1792	1040	675	473	268	173
27,000	3732	1797	1041	676	473	268	173
28,000	3750	1801	1043	677	473	269	173
29,000	3768	1805	1044	677	474	269	173
30,000	3784	1809	1045	678	474	269	173
31,000	3800	1812	1046	678	474	269	173
32,000	3814	1816	1047	679	474	269	173
33,000	3828	1819	1048	679	475	269	173
34,000	3841	1822	1049	679	475	269	173
35,000	3854	1825	1050	680	475	269	173
36,000	3865	1827	1051	680	475	269	173
37,000	3877	1830	1052	681	475	269	173
38,000	3887	1832	1053	681	476	269	173
39,000	3898	1834	1054	681	476	269	173
40,000	3907	1836	1054	682	476	269	173
42,000	3926	1840	1056	682	476	269	173
44,000	3942	1844	1057	683	476	269	173
46,000	3958	1848	1058	683	477	270	173
48,000	3965	1851	1059	683	477	270	173
50,000	3985	1853	1060	684	477	270	173
55,000	4014	1860	1062	685	477	270	173
60,000	4039	1865	1064	685	478	270	173
65,000	4060	1869	1065	686	478	270	173
70,000	4078	1873	1066	686	478	270	173
75,000	4094	1877	1068	687	479	270	173

Population Size	Sample Size for Precision of:						
	±1%	±1.5%	±2%	±2.5%	±3%	±4%	±5%
80,000	4108	1880	1068	687	479	270	173
85,000	4120	1882	1069	688	479	270	173
90,000	4131	1885	1070	688	479	270	173
95,000	4141	1887	1071	688	479	270	173
100,000	4150	1888	1071	688	479	270	173
110,000	4166	1892	1072	689	479	270	173
120,000	4179	1894	1073	689	480	270	173
130,000	4191	1897	1074	690	480	271	173
140,000	4200	1899	1075	690	480	271	173
150,000	4209	1900	1075	690	480	271	173
160,000	4216	1902	1076	690	480	271	173
180,000	4228	1904	1076	691	480	271	174
200,000	4238	1906	1077	691	480	271	174
225,000	4248	1908	1078	691	481	271	174
250,000	4256	1910	1078	691	481	271	174
275,000	4263	1911	1079	692	481	271	174
300,000	4269	1913	1079	692	481	271	174
350,000	4277	1914	1080	692	481	271	174
450,000	4289	1917	1080	692	481	271	174
500,000	4293	1917	1081	692	481	271	174

D

TABLE D-1F Sample Sizes for Sampling Attributes for Random Samples Only—Expected Rate of Occurrence Not over 30% or Expected Rate of Occurrence Not Less than 70%. Confidence Level 90% (Two-sided).

Population Size	Sample Size for Precision of:					
	±1%	±2%	±3%	±4%	±5%	±7%
250					120	80
300					130	84
350					138	88
400				189	145	90
450				199	152	93
500				208	157	95
550				216	161	96
600				224	165	98
650			321	230	169	99
700			332	236	172	100
750			343	242	175	101
800			353	246	178	102
850			363	251	180	103
900			372	255	182	103
950			380	259	184	104
1,000			388	263	186	104
1,050			395	266	187	105
1,100			402	269	189	106
1,150			407	272	190	106
1,200			414	275	192	106
1,250			420	277	193	107
1,300			425	279	194	107
1,350			431	282	195	107
1,400			436	284	196	108
1,450		718	440	286	197	108

TABLE D-1F Samples Sizes for Sampling Attributes for Random Samples Only—Expected Rate of Occurrence Not over 30% or Expected Rate of Occurrence Not Less than 70%. Confidence Level 90% (Two-sided) (Continued).

Population Size	Sample Size for Precision of:					
	±1%	±2%	±3%	±4%	±5%	±7%
1,500		730	445	288	198	108
1,600		753	453	291	200	109
1,700		774	461	294	201	109
1,800		794	468	297	202	109
1,900		813	474	300	204	110
2,000		831	480	302	205	110
2,100		848	486	304	206	110
2,200		864	491	306	207	111
2,300		879	496	308	207	111
2,400		893	500	310	208	111
2,500		906	505	311	205	111
2,700		931	512	314	210	112
2,900		954	519	317	211	112
3,000		965	522	318	212	112
3,100		975	525	319	212	112
3,300		994	530	321	213	113
3,500		1011	535	323	214	113
3,700		1027	540	325	215	113
3,900		1042	544	326	215	113
4,000		1045	546	327	216	113
4,100		1056	548	327	216	113
4,300		1068	551	329	216	113
4,500		1080	554	330	217	114
4,800		1097	559	331	218	114
5,000		1107	561	332	218	114
5,500		1130	567	334	219	114
6,000	2919	1149	572	336	220	114
6,500	3032	1166	576	337	220	114
7,000	3137	1181	580	339	221	115
7,500	3234	1195	583	340	221	115
8,000	3323	1207	586	341	222	115
8,500	3406	1218	588	341	222	115
9,000	3484	1227	591	342	222	115
9,500	3556	1236	593	343	222	115
10,000	3624	1244	594	343	223	115
10,500	3688	1252	596	344	223	115
11,000	3747	1259	598	345	223	115
11,500	3804	1265	599	345	223	115
12,000	3857	1271	600	345	224	115
12,500	3907	1276	602	346	224	115
13,000	3955	1281	603	346	224	115
13,500	4000	1286	604	347	224	115
14,000	4042	1290	605	347	224	116
14,500	4083	1294	606	347	224	116
15,000	4122	1298	606	347	224	116
15,500	4158	1302	607	348	225	116
16,000	4194	1305	608	348	225	116
16,500	4227	1309	609	348	225	116
17,000	4259	1312	609	348	225	116
17,500	4290	1314	610	349	225	116
18,000	4320	1317	611	349	225	116
18,500	4348	1320	611	349	225	116

Population Size	Sample Size for Precision of: ±1%	±2%	±3%	±4%	±5%	±7%
19,000	4375	1322	612	349	225	116
19,500	4401	1325	612	349	225	116
20,000	4426	1328	613	349	225	116
21,000	4473	1331	613	350	225	116
22,000	4517	1335	614	350	225	116
23,000	4557	1339	615	350	226	116
24,000	4595	1342	616	350	226	116
25,000	4631	1345	616	351	226	116
26,000	4664	1348	617	351	226	116
27,000	4695	1350	617	351	226	116
28,000	4724	1353	618	351	226	116
29,000	4752	1355	618	351	226	116
30,000	4778	1357	619	352	226	116
31,000	4803	1359	619	352	226	116
32,000	4826	1361	620	352	226	116
33,000	4848	1363	620	352	226	116
34,000	4869	1364	620	352	226	116
35,000	4889	1366	621	352	226	116
36,000	4908	1367	621	352	226	116
37,000	4927	1369	621	352	226	116
38,000	4944	1370	622	352	226	116
39,000	4960	1371	622	352	226	116
40,000	4976	1372	622	353	227	116
41,000	4991	1374	622	353	227	116
42,000	5006	1375	623	353	227	116
43,000	5020	1376	623	353	227	116
44,000	5033	1377	623	353	227	116
45,000	5046	1378	623	353	227	116
46,000	5058	1379	623	353	227	116
47,000	5070	1379	624	353	227	116
48,000	5082	1380	624	353	227	116
49,000	5093	1381	624	353	227	116
50,000	5103	1382	624	353	227	116
55,000	5151	1385	625	353	227	116
60,000	5192	1388	625	354	227	116
65,000	5226	1391	626	354	227	116
70,000	5256	1393	626	354	227	116
75,000	5283	1395	627	354	227	116
80,000	5306	1396	627	354	227	116
85,000	5327	1398	627	354	227	116
90,000	5346	1399	628	354	227	116
95,000	5362	1400	628	354	227	116
100,000	5378	1401	628	354	227	116
105,000	5391	1402	628	354	227	116
110,000	5404	1403	628	355	227	116
115,000	5416	1404	628	355	227	116
120,000	5426	1405	629	355	227	116
130,000	5445	1406	629	355	227	116
140,000	5461	1407	629	355	227	116
150,000	5476	1408	629	355	227	116
160,000	5488	1409	629	355	227	116
170,000	5499	1409	630	355	228	116
185,000	5514	1410	630	355	228	116
200,000	5526	1411	630	355	228	116
215,000	5537	1412	630	355	228	116

D

TABLE D-1F Sample Sizes for Sampling Attributes for Random Samples Only—Expected Rate of Occurrence Not over 30% or Expected Rate of Occurrence Not Less than 70%. Confidence Level 90% (Two-sided) (Continued).

Population Size	Sample Size for Precision of: ±1%	±2%	±3%	±4%	±5%	±7%
225,000	5543	1412	630	355	228	116
235,000	5549	1413	630	355	228	116
250,000	5557	1413	630	355	228	116
275,000	5568	1414	630	355	228	116
300,000	5578	1414	631	355	228	116
325,000	5585	1415	631	355	228	116
350,000	5592	1415	631	355	228	116
400,000	5604	1416	631	355	228	116
450,000	5612	1417	631	355	228	116
500,000	5619	1417	631	355	228	116

TABLE D-1G Sample Sizes for Sampling Attributes for Random Samples Only—Expected Rate of Occurrence Not over 40% or Expected Rate of Occurrence Not Less than 60%. Confidence Level 90% (Two-sided).

Population Size	Sample Size for Precision of: ±1%	±2%	±3%	±4%	±5%	±7%
100						57
200						80
300					140	92
400				202	158	100
500				225	171	105
600				243	182	109
650				250	186	111
700			356	257	190	112
750			368	264	193	113
800			380	270	197	114
850			391	275	199	115
900			401	280	202	116
950			411	285	204	117
1,000			420	289	207	118
1,050			428	293	209	118
1,100			436	297	211	119
1,150			444	301	212	119
1,200			451	304	214	120
1,250			458	307	216	120
1,300			465	310	217	121
1,350			471	313	218	121
1,400			477	315	220	122
1,450			482	318	221	122
1,500			488	320	222	122
1,550			493	322	223	123
1,600		807	498	324	224	123
1,650		819	503	326	225	123

Population Size	Sample Size for Precision of: ±1%	±2%	±3%	±4%	±5%	±7%
1,700		831	507	328	226	123
1,750		843	511	330	227	124
1,800		854	516	332	228	124
1,850		865	520	333	228	124
1,900		876	523	335	229	124
1,950		886	527	336	230	125
2,000		897	531	338	230	125
2,100		916	538	341	231	125
2,200		935	544	343	233	126
2,300		952	550	346	234	126
2,400		969	555	348	235	126
2,500		985	560	350	236	126
2,600		1000	565	352	237	127
2,700		1014	570	353	237	127
2,800		1028	574	355	238	127
2,900		1041	578	357	239	127
3,000		1054	582	358	240	127
3,100		1066	586	359	240	128
3,200		1078	589	361	241	128
3,300		1089	593	362	241	128
3,400		1099	596	363	242	128
3,500		1110	599	364	242	128
3,600		1119	602	365	243	128
3,700		1129	604	366	243	128
3,800		1130	607	367	244	129
3,900		1147	609	368	244	129
4,000		1155	612	369	244	129
4,200		1171	616	371	245	129
4,400		1186	620	372	246	129
4,500		1194	622	373	246	129
4,600		1201	624	373	246	129
4,800		1214	628	375	247	129
5,000		1226	631	376	247	130
5,500		1254	638	379	249	130
6,000		1278	645	381	249	130
6,500	3249	1300	650	383	250	130
7,000	3369	1318	655	384	251	131
7,500	3481	1335	659	386	252	131
8,000	3585	1350	662	387	252	131
8,500	3682	1364	666	388	253	131
9,000	3773	1376	669	389	253	131
9,500	3858	1387	671	390	253	131
10,000	3938	1397	674	391	254	131
10,500	4013	1407	676	391	254	131
11,000	4084	1415	678	392	254	131
11,500	4151	1423	680	393	255	132
12,000	4214	1431	681	393	255	132
12,500	4274	1437	683	394	255	132
13,000	4331	1444	684	394	255	132
13,500	4385	1450	685	395	255	132
14,000	4437	1455	687	395	256	132

D

TABLE D-1G Samples Sizes for Sampling Attributes for Random Samples Only—Expected Rate of Occurrence Not over 40% or Expected Rate of Occurrence Not Less than 60%. Confidence Level 90% (Two-sided) (Continued).

Population Size	Sample Size for Precision of:					
	±1%	±2%	±3%	±4%	±5%	±7%
14,500	4486	1461	688	395	256	132
15,000	4533	1466	689	396	256	132
15,500	4577	1470	690	396	256	132
16,000	4620	1475	691	396	256	132
16,500	4661	1479	692	397	256	132
17,000	4700	1483	693	397	256	132
17,500	4737	1486	694	397	256	132
18,000	4773	1490	694	397	257	132
18,500	4807	1493	695	398	257	132
19,000	4841	1496	696	398	257	132
19,500	4872	1499	696	398	257	132
20,000	4903	1502	697	398	257	132
21,000	4961	1508	698	399	257	132
22,000	5015	1513	699	399	257	132
23,000	5065	1517	700	399	257	132
24,000	5112	1521	701	400	257	132
25,000	5156	1525	702	400	258	132
26,000	5197	1529	703	400	258	132
27,000	5236	1532	703	400	258	132
28,000	5272	1535	704	401	258	132
29,000	5307	1538	705	401	258	132
30,000	5339	1541	705	401	258	132
31,000	5370	1543	706	401	258	132
32,000	5399	1546	706	401	258	132
33,000	5427	1548	707	401	258	133
34,000	5453	1550	707	402	258	133
35,000	5478	1552	708	402	258	133
36,000	5502	1554	708	402	258	133
37,000	5525	1556	708	402	258	133
38,000	5547	1558	709	402	259	133
39,000	5568	1559	709	402	259	133
40,000	5588	1561	709	402	259	133
41,000	5607	1562	710	402	259	133
42,000	5625	1564	710	403	259	133
43,000	5643	1565	710	403	259	133
44,000	5660	1566	710	403	259	133
45,000	5676	1568	711	403	259	133
46,000	5691	1569	711	403	259	133
47,000	5707	1570	711	403	259	133
48,000	5721	1571	711	403	259	133
49,000	5735	1572	712	403	259	133
50,000	5748	1573	712	403	259	133
55,000	5809	1578	713	403	259	133

Population Size	Sample Size for Precision of: ±1%	±2%	±3%	±4%	±5%	±7%
60,000	5861	1581	714	404	259	133
65,000	5905	1585	714	404	259	133
70,000	5944	1587	715	404	259	133
75,000	5977	1590	715	404	259	133
80,000	6007	1592	716	404	259	133
85,000	6034	1594	716	404	259	133
90,000	6058	1595	716	405	260	133
95,000	6079	1597	717	405	260	133
100,000	6099	1598	717	405	260	133
105,000	6117	1599	717	405	260	133
110,000	6133	1600	717	405	260	133
115,000	6148	1602	718	405	260	133
120,000	6162	1602	718	405	260	133
125,000	6174	1603	718	405	260	133
130,000	6186	1604	718	405	260	133
135,000	6197	1605	718	405	260	133
145,000	6217	1606	719	405	260	133
150,000	6225	1607	719	405	260	133
155,000	6234	1607	719	405	260	133
165,000	6249	1608	719	405	260	133
175,000	6263	1609	719	405	260	133
185,000	6275	1610	719	406	260	133
195,000	6286	1611	719	406	260	133
200,000	6291	1611	720	406	260	133
210,000	6300	1612	720	406	260	133
225,000	6313	1612	720	406	260	133
240,000	6324	1613	720	406	260	133
250,000	6331	1614	720	406	260	133
260,000	6337	1614	720	406	260	133
280,000	6348	1615	720	406	260	133
300,000	6357	1615	720	406	260	133
330,000	6370	1616	721	406	260	133
350,000	6377	1617	721	406	260	133
375,000	6384	1617	721	406	260	133
400,000	6391	1618	721	406	260	133
450,000	6403	1618	721	406	260	133
500,000	6412	1619	721	406	260	133

TABLE D-1H Sample Sizes for Sampling Attributes for Random Samples Only—Expected Rate of Occurrence 50%. Confidence Level 90% (Two-sided).

Population Size	Sample Size for Precision of: ±1%	±2%	±3%	±4%	±5%	±7%
250					130	89
300					143	95
350					153	100
400					162	103
450				218	169	106
500				230	176	109
550				240	182	111

TABLE D-1H Sample Sizes for Sampling Attributes for Random Samples Only—Expected Rate of Occurrence 50%. Confidence Level 90% (Two-sided) (Continued).

Population Size	±1%	±2%	±3%	±4%	±5%	±7%
600				249	187	113
650				257	192	114
700				264	196	116
750				271	199	117
800			388	277	203	118
850			399	283	206	119
900			410	288	209	120
950			420	293	211	121
1,000			430	298	213	122
1,050			439	302	216	123
1,100			447	306	218	123
1,150			455	310	220	124
1,200			463	313	221	124
1,250			470	316	223	125
1,300			477	320	224	125
1,350			483	322	226	126
1,400			490	325	227	126
1,450			496	328	229	127
1,500			501	330	230	127
1,550			507	333	231	127
1,600			512	335	232	128
1,650			517	337	233	128
1,700		848	522	339	234	128
1,750		861	526	341	235	128
1,800		872	531	343	236	129
1,850		884	535	345	237	129
1,900		895	539	346	237	129
1,950		906	543	348	238	129
2,000		917	547	350	239	130
2,100		937	554	352	240	130
2,200		957	561	355	241	130
2,300		975	567	358	243	131
2,400		993	573	360	244	131
2,500		1009	578	362	245	131
2,600		1025	584	364	246	132
2,700		1040	588	366	246	132
2,800		1055	593	368	247	132
2,900		1069	597	370	248	132
3,000		1082	602	371	249	132
3,100		1095	605	373	249	133
3,200		1107	609	374	250	133
3,300		1119	613	375	251	133
3,400		1130	616	377	251	133
3,500		1141	619	378	252	133
3,600		1151	622	379	252	133
3,700		1161	625	380	253	134
3,800		1171	628	381	253	134
3,900		1180	631	382	254	134

Population Size	Sample Size for Precision of: ±1%	±2%	±3%	±4%	±5%	±7%
4,000		1189	633	383	254	134
4,200		1206	638	385	255	134
4,400		1222	642	386	255	134
4,500		1230	645	387	256	134
4,600		1237	647	388	256	135
4,800		1251	650	389	257	135
5,000		1264	654	390	257	135
5,500		1294	662	393	258	135
6,000		1320	668	395	259	135
6,500		1343	674	397	260	136
7,000	3441	1363	679	399	261	136
7,500	3557	1381	684	401	262	136
8,000	3666	1397	688	402	262	136
8,500	3767	1411	691	403	263	136
9,000	3863	1424	694	404	263	136
9,500	3952	1436	697	405	264	137
10,000	4036	1447	700	406	264	137
10,500	4115	1457	702	407	264	137
11,000	4189	1466	704	408	265	137
11,500	4260	1475	706	408	265	137
12,000	4327	1483	708	409	265	137
12,500	4390	1490	710	409	265	137
13,000	4450	1497	711	410	266	137
13,500	4507	1503	713	410	266	137
14,000	4571	1509	714	411	266	137
14,500	4613	1515	715	411	266	137
15,000	4663	1520	716	412	266	137
15,500	4710	1525	717	412	266	137
16,000	4755	1530	718	412	267	137
16,500	4798	1535	719	413	267	137
17,000	4840	1539	720	413	267	137
17,500	4879	1543	721	413	267	137
18,000	4918	1547	722	414	267	138
18,500	4954	1550	723	414	267	138
19,000	4989	1554	724	414	267	138
19,500	5023	1557	724	414	267	138
20,000	5056	1560	725	415	267	138
21,000	5117	1566	726	415	268	138
22,000	5175	1571	727	415	268	138
23,000	5228	1576	728	416	268	138
24,000	5278	1580	729	416	268	138
25,000	5325	1585	730	416	268	138
26,000	5361	1588	731	417	268	138
27,000	5410	1592	732	417	268	138
28,000	5449	1595	733	417	269	138
29,000	5486	1599	733	417	269	138
30,000	5521	1602	734	417	269	138
31,000	5554	1604	734	418	269	138
32,000	5585	1607	735	418	269	138
33,000	5615	1609	735	418	269	138
34,000	5643	1612	736	418	269	138

TABLE D-1H Sample Sizes for Sampling Attributes for Random Samples Only—Expected Rate of Occurrence 50%. Confidence Level 90% (Two-sided) (Continued).

Population Size	Sample Size for Precision of: ±1%	±2%	±3%	±4%	±5%	±7%
35,000	5670	1614	736	418	269	138
36,000	5695	1616	737	418	269	138
37,000	5720	1618	737	419	269	138
38,000	5743	1620	738	419	269	138
39,000	5766	1621	738	419	269	138
40,000	5787	1623	738	419	269	138
41,000	5807	1625	739	419	269	138
42,000	5827	1626	739	419	269	138
43,000	5846	1628	739	419	269	138
44,000	5864	1629	740	419	269	138
45,000	5881	1631	740	419	269	138
46,000	5903	1632	740	419	270	138
47,000	5914	1633	740	420	270	138
48,000	5930	1634	741	420	270	138
49,000	5945	1635	741	420	270	138
50,000	5959	1636	741	420	270	138
55,000	6025	1641	742	420	270	138
60,000	6080	1645	743	420	270	138
65,000	6128	1649	744	421	270	138
70,000	6169	1652	744	421	270	138
75,000	6206	1654	745	421	270	138
80,000	6238	1657	745	421	270	138
85,000	6267	1659	746	421	270	138
90,000	6293	1661	746	421	270	138
95,000	6316	1662	746	421	270	138
100,000	6337	1664	747	422	270	138
105,000	6356	1665	747	422	270	138
110,000	6374	1666	747	422	270	138
115,000	6390	1667	747	422	270	138
120,000	6405	1668	747	422	270	138
125,000	6418	1669	748	422	271	138
130,000	6431	1670	748	422	271	138
135,000	6443	1671	748	422	271	138
140,000	6454	1672	748	422	271	138
150,000	6474	1673	748	422	271	138
160,000	6491	1674	749	422	271	138
170,000	6507	1675	749	422	271	138
180,000	6521	1676	749	422	271	138
190,000	6533	1677	749	422	271	138
200,000	6544	1678	749	422	271	138
210,000	6554	1678	749	422	271	138
225,000	6568	1679	750	423	271	138
240,000	6580	1680	750	423	271	138
250,000	6587	1680	750	423	271	138
275,000	6603	1681	750	423	271	138

Population Size	±1%	±2%	±3%	±4%	±5%	±7%
			Sample Size for Precision of:			
300,000	6616	1682	750	423	271	138
325,000	6632	1683	750	423	271	139
350,000	6637	1684	751	423	271	139
375,000	6646	1684	751	423	271	139
400,000	6653	1685	751	423	271	139
450,000	6665	1685	751	423	271	139
500,000	6675	1686	751	423	271	139

D

TABLE D-2A Sample Sizes for Sampling Attributes for Random Samples Only—Expected Rate of Occurrence Not over 2% or Expected Rate of Occurrence Not Less than 98%. Confidence Level 95% (Two-sided).

Population Size	±.5%	±.75%	±1%	±1.25%	±1.5%	±2%
			Sample Size for Precision of:			
200						97
250						108
300						116
350					172	123
400					182	129
450					192	133
500				246	201	137
550				257	209	141
600				268	215	144
650				277	221	146
700				286	227	149
750				294	232	151
800				301	236	153
850				308	241	155
900				314	244	156
950				320	248	158
1,000			430	326	251	159
1,050			439	331	254	160
1,100			447	336	257	161
1,150			456	340	260	162
1,200			463	344	262	163
1,250			470	348	264	164
1,300			477	352	267	165
1,350		673	484	356	269	166
1,400		685	490	359	271	166
1,450		697	496	362	272	167
1,500		708	501	365	274	168
1,550		719	507	368	276	168
1,600		729	513	371	277	169
1,650		740	518	373	279	169
1,700		749	522	376	280	170
1,750		759	527	378	281	170
1,800		768	531	381	283	171
1,850		777	536	383	284	171
1,900		786	540	385	285	172
1,950		794	544	387	286	172

TABLE D-2A Sample Sizes for Sampling Attributes for Random Samples Only—Expected Rate of Occurrence Not over 2% or Expected Rate of Occurrence Not Less than 98%. Confidence Level 95% (Two-sided) (Continued).

Population Size	Sample Size for Precision of: ±.5%	±.75%	±1%	±1.25%	±1.5%	±2%
2,000		802	547	389	287	173
2,100		818	554	392	289	173
2,200		833	561	396	291	174
2,300		847	568	399	293	174
2,400		860	574	402	294	175
2,500		872	579	405	296	176
2,600		884	584	407	297	176
2,700		895	589	409	298	176
2,800		906	594	412	299	177
2,900		916	598	414	301	177
3,000		925	602	416	302	178
3,100	1528	935	606	418	303	178
3,200	1551	944	610	419	303	178
3,300	1575	953	614	421	304	179
3,400	1597	961	617	423	305	179
3,500	1619	969	620	424	306	179
3,600	1640	976	623	426	307	179
3,700	1661	983	626	427	307	180
3,800	1681	990	629	428	308	180
3,900	1700	997	632	429	309	180
4,000	1719	1003	634	431	309	180
4,100	1737	1010	637	432	310	180
4,200	1754	1016	639	433	310	181
4,300	1772	1021	641	434	311	181
4,400	1789	1027	643	435	311	181
4,500	1805	1032	645	436	312	181
4,600	1821	1037	648	437	312	181
4,700	1836	1042	649	438	313	181
4,800	1851	1047	651	438	313	182
4,900	1866	1052	653	439	314	182
5,000	1880	1056	654	440	314	182
5,500	1947	1077	663	444	316	183
6,000	2006	1095	669	447	317	183
6,500	2059	1110	675	449	319	183
7,000	2106	1124	680	451	320	184
7,500	2149	1136	685	453	320	184
8,000	2189	1147	688	455	322	184
8,500	2224	1157	692	457	322	185
9,000	2257	1166	695	458	323	185
9,500	2287	1174	698	459	324	185
10,000	2315	1181	700	460	324	185
10,500	2341	1188	703	461	325	185
11,000	2365	1194	705	462	325	186
11,500	2387	1200	707	463	326	186
12,000	2408	1205	709	464	326	186
12,500	2428	1210	711	465	326	186
13,000	2446	1214	712	465	327	186
13,500	2463	1218	714	466	327	186
14,000	2479	1222	715	466	327	186
14,500	2495	1226	716	467	328	186
15,000	2509	1229	717	467	328	186
15,500	2522	1232	719	468	328	186
16,500	2548	1239	721	469	328	187
17,500	2570	1244	722	469	329	187

Population Size	±.5%	±.75%	±1%	±1.25%	±1.5%	±2%
18,500	2591	1251	724	470	329	187
19,500	2609	1253	725	471	329	187
20,000	2619	1255	726	471	330	187
22,000	2650	1262	729	472	330	187
24,000	2676	1268	731	473	331	187
25,000	2711	1271	731	473	331	187
26,000	2699	1274	732	474	331	187
28,000	2720	1278	734	474	331	187
30,000	2738	1282	735	475	331	188
32,000	2753	1285	736	475	332	188
34,000	2768	1288	737	476	332	188
36,000	2780	1291	738	476	332	188
38,000	2791	1294	739	476	332	188
40,000	2801	1296	740	477	332	188
42,000	2811	1298	740	477	333	188
45,000	2823	1300	741	477	333	188
47,000	2831	1302	742	477	333	188
50,000	2841	1304	742	478	333	188
55,000	2856	1307	743	478	333	188
60,000	2868	1310	744	479	333	188
65,000	2879	1312	745	479	333	188
70,000	2888	1314	745	479	334	188
75,000	2896	1316	746	479	334	188
80,000	2903	1317	746	480	334	188
85,000	2909	1318	747	480	334	188
90,000	2915	1319	747	480	334	188
95,000	2920	1320	747	480	334	188
100,000	2925	1321	747	480	334	188
110,000	2937	1323	748	480	334	188
125,000	2941	1325	749	481	334	188
135,000	2946	1326	749	481	334	188
150,000	2953	1327	750	481	334	189
175,000	2959	1329	750	481	335	189
200,000	2968	1330	751	481	335	189
250,000	2976	1332	751	481	335	189
300,000	2982	1333	752	482	335	189
350,000	2987	1334	752	482	335	189
400,000	2990	1335	752	482	335	189
450,000	2992	1335	752	482	335	189
500,000	2994	1336	752	482	335	189

Sample Size for Precision of

D

TABLE D-2B Sample Sizes for Sampling Attributes for Random Samples Only—Expected Rate of Occurrence Not over 5% or Expected Rate of Occurrence Not Less than 95%. Confidence Level 95% (Two-sided).

Sample Size for Precision of:

Population Size	±.5%	±1%	±1.5%	±2%	±2.5%	±3%	±4%
150							65
200							73
250						112	79
300					148	121	83
350					160	129	86
400					169	135	89
450					178	140	91

TABLE D-2B Sample Sizes for Sampling Attributes for Random Samples Only—Expected Rate of Occurrence Not over 5% or Expected Rate of Occurrence Not Less than 95%. Confidence Level 95% (Two-sided) (Continued).

Population Size	Sample Size for Precision of: ±.5%	±1%	±1.5%	±2%	±2.5%	±3%	±4%
500				239	185	144	93
550				250	191	148	95
600				259	197	152	96
650				268	202	155	97
700				276	207	157	98
750				284	211	160	99
800				291	214	162	100
850			416	297	218	164	101
900			427	303	221	166	101
950			438	308	224	167	102
1,000			448	314	226	169	102
1,100			467	323	231	171	103
1,200			484	331	235	174	104
1,300			500	338	239	176	105
1,400			514	344	242	177	106
1,500			527	350	245	179	106
1,600			539	355	247	180	107
1,700			550	360	250	181	107
1,750			555	362	251	182	107
1,800		907	560	364	252	182	107
1,850		919	564	366	253	183	107
1,900		931	569	368	254	183	108
1,950		943	573	370	254	184	108
2,000		954	578	372	255	184	108
2,100		977	586	375	257	185	108
2,200		998	593	378	258	186	108
2,300		1018	600	381	260	186	109
2,400		1037	607	384	261	187	109
2,500		1055	613	386	262	188	109
2,600		1073	619	388	263	188	109
2,700		1089	624	390	264	189	109
2,800		1105	629	392	265	189	110
2,900		1120	634	394	266	190	110
3,000		1135	639	396	267	190	110
3,100		1149	643	398	267	190	110
3,300		1175	652	401	269	191	110
3,500		1200	659	404	270	192	110
3,700		1222	666	406	271	192	111
3,900		1243	672	409	272	193	111
4,000		1253	675	410	273	193	111
4,500		1299	688	414	275	194	111
4,700		1315	692	416	275	194	111
5,000		1337	698	418	276	195	112
5,500		1370	707	421	278	196	112
6,000		1400	715	424	279	196	112
6,500		1425	722	426	280	197	112
7,000		1448	727	428	281	197	112
7,500	3700	1468	732	430	282	197	112
8,000	3817	1486	737	432	282	198	112
8,500	3932	1503	741	433	283	198	113
9,000	4031	1517	744	434	283	198	113
9,500	4128	1531	748	435	284	199	113

Population Size	Sample Size for Precision of: ±.5%	±1%	±1.5%	±2%	±2.5%	±3%	±4%
10,000	4220	1543	751	436	284	199	113
10,500	4306	1555	753	437	285	199	113
11,500	4465	1575	758	439	285	199	113
13,000	4675	1600	764	441	286	200	113
14,500	4856	1621	769	442	287	200	113
15,000	4851	1627	770	443	287	200	113
16,500	5061	1643	774	443	287	200	113
19,000	5274	1665	778	446	288	201	113
20,000	5348	1672	780	446	288	201	113
22,000	5482	1685	783	447	289	201	113
24,000	5595	1696	785	448	289	201	114
26,000	5699	1705	787	448	289	201	114
28,000	5790	1713	789	449	289	201	114
30,000	5871	1720	790	449	290	201	114
32,000	5944	1727	791	450	290	202	114
34,000	6010	1732	793	450	290	202	114
36,000	6069	1737	794	451	290	202	114
38,000	6123	1741	795	451	290	202	114
40,000	6173	1745	795	451	290	202	114
45,000	6282	1754	797	452	291	202	114
50,000	6370	1761	799	452	291	202	114
60,000	6508	1771	801	453	291	202	114
70,000	6610	1779	802	453	291	202	114
80,000	6689	1784	803	454	291	202	114
90,000	6752	1789	804	454	291	202	114
100,000	6803	1792	805	454	292	202	114
150,000	6961	1803	807	455	292	203	114
200,000	7043	1809	808	455	292	203	114
250,000	7092	1812	809	455	292	203	114
300,000	7126	1814	809	456	292	203	114
400,000	7169	1817	810	456	292	203	114
500,000	7196	1818	810	456	292	203	114

D

TABLE D-2C Sample Sizes for Sampling Attributes for Random Samples Only—Expected Rate of Occurrence Not over 10% or Expected Rate of Occurrence Not Less than 90%. Confidence Level 95% (Two-sided).

Population Size	Sample Size for Precision of: ±.5%	±1%	±1.5%	±2%	±2.5%	±3%	±4%
250							116
300							126
350							134
400						196	141
450						207	146
500						217	151
550						226	155
600					283	234	159
650					299	242	162
700					309	248	165
750					319	254	168
800					328	260	170
850					336	265	172
900				441	343	269	174
950				453	350	274	176

TABLE D-2C Sample Sizes for Sampling Attributes for Random Samples Only—Expected Rate of Occurrence Not over 10% or Expected Rate of Occurrence Not Less than 90%. Confidence Level 95% (Two-sided) (Continued).

Population Size	Sample Size for Precision of: ±.5%	±1%	±1.5%	±2%	±2.5%	±3%	±4%
1,000				464	357	278	178
1,050				474	363	281	179
1,100				484	369	285	181
1,150				494	374	288	182
1,200				503	379	291	183
1,250				511	384	294	184
1,300				519	389	297	185
1,350				527	393	299	186
1,400				535	397	302	187
1,450				542	401	304	188
1,500				549	405	306	189
1,550			772	555	408	308	190
1,600			784	561	412	310	190
1,650			796	567	415	312	191
1,700			808	573	418	313	192
1,750			819	579	421	315	192
1,800			829	584	424	317	193
1,850			840	589	426	318	194
1,900			850	594	429	320	194
1,950			860	599	431	321	195
2,000			869	604	434	322	195
2,100			888	612	438	325	196
2,200			905	621	443	327	197
2,300			922	628	446	329	198
2,400			937	636	450	331	198
2,500			952	642	453	333	199
2,600			969	649	457	335	200
2,700			983	655	460	336	200
2,800			996	661	462	338	201
2,900			1008	666	465	339	201
3,000			1020	671	468	341	202
3,100			1031	676	470	342	202
3,200			1042	681	472	343	202
3,300			1052	685	474	344	203
3,400			1062	689	476	345	203
3,500		1739	1068	693	478	346	204
3,600		1764	1077	697	480	347	204
3,700		1787	1086	701	482	348	204
3,800		1810	1095	704	483	349	204
3,900		1833	1103	708	485	350	205
4,000		1855	1111	711	486	351	205
4,100		1876	1118	714	488	351	205
4,200		1896	1126	717	489	352	206
4,300		1917	1133	720	491	353	206
4,500		1955	1146	725	493	354	206
4,700		1992	1159	730	495	355	207
4,900		2027	1170	735	498	356	207
5,000		2044	1176	737	499	357	207
5,500		2123	1202	747	503	359	208

Population Size	±.5%	±1%	±1.5%	±2%	±2.5%	±3%	±4%
	Sample Size for Precision of:						
6,000		2194	1224	756	507	361	209
6,500		2257	1243	763	510	363	209
7,000		2314	1261	769	513	364	210
7,500		2367	1276	775	516	365	210
8,000		2414	1290	780	518	367	210
8,500		2453	1302	785	520	368	211
9,000		2493	1313	789	522	368	211
9,500		2535	1323	792	523	369	211
10,000		2569	1332	796	525	370	212
10,500		2601	1341	799	526	371	212
11,000		2631	1349	801	527	371	212
11,500		2658	1356	804	528	372	212
12,000		2684	1363	806	529	372	212
12,500		2708	1369	808	530	373	212
13,000		2731	1375	810	531	373	213
13,500		2752	1380	812	532	374	213
14,000	6957	2773	1385	814	533	374	213
14,500	7079	2792	1390	816	533	375	213
15,000	7196	2810	1394	817	534	375	213
16,000	7418	2843	1402	820	535	375	213
17,000	7626	2873	1410	822	536	376	213
18,000	7821	2900	1416	825	537	376	214
19,000	8004	2925	1422	827	538	377	214
20,000	8176	2948	1427	828	539	377	214
22,000	8491	2988	1437	832	540	378	214
24,000	8774	3022	1445	834	541	378	214
26,000	9028	3055	1451	836	542	379	214
28,000	9257	3077	1457	838	543	379	214
30,000	9465	3100	1462	840	544	379	215
32,000	9658	3120	1467	842	544	380	215
35,000	9913	3146	1472	843	545	380	215
38,000	10140	3169	1477	845	546	380	215
40,000	10277	3182	1480	846	546	380	215
42,000	10405	3194	1483	847	546	381	215
45,000	10579	3210	1486	848	547	381	215
50,000	10834	3234	1491	850	548	381	215
55,000	11050	3253	1495	851	548	381	215
65,000	11404	3282	1502	853	549	382	215
75,000	11677	3305	1506	854	550	382	215
90,000	11989	3329	1511	856	550	382	216
100,000	12150	3242	1514	857	551	383	216
110,000	12287	3352	1516	858	551	383	216
125,000	12453	3365	1518	859	551	383	216
140,000	12587	3374	1520	859	552	383	216
150,000	12663	3379	1522	859	552	383	216
200,000	12936	3398	1525	861	552	383	216
275,000	13167	3414	1529	862	553	384	216
350,000	13303	3423	1530	862	553	384	216
425,000	13340	3430	1532	863	553	384	216
500,000	13459	3433	1532	863	553	384	216

D

TABLE D-2D Sample Sizes for Sampling Attributes for Random Samples Only—Expected Rate of Occurrence Not over 15% or Expected Rate of Occurrence Not Less than 85%. Confidence Level 95% (Two-sided).

Population Size	Sample Size for Precision of:						
	±1%	±1.5%	±2%	±2.5%	±3%	±3.5%	±4%
350							164
400						200	174
450						212	182
500						223	190
550					274	232	197
600					286	240	203
650					296	248	208
700					306	255	213
750					316	261	218
800				396	324	267	222
850				408	332	272	225
900				419	339	277	229
950				430	346	281	232
1,000				440	353	286	235
1,050				449	359	290	237
1,100				459	364	294	240
1,150				467	370	297	242
1,200				475	375	300	244
1,250			619	482	379	303	246
1,300			631	489	384	306	248
1,350			642	496	388	309	250
1,400			653	503	392	312	251
1,450			664	509	396	314	253
1,500			674	515	400	316	254
1,550			684	521	403	318	256
1,600			694	527	406	320	257
1,650			703	532	409	322	258
1,700			712	538	412	324	260
1,750			721	542	415	326	261
1,800			729	546	418	328	262
1,850			737	551	421	329	263
1,900			745	555	423	331	264
1,950			752	560	426	332	265
2,000			760	564	428	334	266
2,100			774	571	432	336	267
2,200		1095	787	578	436	339	269
2,300		1119	799	585	440	341	270
2,400		1142	811	591	444	343	272
2,500		1164	822	597	447	345	273
2,600		1185	833	603	450	347	274
2,700		1206	843	608	453	349	275
2,800		1225	852	613	456	350	276
2,900		1244	861	617	458	352	277
3,000		1262	870	622	461	353	278
3,100		1279	878	626	463	353	279
3,200		1296	886	630	465	356	279
3,300		1312	893	634	467	357	280
3,400		1328	900	637	469	358	281
3,500		1343	907	641	471	359	282
3,600		1357	914	644	473	360	282
3,700		1371	920	647	475	361	283
3,800		1385	926	650	476	362	283
3.900		1398	932	653	478	363	284

Population Size	Sample Size for Precision of: ±1%	±1.5%	±2%	±2.5%	±3%	±3.5%	±4%
4,000		1410	938	656	479	364	284
4,100		1422	943	658	481	365	285
4,200		1434	948	661	482	366	285
4,300		1446	953	663	483	366	286
4,400		1457	958	666	484	367	286
4,500		1468	963	668	486	368	287
4,600		1478	967	670	487	368	287
4,700		1488	972	672	488	369	287
4,800		1498	976	674	489	370	288
4,900		1508	980	676	490	370	288
5,000	2474	1517	984	678	491	371	289
5,500	2591	1560	1002	686	495	373	290
6,000	2697	1598	1017	694	499	375	291
6,500	2793	1631	1031	700	502	377	292
7,000	2882	1661	1042	705	505	379	293
7,500	2963	1688	1053	710	507	380	294
8,000	3038	1712	1062	714	510	381	295
8,500	3108	1727	1070	717	512	382	296
9,000	3172	1753	1078	721	513	383	296
9,500	3232	1772	1085	724	515	384	297
10,000	3288	1788	1091	727	516	385	297
10,500	3340	1804	1097	730	517	386	297
11,000	3389	1818	1102	732	519	386	298
11,500	3435	1831	1107	734	520	387	298
12,000	3478	1843	1111	736	521	387	299
12,500	3519	1855	1115	738	522	388	299
13,000	3558	1865	1119	740	522	388	299
13,500	3594	1875	1123	741	523	389	299
14,000	3629	1884	1126	743	524	389	300
14,500	3661	1893	1129	744	525	390	300
15,000	3693	1902	1132	745	525	390	300
15,500	3722	1909	1135	746	526	390	300
16,000	3750	1917	1138	748	526	391	300
16,500	3777	1924	1140	749	527	391	301
17,000	3803	1930	1142	750	527	391	301
17,500	3827	1937	1144	751	528	391	301
18,000	3850	1943	1147	751	528	392	301
18,500	3873	1948	1149	752	529	392	301
19,000	3894	1954	1150	753	529	392	301
19,500	3915	1959	1152	754	529	392	301
20,000	3935	1964	1154	755	530	393	302
21,000	3972	1973	1157	756	530	393	302
22,000	4006	1981	1160	757	531	393	302
23,000	4038	1989	1163	758	532	394	302
24,000	4068	1996	1165	759	532	394	302
25,000	4096	2003	1167	760	533	394	302
26,000	4122	2009	1169	761	533	394	303
27,000	4146	2015	1171	762	533	395	303
28,000	4169	2020	1173	763	534	395	303
29,000	4190	2025	1175	764	534	395	303
30,000	4211	2030	1177	764	535	395	303
32,000	4248	2039	1179	765	535	395	303
34,000	4281	2046	1182	767	536	396	303
36,000	4312	2053	1184	767	536	396	304
38,000	4339	2059	1186	768	537	396	304

TABLE D-2D Sample Sizes for Sampling Attributes for Random Samples Only—Expected Rate of Occurrence Not over 15% or Expected Rate of Occurrence Not Less than 85%. Confidence Level 95% (Two-sided) (Continued).

Population Size	Sample Size for Precision of: ±1%	±1.5%	±2%	±2.5%	±3%	±3.5%	±4%
40,000	4364	2065	1188	769	537	396	304
42,000	4387	2070	1190	770	537	397	304
44,000	4407	2075	1191	770	538	397	304
46,000	4427	2079	1193	771	538	397	304
48,000	4445	2083	1194	772	538	397	304
50,000	4461	2087	1195	772	538	397	304
55,000	4498	2094	1198	773	539	397	304
60,000	4528	2101	1200	774	539	398	305
65,000	4555	2107	1202	775	540	398	305
70,000	4578	2112	1203	776	540	398	305
75,000	4598	2116	1205	776	540	398	305
85,000	4631	2123	1207	777	541	398	305
95,000	4658	2129	1209	778	541	399	305
100,000	4669	2131	1210	778	541	399	305
120,000	4706	2137	1212	779	542	399	305
135,000	4727	2142	1214	779	542	399	305
150,000	4743	2146	1215	780	542	399	306
175,000	4765	2151	1216	781	543	399	306
200,000	4781	2154	1217	781	543	400	306
250,000	4804	2159	1219	782	543	400	306
300,000	4819	2162	1220	782	543	400	306
350,000	4830	2164	1220	782	543	400	306
450,000	4845	2167	1221	783	544	400	306
500,000	4850	2168	1222	783	544	400	306

TABLE D-2E Sample Sizes for Sampling Attributes for Random Samples Only—Expected Rate of Occurrence Not over 20% or Expected Rate of Occurrence Not Less than 80%. Confidence Level 95% (Two-sided).

Population Size	Sample Size for Precision of: ±1%	±1.5%	±2%	±2.5%	±3%	±4%	±5%
400						196	153
450						207	159
500						218	165
550						226	170
600						234	175
650						242	179
700					346	248	182
750					358	254	185
800					369	260	188
850					379	265	191
900					389	269	193
950					398	274	195
1,000				496	406	278	198
1,050				508	414	281	199
1,100				520	422	285	201
1,150				531	429	288	203
1,200				541	435	291	204
1,250				551	442	294	206

Population Size	Sample Size for Precision of: ±1%	±1.5%	±2%	±2.5%	±3%	±4%	±5%
1,300				560	448	297	207
1,350				569	454	299	208
1,400				578	459	302	209
1,450				587	465	304	210
1,500				595	470	306	211
1,550			772	602	474	308	212
1,600			784	610	479	310	213
1,650			796	617	483	312	214
1,700			807	624	487	314	215
1,750			818	630	491	315	216
1,800			829	636	495	317	216
1,850			840	643	499	318	217
1,900			850	649	503	320	218
1,950			860	654	506	321	218
2,000			869	660	509	322	219
2,100			888	670	516	325	220
2,200			905	680	521	327	221
2,300			921	689	527	329	222
2,400			937	698	532	331	223
2,500			952	706	537	333	224
2,600			966	714	541	335	225
2,700			980	721	545	336	225
2,800		1383	992	728	549	338	226
2,900		1407	1005	735	553	339	227
3,000		1430	1016	741	556	341	227
3,100		1453	1028	747	560	342	228
3,200		1474	1038	753	563	343	228
3,300		1495	1049	758	566	344	229
3,400		1515	1059	763	569	345	229
3,500		1535	1068	768	572	346	230
3,600		1554	1077	773	574	347	230
3,700		1572	1086	777	577	348	231
3,800		1590	1094	782	579	349	231
3,900		1607	1103	786	581	350	231
4,000		1624	1110	790	584	351	232
4,100		1640	1118	794	586	351	232
4,200		1656	1125	797	588	352	232
4,300		1671	1132	801	590	353	233
4,400		1686	1139	804	591	353	233
4,500		1700	1146	808	593	354	233
4,600		1714	1152	811	595	355	233
4,700		1728	1158	814	596	355	234
4,800		1741	1164	817	598	356	234
4,900		1754	1170	820	600	356	234
5,000		1767	1176	822	601	357	234
5,500		1826	1201	835	608	359	235
6,000		1878	1224	845	613	361	236
6,500	3160	1924	1243	855	618	363	237
7,000	3273	1965	1260	863	622	364	238
7,500	3378	2003	1276	870	626	366	238
8,000	3476	2037	1289	876	629	367	239
8,500	3567	2068	1302	882	632	368	239
9,000	3653	2096	1313	887	635	368	239
9,500	3732	2122	1323	892	637	369	240
10,000	3807	2146	1332	896	639	370	240

D

TABLE D-2E Sample Sizes for Sampling Attributes for Random Samples Only--Expected Rate of Occurrence Not over 20% or Expected Rate of Occurrence Not Less than 80%. Confidence Level 95% (Two-sided) (Continued).

Population Size	Sample Size for Precision of: ±1%	±1.5%	±2%	±2.5%	±3%	±4%	±5%
10,500	3877	2168	1341	900	641	371	240
11,000	3944	2189	1348	903	643	371	241
11,500	4006	2208	1356	906	645	372	241
12,000	4065	2226	1362	909	646	372	241
12,500	4121	2242	1369	912	648	373	241
13,000	4174	2258	1374	915	649	373	241
13,500	4224	2273	1380	917	650	374	241
14,000	4272	2286	1385	919	651	374	242
14,500	4317	2299	1390	921	652	374	242
15,000	4360	2311	1394	923	653	375	242
15,500	4402	2323	1398	925	654	375	242
16,000	4441	2334	1402	927	655	375	242
16,500	4479	2344	1406	928	656	375	242
17,000	4515	2354	1409	930	657	376	242
17,500	4549	2363	1413	932	657	376	242
18,000	4582	2372	1416	933	658	376	243
18,500	4614	2381	1419	934	659	376	243
19,000	4645	2389	1422	936	659	377	243
19,500	4674	2397	1425	937	660	377	243
20,000	4702	2404	1427	938	660	377	243
21,000	4755	2418	1432	940	662	377	243
22,000	4805	2430	1436	942	662	378	243
23,000	4851	2442	1441	944	663	378	243
24,000	4894	2453	1444	945	664	378	243
25,000	4934	2463	1448	947	665	378	243
26,000	4972	2473	1451	948	666	379	244
27,000	5007	2481	1454	949	666	379	244
28,000	5041	2489	1457	951	667	379	244
29,000	5072	2497	1459	952	667	379	244
30,000	5102	2504	1462	953	668	379	244
31,000	5130	2511	1464	954	668	379	244
32,000	5157	2517	1466	955	669	380	244
33,000	5182	2523	1468	955	669	380	244
34,000	5206	2529	1470	956	670	380	244
35,000	5229	2534	1472	957	670	380	244
36,000	5251	2540	1474	958	670	380	244
37,000	5271	2545	1476	958	671	380	244
38,000	5291	2549	1477	959	671	380	244
39,000	5310	2552	1479	960	672	381	244
40,000	5328	2558	1480	960	672	381	244
42,000	5362	2565	1483	961	672	381	244
44,000	5394	2573	1485	962	673	381	245
46,000	5423	2579	1487	963	673	381	245
48,000	5449	2585	1489	964	673	381	245
50,000	5474	2591	1491	965	674	381	245
55,000	5529	2603	1495	967	675	382	245
60,000	5576	2613	1498	968	675	382	245
65,000	5616	2622	1501	969	676	382	245
70,000	5651	2630	1504	970	676	382	245
75,000	5681	2636	1506	971	677	382	245
80,000	5708	2642	1508	972	677	382	245
85,000	5733	2647	1509	973	678	382	245
90,000	5754	2652	1511	973	678	383	245
95,000	5773	2656	1513	974	679	383	245

Population Size	Sample Size for Precision of: ±1%	±1.5%	±2%	±2.5%	±3%	±4%	±5%
100,000	5791	2660	1514	974	678	383	245
110,000	5822	2666	1516	975	679	383	245
120,000	5848	2672	1517	976	679	383	245
130,000	5870	2676	1519	977	679	383	245
140,000	5889	2680	1520	977	680	383	245
150,000	5905	2683	1522	978	680	383	245
160,000	5920	2686	1522	978	680	383	246
180,000	5944	2691	1524	979	680	383	246
200,000	5964	2696	1525	979	681	383	246
225,000	5984	2700	1526	980	681	384	246
250,000	6000	2703	1528	980	682	384	246
275,000	6013	2705	1529	980	682	384	246
300,000	6024	2708	1529	981	682	384	246
350,000	6041	2711	1530	981	682	384	246
450,000	6064	2716	1532	982	682	384	246
500,000	6072	2717	1532	982	682	384	246

D

TABLE D-2F Sample Sizes for Sampling Attributes for Random Samples Only—Expected Rate of Occurrence Not over 30% or Expected Rate of Occurrence Not Less than 70%. Confidence Level 95% (Two-sided).

Population Size	Sample Size for Precision of: ±1%	±2%	±3%	±4%	±5%	±7%
450					188	121
550				263	204	127
650				284	216	132
800				310	230	137
850				317	234	138
950			461	330	241	141
1,000			473	335	244	142
1,050			484	341	247	143
1,150			504	351	252	145
1,300			531	363	259	147
1,450			554	374	264	148
1,500			561	378	266	149
1,600			575	384	269	150
1,800			599	394	274	151
2,000			619	403	278	153
2,100		1029	628	407	280	153
2,200		1052	637	410	282	154
2,300		1075	645	414	283	154
2,400		1096	653	417	285	155
2,500		1117	660	420	286	155
2,700		1155	673	425	288	156
2,900		1190	685	430	290	156
3,000		1206	690	432	291	157
3,100		1222	695	434	292	157
3,300		1252	705	437	294	157
3,500		1280	714	441	296	158
3,700		1306	722	444	297	158
3,900		1330	729	447	298	158
4,000		1341	732	448	299	159
4,100		1352	736	449	299	159
4,300		1373	742	451	300	159

TABLE D-2F Sample Sizes for Sampling Attributes for Random Samples Only—Expected Rate of Occurrence Not over 30% or Expected Rate of Occurrence Not Less than 70%. Confidence Level 95% (Two-sided) (Continued).

Population Size	Sample Size for Precision of: ±1%	±2%	±3%	±4%	±5%	7%
4,500		1393	748	453	301	159
4,800		1420	755	456	302	160
5,000		1437	760	458	303	160
5,500		1476	771	462	305	160
6,000		1510	780	465	306	161
6,500		1539	788	468	307	161
7,000		1566	795	470	309	161
7,500		1590	801	472	309	162
8,000		1611	806	474	310	162
8,500	4139	1630	811	476	311	162
9,000	4254	1648	815	477	312	162
9,500	4363	1664	819	479	312	162
10,000	4465	1678	823	480	313	162
10,500	4562	1692	826	481	313	163
11,000	4654	1704	829	482	314	163
11,500	4741	1716	832	483	314	163
12,000	4824	1727	834	484	314	163
12,500	4903	1737	836	485	315	163
13,000	4978	1746	839	485	315	163
13,500	5050	1755	841	486	315	163
14,000	5118	1763	842	487	315	163
14,500	5184	1771	844	487	316	163
15,000	5246	1778	846	488	316	163
15,500	5306	1785	847	488	316	163
16,000	5363	1791	849	489	316	163
16,500	5418	1797	850	489	317	164
17,000	5471	1803	851	490	317	164
17,500	5522	1808	853	490	317	164
18,000	5571	1814	854	490	317	164
18,500	5618	1819	855	491	317	164
19,000	5663	1823	856	491	317	164
19,500	5707	1828	857	492	317	164
20,000	5749	1832	858	492	318	164
21,000	5828	1840	860	492	318	164
22,000	5903	1847	861	493	318	164
23,000	5972	1854	863	493	318	164
24,000	6038	1860	864	494	318	164
25,000	6099	1866	865	494	319	164
26,000	6157	1872	866	495	319	164
27,000	6211	1877	868	495	319	164
28,000	6263	1881	869	495	319	164
29,000	6312	1886	869	496	319	164
30,000	6358	1890	870	496	319	164
31,000	6401	1894	871	496	319	164
32,000	6443	1897	872	496	319	164
33,000	6483	1901	873	497	320	164
34,000	6520	1904	873	497	320	164
35,000	6556	1907	874	497	320	164
36,000	6590	1910	875	497	320	164
37,000	6623	1913	875	497	320	164
38,000	6654	1915	876	498	320	164
39,000	6685	1918	876	498	320	164

Population Size	Sample Size for Precision of: ±1%	±2%	±3%	±4%	±5%	±7%
40,000	6713	1920	877	498	320	164
41,000	6741	1922	877	498	320	164
42,000	6767	1924	878	498	320	164
43,000	6793	1926	878	498	320	165
44,000	6817	1928	878	498	320	165
45,000	6841	1930	879	499	320	165
46,000	6864	1932	879	499	320	165
47,000	6835	1934	880	499	320	165
48,000	6906	1935	880	499	321	165
49,000	6927	1937	880	499	321	165
50,000	6946	1939	881	499	321	165
55,000	7035	1945	882	500	321	165
60,000	7111	1951	883	500	321	165
65,000	7176	1956	884	500	321	165
70,000	7233	1960	885	501	321	165
75,000	7284	1964	886	501	321	165
80,000	7328	1967	886	501	321	165
85,000	7368	1970	887	501	321	165
90,000	7403	1973	888	501	322	165
95,000	7436	1975	888	502	322	165
100,000	7465	1977	888	502	322	165
105,000	7492	1979	889	502	322	165
110,000	7516	1980	889	502	322	165
115,000	7538	1982	889	502	322	165
120,000	7559	1983	890	502	322	165
130,000	7596	1986	890	502	322	165
140,000	7628	1988	891	502	322	165
150,000	7655	1990	891	503	322	165
160,000	7680	1992	891	503	322	165
170,000	7702	1993	892	503	322	165
185,000	7730	1995	892	503	322	165
200,000	7754	1997	892	503	322	165
215,000	7775	1998	893	503	322	165
225,000	7788	1999	893	503	322	165
235,000	7799	2000	893	503	322	165
250,000	7815	2001	893	503	322	165
275,000	7837	2002	893	503	322	165
300,000	7856	2003	894	503	322	165
325,000	7872	2004	894	503	322	165
350,000	7885	2005	894	503	322	165
400,000	7908	2007	894	504	322	165
450,000	7925	2008	895	504	322	165
500,000	7939	2009	895	504	322	165

TABLE D-2G Sample Sizes for Sampling Attributes for Random Samples Only—Expected Rate of Occurrence Not over 40% or Expected Rate of Occurrence Not Less than 60%. Confidence Level 95% (Two-sided).

Population Size	Sample Size for Precision of:					
	±1%	±2%	±3%	±4%	±5%	±7%
500					213	137
600				294	229	144
700				316	242	149
850				344	258	155
1,000				366	262	159
1,050			519	372	273	160
1,150			542	384	280	162
1,250			563	395	285	164
1,350			583	404	290	166
1,500			609	417	297	168
1,650			632	427	302	169
1,800			653	437	307	171
2,000			678	448	312	172
2,200			699	457	316	174
2,400		1176	718	465	320	175
2,500		1200	727	468	322	175
2,600		1222	735	472	323	176
2,700		1244	743	475	325	176
2,800		1264	750	478	326	177
2,900		1284	757	481	328	177
3,000		1304	764	484	329	178
3,200		1340	776	488	331	178
3,400		1374	787	493	333	179
3,600		1405	798	497	335	179
3,800		1435	807	500	337	180
4,000		1463	816	504	338	180
4,200		1488	824	507	340	181
4,400		1513	831	510	341	181
4,600		1536	838	512	342	181
4,800		1557	844	515	343	182
5,000		1578	850	517	344	182
5,500		1624	864	522	346	182
6,000		1665	875	526	348	183
6,500		1702	885	529	349	183
7,000		1734	894	532	351	184
7,500		1763	901	535	352	184
8,000		1790	908	538	353	184
8,500		1813	914	540	354	185
9,000		1835	920	542	355	185
9,500	4679	1855	925	543	356	185
10,000	4797	1873	929	545	356	185
10,500	4909	1890	933	546	357	185
11,000	5016	1906	937	548	357	185
11,500	5118	1920	941	549	358	186
12,000	5214	1934	944	550	358	186
12,500	5306	1946	947	551	359	186

Population Size	Sample Size for Precision of: ±1%	±2%	±3%	±4%	±5%	±7%
13,000	5394	1958	950	552	359	186
13,500	5479	1969	952	553	359	186
14,000	5559	1979	955	554	360	186
14,500	5636	1989	957	554	360	186
15,000	5710	1998	959	555	360	186
15,500	5781	2007	961	556	361	186
16,000	5850	2015	963	556	361	186
16,500	5915	2023	965	557	361	187
17,000	5978	2030	966	557	361	187
17,500	6039	2037	968	558	362	187
18,000	6097	2043	969	558	362	187
18,500	6154	2050	971	559	362	187
19,000	6208	2056	972	559	362	187
19,500	6260	2061	973	560	362	187
20,000	6311	2067	975	560	363	187
21,000	6407	2077	977	561	363	187
22,000	6497	2086	979	562	363	187
23,000	6582	2095	981	562	363	187
24,000	6661	2103	983	563	364	187
25,000	6736	2110	984	563	364	187
26,000	6807	2117	986	564	364	187
27,000	6873	2124	987	564	364	187
28,000	6936	2130	988	565	364	187
29,000	6996	2135	990	565	365	187
30,000	7053	2141	991	565	365	187
31,000	7107	2146	992	566	365	188
32,000	7158	2150	993	566	365	188
33,000	7207	2155	994	566	365	188
34,000	7253	2159	995	567	365	188
35,000	7298	2163	995	567	365	188
36,000	7340	2166	996	567	366	188
37,000	7381	2170	997	567	366	188
38,000	7420	2173	998	568	366	188
39,000	7457	2176	998	568	366	188
40,000	7493	2179	999	568	366	188
41,000	7527	2182	999	568	366	188
42,000	7560	2185	1000	568	366	188
43,000	7592	2188	1001	569	366	188
44,000	7623	2190	1001	569	366	188
45,000	7652	2193	1002	569	366	188
46,000	7681	2195	1002	569	366	188
47,000	7708	2197	1003	569	366	188
48,000	7734	2199	1003	569	366	188
49,000	7760	2201	1003	570	367	188
50,000	7785	2203	1004	570	367	188
55,000	7896	2212	1006	570	367	188
60,000	7992	2220	1007	571	367	188
65,000	8075	2226	1009	571	367	188
70,000	8147	2232	1010	572	367	188
75,000	8211	2236	1011	572	367	188

D

TABLE D-2G Sample Sizes for Sampling Attributes for Random Samples Only—Expected Rate of Occurrence Not over 40% or Expected Rate of Occurrence Not Less than 60%. Confidence Level 95% (Two-sided) (Continued).

Population Size	Sample Size for Precision of: ±1%	±2%	±3%	±4%	±5%	±7%
80,000	8267	2240	1012	572	368	188
85,000	8318	2244	1012	572	368	188
90,000	8363	2247	1013	573	368	188
95,000	8404	2250	1014	573	368	188
100,000	8442	2253	1014	573	368	188
105,000	8476	2256	1015	573	368	188
110,000	8507	2258	1015	573	368	188
115,000	8536	2260	1015	573	368	188
120,000	8562	2262	1016	574	368	188
125,000	8587	2263	1016	574	368	188
130,000	8609	2265	1016	574	368	188
135,000	8631	2266	1017	574	368	188
140,000	8651	2268	1017	574	368	188
145,000	8669	2269	1017	574	368	188
150,000	8686	2271	1018	574	368	188
155,000	8702	2271	1018	574	368	188
165,000	8732	2273	1018	574	368	188
175,000	8759	2275	1018	574	369	188
185,000	8782	2277	1019	574	369	188
195,000	8804	2278	1019	575	369	188
200,000	8814	2279	1019	575	369	188
210,000	8832	2280	1019	575	369	188
225,000	8857	2282	1020	575	369	189
240,000	8879	2283	1020	575	369	189
250,000	8892	2284	1020	575	369	189
260,000	8904	2285	1020	575	369	189
280,000	8926	2286	1021	575	369	189
300,000	8945	2288	1021	575	369	189
330.000	8969	2289	1021	575	369	189
350,000	8984	2290	1022	576	369	189
375,000	8999	2291	1022	576	369	189
400,000	9013	2292	1022	576	369	189
450,000	9035	2294	1023	576	369	189
500,000	9053	2294	1023	576	369	189

TABLE D-2H Sample Sizes for Sampling Attributes for Random Samples Only—Expected Rate of Occurrence 50%. Confidence Level 95% (Two-sided).

Population Size	±1%	±2%	±3%	±4%	±5%	±7%
			Sample Size for Precision of:			
500					217	141
600				300	234	148
700				323	248	154
800				343	260	158
950				368	274	163
1,000				375	278	164
1,100			542	389	285	167
1,200			565	400	291	169
1,300			586	411	297	171
1,400			606	420	302	172
1,500			624	429	306	174
1,550			632	433	308	174
1,700			656	444	314	176
1,850			677	453	318	178
2,100			708	467	325	180
2,300			729	476	329	181
2,500		1225	748	484	333	182
2,600		1249	757	488	335	183
2,700		1271	765	491	336	183
2,800		1293	773	494	338	184
2,900		1314	780	497	339	184
3,000		1334	787	500	341	184
3,200		1372	800	506	343	185
3,400		1407	812	510	345	186
3,600		1441	823	515	347	186
3,800		1472	833	518	349	187
4,000		1501	843	522	351	187
4,200		1528	851	525	352	188
4,400		1554	859	528	353	188
4,600		1578	866	531	355	188
4,800		1601	873	534	356	189
5,000		1622	880	536	357	189
5,500		1672	894	541	359	190
6,000		1715	906	546	361	190
6,500		1754	917	550	363	191
7,000		1788	926	553	364	191
7,500		1819	934	556	365	192
8,000		1847	942	558	367	192
8,500		1872	948	561	368	192
9,000		1896	954	563	368	192
9,500		1917	959	565	369	193
10,000	4899	1936	964	566	370	193
10,500	5016	1954	969	568	371	193
11,000	5128	1971	973	569	371	193
11,500	5234	1986	977	571	372	193
12,000	5335	2001	980	572	372	193
12,500	5431	2014	983	573	373	193
13,000	5524	2027	986	574	373	194
13,500	5612	2039	989	575	374	194

TABLE D-2H Sample Sizes for Sampling Attributes for Random Samples Only—Expected Rate of Occurrence 50%. Confidence Level 95% (Two-sided) (Continued).

Population Size	Sample Size for Precision of: ±1%	±2%	±3%	±4%	±5%	±7%
14,000	5697	2050	992	576	374	194
14,500	5778	2060	994	576	374	194
15,000	5855	2070	996	577	375	194
15,500	5930	2079	998	578	375	194
16,000	6002	2088	1000	579	375	194
16,500	6071	2096	1002	579	375	194
17,000	6137	2104	1004	580	376	194
17,500	6201	2111	1006	580	376	194
18,000	6263	2119	1007	581	376	194
18,500	6322	2125	1009	581	376	194
19,000	6380	2132	1010	582	377	194
19,500	6435	2138	1012	582	377	195
20,000	6489	2144	1013	583	377	195
21,000	6590	2155	1016	584	377	195
22,000	6686	2165	1018	584	378	195
23,000	6775	2174	1020	585	378	195
24,000	6859	2183	1022	586	378	195
25,000	6939	2191	1023	586	378	195
26,000	7014	2198	1025	587	379	195
27,000	7084	2205	1027	587	379	195
28,000	7151	2211	1028	588	379	195
29,000	7215	2217	1029	588	379	195
30,000	7275	2223	1030	588	379	195
31,000	7333	2228	1032	589	379	195
32,000	7387	2233	1033	589	380	195
33,000	7439	2238	1034	590	380	195
34,000	7489	2243	1035	590	380	195
35,000	7536	2247	1036	590	380	195
36,000	7582	2251	1036	590	380	195
37,000	7625	2255	1037	591	380	195
38,000	7667	2258	1038	591	380	195
39,000	7706	2262	1039	591	380	196
40,000	7745	2265	1039	591	381	196
41,000	7781	2268	1040	592	381	196
42,000	7817	2271	1041	592	381	196
43,000	7851	2274	1041	592	381	196
44,000	7883	2277	1042	592	381	196
45,000	7915	2279	1042	592	381	196
46,000	7945	2282	1043	593	381	196
47,000	7975	2284	1043	593	381	196
48,000	8003	2287	1044	593	381	196
49,000	8030	2289	1044	593	381	196

Population Size	Sample Size for Precision of: ±1%	±2%	±3%	±4%	±5%	±7%
50,000	8057	2291	1045	593	381	196
55,000	8176	2301	1047	594	382	196
60,000	8279	2309	1048	594	382	196
65,000	8368	2316	1050	595	382	196
70,000	8445	2321	1051	595	382	196
75,000	8514	2327	1052	595	382	196
80,000	8575	2331	1053	596	382	196
85,000	8629	2335	1054	596	382	196
90,000	8678	2339	1055	596	383	196
95,000	8722	2342	1055	596	383	196
100,000	8763	2345	1056	597	383	196
105,000	8799	2347	1056	597	383	196
110,000	8833	2350	1057	597	383	196
115,000	8864	2352	1057	597	383	196
120,000	8892	2354	1058	597	383	196
125,000	8919	2356	1058	597	383	196
130,000	8943	2357	1058	597	383	196
135,000	8966	2359	1059	598	383	196
140,000	8988	2361	1059	598	383	196
150,000	9026	2363	1060	598	383	196
160,000	9060	2366	1060	598	383	196
170,000	9090	2368	1060	598	383	196
180,000	9118	2369	1061	598	383	196
190,000	9142	2371	1061	598	383	196
200,000	9164	2373	1061	598	383	196
210,000	9184	2374	1062	599	383	196
225,000	9211	2376	1062	599	384	196
240,000	9235	2377	1062	599	384	196
250,000	9249	2378	1063	599	384	196
275,000	9280	2380	1063	599	384	196
300,000	9306	2382	1063	599	384	196
325,000	9328	2383	1064	599	384	196
350,000	9348	2385	1064	599	384	196
375,000	9364	2386	1064	599	384	196
400,000	9379	2387	1064	599	384	196
450,000	9403	2388	1065	599	384	196
500,000	9423	2390	1065	600	384	196

D

TABLE D-3A Sample Sizes for Sampling Attributes for Random Samples Only—Expected Rate of Occurrence Not over 2% or Expected Rate of Occurrence Not Less than 98%. Confidence Level 99% (Two-sided).

Population Size	Sample Size for Precision of: ±.5%	±.75%	±1%	±1.25%	±1.5%	±2%
400						180
450						189
500						197
550						205
600					295	211
650					306	217

TABLE D-3A Sample Sizes for Sampling Attributes for Random Samples Only—Expected Rate of Occurrence Not over 2% or Expected Rate of Occurrence Not Less than 98%. Confidence Level 99% (Two-sided) (Continued).

Population Size	±.5%	±.75%	±1%	±1.25%	±1.5%	±2%
700					317	222
750					327	227
800				408	336	232
850				421	344	236
900				433	352	239
950				444	360	243
1,000				455	367	246
1,050				465	373	249
1,100				474	379	251
1,150				483	385	254
1,200				492	390	256
1,250				500	396	258
1,300			650	508	400	260
1,350			663	515	405	262
1,400			674	522	409	264
1,450			686	529	414	266
1,500			697	536	418	268
1,550			707	542	421	269
1,600			718	548	425	271
1,650			728	553	428	272
1,700			737	559	432	273
1,750			746	564	435	275
1,800			755	569	438	276
1,850			764	574	441	277
1,900			772	579	443	278
1,950			780	584	446	279
2,000			788	587	449	280
2,100			803	596	453	282
2,200			818	604	458	284
2,300		1153	831	611	462	285
2,400		1178	844	618	466	287
2,500		1201	856	625	470	288
2,600		1224	867	631	473	289
2,700		1246	878	636	476	291
2,800		1266	888	642	479	292
2,900		1286	898	647	482	293
3,000		1306	907	652	485	294
3,100		1324	916	656	487	295
3,200		1342	925	661	490	295
3,300		1359	933	665	492	296
3,400		1376	941	669	494	297
3,500		1392	948	673	496	298
3,600		1408	955	676	498	299
3,700		1423	962	680	500	299
3,800		1437	969	683	502	300
3,900		1451	975	686	504	300
4,000		1465	981	689	505	301
4,100		1478	987	692	507	302
4,200		1491	993	695	508	302
4,300		1503	999	697	510	303
4,400		1515	1004	700	511	303

Population Size	Sample Size for Precision of: ±.5%	±.75%	±1%	±1.25%	±1.5%	±2%
4,500		1527	1009	702	512	304
4,600		1538	1014	705	514	304
4,700		1549	1019	707	515	304
4,800		1560	1023	709	516	305
4,900		1571	1028	712	517	305
5,000		1581	1032	714	518	306
5,500	2673	1627	1052	723	523	307
6,000	2786	1669	1069	731	527	309
6,500	2889	1705	1084	738	531	310
7,000	2984	1738	1097	744	534	311
7,500	3071	1767	1108	749	537	312
8,000	3151	1793	1118	754	539	313
8,500	3226	1817	1128	758	541	313
9,000	3296	1839	1136	762	543	314
9,500	3360	1859	1144	765	545	315
10,000	3421	1877	1151	768	547	315
10,500	3477	1894	1157	771	548	316
11,000	3531	1910	1162	774	549	316
11,500	3581	1924	1168	776	550	316
12,000	3628	1938	1173	778	552	317
12,500	3672	1950	1178	780	553	317
13,000	3714	1962	1182	782	554	317
13,500	3753	1973	1185	784	554	318
14,000	3792	1984	1190	786	555	318
14,500	3827	1992	1193	787	556	318
15,000	3861	2003	1197	789	557	319
15,500	3894	2011	1200	790	557	319
16,000	3924	2019	1202	791	558	319
16,500	3953	2027	1205	792	559	319
17,000	3982	2034	1208	793	559	319
17,500	4008	2041	1210	795	560	319
18,000	4034	2048	1213	796	560	320
18,500	4059	2054	1215	796	561	320
19,000	4082	2060	1217	797	561	320
19,500	4104	2066	1219	798	561	320
20,000	4126	2072	1221	799	562	320
21,000	4167	2082	1224	801	563	320
22,000	4205	2091	1228	802	564	321
23,000	4241	2100	1231	803	565	321
24,000	4273	2108	1233	804	565	321
25,000	4304	2115	1236	805	565	321
26,000	4333	2122	1238	806	566	321
27,000	4360	2129	1240	807	566	322
28,000	4385	2135	1242	808	566	322
29,000	4409	2140	1244	809	567	322
30,000	4431	2146	1246	810	567	322
31,000	4453	2151	1248	811	568	322
32,000	4473	2155	1249	811	568	322
34,000	4510	2164	1252	812	568	322
36,000	4543	2172	1255	813	569	322
38,000	4573	2178	1257	814	569	323
40,000	4601	2185	1259	815	570	323
42,000	4627	2190	1261	816	570	323
44,000	4650	2196	1263	817	570	323
46,000	4670	2200	1264	817	571	323
48,000	4691	2205	1266	818	571	323

D

TABLE D-3A Sample Sizes for Sampling Attributes for Random Samples Only—Expected Rate of Occurrence Not over 2% or Expected Rate of Occurrence Not Less than 98%. Confidence Level 99% (Two-sided) (Continued).

Population Size	Sample Size for Precision of: ±.5%	±.75%	±1%	±1.25%	±1.5%	±2%
50,000	4709	2209	1267	819	572	323
55,000	4751	2218	1270	820	572	323
60,000	4784	2225	1273	821	573	324
65,000	4814	2232	1275	822	573	324
70,000	4839	2237	1276	822	573	324
75,000	4862	2242	1278	823	574	324
80,000	4883	2246	1279	824	574	324
90,000	4916	2253	1282	825	574	324
100,000	4942	2259	1283	825	575	324
110,000	4965	2263	1285	826	575	324
125,000	4991	2269	1287	827	575	325
140,000	5012	2273	1288	827	576	325
150,000	5025	2276	1289	828	576	325
175,000	5049	2281	1291	828	576	325
200,000	5067	2285	1292	829	576	325
250,000	5093	2290	1293	829	577	325
300,000	5110	2293	1294	830	577	325
350,000	5122	2296	1295	830	577	325
400,000	5132	2298	1296	831	577	325
450,000	5140	2299	1296	831	577	325
500,000	5145	2300	1297	831	577	325

TABLE D-3B Sample Sizes for Sampling Attributes for Random Samples Only—Expected Rate of Occurrence Not over 5% or Expected Rate of Occurrence Not Less than 95%. Confidence Level 99% (Two-sided).

Population Size	Sample Size for Precision of: ±.5%	±1%	±1.5%	±2%	±2.5%	±3%	±4%
200							99
250							110
300							119
350						175	126
400						187	132
450						197	137
500						206	142
550					263	214	145
600					274	221	148
650					284	228	151
700					293	234	154
750					302	239	156
800				397	310	244	158
850				409	318	248	160
900				420	324	252	162
950				431	330	256	163
1,000				441	336	260	165

Population Size	Sample Size for Precision of:						
	±.5%	±1%	±1.5%	±2%	±2.5%	±3%	±4%
1,050				450	341	263	166
1,100				459	346	266	167
1,150				468	351	269	168
1,200				476	355	271	169
1,250				484	360	274	170
1,300				491	364	276	171
1,350				498	367	278	172
1,400			700	504	371	280	173
1,450			713	511	374	282	174
1,500			725	517	378	284	174
1,550			736	523	381	286	175
1,600			747	528	384	287	176
1,650			758	534	387	289	176
1,700			768	539	389	291	177
1,750			778	544	392	292	177
1,800			788	548	394	293	178
1,850			797	553	397	295	178
1,900			806	557	399	296	179
1,950			860	561	401	297	179
2,000			824	565	403	298	179
2,100			840	573	407	300	180
2,200			856	580	411	302	181
2,300			871	587	414	304	182
2,400			885	593	417	306	182
2,500			898	599	420	307	183
2,600			910	605	423	309	183
2,700			922	610	425	310	184
2,800			934	615	428	311	184
2,900			947	620	430	313	185
3,000			955	624	432	314	185
3,100			965	628	434	315	185
3,200		1588	974	632	436	316	186
3,300		1612	983	636	438	317	186
3,400		1636	993	640	439	318	186
3,500		1659	1000	643	441	318	187
3,600		1681	1008	647	443	319	187
3,700		1702	1016	650	444	320	187
3,800		1723	1023	653	445	321	187
3,900		1743	1031	656	447	321	188
4,000		1763	1037	658	448	322	188
4,200		1801	1050	664	450	323	188
4,400		1837	1062	668	452	324	189
4,600		1871	1074	673	455	326	189
4,800		1903	1084	677	457	326	189
5,000		1934	1094	681	458	327	190
5,500		2004	1116	689	462	329	190
6,000		2067	1136	697	465	331	191
6,500		2123	1152	703	468	332	191
7,000		2174	1167	708	471	334	192
7,500		2220	1180	713	473	335	192
8,000		2261	1192	717	475	336	192
8,500		2300	1202	721	476	336	193
9,000		2335	1212	725	478	337	193
9,500		2367	1221	728	479	338	193
10,000		2397	1228	731	480	338	193
10,500		2424	1236	733	481	339	193
11,000		2450	1242	735	482	339	194
11,500		2474	1248	738	483	340	194

D

TABLE D-3B Sample Sizes for Sampling Attributes for Random Samples Only—Expected Rate of Occurrence Not over 5% or Expected Rate of Occurrence Not Less than 95%. Confidence Level 99% (Two-sided) (Continued).

Population Size	±.5%	±1%	±1.5%	±2%	±2.5%	±3%	±4%
	Sample Size for Precision of:						
12,000		2496	1254	740	484	340	194
12,500	6274	2517	1259	741	485	341	194
13,000	6398	2537	1264	743	486	341	194
14,000	6631	2573	1273	746	487	342	194
15,000	6847	2605	1281	749	488	342	194
16,000	7050	2633	1288	751	489	343	195
17,000	7236	2659	1294	753	490	343	195
18,000	7411	2682	1299	755	491	344	195
19,000	7575	2704	1304	757	491	344	195
20,000	7730	2721	1309	758	492	344	195
21,000	7874	2741	1313	760	493	344	195
23,000	8141	2772	1320	762	494	345	195
25,000	8377	2799	1326	764	494	345	195
27,000	8592	2823	1331	766	495	346	196
29,000	8783	2843	1336	767	496	346	196
30,000	8873	2851	1338	768	496	346	196
32,000	9041	2869	1342	769	497	346	196
35,000	9264	2892	1346	771	497	347	196
38,000	9462	2909	1351	772	498	347	196
40,000	9581	2920	1353	773	498	347	196
43,000	9745	2937	1356	774	498	347	196
45,000	9843	2944	1358	774	499	348	196
48,000	9980	2958	1361	775	499	348	196
50,000	10063	2963	1362	776	499	348	196
55,000	10250	2981	1366	777	500	348	196
65,000	10552	3006	1371	779	501	348	196
80,000	10884	3033	1376	780	501	349	197
100,000	11189	3056	1381	782	502	349	197
130,000	11487	3077	1385	783	502	349	197
150,000	11623	3085	1387	784	503	349	197
180,000	11775	3098	1389	785	503	350	197
200,000	11852	3101	1391	785	503	350	197
250,000	11994	3111	1393	785	503	350	197
375,000	12189	3124	1395	786	504	350	197
500,000	12289	3132	1396	787	504	350	197

TABLE D-3C Sample Sizes for Sampling Attributes for Random Samples Only—Expected Rate of Occurrence Not over 10% or Expected Rate of Occurrence Not Less than 90%. Confidence Level 99% (Two-sided).

Population Size	±.5%	±1%	±1.5%	±2%	±2.5%	±3%	±4%
	Sample Size for Precision of:						
400							193
450							204
500							214
550							223
600							230
650							237

Population Size	Sample Size for Precision of: ±.5%	±1%	±1.5%	±2%	±2.5%	±3%	±4%
700						341	244
750						352	249
800						363	255
850						373	260
900						382	264
950						391	268
1,000					489	399	272
1,050					501	407	276
1,100					512	414	279
1,150					522	421	282
1,200					532	428	285
1,250					542	434	288
1,300					551	440	290
1,350					560	445	293
1,400					568	450	295
1,450					576	455	297
1,500				748	584	460	299
1,550				761	591	465	301
1,600				773	598	469	303
1,650				784	605	473	305
1,700				795	612	477	306
1,750				806	618	481	308
1,800				816	624	485	309
1,850				826	630	489	311
1,900				836	636	492	312
1,950				846	641	495	313
2,000				855	647	498	315
2,100				873	657	504	317
2,200				890	666	510	319
2,300				906	675	515	321
2,400				921	684	520	323
2,500				935	691	525	325
2,600				949	699	529	327
2,700			1338	962	706	533	328
2,800			1363	974	713	537	329
2,900			1386	986	719	540	331
3,000			1407	997	725	544	332
3,100			1430	1008	730	547	333
3,200			1451	1018	736	550	334
3,300			1471	1028	741	553	335
3,400			1490	1038	746	555	336
3,500			1508	1047	751	558	337
3,600			1528	1056	755	560	338
3,700			1545	1064	759	563	339
3,800			1563	1072	764	565	340
3,900			1579	1080	768	567	341
4,000			1595	1087	771	569	341
4,100			1611	1095	775	571	342
4,200			1626	1102	778	573	343
4,300			1641	1108	782	575	344
4,400			1655	1115	785	577	344
4,500			1669	1121	788	578	345
4,600			1683	1127	791	580	345
4,700			1696	1133	794	582	346
4,800			1709	1139	797	583	346
4,900			1721	1145	800	585	347
5,000			1733	1150	802	586	347

D

TABLE D-3C Sample Sizes for Sampling Attributes for Random Samples Only—Expected Rate of Occurrence Not over 10% or Expected Rate of Occurrence Not Less than 90%. Confidence Level 99% (Two-sided) (Continued).

Population Size	Sample Size for Precision of: ±.5%	±1%	±1.5%	±2%	±2.5%	±3%	±4%
5,500			1790	1174	814	592	350
6,000		2993	1840	1196	824	598	351
6,500		3113	1884	1214	833	602	353
7,000		3223	1924	1231	841	606	354
7,500		3325	1960	1245	847	610	356
8,000		3420	1992	1258	854	613	357
8,500		3508	2022	1270	859	616	358
9,000		3590	2049	1281	864	618	358
9,500		3667	2074	1290	868	620	359
10,000		3739	2097	1299	872	622	360
10,500		3807	2118	1307	876	624	360
11,000		3871	2137	1315	879	626	361
11,500		3931	2156	1322	882	627	362
12,000		3988	2173	1328	885	629	362
12,500		4041	2189	1334	888	630	362
13,000		4092	2195	1339	890	631	363
13,500		4141	2217	1334	892	633	363
14,000		4186	2230	1349	894	634	364
14,500		4230	2243	1354	896	635	364
15,000		4272	2254	1358	898	635	364
15,500		4311	2265	1362	900	636	364
16,000		4349	2276	1366	902	637	365
16,500		4385	2285	1369	903	638	365
17,000		4420	2295	1373	905	639	365
17.500		4453	2304	1376	906	639	365
18,000		4484	2312	1379	907	640	366
18,500		4515	2320	1382	908	641	366
19,000		4544	2328	1384	910	641	366
19,500		4572	2335	1387	911	642	366
20,000		4599	2342	1389	912	642	366
21,000		4650	2355	1394	914	643	367
22,000		4697	2367	1398	916	644	367
23,000	11713	4741	2378	1402	917	645	367
24,000	11969	4782	2389	1406	919	646	368
25,000	12212	4821	2398	1409	920	646	368
26,000	12446	4857	2407	1412	921	647	368
27,000	12670	4890	2416	1415	923	648	368
28,000	12887	4922	2423	1417	924	648	368
29,000	13093	4952	2430	1420	925	649	369
30,000	13294	4981	2437	1422	926	649	369
31,000	13487	5007	2443	1424	927	650	369
32,000	13672	5033	2450	1426	928	650	369
33,000	13853	5057	2455	1428	928	650	369
34,000	14025	5080	2461	1430	929	651	369
35,000	14192	5102	2466	1432	930	651	369
36,000	14352	5122	2471	1434	931	652	369
37,000	14510	5142	2475	1435	931	652	370
39,000	14808	5179	2484	1438	931	652	370
40,000	14950	5193	2488	1439	933	653	370
41,000	15085	5213	2492	1441	934	653	370
43,000	15349	5244	2499	1443	935	653	370
45,000	15598	5272	2505	1445	935	654	370

Population Size	±.5%	±1%	±1.5%	±2%	±2.5%	±3%	±4%
	Sample Size for Precision of:						
47,000	15830	5299	2511	1447	936	654	370
49,000	16051	5323	2517	1449	937	655	370
50,000	16157	5332	2519	1450	937	655	371
55,000	16646	5387	2531	1454	939	656	371
60,000	17075	5431	2540	1457	940	656	371
65,000	17460	5470	2549	1459	941	657	371
70,000	17798	5503	2556	1462	942	657	371
75,000	18106	5532	2562	1464	943	658	371
80,000	18385	5557	2568	1466	944	658	372
85,000	18637	5580	2573	1467	945	658	372
90,000	18867	5600	2577	1469	945	659	372
100,000	19269	5636	2584	1471	946	659	372
110,000	19618	5665	2590	1473	947	660	372
120,000	19912	5689	2595	1475	948	660	372
130,000	20100	5710	2599	1476	948	660	372
150,000	20594	5740	2607	1478	949	661	372
160,000	20772	5757	2609	1479	950	661	372
180,000	21072	5780	2614	1481	950	661	372
200,000	21326	5795	2618	1481	951	661	373
250,000	21790	5829	2625	1484	952	662	373
300,000	22111	5852	2630	1485	952	662	373
350,000	22347	5868	2633	1486	953	662	373
400,000	22526	5880	2635	1487	953	662	373
500,000	22786	5902	2639	1489	953	663	373

D

TABLE D-3D Sample Sizes for Sampling Attributes for Random Samples Only—Expected Rate of Occurrence Not over 15% or Expected Rate of Occurrence Not Less than 85%. Confidence Level 99% (Two-sided).

Population Size	±1%	±1.5%	±2%	±2.5%	±3%	±3.5%	±4%
	Sample Size for Precision of:						
550							270
600							281
650							292
700						348	301
750						360	310
800						371	319
850						381	326
900						391	333
950					473	400	340
1,000					485	409	346
1,050					496	417	352
1,100					507	425	357
1,150					518	432	362
1,200					527	439	367
1,250					537	445	372
1,300					546	451	376
1,350					554	457	380
1,400				688	563	463	384
1,450				695	571	468	388
1,500				712	578	473	391
1,550				723	585	478	394
1,600				733	592	483	398
1,650				744	599	487	401

TABLE D-3D Sample Sizes for Sampling Attributes for Random Samples Only—Expected Rate of Occurrence Not over 15% or Expected Rate of Occurrence Not Less than 85%. Confidence Level 99% (Two-sided) (Continued).

Population Size	Sample Size for Precision of: ±1%	±1.5%	±2%	±2.5%	±3%	±3.5%	±4%
1,700				754	606	491	404
1,750				763	612	495	406
1,800				773	618	499	409
1,850				782	624	503	411
1,900				791	629	507	414
1,950				799	635	510	416
2,000				807	640	514	418
2,100				823	650	520	423
2,200			1079	838	659	526	426
2,300			1102	852	668	531	430
2,400			1125	866	676	536	433
2,500			1146	878	683	541	437
2,600			1167	890	691	546	440
2,700			1186	902	698	551	442
2,800			1205	913	704	554	445
2,900			1223	923	710	558	447
3,000			1241	933	716	562	450
3,100			1258	942	722	565	452
3,200			1274	951	727	568	454
3,300			1289	960	732	571	456
3,400			1304	968	737	574	458
3,500			1319	976	741	577	460
3,600			1333	984	746	580	461
3,700			1346	991	750	582	463
3,800		1890	1359	998	754	585	464
3,900		1914	1372	1005	758	587	466
4,000		1938	1384	1011	761	589	467
4,100		1962	1396	1018	765	591	469
4,200		1984	1407	1024	768	593	470
4,300		2006	1418	1029	772	595	471
4,400		2027	1429	1035	775	597	472
4,500		2048	1439	1041	778	599	473
4,600		2069	1449	1046	781	601	474
4,700		2089	1459	1051	784	602	475
4,800		2108	1468	1056	786	604	476
4,900		2127	1478	1061	789	605	477
5,000		2146	1487	1065	791	607	478
5,500		2233	1528	1086	803	614	483
6,000		2311	1564	1104	813	619	486
6,500		2382	1596	1120	821	624	489
7,000		2445	1625	1134	829	629	492
7,500		2504	1650	1146	835	632	494
8,000		2557	1673	1158	841	636	496
8,500	4240	2606	1694	1167	847	639	498
9,000	4361	2651	1713	1176	851	641	500
9,500	4475	2693	1730	1185	856	644	501
10,000	4583	2732	1746	1192	859	646	502
10,500	4686	2768	1761	1199	863	648	504
11,000	4783	2801	1774	1205	866	650	505
11,500	4875	2833	1787	1211	869	652	506
12,000	4962	2862	1798	1216	872	653	507
12,500	5046	2889	1809	1221	874	655	507

Population Size	±1%	±1.5%	±2%	±2.5%	±3%	±3.5%	±4%
13,000	5125	2915	1819	1226	877	656	508
13,500	5201	2940	1829	1230	879	657	509
14,000	5274	2963	1838	1234	881	658	510
14,500	5343	2985	1846	1238	883	659	510
15,000	5410	3005	1854	1241	885	660	511
15,500	5474	3025	1861	1245	886	661	511
16,000	5535	3043	1868	1248	888	662	512
16,500	5593	3061	1875	1251	889	663	512
17,000	5650	3078	1881	1253	891	664	513
17,500	5704	3094	1887	1256	892	664	513
18,000	5756	3109	1893	1259	893	665	514
18,500	5806	3124	1898	1261	895	666	514
19,000	5854	3137	1903	1263	896	666	515
19,500	5901	3151	1908	1265	897	667	515
20,000	5946	3164	1913	1267	898	668	515
21,000	6031	3188	1922	1271	900	669	516
22,000	6111	3210	1930	1275	902	670	516
23,000	6186	3230	1937	1278	903	671	517
24,000	6256	3249	1944	1281	905	671	517
25,000	6322	3267	1950	1284	906	672	518
26,000	6384	3283	1956	1286	907	673	518
27,000	6442	3299	1962	1289	909	673	519
28,000	6498	3313	1967	1291	910	674	519
29,000	6550	3327	1972	1293	911	675	519
30,000	6600	3340	1976	1295	912	675	520
31,000	6647	3352	1980	1297	912	676	520
32,000	6692	3363	1984	1298	913	676	520
33,000	6735	3374	1988	1300	914	676	520
34,000	6775	3384	1991	1301	915	677	521
35,000	6814	3394	1995	1303	916	677	521
36,000	6851	3403	1998	1304	916	678	521
37,000	6886	3411	2001	1305	917	678	521
38,000	6920	3420	2004	1307	917	678	522
39,000	6953	3428	2006	1308	918	679	522
40,000	6984	3435	2009	1309	919	679	522
41,000	7014	3442	2012	1310	919	679	522
42,000	7042	3449	2014	1311	920	679	522
43,000	7070	3456	2016	1312	920	680	522
44,000	7097	3462	2018	1313	920	680	523
45,000	7122	3468	2020	1314	921	680	523
46,000	7147	3474	2022	1315	921	680	523
47,000	7170	3480	2024	1315	922	681	523
48,000	7193	3485	2026	1316	922	681	523
49,000	7215	3490	2028	1317	922	681	523
50,000	7237	3495	2029	1318	923	681	523
55,000	7333	3518	2037	1321	924	682	524
60,000	7415	3536	2043	1323	926	683	524
65,000	7487	3552	2049	1326	927	683	525
70,000	7549	3566	2053	1327	928	684	525
75,000	7603	3579	2057	1329	928	684	525
80,000	7652	3589	2061	1331	929	685	525
85,000	7695	3599	2064	1332	930	685	526
90,000	7734	3607	2067	1333	930	685	526
95,000	7769	3615	2069	1334	931	686	526

D

TABLE D-3D Sample Sizes for Sampling Attributes for Random Samples Only—Expected Rate of Occurrence Not over 15% or Expected Rate of Occurrence Not Less than 85%. Confidence Level 99% (Two-sided) (Continued).

Population Size	Sample Size for Precision of: ±1%	±1.5%	±2%	±2.5%	±3%	±3.5%	±4%
100,000	7801	3622	2071	1335	931	686	526
105,000	7830	3628	2073	1336	932	686	526
110,000	7857	3634	2075	1337	932	686	526
115,000	7881	3639	2077	1337	932	687	526
120,000	7904	3644	2079	1338	933	687	526
125,000	7925	3648	2080	1339	933	687	527
135,000	7962	3656	2083	1340	934	687	527
145,000	7995	3663	2085	1341	934	687	527
150,000	8009	3666	2086	1341	934	687	527
155,000	8023	3669	2087	1341	934	688	527
165,000	8048	3674	2088	1342	935	688	527
175,000	8071	3679	2090	1343	935	688	527
185,000	8091	3683	2091	1343	935	688	527
200,000	8118	3689	2093	1344	936	688	527
215,000	8141	3693	2095	1345	936	688	528
230,000	8161	3697	2096	1345	936	689	528
250,000	8184	3702	2098	1346	937	689	528
270,000	8204	3706	2099	1346	937	689	528
300,000	8229	3711	2100	1347	937	689	528
325,000	8246	3715	2102	1348	937	689	528
350,000	8261	3718	2103	1348	938	689	528
400,000	8286	3723	2104	1349	938	689	528
450,000	8305	3727	2105	1349	938	690	528
500,000	8320	3730	2106	1349	938	690	528

TABLE D-3E Sample Sizes for Sampling Attributes for Random Samples Only—Expected Rate of Occurrence Not over 20% or Expected Rate of Occurrence Not Less than 80%. Confidence Level 99% (Two-sided).

Population Size	Sample Size for Precision of: ±1%	±1.5%	±2%	±2.5%	±3%	±4%	±5%
450							219
500							230
550							240
600							249
650							257
700						341	265
750						352	271
800						363	278
850						373	283
900						382	289
950						391	294
1,000						399	298
1,050						407	303
1,100						414	307
1,150						421	310
1,200					595	428	314
1,250					607	434	317

Population Size	Sample Size for Precision of: ±1%	±1.5%	±2%	±2.5%	±3%	±4%	±5%
1,300					619	440	320
1,350					630	445	323
1,400					640	450	326
1,450					651	455	329
1,500					661	460	331
1,550					670	465	334
1,600					679	469	336
1,650					688	473	338
1,700				850	697	477	340
1,750				862	705	481	342
1,800				874	713	485	344
1,850				886	721	489	346
1,900				897	728	492	347
1,950				908	735	495	349
2,000				919	742	498	350
2,100				939	756	504	353
2,200				959	768	510	356
2,300				977	780	515	359
2,400				995	791	520	361
2,500				1011	802	525	363
2,600				1027	812	529	365
2,700			1339	1043	821	533	367
2,800			1363	1057	830	537	369
2,900			1386	1071	839	540	371
3,000			1409	1085	847	544	372
3,100			1430	1097	855	547	374
3,200			1451	1110	862	550	375
3,300			1471	1121	869	553	376
3,400			1491	1133	876	555	378
3,500			1510	1144	882	558	379
3,600			1528	1154	889	560	380
3,700			1546	1164	895	563	381
3,800			1563	1174	900	565	382
3,900			1580	1183	906	567	383
4,000			1596	1192	911	569	384
4,100			1611	1201	916	571	385
4,200			1627	1209	921	573	386
4,300			1641	1218	926	575	387
4,400			1656	1225	930	577	387
4,500			1670	1233	935	578	388
4,600			1683	1240	939	580	389
4,700		2354	1697	1248	943	582	390
4,800		2379	1709	1254	947	583	390
4,900		2403	1722	1261	951	585	391
5,000		2427	1734	1268	955	586	392
5,500		2539	1790	1298	971	592	394
6,000		2641	1840	1324	986	598	397
6,500		2733	1885	1346	999	602	399
7,000		2818	1925	1367	1010	606	400
7,500		2896	1961	1385	1019	610	402
8,000		2967	1993	1401	1028	613	403
8,500		3033	2023	1415	1036	616	405
9,000		3095	2050	1429	1043	618	406
9,500		3152	2075	1441	1049	620	407
10,000		3204	2098	1452	1055	622	407

TABLE D-3E Sample Sizes for Sampling Attributes for Random Samples Only—Expected Rate of Occurrence Not over 20% or Expected Rate of Occurrence Not Less than 80%. Confidence Level 99% (Two-sided) (Continued).

Population Size	Sample Size for Precision of: ±1%	±1.5%	±2%	±2.5%	±3%	±4%	±5%
10,500		3254	2119	1462	1061	624	408
11,000	5403	3301	2138	1471	1065	626	409
11,500	5521	3345	2157	1480	1070	627	410
12,000	5633	3386	2174	1488	1074	629	410
12,500	5741	3424	2190	1495	1078	630	411
13,000	5844	3461	2204	1502	1082	631	411
13,500	5943	3495	2218	1508	1085	633	412
14,000	6038	3530	2231	1515	1088	634	412
14,500	6129	3559	2244	1520	1091	635	413
15,000	6217	3588	2255	1525	1094	635	413
15,500	6301	3616	2266	1530	1096	636	413
16,000	6382	3642	2277	1535	1099	637	414
16,500	6460	3668	2287	1540	1101	638	414
17,000	6536	3692	2296	1544	1103	639	414
17,500	6608	3715	2305	1548	1105	639	415
18,000	6678	3737	2313	1552	1107	640	415
18,500	6746	3758	2321	1555	1109	641	415
19,000	6811	3778	2329	1559	1111	641	415
19,500	6874	3797	2336	1562	1112	642	416
20,000	6936	3816	2343	1565	1114	642	416
21,000	7052	3851	2357	1571	1117	643	416
22,000	7161	3883	2369	1576	1120	644	417
23,000	7264	3913	2380	1581	1122	645	417
24,000	7361	3941	2390	1586	1124	646	417
25,000	7452	3967	2400	1590	1127	646	418
26,000	7539	3992	2408	1594	1129	647	418
27,000	7621	4015	2417	1598	1130	648	418
28,000	7698	4036	2425	1601	1132	648	418
29,000	7772	4056	2432	1604	1134	649	419
30,000	7842	4075	2439	1607	1135	649	419
31,000	7909	4093	2445	1610	1136	650	419
32,000	7972	4110	2451	1612	1138	650	419
33,000	8033	4126	2457	1615	1139	651	419
34,000	8091	4141	2462	1618	1140	651	419
35,000	8146	4156	2467	1619	1141	651	420
36,000	8199	4170	2472	1622	1142	652	420
37,000	8250	4183	2477	1623	1143	652	420
38,000	8299	4195	2481	1625	1144	652	420
39,000	8345	4207	2485	1627	1145	652	420
40,000	8390	4218	2489	1629	1146	653	420
42,000	8475	4240	2497	1632	1147	653	420
44,000	8553	4259	2503	1635	1149	654	421
46,000	8626	4277	2510	1638	1150	654	421
48,000	8694	4294	2515	1640	1151	655	421
50,000	8758	4309	2520	1642	1152	655	421
55,000	8899	4343	2532	1647	1155	656	421
60,000	9021	4372	2542	1651	1157	656	422
65,000	9126	4397	2550	1655	1159	657	422
70,000	9219	4418	2557	1658	1160	657	422
75,000	9301	4437	2564	1660	1161	658	422
80,000	9373	4453	2569	1663	1163	658	422
85,000	9438	4468	2574	1665	1164	658	423
90,000	9497	4481	2578	1667	1164	659	423

Population Size	±1%	±1.5%	±2%	±2.5%	±3%	±4%	±5%
100,000	9598	4503	2586	1670	1166	659	423
110,000	9683	4522	2592	1672	1167	660	423
120,000	9754	4537	2597	1674	1168	660	423
130,000	9815	4551	2601	1676	1169	660	423
140,000	9869	4562	2605	1678	1170	660	423
150,000	9915	4572	2608	1679	1170	661	423
160,000	9956	4581	2611	1680	1171	661	424
180,000	10026	4595	2616	1682	1172	661	424
200,000	10082	4607	2619	1684	1173	661	424
210,000	10106	4612	2621	1684	1173	661	424
220,000	10128	4617	2623	1685	1173	662	424
230,000	10149	4621	2624	1686	1174	662	424
245,000	10176	4627	2626	1686	1174	662	424
260,000	10201	4632	2627	1687	1174	662	424
275,000	10222	4636	2629	1688	1175	662	424
290,000	10242	4640	2630	1688	1175	662	424
300,000	10254	4643	2631	1688	1175	662	424
310,000	10265	4645	2632	1689	1175	662	424
330,000	10286	4649	2633	1689	1175	662	424
350,000	10304	4653	2634	1690	1176	662	424
375,000	10325	4657	2636	1690	1176	662	424
400,000	10343	4661	2637	1691	1176	662	424
450,000	10372	4667	2639	1692	1177	663	424
500,000	10396	4672	2640	1692	1177	663	424

D

TABLE D-3F Sample Sizes for Sampling Attributes for Random Samples Only—Expected Rate of Occurrence Not over 30% or Expected Rate of Occurrence Not Less than 70%. Confidence Level 99% (Two-sided).

Population Size	±1%	±2%	±3%	±4%	±5%	±7%
600					289	193
700					311	203
800					329	210
900					344	216
950				455	352	219
1,050				476	364	224
1,150				496	376	228
1,300				522	390	234
1,450				544	403	238
1,500				551	407	239
1,600			787	564	414	242
1,700			811	576	420	244
1,800			833	587	426	246
1,900			853	597	431	248
2,000			873	607	436	249
2,200			909	624	445	252
2,400			941	639	452	255
2,600			971	653	459	257
2,800			997	664	465	258

TABLE D-3F Sample Sizes for Sampling Attributes for Random Samples Only—Expected Rate of Occurrence Not over 30% or Expected Rate of Occurrence Not Less than 70%. Confidence Level 99% (Two-sided) (Continued).

Population Size	Sample Size for Precision of: ±1%	±2%	±3%	±4%	±5%	±7%
3,000			1021	675	470	260
3,200			1044	685	475	261
3,400			1064	693	479	263
3,500		1746	1074	698	481	263
3,600		1771	1083	701	483	264
3,700		1795	1092	705	485	264
3,800		1818	1100	709	486	265
3,900		1840	1109	712	488	265
4,000		1862	1116	715	489	266
4,100		1884	1124	718	491	266
4,200		1904	1131	721	492	267
4,300		1925	1139	724	494	267
4,400		1945	1145	727	495	267
4,500		1964	1152	730	496	268
4,600		1983	1159	732	497	268
4,800		2019	1171	737	499	269
5,000		2053	1182	742	502	269
5,500		2133	1208	752	506	271
6,000		2204	1231	761	510	272
6,500		2268	1251	768	513	273
7,000		2326	1268	775	516	274
7,500		2379	1284	780	519	274
8,000		2427	1297	786	521	275
8,500		2471	1310	790	523	275
9,000		2512	1321	794	525	276
9,500		2549	1331	798	527	276
10,000		2584	1341	801	528	277
10,500		2616	1349	804	529	277
11,000		2646	1357	807	531	278
11,500		2674	1365	810	532	278
12,000		2700	1371	812	533	278
12,500		2725	1378	814	534	278
13,000		2748	1384	816	535	279
13,500		2769	1389	818	535	279
14,000	6984	2790	1394	820	536	279
14,500	7106	2809	1399	822	537	279
15,000	7224	2827	1404	823	537	279
15,500	7338	2845	1408	825	538	280
16,000	7448	2861	1412	826	539	280
16,500	7555	2877	1416	827	539	280
17,000	7658	2891	1419	829	540	280
17,500	7758	2906	1423	830	540	280
18,000	7855	2919	1426	831	541	280
18,500	7948	2932	1429	832	541	280
19,000	8039	2944	1432	833	542	280
19,500	8127	2956	1435	834	542	281

Population Size	Sample Size for Precision of: ±1%	±2%	±3%	±4%	±5%	±7%
20,000	8213	2967	1437	835	542	281
21,000	8377	2988	1442	836	543	281
22,000	8531	3008	1447	838	544	281
23,000	8678	3026	1451	839	544	281
24,000	8816	3042	1455	840	545	281
25,000	8948	3058	1458	842	545	281
26,000	9073	3072	1461	843	546	282
27,000	9192	3086	1464	844	546	282
28,000	9305	3098	1467	845	547	282
29,000	9412	3110	1470	846	547	282
30,000	9515	3121	1472	846	547	282
31,000	9614	3132	1475	847	548	282
32,000	9708	3142	1477	848	548	282
33,000	9798	3151	1479	849	548	282
34,000	9884	3160	1481	849	548	282
35,000	9967	3168	1483	850	549	282
36,000	10046	3176	1485	850	549	282
37,000	10123	3184	1486	851	549	283
38,000	10196	3191	1488	851	549	283
39,000	10267	3198	1489	852	550	283
40,000	10335	3205	1491	852	550	283
41,000	10400	3211	1492	853	550	283
42,000	10464	3217	1493	853	550	283
43,000	10525	3223	1495	854	550	283
44,000	10583	3228	1496	854	550	283
45,000	10640	3233	1497	854	551	283
46,000	10695	3239	1498	855	551	283
48,000	10800	3248	1500	855	551	283
49,000	10850	3253	1501	856	551	283
50,000	10898	3257	1502	856	551	283
55,000	11118	3276	1506	857	552	283
60,000	11309	3293	1509	858	552	283
65,000	11475	3307	1512	859	553	283
70,000	11622	3319	1515	860	553	284
75,000	11752	3329	1517	861	553	284
80,000	11868	3338	1519	862	554	284
85,000	11972	3347	1521	862	554	284
90,000	12067	3354	1522	863	554	284
95,000	12153	3361	1524	863	554	284
100,000	12231	3367	1525	863	554	284
105,000	12302	3372	1526	864	554	284
110,000	12368	3377	1527	864	555	284
115,000	12429	3381	1528	864	555	284
120,000	12485	3385	1529	865	555	284
125,000	12537	3389	1529	865	555	284
130,000	12586	3393	1530	865	555	284
135,000	12631	3396	1531	865	555	284
140,000	12674	3399	1531	866	555	284
145,000	12713	3402	1532	866	555	284
150,000	12751	3405	1533	866	555	284
155,000	12786	3407	1533	866	555	284

D

TABLE D-3F Sample Sizes for Sampling Attributes for Random Samples Only—Expected Rate of Occurrence Not over 30% or Expected Rate of Occurrence Not Less than 70%. Confidence Level 99% (Two-sided) (Continued).

Population Size	Sample Size for Precision of: ±1%	±2%	±3%	±4%	±5%	±7%
160,000	12819	3410	1534	866	555	284
165,000	12850	3412	1534	866	556	284
170,000	12879	3414	1534	867	556	284
175,000	12907	3416	1535	867	556	284
180,000	12934	3418	1535	867	556	284
185,000	12959	3419	1535	867	556	284
190,000	12983	3421	1536	867	556	284
195,000	13006	3423	1536	867	556	284
200,000	13027	3424	1536	867	556	284
205,000	13048	3426	1537	867	556	284
210,000	13068	3427	1537	867	556	284
220,000	13105	3429	1538	868	556	284
230,000	13139	3432	1538	868	556	284
240,000	13170	3434	1538	868	556	284
250,000	13199	3436	1539	868	556	284
260,000	13226	3438	1539	868	556	284
270,000	13251	3439	1540	868	556	284
280,000	13274	3441	1540	868	556	284
290,000	13296	3442	1540	868	556	284
300,000	13316	3444	1540	868	556	284
310,000	13336	3445	1541	869	556	284
325,000	13362	3447	1541	869	556	284
340,000	13386	3448	1541	869	556	284
350,000	13401	3449	1542	869	557	284
375,000	13436	3452	1542	869	557	284
400,000	13466	3454	1542	869	557	284
450,000	13516	3457	1543	869	557	284
500,000	13557	3460	1544	869	557	285

TABLE D-3G Sample Sizes for Sampling Attributes for Random Samples Only—Expected Rate of Occurrence Not over 40% or Expected Rate of Occurrence Not Less than 60%. Confidence Level 99% (Two-sided).

Population Size	Sample Size for Precision of: ±1%	±2%	±3%	±4%	±5%	±7%
1,000				499	389	245
1,100				523	404	251
1,200				544	416	256
1,300				564	428	260
1,450				590	443	266
1,500				599	447	267
1,600				614	456	270
1,750				635	467	274
1,800			893	641	471	276
1,900			916	653	477	278

Population Size	Sample Size for Precision of: ±1%	±2%	±3%	±4%	±5%	±7%
2,000			939	665	483	280
2,100			961	676	489	282
2,200			981	686	494	283
2,400			1019	704	504	287
2,500			1036	712	508	288
2,600			1053	720	512	289
2,800			1085	735	519	292
3,000			1113	748	526	294
3,200			1140	759	531	295
3,400			1164	770	537	297
3,600			1187	780	541	298
3,800			1208	789	546	300
4,000		1996	1227	797	550	301
4,100		2020	1236	801	551	301
4,200		2044	1245	805	553	302
4,300		2068	1254	808	555	302
4,400		2090	1262	812	557	303
4,500		2113	1270	815	558	303
4,600		2134	1278	818	560	304
4,700		2156	1286	822	561	304
4,800		2177	1293	825	563	305
4,900		2197	1300	827	564	305
5,000		2217	1307	830	565	305
5,500		2310	1339	843	571	307
6,000		2394	1367	854	576	309
6,500		2469	1391	863	580	310
7,000		2538	1413	872	584	311
7,500		2601	1432	879	587	312
8,000		2659	1449	885	590	313
8,500		2712	1465	891	593	313
9,000		2761	1479	896	595	314
9,500		2806	1492	901	597	315
10,000		2848	1504	905	599	315
10,500		2887	1514	909	601	316
11,000		2924	1524	913	602	316
11,500		2958	1534	916	604	316
12,000		2990	1542	919	605	317
12,500		3020	1550	922	606	317
13,000		3048	1558	925	607	317
13,500		3075	1565	927	608	318
14,000		3100	1571	929	609	318
14,500		3124	1577	931	610	318
15,000		3147	1583	933	611	318
15,500		3168	1588	935	612	319
16,000	7982	3188	1593	937	613	319
16,500	8104	3208	1598	939	613	319
17,000	8223	3226	1603	940	614	319
17,500	8338	3244	1607	942	615	319
18,000	8450	3260	1611	943	615	320
18,500	8559	3277	1615	945	616	320
19,000	8664	3292	1619	946	616	320
19,500	8767	3307	1622	947	617	320

D

TABLE D-3G Sample Sizes for Sampling Attributes for Random Samples Only—Expected Rate of Occurrence Not over 40% or Expected Rate of Occurrence Not Less than 60%. Confidence Level 99% (Two-sided) (Continued).

Population Size	±1%	±2%	±3%	±4%	±5%	±7%
20,000	8866	3321	1626	948	617	320
21,000	9057	3347	1632	950	618	320
22,000	9239	3371	1638	952	619	321
23,000	9410	3394	1643	954	620	321
24,000	9574	3415	1648	956	621	321
25,000	9729	3435	1653	957	621	321
26,000	9877	3453	1657	959	622	321
27,000	10018	3470	1661	960	622	321
28,000	10152	3486	1664	961	623	322
29,000	10281	3501	1668	962	623	322
30,000	10403	3515	1671	963	624	322
31,000	10521	3528	1674	964	624	322
32,000	10634	3541	1677	965	625	322
33,000	10742	3553	1680	966	625	322
34,000	10846	3564	1682	967	625	322
35,000	10946	3575	1684	968	626	322
36,000	11042	3585	1687	969	626	322
37,000	11134	3595	1689	969	626	322
38,000	11223	3604	1691	970	627	323
39,000	11308	3613	1693	971	627	323
40,000	11391	3621	1695	971	627	323
41,000	11471	3629	1696	972	627	323
42,000	11548	3637	1698	972	628	323
43,000	11622	3644	1700	973	628	323
44,000	11694	3651	1701	973	628	323
45,000	11763	3658	1703	974	628	323
46,000	11830	3664	1704	974	628	323
47,000	11895	3671	1705	975	629	323
48,000	11959	3677	1707	975	629	323
49,000	12020	3682	1708	976	629	323
50,000	12079	3688	1709	976	629	323
55,000	12350	3713	1714	978	630	323
60,000	12586	3734	1719	979	630	324
65,000	12792	3752	1723	980	631	324
70,000	12974	3767	1726	981	631	324
75,000	13137	3781	1729	982	632	324
80,000	13282	3793	1731	983	632	324
85,000	13413	3803	1733	984	632	324
90,000	13532	3813	1735	984	633	324
95,000	13640	3821	1737	985	633	324
100,000	13738	3829	1739	986	633	324
105,000	13829	3836	1740	986	633	324
110,000	13912	3842	1742	986	633	324
115,000	13989	3848	1743	987	634	324
120,000	14060	3854	1744	987	634	324
125,000	14126	3859	1745	988	634	324

Population Size	Sample Size for Precision of: ±1%	±2%	±3%	±4%	±5%	±7%
130,000	14188	3863	1746	988	634	324
135,000	14246	3867	1747	988	634	324
140,000	14299	3871	1747	988	634	325
145,000	14350	3875	1748	989	634	325
150,000	14397	3879	1749	989	634	325
155,000	14442	3882	1750	989	634	325
160,000	14484	3885	1750	989	635	325
165,000	14524	3888	1751	989	635	325
170,000	14562	3890	1751	990	635	325
175,000	14598	3893	1752	990	635	325
180,000	14632	3895	1752	990	635	325
185,000	14664	3898	1753	990	635	325
190,000	14694	3900	1753	990	635	325
195,000	14724	3902	1754	990	635	325
200,000	14751	3904	1754	990	635	325
205,000	14778	3906	1754	991	635	325
210,000	14803	3907	1755	991	635	325
215,000	14828	3909	1755	991	635	325
220,000	14851	3911	1755	991	635	325
225,000	14873	3912	1756	991	635	325
230,000	14895	3914	1756	991	635	325
235,000	14915	3915	1756	991	635	325
240,000	14935	3917	1757	991	635	325
250,000	14972	3919	1757	991	635	325
260,000	15007	3921	1758	992	635	325
270,000	15039	3924	1758	992	636	325
280,000	15069	3926	1758	992	636	325
290,000	15097	3928	1759	992	636	325
300,000	15123	3929	1759	992	636	325
310,000	15148	3931	1760	992	636	325
320,000	15171	3933	1760	992	636	325
330,000	15193	3934	1760	992	636	325
340,000	15213	3935	1760	992	636	325
350,000	15233	3937	1761	993	636	325
365,000	15260	3939	1761	993	636	325
380,000	15285	3940	1761	993	636	325
395,000	15309	3942	1762	993	636	325
400,000	15316	3942	1762	993	636	325
410,000	15331	3943	1762	993	636	325
425,000	15351	3945	1762	993	636	325
450,000	15382	3947	1763	993	636	325
465,000	15399	3948	1763	993	636	325
475,000	15409	3948	1763	993	636	325
485,000	15420	3949	1763	993	636	325
500,000	15434	3950	1763	993	636	325

D

TABLE D-3H Sample Sizes for Sampling Attributes for Random Samples Only—Expected Rate of Occurrence 50%. Confidence Level 99% (Two-sided).

Population Size	Sample Size for Precision of:					
	±1%	±2%	±3%	±4%	±5%	±7%
1,050				522	407	256
1,150				545	421	262
1,250				567	434	267
1,350				587	445	271
1,500				613	460	277
1,650				637	473	281
1,800				658	485	285
1,850			924	665	489	286
1,950			948	677	495	289
2,000			959	683	498	290
2,100			982	694	504	292
2,200			1003	705	510	294
2,300			1023	715	515	295
2,400			1043	724	520	297
2,500			1061	733	525	298
2,600			1079	741	529	300
2,800			1112	757	537	302
3,000			1142	771	544	305
3,200			1170	783	550	306
3,400			1195	795	555	308
3,600			1219	805	560	310
3,800			1241	815	565	311
4,000			1262	824	569	312
4,100		2062	1272	828	571	313
4,200		2087	1281	832	573	314
4,300		2111	1290	836	575	314
4,400		2135	1299	839	577	315
4,500		2158	1308	843	578	315
4,600		2181	1316	846	580	316
4,700		2203	1324	850	582	316
4,800		2225	1332	853	583	317
4,900		2246	1340	856	585	317
5,000		2267	1347	859	586	317
5,500		2365	1381	872	592	319
6,000		2452	1410	884	598	321
6,500		2532	1436	894	602	322
7,000		2605	1459	903	606	323
7,500		2671	1480	911	610	324
8,000		2732	1498	918	613	325
8,500		2788	1515	924	616	326
9,000		2839	1530	930	618	327
9,500		2887	1544	935	620	327
10,000		2932	1556	939	622	328
10,500		2973	1568	944	624	328
11,000		3012	1579	948	626	329
11,500		3048	1589	951	627	329

Population Size	±1%	±2%	±3%	±4%	±5%	±7%
	Sample Size for Precision of:					
12,000		3082	1598	954	629	330
12,500		3114	1606	957	630	330
13,000		3144	1614	960	631	330
13,500		3173	1622	963	633	331
14,000		3200	1629	965	634	331
14,500		3225	1635	968	635	331
15,000		3249	1642	970	635	331
15,500		3272	1647	972	636	332
16,000		3294	1653	974	637	332
16,500		3314	1658	976	638	332
17,000	8396	3334	1663	977	639	332
17,500	8516	3353	1668	979	639	332
18,000	8633	3371	1672	980	640	333
18,500	8746	3388	1676	982	641	333
19,000	8857	3404	1680	983	641	333
19,500	8964	3420	1684	985	642	333
20,000	9068	3435	1688	986	642	333
21,000	9268	3463	1695	988	643	333
22,000	9458	3490	1701	990	644	334
23,000	9638	3514	1707	992	645	334
24,000	9809	3536	1712	994	646	334
25,000	9972	3557	1717	996	646	334
26,000	10128	3577	1721	997	647	334
27,000	10276	3595	1725	999	648	335
28,000	10417	3612	1729	1000	648	335
29,000	10553	3628	1733	1001	649	335
30,000	10682	3644	1737	1002	649	335
31,000	10806	3658	1740	1003	650	335
32,000	10925	3672	1743	1004	650	335
33,000	11040	3684	1746	1005	650	335
34,000	11149	3696	1748	1006	651	335
35,000	11255	3708	1751	1007	651	336
36,000	11356	3719	1753	1008	652	336
37,000	11454	3729	1756	1009	652	336
38,000	11548	3739	1758	1009	652	336
39,000	11639	3749	1760	1010	652	336
40,000	11726	3758	1762	1011	653	336
41,000	11811	3766	1764	1011	653	336
42,000	11892	3775	1766	1012	653	336
43,000	11971	3783	1767	1012	653	336
44,000	12047	3790	1769	1013	654	336
45,000	12121	3797	1771	1013	654	336
46,000	12192	3804	1772	1014	654	336
47,000	12261	3811	1774	1014	654	336
48,000	12328	3817	1775	1015	655	336
49,000	12393	3824	1776	1015	655	336
50,000	12456	3830	1778	1016	655	337
55,000	12745	3857	1783	1018	656	337
60,000	12996	3879	1788	1019	656	337
65,000	13216	3899	1792	1021	657	337
70,000	13411	3915	1796	1022	657	337
75,000	13584	3930	1799	1023	658	337

D

TABLE D-3H Sample Sizes for Sampling Attributes for Random Samples Only—Expected Rate of Occurrence 50%. Confidence Level 99% (Two-sided) (Continued).

Population Size	Sample Size for Precision of: ±1%	±2%	±3%	±4%	±5%	±7%
80,000	13740	3943	1802	1024	658	337
85,000	13880	3954	1804	1024	658	337
90,000	14007	3965	1806	1025	659	338
95,000	14123	3974	1808	1026	659	338
100,000	14229	3982	1810	1026	659	338
105,000	14326	3990	1811	1027	659	338
110,000	14415	3997	1813	1027	660	338
115,000	14498	4003	1814	1028	660	338
120,000	14574	4009	1815	1028	660	338
125,000	14645	4014	1816	1028	660	338
130,000	14712	4019	1817	1029	660	338
135,000	14774	4024	1818	1029	660	338
140,000	14832	4028	1819	1029	660	338
145,000	14886	4032	1820	1029	661	338
150,000	14937	4036	1821	1030	661	338
155,000	14985	4039	1822	1030	661	338
160,000	15031	4042	1822	1030	661	338
165,000	15074	4046	1823	1030	661	338
170,000	15114	4049	1823	1031	661	338
175,000	15153	4051	1824	1031	661	338
180,000	15189	4054	1825	1031	661	338
185,000	15224	4056	1825	1031	661	338
190,000	15257	4059	1826	1031	661	338
195,000	15288	4061	1826	1031	661	338
200,000	15318	4063	1826	1031	661	338
205,000	15347	4065	1827	1032	661	338
210,000	15375	4067	1827	1032	661	338
215,000	15401	4069	1828	1032	662	338
220,000	15426	4071	1828	1032	662	338
225,000	15450	4072	1828	1032	662	338
230,000	15473	4074	1829	1032	662	338
235,000	15495	4075	1829	1032	662	338
240,000	15517	4077	1829	1032	662	338
245,000	15537	4078	1829	1032	662	338
250,000	15557	4080	1830	1033	662	338
260,000	15594	4082	1830	1033	662	338
270,000	15629	4085	1831	1033	662	338
280,000	15661	4087	1831	1033	662	338
290,000	15691	4089	1832	1033	662	338
300,000	15720	4091	1832	1033	662	338
310,000	15746	4093	1832	1033	662	338
320,000	15771	4094	1833	1033	662	338
330,000	15795	4086	1833	1034	662	338
340,000	15817	4097	1833	1034	662	338
350,000	15838	4099	1834	1034	662	338
360,000	15858	4100	1834	1034	662	338
375,000	15886	4102	1834	1034	662	338
390,000	15912	4104	1835	1034	662	339

Population Size	Sample Size for Precision of:					
	±1%	±2%	±3%	±4%	±5%	±7%
400,000	15928	4105	1835	1034	662	339
420,000	15959	4107	1835	1034	663	339
435,000	15980	4108	1835	1034	663	339
450,000	15999	4109	1836	1034	663	339
465,000	16018	4111	1836	1035	663	339
475,000	16029	4111	1836	1035	663	339
490,000	16046	4112	1836	1035	663	339
500,000	16056	4113	1836	1035	663	339

D

APPENDIX E
ESTIMATING SAMPLE SIZE–VARIABLES

TABLE E-1 Sample Sizes for Estimating Average Values (Variables) for Random Samples Only

Ratio of Sampling Error to Standard Deviation (Sampling Error/Standard Deviation)	Sample Size Required with Confidence Levels (Two-sided) of			
	90%	95%	99%	99.9%
Field Size is 500				
.09	200	244	-	-
.10	176	217	-	-
.11	155	195	-	-
.12	137	174	241	-
.13	121	157	221	-
.14	108	141	203	-
.15	97	127	187	246
.16	88	118	172	230
.17	79	106	158	215
.18	72	96	146	201
.19	65	88	135	189
.20	60	81	125	176
.21	55	75	116	166
.22	51	69	108	156
.23	47	64	101	146
.24	43	59	94	138
.25	40	55	88	129
.30	-	-	64	97
.35	-	-	50	76
.40	-	-	-	60
Field Size is 1,000				
.07	356	440	-	-
.08	297	376	-	-
.09	250	322	452	-
.10	213	278	400	-
.11	183	241	335	474
.12	158	211	317	431
.13	138	186	283	392
.14	121	164	254	358
.15	107	146	228	326
.16	96	131	209	299
.17	86	118	188	274
.18	78	106	171	252
.19	70	97	156	232
.20	64	88	143	214
.21	58	81	132	199
.22	53	74	121	184
.23	49	68	112	171
.24	45	63	104	160
.25	42	58	96	148
.30	-	41	69	108
.35	-	-	52	82
.40	-	-	40	64
Field Size is 1,500				
.05	629	-	-	-
.06	501	624	829	-
.07	404	515	713	-
.08	330	429	615	798
.09	273	361	531	709
.10	229	306	462	631
.11	195	263	403	563
.12	167	227	354	503
.13	145	198	312	451
.14	126	174	277	406
.15	111	154	248	366
.16	99	137	222	332
.17	89	123	200	302
.18	80	110	181	275
.19	72	100	165	252
.20	65	91	150	231

Ratio of Sampling Error to Standard Deviation (Sampling Error/Standard Deviation)	Sample Size Required with Confidence Levels (Two-sided) of 90%	95%	99%	99.9%
Field Size is 1,500 (Con't.)				
.21	59	83	138	213
.22	54	76	126	196
.23	50	70	117	182
.24	46	64	108	168
.25	43	60	100	157
.30		42	71	112
.35			53	84
.40			41	65
Field Size is 2,000				
.04	916	-	-	-
.05	695	869	-	-
.06	546	696	961	-
.07	433	564	809	-
.08	349	462	685	920
.09	286	384	583	804
.10	238	322	500	705
.11	201	274	432	621
.12	172	235	376	549
.13	148	205	330	488
.14	129	179	291	435
.15	113	157	258	390
.16	101	140	231	351
.17	90	125	207	318
.18	81	112	187	288
.19	73	102	169	263
.20	66	92	154	240
.21	60	84	141	220
.22	55	77	129	203
.23	50	71	119	187
.24	46	65	110	173
.25	43	60	101	160
.30		42	71	114
.35			53	86
.40			41	66
Field Size is 2,500				
.04	1009	1225	-	-
.05	755	952	-	-
.06	587	748	1063	-
.07	452	597	881	1177
.08	362	485	735	1013
.09	295	399	619	875
.10	244	332	526	759
.11	205	282	451	662
.12	175	242	391	581
.13	150	209	341	513
.14	131	182	299	455
.15	115	160	265	406
.16	102	142	236	364
.17	91	127	211	328
.18	81	114	190	297
.19	73	103	172	270
.20	66	93	157	246
.21	60	85	143	225
.22	55	77	131	207
.23	51	71	121	191
.24	47	65	111	176
.25	43	60	103	163
.30		42	72	116
.35			54	86
.40			41	67
Field Size is 3,000				
.04	1082	1334	-	-
.05	795	1016	1411	-
.06	601	788	1144	-
.07	466	622	936	1277
.08	371	501	773	1086
.09	301	410	646	929
.10	248	341	545	799

TABLE E-1 Sample Sizes for Estimating Average Values (Variables) for Random Samples Only (Continued)

Ratio of Sampling Error to Standard Deviation (Sampling Error/Standard Deviation)	Sample Size Required with Confidence Levels (Two-sided) of 90%	95%	99%	99.9%
Field Size is 3,000 (Con't.)				
.11	208	288	465	693
.12	177	245	401	604
.13	152	212	349	531
.14	132	184	306	469
.15	116	162	269	417
.16	103	143	240	373
.17	91	128	214	335
.18	82	115	193	303
.19	74	103	174	275
.20	66	93	158	250
.21	61	85	144	229
.22	56	78	132	210
.23	51	71	122	193
.24	47	66	112	178
.25	43	60	103	165
.30		42	72	116
.35			54	87
.40			42	67
Field Size is 4,000				
.03	1716	-	-	-
.04	1189	1500	-	-
.05	852	1110	1598	-
.06	633	843	1265	1723
.07	485	656	1015	1429
.08	382	522	826	1194
.09	308	424	682	1007
.10	253	351	571	856
.11	212	295	484	735
.12	179	251	413	637
.13	154	216	359	555
.14	133	187	314	488
.15	117	164	275	432
.16	103	145	245	385
.17	92	129	218	345
.18	82	116	196	311
.19	74	104	177	281
.20	67	94	160	255
.21	61	86	146	233
.22	56	78	133	214
.23	51	72	123	196
.24	47	66	113	181
.25	43	61	104	167
.30	-	42	73	117
.35	-	-	54	87
.40	-	-	42	67
Field Size is 5,000				
.03	1878	2303	-	-
.04	1264	1622	2271	-
.05	890	1175	1737	2328
.06	653	880	1350	1885
.07	497	678	1069	1539
.08	390	536	861	1270
.09	313	434	706	1060
.10	257	357	588	894
.11	214	299	496	763
.12	181	254	424	657
.13	155	218	366	571
.14	134	189	319	501
.15	117	165	279	441
.16	104	146	248	393
.17	92	130	221	351

Ratio of Sampling Error to Standard Deviation (Sampling Error/Standard Deviation)	Sample Size Required with Confidence Levels (Two-sided) of 90%	95%	99%	99.9%
Field Size is 5,000 (Con't.)				
.18	83	116	198	315
.19	74	105	178	285
.20	67	94	161	258
.21	61	86	147	236
.22	56	79	134	216
.23	51	72	124	198
.24	47	66	113	183
.25	43	61	105	169
.30		42	73	118
.35			54	88
.40			42	68
Field Size is 6,000				
.03	2003	2495	-	-
.04	1319	1715	2457	-
.05	917	1224	1845	2524
.06	668	906	1414	2012
.07	506	694	1108	1622
.08	395	546	887	1326
.09	316	440	723	1099
.10	259	362	600	922
.11	217	302	504	783
.12	182	256	430	672
.13	156	220	370	582
.14	135	190	322	509
.15	118	167	282	448
.16	104	147	250	398
.17	93	131	222	355
.18	83	117	199	319
.19	75	105	179	288
.20	67	95	162	261
.21	61	86	148	238
.22	58	79	135	217
.23	51	72	124	200
.24	47	66	114	184
.25	43	61	105	170
.30		43	74	119
.35			54	88
.40			42	68
Field Size is 7,000				
.02	3440	-	-	-
.03	2103	2652	-	-
.04	1362	1788	2610	3451
.05	937	1261	1929	2686
.06	679	926	1463	2113
.07	512	706	1138	1687
.08	399	553	906	1369
.09	319	445	736	1128
.10	261	365	608	943
.11	217	304	511	798
.12	183	257	434	683
.13	157	221	373	591
.14	135	191	324	515
.15	118	167	284	453
.16	105	147	251	402
.17	93	131	223	358
.18	83	117	200	321
.19	75	105	180	290
.20	68	95	163	263
.21	61	86	148	239
.22	56	79	135	218
.23	51	72	124	200
.24	47	67	114	185
.25	44	61	105	171
.30		43	74	119
.35			54	88
.40			42	68

E

TABLE E-1 Sample Sizes for Estimating Average Values (Variables) for Random Samples Only (Continued)

Ratio of Sampling Error to Standard Deviation (Sampling Error/Standard Deviation)	Sample Size Required with Confidence Levels (Two-sided) of 90%	95%	99%	99.9%
Field Size is 8,000				
.02	3665	-	-	-
.03	2185	2784	3844	-
.04	1394	1847	2737	3678
.05	953	1290	1998	2821
.06	688	942	1502	2196
.07	517	715	1162	1740
.08	402	559	921	1404
.09	321	448	746	1152
.10	262	367	615	959
.11	218	306	515	809
.12	184	259	437	691
.13	157	222	376	597
.14	136	192	326	520
.15	118	168	286	457
.16	105	148	252	404
.17	93	131	224	360
.18	83	117	201	323
.19	75	106	181	291
.20	68	95	164	264
.21	61	87	149	240
.22	56	79	136	219
.23	51	72	125	201
.24	47	67	114	185
.25	44	61	106	171
.30		43	74	120
.35			54	88
.40			42	68
Field Size is 9,000				
.02	3862	-	-	-
.03	2254	2896	4060	-
.04	1424	1896	2846	3876
.05	966	1313	2055	2936
.06	694	954	1534	2265
.07	520	722	1181	1783
.08	404	563	933	1432
.09	322	451	754	1170
.10	263	369	620	972
.11	218	307	519	819
.12	184	260	440	698
.13	157	222	378	602
.14	136	192	328	524
.15	119	168	287	460
.16	105	148	253	407
.17	93	131	225	362
.18	83	118	201	325
.19	75	106	181	292
.20	68	96	164	265
.21	61	87	149	241
.22	56	79	136	219
.23	51	73	125	202
.24	47	67	115	186
.25	44	62	106	171
.30		43	74	120
.35			55	89
.40			42	68
Field Size is 10,000				
.02	4035	4900	-	-
.03	2312	2991	4252	-
.04	1447	1936	2938	4050
.05	977	1332	2103	3034
.06	699	965	1561	2323
.07	523	728	1196	1819

Ratio of Sampling Error to Standard Deviation (Sampling Error/Standard Deviation)	Sample Size Required with Confidence Levels (Two-sided) of 90%	95%	99%	99.9%
Field Size is 10,000 (Con't.)				
.08	406	567	943	1455
.09	323	453	760	1186
.10	263	370	624	982
.11	219	308	522	826
.12	184	260	442	704
.13	158	223	379	606
.14	136	193	329	527
.15	119	168	287	462
.16	105	148	254	409
.17	93	132	226	364
.18	83	118	202	326
.19	75	106	182	293
.20	68	96	164	265
.21	61	87	149	241
.22	56	79	136	221
.23	52	73	125	202
.24	47	67	115	186
.25	44	62	106	171
.30		43	74	120
.35			55	89
.40			42	68
Field Size is 15,000				
.02	4662	5856	-	-
.03	2505	3323	4954	6698
.04	1520	2070	3257	4682
.05	1010	1394	2262	3376
.06	716	997	1647	2518
.07	533	746	1246	1936
.08	411	578	973	1529
.09	327	460	780	1234
.10	266	375	638	1016
.11	221	311	531	850
.12	186	263	449	720
.13	158	224	384	618
.14	137	194	333	536
.15	119	169	291	469
.16	105	149	256	414
.17	94	132	227	368
.18	84	118	203	329
.19	75	106	183	296
.20	68	96	165	268
.21	62	87	150	243
.22	56	79	137	222
.23	52	73	126	204
.24	47	67	115	187
.25	44	62	106	173
.30		43	74	121
.35			55	89
.40			42	68
Field Size is 20,000				
.02	5055	6489	9083	
.03	2614	3517	5400	7541
.04	1559	2144	3444	5079
.05	1031	1427	2350	3577
.06	724	1014	1693	2628
.07	537	755	1273	2001
.08	414	583	989	1569
.09	329	464	790	1260
.10	267	377	644	1033
.11	221	313	536	862
.12	186	264	452	729
.13	159	225	387	625
.14	137	195	334	541
.15	120	169	292	473
.16	106	149	257	417
.17	94	133	228	370

E

TABLE E-1 Sample Sizes for Estimating Average Values (Variables) for Random Samples Only (Continued)

Ratio of Sampling Error to Standard Deviation (Sampling Error/Standard Deviation)	Sample Size Required with Confidence Levels (Two-sided) of 90%	95%	99%	99.9%
	Field Size is 20,000 (Con't.)			
.18	84	118	204	331
.19	75	106	183	298
.20	68	96	165	269
.21	62	87	150	244
.22	56	80	137	223
.23	52	73	126	204
.24	47	67	115	188
.25	44	62	106	173
.30		43	74	121
.35			55	89
.40			42	68
	Field Size is 25,000			
.02	5321	6939	9992	-
.03	2684	3646	5708	8154
.04	1584	2191	3567	5350
.05	1037	1448	2407	3710
.06	728	1024	1722	2699
.07	540	761	1289	2042
.08	416	587	999	1594
.09	330	466	796	1276
.10	268	379	649	1044
.11	222	314	539	869
.12	187	264	454	735
.13	159	226	388	629
.14	137	195	336	544
.15	120	170	293	475
.16	106	150	258	419
.17	94	133	229	372
.18	84	119	204	332
.19	75	106	184	299
.20	68	96	166	270
.21	62	87	151	245
.22	56	80	137	223
.23	52	73	126	205
.24	47	67	116	188
.25	44	62	107	174
.30		43	74	121
.35			55	89
.40			42	68
	Field Size is 30,000			
.01	14229	-	-	-
.02	5520	7276	10704	14273
.03	2733	3737	5932	8623
.04	1601	2224	3654	5548
.05	1045	1462	2446	3804
.06	733	1031	1742	2748
.07	542	765	1300	2070
.08	417	589	1006	1611
.09	330	467	800	1287
.10	268	380	652	1051
.11	222	315	541	874
.12	187	265	456	738
.13	159	226	389	631
.14	137	195	336	546
.15	120	170	293	477
.16	106	150	258	420
.17	94	133	229	373
.18	84	119	205	333
.19	75	107	184	299
.20	68	96	166	270

Ratio of Sampling Error to Standard Deviation (Sampling Error/Standard Deviation)	Sample Size Required with Confidence Levels (Two-sided) of 90%	95%	99%	99.9%
Field Size is 30,000 (Con't.)				
.21	62	87	151	245
.22	56	80	137	224
.23	52	73	126	205
.24	47	67	116	188
.25	44	62	107	174
.30		43	74	121
.35			55	89
.40			42	68
Field Size is 40,000				
.01	16142	19597	-	-
.02	5786	7745	11576	16200
.03	2796	3857	6242	9290
.04	1623	2266	3769	5817
.05	1054	1480	2497	3929
.06	738	1040	1768	2813
.07	545	769	1314	2106
.08	418	592	1014	1633
.09	331	469	806	1301
.10	269	381	655	1061
.11	222	315	543	881
.12	187	266	457	743
.13	159	227	391	635
.14	138	196	337	549
.15	120	170	294	479
.16	106	150	259	421
.17	94	133	230	374
.18	84	119	205	334
.19	75	107	184	300
.20	68	96	166	271
.21	62	87	151	246
.22	56	80	138	224
.23	52	73	126	205
.24	47	67	116	189
.25	44	62	107	174
.30		43	74	121
.35			55	89
.40			42	68
Field Size is 50,000				
.01	17559	21725	-	-
.02	5959	8057	12486	17628
.03	2836	3933	6443	9743
.04	1636	2291	3841	5991
.05	1059	1491	2528	4007
.06	741	1045	1784	2852
.07	546	772	1323	2128
.08	419	594	1019	1646
.09	332	470	809	1310
.10	269	382	657	1066
.11	223	316	545	885
.12	187	266	459	745
.13	160	227	391	637
.14	138	196	338	550
.15	120	170	295	480
.16	106	150	259	422
.17	94	133	230	374
.18	84	119	205	334
.19	75	107	184	300
.20	68	96	166	271
.21	62	87	151	246
.22	56	80	138	224
.23	52	73	126	206
.24	47	67	116	189
.25	44	62	107	174
.30		43	74	121
.35			55	89
.40			42	68

E

TABLE E-1 Sample Sizes for Estimating Average Values (Variables) for Random Samples Only (Continued)

Ratio of Sampling Error to Standard Deviation (Sampling Error/Standard Deviation)	Sample Size Required with Confidence Levels (Two-sided) of 90%	95%	99%	99.9%
Field Size is 70,000				
.01	19516	24804	-	-
.02	6169	8445	13445	19602
.03	2883	4024	6690	10317
.04	1651	2322	3927	6204
.05	1066	1504	2565	4101
.06	744	1052	1802	2900
.07	548	776	1332	2155
.08	420	596	1025	1662
.09	332	472	813	1320
.10	270	383	660	1073
.11	223	317	546	889
.12	187	266	460	749
.13	160	227	392	639
.14	138	196	338	552
.15	120	171	295	481
.16	106	150	260	423
.17	94	133	230	375
.18	84	119	205	335
.19	75	107	184	301
.20	68	96	167	272
.21	62	88	151	247
.22	56	80	138	225
.23	52	73	126	206
24	47	67	116	189
.25	44	62	107	174
.30		43	74	121
.35			55	89
.40			42	68
Field Size is 80,000				
.01	20222	25953	36334	-
.02	6238	8574	13776	20313
.03	2897	4053	6770	10511
.04	1656	2332	3955	6273
.05	1068	1508	2577	4132
.06	745	1054	1808	2915
.07	548	777	1336	2163
.08	421	596	1026	1693
.09	333	472	814	1323
.10	270	383	661	1075
.11	223	317	547	890
.12	187	266	460	750
.13	160	227	392	640
.14	138	196	339	552
.15	120	171	295	482
.16	106	150	260	424
.17	94	133	230	376
.18	84	119	205	335
.19	75	107	184	301
.20	68	96	167	272
.21	62	88	151	247
.22	56	80	138	225
.23	52	73	126	206
.24	47	67	116	189
.25	44	62	107	174
.30		43	74	121
.35			55	89
.40			42	69

Ratio of Sampling Error to Standard Deviation (Sampling Error/Standard Deviation)	Sample Size Required with Confidence Levels (Two-sided) of 90%	95%	99%	99.9%
Field Size is 100,000				
.01	21299	27755	39968	
.02	6336	8764	14265	21413
.03	2919	4093	6887	10799
.04	1663	2345	3994	6373
.05	1071	1513	2593	4174
.06	746	1056	1816	2937
.07	549	778	1341	2175
.08	421	597	1030	1674
.09	333	473	816	1327
.10	270	383	661	1077
.11	223	317	548	892
.12	188	267	461	751
.13	160	227	393	641
.14	138	196	339	553
.15	120	171	295	482
.16	106	150	260	424
.17	94	133	230	376
.18	84	119	206	335
.19	75	107	185	301
.20	68	96	167	272
.21	62	88	151	247
.22	56	80	138	225
.23	52	73	126	206
.24	47	67	116	189
.25	44	62	107	174
.30		43	74	121
.35			55	89
.40			42	69
Field Size is 500,000				
.01	25674	35676	58744	89424
.02	6675	9424	16105	25820
.03	2989	4233	7289	11815
.04	1686	2390	4126	6715
.05	1080	1532	2649	4319
.06	751	1065	1843	3007
.07	552	783	1355	2213
.08	422	600	1038	1696
.09	334	474	821	1341
.10	270	384	665	1087
.11	224	318	550	899
.12	188	267	462	756
.13	160	228	394	644
.14	138	196	340	555
.15	120	171	296	484
.16	106	151	260	426
.17	94	133	231	377
.18	84	119	206	336
.19	75	107	185	302
.20	68	97	167	273
.21	62	88	151	247
.22	56	80	138	225
.23	52	73	127	206
.24	47	67	116	189
.25	44	62	107	174
.30		43	74	121
.35			55	89
.40			42	69
Field Size is 1,000,000				
.01	26350	36996	62422	98206
.02	6719	9513	16370	26504
.03	2998	4251	7342	11956
.04	1688	2396	4143	6761
.05	1081	1535	2656	4338
.06	751	1066	1846	3016
.07	552	784	1357	2218

TABLE E-1 Sample Sizes for Estimating Average Values (Variables) for Random Samples Only (Continued)

Ratio of Sampling Error to Standard Deviation (Sampling Error/Standard Deviation)	Sample Size Required with Confidence Levels (Two-sided) of			
	90%	95%	99%	99.9%
Field Size is 1,000,000 (Con't.)				
.08	423	600	1039	1699
.09	334	475	822	1343
.10	271	385	666	1088
.11	224	318	550	900
.12	188	267	463	756
.13	160	228	394	644
.14	138	196	340	556
.15	120	171	296	484
.16	106	151	260	426
.17	94	133	231	377
.18	84	119	206	336
.19	75	107	185	302
.20	68	97	167	273
.21	62	88	151	247
.22	56	80	138	225
.23	52	73	127	206
.24	47	67	116	190
.25	44	62	107	175
.30		43	74	121
.35			55	89
.40			42	69

TABLE E-2 Factors for Estimating the Standard Deviation

$$\text{Estimated standard deviation} = \frac{\text{Average range}}{d_2 \text{ factor}}$$

Group size	d_2 factor
6	2.534
7	2.704
8	2.847

APPENDIX F
SAMPLE PRECISION
FOR RELATIVE FREQUENCIES

Rate of Occurrence in Sample	Table
1%*	F-1
2%	F-2
3%	F-3
4%	F-4
5%	F-5
6%	F-6
7%	F-7
8%	F-8
9%	F-9
10%	F-10
11%	F-11
12%	F-12
13%	F-13
14%	F-14
15%	F-15
16%	F-16
17%	F-17
18%	F-18
19%	F-19
20%	F-20
25%	F-21
30%	F-22
35%	F-23
40%	F-24
45%	F-25
50%	F-26
0%	F-27

*90, 95,and 99% Confidence Levels on succeeding pages.

TABLE F-1 Sample Precision for Relative Frequencies for Random Samples Only—Rate of Occurrence in Sample 1%

For Field Size of:

And Sample Size is:	500 Lower Limit	500 Upper Limit	1,000 Lower Limit	1,000 Upper Limit	1,500 Lower Limit	1,500 Upper Limit	2,000 Lower Limit	2,000 Upper Limit	10,000 Lower Limit	10,000 Upper Limit	50,000 Lower Limit	50,000 Upper Limit	100,000 and over Lower Limit	100,000 and over Upper Limit
Confidence Level 90% (Two-sided) Confidence Level 95% (One-sided)														
100	.2%	4.3%	.1%	4.5%	.1%	4.5%	.1%	4.6%	.1%	4.6%	.1%	4.7%	.1%	4.7%
200	.4	2.6	.3	2.9	.2	3.0	.2	3.0	.2	3.1	.2	3.1	.2	3.1
300			.4	2.3	.4	2.4	.3	2.4	.3	2.5	.3	2.6	.3	2.6
400			.5	2.0	.4	2.1	.4	2.1	.4	2.2	.3	2.3	.3	2.3
500					.5	1.9	.5	1.9	.4	2.1	.4	2.1	.4	2.1
600					.6	1.7	.5	1.8	.5	1.9	.4	2.0	.4	2.0
700					.6	1.6	.6	1.7	.5	1.8	.5	1.9	.5	1.9
800					.7	1.5	.6	1.6	.5	1.8	.5	1.8	.5	1.8
900									.5	1.7	.5	1.7	.5	1.7
1,000									.6	1.7	.6	1.7	.6	1.7
1,500									.7	1.5	.6	1.5	.6	1.5
2,000									.7	1.4	.7	1.4	.7	1.4
3,000									.8	1.3	.7	1.3	.7	1.3

F

TABLE F-1 Sample Precision for Relative Frequencies for Random Samples Only—Rate of Occurrence in Sample 1% (Continued)

And Sample Size is:	For Field Size of: 500 Lower Limit	500 Upper Limit	1,000 Lower Limit	1,000 Upper Limit	1,500 Lower Limit	1,500 Upper Limit	2,000 Lower Limit	2,000 Upper Limit	10,000 Lower Limit	10,000 Upper Limit	50,000 Lower Limit	50,000 Upper Limit	100,000 and over Lower Limit	100,000 and over Upper Limit
	Confidence Level 95% (Two-sided) Confidence Level 97.5% (One-sided)													
100	.2%	5.0%	.1%	5.2%	.1%	5.3%	.1%	5.3%	.0*	5.4%	.0*	5.5%	.0*	5.5%
120	.2	4.3	.1	4.6	.1	4.7	.1	4.7	.1	4.8	.1	4.8	.1	4.9
140	.2	3.9	.2	4.2	.1	4.3	.1	4.3	.1	4.4	.1	4.4	.1	4.4
150	.2	3.7	.2	4.0	.1	4.0	.1	4.1	.1	4.2	.1	4.2	.1	4.3
160	.3	3.5	.2	3.8	.1	3.9	.1	4.0	.1	4.1	.1	4.1	.1	4.1
180	.3	3.3	.2	3.6	.2	3.6	.2	3.7	.1	3.8	.1	3.8	.1	3.8
200	.4	3.0	.2	3.3	.2	3.4	.2	3.4	.1	3.5	.1	3.6	.1	3.6
250	.4	2.6	.3	3.0	.3	3.1	.2	3.1	.2	3.3	.2	3.3	.2	3.3
300			.3	2.6	.3	2.7	.3	2.8	.2	2.9	.2	2.9	.2	2.9
400			.4	2.2	.4	2.3	.4	2.4	.3	2.5	.3	2.5	.3	2.4
500					.5	2.1	.4	2.1	.3	2.3	.3	2.3	.3	2.3
600					.5	1.9	.5	1.9	.4	2.1	.4	2.2	.4	2.2
700					.6	1.8	.6	1.8	.4	2.1	.4	2.1	.4	2.1
800									.5	1.9	.4	2.0	.4	2.0
900									.5	1.9	.5	1.9	.5	1.9
1,000									.5	1.8	.5	1.8	.5	1.8
1,500									.6	1.6	.6	1.6	.6	1.6
2,000									.7	1.5	.6	1.5	.6	1.5
3,000									.7	1.4	.7	1.4	.7	1.4

*Less than 0.05%.

And Sample Size is:	500 Lower Limit	500 Upper Limit	1,000 Lower Limit	1,000 Upper Limit	1,500 Lower Limit	1,500 Upper Limit	2,000 Lower Limit	2,000 Upper Limit	10,000 Lower Limit	10,000 Upper Limit	50,000 Lower Limit	50,000 Upper Limit	100,000 and over Lower Limit	100,000 and over Upper Limit
Confidence Level 99% (Two-sided) Confidence Level 99.5% (One-sided)														
100	.1%	6.6%	.1%	6.9%	.0*	7.0%	.0*	7.1%	.0*	7.2%	.0*	7.2%	.0*	7.2%
120	.1	5.6	.1	6.0	.1	6.1	.0*	6.2	.0*	6.3	.0*	6.3	.0*	6.3
140	.2	5.0	.1	5.4	.1	5.5	.1	5.6	.0*	5.7	.0*	5.8	.0*	5.8
150	.2	4.7	.1	5.1	.1	5.2	.1	5.3	.0*	5.4	.0*	5.4	.0*	5.5
160	.2	4.5	.1	4.9	.1	5.0	.1	5.1	.0*	5.2	.0*	5.3	.0*	5.3
180	.2	4.2	.1	4.6	.1	4.7	.1	4.8	.1	4.9	.1	4.9	.1	5.0
200	.3	3.8	.2	4.2	.1	4.3	.1	4.4	.1	4.5	.1	4.5	.1	4.6
250	.4	3.2	.2	3.7	.2	3.9	.1	3.9	.1	4.1	.1	4.1	.1	4.2
300			.3	3.2	.2	3.3	.2	3.4	.1	3.6	.1	3.6	.1	3.6
400			.4	2.6	.3	2.8	.3	2.9	.2	3.1	.2	3.1	.2	3.1
500					.4	2.5	.3	2.6	.2	2.8	.2	2.8	.2	2.8
600					.4	2.2	.4	2.3	.3	2.5	.3	2.6	.3	2.6
700					.5	2.0	.4	2.2	.3	2.4	.3	2.4	.3	2.4
800							.5	2.0	.4	2.3	.3	2.3	.3	2.3
900							.5	1.9	.4	2.2	.3	2.2	.3	2.2
1,000									.4	2.1	.4	2.1	.4	2.1
1,500									.5	1.8	.5	1.9	.5	1.9
2,000									.6	1.7	.5	1.7	.5	1.7
3,000									.7	1.5	.6	1.6	.6	1.6

*Less than 0.05%.

F

TABLE F-2 Sample Precision for Relative Frequencies for Random Samples Only—Rate of Occurrence in Sample 2%

And Sample Size is:	For Field Size of: 500 Lower Limit	500 Upper Limit	1,000 Lower Limit	1,000 Upper Limit	1,500 Lower Limit	1,500 Upper Limit	2,000 Lower Limit	2,000 Upper Limit	10,000 Lower Limit	10,000 Upper Limit	50,000 Lower Limit	50,000 Upper Limit	100,000 and over Lower Limit	100,000 and over Upper Limit
Confidence Level 90% (Two-sided) Confidence Level 95% (One-sided)														
50	.2%	8.9%	.2%	9.1%	.1%	9.1%	.1%	9.2%	.1%	9.3%	.1%	9.3%	.1%	9.3%
80	.4	6.6	.4	6.8	.3	6.9	.3	6.9	.3	7.0	.3	7.0	.3	7.0
90	.5	6.1	.4	6.4	.4	6.4	.4	6.5	.3	6.6	.3	6.6	.3	6.6
100	.5	5.8	.4	6.0	.4	6.1	.4	6.1	.4	6.2	.4	6.2	.4	6.2
120	.7	5.2	.6	5.5	.5	5.5	.5	5.6	.5	5.7	.5	5.7	.5	5.7
140	.8	4.8	.6	5.1	.6	5.2	.6	5.2	.5	5.3	.5	5.3	.5	5.3
150	.8	4.6	.7	4.9	.6	5.0	.6	5.0	.6	5.1	.6	5.1	.6	5.1
160	.8	4.5	.7	4.8	.7	4.9	.7	4.9	.6	5.0	.6	5.0	.6	5.1
180	.9	4.3	.8	4.6	.8	4.7	.7	4.7	.7	4.8	.7	4.8	.7	4.8
200	1.0	4.0	.8	4.3	.8	4.4	.8	4.4	.7	4.5	.7	4.5	.7	4.6
250	1.2	3.7	1.0	4.0	.9	4.1	.9	4.2	.9	4.3	.9	4.3	.8	4.3
300			1.2	3.5	1.1	3.7	1.1	3.7	1.0	3.8	1.0	3.8	1.0	3.8
400			1.3	3.2	1.3	3.3	1.2	3.4	1.1	3.5	1.1	3.5	1.1	3.5
500			1.4	2.9	1.4	3.1	1.3	3.2	1.2	3.3	1.2	3.3	1.2	3.3
600					1.4	2.9	1.4	3.0	1.3	3.1	1.3	3.2	1.3	3.2
700					1.5	2.8	1.4	2.9	1.3	3.0	1.3	3.1	1.3	3.1
800							1.5	2.8	1.4	2.9	1.4	3.0	1.3	3.0
900							1.5	2.7	1.4	2.9	1.4	2.9	1.4	2.9
1,000							1.6	2.6	1.4	2.8	1.4	2.8	1.4	2.8
1,500									1.5	2.6	1.5	2.7	1.5	2.7
2,000									1.6	2.5	1.6	2.6	1.6	2.6
3,000									1.7	2.4	1.7	2.4	1.6	2.4

And Sample Size is:	For Field Size of: 500 Lower Limit	500 Upper Limit	1,000 Lower Limit	1,000 Upper Limit	1,500 Lower Limit	1,500 Upper Limit	2,000 Lower Limit	2,000 Upper Limit	10,000 Lower Limit	10,000 Upper Limit	50,000 Lower Limit	50,000 Upper Limit	100,000 and over Lower Limit	100,000 and over Upper Limit
	Confidence Level 95% (Two-sided) Confidence Level 97.5% (One-sided)													
50	.2%	10.2%	.1%	10.4%	.1%	10.5%	.1%	10.6%	.1%	10.6%	.1%	10.7%	.1%	10.7%
80	.3	7.5	.3	7.7	.2	7.8	.2	7.8	.2	7.9	.2	8.0	.2	8.0
90	.4	6.9	.3	7.2	.3	7.3	.3	7.3	.2	7.4	.2	7.4	.2	7.4
100	.4	6.5	.3	6.8	.3	6.9	.3	6.9	.3	7.0	.2	7.0	.2	7.0
120	.5	5.8	.4	6.1	.4	6.2	.4	6.3	.3	6.4	.3	6.4	.3	6.4
140	.6	5.4	.5	5.7	.5	5.8	.4	5.8	.4	6.0	.4	6.0	.4	6.0
150	.7	5.1	.5	5.4	.5	5.5	.5	5.6	.4	5.7	.4	5.7	.4	5.7
160	.7	5.0	.6	5.3	.5	5.4	.5	5.5	.5	5.6	.5	5.6	.5	5.6
180	.8	4.7	.7	5.1	.6	5.1	.6	5.2	.5	5.3	.5	5.4	.5	5.4
200	.9	4.4	.7	4.7	.7	4.8	.6	4.9	.6	5.0	.6	5.0	.6	5.0
250	1.1	4.0	.9	4.4	.8	4.5	.8	4.6	.7	4.8	.7	4.8	.7	4.8
300			1.1	3.8	1.0	4.0	1.0	4.0	.9	4.2	.9	4.2	.9	4.2
400			1.2	3.4	1.1	3.5	1.1	3.6	1.0	3.8	1.0	3.8	1.0	3.8
500					1.2	3.3	1.2	3.4	1.1	3.5	1.1	3.6	1.1	3.6
600					1.3	3.1	1.3	3.2	1.2	3.3	1.1	3.4	1.1	3.4
700					1.4	2.9	1.3	3.0	1.2	3.2	1.2	3.3	1.2	3.3
800							1.4	2.9	1.3	3.1	1.2	3.2	1.2	3.2
900							1.5	2.8	1.3	3.0	1.3	3.1	1.3	3.1
1,000									1.3	3.0	1.3	3.0	1.3	3.0
1,500									1.5	2.7	1.5	2.8	1.5	2.8
2,000									1.5	2.6	1.5	2.7	1.5	2.7
3,000									1.6	2.4	1.6	2.5	1.6	2.5

F

TABLE F-2 Sample Precision for Relative Frequencies for Random Samples Only—Rate of Occurrence in Sample 2% (Continued)

And Sample Size is:	For Field Size of: 500 Lower Limit	500 Upper Limit	1,000 Lower Limit	1,000 Upper Limit	1,500 Lower Limit	1,500 Upper Limit	2,000 Lower Limit	2,000 Upper Limit	10,000 Lower Limit	10,000 Upper Limit	50,000 Lower Limit	50,000 Upper Limit	100,000 and over Lower Limit	100,000 and over Upper Limit
	Confidence Level 99% (Two-sided) Confidence Level 99.5% (One-sided)													
50	.2%	13.4%	.1%	13.7%	.0*	13.8%	.0*	13.8%	.0*	14.0%	.0*	14.0%	.0*	14.0%
80	.2	9.5	.1	9.9	.1	10.0	.1	10.1	.1	10.2	.1	10.2	.1	10.2
90	.3	8.8	.2	9.2	.2	9.3	.1	9.3	.1	9.5	.1	9.5	.1	9.5
100	.4	8.2	.2	8.6	.2	8.7	.2	8.8	.1	8.9	.1	8.9	.1	8.9
120	.4	7.3	.3	7.7	.2	7.8	.2	7.9	.2	8.0	.2	8.0	.2	8.0
140	.5	6.6	.3	7.1	.3	7.2	.3	7.3	.2	7.4	.2	7.5	.2	7.5
150	.6	6.3	.4	6.7	.3	6.9	.3	6.9	.2	7.1	.2	7.1	.2	7.1
160	.6	6.1	.4	6.6	.4	6.7	.3	6.8	.3	7.0	.3	7.0	.3	7.0
180	.6	5.7	.5	6.2	.4	6.3	.4	6.4	.3	6.6	.3	6.6	.3	6.6
200	.8	5.2	.5	5.7	.5	5.9	.4	6.0	.4	6.1	.3	6.2	.3	6.2
250	.9	4.7	.7	5.3	.6	5.5	.6	5.5	.5	5.7	.5	5.8	.5	5.8
300			.9	4.5	.8	4.7	.8	4.8	.7	5.0	.7	5.0	.7	5.0
400			1.1	3.9	1.0	4.1	.9	4.2	.8	4.4	.8	4.4	.8	4.4
500					1.1	3.7	1.0	3.8	.9	4.1	.9	4.1	.9	4.1
600					1.2	3.5	1.1	3.6	1.0	3.8	.9	3.8	.9	3.8
700					1.3	3.2	1.2	3.4	1.0	3.6	1.0	3.7	1.0	3.7
800							1.3	3.2	1.1	3.5	1.1	3.5	1.0	3.5
900							1.3	3.1	1.1	3.4	1.1	3.4	1.1	3.5
1,000									1.2	3.3	1.1	3.4	1.1	3.4
1,500									1.3	3.0	1.3	3.0	1.3	3.1
2,000									1.4	2.8	1.4	2.9	1.4	2.9
3,000									1.4	2.7	1.4	2.8	1.4	2.8

*Less than 0.05%.

TABLE F-3 Sample Precision for Relative Frequencies for Random Samples Only—Rate of Occurrence in Sample 3%

And Sample Size is:	For Field Size of: 500 Lower Limit	500 Upper Limit	1,000 Lower Limit	1,000 Upper Limit	1,500 Lower Limit	1,500 Upper Limit	2,000 Lower Limit	2,000 Upper Limit	10,000 Lower Limit	10,000 Upper Limit	50,000 Lower Limit	50,000 Upper Limit	100,000 and over Lower Limit	100,000 and over Upper Limit
	Confidence Level 90% (Two-sided) Confidence Level 95% (One-sided)													
80	.9%	8.0%	.8%	8.2%	.7%	8.3%	.7%	8.3%	.7%	8.4%	.7%	8.4%	.7%	8.4%
90	1.0	7.5	.9	7.8	.8	7.8	.8	7.9	.8	8.0	.8	8.0	.8	8.0
100	1.0	7.2	.9	7.4	.9	7.5	.9	7.5	.8	7.6	.8	7.6	.8	7.6
120	1.2	6.5	1.1	6.8	1.1	6.9	1.0	6.9	1.0	7.0	1.0	7.0	1.0	7.0
140	1.4	6.1	1.2	6.4	1.2	6.5	1.2	6.6	1.1	6.7	1.1	6.7	1.1	6.7
150	1.4	5.9	1.3	6.2	1.2	6.3	1.2	6.4	1.1	6.5	1.1	6.5	1.1	6.5
160	1.5	5.8	1.3	6.1	1.3	6.2	1.3	6.3	1.2	6.4	1.2	6.4	1.2	6.4
180	1.6	5.5	1.4	5.9	1.4	6.0	1.4	6.0	1.3	6.2	1.3	6.2	1.3	6.2
200	1.7	5.2	1.5	5.6	1.5	5.7	1.4	5.7	1.4	5.8	1.3	5.9	1.3	5.9
250	2.0	4.9	1.7	5.3	1.7	5.4	1.6	5.5	1.6	5.6	1.5	5.7	1.5	5.7
300			1.9	4.8	1.9	4.9	1.8	4.9	1.7	5.1	1.7	5.1	1.7	5.1
400			2.1	4.4	2.0	4.5	2.0	4.6	1.9	4.7	1.9	4.7	1.9	4.7
500			2.3	4.1	2.2	4.2	2.1	4.3	2.0	4.5	2.0	4.5	2.0	4.5
600					2.2	4.0	2.2	4.1	2.1	4.3	2.1	4.3	2.1	4.4
700					2.4	3.9	2.3	4.0	2.2	4.2	2.1	4.2	2.1	4.2
800							2.4	3.9	2.2	4.1	2.2	4.1	2.2	4.1
900							2.4	3.8	2.2	4.0	2.2	4.0	2.2	4.1
1,000							2.5	3.7	2.3	3.9	2.3	4.0	2.3	4.0
1,500									2.4	3.7	2.4	3.8	2.4	3.8
2,000									2.5	3.6	2.5	3.6	2.5	3.7
3,000									2.6	3.4	2.6	3.5	2.5	3.5

F

TABLE F-3 Sample Precision for Relative Frequencies for Random Samples Only—Rate of Occurrence in Sample 3% (Continued)

And Sample Size is:	For Field Size of: 500 Lower Limit	500 Upper Limit	1,000 Lower Limit	1,000 Upper Limit	1,500 Lower Limit	1,500 Upper Limit	2,000 Lower Limit	2,000 Upper Limit	10,000 Lower Limit	10,000 Upper Limit	50,000 Lower Limit	50,000 Upper Limit	100,000 and over Lower Limit	100,000 and over Upper Limit
	Confidence Level 95% (Two-sided) Confidence Level 97.5% (One-sided)													
80	.7%	8.9%	.6%	9.2%	.6%	9.3%	.6%	9.3%	.5%	9.5%	.5%	9.5%	.5%	9.5%
90	.8	8.4	.7	8.7	.6	8.8	.6	8.8	.6	8.9	.6	8.9	.6	9.0
100	.9	8.0	.7	8.3	.7	8.3	.7	8.4	.6	8.5	.6	8.5	.6	8.5
120	1.0	7.2	.9	7.5	.9	7.6	.8	7.6	.8	7.8	.8	7.8	.8	7.8
140	1.2	6.7	1.0	7.1	1.0	7.2	.9	7.3	.9	7.4	.9	7.4	.9	7.4
150	1.3	6.5	1.1	6.8	1.0	6.9	1.0	7.0	.9	7.1	.9	7.1	.9	7.2
160	1.3	6.4	1.1	6.7	1.1	6.8	1.1	6.9	1.0	7.0	1.0	7.1	1.0	7.1
180	1.4	6.0	1.2	6.4	1.2	6.5	1.1	6.6	1.1	6.8	1.1	6.8	1.1	6.8
200	1.5	5.7	1.3	6.1	1.2	6.2	1.2	6.2	1.1	6.4	1.1	6.4	1.1	6.4
250	1.8	5.2	1.5	5.8	1.5	5.9	1.4	6.0	1.3	6.1	1.3	6.2	1.3	6.2
300			1.8	5.1	1.7	5.2	1.6	5.3	1.5	5.5	1.5	5.5	1.5	5.5
400			1.9	4.7	1.8	4.9	1.7	4.9	1.6	5.1	1.6	5.2	1.6	5.2
500					2.0	4.5	2.0	4.6	1.8	4.8	1.8	4.8	1.8	4.8
600					2.1	4.2	2.1	4.3	1.9	4.6	1.9	4.6	1.9	4.6
700					2.2	4.1	2.1	4.2	2.0	4.4	2.0	4.5	2.0	4.5
800							2.2	4.0	2.1	4.3	2.0	4.3	2.0	4.4
900							2.3	3.9	2.1	4.2	2.1	4.2	2.1	4.3
1,000									2.2	4.1	2.1	4.2	2.1	4.2
1,500									2.3	3.9	2.3	3.9	2.3	3.9
2,000									2.4	3.7	2.4	3.8	2.4	3.8
3,000									2.5	3.5	2.5	3.6	2.5	3.6

And Sample Size is:	For Field Size of: 500 Lower Limit	500 Upper Limit	1,000 Lower Limit	1,000 Upper Limit	1,500 Lower Limit	1,500 Upper Limit	2,000 Lower Limit	2,000 Upper Limit	10,000 Lower Limit	10,000 Upper Limit	50,000 Lower Limit	50,000 Upper Limit	100,000 and over Lower Limit	100,000 and over Upper Limit
	Confidence Level 99% (Two-sided) Confidence Level 99.5% (One-sided)													
80	.5%	11.1%	.4%	11.5%	.3%	11.6%	.3%	11.7%	.3%	11.8%	.3%	11.9%	.2%	11.9%
90	.6	10.4	.4	10.8	.4	10.9	.4	11.0	.3	11.1	.3	11.1	.3	11.2
100	.6	9.8	.5	10.2	.4	10.3	.4	10.4	.4	10.5	.3	10.6	.3	10.6
120	.8	8.8	.6	9.2	.6	9.3	.5	9.4	.5	9.6	.5	9.6	.4	9.6
140	.9	8.1	.7	8.6	.7	8.8	.6	8.8	.6	9.0	.6	9.0	.5	9.0
150	1.0	7.7	.8	8.2	.7	8.4	.7	8.5	.6	8.6	.6	8.7	.6	8.7
160	1.1	7.6	.8	8.1	.8	8.2	.7	8.3	.7	8.5	.6	8.5	.6	8.5
180	1.2	7.1	.9	7.7	.9	7.8	.8	7.9	.7	8.1	.7	8.1	.7	8.2
200	1.3	6.6	1.0	7.2	.9	7.3	.9	7.4	.8	7.6	.8	7.6	.8	7.7
250	1.6	6.0	1.2	6.7	1.1	6.9	1.1	7.0	1.0	7.2	1.0	7.3	1.0	7.3
300			1.5	5.8	1.5	6.0	1.4	6.1	1.3	6.4	1.2	6.4	1.2	6.4
400			1.6	5.3	1.5	5.5	1.4	5.6	1.3	5.9	1.2	5.9	1.2	5.9
500					1.8	5.0	1.7	5.1	1.6	5.4	1.5	5.4	1.5	5.4
600					1.9	4.7	1.8	4.8	1.7	5.1	1.6	5.2	1.6	5.2
700					2.1	4.4	2.0	4.6	1.8	4.9	1.7	5.0	1.7	5.0
800							2.0	4.4	1.8	4.7	1.8	4.8	1.8	4.8
900							2.1	4.3	1.9	4.6	1.8	4.7	1.8	4.7
1,000									1.9	4.5	1.9	4.6	1.9	4.6
1,500									2.1	4.2	2.1	4.2	2.1	4.3
2,000									2.3	4.0	2.2	4.0	2.2	4.1
3,000									2.4	3.7	2.3	3.8	2.3	3.8

F

4%

TABLE F-4 Sample Precision for Relative Frequencies for Random Samples Only—Rate of Occurrence in Sample 4%

And Sample Size is:	For Field Size of: 500 Lower Limit	500 Upper Limit	1,000 Lower Limit	1,000 Upper Limit	1,500 Lower Limit	1,500 Upper Limit	2,000 Lower Limit	2,000 Upper Limit	10,000 Lower Limit	10,000 Upper Limit	50,000 Lower Limit	50,000 Upper Limit	100,000 and over Lower Limit	100,000 and over Upper Limit
	Confidence Level 90% (Two-sided) Confidence Level 95% (One-sided)													
50	.9%	11.7%	.8%	12.0%	.8%	12.0%	.8%	12.1%	.7%	12.1%	.7%	12.2%	.7%	12.2%
80	1.4	9.3	1.3	9.6	1.2	9.7	1.2	9.7	1.2	9.8	1.2	9.8	1.2	9.8
90	1.5	8.9	1.4	9.1	1.4	9.2	1.3	9.2	1.3	9.3	1.3	9.4	1.3	9.4
100	1.7	8.5	1.5	8.7	1.5	8.8	1.4	8.9	1.4	9.0	1.4	9.0	1.4	9.0
120	1.9	7.8	1.7	8.1	1.7	8.2	1.6	8.2	1.6	8.3	1.6	8.4	1.6	8.4
140	2.1	7.4	1.9	7.7	1.8	7.8	1.8	7.9	1.7	8.0	1.7	8.0	1.7	8.0
150	2.1	7.2	1.9	7.5	1.9	7.6	1.9	7.6	1.8	7.8	1.8	7.8	1.8	7.8
160	2.2	7.1	2.0	7.4	2.0	7.5	1.9	7.6	1.9	7.7	1.8	7.7	1.8	7.7
180	2.4	6.8	2.2	7.2	2.1	7.3	2.1	7.3	2.0	7.5	2.0	7.5	2.0	7.5
200	2.5	6.4	2.2	6.8	2.2	6.9	2.1	7.0	2.1	7.1	2.0	7.1	2.0	7.1
250	2.7	5.9	2.5	6.3	2.4	6.5	2.3	6.5	2.3	6.7	2.2	6.7	2.2	6.7
300			2.7	6.0	2.6	6.1	2.5	6.2	2.5	6.3	2.4	6.4	2.4	6.4
400			2.9	5.5	2.8	5.7	2.8	5.8	2.7	5.9	2.6	6.0	2.6	6.0
500			3.1	5.2	3.0	5.4	2.9	5.5	2.8	5.7	2.8	5.7	2.8	5.7
600					3.1	5.2	3.0	5.3	2.9	5.5	2.9	5.5	2.9	5.5
700					3.2	5.0	3.1	5.1	3.0	5.4	2.9	5.4	2.9	5.4
800							3.2	5.0	3.0	5.2	3.0	5.3	3.0	5.3
900							3.3	4.9	3.1	5.2	3.1	5.2	3.1	5.2
1,000							3.4	4.8	3.1	5.1	3.1	5.1	3.1	5.1
1,500									3.3	4.8	3.3	4.9	3.2	4.9
2,000									3.4	4.7	3.4	4.8	3.3	4.8
3,000									3.5	4.5	3.5	4.6	3.5	4.6

And Sample Size is:	For Field Size of: 500 Lower Limit	Upper Limit	1,000 Lower Limit	Upper Limit	1,500 Lower Limit	Upper Limit	2,000 Lower Limit	Upper Limit	10,000 Lower Limit	Upper Limit	50,000 Lower Limit	Upper Limit	100,000 and over Lower Limit	Upper Limit
	Confidence Level 95% (Two-sided) Confidence Level 97.5% (One-sided)													
50	.7%	13.2%	.6%	13.5%	.6%	13.6%	.5%	13.6%	.5%	13.7%	.5%	13.7%	.5%	13.7%
80	1.2	10.4	1.0	10.6	1.0	10.7	1.0	10.8	.9	10.9	.9	10.9	.9	10.9
90	1.3	9.8	1.1	10.1	1.1	10.2	1.1	10.2	1.0	10.4	1.0	10.4	1.0	10.4
100	1.4	9.3	1.3	9.6	1.2	9.7	1.2	9.8	1.1	9.9	1.1	9.9	1.1	9.9
120	1.6	8.5	1.4	8.9	1.4	9.0	1.4	9.1	1.3	9.2	1.3	9.2	1.3	9.2
140	1.8	8.1	1.6	8.5	1.6	8.6	1.5	8.6	1.5	8.8	1.4	8.8	1.4	8.8
150	1.9	7.8	1.7	8.6	1.6	8.3	1.6	8.3	1.5	8.5	1.5	8.5	1.5	8.5
160	2.0	7.6	1.8	8.1	1.7	8.2	1.7	8.2	1.6	8.4	1.6	8.4	1.6	8.4
180	2.1	7.3	1.9	7.8	1.8	7.9	1.8	8.0	1.7	8.1	1.7	8.1	1.7	8.2
200	2.3	6.9	2.0	7.3	1.9	7.5	1.9	7.5	1.8	7.7	1.7	7.7	1.7	7.7
250	2.5	6.3	2.2	6.8	2.1	6.9	2.1	7.0	2.0	7.2	1.9	7.2	1.9	7.2
300			2.5	6.4	2.4	6.5	2.3	6.6	2.2	6.8	2.2	6.8	2.2	6.8
400			2.7	5.8	2.6	6.0	2.6	6.1	2.4	6.3	2.4	6.3	2.4	6.4
500					2.8	5.7	2.7	5.8	2.6	6.0	2.5	6.0	2.5	6.0
600					2.9	5.4	2.9	5.5	2.7	5.8	2.6	5.8	2.6	5.8
700					3.1	5.2	3.0	5.4	2.8	5.6	2.7	5.7	2.7	5.7
800							3.1	5.2	2.8	5.5	2.8	5.5	2.8	5.6
900							3.2	5.1	2.9	5.4	2.9	5.4	2.9	5.5
1,000									3.0	5.3	2.9	5.4	2.9	5.4
1,500									3.2	5.0	3.1	5.1	3.1	5.1
2,000									3.3	4.8	3.2	4.9	3.2	4.9
3,000									3.5	4.6	3.4	4.7	3.4	4.7

F

TABLE F-4 Sample Precision for Relative Frequencies for Random Samples Only—Rate of Occurrence in Sample 4% (Continued)

And Sample Size is:	For Field Size of: 500 Lower Limit	500 Upper Limit	1,000 Lower Limit	1,000 Upper Limit	1,500 Lower Limit	1,500 Upper Limit	2,000 Lower Limit	2,000 Upper Limit	10,000 Lower Limit	10,000 Upper Limit	50,000 Lower Limit	50,000 Upper Limit	100,000 and over Lower Limit	100,000 and over Upper Limit
	Confidence Level 99% (Two-sided) Confidence Level 99.5% (One-sided)													
50	.4%	16.5%	.3%	16.9%	.3%	17.0%	.3%	17.0%	.2%	17.2%	.2%	17.2%	.2%	17.2%
80	.8	12.7	.7	13.1	.6	13.2	.6	13.3	.5	13.4	.5	13.4	.5	13.5
90	.9	11.9	.8	12.3	.7	12.4	.7	12.5	.6	12.7	.6	12.7	.6	12.7
100	1.0	11.2	.9	11.7	.8	11.8	.8	11.9	.7	12.0	.7	12.1	.7	12.1
120	1.2	10.2	1.0	10.7	1.0	10.8	.9	10.9	.9	11.1	.9	11.1	.8	11.1
140	1.4	9.5	1.2	10.0	1.1	10.2	1.1	10.3	1.0	10.5	1.0	10.5	1.0	10.5
150	1.5	9.1	1.3	9.6	1.2	9.8	1.2	9.9	1.1	10.1	1.0	10.1	1.0	10.1
160	1.6	8.9	1.4	9.5	1.3	9.7	1.2	9.7	1.1	9.9	1.1	10.0	1.1	10.0
180	1.8	8.5	1.5	9.1	1.4	9.2	1.4	9.3	1.3	9.5	1.2	9.6	1.2	9.6
200	1.9	7.9	1.6	8.5	1.5	8.7	1.5	8.8	1.3	9.0	1.3	9.0	1.3	9.0
250	2.2	7.1	1.8	7.8	1.7	8.0	1.7	8.1	1.5	8.3	1.5	8.4	1.5	8:4
300			2.1	7.2	2.0	7.4	1.9	7.5	1.8	7.7	1.8	7.8	1.8	7.8
400			2.5	6.4	2.3	6.7	2.2	6.8	2.0	7.1	2.0	7.1	2.0	7.2
500					2.5	6.3	2.4	6.4	2.2	6.7	2.2	6.7	2.2	6.7
600					2.7	5.9	2.6	6.1	2.4	6.4	2.3	6.4	2.3	6.5
700					2.8	5.6	2.7	5.8	2.5	6.2	2.4	6.2	2.4	6.3
800							2.8	5.6	2.6	6.0	2.5	6.1	2.5	6.1
900							2.9	5.4	2.6	5.9	2.6	5.9	2.6	5.9
1,000									2.7	5.7	2.7	5.8	2.7	5.8
1,500									2.9	5.3	2.9	5.4	2.9	5.4
2,000									3.1	5.1	3.0	5.2	3.0	5.2
3,000									3.3	4.8	3.2	5.0	3.2	5.0

TABLE F-5 Sample Precision for Relative Frequencies for Random Samples Only—Rate of Occurrence in Sample 5%

And Sample Size is:	For Field Size of: 500		1,000		1,500		2,000		10,000		50,000		100,000 and over	
	Lower Limit	Upper Limit	Lower Limit	Upper Limit	Lower Limit	Upper Limit	Lower Limit	Upper Limit	Lower Limit	Upper Limit	Lower Limit	Upper Limit	Lower Limit	Upper Limit
	Confidence Level 90% (Two-sided) Confidence Level 95% (One-sided)													
80	2.0%	10.6%	1.8%	10.9%	1.8%	11.0%	1.8%	11.0%	1.7%	11.1%	1.7%	11.1%	1.7%	11.1%
90	2.2	10.1	2.0	10.4	2.0	10.5	1.9	10.5	1.9	10.6	1.9	10.7	1.9	10.7
100	2.3	9.7	2.1	10.0	2.1	10.1	2.1	10.1	2.0	10.3	2.0	10.3	2.0	10.3
120	2.6	9.1	2.4	9.4	2.3	9.5	2.3	9.5	2.2	9.6	2.2	9.7	2.2	9.7
140	2.8	8.7	2.6	9.0	2.5	9.1	2.5	9.2	2.4	9.3	2.4	9.3	2.4	9.3
150	2.9	8.4	2.7	8.7	2.6	8.8	2.6	8.9	2.5	9.0	2.5	9.0	2.5	9.0
160	3.0	8.2	2.7	8.5	2.7	8.7	2.6	8.7	2.5	8.8	2.5	8.9	2.5	8.9
180	3.1	7.9	2.9	8.3	2.8	8.4	2.8	8.4	2.7	8.6	2.7	8.6	2.7	8.6
200	3.3	7.6	3.0	8.0	2.9	8.1	2.9	8.2	2.8	8.3	2.8	8.4	2.8	8.4
250	3.6	7.1	3.3	7.5	3.2	7.7	3.1	7.7	3.0	7.9	3.0	7.9	3.0	7.9
300			3.4	7.2	3.3	7.3	3.3	7.4	3.2	7.6	3.2	7.6	3.1	7.6
400			3.7	6.7	3.6	6.9	3.5	7.0	3.4	7.2	3.4	7.2	3.4	7.2
500			4.0	6.4	3.8	6.6	3.7	6.7	3.6	6.9	3.5	6.9	3.5	6.9
600					4.0	6.3	3.9	6.4	3.7	6.7	3.7	6.7	3.7	6.7
700					4.1	6.2	4.0	6.3	3.8	6.5	3.8	6.6	3.7	6.6
800							4.1	6.1	3.9	6.4	3.8	6.5	3.8	6.5
900							4.2	6.0	3.9	6.3	3.9	6.4	3.9	6.4
1,000							4.2	5.9	4.0	6.2	3.9	6.3	3.9	6.3
1,500									4.2	5.9	4.1	6.0	4.1	6.0
2,000									4.3	5.8	4.2	5.9	4.2	5.9
3,000									4.5	5.6	4.4	5.7	4.4	5.7

F

TABLE F-5 Sample Precision for Relative Frequencies for Random Samples Only—Rate of Occurrence in Sample 5% (Continued)

And Sample Size is:	500 Lower Limit	500 Upper Limit	1,000 Lower Limit	1,000 Upper Limit	1,500 Lower Limit	1,500 Upper Limit	2,000 Lower Limit	2,000 Upper Limit	10,000 Lower Limit	10,000 Upper Limit	50,000 Lower Limit	50,000 Upper Limit	100,000 and over Lower Limit	100,000 and over Upper Limit
	For Field Size of:													
	Confidence Level 95% (Two-sided) Confidence Level 97.5% (One-sided)													
80	1.7%	11.7%	1.5%	12.0%	1.5%	12.1%	1.5%	12.2%	1.4%	12.3%	1.4%	12.3%	1.4%	12.3%
90	1.8	11.1	1.7	11.4	1.6	11.5	1.6	11.6	1.5	11.7	1.5	11.7	1.5	11.8
100	2.0	10.6	1.8	11.0	1.8	11.1	1.7	11.1	1.7	11.3	1.6	11.3	1.6	11.3
120	2.3	9.8	2.1	10.2	2.0	10.3	2.0	10.4	1.9	10.5	1.9	10.6	1.9	10.6
140	2.5	9.4	2.3	9.8	2.2	9.9	2.2	10.0	2.1	10.1	2.1	10.1	2.1	10.1
150	2.6	9.0	2.3	9.4	2.3	9.6	2.2	9.6	2.1	9.8	2.1	9.8	2.1	9.8
160	2.7	8.8	2.4	9.2	2.3	9.4	2.3	9.4	2.2	9.6	2.2	9.6	2.2	9.6
180	2.8	8.4	2.6	8.9	2.5	9.0	2.4	9.1	2.3	9.2	2.3	9.3	2.3	9.3
200	3.0	8.1	2.7	8.6	2.6	8.7	2.6	8.8	2.5	9.0	2.4	9.0	2.4	9.0
250	3.3	7.5	3.0	8.0	2.9	8.2	2.8	8.3	2.7	8.4	2.7	8.5	2.6	8.5
300			3.2	7.6	3.1	7.8	3.0	7.9	2.9	8.1	2.8	8.1	2.8	8.1
400			3.5	7.0	3.4	7.2	3.3	7.3	3.1	7.6	3.1	7.6	3.1	7.6
500					3.6	6.9	3.5	7.0	3.3	7.2	3.3	7.3	3.3	7.3
600					3.8	6.6	3.7	6.7	3.4	7.0	3.4	7.0	3.4	7.1
700					3.9	6.4	3.8	6.5	3.6	6.8	3.5	6.9	3.5	6.9
800							3.9	6.4	3.7	6.7	3.6	6.7	3.6	6.7
900							4.0	6.2	3.7	6.6	3.7	6.6	3.7	6.6
1,000									3.8	6.5	3.8	6.5	3.7	6.5
1,500									4.0	6.1	4.0	6.2	4.0	6.2
2,000									4.2	5.9	4.1	6.0	4.1	6.0
3,000									4.4	5.7	4.3	5.8	4.2	5.8

And Sample Size is:	For Field Size of: 500 Lower Limit	500 Upper Limit	1,000 Lower Limit	1,000 Upper Limit	1,500 Lower Limit	1,500 Upper Limit	2,000 Lower Limit	2,000 Upper Limit	10,000 Lower Limit	10,000 Upper Limit	50,000 Lower Limit	50,000 Upper Limit	100,000 and over Lower Limit	100,000 and over Upper Limit
	Confidence Level 99% (Two-sided) Confidence Level 99.5% (One-sided)													
80	1.2%	14.1%	1.0%	14.5%	1.0%	14.7%	.9%	14.7%	.9%	14.9%	.9%	14.9%	.9%	14.9%
90	1.4	13.3	1.2	13.7	1.1	13.9	1.1	14.0	1.0	14.1	1.0	14.2	1.0	14.2
100	1.5	12.6	1.3	13.1	1.2	13.2	1.2	13.3	1.1	13.5	1.1	13.5	1.1	13.5
120	1.8	11.6	1.5	12.1	1.5	12.2	1.4	12.3	1.3	12.5	1.3	12.5	1.3	12.5
140	2.0	10.9	1.8	11.4	1.7	11.6	1.6	11.7	1.5	11.9	1.5	11.9	1.5	11.9
150	2.1	10.4	1.8	11.0	1.7	11.2	1.7	11.3	1.6	11.5	1.6	11.5	1.6	11.5
160	2.2	10.1	1.9	10.7	1.8	10.9	1.8	11.0	1.7	11.2	1.6	11.2	1.6	11.2
180	2.4	9.6	2.1	10.2	2.0	10.4	1.9	10.5	1.8	10.7	1.8	10.8	1.8	10.8
200	2.6	9.2	2.2	9.8	2.1	10.0	2.0	10.1	1.9	10.4	1.9	10.4	1.9	10.4
250	3.0	8.3	2.5	9.1	2.4	9.3	2.3	9.4	2.2	9.6	2.1	9.7	2.1	9.7
300			2.8	8.5	2.6	8.7	2.5	8.9	2.4	9.1	2.3	9.2	2.3	9.2
400			3.2	7.7	3.0	8.0	2.9	8.1	2.7	8.4	2.6	8.5	2.6	8.5
500					3.2	7.5	3.1	7.7	2.9	8.0	2.8	8.1	2.8	8.1
600					3.4	7.1	3.3	7.3	3.1	7.7	3.0	7.7	3.0	7.8
700					3.6	6.8	3.5	7.0	3.2	7.4	3.1	7.5	3.1	7.5
800							3.6	6.8	3.3	7.2	3.2	7.3	3.2	7.3
900							3.7	6.6	3.4	7.1	3.3	7.2	3.3	7.2
1,000									3.5	6.9	3.4	7.0	3.4	7.0
1,500									3.8	6.5	3.7	6.6	3.7	6.6
2,000									4.0	6.2	3.9	6.4	3.8	6.4
3,000									4.2	5.9	4.1	6.1	4.0	6.1

F

TABLE F-6 Sample Precision for Relative Frequencies for Random Samples Only—Rate of Occurrence in Sample 6%

And Sample Size is:	For Field Size of: 500 Lower Limit	500 Upper Limit	1,000 Lower Limit	1,000 Upper Limit	1,500 Lower Limit	1,500 Upper Limit	2,000 Lower Limit	2,000 Upper Limit	10,000 Lower Limit	10,000 Upper Limit	50,000 Lower Limit	50,000 Upper Limit	100,000 and over Lower Limit	100,000 and over Upper Limit
	Confidence Level 90% (Two-sided) Confidence Level 95% (One-sided)													
50	1.9%	14.4%	1.8%	14.6%	1.7%	14.7%	1.7%	14.8%	1.7%	14.8%	1.7%	14.9%	1.7%	14.9%
80	2.6	11.9	2.5	12.2	2.4	12.3	2.4	12.3	2.3	12.4	2.3	12.4	2.3	12.4
90	2.8	11.4	2.7	11.7	2.6	11.8	2.6	11.8	2.5	11.9	2.5	11.9	2.5	11.9
100	3.0	11.0	2.8	11.3	2.8	11.4	2.7	11.4	2.7	11.5	2.7	11.5	2.6	11.5
120	3.3	10.3	3.1	10.6	3.0	10.7	3.0	10.8	2.9	10.9	2.9	10.9	2.9	10.9
140	3.6	9.9	3.3	10.2	3.3	10.3	3.2	10.4	3.1	10.5	3.1	10.6	3.1	10.6
150	3.6	9.6	3.4	9.9	3.3	10.1	3.3	10.1	3.2	10.2	3.2	10.3	3.2	10.3
160	3.8	9.3	3.5	9.7	3.5	9.8	3.4	9.9	3.3	10.0	3.3	10.1	3.3	10.1
180	4.0	9.0	3.7	9.4	3.6	9.5	3.6	9.6	3.5	9.7	3.5	9.8	3.4	9.8
200	4.1	8.7	3.6	9.2	3.7	9.3	3.7	9.4	3.6	9.5	3.6	9.5	3.6	9.5
250	4.4	8.2	4.1	8.7	4.0	8.9	3.9	8.9	3.8	9.1	3.8	9.1	3.8	9.1
300			4.3	8.3	4.2	8.5	4.1	8.5	4.0	8.7	4.0	8.7	4.0	8.8
400			4.6	7.8	4.5	8.0	4.4	8.1	4.3	8.3	4.2	8.3	4.2	8.3
500			4.9	7.4	4.7	7.7	4.6	7.8	4.5	8.0	4.4	8.0	4.4	8.0
600					4.9	7.4	4.8	7.5	4.6	7.8	4.5	7.8	4.5	7.8
700					5.0	7.2	4.9	7.4	4.7	7.6	4.6	7.7	4.6	7.7
800							5.0	7.2	4.8	7.5	4.7	7.5	4.7	7.6
900							5.1	7.1	4.8	7.4	4.8	7.4	4.8	7.5
1,000							5.2	7.0	4.9	7.3	4.9	7.4	4.9	7.4
1,500									5.1	7.0	5.1	7.1	5.1	7.1
2,000									5.3	6.8	5.2	6.9	5.2	6.9
3,000									5.4	6.6	5.3	6.7	5.3	6.8

And Sample Size is:	For Field Size of: 500 Lower Limit	Upper Limit	1,000 Lower Limit	Upper Limit	1,500 Lower Limit	Upper Limit	2,000 Lower Limit	Upper Limit	10,000 Lower Limit	Upper Limit	50,000 Lower Limit	Upper Limit	100,000 and over Lower Limit	Upper Limit
	Confidence Level 95% (Two-sided) Confidence Level 97.5% (One-sided)													
50	1.5%	16.0%	1.4%	16.3%	1.3%	16.4%	1.3%	16.4%	1.3%	16.5%	1.3%	16.6%	1.3%	16.6%
80	2.3	13.0	2.1	13.3	2.0	13.5	2.0	13.5	1.9	13.6	1.9	13.7	1.9	13.7
90	2.5	12.4	2.3	12.8	2.2	12.9	2.2	12.9	2.1	13.0	2.1	13.1	2.1	13.1
100	2.6	11.9	2.4	12.3	2.4	12.4	2.3	12.4	2.3	12.6	2.2	12.6	2.2	12.6
120	2.9	11.1	2.7	11.5	2.6	11.6	2.6	11.7	2.5	11.8	2.5	11.9	2.5	11.9
140	3.2	10.6	3.0	11.0	2.9	11.2	2.8	11.2	2.7	11.4	2.7	11.4	2.7	11.4
150	3.3	10.3	3.0	10.7	2.9	10.8	2.9	10.9	2.8	11.1	2.8	11.1	2.8	11.1
160	3.5	10.0	3.2	10.4	3.1	10.6	3.0	10.6	2.9	10.8	2.9	10.8	2.9	10.8
180	3.6	9.6	3.3	10.1	3.3	10.2	3.2	10.3	3.1	10.4	3.1	10.5	3.1	10.5
200	3.8	9.3	3.5	9.8	3.4	9.9	3.3	10.0	3.2	10.2	3.2	10.2	3.2	10.2
250	4.2	8.7	3.8	9.2	3.6	9.4	3.6	9.5	3.4	9.7	3.4	9.7	3.4	9.8
300			4.0	8.7	3.9	8.9	3.8	9.0	3.7	9.2	3.6	9.3	3.6	9.3
400			4.4	8.1	4.2	8.4	4.1	8.5	4.0	8.7	3.9	8.8	3.9	8.8
500					4.5	8.0	4.4	8.1	4.2	8.4	4.1	8.4	4.1	8.4
600					4.7	7.7	4.5	7.8	4.3	8.1	4.3	8.2	4.3	8.2
700					4.8	7.5	4.7	7.6	4.4	7.9	4.4	8.0	4.4	8.0
800							4.8	7.4	4.5	7.8	4.5	7.8	4.5	7.9
900							4.9	7.3	4.6	7.7	4.6	7.7	4.6	7.7
1,000									4.6	7.6	4.6	7.6	4.6	7.6
1,500									5.0	7.2	4.9	7.3	4.9	7.3
2,000									5.1	7.1	5.0	7.1	5.0	7.1
3,000									5.3	6.8	5.2	6.9	5.2	6.9

F

TABLE F-6 Sample Precision for Relative Frequencies for Random Samples Only—Rate of Occurrence in Sample 6% (Continued)

And Sample Size is:	For Field Size of: 500 Lower Limit	500 Upper Limit	1,000 Lower Limit	1,000 Upper Limit	1,500 Lower Limit	1,500 Upper Limit	2,000 Lower Limit	2,000 Upper Limit	10,000 Lower Limit	10,000 Upper Limit	50,000 Lower Limit	50,000 Upper Limit	100,000 and over Lower Limit	100,000 and over Upper Limit
	Confidence Level 99% (Two-sided) Confidence Level 99.5% (One-sided)													
50	1.0%	19.6%	.8%	20.0%	.8%	20.1%	.8%	20.1%	.7%	20.3%	.7%	20.3%	.7%	20.3%
80	1.7	15.5	1.5	15.9	1.4	16.1	1.4	16.2	1.3	16.3	1.3	16.4	1.3	16.4
90	1.9	14.7	1.6	15.1	1.6	15.3	1.5	15.4	1.5	15.5	1.4	15.6	1.4	15.6
100	2.0	14.0	1.8	14.5	1.7	14.6	1.7	14.7	1.6	14.9	1.6	14.9	1.6	14.9
120	2.4	12.9	2.1	13.4	2.0	13.6	1.9	13.7	1.8	13.9	1.8	13.9	1.8	13.9
140	2.6	12.2	2.3	12.8	2.2	13.0	2.2	13.0	2.1	13.2	2.1	13.3	2.1	13.3
150	2.8	11.7	2.4	12.3	2.3	12.5	2.3	12.6	2.1	12.8	2.1	12.8	2.1	12.9
160	2.9	11.4	2.6	12.0	2.5	12.2	2.4	12.2	2.3	12.5	2.3	12.5	2.3	12.5
180	3.1	10.8	2.8	11.5	2.7	11.7	2.6	11.8	2.5	12.0	2.4	12.0	2.4	12.1
200	3.3	10.4	2.9	11.1	2.8	11.3	2.8	11.4	2.6	11.6	2.6	11.7	2.6	11.7
250	3.8	9.6	3.2	10.4	3.1	10.6	3.0	10.7	2.9	11.0	2.8	11.0	2.8	11.0
300			3.6	9.7	3.4	9.9	3.3	10.1	3.1	10.3	3.1	10.4	3.1	10.4
400			4.0	8.9	3.8	9.2	3.7	9.3	3.4	9.6	3.4	9.7	3.4	9.7
500					4.1	8.7	4.0	8.8	3.7	9.2	3.6	9.2	3.6	9.2
600					4.3	8.3	4.2	8.4	3.9	8.8	3.8	8.9	3.8	8.9
700					4.5	7.9	4.3	8.2	4.0	8.6	4.0	8.7	3.9	8.7
800							4.5	7.9	4.1	8.4	4.1	8.5	4.1	8.5
900							4.6	7.7	4.3	8.2	4.2	8.3	4.2	8.3
1,000									4.3	8.1	4.3	8.2	4.3	8.2
1,500									4.7	7.6	4.6	7.7	4.5	7.7
2,000									4.9	7.3	4.8	7.5	4.7	7.5
3,000									5.1	7.0	5.0	7.2	4.9	7.2

TABLE F-7 Sample Precision for Relative Frequencies for Random Samples Only—Rate of Occurrence in Sample 7%

And Sample Size is:	For Field Size of: 500		1,000		1,500		2,000		10,000		50,000		100,000 and over	
	Lower Limit	Upper Limit	Lower Limit	Upper Limit	Lower Limit	Upper Limit	Lower Limit	Upper Limit	Lower Limit	Upper Limit	Lower Limit	Upper Limit	Lower Limit	Upper Limit
	Confidence Level 90% (Two-sided) Confidence Level 95% (One-sided)													
80	3.3%	13.1%	3.1%	13.4%	3.1%	13.5%	3.1%	13.5%	3.0%	13.7%	3.0%	13.7%	3.0%	13.7%
90	3.5	12.6	3.3	12.9	3.3	13.0	3.3	13.0	3.2	13.2	3.2	13.2	3.2	13.2
100	3.7	12.1	3.5	12.4	3.4	12.5	3.4	12.6	3.3	12.7	3.3	12.7	3.3	12.7
120	4.0	11.5	3.8	11.8	3.7	11.9	3.7	12.0	3.6	12.1	3.6	12.1	3.6	12.1
140	4.3	11.0	4.1	11.4	4.0	11.5	4.0	11.6	3.9	11.7	3.9	11.7	3.9	11.7
150	4.5	10.7	4.2	11.1	4.1	11.2	4.1	11.3	4.0	11.4	4.0	11.4	4.0	11.4
160	4.6	10.5	4.3	10.9	4.2	11.0	4.2	11.1	4.1	11.2	4.1	11.2	4.1	11.2
180	4.8	10.2	4.5	10.6	4.4	10.7	4.4	10.7	4.3	10.9	4.2	10.9	4.2	10.9
200	5.0	9.9	4.6	10.3	4.5	10.4	4.5	10.5	4.4	10.7	4.4	10.7	4.4	10.7
250	5.3	9.3	4.9	9.9	4.8	10.0	4.8	10.1	4.6	10.3	4.6	10.3	4.6	10.3
300			5.2	9.4	5.1	9.6	5.0	9.7	4.9	9.9	4.8	9.9	4.8	9.9
400			5.5	8.9	5.4	9.1	5.3	9.2	5.1	9.4	5.1	9.4	5.1	9.5
500			5.8	8.5	5.6	8.8	5.5	8.9	5.3	9.1	5.3	9.1	5.3	9.1
600					5.8	8.5	5.7	8.6	5.5	8.9	5.4	8.9	5.4	8.9
700					5.9	8.3	5.8	8.4	5.6	8.7	5.6	8.8	5.5	8.8
800							5.9	8.3	5.7	8.6	5.6	8.6	5.6	8.6
900							6.0	8.1	5.8	8.5	5.7	8.5	5.7	8.5
1,000							6.1	8.0	5.8	8.4	5.8	8.4	5.8	8.5
1,500									6.1	8.1	6.0	8.1	6.0	8.2
2,000									6.2	7.9	6.1	8.0	6.1	8.0
3,000									6.4	7.7	6.3	7.8	6.3	7.8

F

TABLE F-7 Sample Precision for Relative Frequencies for Random Samples Only—Rate of Occurrence in Sample 7% (Continued)

And Sample Size is:	For Field Size of: 500 Lower Limit	500 Upper Limit	1,000 Lower Limit	1,000 Upper Limit	1,500 Lower Limit	1,500 Upper Limit	2,000 Lower Limit	2,000 Upper Limit	10,000 Lower Limit	10,000 Upper Limit	50,000 Lower Limit	50,000 Upper Limit	100,000 and over Lower Limit	100,000 and over Upper Limit
	Confidence Level 95% (Two-sided) Confidence Level 97.5% (One-sided)													
80	2.9%	14.3%	2.7%	14.6%	2.6%	14.7%	2.6%	14.8%	2.5%	14.9%	2.5%	15.0%	2.5%	15.0%
90	3.1	13.7	2.9	14.0	2.8	14.2	2.8	14.2	2.7	14.3	2.7	14.4	2.7	14.4
100	3.3	13.2	3.1	13.6	3.0	13.7	3.0	13.7	2.9	13.9	2.9	13.9	2.9	13.9
120	3.6	12.3	3.4	12.8	3.3	12.9	3.3	12.9	3.2	13.1	3.2	13.1	3.1	13.1
140	3.9	11.8	3.7	12.2	3.6	12.4	3.5	12.4	3.4	12.6	3.4	12.6	3.4	12.6
150	4.1	11.4	3.8	11.9	3.7	12.0	3.7	12.1	3.6	12.2	3.6	12.3	3.5	12.3
160	4.2	11.2	3.9	11.6	3.8	11.8	3.8	11.9	3.7	12.0	3.6	12.1	3.6	12.1
180	4.4	10.8	4.1	11.3	4.0	11.4	3.9	11.5	3.8	11.7	3.8	11.7	3.8	11.7
200	4.6	10.4	4.3	10.9	4.2	11.1	4.1	11.2	4.0	11.4	4.0	11.4	3.9	11.4
250	5.0	9.8	4.6	10.4	4.4	10.6	4.4	10.7	4.2	10.9	4.2	10.9	4.2	10.9
300			4.9	9.9	4.7	10.1	4.6	10.2	4.5	10.4	4.5	10.4	4.4	10.4
400			5.3	9.3	5.0	9.5	4.9	9.6	4.8	9.9	4.8	9.9	4.8	9.9
500					5.3	9.1	5.2	9.2	5.0	9.5	5.0	9.6	5.0	9.6
600					5.6	8.8	5.4	8.9	5.2	9.2	5.1	9.3	5.1	9.3
700					5.7	8.5	5.6	8.7	5.3	9.0	5.3	9.1	5.3	9.1
800							5.7	8.5	5.4	8.9	5.4	8.9	5.4	9.0
900							5.9	8.4	5.5	8.8	5.5	8.8	5.5	8.8
1,000									5.6	8.6	5.5	8.7	5.5	8.7
1,500									5.9	8.3	5.8	8.4	5.8	8.4
2,000									6.1	8.1	6.0	8.2	6.0	8.2
3,000									6.3	7.8	6.2	7.9	6.1	8.0

And Sample Size is:	For Field Size of: 500 Lower Limit	500 Upper Limit	1,000 Lower Limit	1,000 Upper Limit	1,500 Lower Limit	1,500 Upper Limit	2,000 Lower Limit	2,000 Upper Limit	10,000 Lower Limit	10,000 Upper Limit	50,000 Lower Limit	50,000 Upper Limit	100,000 and over Lower Limit	100,000 and over Upper Limit
Confidence Level 99% (Two-sided) Confidence Level 99.5% (One-sided)														
80	2.2%	16.8%	1.9%	17.3%	1.9%	17.4%	1.8%	17.5%	1.7%	17.7%	1.7%	17.7%	1.7%	17.7%
90	2.4	16.0	2.1	16.5	2.1	16.6	2.0	16.7	1.9	16.9	1.9	16.9	1.9	16.9
100	2.6	15.3	2.3	15.8	2.3	16.0	2.2	16.1	2.1	16.2	2.1	16.3	2.1	16.3
120	3.0	14.2	2.7	14.7	2.6	14.9	2.5	15.0	2.4	15.2	2.4	15.2	2.4	15.2
140	3.3	13.4	3.0	14.0	2.8	14.2	2.8	14.3	2.7	14.5	2.6	14.6	2.6	14.6
150	3.5	12.9	3.1	13.5	3.0	13.7	3.0	13.8	2.9	14.0	2.8	14.1	2.8	14.1
160	3.6	12.6	3.3	13.2	3.1	13.4	3.1	13.5	3.0	13.7	2.9	13.8	2.9	13.8
180	3.9	12.1	3.5	12.7	3.4	12.9	3.3	13.0	3.1	13.3	3.1	13.3	3.1	13.3
200	4.1	11.6	3.7	12.3	3.5	12.5	3.4	12.6	3.3	12.9	3.3	12.9	3.3	12.9
250	4.5	10.7	4.0	11.6	3.8	11.8	3.8	11.9	3.6	12.2	3.5	12.3	3.5	12.3
300			4.3	10.9	4.2	11.1	4.1	11.3	3.9	11.6	3.8	11.6	3.8	11.6
400			4.8	10.0	4.6	10.3	4.5	10.5	4.2	10.8	4.2	10.9	4.2	10.9
500					4.9	9.8	4.8	10.0	4.5	10.3	4.4	10.4	4.4	10.4
600					5.2	9.4	5.0	9.6	4.7	10.0	4.6	10.1	4.6	10.1
700					5.4	9.1	5.2	9.3	4.9	9.7	4.8	9.8	4.8	9.8
800							5.4	9.0	5.0	9.5	4.9	9.6	4.9	9.6
900							5.5	8.8	5.1	9.3	5.0	9.4	5.0	9.4
1,000									5.2	9.2	5.1	9.3	5.1	9.3
1,500									5.6	8.7	5.5	8.8	5.4	8.8
2,000									5.8	8.4	5.7	8.5	5.6	8.6
3,000									6.1	8.1	5.9	8.2	5.9	8.3

F

TABLE F-8 Sample Precision for Relative Frequencies for Random Samples Only—Rate of Occurrence in Sample 8%

And Sample Size is:	For Field Size of: 500 Lower Limit	500 Upper Limit	1,000 Lower Limit	1,000 Upper Limit	1,500 Lower Limit	1,500 Upper Limit	2,000 Lower Limit	2,000 Upper Limit	10,000 Lower Limit	10,000 Upper Limit	50,000 Lower Limit	50,000 Upper Limit	100,000 and over Lower Limit	100,000 and over Upper Limit
	Confidence Level 90% (Two-sided) Confidence Level 95% (One-sided)													
50	3.0%	17.0%	2.9%	17.2%	2.9%	17.3%	2.8%	17.3%	2.8%	17.4%	2.8%	17.4%	2.8%	17.4%
80	4.0	14.3	3.8	14.6	3.8	14.7	3.7	14.8	3.7	14.9	3.7	14.9	3.7	14.9
90	4.3	13.8	4.1	14.1	4.0	14.2	4.0	14.3	3.9	14.4	3.9	14.4	3.9	14.4
100	4.5	13.4	4.2	13.7	4.2	13.8	4.1	13.9	4.0	14.0	4.0	14.0	4.0	14.0
120	4.8	12.7	4.6	13.0	4.5	13.1	4.5	13.2	4.4	13.3	4.4	13.3	4.4	13.3
140	5.1	12.2	4.9	12.6	4.8	12.7	4.7	12.7	4.6	12.9	4.6	12.9	4.6	12.9
150	5.2	11.9	5.0	12.3	4.9	12.4	4.8	12.5	4.7	12.6	4.7	12.7	4.7	12.7
160	5.4	11.7	5.1	12.1	5.0	12.2	5.0	12.3	4.9	12.4	4.9	12.4	4.9	12.4
180	5.6	11.3	5.3	11.7	5.2	11.9	5.2	11.9	5.1	12.1	5.0	12.1	5.0	12.1
200	5.8	11.0	5.5	11.5	5.4	11.6	5.3	11.7	5.2	11.8	5.2	11.9	5.2	11.9
250	6.2	10.4	5.8	11.0	5.6	11.2	5.6	11.2	5.5	11.4	5.4	11.4	5.4	11.5
300			6.0	10.5	5.9	10.7	5.8	10.8	5.7	11.0	5.7	11.0	5.7	11.0
400			6.4	10.0	6.3	10.2	6.2	10.3	6.0	10.5	6.0	10.6	6.0	10.6
500			6.7	9.6	6.5	9.9	6.4	10.0	6.2	10.2	6.2	10.3	6.2	10.3
600					6.7	9.6	6.6	9.7	6.4	10.0	6.3	10.0	6.3	10.0
700					6.9	9.4	6.7	9.5	6.5	9.8	6.4	9.9	6.4	9.9
800							6.9	9.3	6.6	9.7	6.5	9.7	6.5	9.7
900							7.0	9.2	6.7	9.6	6.6	9.6	6.6	9.6
1,000							7.1	9.1	6.7	9.5	6.7	9.5	6.7	9.5
1,500									7.0	9.1	6.9	9.2	6.9	9.2
2,000									7.2	8.9	7.1	9.0	7.1	9.0
3,000									7.3	8.7	7.2	8.8	7.2	8.8

And Sample Size is:	For Field Size of: 500 Lower Limit	500 Upper Limit	1,000 Lower Limit	1,000 Upper Limit	1,500 Lower Limit	1,500 Upper Limit	2,000 Lower Limit	2,000 Upper Limit	10,000 Lower Limit	10,000 Upper Limit	50,000 Lower Limit	50,000 Upper Limit	100,000 and over Lower Limit	100,000 and over Upper Limit
	Confidence Level 95% (Two-sided) Confidence Level 97.5% (One-sided)													
50	2.5%	13.7%	2.4%	19.0%	2.3%	19.1%	2.3%	19.1%	2.2%	19.2%	2.2%	19.2%	2.2%	19.3%
80	3.5	15.6	3.3	15.9	3.3	16.0	3.2	16.1	3.1	16.2	3.1	16.2	3.1	16.3
90	3.3	14.9	3.5	15.3	3.5	15.4	3.4	15.5	3.4	15.6	3.3	15.6	3.3	15.7
100	4.0	14.4	3.7	14.8	3.7	14.9	3.6	15.0	3.5	15.1	3.5	15.2	3.5	15.2
120	4.4	13.6	4.1	14.0	4.0	14.1	4.0	14.2	3.9	14.3	3.8	14.4	3.8	14.4
140	4.7	13.0	4.4	13.4	4.3	13.6	4.2	13.7	4.1	13.8	4.1	13.9	4.1	13.9
150	4.9	12.6	4.6	13.1	4.5	13.2	4.4	13.3	4.3	13.5	4.3	13.5	4.3	13.5
160	5.0	12.4	4.7	12.8	4.6	13.0	4.5	13.1	4.4	13.2	4.4	13.3	4.4	13.3
180	5.2	11.9	4.9	12.5	4.8	12.6	4.7	12.7	4.6	12.9	4.6	12.9	4.6	12.9
200	5.4	11.6	5.1	12.1	4.9	12.3	4.9	12.4	4.7	12.6	4.7	12.6	4.7	12.6
250	5.9	10.9	5.4	11.6	5.2	11.8	5.2	11.9	5.0	12.1	5.0	12.1	5.0	12.1
300			5.7	11.0	5.5	11.2	5.5	11.3	5.3	11.6	5.3	11.6	5.2	11.6
400			6.1	10.4	5.9	10.6	5.8	10.7	5.6	11.0	5.6	11.1	5.6	11.1
500					6.2	10.2	6.1	10.3	5.9	10.6	5.8	10.7	5.8	10.7
600					6.4	9.9	6.3	10.0	6.1	10.4	6.0	10.4	6.0	10.4
700					6.6	9.6	6.5	9.8	6.2	10.2	6.1	10.2	6.1	10.2
800							6.6	9.6	6.3	10.0	6.3	10.1	6.2	10.1
900							6.8	9.4	6.4	9.9	6.4	9.9	6.3	9.9
1,000									6.5	9.7	6.4	9.8	6.4	9.8
1,500									6.8	9.4	6.7	9.4	6.7	9.5
2,000									7.0	9.1	6.9	9.2	6.9	9.3
3,000									7.2	8.8	7.1	9.0	7.1	9.0

F

TABLE F-8 Sample Precision for Relative Frequencies for Random Samples Only—Rate of Occurrence in Sample 8% (Continued)

And Sample Size is:	For Field Size of: 500 Lower Limit	500 Upper Limit	1,000 Lower Limit	1,000 Upper Limit	1,500 Lower Limit	1,500 Upper Limit	2,000 Lower Limit	2,000 Upper Limit	10,000 Lower Limit	10,000 Upper Limit	50,000 Lower Limit	50,000 Upper Limit	100,000 and over Lower Limit	100,000 and over Upper Limit
Confidence Level 99% (Two-sided) Confidence Level 99.5% (One-sided)														
50	1.7%	22.4%	1.6%	22.8%	1.5%	22.9%	1.5%	22.9%	1.4%	23.1%	1.4%	23.1%	1.4%	23.1%
80	2.7	18.2	2.5	18.6	2.4	18.8	2.3	18.9	2.2	19.0	2.2	19.1	2.2	19.1
90	3.0	17.3	2.7	17.8	2.6	18.0	2.6	18.0	2.5	18.2	2.4	18.3	2.4	18.3
100	3.2	16.6	2.9	17.1	2.8	17.3	2.8	17.4	2.7	17.6	2.6	17.6	2.6	17.6
120	3.6	15.5	3.3	16.0	3.2	16.2	3.1	16.3	3.0	16.5	3.0	16.5	3.0	16.6
140	4.0	14.7	3.6	15.3	3.5	15.5	3.4	15.6	3.3	15.8	3.3	15.8	3.3	15.9
150	4.2	14.2	3.8	14.8	3.7	15.0	3.6	15.1	3.5	15.3	3.5	15.4	3.5	15.4
160	4.3	13.8	3.9	14.5	3.8	14.7	3.7	14.8	3.6	15.0	3.6	15.1	3.6	15.1
180	4.6	13.3	4.2	14.0	4.1	14.1	3.9	14.3	3.8	14.5	3.8	14.6	3.8	14.6
200	4.9	12.8	4.4	13.5	4.2	13.8	4.1	13.9	4.0	14.1	3.9	14.2	3.9	14.2
250	5.3	11.9	4.7	12.8	4.6	13.0	4.5	13.2	4.3	13.4	4.2	13.5	4.2	13.5
300			5.1	12.1	4.9	12.3	4.8	12.5	4.6	12.8	4.6	12.8	4.6	12.8
400			5.6	11.2	5.4	11.5	5.3	11.7	5.0	12.0	5.0	12.1	5.0	12.1
500					5.7	10.9	5.6	11.1	5.3	11.5	5.2	11.6	5.2	11.6
600					6.0	10.5	5.9	10.7	5.5	11.1	5.5	11.2	5.5	11.2
700					6.3	10.2	6.1	10.4	5.7	10.9	5.6	10.9	5.6	11.0
800							6.3	10.1	5.9	10.6	5.8	10.7	5.8	10.8
900							6.4	9.9	6.0	10.5	5.9	10.6	5.9	10.6
1,000									6.1	10.3	6.0	10.4	6.0	10.4
1,500									6.5	9.8	6.4	9.9	6.3	10.0
2,000									6.7	9.5	6.6	9.6	6.6	9.7
3,000									7.0	9.1	6.8	9.3	6.8	9.3

TABLE F-9 Sample Precision for Relative Frequencies for Random Samples Only—Rate of Occurrence in Sample 9%

Confidence Level 90% (Two-sided)
Confidence Level 95% (One-sided)

And Sample Size is:	For Field Size of: 500 Lower Limit	500 Upper Limit	1,000 Lower Limit	1,000 Upper Limit	1,500 Lower Limit	1,500 Upper Limit	2,000 Lower Limit	2,000 Upper Limit	10,000 Lower Limit	10,000 Upper Limit	50,000 Lower Limit	50,000 Upper Limit	100,000 and over Lower Limit	100,000 and over Upper Limit
80	4.7%	15.6%	4.5%	15.9%	4.5%	16.0%	4.4%	16.0%	4.4%	16.1%	4.4%	16.1%	4.4%	16.2%
90	5.0	15.0	4.8	15.3	4.7	15.4	4.7	15.5	4.6	15.6	4.6	15.6	4.6	15.6
100	5.2	14.6	5.0	14.9	4.9	15.0	4.9	15.1	4.8	15.2	4.8	15.2	4.8	15.2
120	5.6	13.8	5.3	14.2	5.3	14.3	5.2	14.4	5.1	14.5	5.1	14.5	5.1	14.5
140	6.0	13.3	5.8	13.7	5.7	13.9	5.6	13.9	5.5	14.1	5.5	14.1	5.5	14.1
150	6.1	13.0	5.8	13.4	5.7	13.6	5.7	13.6	5.6	13.8	5.5	13.8	5.5	13.8
160	6.2	12.8	5.9	13.2	5.8	13.4	5.8	13.4	5.7	13.6	5.6	13.6	5.6	13.6
180	6.4	12.4	6.1	12.9	6.0	13.0	6.0	13.1	5.8	13.3	5.8	13.3	5.8	13.3
200	6.6	12.1	6.3	12.6	6.2	12.8	6.1	12.8	6.0	13.0	6.0	13.0	6.0	13.0
250	7.0	11.6	6.6	12.1	6.5	12.3	6.4	12.4	6.3	12.6	6.2	13.6	6.2	12.6
300			6.9	11.7	6.8	11.9	6.7	11.9	6.5	12.1	6.5	12.2	6.5	12.2
400			7.3	11.1	7.1	11.3	7.0	11.4	6.9	11.6	6.8	11.7	6.8	11.7
500			7.6	10.7	7.4	10.9	7.3	11.1	7.1	11.3	7.0	11.4	7.0	11.4
600					7.6	10.7	7.5	10.8	7.3	11.1	7.2	11.1	7.2	11.1
700					7.8	10.4	7.6	10.6	7.4	10.9	7.3	11.0	7.3	11.0
800							7.8	10.4	7.5	10.8	7.4	10.8	7.4	10.8
900							7.9	10.3	7.6	10.6	7.5	10.7	7.5	10.7
1,000							8.0	10.1	7.7	10.5	7.6	10.6	7.6	10.6
1,500									7.9	10.2	7.9	10.3	7.8	10.3
2,000									8.1	10.0	8.0	10.1	8.0	10.1
3,000									8.2	9.8	8.1	9.9	8.1	9.9

F

TABLE F-9 Sample Precision for Relative Frequencies for Random Samples Only—Rate of Occurrence in Sample 9% (Continued)

And Sample Size is:	For Field Size of: 500 Lower Limit	500 Upper Limit	1,000 Lower Limit	1,000 Upper Limit	1,500 Lower Limit	1,500 Upper Limit	2,000 Lower Limit	2,000 Upper Limit	10,000 Lower Limit	10,000 Upper Limit	50,000 Lower Limit	50,000 Upper Limit	100,000 and over Lower Limit	100,000 and over Upper Limit
	Confidence Level 95% (Two-sided) Confidence Level 97.5% (One-sided)													
80	4.2%	16.8%	4.0%	17.2%	3.9%	17.3%	3.9%	17.3%	3.8%	17.5%	3.8%	17.5%	3.8%	17.5%
90	4.5	16.2	4.2	16.5	4.1	16.7	4.1	16.7	4.0	16.9	4.0	16.9	4.0	16.9
100	4.7	15.6	4.5	16.0	4.4	16.2	4.3	16.2	4.2	16.4	4.2	16.4	4.2	16.4
120	5.1	14.8	4.8	15.2	4.7	15.3	4.7	15.4	4.6	15.6	4.6	15.6	4.5	15.6
140	5.5	14.2	5.2	14.6	5.0	14.8	5.0	14.9	4.9	15.0	4.9	15.0	4.9	15.0
150	5.6	13.8	5.3	14.3	5.2	14.4	5.1	14.5	5.0	14.7	5.0	14.7	5.0	14.7
160	5.8	13.5	5.4	14.0	5.3	14.2	5.3	14.3	5.1	14.5	5.1	14.5	5.1	14.5
180	6.0	13.1	5.6	13.6	5.6	13.8	5.5	13.9	5.3	14.1	5.3	14.1	5.3	14.1
200	6.3	12.7	5.8	13.3	5.7	13.5	5.6	13.6	5.5	13.8	5.5	13.8	5.5	13.8
250	6.7	12.0	6.2	12.7	6.0	12.9	6.0	13.0	5.8	13.3	5.8	13.3	5.8	13.3
300			6.5	12.2	6.4	12.4	6.3	12.5	6.1	12.7	6.1	12.8	6.1	12.8
400			7.0	11.5	6.8	11.8	6.7	11.9	6.5	12.2	6.4	12.2	6.4	12.2
500					7.1	11.3	7.0	11.5	6.7	11.8	6.7	11.8	6.7	11.8
600					7.3	11.0	7.2	11.1	6.9	11.5	6.9	11.5	6.9	11.6
700					7.5	10.7	7.4	10.9	7.1	11.3	7.0	11.3	7.0	11.3
800							7.6	10.7	7.2	11.1	7.1	11.2	7.1	11.2
900							7.7	10.5	7.3	11.0	7.2	11.0	7.2	11.1
1,000									7.4	10.8	7.3	10.9	7.3	10.9
1,500									7.7	10.4	7.6	10.5	7.6	10.6
2,000									7.9	10.2	7.8	10.3	7.8	10.3
3,000									8.2	9.9	8.1	10.0	8.0	10.1

And Sample Size is:	For Field Size of: 500 Lower Limit	500 Upper Limit	1,000 Lower Limit	1,000 Upper Limit	1,500 Lower Limit	1,500 Upper Limit	2,000 Lower Limit	2,000 Upper Limit	10,000 Lower Limit	10,000 Upper Limit	50,000 Lower Limit	50,000 Upper Limit	100,000 and over Lower Limit	100,000 and over Upper Limit
Confidence Level 99% (Two-sided) Confidence Level 99.5% (One-sided)														
80	3.3%	19.5%	3.0%	19.9%	2.9%	20.1%	2.9%	20.2%	2.8%	20.4%	2.8%	20.4%	2.8%	20.4%
90	3.6	18.6	3.3	19.1	3.2	19.3	3.1	19.3	3.0	19.5	3.0	19.6	3.0	19.6
100	3.8	17.9	3.5	18.4	3.4	18.6	3.4	18.7	3.2	18.9	3.2	18.9	3.2	18.9
120	4.3	16.7	3.9	17.3	3.8	17.5	3.8	17.6	3.6	17.8	3.6	17.8	3.6	17.8
140	4.7	15.9	4.3	16.5	4.2	16.7	4.1	16.8	3.9	17.1	3.9	17.1	3.9	17.1
150	4.9	15.4	4.5	16.1	4.3	16.3	4.3	16.4	4.1	16.6	4.1	16.6	4.1	16.7
160	5.0	15.1	4.6	15.8	4.5	16.0	4.4	16.1	4.2	16.3	4.2	16.4	4.2	16.4
180	5.3	14.5	4.9	15.2	4.7	15.4	4.6	15.5	4.5	15.8	4.4	15.8	4.4	15.9
200	5.6	14.0	5.1	14.8	4.9	15.0	4.8	15.1	4.7	15.4	4.6	15.4	4.6	15.4
250	6.1	13.1	5.5	14.0	5.3	14.2	5.2	14.4	5.0	14.7	5.0	14.7	4.9	14.8
300			5.9	13.2	5.7	13.5	5.6	13.7	5.4	14.0	5.3	14.0	5.3	14.1
400			6.5	12.3	6.2	12.7	6.1	12.8	5.8	13.2	5.7	13.3	5.7	13.3
500					6.6	12.1	6.4	12.3	6.1	12.7	6.1	12.7	6.1	12.8
600					6.9	11.6	6.7	11.8	6.4	12.3	6.3	12.4	6.3	12.4
700					7.1	11.3	6.9	11.5	6.5	12.0	6.5	12.1	6.5	12.1
800							7.1	11.1	6.7	11.8	6.6	11.9	6.6	11.9
900							7.3	11.0	6.8	11.6	6.8	11.7	6.7	11.7
1,000									7.0	11.4	6.9	11.5	6.9	11.6
1,500									7.3	10.9	7.2	11.0	7.2	11.1
2,000									7.6	10.6	7.5	10.7	7.5	10.7
3,000									7.9	10.2	7.8	10.4	7.7	10.4

F

TABLE F-10 Sample Precision for Relative Frequencies for Random Samples Only—Rate of Occurrence in Sample 10%

And Sample Size is:	For Field Size of: 500 Lower Limit	500 Upper Limit	1,000 Lower Limit	1,000 Upper Limit	1,500 Lower Limit	1,500 Upper Limit	2,000 Lower Limit	2,000 Upper Limit	10,000 Lower Limit	10,000 Upper Limit	50,000 Lower Limit	50,000 Upper Limit	100,000 and over Lower Limit	100,000 and over Upper Limit
	Confidence Level 90% (Two-sided) Confidence Level 95% (One-sided)													
50	4.3%	19.4%	4.2%	19.7%	4.1%	19.8%	4.1%	19.8%	4.0%	19.8%	4.0%	19.9%	4.0%	19.9%
80	5.5	16.7	5.3	17.1	5.2	17.2	5.2	17.2	5.1	17.3	5.1	17.3	5.1	17.4
90	5.8	16.2	5.6	16.5	5.5	16.6	5.5	16.7	5.4	16.8	5.4	16.8	5.4	16.8
100	6.0	15.7	5.8	16.1	5.7	16.2	5.6	16.2	5.6	16.4	5.5	16.4	5.5	16.4
120	6.4	15.0	6.1	15.4	6.0	15.5	6.0	15.5	5.9	15.7	5.9	15.7	5.9	15.7
140	6.8	14.4	6.4	14.8	6.4	15.0	6.3	15.0	6.2	15.2	6.2	15.2	6.2	15.2
150	6.9	14.0	6.6	14.4	6.5	14.6	6.4	14.6	6.3	14.8	6.3	14.8	6.3	14.8
160	7.0	14.0	6.7	14.4	6.6	14.5	6.5	14.6	6.4	14.8	6.4	14.8	6.4	14.8
180	7.3	13.6	6.9	14.1	6.8	14.2	6.7	14.3	6.6	14.4	6.6	14.5	6.6	14.5
200	7.5	13.3	7.1	13.8	7.0	13.9	6.9	14.0	6.8	14.2	6.8	14.2	6.8	14.2
250	7.9	12.6	7.5	13.2	7.3	13.4	7.3	13.5	7.1	13.7	7.1	13.7	7.1	13.7
300			7.8	12.8	7.6	13.0	7.5	13.1	7.4	13.3	7.3	13.3	7.3	13.3
400			8.2	12.2	8.0	12.4	7.9	12.5	7.7	12.8	7.7	12.8	7.7	12.8
500			8.5	11.8	8.3	12.0	8.2	12.2	8.0	12.4	7.9	12.5	7.9	12.5
600					8.5	11.7	8.4	11.9	8.1	12.2	8.1	12.2	8.1	12.2
700					8.7	11.5	8.6	11.7	8.3	12.0	8.2	12.1	8.2	12.1
800							8.7	11.5	8.4	11.8	8.3	11.9	8.3	11.9
900							8.8	11.3	8.5	11.7	8.4	11.8	8.4	11.8
1,000							8.9	11.2	8.6	11.6	8.5	11.7	8.5	11.7
1,500									8.9	11.3	8.8	11.3	8.8	11.4
2,000									9.0	11.1	8.9	11.2	8.9	11.2
3,000									9.3	10.8	9.2	10.9	9.2	10.9

And Sample Size is:	For Field Size of: 500 Lower Limit	500 Upper Limit	1,000 Lower Limit	1,000 Upper Limit	1,500 Lower Limit	1,500 Upper Limit	2,000 Lower Limit	2,000 Upper Limit	10,000 Lower Limit	10,000 Upper Limit	50,000 Lower Limit	50,000 Upper Limit	100,000 and over Lower Limit	100,000 and over Upper Limit
	Confidence Level 95% (Two-sided) Confidence Level 97.5% (One-sided)													
50	3.7%	21.2%	3.5%	21.5%	3.4%	21.6%	3.4%	21.7%	3.3%	21.8%	3.3%	21.8%	3.3%	21.8%
80	4.9	18.0	4.6	18.4	4.6	18.5	4.5	18.6	4.4	18.7	4.4	18.8	4.4	18.8
90	5.2	17.4	4.9	17.8	4.8	17.9	4.8	17.9	4.7	18.1	4.7	18.1	4.7	18.1
100	5.4	16.8	5.2	17.3	5.1	17.4	5.0	17.4	4.9	17.6	4.9	17.6	4.9	17.6
120	5.9	15.9	5.6	16.4	5.5	16.5	5.4	16.6	5.3	16.8	5.3	16.8	5.3	16.8
140	6.2	15.3	5.9	15.8	5.8	15.9	5.7	16.0	5.6	16.2	5.6	16.2	5.6	16.2
150	6.4	15.0	6.0	15.5	5.9	15.6	5.9	15.7	5.7	15.9	5.7	15.9	5.7	16.0
160	6.6	14.7	6.2	15.3	6.1	15.4	6.0	15.5	5.9	15.7	5.8	15.7	5.8	15.7
180	6.8	14.3	6.4	14.8	6.3	15.0	6.2	15.1	6.1	15.3	6.0	15.3	6.0	15.3
200	7.1	13.9	6.6	14.5	6.5	14.7	6.4	14.8	6.3	15.0	6.2	15.0	6.2	15.0
250	7.6	13.1	7.0	13.8	6.9	14.0	6.8	14.1	6.6	14.4	6.6	14.4	6.6	14.4
300			7.4	13.3	7.2	13.6	7.1	13.7	6.9	13.9	6.9	14.0	6.9	14.0
400			7.9	12.6	7.6	12.9	7.5	13.0	7.3	13.3	7.3	13.4	7.2	13.4
500					8.0	12.4	7.9	12.6	7.6	12.9	7.5	13.0	7.5	13.0
600					8.2	12.1	8.1	12.2	7.8	12.6	7.7	12.7	7.7	12.7
700					8.5	11.8	8.3	12.0	8.0	12.4	7.9	12.5	7.9	12.5
800							8.5	11.8	8.1	12.2	8.0	12.3	8.0	12.3
900							8.6	11.6	8.2	12.1	8.1	12.1	8.1	12.2
1,000									8.3	11.9	8.2	12.0	8.2	12.0
1,500									8.6	11.5	8.6	11.6	8.5	11.6
2,000									8.9	11.3	8.7	11.4	8.7	11.4
3,000									9.1	10.9	9.0	11.1	9.0	11.1

F

TABLE F-10 Sample Precision for Relative Frequencies for Random Samples Only—Rate of Occurrence in Sample 10% (Continued)

And Sample Size is:	For Field Size of: 500 Lower Limit	500 Upper Limit	1,000 Lower Limit	1,000 Upper Limit	1,500 Lower Limit	1,500 Upper Limit	2,000 Lower Limit	2,000 Upper Limit	10,000 Lower Limit	10,000 Upper Limit	50,000 Lower Limit	50,000 Upper Limit	100,000 and over Lower Limit	100,000 and over Upper Limit
	Confidence Level 99% (Two-sided) Confidence Level 99.5% (One-sided)													
50	2.6%	25.0%	2.4%	25.4%	2.4%	25.5%	2.3%	25.6%	2.2%	25.8%	2.2%	25.8%	2.2%	25.8%
80	3.9	20.7	3.6	21.2	3.5	21.4	3.4	21.5	3.3	21.7	3.3	21.7	3.3	21.7
90	4.2	19.9	3.9	20.4	3.8	20.6	3.7	20.6	3.6	20.8	3.6	20.9	3.6	20.9
100	4.5	19.1	4.1	19.7	4.0	19.9	4.0	19.9	3.9	20.2	3.8	20.2	3.8	20.2
120	5.0	17.9	4.6	18.5	4.5	18.7	4.4	18.8	4.3	19.1	4.2	19.1	4.2	19.1
140	5.4	17.0	5.0	17.7	4.8	17.9	4.8	18.0	4.6	18.2	4.6	18.3	4.6	18.3
150	5.6	16.7	5.1	17.3	5.0	17.6	4.9	17.7	4.7	17.9	4.7	17.9	4.7	18.0
160	5.7	16.3	5.3	17.0	5.1	17.2	5.1	17.3	4.9	17.6	4.8	17.6	4.8	17.7
180	6.1	15.7	5.5	16.5	5.4	16.6	5.3	16.8	5.1	17.1	5.1	17.1	5.1	17.1
200	6.4	15.2	5.8	16.0	5.6	16.2	5.5	16.4	5.3	16.6	5.3	16.7	5.3	16.7
250	7.0	14.2	6.3	15.1	6.1	15.4	6.0	15.5	5.8	15.8	5.7	15.9	5.7	15.9
300			6.7	14.4	6.5	14.7	6.4	14.9	6.1	15.2	6.1	15.3	6.0	15.3
400			7.3	13.5	7.0	13.8	6.9	14.0	6.6	14.4	6.5	14.5	6.5	14.5
500					7.4	13.2	7.3	13.4	6.9	13.9	6.9	13.9	6.9	13.9
600					7.7	12.8	7.6	13.0	7.2	13.5	7.1	13.5	7.1	13.6
700					8.0	12.4	7.8	12.6	7.4	13.2	7.3	13.2	7.3	13.3
800							8.0	12.4	7.6	12.9	7.5	13.0	7.5	13.0
900							8.2	12.1	7.7	12.7	7.6	12.8	7.6	12.9
1,000									7.8	12.6	7.7	12.7	7.7	12.7
1,500									8.2	12.0	8.1	12.1	8.1	12.2
2,000									8.5	11.7	8.4	11.8	8.4	11.8
3,000									8.9	11.2	8.7	11.4	8.6	11.5

TABLE F-11 Sample Precision for Relative Frequencies for Random Samples Only—Rate of Occurrence in Sample 11%

Confidence Level 90% (Two-sided)
Confidence Level 95% (One-sided)

And Sample Size is:	For Field Size of: 500 Lower Limit	500 Upper Limit	1,000 Lower Limit	1,000 Upper Limit	1,500 Lower Limit	1,500 Upper Limit	2,000 Lower Limit	2,000 Upper Limit	10,000 Lower Limit	10,000 Upper Limit	50,000 Lower Limit	50,000 Upper Limit	100,000 and over Lower Limit	100,000 and over Upper Limit
80	6.2%	17.9%	6.0%	18.2%	5.9%	18.3%	5.9%	18.4%	5.8%	18.5%	5.8%	18.5%	5.8%	18.5%
90	6.5	17.3	6.3	17.7	6.2	17.8	6.2	17.8	6.1	18.0	6.1	18.0	6.1	18.0
100	6.8	16.9	6.6	17.2	6.5	17.3	6.4	17.4	6.3	17.5	6.3	17.5	6.3	17.5
120	7.2	16.1	7.0	16.5	6.9	16.6	6.8	16.7	6.7	16.8	6.7	16.9	6.7	16.9
140	7.6	15.5	7.3	16.0	7.2	16.1	7.1	16.2	7.0	16.3	7.0	16.3	7.0	16.3
150	7.8	15.3	7.4	15.7	7.3	15.9	7.3	15.9	7.2	16.1	7.1	16.1	7.1	16.1
160	7.9	15.1	7.5	15.5	7.4	15.7	7.4	15.7	7.3	15.9	7.2	15.9	7.2	15.9
180	8.1	14.7	7.8	15.2	7.7	15.3	7.6	15.4	7.5	15.6	7.4	15.6	7.4	15.6
200	8.4	14.4	8.0	14.9	7.9	15.0	7.8	15.1	7.7	15.3	7.6	15.3	7.6	15.3
250	8.9	13.7	8.4	14.3	8.2	14.5	8.2	14.6	8.0	14.8	8.0	14.8	8.0	14.8
300			8.7	13.9	8.5	14.1	8.4	14.2	8.3	14.4	8.2	14.4	8.2	14.4
400			9.1	13.3	8.9	13.5	8.8	13.6	8.6	13.9	8.6	13.9	8.6	13.9
500			9.5	12.8	9.2	13.1	9.1	13.3	8.9	13.5	8.8	13.6	8.8	13.6
600					9.5	12.8	9.3	12.9	9.1	13.3	9.0	13.3	9.0	13.3
700					9.6	12.6	9.5	12.7	9.2	13.1	9.2	13.1	9.1	13.1
800							9.7	12.5	9.3	12.9	9.3	13.0	9.3	13.0
900							9.8	12.4	9.4	12.8	9.4	12.8	9.4	12.9
1,000							9.9	12.2	9.5	12.7	9.5	12.7	9.4	12.8
1,500									9.8	12.3	9.7	12.4	9.7	12.4
2,000									10.0	12.1	9.9	12.2	9.9	12.2
3,000									10.2	11.8	10.1	12.0	10.1	12.0

F

TABLE F-11 Sample Precision for Relative Frequencies for Random Samples Only—Rate of Occurrence in Sample 11% (Continued)

And Sample Size is:	For Field Size of: 500 Lower Limit	500 Upper Limit	1,000 Lower Limit	1,000 Upper Limit	1,500 Lower Limit	1,500 Upper Limit	2,000 Lower Limit	2,000 Upper Limit	10,000 Lower Limit	10,000 Upper Limit	50,000 Lower Limit	50,000 Upper Limit	100,000 and over Lower Limit	100,000 and over Upper Limit
	Confidence Level 95% (Two-sided) Confidence Level 97.5% (One-sided)													
80	5.6%	19.2%	5.3%	19.6%	5.3%	19.7%	5.2%	19.8%	5.1%	19.9%	5.1%	20.0%	5.1%	20.0%
90	5.9	18.6	5.6	19.0	5.6	19.1	5.5	19.2	5.4	19.3	5.4	19.3	5.4	19.3
100	6.2	18.0	5.9	18.4	5.8	18.5	5.8	18.6	5.7	18.7	5.7	18.8	5.7	18.8
120	6.7	17.1	6.4	17.5	6.3	17.7	6.2	17.8	6.1	17.9	6.0	18.0	6.0	18.0
140	7.1	16.4	6.7	16.9	6.6	17.1	6.5	17.1	6.4	17.3	6.4	17.4	6.4	17.4
150	7.2	16.1	6.9	16.6	6.7	16.8	6.7	16.9	6.5	17.1	6.5	17.1	6.5	17.1
160	7.4	15.8	7.0	16.4	6.9	16.6	6.8	16.6	6.7	16.8	6.6	16.9	6.6	16.9
180	7.7	15.4	7.2	16.0	7.1	16.1	7.0	16.2	6.9	16.4	6.9	16.5	6.8	16.5
200	7.9	15.0	7.5	15.6	7.3	15.8	7.3	15.9	7.1	16.1	7.1	16.2	7.1	16.2
250	8.5	14.2	7.9	14.9	7.7	15.1	7.7	15.2	7.5	15.5	7.4	15.5	7.4	15.5
300			8.3	14.4	8.1	14.7	8.0	14.8	7.8	15.0	7.7	15.1	7.7	15.1
400			8.8	13.7	8.5	14.0	8.4	14.1	8.2	14.3	8.1	14.5	8.1	14.5
500					8.9	13.5	8.8	13.7	8.5	13.9	8.4	14.0	8.4	14.1
600					9.2	13.1	9.0	13.3	8.8	13.6	8.6	13.8	8.6	13.8
700					9.4	12.9	9.2	13.0	9.0	13.4	8.8	13.5	8.8	13.5
800							9.4	12.8	9.1	13.2	8.9	13.4	8.9	13.4
900							9.5	12.6	9.2	13.0	9.1	13.2	9.0	13.2
1,000									9.3	12.9	9.2	13.1	9.2	13.1
1,500									9.6	12.6	9.5	12.7	9.5	12.7
2,000									10.0	12.1	9.7	12.4	9.7	12.4
3,000									10.1	12.0	9.9	12.1	9.9	12.2

And Sample Size is:	For Field Size of: 500 Lower Limit	500 Upper Limit	1,000 Lower Limit	1,000 Upper Limit	1,500 Lower Limit	1,500 Upper Limit	2,000 Lower Limit	2,000 Upper Limit	10,000 Lower Limit	10,000 Upper Limit	50,000 Lower Limit	50,000 Upper Limit	100,000 and over Lower Limit	100,000 and over Upper Limit
	Confidence Level 99% (Two-sided) Confidence Level 99.5% (One-sided)													
80	4.5%	22.0%	4.2%	22.5%	4.1%	22.7%	4.0%	22.8%	3.9%	23.0%	3.9%	23.0%	3.9%	23.0%
90	4.8	21.1	4.5	21.6	4.4	21.8	4.3	21.9	4.2	22.1	4.2	22.1	4.2	22.2
100	5.2	20.3	4.8	20.9	4.7	21.1	4.6	21.2	4.5	21.4	4.5	21.4	4.5	21.4
120	5.7	19.1	5.3	19.8	5.2	19.9	5.1	20.0	5.0	20.3	4.9	20.3	4.9	20.3
140	6.1	18.2	5.7	18.9	5.6	19.1	5.5	19.2	5.3	19.4	5.3	19.5	5.3	19.5
150	6.3	17.8	5.9	18.5	5.7	18.7	5.7	18.8	5.5	19.1	5.4	19.1	5.4	19.2
160	6.5	17.5	6.0	18.2	5.9	18.4	5.8	18.5	5.6	18.8	5.6	18.8	5.6	18.9
180	6.9	16.9	6.3	17.6	6.2	17.8	6.1	18.0	5.9	18.3	5.8	18.3	5.8	18.3
200	7.2	16.3	6.6	17.1	6.4	17.4	6.3	17.5	6.1	17.8	6.1	17.9	6.1	17.9
250	7.8	15.3	7.1	16.2	6.9	16.5	6.8	16.6	6.6	17.0	6.5	17.0	6.5	17.0
300			7.5	15.5	7.3	15.9	7.2	16.0	6.9	16.4	6.9	16.4	6.9	16.4
400			8.2	14.6	7.9	14.9	7.7	15.1	7.4	15.5	7.4	15.6	7.4	15.6
500					8.3	14.3	8.1	14.5	7.8	15.0	7.7	15.1	7.7	15.1
600					8.6	13.8	8.5	14.1	8.1	14.6	8.0	14.6	8.0	14.6
700					8.9	13.5	8.7	13.7	8.3	14.3	8.2	14.3	8.2	14.3
800							8.9	13.4	8.4	14.0	8.4	14.1	8.3	14.1
900							9.1	13.2	8.6	13.8	8.5	13.9	8.5	13.9
1,000									8.7	13.6	8.6	13.8	8.6	13.8
1,500									9.2	13.1	9.0	13.2	9.0	13.2
2,000									9.5	12.7	9.3	12.9	9.3	12.9
3,000									9.8	12.3	9.6	12.5	9.6	12.5

TABLE F-12 Sample Precision for Relative Frequencies for Random Samples Only—Rate of Occurrence in Sample 12%

And Sample Size is:	For Field Size of: 500 Lower Limit	500 Upper Limit	1,000 Lower Limit	1,000 Upper Limit	1,500 Lower Limit	1,500 Upper Limit	2,000 Lower Limit	2,000 Upper Limit	10,000 Lower Limit	10,000 Upper Limit	50,000 Lower Limit	50,000 Upper Limit	100,000 and over Lower Limit	100,000 and over Upper Limit
	Confidence Level 90% (Two-sided) Confidence Level 95% (One-sided)													
50	5.7%	21.8%	5.5%	22.1%	5.5%	22.2%	5.4%	22.2%	5.4%	22.3%	5.4%	22.3%	5.4%	22.3%
80	7.0	19.1	6.8	19.4	6.7	19.5	6.7	19.6	6.6	19.7	6.6	19.7	6.6	19.7
90	7.3	18.5	7.1	18.8	7.0	19.0	6.9	19.0	6.8	19.1	6.8	19.2	6.8	19.2
100	7.6	18.0	7.4	18.4	7.3	18.5	7.2	18.5	7.1	18.7	7.1	18.7	7.1	18.7
120	8.1	17.2	7.8	17.6	7.7	17.8	7.6	17.8	7.5	18.0	7.5	18.0	7.5	18.0
140	8.4	16.7	8.1	17.1	8.0	17.2	8.0	17.3	7.8	17.4	7.8	17.5	7.8	17.5
150	8.6	16.4	8.3	16.9	8.1	17.0	8.1	17.1	8.0	17.2	7.8	17.3	7.9	17.3
160	8.8	16.2	8.4	16.6	8.3	16.8	8.2	16.9	8.1	17.0	8.1	17.1	8.1	17.1
180	9.0	15.8	8.6	16.3	8.5	16.4	8.5	16.5	8.3	16.7	8.3	16.7	8.3	16.7
200	9.3	15.4	8.8	16.0	8.7	16.1	8.6	16.2	8.5	16.4	8.5	16.4	8.5	16.4
250	9.8	14.8	9.3	15.4	9.1	15.6	9.0	15.7	8.9	15.9	8.8	15.9	8.8	15.9
300			9.6	14.9	9.4	15.2	9.3	15.2	9.1	15.5	9.1	15.5	9.1	15.5
400			10.0	14.3	9.8	14.6	9.7	14.7	9.5	14.9	9.5	15.0	9.5	15.0
500			10.4	13.9	10.1	14.2	10.0	14.3	9.8	14.6	9.7	14.6	9.7	14.7
600					10.4	13.9	10.3	14.0	10.0	14.3	9.9	14.4	9.9	14.4
700					10.6	13.6	10.4	13.8	10.1	14.1	10.1	14.2	10.1	14.2
800							10.6	13.6	10.3	14.0	10.2	14.0	10.2	14.0
900							10.7	13.4	10.4	13.8	10.3	13.9	10.3	13.9
1,000							10.8	13.3	10.5	13.7	10.4	13.8	10.4	13.8
1,500									10.8	13.3	10.7	13.4	10.7	13.5
2,000									11.0	13.1	10.9	13.2	10.8	13.3
3,000									11.2	12.8	11.1	13.0	11.1	13.0

And Sample Size is:	For Field Size of: 500 Lower Limit	500 Upper Limit	1,000 Lower Limit	1,000 Upper Limit	1,500 Lower Limit	1,500 Upper Limit	2,000 Lower Limit	2,000 Upper Limit	10,000 Lower Limit	10,000 Upper Limit	50,000 Lower Limit	50,000 Upper Limit	100,000 and over Lower Limit	100,000 and over Upper Limit
	Confidence Level 95% (Two-sided) Confidence Level 97.5% (One-sided)													
50	4.9%	23.7%	4.7%	24.0%	4.7%	24.1%	4.6%	24.2%	4.6%	24.3%	4.5%	24.3%	4.5%	24.3%
80	6.3	20.4	6.1	20.8	6.0	20.9	5.9	21.0	5.8	21.1	5.8	21.2	5.8	21.2
90	6.7	19.7	6.4	20.2	6.3	20.3	6.2	20.4	6.1	20.5	6.1	20.5	6.1	20.6
100	7.0	19.1	6.7	19.6	6.6	19.7	6.5	19.8	6.4	19.9	6.4	20.0	6.4	20.0
120	7.5	18.2	7.1	18.7	7.0	18.9	7.0	18.9	6.9	19.1	6.8	19.2	6.8	19.2
140	7.9	17.5	7.5	18.1	7.4	18.2	7.3	18.3	7.2	18.5	7.2	18.5	7.2	18.5
150	8.1	17.2	7.7	17.8	7.5	17.9	7.5	18.0	7.3	18.2	7.3	18.3	7.3	18.3
160	8.2	17.0	7.8	17.5	7.7	17.7	7.6	17.8	7.5	18.0	7.4	18.0	7.4	18.0
180	8.5	16.5	8.1	17.1	8.0	17.2	7.9	17.4	7.7	17.6	7.7	17.6	7.7	17.6
200	8.8	16.1	8.3	16.7	8.2	16.9	8.1	17.0	7.9	17.3	7.9	17.3	7.9	17.3
250	9.4	15.3	8.8	16.0	8.6	16.3	8.5	16.4	8.3	16.6	8.3	16.6	8.3	16.7
300			9.1	15.5	8.9	15.8	8.8	15.9	8.6	16.1	8.6	16.2	8.6	16.2
400			9.7	14.8	9.4	15.1	9.3	15.2	9.1	15.5	9.0	15.6	9.0	15.6
500					9.8	14.6	9.7	14.7	9.4	15.1	9.3	15.1	9.3	15.2
600					10.1	14.2	9.9	14.4	9.6	14.8	9.5	14.8	9.5	14.9
700					10.3	13.9	10.1	14.1	9.8	14.5	9.7	14.6	9.7	14.6
800							10.3	13.9	9.9	14.3	9.9	14.4	9.8	14.4
900							10.5	13.7	10.1	14.2	10.0	14.3	10.0	14.3
1,000									10.2	14.1	10.1	14.1	10.1	14.2
1,500									10.5	13.6	10.4	13.7	10.4	13.7
2,000									10.8	13.3	10.7	13.5	10.6	13.5
3,000									11.1	13.0	10.9	13.2	10.9	13.2

F

TABLE F-12 Sample Precision for Relative Frequencies for Random Samples Only—Rate of Occurrence in Sample 12% (Continued)

Sample Size is:	For Field Size of: 500 Lower Limit	500 Upper Limit	1,000 Lower Limit	1,000 Upper Limit	1,500 Lower Limit	1,500 Upper Limit	2,000 Lower Limit	2,000 Upper Limit	10,000 Lower Limit	10,000 Upper Limit	50,000 Lower Limit	50,000 Upper Limit	100,000 and over Lower Limit	100,000 and over Upper Limit
	Confidence Level 99% (Two-sided) Confidence Level 99.5% (One-sided)													
50	3.6%	27.6%	3.4%	28.0%	3.3%	28.1%	3.3%	28.2%	3.2%	28.4%	3.2%	28.4%	3.2%	28.4%
80	5.1	23.2	4.8	23.8	4.7	23.9	4.7	24.0	4.5	24.2	4.5	24.3	4.5	24.3
90	5.5	22.3	5.2	22.9	5.0	23.1	5.0	23.1	4.9	23.3	4.8	23.4	4.8	23.4
100	5.9	21.5	5.5	22.1	5.4	22.3	5.3	22.4	5.2	22.6	5.2	22.6	5.2	22.6
120	6.4	20.3	6.0	20.9	5.9	21.2	5.8	21.2	5.7	21.5	5.6	21.5	5.6	21.5
140	6.9	19.4	6.4	20.1	6.3	20.3	6.2	20.4	6.0	20.6	6.0	20.7	6.0	20.7
150	7.1	19.0	6.6	19.7	6.5	19.9	6.4	20.0	6.2	20.3	6.2	20.3	6.2	20.4
160	7.3	18.6	6.8	19.4	6.6	19.6	6.6	19.7	6.4	20.0	6.3	20.0	6.3	20.0
180	7.7	18.0	7.1	18.8	7.0	19.0	6.8	19.2	6.6	19.4	6.6	19.5	6.6	19.5
200	8.0	17.5	7.4	18.3	7.2	18.6	7.1	18.7	6.9	19.0	6.8	19.0	6.8	19.0
250	8.7	16.4	7.9	17.4	7.7	17.7	7.6	17.8	7.4	18.1	7.3	18.2	7.3	18.2
300			8.4	16.7	8.1	17.0	8.0	17.1	7.7	17.5	7.7	17.6	7.7	17.6
400			9.0	15.7	8.7	16.1	8.6	16.2	8.3	16.6	8.2	16.7	8.2	16.7
500					9.2	15.4	9.0	15.6	8.7	16.1	8.6	16.2	8.6	16.2
600					9.6	14.9	9.4	15.2	8.9	15.7	8.9	15.8	8.8	15.8
700					9.8	14.5	9.6	14.3	9.2	15.4	9.1	15.5	9.0	15.5
800							9.9	14.6	9.4	15.2	9.3	15.3	9.2	15.3
900							10.1	14.2	9.5	14.9	9.4	15.0	9.4	15.0
1,000									9.6	14.7	9.5	14.8	9.5	14.9
1,500									10.1	14.1	10.0	14.3	9.9	14.3
2,000									10.4	13.8	10.3	13.9	10.2	14.0
3,000									10.8	13.3	10.6	13.6	10.5	13.6

TABLE F-13 Sample Precision for Relative Frequencies for Random Samples Only—Rate of Occurrence in Sample 13%

And Sample Size is:	For Field Size of: 500 Lower Limit	500 Upper Limit	1,000 Lower Limit	1,000 Upper Limit	1,500 Lower Limit	1,500 Upper Limit	2,000 Lower Limit	2,000 Upper Limit	10,000 Lower Limit	10,000 Upper Limit	50,000 Lower Limit	50,000 Upper Limit	100,000 and over Lower Limit	100,000 and over Upper Limit
	Confidence Level 90% (Two-sided) Confidence Level 95% (One-sided)													
80	7.8%	20.2%	7.5%	20.6%	7.5%	20.7%	7.4%	20.7%	7.3%	20.8%	7.3%	20.9%	7.3%	20.9%
90	8.1	19.6	7.9	20.0	7.8	20.1	7.7	20.2	7.6	20.3	7.6	20.3	7.6	20.3
100	8.4	19.1	8.2	19.5	8.1	19.6	8.0	19.7	7.9	19.8	7.9	19.8	7.9	19.9
120	8.9	18.4	8.6	18.6	8.5	18.9	8.5	19.0	8.3	19.1	8.3	19.1	8.3	19.2
140	9.3	17.8	9.0	18.2	8.8	18.3	8.8	18.4	8.7	18.6	8.6	18.6	8.6	18.6
150	9.5	17.5	9.1	18.0	9.0	18.1	8.9	18.2	8.8	18.3	8.8	18.4	8.8	18.4
160	9.6	17.3	9.2	17.8	9.1	17.9	9.1	18.0	8.9	18.2	8.9	18.2	8.9	18.2
180	9.9	16.9	9.5	17.5	9.4	17.6	9.3	17.7	9.2	17.9	9.1	17.9	9.1	17.9
200	10.2	16.5	9.7	17.1	9.6	17.3	9.5	17.3	9.4	17.5	9.3	17.6	9.3	17.6
250	10.7	15.8	10.1	16.5	10.0	16.7	9.9	16.7	9.7	17.0	9.7	17.0	9.7	17.0
300			10.5	16.0	10.3	16.2	10.2	16.3	10.0	16.6	10.0	16.6	10.0	16.6
400			11.0	15.4	10.8	15.6	10.7	15.8	10.4	16.0	10.4	16.1	10.4	16.1
500			11.3	14.9	11.1	15.2	11.0	15.4	10.7	15.7	10.7	15.7	10.7	15.7
600					11.3	14.9	11.2	15.1	10.9	15.4	10.9	15.5	10.8	15.5
700					11.5	14.7	11.4	14.8	11.1	15.2	11.0	15.3	11.0	15.3
800							11.5	14.6	11.2	15.0	11.1	15.1	11.1	15.1
900							11.7	14.5	11.3	14.9	11.2	15.0	11.2	15.0
1,000							11.8	14.3	11.4	14.8	11.3	14.9	11.3	14.9
1,500									11.7	14.4	11.6	14.5	11.6	14.5
2,000									11.9	14.2	11.8	14.3	11.8	14.3
3,000									12.2	13.9	12.0	14.0	12.0	14.0

F

TABLE F-13 Sample Precision for Relative Frequencies for Random Samples Only—Rate of Occurrence in Sample 13% (Continued)

And Sample Size is:	For Field Size of: 500 Lower Limit	500 Upper Limit	1,000 Lower Limit	1,000 Upper Limit	1,500 Lower Limit	1,500 Upper Limit	2,000 Lower Limit	2,000 Upper Limit	10,000 Lower Limit	10,000 Upper Limit	50,000 Lower Limit	50,000 Upper Limit	100,000 and over Lower Limit	100,000 and over Upper Limit
	Confidence Level 95% (Two-sided) Confidence Level 97.5% (One-sided)													
80	7.1%	21.6%	6.8%	22.0%	6.7%	22.1%	6.7%	22.2%	6.6%	22.3%	6.5%	22.4%	6.5%	22.4%
90	7.4	20.9	7.1	21.3	7.0	21.5	7.0	21.5	6.9	21.7	6.8	21.7	6.8	21.7
100	7.8	20.3	7.5	20.8	7.4	20.9	7.3	21.0	7.2	21.1	7.2	21.2	7.2	21.2
120	8.3	19.4	7.9	19.9	7.8	20.0	7.8	20.1	7.6	20.3	7.6	20.3	7.6	20.3
140	8.7	18.7	8.3	19.2	8.2	19.4	8.1	19.5	8.0	19.6	8.0	19.7	8.0	19.7
150	8.9	18.4	8.5	18.9	8.4	19.1	8.3	19.2	8.1	19.4	8.1	19.4	8.1	19.4
160	9.1	18.1	8.6	18.7	8.5	18.9	8.4	18.9	8.3	19.1	8.2	19.2	8.2	19.2
180	9.4	17.6	8.9	18.2	8.8	18.4	8.7	18.5	8.5	18.7	8.5	18.8	8.5	18.8
200	9.7	17.2	9.2	17.9	9.0	18.1	8.9	18.2	8.7	18.4	8.7	18.4	8.7	18.4
250	10.3	16.4	9.6	17.1	9.5	17.4	9.4	17.5	9.2	17.7	9.1	17.8	9.1	17.8
300			10.6	16.6	9.8	16.9	9.7	17.0	9.5	17.3	9.4	17.3	9.4	17.3
400			10.6	15.9	10.3	16.2	10.2	16.3	9.9	16.6	9.9	16.7	9.9	16.7
500					10.7	15.7	10.6	15.8	10.3	16.2	10.2	16.2	10.2	16.2
600					11.0	15.3	10.8	15.5	10.5	15.9	10.4	15.9	10.4	15.9
700					11.3	15.0	11.1	15.2	10.7	15.6	10.6	15.7	10.6	15.7
800							11.3	15.0	10.9	15.4	10.8	15.5	10.8	15.5
900							11.4	14.8	11.0	15.3	10.9	15.3	10.9	15.4
1,000									11.1	15.1	11.0	15.2	11.0	15.2
1,500									11.5	14.7	11.4	14.8	11.4	14.8
2,000									11.7	14.4	11.6	14.5	11.6	14.5
3,000									12.0	14.0	11.9	14.2	11.8	14.3

And Sample Size is:	For Field Size of: 500		1,000		1,500		2,000		10,000		50,000		100,000 and over	
	Lower Limit	Upper Limit	Lower Limit	Upper Limit	Lower Limit	Upper Limit	Lower Limit	Upper Limit	Lower Limit	Upper Limit	Lower Limit	Upper Limit	Lower Limit	Upper Limit
	Confidence Level 99% (Two-sided) Confidence Level 99.5% (One-sided)													
80	5.8%	24.4%	5.5%	25.0%	5.3%	25.2%	5.3%	25.2%	5.2%	25.4%	5.1%	25.5%	5.1%	25.5%
90	6.2	23.5	5.8	24.1	5.7	24.3	5.6	24.4	5.5	24.6	5.5	24.6	5.5	24.6
100	6.6	22.7	6.2	23.3	6.1	23.5	6.0	23.6	5.9	23.8	5.8	23.9	5.8	23.9
120	7.2	21.5	6.7	22.1	6.6	22.4	6.5	22.5	6.4	22.7	6.3	22.7	6.3	22.8
140	7.7	20.6	7.2	21.3	7.0	21.5	7.0	21.6	6.8	21.8	6.7	21.9	6.7	21.9
150	7.9	20.2	7.4	20.9	7.2	21.1	7.1	21.2	6.9	21.5	6.9	21.5	6.9	21.6
160	8.1	19.8	7.7	20.5	7.4	20.8	7.3	20.9	7.1	21.2	7.1	21.2	7.1	21.2
180	8.5	19.1	7.9	20.0	7.8	20.1	7.6	20.3	7.4	20.6	7.4	20.7	7.4	20.7
200	8.8	18.6	8.2	19.5	7.9	19.7	7.9	19.9	7.7	20.2	7.6	20.2	7.6	20.2
250	9.5	17.5	8.8	18.5	8.5	18.8	8.4	18.9	8.2	19.3	8.1	19.3	8.1	19.4
300			9.2	17.8	9.0	18.1	8.8	18.3	8.6	18.6	8.5	18.7	8.5	18.7
400			9.9	16.8	9.6	17.2	9.4	17.4	9.1	17.8	9.0	17.9	9.0	17.9
500					10.1	16.5	9.9	16.7	9.5	17.2	9.4	17.3	9.4	17.3
600					10.5	16.0	10.2	16.3	9.8	16.8	9.7	16.9	9.7	16.9
700					10.8	15.6	10.5	15.9	10.0	16.5	10.0	16.6	9.9	16.6
800							10.8	15.6	10.2	16.2	10.1	16.3	10.1	16.3
900							11.0	15.3	10.4	16.0	10.3	16.1	10.3	16.1
1,000									10.5	15.8	10.4	15.9	10.4	15.9
1,500									11.0	15.2	10.9	15.3	10.9	15.4
2,000									11.3	14.8	11.2	15.0	11.2	15.0
3,000									11.7	14.4	11.5	14.6	11.5	14.7

F

TABLE F-14 Sample Precision for Relative Frequencies for Random Samples Only—Rate of Occurrence in Sample 14%

And Sample Size is:	For Field Size of: 500 Lower Limit	500 Upper Limit	1,000 Lower Limit	1,000 Upper Limit	1,500 Lower Limit	1,500 Upper Limit	2,000 Lower Limit	2,000 Upper Limit	10,000 Lower Limit	10,000 Upper Limit	50,000 Lower Limit	50,000 Upper Limit	100,000 and over Lower Limit	100,000 and over Upper Limit
	Confidence Level 90% (Two-sided) Confidence Level 95% (One-sided)													
50	7.1%	24.2%	6.9%	24.4%	6.9%	24.5%	6.9%	24.6%	6.8%	24.7%	6.8%	24.7%	6.8%	24.7%
80	8.6	21.4	8.3	21.7	8.3	21.8	8.2	21.9	8.1	22.0	8.1	22.0	8.1	22.0
90	8.9	20.9	8.7	21.2	8.6	21.3	8.5	21.3	8.4	21.4	8.4	21.5	8.4	21.5
100	9.3	20.3	9.0	20.6	8.9	20.8	8.8	20.8	8.7	21.0	8.7	21.0	8.7	21.0
120	9.8	19.5	9.4	20.0	9.3	20.0	9.3	20.1	9.2	20.3	9.1	20.3	9.1	20.3
140	10.2	18.9	9.8	19.4	9.7	19.5	9.6	19.5	9.5	19.7	9.5	19.7	9.5	19.7
150	10.3	18.6	10.0	19.1	9.8	19.2	9.8	19.3	9.6	19.5	9.6	19.5	9.6	19.5
160	10.5	18.4	10.1	18.9	10.0	19.0	9.9	19.1	9.8	19.3	9.8	19.3	9.8	19.3
180	10.8	18.0	10.4	18.5	10.2	18.7	10.2	18.8	10.0	18.9	10.0	19.0	10.0	19.0
200	11.0	17.6	10.6	18.2	10.5	18.4	10.4	18.4	10.2	18.6	10.2	18.7	10.2	18.7
250	11.6	16.9	11.0	17.6	10.9	17.8	10.8	17.9	10.6	18.1	10.6	18.1	10.6	18.1
300			11.4	17.1	11.2	17.3	11.1	17.4	10.9	17.7	10.9	17.7	10.9	17.7
400			11.9	16.5	11.7	16.7	11.6	16.9	11.3	17.1	11.3	17.2	11.3	17.2
500			12.3	16.0	12.0	16.3	11.9	16.5	11.6	16.7	11.6	16.8	11.6	16.8
600					12.3	16.0	12.1	16.1	11.8	16.5	11.8	16.5	11.8	16.5
700					12.5	15.7	12.3	15.9	12.0	16.3	11.9	16.3	11.9	16.3
800							12.5	15.7	12.1	16.1	12.1	16.2	12.1	16.2
900							12.6	15.5	12.2	15.9	12.2	16.0	12.2	16.0
1,000							12.8	15.4	12.3	15.8	12.3	15.9	12.3	15.9
1,500									12.7	15.4	12.6	15.5	12.6	15.6
2,000									12.9	15.2	12.8	15.3	12.8	15.3
3,000									13.1	14.9	13.0	15.1	13.0	15.1

And sample size is:	For Field Size of: 500		1,000		1,500		2,000		10,000		50,000		100,000 and over	
	Lower Limit	Upper Limit	Lower Limit	Upper Limit	Lower Limit	Upper Limit	Lower Limit	Upper Limit	Lower Limit	Upper Limit	Lower Limit	Upper Limit	Lower Limit	Upper Limit
	Confidence Level 95% (Two-sided) Confidence Level 97.5% (One-sided)													
50	6.3%	26.1%	6.0%	26.4%	6.0%	26.5%	5.9%	26.6%	5.8%	26.7%	5.8%	26.7%	5.8%	26.8%
80	7.8	22.8	7.5	23.2	7.4	23.3	7.4	23.4	7.3	23.5	7.3	23.6	7.3	23.6
90	8.2	22.1	7.9	22.5	7.8	22.6	7.7	22.7	7.6	22.9	7.6	22.9	7.6	22.9
100	8.5	21.5	8.2	21.9	8.1	22.1	8.1	22.1	7.9	22.3	7.9	22.3	7.9	22.4
120	9.1	20.5	8.7	21.0	8.6	21.2	8.5	21.3	8.4	21.5	8.4	21.5	8.4	21.5
140	9.5	19.8	9.1	20.4	9.0	20.5	8.9	20.6	8.8	20.8	8.7	20.8	8.7	20.9
150	9.7	19.5	9.3	20.1	9.2	20.2	9.1	20.3	8.9	20.5	8.9	20.6	8.9	20.6
160	9.9	19.2	9.5	19.8	9.3	20.0	9.3	20.1	9.1	20.3	9.1	20.3	9.1	20.3
180	10.2	18.7	9.8	19.4	9.6	19.5	9.5	19.6	9.4	19.9	9.3	19.9	9.3	19.9
200	10.5	18.3	10.0	19.0	9.8	19.2	9.8	19.3	9.6	19.5	9.5	19.6	9.5	19.6
250	11.2	17.5	10.5	18.3	10.3	18.5	10.2	18.6	10.0	18.8	10.0	18.9	10.0	18.9
300			10.9	17.7	10.7	18.0	10.6	18.1	10.4	18.4	10.3	18.4	10.3	18.4
400			11.5	16.9	11.2	17.2	11.1	17.4	10.8	17.7	10.8	17.8	10.8	17.8
500					11.6	16.7	11.5	16.9	11.2	17.3	11.1	17.3	11.1	17.3
600					11.9	16.3	11.8	16.5	11.4	16.9	11.3	17.0	11.3	17.0
700					12.2	16.0	12.0	16.2	11.6	16.7	11.5	16.8	11.5	16.8
800							12.2	16.0	11.8	16.5	11.7	16.6	11.7	16.6
900							12.4	15.8	11.9	16.3	11.8	16.4	11.8	16.4
1,000									12.0	16.2	11.9	16.3	11.9	16.3
1,500									12.4	15.7	12.3	15.8	12.3	15.9
2,000									12.7	15.4	12.5	15.6	12.5	15.6
3,000									13.0	15.1	12.8	15.3	12.8	15.3

F

TABLE F-14 Sample Precision for Relative Frequencies for Random Samples Only—Rate of Occurrence in Sample 14% (Continued)

And Sample Size is:	For Field Size of: 500 Lower Limit	500 Upper Limit	1,000 Lower Limit	1,000 Upper Limit	1,500 Lower Limit	1,500 Upper Limit	2,000 Lower Limit	2,000 Upper Limit	10,000 Lower Limit	10,000 Upper Limit	50,000 Lower Limit	50,000 Upper Limit	100,000 and over Lower Limit	100,000 and over Upper Limit
	Confidence Level 99% (Two-sided) Confidence Level 99.5% (One-sided)													
50	4.8%	30.1%	4.5%	30.5%	4.4%	30.6%	4.4%	30.7%	4.3%	30.9%	4.3%	30.9%	4.3%	30.9%
80	6.5	25.6	6.1	26.2	6.0	26.4	5.9	26.5	5.8	26.7	5.8	26.7	5.8	26.7
90	6.9	24.7	6.5	25.3	6.4	25.5	6.3	25.6	6.2	25.8	6.1	25.8	6.1	25.8
100	7.3	23.9	6.9	24.5	6.7	24.7	6.7	24.8	6.5	25.0	6.5	25.1	6.5	25.1
120	7.9	22.7	7.5	23.4	7.3	23.6	7.2	23.7	7.1	23.9	7.0	24.0	7.0	24.0
140	8.4	21.7	7.9	22.4	7.8	22.7	7.7	22.8	7.5	23.0	7.5	23.1	7.5	23.1
150	8.7	21.3	8.2	22.1	8.0	22.3	7.9	22.4	7.7	22.7	7.7	22.7	7.7	22.7
160	8.9	20.9	8.3	21.7	8.1	22.0	8.1	22.1	7.9	22.4	7.8	22.4	7.8	22.4
180	9.3	20.3	8.7	21.1	8.5	21.3	8.4	21.5	8.2	21.8	8.1	21.9	8.1	21.9
200	9.7	19.7	9.0	20.6	8.8	20.9	8.7	21.0	8.4	21.3	8.4	21.4	8.4	21.4
250			9.6	19.6	9.3	20.0	9.2	20.1	9.0	20.4	8.9	20.5	8.9	20.5
300			10.1	18.9	9.8	19.3	9.7	19.4	9.4	19.8	9.3	19.9	9.3	19.9
400			10.8	17.9	10.5	18.3	10.3	18.5	10.0	18.9	9.9	19.0	9.9	19.0
500					11.0	17.6	10.8	17.8	10.4	18.3	10.3	18.4	10.3	18.4
600					11.4	17.1	11.1	17.4	10.7	17.9	10.6	18.0	10.6	18.0
700					11.7	16.7	11.4	17.0	10.9	17.5	10.8	17.7	10.8	17.7
800							11.7	16.7	11.1	17.3	11.0	17.4	11.0	17.4
900							11.9	16.4	11.3	17.1	11.2	17.2	11.2	17.2
1,000									11.5	16.9	11.3	17.0	11.3	17.0
1,500									12.0	16.3	11.8	16.4	11.8	16.5
2,000									12.3	15.9	12.1	16.1	12.1	16.1
3,000									12.7	15.4	12.5	15.6	12.4	15.7

TABLE F-15 Sample Precision for Relative Frequencies for Random Samples Only—Rate of Occurrence in Sample 15%

Confidence Level 90% (Two-sided)
Confidence Level 95% (One-sided)

And Sample Size is:	For Field Size of: 500		1,000		1,500		2,000		10,000		50,000		100,000 and over	
	Lower Limit	Upper Limit	Lower Limit	Upper Limit	Lower Limit	Upper Limit	Lower Limit	Upper Limit	Lower Limit	Upper Limit	Lower Limit	Upper Limit	Lower Limit	Upper Limit
50	7.9%	25.3%	7.7%	25.6%	7.6%	25.7%	7.6%	25.7%	7.5%	25.8%	7.5%	25.9%	7.5%	25.9%
80	9.4	22.5	9.1	22.8	9.0	23.0	9.0	23.0	8.9	23.1	8.9	23.2	8.9	23.2
90	9.7	21.9	9.5	22.3	9.4	22.4	9.3	22.6	9.2	22.6	9.2	22.6	9.2	22.6
100	10.1	21.4	9.8	21.8	9.7	21.9	9.6	22.0	9.5	22.1	9.5	22.2	9.5	22.2
120	10.6	20.6	10.2	21.0	10.1	21.2	10.1	21.2	10.0	21.4	9.9	21.4	9.9	21.4
140	11.0	20.0	10.6	20.5	10.5	20.6	10.5	20.7	10.3	20.8	10.3	20.9	10.3	20.9
150	11.2	19.7	10.8	20.2	10.7	20.4	10.6	20.4	10.5	20.6	10.5	20.6	10.4	20.7
160	11.4	19.5	11.0	20.0	10.8	20.1	10.8	20.2	10.6	20.4	10.6	20.4	10.6	20.4
180	11.7	19.1	11.2	19.6	11.1	19.8	11.0	19.9	10.8	20.0	10.8	20.1	10.8	20.1
200	11.9	18.7	11.5	19.3	11.3	19.5	11.2	19.6	11.1	19.8	11.1	19.8	11.0	19.8
250	12.5	18.0	11.9	18.7	11.8	18.9	11.7	19.0	11.5	19.2	11.5	19.2	11.4	19.2
300			12.3	18.2	12.1	18.4	12.0	18.5	11.8	18.8	11.8	18.8	11.8	18.8
400			12.8	17.5	12.6	17.8	12.5	17.9	12.2	18.2	12.2	18.2	12.2	18.3
500			13.2	17.0	12.9	17.4	12.8	17.5	12.5	17.8	12.5	17.9	12.5	17.9
600					13.2	17.0	13.1	17.2	12.8	17.5	12.7	17.6	12.7	17.6
700					13.4	16.8	13.3	16.9	12.9	17.3	12.9	17.4	12.9	17.4
800							13.4	16.7	13.1	17.1	13.0	17.2	13.0	17.2
900							13.6	16.6	13.2	17.0	13.1	17.1	13.1	17.1
1,000							13.7	16.4	13.3	16.9	13.2	17.0	13.2	17.0
1,500									13.6	16.5	13.5	16.6	13.5	16.6
2,000									13.8	16.2	13.7	16.3	13.7	16.4
3,000									14.1	15.9	14.0	16.1	13.9	16.1

F

TABLE F-15 Sample Precision for Relative Frequencies for Random Samples Only—Rate of Occurrence in Sample 15% (Continued)

And Sample Size is:	For Field Size of: 500 Lower Limit	500 Upper Limit	1,000 Lower Limit	1,000 Upper Limit	1,500 Lower Limit	1,500 Upper Limit	2,000 Lower Limit	2,000 Upper Limit	10,000 Lower Limit	10,000 Upper Limit	50,000 Lower Limit	50,000 Upper Limit	100,000 and over Lower Limit	100,000 and over Upper Limit
	Confidence Level 95% (Two-sided) Confidence Level 97.5% (One-sided)													
80	8.6%	23.9%	8.3%	24.3%	8.2%	24.5%	8.1%	24.5%	8.0%	24.7%	8.0%	24.7%	8.0%	24.7%
90	9.0	23.2	8.7	23.7	8.5	23.8	8.5	23.9	8.4	24.0	8.4	24.1	8.4	24.1
100	9.3	22.6	9.0	23.1	8.9	23.2	8.8	23.3	8.7	23.5	8.7	23.5	8.7	23.5
120	9.9	21.7	9.5	22.2	9.4	22.4	9.3	22.4	9.2	22.6	9.1	22.7	9.1	22.7
140	10.4	20.9	9.9	21.5	9.8	21.7	9.7	21.8	9.6	22.0	9.5	22.0	9.5	22.0
150	10.6	20.6	10.1	21.2	10.0	21.4	9.9	21.5	9.7	21.7	9.7	21.7	9.7	21.7
160	10.8	20.4	10.3	20.9	10.1	21.1	10.1	21.2	9.9	21.6	9.9	21.5	9.9	21.5
180	11.0	19.9	10.6	20.5	10.5	20.6	10.3	20.8	10.2	21.0	10.1	21.1	10.1	21.1
200	11.4	19.4	10.9	20.1	10.7	20.3	10.6	20.4	10.4	20.7	10.4	20.7	10.4	20.7
250	12.0	18.6	11.4	19.4	11.2	19.6	11.1	19.7	10.9	20.0	10.8	20.0	10.8	20.0
300			11.8	18.8	11.6	19.1	11.5	19.2	11.2	19.5	11.2	19.5	11.2	19.5
400			12.4	18.0	12.1	18.3	12.0	18.5	11.7	18.8	11.7	18.9	11.7	18.9
500					12.5	17.8	12.4	18.0	12.1	18.4	12.0	18.4	12.0	18.4
600					12.9	17.4	12.7	17.6	12.3	18.0	12.3	18.1	12.2	18.1
700					13.1	17.1	12.9	17.3	12.5	17.8	12.5	17.8	12.4	17.9
800							13.1	17.1	12.7	17.6	12.6	17.6	12.6	17.7
900							13.3	16.9	12.8	17.4	12.8	17.5	12.7	17.5
1,000									13.0	17.3	12.9	17.4	12.9	17.4
1,500									13.4	16.8	13.3	16.9	13.2	16.9
2,000									13.6	16.5	13.5	16.6	13.5	16.6
3,000									13.9	16.1	13.8	16.3	13.7	16.3

And Sample Size is:	For Field Size of: 500 Lower Limit	500 Upper Limit	1,000 Lower Limit	1,000 Upper Limit	1,500 Lower Limit	1,500 Upper Limit	2,000 Lower Limit	2,000 Upper Limit	10,000 Lower Limit	10,000 Upper Limit	50,000 Lower Limit	50,000 Upper Limit	100,000 and over Lower Limit	100,000 and over Upper Limit
Confidence Level 99% (Two-sided) Confidence Level 99.5% (One-sided)														
50	5.3%	31.3%	5.1%	31.7%	5.0%	31.9%	4.9%	31.9%	4.8%	32.1%	4.8%	32.1%	4.8%	32.1%
80	7.1	26.9	6.8	27.4	6.7	27.6	6.6	27.6	6.5	27.9	6.4	27.9	6.4	27.9
90	7.6	25.9	7.2	26.5	7.1	26.7	7.0	26.8	6.8	27.0	6.8	27.0	6.8	27.1
100	8.0	25.1	7.6	25.8	7.4	26.0	7.4	26.0	7.2	26.3	7.2	26.3	7.2	26.3
120	8.7	23.9	8.2	24.5	8.0	24.8	7.9	24.9	7.8	25.1	7.7	25.2	7.7	25.2
140	9.2	22.9	8.7	23.6	8.5	23.9	8.4	24.0	8.2	24.2	8.2	24.3	8.2	24.3
150	9.5	22.5	8.9	23.2	8.7	23.5	8.6	23.6	8.4	23.9	8.4	23.9	8.4	23.9
160	9.7	22.1	9.1	22.9	8.9	23.1	8.8	23.3	8.6	23.5	8.6	23.6	8.6	23.6
180	10.1	21.4	9.5	22.3	9.3	22.5	9.2	22.7	8.9	23.0	8.9	23.0	8.9	23.1
200	10.5	20.9	9.8	21.8	9.6	22.1	9.5	22.2	9.2	22.5	9.2	22.6	9.2	22.6
250	11.3	19.7	10.4	20.7	10.2	21.1	10.0	21.2	9.8	21.6	9.7	21.7	9.7	21.7
300			10.9	20.1	10.6	20.4	10.5	20.6	10.2	20.9	10.1	21.0	10.1	21.0
400			11.7	19.0	11.3	19.4	11.2	19.6	10.8	20.0	10.7	20.1	10.7	20.1
500					11.9	18.7	11.7	18.9	11.2	19.4	11.2	19.5	11.2	19.5
600					12.3	18.2	12.0	18.4	11.6	19.0	11.5	19.1	11.4	19.1
700					12.6	17.8	12.3	18.1	11.8	18.7	11.7	18.8	11.7	18.8
800							12.6	17.7	12.0	18.4	11.9	18.5	11.9	18.5
900							12.8	17.5	12.2	18.2	12.1	18.3	12.1	18.3
1,000									12.4	18.0	12.2	18.1	12.2	18.1
1,500									12.9	17.3	12.7	17.5	12.7	17.5
2,000									13.2	16.9	13.0	17.1	13.0	17.2
3,000									13.6	16.5	13.4	16.7	13.4	16.8

F

TABLE F-16 Sample Precision for Relative Frequencies for Random Samples Only—Rate of Occurrence in Sample 16%

And Sample Size is:	For Field Size of: 500 Lower Limit	500 Upper Limit	1,000 Lower Limit	1,000 Upper Limit	1,500 Lower Limit	1,500 Upper Limit	2,000 Lower Limit	2,000 Upper Limit	10,000 Lower Limit	10,000 Upper Limit	50,000 Lower Limit	50,000 Upper Limit	100,000 and over Lower Limit	100,000 and over Upper Limit
	Confidence Level 90% (Two-sided) Confidence Level 95% (One-sided)													
50	8.6%	26.4%	8.4%	26.7%	8.3%	26.8%	8.3%	26.9%	8.2%	27.0%	8.2%	27.0%	8.2%	27.0%
80	10.2	23.6	10.0	24.0	9.9	24.1	9.8	24.1	9.7	24.3	9.7	24.3	9.7	24.3
90	10.6	23.1	10.3	22.6	10.2	22.7	10.2	22.7	10.1	22.9	10.0	22.9	10.0	22.9
100	10.9	22.5	10.6	22.9	10.5	23.0	10.5	23.1	10.3	23.2	10.3	23.3	10.3	23.3
120	11.5	21.7	11.1	22.1	11.0	22.3	10.9	22.3	10.8	22.5	10.8	22.5	10.8	22.5
140	11.9	21.1	11.5	21.5	11.4	21.7	11.3	21.8	11.2	21.9	11.2	22.0	11.2	22.0
150	12.1	20.8	11.7	21.3	11.6	21.5	11.5	21.5	11.3	21.7	11.3	21.7	11.3	21.7
160	12.3	20.6	11.8	21.1	11.7	21.2	11.6	21.5	11.5	21.5	11.5	21.5	11.5	21.5
180	12.6	20.1	12.1	20.7	12.0	20.9	11.9	20.9	11.7	21.1	11.7	21.2	11.7	21.2
200	12.8	19.8	12.4	20.4	12.2	20.5	12.1	20.6	12.0	20.8	11.9	20.9	11.9	20.9
250	13.4	19.0	12.8	19.7	12.7	19.9	12.6	20.0	12.4	20.3	12.4	20.3	12.4	20.3
300			13.2	19.3	13.0	19.5	12.9	19.6	12.7	19.8	12.7	19.9	12.7	19.9
400			13.8	18.6	13.5	18.8	13.4	19.0	13.2	19.3	13.1	19.3	13.1	19.3
500			14.2	18.1	13.9	18.4	13.7	18.6	13.5	18.9	13.4	18.9	13.4	18.9
600					14.2	18.1	14.0	18.2	13.7	18.6	13.6	18.7	13.6	18.7
700					14.4	17.8	14.2	18.0	13.9	18.4	13.8	18.4	13.8	18.5
800							14.4	17.8	14.0	18.2	13.9	18.3	13.9	18.3
900							14.5	17.6	14.1	18.0	14.1	18.1	14.0	18.1
1,000							14.7	17.4	14.2	17.9	14.2	18.0	14.1	18.0
1,500									14.6	17.5	14.5	17.6	14.5	17.6
2,000									14.8	17.3	14.7	17.4	14.7	17.4
3,000									15.1	17.0	15.0	17.1	14.9	17.1

And Sample Size is:	For Field Size of: 500 Lower Limit	500 Upper Limit	1,000 Lower Limit	1,000 Upper Limit	1,500 Lower Limit	1,500 Upper Limit	2,000 Lower Limit	2,000 Upper Limit	10,000 Lower Limit	10,000 Upper Limit	50,000 Lower Limit	50,000 Upper Limit	100,000 and over Lower Limit	100,000 and over Upper Limit
Confidence Level 95% (Two-sided) Confidence Level 97.5% (One-sided)														
50	7.6%	28.4%	7.4%	28.8%	7.3%	28.9%	7.3%	29.0%	7.2%	29.1%	7.2%	29.1%	7.2%	29.1%
80	9.4	25.1	9.1	25.5	9.0	25.6	8.9	25.7	8.8	25.8	8.8	25.9	8.8	25.9
90	9.8	24.3	9.5	24.8	9.3	24.9	9.3	25.0	9.2	25.2	9.1	25.2	9.1	25.2
100	10.1	23.7	9.8	24.2	9.7	24.4	9.6	24.4	9.5	24.6	9.5	24.6	9.5	24.6
120	10.7	22.8	10.3	23.3	10.2	23.5	10.1	23.6	10.0	23.7	10.0	23.8	10.0	23.8
140	11.2	22.0	10.8	22.6	10.6	22.8	10.6	22.9	10.4	23.1	10.4	23.1	10.4	23.1
150	11.4	21.7	11.0	22.3	10.8	22.5	10.7	22.6	10.6	22.8	10.5	22.8	10.5	22.9
160	11.6	21.4	11.1	22.0	11.0	22.2	10.9	22.3	10.7	22.5	10.7	22.6	10.7	22.6
180	12.0	20.9	11.5	21.6	11.3	21.7	11.2	21.9	11.0	22.1	11.0	22.2	11.0	22.2
200	12.3	20.5	11.7	21.2	11.5	21.4	11.5	21.5	11.3	21.8	11.2	21.8	11.2	21.8
250	13.0	19.6	12.3	20.4	12.1	20.7	12.0	20.8	11.8	21.1	11.7	21.1	11.7	21.1
300			12.7	19.9	12.5	20.2	12.4	20.3	12.1	20.6	12.1	20.6	12.1	20.6
400			13.3	19.1	13.0	19.4	12.9	19.5	12.6	19.9	12.6	19.9	12.6	20.0
500					13.5	18.9	13.3	19.0	13.0	19.4	12.9	19.5	12.9	19.5
600					13.8	18.5	13.6	18.7	13.2	19.1	13.2	19.2	13.2	19.2
700					14.1	18.1	13.9	18.4	13.5	18.8	13.4	18.9	13.4	18.9
800							14.1	18.1	13.6	18.6	13.5	18.7	13.5	18.7
900							14.3	17.9	13.8	18.4	13.7	18.5	13.7	18.6
1,000									13.9	18.3	13.8	18.4	13.8	18.4
1,500									14.3	17.8	14.2	17.9	14.2	18.0
2,000									14.6	17.5	14.5	17.6	14.4	17.7
3,000									14.9	17.1	14.8	17.3	14.7	17.4

F

TABLE F-16 Sample Precision for Relative Frequencies for Random Samples Only—Rate of Occurrence in Sample 16% (Continued)

And Sample Size is:	For Field Size of: 500 Lower Limit	500 Upper Limit	1,000 Lower Limit	1,000 Upper Limit	1,500 Lower Limit	1,500 Upper Limit	2,000 Lower Limit	2,000 Upper Limit	10,000 Lower Limit	10,000 Upper Limit	50,000 Lower Limit	50,000 Upper Limit	100,000 and over Lower Limit	100,000 and over Upper Limit
	Confidence Level 99% (Two-sided) Confidence Level 99.5% (One-sided)													
50	5.9%	32.5%	5.7%	32.9%	5.6%	33.1%	5.5%	33.1%	5.4%	33.3%	5.4%	33.4%	5.4%	33.4%
80	7.9	28.0	7.5	28.6	7.4	28.7	7.3	28.8	7.2	29.0	7.1	29.1	7.1	29.1
90	8.3	27.1	7.9	27.7	7.8	27.8	7.7	27.9	7.6	28.2	7.5	28.2	7.5	28.2
100	8.7	26.3	8.3	26.9	8.2	27.1	8.1	27.2	7.9	27.4	7.9	27.5	7.9	27.5
120	9.4	25.0	8.9	25.7	8.8	25.9	8.7	26.0	8.5	26.3	8.5	26.3	8.5	26.3
140	10.0	24.0	9.5	24.8	9.3	25.0	9.2	25.1	9.0	25.4	9.0	25.4	9.0	25.5
150	10.3	23.6	9.7	24.4	9.5	24.6	9.4	24.7	9.2	25.0	9.2	25.1	9.2	25.1
160	10.5	23.2	9.9	24.0	9.7	24.3	9.6	24.4	9.4	24.7	9.4	24.7	9.3	24.8
180	10.9	22.5	10.3	23.4	10.1	23.6	10.0	23.8	9.7	24.1	9.7	24.2	9.7	24.2
200	11.3	22.0	10.6	22.9	10.4	23.2	10.3	23.3	10.0	23.7	10.0	23.7	10.0	23.7
250	12.1	20.8	11.3	21.9	11.0	22.2	10.9	22.4	10.6	22.7	10.6	22.8	10.5	22.8
300			11.8	21.1	11.5	21.5	11.4	21.7	11.0	22.0	11.0	22.1	11.0	22.1
400			12.6	20.1	12.2	20.5	12.1	20.7	11.7	21.1	11.6	21.2	11.6	21.2
500					12.8	19.8	12.6	20.0	12.1	20.5	12.0	20.6	12.0	20.6
600					13.2	19.3	12.9	19.5	12.5	20.1	12.4	20.2	12.3	20.2
700					13.5	18.8	13.3	19.1	12.7	19.7	12.6	19.8	12.6	19.9
800							13.5	18.8	13.0	19.4	12.8	19.6	12.8	19.6
900							13.8	18.5	13.1	19.2	13.0	19.3	13.0	19.4
1,000									13.3	19.0	13.2	19.2	13.2	19.2
1,500									13.8	18.4	13.7	18.5	13.7	18.6
2,000									14.2	18.0	14.0	18.2	14.0	18.2
3,000									14.6	17.5	14.4	17.7	14.3	17.8

TABLE F-17 Sample Precision for Relative Frequencies for Random Samples Only—Rate of Occurrence in Sample 17%

Confidence Level 90% (Two-sided)
Confidence Level 95% (One-sided)

And Sample Size is:	For Field Size of: 500 Lower Limit	500 Upper Limit	1,000 Lower Limit	1,000 Upper Limit	1,500 Lower Limit	1,500 Upper Limit	2,000 Lower Limit	2,000 Upper Limit	10,000 Lower Limit	10,000 Upper Limit	50,000 Lower Limit	50,000 Upper Limit	100,000 and over Lower Limit	100,000 and over Upper Limit
50	9.4%	27.6%	9.2%	27.9%	9.1%	28.0%	9.1%	28.0%	9.0%	28.1%	9.0%	28.1%	9.0%	28.1%
80	11.1	24.7	10.8	25.1	10.7	25.2	10.6	25.2	10.5	25.4	10.5	25.4	10.5	25.4
90	11.4	24.1	11.1	24.5	11.0	24.6	11.0	24.7	10.9	24.8	10.9	24.8	10.9	24.8
100	11.8	23.6	11.5	24.0	11.3	24.1	11.3	24.2	11.2	24.3	11.2	24.4	11.1	24.4
120	12.3	22.8	12.0	23.2	11.9	23.4	11.8	23.4	11.7	23.6	11.6	23.6	11.6	23.6
140	12.8	22.2	12.4	22.6	12.3	22.8	12.2	22.9	12.1	23.0	12.0	23.1	12.0	23.1
150	13.0	21.9	12.6	22.4	12.4	22.5	12.4	22.6	12.2	22.8	12.2	22.8	12.2	22.8
160	13.2	21.6	12.7	22.2	12.6	22.3	12.5	22.4	12.4	22.6	12.3	22.6	12.3	22.6
180	13.5	21.2	13.0	21.8	12.9	21.9	12.8	22.0	12.6	22.2	12.6	22.3	12.6	22.3
200	13.8	20.8	13.3	21.4	13.1	21.6	13.0	21.7	12.9	21.9	12.8	22.0	12.8	22.0
250	14.3	20.1	13.8	20.8	13.6	21.0	13.5	21.1	13.3	21.3	13.3	21.4	13.3	21.4
300			14.1	20.3	13.9	20.5	13.8	20.7	13.6	20.9	13.6	20.9	13.6	21.0
400			14.7	19.6	14.5	19.9	14.3	20.0	14.1	20.3	14.0	20.4	14.0	20.4
500			15.1	19.1	14.8	19.4	14.7	19.6	14.4	19.9	14.3	20.0	14.3	20.0
600					15.1	19.1	15.0	19.3	14.6	19.6	14.6	19.7	14.6	19.7
700					15.3	18.8	15.2	19.0	14.8	19.4	14.7	19.5	14.7	19.5
800							15.4	18.8	15.0	19.2	14.9	19.3	14.9	19.3
900							15.5	18.6	15.1	19.1	15.0	19.2	15.0	19.2
1,000							15.7	18.5	15.2	19.0	15.1	19.1	15.1	19.1
1,500									15.6	18.5	15.5	18.6	15.4	18.7
2,000									15.8	18.3	15.7	18.4	15.6	18.4
3,000									16.1	18.0	15.9	18.1	15.9	18.2

TABLE F-17 Sample Precision for Relative Frequencies for Random Samples Only—Rate of Occurrence in Sample 17% (Continued)

And Sample Size is:	For Field Size of: 500 Lower Limit	Upper Limit	1,000 Lower Limit	Upper Limit	1,500 Lower Limit	Upper Limit	2,000 Lower Limit	Upper Limit	10,000 Lower Limit	Upper Limit	50,000 Lower Limit	Upper Limit	100,000 and over Lower Limit	Upper Limit
	Confidence Level 95% (Two-sided) Confidence Level 97.5% (One-sided)													
50	8.3%	29.6%	8.1%	29.9%	8.0%	30.1%	8.0%	30.1%	7.9%	30.2%	7.9%	30.3%	7.9%	30.3%
80	10.2	26.2	9.9	26.6	9.8	26.7	9.7	26.8	9.6	27.0	9.6	27.0	9.6	27.0
90	10.6	25.6	10.3	26.0	10.1	26.1	10.1	26.2	10.0	26.3	9.9	26.3	9.9	26.4
100	11.0	24.9	10.6	25.3	10.5	25.5	10.4	25.6	10.3	25.7	10.3	25.8	10.3	25.8
120	11.6	23.9	11.2	24.4	11.0	24.6	11.0	24.7	10.8	24.9	10.8	24.9	10.8	24.9
140	12.1	23.1	11.6	23.6	11.5	23.9	11.4	24.0	11.3	24.2	11.2	24.2	11.2	24.2
150	12.3	23.1	11.8	23.7	11.7	23.9	11.6	24.0	11.4	24.0	11.4	24.0	11.4	24.0
160	12.5	22.5	12.0	23.1	11.8	23.3	11.8	23.4	11.6	23.7	11.6	23.7	11.6	23.7
180	12.9	22.0	12.3	22.7	12.2	22.8	12.1	23.0	11.9	23.2	11.8	23.3	11.8	23.3
200	13.2	21.6	12.6	22.3	12.4	22.5	12.3	22.6	12.1	22.9	12.1	22.9	12.1	22.9
250	13.9	20.0	13.2	20.7	13.0	20.9	12.9	21.0	12.6	21.2	12.6	21.2	12.6	21.2
300			13.6	20.9	13.4	21.2	13.3	21.4	13.0	21.6	13.0	21.7	12.9	21.7
400			14.3	20.1	14.0	20.5	13.8	20.6	13.5	20.9	13.5	21.0	13.5	21.0
500					14.4	19.9	14.2	20.1	13.9	20.5	13.8	20.6	13.8	20.6
600					14.7	19.5	14.6	19.7	14.2	20.1	14.1	20.2	14.1	20.2
700					15.0	19.2	14.8	19.4	14.4	19.9	14.3	20.0	14.3	20.0
800							15.0	19.2	14.6	19.7	14.5	19.8	14.5	19.8
900							15.2	18.9	14.7	19.5	14.6	19.6	14.6	19.6
1,000									14.8	19.3	14.8	19.4	14.7	19.5
1,500									15.3	18.8	15.2	19.0	15.1	19.0
2,000									15.6	18.5	15.4	18.7	15.4	18.7
3,000									15.9	18.2	15.7	18.3	15.7	18.4

And Sample Size is:	For Field Size of: 500 Lower Limit	500 Upper Limit	1,000 Lower Limit	1,000 Upper Limit	1,500 Lower Limit	1,500 Upper Limit	2,000 Lower Limit	2,000 Upper Limit	10,000 Lower Limit	10,000 Upper Limit	50,000 Lower Limit	50,000 Upper Limit	100,000 and over Lower Limit	100,000 and over Upper Limit
	Confidence Level 99% (Two-sided) Confidence Level 99.5% (One-sided)													
50	6.6%	33.6%	6.3%	34.1%	6.2%	34.3%	6.1%	34.3%	6.0%	34.5%	6.0%	34.5%	6.0%	34.5%
80	8.6	29.2	8.2	29.7	8.1	29.9	8.0	30.0	7.9	30.2	7.8	30.3	7.8	30.3
90	9.1	28.2	8.7	28.8	8.5	29.0	8.5	29.1	8.3	29.3	8.3	29.4	8.3	29.4
100	9.5	27.4	9.1	28.1	8.9	28.3	8.8	28.4	8.7	28.6	8.6	28.6	8.6	28.7
120	10.2	26.1	9.7	26.8	9.6	27.1	9.5	27.2	9.3	27.4	9.2	27.5	9.2	27.5
140	10.8	25.1	10.3	25.9	10.1	26.1	10.0	26.2	9.8	26.5	9.8	26.6	9.7	26.6
150	11.1	24.7	10.5	25.5	10.3	25.7	10.2	25.9	10.0	26.2	10.0	26.2	9.9	26.2
160	11.4	24.3	10.7	25.1	10.5	25.4	10.4	25.5	10.2	25.8	10.2	25.9	10.2	25.9
180	11.8	23.7	11.1	24.5	11.0	24.7	10.8	24.9	10.5	25.2	10.5	25.3	10.5	25.3
200	12.2	23.1	11.4	24.0	11.2	24.3	11.1	24.4	10.9	24.8	10.8	24.8	10.8	24.8
250	13.0	21.9	12.1	23.0	11.9	23.3	11.7	23.5	11.5	23.8	11.4	23.9	11.4	23.9
300			12.7	22.2	12.4	22.6	12.2	22.8	11.9	23.2	11.8	23.2	11.8	23.3
400			13.5	21.1	13.1	21.6	12.9	21.8	12.6	22.2	12.5	22.3	12.5	22.3
500					13.7	20.9	13.5	21.1	13.0	21.6	12.9	21.7	12.9	21.7
600					14.1	20.3	13.9	20.6	13.4	21.1	13.3	21.3	13.3	21.3
700					14.5	19.9	14.3	20.2	13.6	20.8	13.5	20.9	13.5	20.9
800							14.5	19.8	13.9	20.5	13.8	20.6	13.7	20.7
900							14.7	19.6	14.1	20.3	13.9	20.4	13.9	20.4
1,000									14.2	20.1	14.1	20.2	14.1	20.3
1,500									14.8	19.4	14.6	19.6	14.6	19.6
2,000									15.1	19.0	14.9	19.2	14.9	19.3
3,000									15.6	18.5	15.3	18.8	15.3	18.8

F

TABLE F-18 Sample Precision for Relative Frequencies for Random Samples Only—Rate of Occurrence in Sample 18%

And Sample Size is:	For Field Size of: 500 Lower Limit	500 Upper Limit	1,000 Lower Limit	1,000 Upper Limit	1,500 Lower Limit	1,500 Upper Limit	2,000 Lower Limit	2,000 Upper Limit	10,000 Lower Limit	10,000 Upper Limit	50,000 Lower Limit	50,000 Upper Limit	100,000 and over Lower Limit	100,000 and over Upper Limit
	Confidence Level 90% (Two-sided) Confidence Level 95% (One-sided)													
50	10.1%	28.7%	9.9%	29.0%	9.9%	29.1%	9.8%	29.1%	9.7%	29.3%	9.7%	29.3%	9.7%	29.3%
80	11.9	25.8	11.6	26.2	11.5	26.3	11.5	26.4	11.4	26.5	11.3	26.5	11.3	26.5
90	12.3	25.2	12.0	25.6	11.9	25.7	11.8	25.8	11.7	25.9	11.7	26.0	11.7	26.0
100	12.6	24.8	12.3	25.1	12.2	25.2	12.1	25.3	12.0	25.4	12.0	25.5	12.0	25.5
120	13.2	23.9	12.8	24.3	12.7	24.5	12.7	24.5	12.5	24.7	12.5	24.7	12.5	24.7
140	13.7	23.2	13.3	23.7	13.1	23.9	13.1	24.0	12.9	24.1	12.9	24.2	12.9	24.2
150	13.9	23.0	13.4	23.5	13.3	23.6	13.2	23.7	13.1	23.9	13.1	23.9	13.1	23.9
160	14.1	22.7	13.6	23.2	13.5	23.4	13.4	23.5	13.2	23.7	13.2	23.7	13.2	23.7
180	14.4	22.3	13.9	22.9	13.8	23.0	13.7	23.1	13.5	23.3	13.5	23.4	13.5	23.4
200	14.7	21.9	14.2	22.5	14.0	22.7	13.9	22.8	13.8	23.0	13.7	23.0	13.7	23.1
250	15.3	21.2	14.7	21.9	14.5	22.1	14.4	22.2	14.2	22.4	14.2	22.5	14.2	22.5
300			15.1	21.4	14.9	21.6	14.8	21.7	14.5	22.0	14.5	22.0	14.5	22.0
400			15.6	20.7	15.4	21.0	15.3	21.1	15.0	21.4	15.0	21.4	15.0	21.4
500			15.9	20.1	15.8	20.5	15.6	20.7	15.3	21.0	15.3	21.0	15.3	21.1
600					16.1	20.1	15.9	20.3	15.6	20.7	15.5	20.8	15.5	20.8
700					16.3	19.9	16.1	20.1	15.8	20.5	15.7	20.5	15.7	20.6
800							16.3	19.8	15.9	20.4	15.8	20.4	15.8	20.4
900							16.5	19.7	16.0	20.1	16.0	20.2	15.9	20.2
1,000							16.6	19.5	16.1	20.0	16.1	20.1	16.0	20.1
1,500									16.5	19.6	16.4	19.7	16.4	19.7
2,000									16.8	19.3	16.6	19.4	16.6	19.6
3,000									17.1	19.0	16.9	19.2	16.9	19.2

And Sample Size is:	For Field Size of: 500		1,000		1,500		2,000		10,000		50,000		100,000 and over	
	Lower Limit	Upper Limit	Lower Limit	Upper Limit	Lower Limit	Upper Limit	Lower Limit	Upper Limit	Lower Limit	Upper Limit	Lower Limit	Upper Limit	Lower Limit	Upper Limit
	Confidence Level 95% (Two-sided) Confidence Level 97.5% (One-sided)													
50	9.1%	30.8%	8.8%	31.1%	8.7%	31.2%	8.7%	31.3%	8.6%	31.4%	8.6%	31.4%	8.6%	31.4%
80	11.0	27.3	10.6	27.7	10.5	27.9	10.5	28.0	10.4	30.1	10.4	30.2	10.3	28.2
90	11.4	26.6	11.1	27.1	10.9	27.2	10.9	27.3	10.8	27.4	10.7	27.5	10.7	27.5
100	11.8	26.0	11.4	26.5	11.3	26.6	11.2	26.7	11.1	26.9	11.1	26.9	11.1	26.9
120	12.4	25.0	12.0	25.5	11.9	25.7	11.8	25.8	11.6	26.0	11.6	26.0	11.6	26.0
140	12.9	24.2	12.5	24.8	12.3	25.0	12.3	25.1	12.1	25.3	12.0	25.3	12.0	25.4
150	13.2	23.9	12.7	24.5	12.5	24.7	12.5	24.8	12.3	25.0	12.2	25.1	12.2	25.1
160	13.4	23.6	12.9	24.3	12.7	24.4	12.6	24.5	12.4	24.7	12.4	24.8	12.4	24.8
180	13.8	23.1	13.2	23.8	13.1	23.9	13.0	24.1	12.8	24.3	12.7	24.4	12.7	24.4
200	14.1	22.7	13.5	23.4	13.3	23.6	13.2	23.7	13.0	24.0	13.0	24.0	13.0	24.0
250	14.8	21.8	14.1	22.6	13.9	22.9	13.8	23.0	13.5	23.3	13.5	23.3	13.5	23.3
300			14.5	22.0	14.3	22.3	14.2	22.4	13.9	22.7	13.9	22.8	13.8	22.8
400			15.2	21.2	14.9	21.5	14.8	21.7	14.4	22.0	14.4	22.1	14.4	22.1
500					15.3	21.0	15.2	21.2	14.8	21.5	14.8	21.6	14.7	21.6
600					15.7	20.6	15.5	20.8	15.1	21.2	15.0	21.3	15.0	21.3
700					16.0	20.2	15.8	20.5	15.3	20.9	15.2	21.0	15.2	21.0
800							16.0	20.2	15.5	20.7	15.4	20.8	15.4	20.8
900							16.2	20.0	15.7	20.5	15.6	20.6	15.6	20.6
1,000									15.8	20.4	15.7	20.5	15.7	20.5
1,500									16.2	19.9	16.1	20.0	16.1	20.0
2,000									16.5	19.6	16.4	19.7	16.4	19.8
3,000									16.9	19.2	16.7	19.4	16.6	19.4

F

TABLE F-18 Sample Precision for Relative Frequencies for Random Samples Only—Rate of Occurrence in Sample 18% (Continued)

And Sample Size is:	For Field Size of: 500 Lower Limit	500 Upper Limit	1,000 Lower Limit	1,000 Upper Limit	1,500 Lower Limit	1,500 Upper Limit	2,000 Lower Limit	2,000 Upper Limit	10,000 Lower Limit	10,000 Upper Limit	50,000 Lower Limit	50,000 Upper Limit	100,000 and over Lower Limit	100,000 and over Upper Limit
	Confidence Level 99% (Two-sided) Confidence Level 99.5% (One-sided)													
50	7.2%	34.8%	6.9%	35.3%	6.8%	35.4%	6.7%	35.5%	6.6%	35.7%	6.6%	35.7%	6.6%	35.7%
80	9.3	30.3	8.9	30.9	8.8	31.1	8.7	31.2	8.6	31.4	8.5	31.4	8.5	31.4
90	9.8	29.4	9.4	30.0	9.3	30.2	9.2	30.3	9.0	30.5	9.0	30.5	9.0	30.6
100	10.3	28.6	9.8	29.2	9.7	29.4	9.6	29.5	9.4	29.7	9.4	29.8	9.4	29.8
120	11.0	27.3	10.5	28.0	10.3	28.2	10.3	28.3	10.1	28.6	10.0	28.6	10.0	28.6
140	11.7	26.3	11.1	27.0	10.9	27.3	10.8	27.4	10.6	27.7	10.5	27.7	10.5	27.7
150	11.9	25.8	11.3	26.6	11.1	26.9	11.0	27.0	10.8	27.3	10.8	27.3	10.7	27.4
160	12.2	25.4	11.5	26.3	11.3	26.5	11.2	26.7	11.0	27.0	11.0	27.0	11.0	27.0
180	12.6	24.8	11.9	25.7	11.8	25.8	11.6	26.1	11.4	26.4	11.3	26.4	11.3	26.5
200	13.1	24.2	12.3	25.1	12.1	25.4	11.9	25.6	11.7	25.9	11.6	25.9	11.6	26.0
250	13.9	23.0	13.0	24.1	12.7	24.4	12.6	24.6	12.3	24.9	12.2	25.0	12.2	25.0
300			13.6	23.3	13.3	23.7	13.1	23.9	12.8	24.3	12.7	24.3	12.7	24.4
400			14.4	22.2	14.0	22.6	13.8	22.9	13.4	23.3	13.4	23.4	13.4	23.4
500					14.6	21.9	14.4	22.2	13.9	22.7	13.8	22.8	13.8	22.8
600					15.0	21.4	14.8	21.6	14.3	22.2	14.2	22.3	14.2	22.4
700					15.4	20.9	15.1	21.2	14.6	21.9	14.5	22.0	14.4	22.0
800							15.4	20.9	14.8	21.6	14.7	21.7	14.7	21.8
900							15.6	20.6	15.0	21.3	14.9	21.5	14.8	21.5
1,000									15.1	21.1	15.0	21.3	15.0	21.3
1,500									15.7	20.5	15.6	20.6	15.5	20.7
2,000									16.1	20.1	15.9	20.3	15.9	20.3
3,000									16.5	19.6	16.3	19.8	16.2	19.9

TABLE F-19 Sample Precision for Relative Frequencies for Random Samples Only—Rate of Occurrence in Sample 19%

And Sample Size is:	For Field Size of: 500		1,000		1,500		2,000		10,000		50,000		100,000 and over	
	Lower Limit	Upper Limit	Lower Limit	Upper Limit	Lower Limit	Upper Limit	Lower Limit	Upper Limit	Lower Limit	Upper Limit	Lower Limit	Upper Limit	Lower Limit	Upper Limit
	Confidence Level 90% (Two-sided) Confidence Level 95% (One-sided)													
50	10.9%	29.8%	10.7%	30.1%	10.6%	30.2%	10.6%	30.3%	10.5%	30.4%	10.5%	30.4%	10.5%	30.4%
80	12.7	26.9	12.4	27.3	12.3	27.4	12.3	27.5	12.2	27.6	12.1	27.6	12.1	27.6
90	13.1	26.3	12.8	26.7	12.7	26.8	12.7	26.9	12.5	27.0	12.5	27.1	12.5	27.1
100	13.5	25.8	13.1	26.2	13.0	26.3	13.0	26.4	12.9	26.6	12.8	26.6	12.8	26.6
120	14.1	25.0	13.7	25.4	13.6	25.6	13.5	25.6	13.4	25.8	13.4	25.8	13.3	25.8
140	14.5	24.3	14.1	24.8	14.0	25.0	13.9	25.1	13.8	25.2	13.8	25.3	13.8	25.3
150	14.8	24.0	14.3	24.6	14.2	24.7	14.1	24.8	14.0	25.0	13.9	25.0	13.9	25.0
160	14.9	23.8	14.5	24.3	14.4	24.5	14.3	24.6	14.1	24.8	14.1	24.8	14.1	24.8
180	15.3	23.4	14.8	23.9	14.6	24.1	14.6	24.2	14.4	24.4	14.4	24.4	14.4	24.4
200	15.6	23.0	15.1	23.6	14.9	23.8	14.8	23.9	14.6	24.1	14.6	24.1	14.6	24.1
250	16.2	22.2	15.6	22.9	15.4	23.1	15.3	23.2	15.1	23.5	15.1	23.5	15.1	23.5
300			16.0	22.5	15.8	22.7	15.6	22.8	15.4	23.1	15.4	23.2	15.4	23.2
400			16.6	21.7	16.3	22.0	16.2	22.2	15.9	22.4	15.9	22.5	15.9	22.5
500			17.0	21.2	16.7	21.5	16.6	21.7	16.3	22.0	16.2	22.1	16.2	22.1
600					17.0	21.2	16.9	21.4	16.5	21.7	16.4	21.8	16.4	21.8
700					17.3	20.9	17.1	21.1	16.7	21.5	16.6	21.6	16.6	21.6
800							17.3	20.9	16.9	21.3	16.8	21.4	16.8	21.4
900							17.4	20.7	17.0	21.2	16.9	21.3	16.9	21.3
1,000							17.6	20.5	17.1	21.0	17.0	21.1	17.0	21.2
1,500									17.5	20.6	17.4	20.7	17.4	20.7
2,000									17.7	20.4	17.6	20.5	17.6	20.5
3,000									18.0	20.0	17.9	20.2	17.8	20.2

F

TABLE F-19 Sample Precision for Relative Frequencies for Random Samples Only—Rate of Occurrence in Sample 19% (Continued)

And Sample Size is:	500 Lower Limit	500 Upper Limit	1,000 Lower Limit	1,000 Upper Limit	1,500 Lower Limit	1,500 Upper Limit	2,000 Lower Limit	2,000 Upper Limit	10,000 Lower Limit	10,000 Upper Limit	50,000 Lower Limit	50,000 Upper Limit	100,000 and over Lower Limit	100,000 and over Upper Limit
	For Field Size of:													
	Confidence Level 95% (Two-sided) Confidence Level 97.5% (One-sided)													
50	9.8%	31.9%	9.6%	32.2%	9.5%	32.4%	9.4%	32.4%	9.3%	32.5%	9.3%	32.6%	9.3%	32.6%
80	11.8	28.4	11.5	28.9	11.4	29.0	11.3	29.1	11.1	29.3	11.1	29.3	11.1	29.3
90	12.1	27.4	11.8	27.9	11.7	28.0	11.7	28.1	11.5	28.3	11.5	28.3	11.5	28.3
100	12.6	27.1	12.2	27.6	12.1	27.8	12.0	27.8	11.9	28.0	11.9	28.1	11.9	28.1
120	13.3	26.1	12.8	26.7	12.7	26.8	12.6	26.9	12.5	27.1	12.4	27.2	12.4	27.2
140	13.8	25.3	13.3	25.9	13.2	26.1	13.1	26.2	12.9	26.4	12.9	26.5	12.9	26.5
150	14.0	25.0	13.5	25.6	13.4	25.8	13.3	25.9	13.1	26.1	13.1	26.2	13.1	26.2
160	14.3	24.7	13.7	25.4	13.6	25.6	13.5	25.7	13.3	25.9	13.3	25.9	13.2	25.9
180	14.6	24.2	14.1	24.9	14.0	25.0	13.8	25.2	13.6	25.4	13.6	25.5	13.6	25.5
200	15.0	23.7	14.4	24.5	14.2	24.7	14.1	24.8	13.9	25.1	13.8	25.1	13.8	25.1
250	15.7	22.8	15.0	23.7	14.7	23.9	14.6	24.1	14.4	24.3	14.4	24.4	14.3	24.1
300			15.4	23.1	15.2	23.4	15.1	23.5	14.8	23.8	14.7	23.9	14.7	23.9
400			16.1	22.2	15.8	22.6	15.7	22.7	15.4	23.1	15.3	23.2	15.3	23.2
500					16.3	22.0	16.1	22.2	15.7	22.6	15.7	22.7	15.7	22.7
600					16.6	21.6	16.4	21.8	16.0	22.3	16.0	22.4	15.9	22.4
700					16.9	21.3	16.7	21.5	16.3	22.0	16.2	22.1	16.2	22.1
800							16.9	21.2	16.4	21.8	16.4	21.9	16.3	21.9
900							17.1	21.0	16.6	21.6	16.5	21.7	16.5	21.7
1,000									16.7	21.4	16.6	21.5	16.6	21.6
1,500									17.2	20.9	17.1	21.0	17.0	21.1
2,000									17.5	20.6	17.3	20.8	17.3	20.8
3,000									17.8	20.2	17.7	20.4	17.6	20.5

And Sample Size is:	For Field Size of: 500		1,000		1,500		2,000		10,000		50,000		100,000 and over	
	Lower Limit	Upper Limit	Lower Limit	Upper Limit	Lower Limit	Upper Limit	Lower Limit	Upper Limit	Lower Limit	Upper Limit	Lower Limit	Upper Limit	Lower Limit	Upper Limit
	Confidence Level 99% (Two-sided) Confidence Level 99.5% (One-sided)													
50	7.8%	37.0%	7.5%	37.4%	7.4%	37.6%	7.4%	37.7%	7.3%	37.8%	7.2%	37.9%	7.2%	37.9%
80	10.1	31.5	9.6	32.0	9.5	32.2	9.4	32.3	9.3	32.5	9.2	32.6	9.2	32.6
90	10.6	30.5	10.1	31.1	10.0	31.3	9.9	31.4	9.7	31.7	9.7	31.7	9.7	31.7
100	11.0	29.7	10.6	30.3	10.4	30.6	10.3	30.7	10.1	30.9	10.1	30.9	10.1	31.0
120	11.8	28.4	11.3	29.1	11.1	29.3	11.0	29.5	10.8	29.7	10.8	29.8	10.8	29.8
140	12.5	27.3	11.9	28.1	11.7	28.4	11.6	28.5	11.4	28.8	11.3	28.8	11.3	28.8
150	12.7	26.9	12.1	27.8	11.9	28.0	11.8	28.1	11.6	28.4	11.5	28.5	11.5	28.5
160	13.0	26.6	12.3	27.4	12.1	27.7	12.0	27.8	11.8	28.1	11.8	28.2	11.7	28.2
180	13.5	25.9	12.8	26.8	12.6	27.0	12.4	27.2	12.2	27.5	12.1	27.6	12.1	27.6
200	13.9	25.3	13.1	26.2	12.9	26.5	12.8	26.7	12.5	27.0	12.4	27.1	12.4	27.1
250	15.2	24.1	13.9	25.2	13.6	25.5	13.5	25.7	13.1	26.1	13.1	26.1	13.1	26.2
300			14.4	24.4	14.1	24.8	14.0	25.0	13.6	25.4	13.6	25.5	13.6	25.5
400			15.3	23.3	14.9	23.7	14.7	23.9	14.3	24.4	14.2	24.5	14.2	24.5
500					15.5	23.0	15.3	23.2	14.8	23.8	14.7	23.9	14.7	23.9
600					15.9	22.4	15.7	22.7	15.2	23.3	15.1	23.4	15.1	23.4
700					16.3	22.0	16.0	22.3	15.5	22.9	15.4	23.1	15.3	23.1
800							16.3	22.0	15.7	22.7	15.6	22.8	15.6	22.8
900							16.6	21.7	15.9	22.4	15.8	22.5	15.8	22.6
1,000									16.1	22.2	16.0	22.3	15.9	22.3
1,500									16.7	21.5	16.5	21.7	16.5	21.7
2,000									17.0	21.1	16.8	21.3	16.8	21.3
3,000									17.5	20.6	17.2	20.9	17.2	20.9

F

TABLE F-20 Sample Precision for Relative Frequencies for Random Samples Only—Rate of Occurrence in Sample 20%

And Sample Size is:	For Field Size of: 500 Lower Limit	500 Upper Limit	1,000 Lower Limit	1,000 Upper Limit	1,500 Lower Limit	1,500 Upper Limit	2,000 Lower Limit	2,000 Upper Limit	10,000 Lower Limit	10,000 Upper Limit	50,000 Lower Limit	50,000 Upper Limit	100,000 and over Lower Limit	100,000 and over Upper Limit
	Confidence Level 90% (Two-sided) Confidence Level 95% (One-sided)													
50	11.7%	30.9%	11.5%	31.2%	11.4%	31.3%	11.4%	31.4%	11.3%	31.5%	11.3%	31.5%	11.3%	31.5%
80	13.5	28.0	13.2	28.4	13.1	28.5	13.1	28.6	13.0	28.7	13.0	28.8	13.0	28.8
90	14.0	27.4	13.6	27.8	13.5	27.9	13.5	28.0	13.4	28.2	13.3	28.2	13.3	28.2
100	14.3	26.9	14.0	27.3	13.9	27.5	13.8	27.5	13.7	27.7	13.7	27.7	13.7	27.7
120	14.9	26.1	14.6	26.5	14.4	26.7	14.4	26.7	14.2	26.9	14.2	26.9	14.2	26.9
140	15.4	25.4	15.0	25.9	14.9	26.1	14.8	26.1	14.7	26.3	14.6	26.4	14.6	26.4
150	15.6	25.1	15.2	25.7	15.1	25.8	15.0	25.9	14.8	26.1	14.8	26.1	14.8	26.1
160	15.8	24.9	15.4	25.4	15.2	25.6	15.2	25.7	15.0	25.9	15.0	25.9	15.0	25.9
180	16.2	24.4	15.7	25.0	15.5	25.1	15.5	25.3	15.3	25.5	15.3	25.5	15.2	25.5
200	16.5	24.0	16.0	24.7	15.8	24.9	15.7	25.0	15.5	25.2	15.5	25.2	15.5	25.2
250	17.1	23.3	16.5	24.0	16.3	24.2	16.2	24.3	16.0	24.6	16.0	24.6	16.0	24.6
300			16.9	23.6	16.7	23.7	16.6	23.9	16.4	24.1	16.3	24.2	16.3	24.2
400			17.5	22.8	17.3	23.1	17.1	23.2	16.9	23.5	16.8	23.6	16.8	23.6
500			18.0	22.3	17.7	22.6	17.5	22.8	17.2	23.1	17.1	23.2	17.1	23.2
600					18.0	22.2	17.8	22.4	17.5	22.8	17.4	22.9	17.4	22.9
700					18.2	21.9	18.0	22.1	17.7	22.6	17.6	22.6	17.6	22.7
800							18.2	21.9	17.8	22.4	17.7	22.5	17.7	22.5
900							18.4	21.7	17.9	22.2	17.9	22.3	17.8	22.3
1,000							18.6	21.5	18.1	22.1	18.0	22.2	18.0	22.2
1,500									18.5	21.6	18.3	21.7	18.3	21.8
2,000									18.7	21.4	18.6	21.5	18.5	21.5
3,000									19.0	21.0	18.8	21.2	18.8	21.2

And Sample Size is:	For Field Size of: 500 Lower Limit	500 Upper Limit	1,000 Lower Limit	1,000 Upper Limit	1,500 Lower Limit	1,500 Upper Limit	2,000 Lower Limit	2,000 Upper Limit	10,000 Lower Limit	10,000 Upper Limit	50,000 Lower Limit	50,000 Upper Limit	100,000 and over Lower Limit	100,000 and over Upper Limit
Confidence Level 95% (Two-sided) Confidence Level 97.5% (One-sided)														
50	10.6%	33.0%	10.3%	33.4%	10.2%	33.5%	10.2%	33.5%	10.1%	33.7%	10.1%	33.7%	10.1%	33.7%
80	12.6	29.6	12.2	30.0	12.1	30.2	12.0	30.2	11.9	30.3	11.9	30.4	11.9	30.4
90	13.0	28.8	12.7	29.3	12.5	29.5	12.5	29.5	12.3	29.7	12.3	29.8	12.3	29.8
100	13.4	28.2	13.0	28.7	12.9	28.9	12.8	29.0	12.7	29.1	12.7	29.2	12.7	29.2
120	14.1	27.2	13.7	27.8	13.5	27.9	13.5	28.0	13.3	28.2	13.3	28.3	13.3	28.3
140	14.7	26.4	14.2	27.0	14.0	27.2	13.9	27.3	13.8	27.5	13.7	27.6	13.7	27.6
150	14.9	26.1	14.4	26.7	14.2	26.7	14.2	27.0	14.0	27.3	13.9	27.3	13.9	27.3
160	15.1	25.8	14.6	26.5	14.4	26.7	14.3	26.8	14.1	27.0	14.1	27.0	14.1	27.1
180	15.5	25.3	14.9	26.0	14.8	26.1	14.7	26.3	14.5	26.5	14.4	26.6	14.4	26.6
200	15.9	24.8	15.3	25.6	15.1	25.8	15.0	25.9	14.7	26.2	14.7	26.2	14.7	26.2
250	16.6	23.9	15.9	24.8	15.6	25.0	15.5	25.1	15.3	25.4	15.2	25.5	15.2	25.5
300			16.3	24.2	16.1	24.5	16.0	24.6	15.7	24.9	15.6	25.0	15.6	25.0
400			17.0	23.3	16.7	23.6	16.6	23.8	16.3	24.2	16.2	24.2	16.2	24.3
500					17.2	23.1	17.0	23.3	16.7	23.7	16.6	23.8	16.6	23.8
600					17.6	22.7	17.4	22.9	17.0	23.3	16.9	23.4	16.9	23.4
700					17.9	22.3	17.7	22.5	17.2	23.0	17.1	23.1	17.1	23.2
800							17.9	22.3	17.4	22.8	17.3	22.9	17.3	22.9
900							18.1	22.1	17.5	22.6	17.5	22.7	17.4	22.8
1,000									17.7	22.5	17.6	22.6	17.6	22.6
1,500									17.2	22.0	18.0	22.1	18.0	22.1
2,000									18.5	21.6	18.3	21.8	18.3	21.8
3,000									18.8	21.2	18.6	21.4	18.6	21.5

F

TABLE F-20 Sample Precision for Relative Frequencies for Random Samples Only—Rate of Occurrence in Sample 20% (Continued)

And Sample Size is:	For Field Size of: 500 Lower Limit	500 Upper Limit	1,000 Lower Limit	1,000 Upper Limit	1,500 Lower Limit	1,500 Upper Limit	2,000 Lower Limit	2,000 Upper Limit	10,000 Lower Limit	10,000 Upper Limit	50,000 Lower Limit	50,000 Upper Limit	100,000 and over Lower Limit	100,000 and over Upper Limit
	Confidence Level 99% (Two-sided) Confidence Level 99.5% (One-sided)													
50	8.5%	37.1%	8.2%	37.6%	8.1%	37.7%	8.0%	37.8%	7.9%	38.0%	7.9%	38.0%	7.9%	38.0%
80	10.8	32.6	10.4	33.2	10.2	33.4	10.1	33.5	10.0	33.7	9.9	33.8	9.9	33.8
90	11.3	31.7	10.9	32.3	10.7	32.5	10.6	32.6	10.5	32.8	10.4	32.9	10.4	32.9
100	11.8	30.8	11.3	31.5	11.2	31.7	11.1	31.8	10.9	32.1	10.8	32.1	10.8	32.1
120	12.6	29.5	12.1	30.3	11.9	30.5	11.8	30.6	11.6	30.9	11.5	30.9	11.5	30.9
140	13.3	28.5	12.7	29.3	12.5	29.5	12.4	29.7	12.1	29.9	12.1	30.0	12.1	30.0
150	13.6	28.1	12.9	28.9	12.7	29.1	12.6	29.3	12.4	29.6	12.3	29.6	12.3	29.6
160	13.8	27.7	13.2	28.5	12.9	28.8	12.8	28.9	12.6	29.2	12.6	29.3	12.5	29.3
180	14.3	27.0	13.6	27.9	13.4	28.1	13.3	28.3	13.0	28.6	12.9	28.7	12.9	28.7
200	14.8	26.4	14.0	27.4	13.7	27.7	13.6	27.8	13.3	28.1	13.3	28.2	13.3	28.2
250	15.7	25.1	14.7	26.3	14.4	26.6	14.3	26.8	14.0	27.2	13.9	27.3	13.9	27.3
300			15.3	25.5	15.0	25.9	14.8	26.1	14.5	26.5	14.4	26.6	14.4	26.6
400			16.2	24.4	15.8	24.8	15.6	25.0	15.2	25.5	15.1	25.6	15.1	25.6
500					16.4	24.1	16.2	24.3	15.7	24.9	15.6	25.0	15.6	25.0
600					17.0	23.5	16.6	23.8	16.1	24.4	16.0	24.5	16.0	24.5
700					17.3	23.0	17.0	23.4	16.4	24.0	16.3	24.1	16.2	24.2
800							17.3	23.0	16.6	23.7	16.5	23.8	16.5	23.9
900							17.5	22.7	16.8	23.5	16.7	23.6	16.7	23.7
1,000									17.0	23.3	16.9	23.4	16.9	23.4
1,500									17.6	22.6	17.4	22.7	17.4	22.8
2,000									18.0	22.1	17.8	22.4	17.8	22.1
3,000									18.5	21.6	18.2	21.9	18.1	21.9

TABLE F-21 Sample Precision for Relative Frequencies for Random Samples Only—Rate of Occurrence in Sample 25%

And Sample Size is:	For Field Size of: 500 Lower Limit	500 Upper Limit	1,000 Lower Limit	1,000 Upper Limit	1,500 Lower Limit	1,500 Upper Limit	2,000 Lower Limit	2,000 Upper Limit	10,000 Lower Limit	10,000 Upper Limit	50,000 Lower Limit	50,000 Upper Limit	100,000 and over Lower Limit	100,000 and over Upper Limit
	Confidence Level 90% (Two-sided) Confidence Level 95% (One-sided)													
50	15.8%	36.4%	15.5%	36.7%	15.5%	36.8%	15.4%	36.8%	15.3%	36.9%	15.3%	37.0%	15.3%	37.0%
80	17.9	33.4	17.5	33.8	17.4	33.9	17.4	34.0	17.2	34.1	17.2	34.2	17.2	34.2
90	18.3	32.8	18.0	33.2	17.9	33.3	17.8	33.4	17.7	33.6	17.7	33.6	17.6	33.6
100	18.8	32.3	18.4	32.7	18.3	32.8	18.2	32.9	18.0	33.1	18.0	33.1	18.0	33.1
120	19.4	31.4	19.0	31.9	18.9	32.0	18.8	32.1	18.7	32.3	18.6	32.3	18.6	32.3
140	20.0	30.7	19.5	31.2	19.4	31.4	19.3	31.5	19.1	31.7	19.1	31.7	19.1	31.7
150	20.2	30.4	19.7	31.0	19.6	31.1	19.5	31.2	19.3	31.4	19.3	31.5	19.3	31.5
160	20.4	30.2	19.9	30.7	19.8	30.9	19.7	31.0	19.5	31.2	19.5	31.2	19.5	31.3
180	20.8	29.7	20.3	30.3	20.1	30.5	20.0	30.6	19.8	30.8	19.8	30.9	19.8	30.9
200	21.2	29.3	20.6	30.0	20.4	30.2	20.3	30.3	20.1	30.5	20.1	30.5	20.0	30.5
250	21.9	28.5	21.2	29.3	21.0	29.5	20.9	29.6	20.6	29.8	20.6	29.9	20.6	29.9
300			21.6	28.7	21.4	29.0	21.3	29.1	21.0	29.4	21.0	29.4	20.9	29.4
400			22.3	28.0	22.0	28.3	21.9	28.4	21.6	28.7	21.5	28.8	21.5	28.8
500			22.8	27.4	22.4	27.8	22.3	28.0	21.9	28.3	21.9	28.4	21.9	28.4
600					22.8	27.4	22.6	27.6	22.2	28.0	22.1	28.1	22.1	28.1
700					23.1	27.1	22.9	27.3	22.4	27.7	22.4	27.8	22.3	27.8
800							23.1	27.0	22.6	27.5	22.5	27.6	22.5	27.6
900							23.3	26.8	22.8	27.4	22.7	27.5	22.6	27.5
1,000							23.4	26.7	22.9	27.2	22.8	27.3	22.8	27.4
1,500									23.3	26.8	23.2	26.9	23.2	26.9
2,000									23.6	26.5	23.4	26.6	23.4	26.6
3,000									23.9	26.1	23.7	26.3	23.7	26.3

F

TABLE F-21 Sample Precision for Relative Frequencies for Random Samples Only—Rate of Occurrence in Sample 25% (Continued)

And Sample Size is:	For Field Size of: 500 Lower Limit	500 Upper Limit	1,000 Lower Limit	1,000 Upper Limit	1,500 Lower Limit	1,500 Upper Limit	2,000 Lower Limit	2,000 Upper Limit	10,000 Lower Limit	10,000 Upper Limit	50,000 Lower Limit	50,000 Upper Limit	100,000 and over Lower Limit	100,000 and over Upper Limit
	Confidence Level 95% (Two-sided) Confidence Level 97.5% (One-sided)													
80	16.7%	35.0%	16.4%	35.5%	16.2%	35.6%	16.2%	35.7%	16.0%	35.9%	16.0%	35.9%	16.0%	35.9%
90	17.3	34.3	16.9	34.8	16.7	34.9	16.7	35.0	16.5	35.2	16.5	35.2	16.5	35.2
100	17.7	33.6	17.3	34.2	17.2	34.3	17.1	34.4	16.9	34.6	16.9	34.7	16.9	34.7
120	18.5	32.6	18.0	33.2	17.9	33.4	17.8	33.5	17.6	33.7	17.6	33.7	17.6	33.7
140	19.1	31.8	18.6	32.4	18.4	32.6	18.3	32.7	18.1	33.0	18.1	33.0	18.1	33.0
150	19.4	31.5	18.8	32.1	18.6	32.3	18.6	32.4	18.4	32.7	18.3	32.7	18.3	32.7
160	19.6	31.1	19.0	31.8	18.9	32.0	18.8	32.1	18.6	32.4	18.5	32.4	18.5	32.5
180	20.1	30.6	19.4	31.3	19.3	31.5	19.1	31.7	18.9	31.9	18.9	32.0	18.9	32.0
200	20.5	30.1	19.8	30.9	19.6	31.1	19.5	31.3	19.2	31.5	19.2	31.6	19.2	31.6
250	21.3	29.1	20.5	30.1	20.2	30.3	20.1	30.5	19.8	30.8	19.8	30.8	19.8	30.9
300			21.0	29.4	20.7	29.7	20.6	29.9	20.3	30.2	20.2	30.3	20.2	30.3
400			21.8	28.5	21.4	28.9	21.3	29.1	20.9	29.4	20.8	29.5	20.8	29.5
500					21.9	28.3	21.8	28.5	21.4	28.9	21.3	29.0	21.3	29.0
600					22.4	27.8	22.1	28.1	21.7	28.6	21.6	28.6	21.6	28.7
700					22.7	27.5	22.4	27.7	21.9	28.3	21.9	28.4	21.8	28.4
800							22.7	27.4	22.2	28.0	22.1	28.1	22.0	28.1
900							22.9	27.2	22.3	27.8	22.2	27.9	22.2	28.0
1,000									22.5	27.7	22.4	27.8	22.3	27.8
1,500									23.0	27.1	22.9	27.2	22.8	27.3
2,000									23.3	26.8	23.1	26.9	23.1	26.9
3,000									23.7	26.3	23.5	26.5	23.5	26.6

And Sample Size is:	For Field Size of: 500 Lower Limit	Upper Limit	1,000 Lower Limit	Upper Limit	1,500 Lower Limit	Upper Limit	2,000 Lower Limit	Upper Limit	10,000 Lower Limit	Upper Limit	50,000 Lower Limit	Upper Limit	100,000 and over Lower Limit	Upper Limit
	Confidence Level 99% (Two-sided) Confidence Level 99.5% (One-sided)													
50	12.0%	42.7%	11.6%	43.2%	11.5%	43.3%	11.4%	43.4%	11.3%	43.6%	11.3%	43.6%	11.3%	43.7%
80	14.7	38.2	14.2	38.8	14.0	39.0	13.9	39.1	13.7	39.3	13.7	39.3	13.7	39.4
90	15.3	37.2	14.8	37.8	14.6	38.0	14.5	38.1	14.3	38.4	14.3	38.4	14.3	38.5
100	15.9	36.3	15.3	37.0	15.1	37.3	15.0	37.4	14.8	37.6	14.8	37.7	14.8	37.7
120	16.8	35.0	16.2	35.7	16.0	36.0	15.9	36.1	15.6	36.4	15.6	36.4	15.6	36.4
140	17.5	34.0	16.8	34.8	16.6	35.0	16.5	35.2	16.3	35.5	16.2	35.5	16.2	35.5
150	17.9	33.5	17.1	34.4	16.9	34.6	16.8	34.8	16.5	35.1	16.5	35.1	16.5	35.2
160	18.2	33.1	17.4	34.0	17.2	34.3	17.1	34.4	16.8	34.7	16.7	34.8	16.7	34.8
180	18.7	32.4	17.9	33.3	17.7	33.5	17.5	33.8	17.2	34.1	17.2	34.2	17.2	34.2
200	19.2	31.7	18.3	32.8	18.1	33.1	17.9	33.2	17.6	33.6	17.6	33.7	17.5	33.7
250	20.2	30.4	19.2	31.7	18.9	32.0	18.7	32.2	18.4	32.6	18.3	32.7	18.3	32.7
300			19.8	30.8	19.5	31.2	19.3	31.4	18.9	31.9	18.9	32.0	18.8	32.0
400			20.8	29.6	20.4	30.1	20.2	30.3	19.7	30.9	19.7	31.0	19.6	31.0
500					21.1	29.3	20.8	29.6	20.3	30.2	20.2	30.3	20.2	30.3
600					21.6	28.7	21.3	29.0	20.7	29.7	20.6	29.8	20.6	29.8
700					22.0	28.2	21.7	28.6	21.0	29.3	20.9	29.4	20.9	29.5
800							22.0	28.2	21.3	29.0	21.2	29.1	21.2	29.1
900							22.3	27.9	21.5	28.7	21.4	28.9	21.4	28.9
1,000									21.7	28.3	21.6	28.7	21.6	28.7
1,500									22.4	27.8	22.2	27.9	22.2	28.0
2,000									22.8	27.3	22.6	27.5	22.6	27.6
3,000									23.3	26.7	23.1	27.0	23.0	27.1

F

TABLE F-22 Sample Precision for Relative Frequencies for Random Samples Only—Rate of Occurrence in Sample 30%

And Sample Size is:	For Field Size of: 500 Lower Limit	500 Upper Limit	1,000 Lower Limit	1,000 Upper Limit	1,500 Lower Limit	1,500 Upper Limit	2,000 Lower Limit	2,000 Upper Limit	10,000 Lower Limit	10,000 Upper Limit	50,000 Lower Limit	50,000 Upper Limit	100,000 and over Lower Limit	100,000 and over Upper Limit
	Confidence Level 90% (Two-sided) Confidence Level 95% (One-sided)													
50	20.0%	41.6%	19.8%	42.0%	19.7%	42.1%	19.6%	42.2%	19.5%	42.2%	19.5%	42.3%	19.5%	42.3%
80	22.3	38.7	22.0	39.1	21.8	39.2	31.8	39.3	21.7	39.4	21.6	39.5	21.6	39.5
90	22.8	38.0	22.5	38.5	22.3	38.6	22.3	38.7	22.1	38.8	22.1	38.9	22.1	38.9
100	23.3	37.5	22.9	38.0	22.7	38.1	22.7	38.2	22.5	38.3	22.5	38.4	22.5	38.5
120	24.0	36.6	23.6	37.1	23.4	37.3	23.3	37.4	23.1	37.5	23.1	37.6	23.1	37.6
140	24.6	35.9	24.1	36.5	24.0	36.6	23.9	36.7	23.7	36.9	23.7	37.0	23.7	37.0
150	24.9	35.6	24.3	36.2	24.2	36.4	24.1	36.5	23.9	36.7	23.9	36.7	23.9	36.7
160	25.1	35.4	24.6	36.0	24.4	36.1	24.3	36.2	24.1	36.4	24.1	36.5	24.1	36.5
180	25.5	34.9	24.9	35.5	24.7	35.7	24.7	35.8	24.5	36.0	24.4	36.1	24.4	36.1
200	25.9	34.5	25.3	35.2	25.1	35.4	25.0	35.5	24.7	35.7	24.7	35.8	24.7	35.8
250	26.6	33.6	25.9	34.4	25.7	34.7	25.6	34.8	25.3	35.0	25.3	35.1	25.3	35.1
300			26.4	33.9	26.1	34.2	26.0	34.3	25.7	34.7	25.7	34.6	25.7	34.6
400			27.1	33.1	26.8	33.4	26.7	33.6	26.3	33.9	26.3	34.0	26.3	34.0
500			27.6	32.5	27.3	32.9	27.1	33.1	26.7	33.5	26.7	33.5	26.7	33.6
600					27.6	32.5	27.4	32.7	27.0	33.1	27.0	33.2	26.9	33.2
700					27.9	32.2	27.7	32.4	27.3	32.9	27.2	33.0	27.2	33.0
800							27.9	32.2	27.5	32.7	27.4	32.8	27.4	32.8
900							28.1	21.9	27.6	32.5	27.5	32.6	27.5	32.6
1,000							28.3	31.7	27.7	32.3	27.6	32.5	27.6	32.5
1,500									28.2	31.8	28.1	32.0	28.1	32.0
2,000									28.5	31.5	28.4	31.7	28.3	31.7
3,000									28.8	31.2	28.7	31.4	28.6	31.4

And Sample Size is:	For Field Size of: 500 Lower Limit	Upper Limit	1,000 Lower Limit	Upper Limit	1,500 Lower Limit	Upper Limit	2,000 Lower Limit	Upper Limit	10,000 Lower Limit	Upper Limit	50,000 Lower Limit	Upper Limit	100,000 and over Lower Limit	Upper Limit
	Confidence Level 95% (Two-sided) Confidence Level 97.5% (One-sided)													
50	18.5%	43.9%	18.2%	44.2%	18.1%	44.4%	18.0%	44.4%	17.9%	44.6%	17.9%	44.6%	17.9%	44.6%
80	21.1	40.3	20.7	40.8	20.5	41.0	20.5	41.1	20.3	41.2	20.3	41.3	20.3	41.3
90	21.7	39.6	21.2	40.1	21.1	40.2	21.0	40.3	20.8	40.5	20.8	40.6	20.8	40.6
100	22.2	38.9	21.7	39.5	21.5	39.6	21.5	39.7	21.3	39.9	21.2	40.0	21.2	40.0
120	23.0	37.9	22.5	38.5	22.3	38.7	22.2	38.8	22.0	39.0	22.0	39.0	22.0	39.0
140	23.7	37.1	23.1	37.7	22.9	37.9	22.8	38.0	22.6	38.3	22.6	38.3	22.5	38.3
150	24.0	36.7	23.4	37.4	23.2	37.6	23.1	37.7	22.9	37.9	22.8	38,0	22.8	38.0
160	24.2	36.4	23.6	37.1	23.4	37.3	23.3	37.4	23.1	37.7	23.0	37.7	23.0	37.7
180	24.7	35.8	24.0	36.6	23.9	36.7	23.7	36.9	23.5	37.2	23.4	37.2	23.4	37.3
200	25.2	35.3	24.4	36.1	24.2	36.4	24.1	36.5	23.8	36.8	23.8	36.9	23.7	36.9
250	26.0	34.3	25.1	35.3	24.9	35.6	24.8	35.7	24.5	36.0	24.4	36.1	24.4	36.1
300			25.7	34.6	25.4	34.9	25.3	35.1	24.9	35.4	24.9	35.5	24.9	35.5
400			26.6	33.7	26.2	34.1	26.0	34.2	25.6	34.7	25.6	34.7	25.6	34.8
500					26.7	33.5	26.5	33.7	26.1	34.1	26.0	34.2	26.0	34.2
600					27.2	33.0	27.0	33.2	26.5	33.7	26.4	33.8	26.4	33.8
700					27.5	32.6	27.3	32.9	26.7	33.4	26.6	33.5	26.6	33.6
800							27.6	32.6	27.0	33.2	26.9	33.3	26.8	33.3
900							27.8	32.3	27.2	33.0	27.0	33.1	27.0	33.1
1,000									27.3	32.8	27.2	32.9	27.2	33.0
1,500									27.9	32.2	27.7	32.4	27.7	32.4
2,000									28.2	31.8	28.0	32.0	28.0	32.1
3,000									28.6	31.4	28.4	31.6	28.4	31.7

TABLE F-22 Sample Precision for Relative Frequencies for Random Samples Only—Rate of Occurrence in Sample 30% (Continued)

And Sample Size is:	For Field Size of: 500 Lower Limit	500 Upper Limit	1,000 Lower Limit	1,000 Upper Limit	1,500 Lower Limit	1,500 Upper Limit	2,000 Lower Limit	2,000 Upper Limit	10,000 Lower Limit	10,000 Upper Limit	50,000 Lower Limit	50,000 Upper Limit	100,000 and over Lower Limit	100,000 and over Upper Limit
	Confidence Level 99% (Two-sided) Confidence Level 99.5% (One-sided)													
50	15.7%	48.0%	15.3%	48.5%	15.2%	48.7%	15.1%	48.8%	14.9%	48.9%	14.9%	49.0%	14.9%	49.0%
80	18.7	43.5	18.2	44.1	18.0	44.3	18.0	44.4	17.8	44.7	17.7	44.7	17.7	44.7
90	19.5	42.5	18.9	43.2	18.7	43.4	18.6	43.5	18.4	43.8	18.4	43.8	18.4	43.8
100	20.1	41.7	19.5	42.4	19.3	42.6	19.2	42.7	19.0	43.0	18.9	43.0	18.9	43.1
120	21.1	40.3	20.4	41.1	20.2	41.4	20.1	41.5	19.9	41.8	19.8	41.8	19.8	41.8
140	21.9	39.2	21.2	40.1	21.0	40.4	20.8	40.5	20.6	40.8	20.5	40.9	20.5	40.9
150	22.3	38.8	21.5	39.7	21.3	40.0	21.2	40.1	20.9	40.4	20.8	40.5	20.8	40.5
160	22.6	38.4	21.8	39.3	21.6	39.6	21.4	39.7	21.1	40.1	21.1	40.1	21.1	40.2
180	23.2	37.6	22.4	38.6	22.2	38.8	21.9	39.1	21.6	39.4	21.6	39.5	21.6	39.5
200	23.8	37.0	22.8	38.1	22.5	38.4	22.4	38.5	22.1	38.9	22.0	39.0	22.0	39.0
250	24.9	35.7	23.7	36.9	23.4	37.3	23.2	37.5	22.9	37.9	22.8	38.0	22.8	38.0
300			24.5	36.1	24.1	36.5	23.9	36.7	23.5	37.2	23.4	37.2	23.4	37.2
400			25.5	34.8	25.1	35.3	24.8	35.6	24.4	36.1	24.3	36.2	24.3	36.2
500					25.8	34.5	25.5	34.8	25.0	35.4	24.9	35.5	24.8	35.5
600					26.3	33.9	26.0	34.2	25.4	34.9	25.3	35.0	25.3	35.1
700					26.8	33.4	26.5	33.8	25.8	34.5	25.7	34.6	25.6	34.7
800							26.8	33.4	26.1	34.2	25.1	34.3	25.1	34.3
900							27.1	33.0	26.3	33.9	26.2	34.1	26.1	34.1
1,000									26.5	33.7	26.4	33.8	26.3	33.9
1,500									27.2	32.9	27.0	33.1	27.0	33.1
2,000									27.7	32.4	27.4	32.7	27.4	32.7
3,000									28.2	31.8	27.9	32.1	27.9	32.2

TABLE F-23 Sample Precision for Relative Frequencies for Random Samples Only—Rate of Occurrence in Sample 35%

And Sample Size is:	500 Lower Limit	500 Upper Limit	1,000 Lower Limit	1,000 Upper Limit	1,500 Lower Limit	1,500 Upper Limit	2,000 Lower Limit	2,000 Upper Limit	10,000 Lower Limit	10,000 Upper Limit	50,000 Lower Limit	50,000 Upper Limit	100,000 and over Lower Limit	100,000 and over Upper Limit
	For Field Size of:													
	Confidence Level 90% (Two-sided) Confidence Level 95% (One-sided)													
50	24.5%	46.8%	24.2%	47.1%	24.1%	47.2%	24.0%	47.3%	23.9%	47.4%	23.9%	47.4%	23.9%	47.4%
80	26.9	43.8	26.5	44.2	26.4	44.4	26.3	44.4	26.2	44.6	26.1	44.6	26.1	44.6
90	27.4	43.2	27.0	43.6	26.9	43.8	26.8	43.8	26.7	44.0	26.7	44.0	26.6	44.0
100	27.9	42.7	27.5	43.1	27.3	43.3	27.3	43.3	27.1	43.5	27.1	43.6	27.1	43.6
120	28.7	41.8	28.2	42.3	28.1	42.4	28.0	42.5	27.8	42.7	27.8	42.7	27.8	42.8
140	29.3	41.1	28.8	41.6	28.6	41.8	28.6	41.9	28.4	42.1	28.3	42.1	28.3	42.1
150	29.6	40.8	29.0	41.3	28.9	41.5	28.8	41.6	28.6	41.8	28.6	41.9	28.5	41.9
160	29.8	40.5	29.3	41.1	29.1	41.3	29.0	41.4	28.8	41.6	28.8	41.6	28.8	41.7
180	30.3	40.0	29.7	40.7	29.5	40.8	29.4	41.0	29.2	41.2	29.1	41.2	29.1	41.3
200	30.7	39.6	30.0	40.3	29.8	40.5	29.7	40.6	29.5	40.8	29.4	40.9	29.4	40.9
250	31.5	38.7	30.7	39.5	30.5	39.8	30.3	39.9	30.1	40.2	30.0	40.2	30.0	40.3
300			31.2	39.0	31.0	39.3	30.8	39.4	30.5	39.7	30.5	39.8	30.5	39.8
400			32.0	38.2	31.6	38.5	31.5	39.0	31.2	39.1	31.1	39.1	31.1	39.1
500			32.5	37.6	32.1	38.0	32.0	38.2	31.6	38.6	31.5	38.6	31.5	38.7
600					32.5	37.6	32.3	37.8	31.9	38.2	31.8	38.3	31.8	38.3
700					32.8	37.2	32.6	37.5	32.1	38.0	32.0	38.1	32.0	38.1
800							32.8	37.3	32.3	37.8	32.2	37.8	32.2	37.9
900							33.1	37.0	32.5	37.6	32.4	37.7	32.4	37.7
1,000							33.2	36.8	32.6	37.4	32.5	37.5	32.5	37.6
1,500									33.1	36.9	33.0	37.0	33.0	37.1
2,000									33.4	36.6	33.3	36.8	33.2	36.8
3,000									33.8	36.2	33.6	36.4	33.6	35.5

F

TABLE F-23 Sample Precision for Relative Frequencies for Random Samples Only—Rate of Occurrence in Sample 35% (Continued)

And Sample Size is:	500 Lower Limit	500 Upper Limit	1,000 Lower Limit	1,000 Upper Limit	1,500 Lower Limit	1,500 Upper Limit	2,000 Lower Limit	2,000 Upper Limit	10,000 Lower Limit	10,000 Upper Limit	50,000 Lower Limit	50,000 Upper Limit	100,000 and over Lower Limit	100,000 and over Upper Limit
	For Field Size of:													
	Confidence Level 95% (Two-sided) Confidence Level 97.5% (One-sided)													
50	22.7%	49.0%	22.4%	49.4%	22.3%	49.6%	22.2%	49.6%	22.1%	49.8%	22.1%	49.8%	22.1%	49.8%
80	25.5	45.5	25.1	46.0	24.9	46.2	24.9	46.2	24.7	46.4	24.7	46.5	24.7	46.5
90	26.2	44.8	25.7	45.3	25.5	45.5	25.5	45.5	25.3	45.7	25.2	45.8	25.2	45.8
100	26.7	44.1	26.2	44.7	26.0	44.8	26.0	44.9	25.8	45.1	25.7	45.2	25.7	45.2
120	27.6	43.1	27.0	43.7	26.9	43.9	26.8	44.0	26.6	44.2	26.5	44.2	26.5	44.2
140	28.3	42.2	27.7	42.9	27.5	43.1	27.4	43.2	27.2	43.5	27.2	43.5	27.1	43.5
150	28.6	41.9	28.0	42.6	27.8	42.8	27.7	42.9	27.5	43.1	27.4	43.2	27.4	43.2
160	28.9	41.5	28.2	42.3	28.0	42.5	27.9	42.6	27.7	42.9	27.6	42.9	27.6	42.9
180	29.4	41.0	28.7	41.8	28.5	41.9	28.4	42.1	28.1	42.4	28.1	42.4	28.0	42.5
200	29.9	40.5	29.1	41.3	28.9	41.6	28.7	41.7	28.5	42.0	28.4	42.0	28.4	42.0
250	30.8	39.4	29.9	40.4	29.6	40.7	29.5	40.9	29.2	41.2	29.1	41.2	29.1	41.3
300			30.5	39.8	30.2	40.1	30.0	40.2	29.7	40.6	29.6	40.7	29.6	40.7
400			31.4	38.8	31.0	39.2	30.8	39.4	30.4	39.8	30.3	39.9	30.3	39.9
500					31.6	38.6	31.4	38.8	30.9	39.2	30.8	39.3	30.8	39.3
600					32.0	38.1	31.8	38.3	31.3	38.9	31.2	39.0	31.2	39.0
700					32.4	37.7	32.1	38.0	31.6	35.3	31.5	38.6	31.5	38.7
800							32.4	37.6	31.8	38.3	31.7	38.4	31.7	38.4
900							32.7	37.4	32.0	38.1	31.9	38.2	31.9	38.2
1,000									32.2	37.9	32.1	38.0	32.1	38.0
1,500									32.8	37.3	32.6	37.4	32.6	37.5
2,000									33.1	36.9	33.0	37.1	32.9	37.1
3,000									33.8	36.5	33.3	36.7	33.3	36.7

And Sample Size is:	For Field Size of: 500 Lower Limit	500 Upper Limit	1,000 Lower Limit	1,000 Upper Limit	1,500 Lower Limit	1,500 Upper Limit	2,000 Lower Limit	2,000 Upper Limit	10,000 Lower Limit	10,000 Upper Limit	50,000 Lower Limit	50,000 Upper Limit	100,000 and over Lower Limit	100,000 and over Upper Limit
	Confidence Level 99% (Two-sided) Confidence Level 99.5% (One-sided)													
50	19.6%	53.2%	19.2%	53.7%	19.1%	53.8%	19.0%	53.9%	18.8%	54.1%	18.8%	54.1%	18.8%	54.1%
80	23.0	48.7	22.4	49.3	22.2	49.5	22.2	49.6	21.9	49.9	21.9	49.9	21.9	49.9
90	23.8	47.7	23.2	48.4	23.0	48.6	22.9	48.7	22.6	49.0	22.6	49.0	22.6	49.0
100	24.4	46.9	23.8	47.6	23.6	47.8	23.5	47.9	23.2	48.2	23.2	48.3	23.2	48.3
120	25.5	45.5	24.8	46.3	24.6	46.6	24.5	46.7	24.2	47.0	24.2	47.0	24.2	47.1
140	26.5	44.4	25.7	45.3	25.4	45.6	25.3	45.7	25.0	46.0	24.9	46.1	24.9	46.1
150	26.8	44.0	26.0	44.9	25.8	45.2	25.6	45.3	25.3	45.6	25.3	45.7	25.3	45.7
160	27.2	43.6	26.3	44.5	26.1	44.8	25.9	44.9	25.6	45.3	25.6	45.4	25.6	45.4
180	27.9	42.8	26.9	43.8	26.7	44.0	26.5	44.3	26.2	44.7	26.1	44.7	26.1	44.7
200	28.4	42.1	27.4	43.2	27.1	43.6	26.9	43.7	26.6	44.1	26.5	44.2	26.5	44.2
250	29.6	40.8	28.4	42.1	28.0	42.5	27.9	42.7	27.5	43.1	27.4	43.2	27.4	43.2
300			29.2	41.2	28.8	41.7	28.6	41.9	28.1	42.3	28.1	42.4	28.0	42.5
400			30.3	40.0	29.8	40.5	29.6	40.7	29.1	41.3	29.0	41.4	28.9	41.4
500					30.6	39.7	30.3	40.0	29.7	40.6	29.6	40.7	29.6	40.7
600					31.2	39.0	30.8	39.4	30.2	40.0	30.1	40.2	30.0	40.2
700					31.6	38.5	31.3	38.9	30.6	39.6	30.4	39.8	30.4	39.8
800							31.7	38.5	30.9	39.3	30.7	39.5	30.7	39.5
900							32.0	38.1	31.1	39.0	31.0	39.2	30.9	39.2
1,000									31.3	38.8	31.2	39.0	31.1	39.0
1,500									32.1	38.0	31.9	38.2	31.9	38.3
2,000									32.6	37.5	32.3	37.8	32.3	37.8
3,000									33.1	36.9	32.8	37.2	32.8	37.3

TABLE F-24 Sample Precision for Relative Frequencies for Random Samples Only—Rate of Occurrence in Sample 40%

For Field Size of:

Confidence Level 90% (Two-sided)
Confidence Level 95% (One-sided)

And Sample Size is:	500 Lower Limit	500 Upper Limit	1,000 Lower Limit	1,000 Upper Limit	1,500 Lower Limit	1,500 Upper Limit	2,000 Lower Limit	2,000 Upper Limit	10,000 Lower Limit	10,000 Upper Limit	50,000 Lower Limit	50,000 Upper Limit	100,000 and over Lower Limit	100,000 and over Upper Limit
50	28.9%	51.8%	28.6%	52.1%	28.5%	52.2%	28.5%	52.3%	28.3%	52.4%	28.3%	52.4%	28.3%	52.4%
80	31.5	48.9	31.1	49.3	31.0	49.4	30.9	49.5	30.8	49.7	30.8	49.7	30.8	49.7
90	32.1	48.3	31.7	48.7	31.6	48.8	31.5	48.9	31.3	49.1	31.3	49.1	31.3	49.1
100	32.6	47.7	32.2	48.2	32.0	48.4	32.0	48.4	31.8	48.6	31.8	48.6	31.8	48.6
120	33.4	46.8	33.0	47.4	32.8	47.5	32.7	47.6	32.5	47.8	32.5	47.8	32.5	47.8
140	34.1	46.1	33.6	46.7	33.4	46.9	33.3	47.0	33.1	47.2	33.1	47.2	33.1	47.2
150	34.4	45.8	33.8	46.4	33.6	46.6	33.6	46.7	33.3	46.9	33.3	47.0	33.3	47.0
160	34.7	45.6	34.1	46.2	33.9	46.4	33.8	46.5	33.6	46.7	33.5	46.7	33.5	46.7
180	35.1	45.1	34.5	45.7	34.3	45.9	34.2	46.0	33.9	46.3	33.9	46.3	33.9	46.3
200	35.5	44.6	34.8	45.4	34.6	45.6	34.5	45.7	34.3	45.9	34.2	46.0	34.2	46.0
250	36.3	43.8	35.5	44.6	35.3	44.9	35.2	45.0	34.9	45.3	34.9	45.3	34.8	45.3
300			36.1	44.1	35.8	44.3	35.6	44.5	35.4	44.8	35.3	44.9	35.3	44.9
400			36.9	43.2	36.5	43.6	36.4	43.7	36.0	44.1	36.0	44.2	35.9	44.2
500			37.4	42.6	37.0	43.0	36.9	43.3	36.5	43.6	36.4	43.7	36.4	43.7
600					37.4	42.6	37.2	42.8	36.8	43.3	36.7	43.4	36.7	43.4
700					37.8	42.3	37.5	42.5	37.0	43.0	37.0	43.1	36.9	43.1
800							37.8	42.3	37.2	42.8	37.2	42.9	37.1	42.9
900							38.0	42.0	37.4	42.6	37.3	42.7	37.3	42.8
1,000							38.2	41.8	37.6	42.5	37.5	42.6	37.4	42.6
1,500									38.1	42.0	37.9	42.1	37.9	42.1
2,000									38.4	41.7	38.2	41.8	38.2	41.8
3,000									38.8	41.2	38.6	41.4	38.5	41.5

And Sample Size is:	For Field Size of: 500 Lower Limit	500 Upper Limit	1,000 Lower Limit	1,000 Upper Limit	1,500 Lower Limit	1,500 Upper Limit	2,000 Lower Limit	2,000 Upper Limit	10,000 Lower Limit	10,000 Upper Limit	50,000 Lower Limit	50,000 Upper Limit	100,000 and over Lower Limit	100,000 and over Upper Limit
					Confidence Level 95% (Two-sided) Confidence Level 97.5% (One-sided)									
50	27.1%	54.1%	26.8%	54.4%	26.6%	54.6%	26.6%	54.6%	26.4%	54.8%	26.4%	54.8%	26.4%	54.8%
80	30.1	50.6	29.6	51.1	29.5	51.3	29.4	51.3	29.2	51.5	29.2	51.6	29.2	51.6
90	30.8	49.8	30.3	50.4	30.1	50.5	30.0	50.6	29.9	50.8	29.8	50.9	29.8	50.9
100	31.4	49.2	30.8	49.8	30.7	49.9	30.6	50.0	30.4	50.2	30.3	50.3	30.3	50.3
120	32.3	48.1	31.7	48.8	31.5	49.0	31.4	49.1	31.2	49.3	31.2	49.3	31.2	49.3
140	33.1	47.3	32.4	48.0	32.2	48.2	32.1	48.3	31.9	48.6	31.8	49.6	31.8	48.6
150	33.4	46.9	32.7	47.7	32.5	47.9	32.4	48.0	32.2	48.2	32.1	48.3	32.1	48.3
160	33.7	46.6	33.0	47.4	32.8	47.6	32.7	47.7	32.4	48.0	32.4	48.0	32.3	48.0
180	34.2	46.0	33.5	46.8	33.3	47.0	33.1	47.2	32.8	47.5	32.8	47.5	32.8	47.6
200	34.7	45.5	33.9	46.4	33.6	46.6	33.5	46.8	33.2	47.1	33.2	47.1	33.2	47.1
250	35.7	44.5	34.7	45.5	34.4	45.8	34.3	46.0	34.0	46.3	33.9	46.3	33.9	46.4
300			35.3	44.8	35.0	45.2	34.8	45.3	34.5	45.7	34.4	45.8	34.4	45.8
400			36.3	43.9	35.9	44.3	35.6	44.5	35.3	44.9	35.2	45.0	35.2	45.0
500					36.5	43.6	36.3	43.8	35.8	44.3	35.7	44.4	35.7	44.4
600					36.9	43.1	36.7	43.4	36.2	43.9	36.1	44.0	36.0	44.0
700					37.3	42.7	37.1	43.0	36.5	43.6	36.4	43.7	36.3	43.7
800							37.4	42.7	36.7	43.3	36.6	43.5	36.6	43.5
900							37.6	42.4	36.9	43.1	36.8	43.3	36.8	43.3
1,000									37.1	43.0	37.0	43.1	37.0	43.1
1,500									37.7	42.3	37.5	42.5	37.5	42.5
2,000									38.1	42.0	37.9	42.1	37.9	42.2
3,000									38.5	41.5	38.3	41.7	38.2	41.8

F

TABLE F-24 Sample Precision for Relative Frequencies for Random Samples Only—Rate of Occurrence in Sample 40% (Continued)

And Sample Size is:	For Field Size of: 500 Lower Limit	500 Upper Limit	1,000 Lower Limit	1,000 Upper Limit	1,500 Lower Limit	1,500 Upper Limit	2,000 Lower Limit	2,000 Upper Limit	10,000 Lower Limit	10,000 Upper Limit	50,000 Lower Limit	50,000 Upper Limit	100,000 and over Lower Limit	100,000 and over Upper Limit
	Confidence Level 99% (Two-sided) Confidence Level 99.5% (One-sided)													
50	23.7%	58.1%	23.3%	58.6%	23.2%	58.8%	23.1%	58.8%	22.9%	59.0%	22.9%	59.1%	22.9%	59.1%
80	26.9	54.6	26.8	54.4	26.6	54.6	26.5	54.7	26.3	54.9	26.3	55.0	26.2	55.0
90	28.2	52.8	27.6	53.4	27.4	53.7	27.3	53.8	27.0	54.0	27.0	54.1	27.0	54.1
100	28.9	51.9	28.3	52.7	28.0	52.9	27.9	53.0	27.7	53.3	27.6	53.3	27.6	53.4
120	30.1	50.6	29.4	51.4	29.1	51.7	29.0	51.8	28.7	52.1	28.7	52.1	28.7	52.2
140	31.1	49.5	30.2	50.4	30.0	50.7	29.9	50.8	29.6	51.1	29.5	51.2	29.5	51.2
150	31.5	49.1	30.6	50.0	30.4	50.3	30.2	50.4	29.9	50.7	29.8	50.8	29.8	50.8
160	31.9	48.6	31.0	49.6	30.7	49.9	30.5	50.0	30.2	50.4	30.2	50.5	30.1	50.5
180	32.6	47.9	31.6	48.9	31.4	49.1	31.1	49.4	30.8	49.8	30.7	49.8	30.7	49.9
200	33.2	47.2	32.1	48.3	31.8	48.7	31.6	48.9	31.2	49.2	31.2	49.3	31.2	49.3
250	34.4	45.9	31.1	47.2	32.8	47.6	32.6	47.8	32.3	48.2	32.1	48.3	32.1	48.3
300			33.9	46.3	33.5	46.8	33.3	47.0	32.9	47.5	32.8	47.5	32.8	47.6
400			35.1	45.1	34.6	45.6	34.4	45.8	33.8	46.4	33.7	46.5	33.7	46.5
500					35.4	44.8	35.1	45.0	34.5	45.7	34.4	45.8	34.4	45.8
600					36.0	44.1	35.7	44.4	35.0	45.1	34.9	45.3	34.9	45.3
700					36.5	43.6	36.2	44.0	35.4	44.7	35.3	44.9	35.2	44.9
800							36.6	43.5	35.7	44.4	35.6	44.5	35.6	44.6
900							36.9	43.2	36.0	44.1	35.8	44.3	35.8	44.3
1,000									36.2	43.9	36.1	44.0	36.0	44.1
1,500									36.8	43.1	36.8	43.2	36.8	43.2
2,000									37.5	42.6	37.2	42.8	37.2	42.9
3,000									38.1	42.0	37.8	42.3	37.7	42.3

TABLE F-25 Sample Precision for Relative Frequencies for Random Samples Only—Rate of Occurrence in Sample 45%

And Sample Size is:	For Field Size of: 500 Lower Limit	500 Upper Limit	1,000 Lower Limit	1,000 Upper Limit	1,500 Lower Limit	1,500 Upper Limit	2,000 Lower Limit	2,000 Upper Limit	10,000 Lower Limit	10,000 Upper Limit	50,000 Lower Limit	50,000 Upper Limit	100,000 and over Lower Limit	100,000 and over Upper Limit
	Confidence Level 90% (Two-sided) Confidence Level 95% (One-sided)													
50	33.6%	56.7%	33.3%	57.0%	33.2%	57.1%	33.1%	57.2%	33.0%	57.3%	33.0%	57.3%	33.0%	57.4%
80	36.3	53.9	35.9	54.3	35.7	54.4	35.7	54.5	35.5	54.6	35.5	54.7	35.5	54.7
90	36.9	53.2	36.5	53.7	36.3	53.8	36.3	53.9	36.1	54.1	36.1	54.1	36.0	54.1
100	37.4	52.7	37.0	53.2	36.8	53.3	36.7	53.4	36.6	53.6	36.5	53.6	36.5	53.6
120	38.3	51.9	37.8	52.4	37.6	52.5	37.5	52.6	37.3	52.8	37.3	52.8	37.3	52.8
140	39.0	51.2	38.4	51.7	38.2	51.9	38.1	52.0	37.9	52.2	37.9	52.2	37.9	52.2
150	39.2	50.9	38.7	51.4	38.5	51.6	38.4	51.7	38.2	51.9	38.1	52.0	38.1	52.0
160	39.5	50.6	38.9	51.2	38.7	51.4	38.6	51.5	38.4	51.7	38.4	51.7	38.4	51.8
180	40.0	50.1	39.3	50.8	39.1	50.9	39.0	51.1	38.8	51.3	38.8	51.4	38.7	51.5
200	40.4	49.7	39.7	50.4	39.5	50.6	39.4	50.7	39.1	51.0	39.1	51.0	39.1	51.0
250	41.3	48.8	40.4	49.6	40.2	49.9	40.1	50.0	39.8	50.3	39.7	50.3	39.7	50.4
300			41.0	49.1	40.7	49.4	40.6	49.5	40.3	49.8	40.2	49.9	40.2	49.9
400			41.8	48.3	41.4	48.6	41.3	48.8	40.9	49.1	40.9	49.2	40.8	49.2
500			42.4	47.6	42.0	48.1	41.8	48.3	41.4	48.7	41.3	48.7	41.3	48.8
600					42.4	47.7	42.2	47.9	41.7	48.3	41.6	48.4	41.6	48.4
700					42.7	47.3	42.5	47.6	42.0	48.1	41.9	48.1	41.9	48.2
800							42.7	47.3	42.2	47.8	42.1	47.9	42.1	48.0
900							43.0	47.1	42.4	47.7	42.3	47.8	42.2	47.8
1,000							43.2	46.9	42.5	47.5	42.4	47.6	42.4	47.6
1,500									43.0	47.0	42.9	47.1	42.9	47.1
2,000									43.3	46.7	43.2	46.8	43.2	46.9
3,000									43.7	46.3	43.5	46.5	43.5	46.5

F

TABLE F-25 Sample Precision for Relative Frequencies for Random Samples Only—Rate of Occurrence in Sample 45% (Continued)

Confidence Level 95% (Two-sided)
Confidence Level 97.5% (One-sided)

And Sample Size is:	For Field Size of: 500 Lower Limit	500 Upper Limit	1,000 Lower Limit	1,000 Upper Limit	1,500 Lower Limit	1,500 Upper Limit	2,000 Lower Limit	2,000 Upper Limit	10,000 Lower Limit	10,000 Upper Limit	50,000 Lower Limit	50,000 Upper Limit	100,000 and over Lower Limit	100,000 and over Upper Limit
50	31.6%	59.0%	31.3%	59.3%	31.1%	59.5%	31.1%	59.5%	30.9%	59.7%	30.9%	59.7%	30.9%	59.7%
80	34.8	55.6	34.3	56.1	34.2	56.2	34.1	56.3	33.9	56.5	33.9	56.5	33.9	56.5
90	35.5	54.8	35.0	55.3	34.8	55.5	34.7	55.6	34.5	55.8	34.5	55.8	34.5	55.9
100	36.1	54.2	35.5	54.7	35.4	54.9	35.3	55.0	35.1	55.2	35.0	55.3	35.0	55.3
120	37.1	53.1	36.5	53.8	36.3	54.0	36.2	54.1	36.0	54.3	35.9	54.3	35.9	54.3
140	37.9	52.3	37.2	53.0	37.0	53.2	36.9	53.3	36.6	53.6	36.6	53.6	36.6	53.6
150	38.2	52.0	37.5	52.7	37.3	52.9	37.2	53.0	36.9	53.3	36.9	53.3	36.9	53.3
160	38.5	51.6	37.8	52.4	37.6	52.6	37.5	52.7	37.2	53.0	37.2	53.0	37.1	53.1
180	39.1	51.1	38.3	51.9	38.1	53.0	37.9	52.3	37.7	52.5	37.6	52.6	37.6	52.6
200	39.6	50.6	38.7	51.4	38.5	51.7	38.3	51.8	38.0	52.1	38.0	52.2	38.0	52.2
250	40.6	49.5	39.6	50.5	39.3	50.8	39.1	51.0	38.8	51.3	38.7	51.4	38.7	51.4
300			40.2	49.9	39.9	50.2	39.7	50.4	39.4	50.7	39.3	50.8	39.3	50.8
400			41.2	48.9	40.8	49.3	40.6	49.5	40.2	49.9	40.1	50.0	40.1	50.0
500					41.4	48.7	41.2	48.9	40.7	49.4	40.6	49.5	40.6	49.5
600					41.9	48.2	41.6	48.4	41.1	49.0	41.0	49.1	41.0	49.1
700					42.3	47.8	42.0	48.0	41.4	48.6	41.3	48.7	41.3	48.8
800							42.3	47.7	41.7	48.3	41.5	48.5	41.5	48.5
900							42.6	47.5	41.9	48.2	41.7	48.3	41.7	48.3
1,000									42.0	48.0	41.9	48.1	41.9	48.1
1,500									42.7	47.4	42.5	47.5	42.5	47.6
2,000									43.0	47.0	42.8	47.2	42.8	47.2
3,000									43.5	46.5	43.3	46.7	43.2	46.8

And Sample Size is:	For Field Size of: 500 Lower Limit	500 Upper Limit	1,000 Lower Limit	1,000 Upper Limit	1,500 Lower Limit	1,500 Upper Limit	2,000 Lower Limit	2,000 Upper Limit	10,000 Lower Limit	10,000 Upper Limit	50,000 Lower Limit	50,000 Upper Limit	100,000 and over Lower Limit	100,000 and over Upper Limit
	Confidence Level 99% (Two-sided) Confidence Level 99.5% (One-sided)													
50	28.0%	62.9%	27.6%	63.3%	27.4%	63.5%	27.3%	63.6%	27.2%	63.8%	27.1%	63.9%	27.1%	63.9%
80	31.9	58.6	31.3	59.3	31.1	59.5	31.0	59.6	30.8	59.8	30.7	59.9	30.7	59.9
90	32.8	57.7	32.1	58.4	31.9	58.6	31.8	58.7	31.6	59.0	31.5	59.0	31.5	59.0
100	33.5	56.9	32.8	57.6	32.6	57.8	32.5	58.0	32.3	58.2	32.2	58.3	32.2	58.3
120	34.8	55.6	34.0	56.4	33.8	56.6	33.6	56.8	33.4	57.0	33.3	57.1	33.3	57.1
140	35.8	54.5	34.9	55.4	34.7	55.7	34.5	55.8	34.2	56.1	34.2	56.2	34.1	56.2
150	36.2	54.1	35.3	55.0	35.0	55.3	34.9	55.4	34.6	55.7	34.5	55.8	34.5	55.8
160	36.6	53.6	35.7	54.6	35.4	54.9	35.3	55.0	34.9	55.4	34.9	55.5	34.8	55.5
180	37.3	52.9	36.3	53.9	36.1	54.2	35.9	54.4	35.5	54.8	35.4	54.8	35.4	54.9
200	38.0	52.2	36.9	53.4	36.5	53.7	36.4	53.9	36.0	54.2	35.9	54.3	35.9	54.3
250	39.2	50.9	38.0	52.2	37.6	52.6	37.4	52.8	37.0	53.2	36.9	53.3	36.9	53.3
300			38.8	51.4	38.3	51.8	38.1	52.0	37.7	52.5	37.6	52.6	37.6	52.6
400			40.0	50.1	39.5	50.6	39.2	50.9	38.7	51.5	38.6	51.5	38.6	51.6
500					40.3	49.8	40.0	50.1	39.4	50.7	39.3	50.8	39.2	50.9
600					40.9	49.1	40.6	49.5	39.9	50.2	39.8	50.3	39.7	50.3
700					41.4	48.6	41.1	49.0	40.3	49.8	40.2	49.9	40.1	49.9
800							41.5	48.6	40.6	49.4	40.5	49.6	40.5	49.6
900							41.8	48.2	40.9	49.1	40.7	49.3	40.7	49.3
1,000									41.1	48.9	41.0	49.0	40.9	49.1
1,500									41.9	48.1	41.7	48.3	41.7	48.4
2,000									42.4	47.6	42.2	47.8	42.1	47.9
3,000									43.0	47.0	42.7	47.3	42.7	47.4

F

TABLE F-26 Sample Precision for Relative Frequencies for Random Samples Only—Rate of Occurrence in Sample 50%

And Sample Size is:	For Field Size of: 500 Lower Limit	500 Upper Limit	1,000 Lower Limit	1,000 Upper Limit	1,500 Lower Limit	1,500 Upper Limit	2,000 Lower Limit	2,000 Upper Limit	10,000 Lower Limit	10,000 Upper Limit	50,000 Lower Limit	50,000 Upper Limit	100,000 and over Lower Limit	100,000 and over Upper Limit
	Confidence Level 90% (Two-sided) Confidence Level 95% (One-sided)													
50	38.5%	61.5%	38.2%	61.8%	38.1%	61.9%	38.0%	62.0%	37.9%	62.1%	37.9%	62.1%	37.9%	62.1%
80	41.2	58.8	40.8	59.2	40.7	59.3	40.6	59.4	40.5	59.5	40.4	59.6	40.4	59.6
90	41.8	58.2	41.4	58.6	41.3	58.7	41.2	58.8	41.0	59.0	41.0	59.0	41.0	59.0
100	42.4	57.6	41.9	58.1	41.7	58.3	41.7	58.3	41.5	58.5	41.5	58.5	41.5	58.5
120	43.2	56.8	42.7	57.3	42.5	57.5	42.5	57.5	42.3	57.7	42.2	57.8	42.2	57.8
140	43.9	56.1	43.3	56.7	43.2	56.8	43.1	56.9	42.9	57.1	42.8	57.2	42.8	57.2
150	44.2	55.8	43.6	56.4	43.4	56.6	43.3	56.7	43.1	56.9	43.1	56.9	43.1	56.9
160	44.5	55.5	43.8	56.2	43.7	56.3	43.6	56.4	43.3	56.7	43.3	56.7	43.3	56.7
180	44.9	55.1	44.3	55.7	44.1	55.9	44.0	56.0	43.7	56.3	43.7	56.3	43.7	56.3
200	45.4	54.6	44.6	55.4	44.4	55.6	44.3	55.7	44.1	55.9	44.0	56.0	44.0	56.0
250	46.2	53.8	45.4	54.6	45.1	54.9	45.0	55.0	44.7	55.3	44.7	55.3	44.7	55.3
300			45.9	54.1	45.6	54.4	45.5	54.5	45.2	54.8	45.1	54.9	45.1	54.9
400			46.7	53.3	46.4	53.6	46.2	53.8	45.9	54.1	45.8	54.2	45.8	54.2
500			47.4	52.6	46.9	53.1	46.7	53.3	46.3	53.7	46.3	53.7	46.2	53.8
600					47.3	52.7	47.1	52.9	46.7	53.3	46.6	53.4	46.6	53.4
700					47.7	52.3	47.4	52.6	46.9	53.1	46.9	53.1	46.8	53.2
800							47.7	52.3	47.2	52.8	47.1	52.9	47.0	53.0
900							47.9	52.1	47.3	52.7	47.2	52.8	47.2	52.8
1,000							48.1	51.9	47.5	52.5	47.4	52.6	47.4	52.6
1,500									48.0	52.0	47.9	52.1	47.9	52.1
2,000									48.3	51.7	48.2	51.8	48.2	51.9
3,000									48.7	51.3	48.5	51.5	48.5	51.5

And Sample Size is:	For Field Size of: 500 Lower Limit	500 Upper Limit	1,000 Lower Limit	1,000 Upper Limit	1,500 Lower Limit	1,500 Upper Limit	2,000 Lower Limit	2,000 Upper Limit	10,000 Lower Limit	10,000 Upper Limit	50,000 Lower Limit	50,000 Upper Limit	100,000 and over Lower Limit	100,000 and over Upper Limit
	Confidence Level 95% (Two-sided) Confidence Level 97.5% (One-sided)													
50	36.3%	63.7%	35.9%	64.1%	35.8%	64.2%	35.7%	64.3%	35.6%	64.4%	35.5%	64.5%	35.5%	64.5%
80	39.6	60.4	39.1	60.9	38.9	61.1	38.8	61.2	38.7	61.3	38.6	61.4	38.6	61.4
90	40.3	59.7	39.8	60.2	39.6	60.4	39.5	60.5	39.3	60.7	39.3	60.7	39.3	61.7
100	40.9	59.1	40.4	59.6	40.2	59.8	40.1	59.9	39.9	60.1	39.8	60.2	39.8	60.2
120	41.9	58.1	41.3	58.7	41.1	58.9	41.0	59.0	40.8	59.2	40.7	59.3	40.7	59.3
140	42.7	57.3	42.1	57.9	41.8	58.2	41.7	58.3	41.5	58.5	41.4	58.6	41.4	58.6
150	43.1	56.9	42.4	57.6	42.2	57.8	42.0	58.0	41.8	58.2	41.7	58.3	41.7	58.3
160	43.4	56.6	42.7	57.3	42.4	57.6	42.3	57.7	42.1	57.9	42.0	58.0	42.0	58.0
180	44.0	56.0	43.2	56.8	43.0	57.0	42.8	57.2	42.5	57.5	42.5	57.5	42.5	57.5
200	44.5	55.5	43.6	56.4	43.4	56.6	43.2	56.8	42.9	57.1	42.9	57.1	42.9	57.1
250	45.5	54.5	44.5	55.5	44.2	55.8	44.0	56.0	43.7	56.3	43.6	56.4	43.6	56.4
300			45.1	54.9	44.8	55.2	44.7	55.3	44.3	55.7	44.2	55.8	44.2	55.8
400			46.1	53.9	45.7	54.3	45.5	54.5	45.1	54.9	45.0	55.0	45.0	55.0
500					46.4	53.6	46.1	53.9	45.6	54.4	45.6	54.4	45.5	54.5
600					46.8	53.2	46.5	53.4	46.0	54.0	45.9	54.1	45.9	54.1
700					47.2	52.8	47.0	53.0	46.4	53.6	46.3	53.7	46.2	53.8
800							47.3	52.7	46.6	53.4	46.5	53.5	46.5	53.5
900							47.5	52.5	46.8	53.2	46.7	53.3	46.7	53.3
1,000									47.0	53.0	46.9	53.1	46.9	53.1
1,500									47.6	52.4	47.5	52.5	47.4	52.6
2,000									48.0	52.0	47.8	52.2	47.8	52.2
3,000									48.5	51.5	48.2	51.8	48.2	51.8

F

TABLE F-26 Sample Precision for Relative Frequencies for Random Samples Only—Rate of Occurrence in Sample 50% (Continued)

And Sample Size is:	For Field Size of: 500 Lower Limit	500 Upper Limit	1,000 Lower Limit	1,000 Upper Limit	1,500 Lower Limit	1,500 Upper Limit	2,000 Lower Limit	2,000 Upper Limit	10,000 Lower Limit	10,000 Upper Limit	50,000 Lower Limit	50,000 Upper Limit	100,000 and over Lower Limit	100,000 and over Upper Limit
	Confidence Level 99% (Two-sided) Confidence Level 99.5% (One-sided)													
50	32.5%	67.5%	32.0%	68.0%	31.9%	68.1%	31.8%	68.2%	31.6%	68.4%	31.6%	68.4%	31.6%	68.4%
80	36.6	63.4	35.9	64.1	35.7	64.3	35.6	64.4	35.4	64.6	35.4	64.6	35.4	64.7
90	37.5	62.5	36.8	63.2	36.6	63.4	36.5	63.5	36.2	63.8	36.2	63.8	36.2	63.8
100	38.3	61.7	37.6	62.4	37.3	62.7	37.2	62.8	37.0	63.0	36.9	63.1	36.9	63.1
120	39.6	60.4	38.8	61.2	38.5	61.5	38.4	61.6	38.1	61.9	38.0	62.0	38.0	62.0
140	40.6	59.4	39.7	60.3	39.4	60.6	39.3	60.7	39.0	61.0	38.9	61.1	38.9	61.1
150	41.0	59.0	40.1	59.9	39.8	60.2	39.7	60.3	39.4	60.6	39.3	60.7	39.3	60.7
160	41.5	58.5	40.5	59.5	40.2	59.8	40.1	59.9	39.7	60.3	39.7	60.3	39.6	60.4
180	42.2	57.8	41.2	58.8	40.9	59.1	40.7	59.3	40.3	59.7	40.2	59.8	40.2	59.8
200	42.8	57.2	41.7	58.3	41.4	58.6	41.2	58.8	40.8	59.2	40.8	59.2	40.7	59.3
250	44.1	55.9	42.8	57.2	42.4	57.6	42.3	57.7	41.8	58.2	41.7	58.3	41.7	58.3
300			43.7	56.3	43.2	56.8	43.0	57.0	42.6	57.4	42.5	57.5	42.5	57.5
400			44.9	55.1	44.4	55.6	44.2	55.8	43.6	56.4	43.5	56.5	43.5	56.5
500					45.2	54.8	44.9	55.1	44.3	55.7	44.2	55.8	44.2	55.8
600					45.9	54.1	45.5	54.5	44.8	55.2	44.7	55.3	44.7	55.3
700					46.4	53.6	46.0	54.0	45.2	54.8	45.1	54.9	45.1	54.9
800							46.4	53.6	45.6	54.4	45.4	54.6	45.4	54.6
900							46.8	53.2	45.9	54.1	45.7	54.3	45.7	54.3
1,000									46.1	53.9	45.9	54.1	45.9	54.1
1,500									46.9	53.1	46.7	53.3	46.6	53.4
2,000									47.4	52.6	47.2	52.8	47.1	52.9
3,000									48.0	52.0	47.7	52.3	47.6	52.4

TABLE F-27 Sample Precision for Relative Frequencies for Random Samples Only—Rate of Occurrence in Sample 0%

And Sample Size is:	For Field Size of: 500 Upper Limit	1,000 Upper Limit	1,500 Upper Limit	2,000 Upper Limit	10,000 Upper Limit	50,000 Upper Limit	100,000 and over Upper Limit
	Confidence Level 90%						
30	7.2%	7.3%	7.3%	7.3%	7.4%	7.4%	7.4%
40	5.4	5.5	5.5	5.5	5.6	5.6	5.6
50	4.3	4.4	4.4	4.4	4.5	4.5	4.5
60	3.5	3.7	3.7	3.7	3.8	3.8	3.8
70	3.0	3.1	3.2	3.2	3.2	3.2	3.2
80	2.6	2.7	2.8	2.8	2.8	2.8	2.8
90	2.3	2.4	2.5	2.5	2.5	2.5	2.5
100	2.0	2.2	2.2	2.2	2.3	2.3	2.3
150	1.3	1.4	1.5	1.5	1.5	1.5	1.5
200	.9	1.0	1.1	1.1	1.1	1.1	1.2
300		.6	.7	.7	.7	.8	.8
400		.4	.5	.5	.6	.6	.6
500		.3	.4	.4	.5	.5	.5
1,000				.2	.2	.2	.2
2,000					.2	.2	.2

F

TABLE F-27 Sample Precision for Relative Frequencies for Random Samples Only—Rate of Occurrence in Sample 0% (Continued)

And Sample Size is:	For Field Size of: 500 Upper Limit	1,000 Upper Limit	1,500 Upper Limit	2,000 Upper Limit	10,000 Upper Limit	50,000 Upper Limit	100,000 and over Upper Limit
	Confidence Level 95%						
30	9.2%	9.4%	9.4%	9.4%	9.5%	9.5%	9.5%
40	6.9	7.1	7.1	7.1	7.2	7.2	7.2
50	5.5	5.7	5.7	5.7	5.8	5.8	5.8
60	4.6	4.7	4.8	4.8	4.9	4.9	4.9
70	3.9	4.0	4.1	4.1	4.2	4.2	4.2
80	3.4	3.5	3.6	3.6	3.7	3.7	3.7
90	3.0	3.1	3.2	3.2	3.3	3.3	3.3
100	2.6	2.8	2.9	2.9	2.9	3.0	3.0
150	1.7	1.8	1.9	1.9	2.0	2.0	2.0
200	1.2	1.3	1.4	1.4	1.5	1.5	1.5
300		.8	.9	.9	1.0	1.0	1.0
400		.6	.6	.7	.7	.7	.8
500			.5	.5	.6	.6	.6
1,000					.3	.3	.3
2,000					.2	.2	.2

And Sample Size is:	For Field Size of: 500 Upper Limit	1,000 Upper Limit	1,500 Upper Limit	2,000 Upper Limit	10,000 Upper Limit	50,000 Upper Limit	100,000 and over Upper Limit
			Confidence Level 99%				
30	13.8%	14.0%	14.1%	14.1%	14.2%	14.2%	14.2%
40	10.4	10.7	10.7	10.8	10.8	10.9	10.9
50	8.4	8.6	8.7	8.7	8.8	8.8	8.8
60	6.9	7.2	7.2	7.3	7.4	7.4	7.4
70	5.9	6.1	6.2	6.3	6.3	6.4	6.4
80	5.1	5.4	5.4	5.5	5.6	5.6	5.6
90	4.5	4.8	4.8	4.9	5.0	5.0	5.0
100	4.0	4.3	4.4	4.4	4.5	4.5	4.5
150	2.5	2.8	2.9	2.9	3.0	3.0	3.0
200	1.8	2.0	2.1	2.2	2.3	2.3	2.3
300		1.3	1.4	1.4	1.5	1.5	1.5
400		.9	1.0	1.0	1.1	1.1	1.1
500			.8	.8	.9	.9	.9
1,000					.4	.5	.5
2,000					.2	.2	.2

F

APPENDIX G
SAMPLE PRECISION FOR AVERAGE VALUES FOR RANDOM SAMPLES ONLY

When Sample Size is:	For Confidence Levels (Two-sided) of: 90%	95%	99%	99.9%
	Sampling Error as Multiple of Standard Deviation			
	Field Size is 500			
40	±.2494	±.2972	±.3912	±.5005
50	.2207	.2630	.3461	.4414
60	.1992	.2373	.3125	.3996
70	.1824	.2173	.2860	.3658
80	.1685	.2008	.2644	.3382
90	.1570	.1871	.2463	.3150
100	.1471	.1753	.2308	.2943
110	.1386	.1651	.2173	.2778
120	.1309	.1560	.2053	.2626
130	.1241	.1479	.1947	.2490
140	.1180	.1406	.1850	.2367
150	.1124	.1339	.1763	.2248
200	.0914	.1074	.1413	.1802
	Field Size is 1,000			
40	±.2548	±.3036	±.3997	±.5113
50	.2268	.2702	.3556	.4535
60	.2059	.2453	.3229	.4130
70	.1897	.2260	.2982	.3804
80	.1764	.2102	.2767	.3539
90	.1654	.1971	.2595	.3319
100	.1560	.1859	.2448	.3121
110	.1480	.1763	.2321	.2968
120	.1408	.1678	.2209	.2826
130	.1345	.1603	.2088	.2699
140	.1290	.1537	.2022	.2587
150	.1238	.1475	.1942	.2477
200	.1041	.1240	.1632	.2081
300	.0795	.0947	.1246	.1589
400	.0637	.0759	.0999	.1274
	Field Size is 2,000			
40	±.2575	±.3068	±.4038	±.5165
50	.2297	.2737	.3603	.4594
60	.2092	.2492	.3281	.4196
70	.1932	.2302	.3029	.3874
80	.1802	.2147	.2827	.3615
90	.1695	.2019	.2658	.3400
100	.1603	.1910	.2515	.3207
110	.1525	.1817	.2391	.3058
120	.1455	.1734	.2283	.2920
130	.1392	.1658	.2188	.2798

When Sample Size is:	For Confidence Levels (Two-sided) of: 90%	95%	99%	99.9%
	Sampling Error as Multiple of Standard Deviation			
	Field Size is 2,000 (con't)			
140	.1341	.1598	.2102	.2690
150	.1292	.1539	.2026	.2584
200	.1103	.1314	.1729	.2205
300	.0875	.1043	.1373	.1751
400	.0736	.0877	.1154	.1471
500	.0637	.0759	.0999	.1274
600	.0562	.0670	.0881	.1124
700	.0501	.0597	.0786	.1003
800	.0451	.0537	.0707	.0901
900	.0406	.0484	.0638	.0813
	Field Size is 3,000			
40	±.2583	±.3078	±.4052	±.5183
50	.2307	.2749	.3618	.4614
60	.2102	.2504	.3297	.4217
70	.1944	.2316	.3048	.3937
80	.1815	.2162	.2846	.3641
90	.1708	.2035	.2679	.3426
100	.1617	.1927	.2537	.3235
110	.1539	.1834	.2414	.3088
120	.1471	.1753	.2307	.2951
130	.1411	.1681	.2213	.2831
140	.1358	.1618	.2129	.2723
150	.1309	.1560	.2053	.2618
200	.1124	.1339	.1763	.2248
300	.0901	.1074	.1413	.1802
400	.0765	.0912	.1201	.1532
500	.0671	.0800	.1053	.1343
600	.0601	.0716	.0942	.1202
700	.0545	.0649	.0854	.1089
800	.0499	.0594	.0781	.0996
900	.0459	.0547	.0720	.0918
1,000	.0425	.0506	.0666	.0850
	Field Size is 4,000			
40	±.2588	±.3084	±.4059	±.5192
50	.2311	.2754	.3626	.4624
60	.2107	.2511	.3306	.4228
70	.1949	.2322	.3057	.3909
80	.1820	.2169	.2856	.3653
90	.1715	.2043	.2689	.3440
100	.1624	.1935	.2548	.3249
110	.1547	.1843	.2426	.3103
120	.1479	.1762	.2319	.2967
130	.1419	.1691	.2226	.2847

Appendix G
Sample Precision for Average Values for Random Samples Only (Continued)

When Sample Size is:	For Confidence Levels (Two-sided) of: 90%	95%	99%	99.9%
	Sampling Error as Multiple of Standard Deviation			
	Field Size is 4,000 (con't)			
140	.1366	.1628	.2141	.2740
150	.1318	.1570	.2067	.2635
200	.1134	.1351	.1778	.2267
300	.0913	.1088	.1433	.1827
400	.0781	.0930	.1224	.1561
500	.0688	.0820	.1079	.1376
600	.0619	.0738	.0971	.1238
700	.0565	.0673	.0886	.1130
800	.0520	.0620	.0816	.1040
900	.0483	.0575	.0757	.0965
1,000	.0451	.0537	.0707	.0901
1,100	.0422	.0503	.0662	.0845
1,200	.0397	.0473	.0623	.0794
1,300	.0375	.0447	.0588	.0749
1,400	.0354	.0422	.0556	.0709
1,500	.0336	.0400	.0527	.0672
	Field Size is 5,000			
40	±.2591	±.3087	±.4063	±.5198
50	.2315	.2758	.3630	.4629
60	.2111	.2515	.3311	.4234
70	.1953	.2327	.3062	.3916
80	.1824	.2173	.2862	.3660
90	.1718	.2047	.2696	.3448
100	.1628	.1940	.2554	.3257
110	.1551	.1848	.2433	.3111
120	.1483	.1767	.2327	.2976
130	.1423	.1696	.2233	.2856
140	.1371	.1634	.2149	.2750
150	.1323	.1576	.2075	.2646
200	.1140	.1358	.1787	.2279
300	.0921	.1097	.1444	.1842
400	.0789	.0940	.1237	.1578
500	.0698	.0832	.1095	.1396
600	.0630	.0751	.0988	.1260
700	.0577	.0687	.0904	.1153
800	.0533	.0635	.0836	.1066
900	.0497	.0592	.0779	.0993
1,000	.0465	.0554	.0730	.0931
1,100	.0438	.0522	.0687	.0876
1,200	.0414	.0493	.0649	.0828
1,300	.0393	.0468	.0615	.0785
1,400	.0373	.0444	.0585	.0746
1,500	.0356	.0424	.0558	.0711
2,000	.0285	.0339	.0447	.0570

When Sample Size is:	For Confidence Levels (Two-sided) of: 90%	95%	99%	99.9%
	Sampling Error as Multiple of Standard Deviation			
	Field Size is 10,000			
40	±.2596	±.3093	±.4071	±.5208
50	.2321	.2765	.3640	.4641
60	.2117	.2522	.3321	.4247
70	.1960	.2335	.3073	.3930
80	.1831	.2182	.2873	.3675
90	.1726	.2057	.2708	.3463
100	.1637	.1950	.2567	.3274
110	.1560	.1859	.2446	.3129
120	.1492	.1778	.2341	.2994
130	.1434	.1708	.2248	.2875
140	.1381	.1645	.2165	.2769
150	.1333	.1588	.2091	.2666
200	.1152	.1372	.1806	.2303
300	.0935	.1114	.1467	.1871
400	.0806	.0960	.1264	.1612
500	.0717	.0854	.1125	.1434
600	.0651	.0776	.1021	.1302
700	.0600	.0715	.0941	.1199
800	.0558	.0665	.0875	.1116
900	.0523	.0623	.0820	.1046
1,000	.0494	.0588	.0774	.0987
1,100	.0467	.0557	.0734	.0936
1,200	.0446	.0531	.0699	.0891
1,300	.0426	.0507	.0667	.0851
1,400	.0408	.0486	.0639	.0815
1,500	.0392	.0467	.0614	.0783
2,000	.0329	.0392	.0516	.0658
2,500	.0285	.0339	.0447	.0570
	Field Size is 20,000			
40	±.2598	±.3096	±.4075	±.5213
50	.2323	.2768	.3644	.4647
60	.2120	.2526	.3326	.4254
70	.1963	.2339	.3078	.3937
80	.1836	.2187	.2879	.3683
90	.1730	.2061	.2714	.3471
100	.1641	.1955	.2754	.3282
110	.1564	.1864	.2453	.3137
120	.1497	.1784	.2348	.3003
130	.1438	.1713	.2256	.2884
140	.1386	.1651	.2172	.2779
150	.1338	.1594	.2099	.2676
200	.1157	.1379	.1815	.2315
300	.0943	.1123	.1478	.1885
400	.0814	.0970	.1277	.1628
500	.0727	.0866	.1139	.1453
600	.0661	.0788	.1037	.1323
700	.0611	.0728	.0958	.1222
800	.0570	.0679	.0894	.1140
900	.0535	.0638	.0840	.1072

G

Appendix G
Sample Precision for Average Values for Random Samples Only (Continued)

When Sample Size is:	For Confidence Levels (Two-sided) of: 90%	95%	99%	99.9%
	Sampling Error as Multiple of Standard Deviation			
	Field Size is 20,000 (con't)			
1,000	.0507	.0604	.0795	.1014
1,100	.0482	.0574	.0756	.0964
1,200	.0460	.0548	.0722	.0921
1,300	.0441	.0526	.0692	.0882
1,400	.0424	.0505	.0665	.0848
1,500	.0409	.0487	.0641	.0817
2,000	.0349	.0416	.0547	.0698
2,500	.0308	.0367	.0483	.0615
	Field Size is 100,000			
40	±.2600	±.3098	±.4078	±.5217
50	.2326	.2771	.3648	.4652
60	.2123	.2529	.3330	.4259
70	.1966	.2342	.3083	.3943
80	.1838	.2190	.2884	.3689
90	.1733	.2065	.2719	.3478
100	.1644	.1959	.2579	.3288
110	.1568	.1868	.2459	.3144
120	.1501	.1788	.2354	.3010
130	.1442	.1718	.2262	.2892
140	.1390	.1656	.2178	.2787
150	.1342	.1599	.2105	.2684
200	.1162	.1385	.1823	.2324
300	.0948	.1130	.1487	.1897
400	.0821	.0978	.1287	.1642
500	.0734	.0874	.1151	.1468
600	.0670	.0798	.1050	.1339
700	.0619	.0738	.0972	.1239
800	.0579	.0690	.0909	.1159
900	.0546	.0650	.0856	.1092
1,000	.0518	.0617	.0812	.1035
1,100	.0494	.0588	.0774	.0986
1,200	.0472	.0562	.0740	.0944
1,300	.0453	.0540	.0711	.0906
1,400	.0436	.0520	.0685	.0873
1,500	.0421	.0502	.0661	.0843
2,000	.0364	.0434	.0571	.0728
2,500	.0325	.0387	.0509	.0650

APPENDIX H
SAMPLE PRECISION FOR AVERAGE VALUES[1] FOR RANDOM SAMPLES ONLY WHEN FIELD SIZE IS INFINITE

When Sample Size is:	For Confidence Levels (Two-sided) of: 90%	95%	99%	99.9%
	Sampling Error as Multiple of Standard Deviation			
40	±.2601	±.3099	±.4079	±.5218
41	.2569	.3061	.4029	.5154
42	.2538	.3024	.3981	.5092
43	.2509	.2989	.3934	.5032
44	.2480	.2955	.3889	.4975
45	.2452	.2922	.3846	.4919
46	.2426	.2890	.3804	.4866
47	.2400	.2859	.3763	.4814
48	.2374	.2829	.3724	.4763
49	.2350	.2800	.3686	.4714
50	.2327	.2772	.3649	.4667
51	.2304	.2745	.3613	.4620
52	.2281	.2718	.3578	.4576
53	.2259	.2692	.3544	.4533
54	.2238	.2667	.3511	.4491
55	.2218	.2643	.3479	.4450
56	.2198	.2619	.3448	.4410
57	.2179	.2596	.3417	.4371
58	.2160	.2574	.3388	.4333
59	.2142	.2552	.3359	.4296
60	.2123	.2530	.3331	.4260
61	.2107	.2510	.3303	.4225
62	.2089	.2489	.3277	.4191
63	.2072	.2469	.3250	.4158
64	.2056	.2450	.3225	.4125
65	.2040	.2431	.3200	.4093
66	.2025	.2413	.3176	.4062
67	.2010	.2395	.3152	.4032
68	.1995	.2377	.3129	.4002
69	.1981	.2360	.3106	.3973
70	.1966	.2343	.3084	.3944
71	.1952	.2326	.3062	.3916
72	.1939	.2310	.3041	.3889
73	.1925	.2294	.3020	.3862
74	.1912	.2278	.2999	.3836
75	.1899	.2263	.2979	.3811
76	.1887	.2248	.2959	.3785
77	.1875	.2234	.2940	.3761
78	.1862	.2219	.2921	.3737
79	.1851	.2205	.2903	.3713
80	.1839	.2191	.2885	.3690
81	.1828	.2178	.2867	.3667
82	.1816	.2164	.2849	.3644
83	.1805	.2151	.2832	.3622
84	.1795	.2139	.2815	.3601
85	.1784	.2126	.2798	.3579
86	.1774	.2114	.2782	.3558
87	.1763	.2101	.2766	.3538
88	.1753	.2089	.2750	.3518
89	.1744	.2078	.2735	.3498

1. For sample sizes of less than 40, use Appendix L.

Appendix H Sample Precision for Average Values for Random Samples Only—When Field Size Is Infinite (Continued)

When Sample Size is:	For Confidence Levels (Two-sided) of: 90%	95%	99%	99.9%
	Sampling Error as Multiple of Standard Deviation			
90	±.1734	±.2066	±.2720	±.3479
91	.1725	.2055	.2705	.3459
92	.1715	.2043	.2690	.3440
93	.1705	.2032	.2675	.3422
94	.1697	.2022	.2661	.3404
95	.1688	.2011	.2647	.3386
96	.1679	.2000	.2633	.3368
97	.1670	.1990	.2620	.3351
98	.1662	.1980	.2606	.3334
99	.1653	.1970	.2592	.3317
100	.1645	.1960	.2580	.3300
101	.1637	.1950	.2567	.3284
102	.1629	.1941	.2555	.3267
103	.1621	.1931	.2542	.3252
104	.1613	.1922	.2530	.3236
105	.1606	.1913	.2518	.3220
106	.1598	.1904	.2506	.3205
107	.1590	.1895	.2494	.3190
108	.1583	.1886	.2483	.3175
109	.1575	.1877	.2471	.3161
110	.1569	.1869	.2460	.3146
111	.1561	.1860	.2449	.3132
112	.1554	.1852	.2438	.3118
113	.1548	.1844	.2427	.3104
114	.1541	.1836	.2416	.3091
115	.1534	.1828	.2406	.3077
116	.1528	.1820	.2395	.3064
117	.1521	.1812	.2385	.3051
118	.1514	.1804	.2375	.3038
119	.1508	.1797	.2365	.3025
120	.1501	.1789	.2355	.3012
121	.1496	.1782	.2345	.3000
122	.1489	.1774	.2336	.2988
123	.1483	.1767	.2326	.2976
124	.1477	.1760	.2317	.2963
125	.1471	.1753	.2308	.2952
126	.1465	.1746	.2298	.2940
127	.1460	.1739	.2289	.2928
128	.1454	.1732	.2280	.2917
129	.1449	.1726	.2272	.2905
130	.1443	.1719	.2263	.2894
131	.1437	.1712	.2254	.2883
132	.1432	.1706	.2246	.2872
133	.1426	.1699	.2237	.2861
134	.1421	.1693	.2229	.2851
135	.1416	.1687	.2221	.2840
136	.1411	.1681	.2212	.2830
137	.1406	.1675	.2204	.2819
138	.1400	.1668	.2196	.2809
139	.1395	.1662	.2188	.2799

When Sample Size is:	For Confidence Levels (Two-sided) of: 90%	95%	99%	99.9%
	Sampling Error as Multiple of Standard Deviation			
140	±.1391	±.1657	±.2180	±.2789
141	.1386	.1651	.2173	.2779
142	.1381	.1645	.2165	.2769
143	.1376	.1639	.2158	.2760
144	.1371	.1633	.2150	.2750
145	.1366	.1628	.2143	.2741
146	.1361	.1622	.2135	.2731
147	.1357	.1617	.2128	.2722
148	.1352	.1611	.2121	.2713
149	.1348	.1606	.2114	.2703
150	.1343	.1600	.2107	.2694
151	.1339	.1595	.2100	.2686
152	.1334	.1590	.2093	.2677
153	.1330	.1585	.2086	.2668
154	.1325	.1579	.2079	.2659
155	.1321	.1574	.2072	.2651
156	.1317	.1569	.2066	.2642
157	.1313	.1564	.2059	.2634
158	.1308	.1559	.2053	.2625
159	.1304	.1554	.2046	.2617
160	.1301	.1550	.2040	.2609
161	.1297	.1545	.2033	.2601
162	.1293	.1540	.2027	.2593
163	.1288	.1535	.2021	.2585
164	.1285	.1531	.2015	.2577
165	.1281	.1526	.2009	.2569
166	.1277	.1521	.2002	.2561
167	.1273	.1517	.1996	.2554
168	.1269	.1512	.1991	.2546
169	.1266	.1508	.1985	.2538
170	.1261	.1503	.1979	.2531
171	.1258	.1499	.1973	.2524
172	.1254	.1494	.1967	.2516
173	.1251	.1490	.1962	.2509
174	.1247	.1486	.1956	.2502
175	.1244	.1482	.1950	.2495
176	.1240	.1477	.1945	.2487
177	.1236	.1473	.1939	.2480
178	.1233	.1469	.1934	.2473
179	.1230	.1465	.1928	.2467
180	.1226	.1461	.1923	.2460
181	.1223	.1457	.1918	.2453
182	.1219	.1453	.1912	.2446
183	.1216	.1449	.1907	.2439
184	.1213	.1445	.1902	.2433
185	.1209	.1441	.1897	.2426
186	.1206	.1437	.1892	.2420
187	.1203	.1433	.1887	.2413
188	.1199	.1429	.1882	.2407
189	.1197	.1426	.1877	.2400

H

Appendix H Sample Precision for Average Values for Random Samples Only—When Field Size Is Infinite (Continued)

When Sample Size is:	For Confidence Levels (Two-sided) of: 90%	95%	99%	99.9%
	Sampling Error as Multiple of Standard Deviation			
190	±.1193	±.1422	±.1872	±.2394
191	.1190	.1418	.1867	.2388
192	.1188	.1415	.1862	.2382
193	.1184	.1411	.1857	.2375
194	.1181	.1407	.1852	.2369
195	.1178	.1404	.1846	.2363
196	.1175	.1400	.1843	.2357
197	.1172	.1396	.1838	.2351
198	.1169	.1393	.1834	.2345
199	.1166	.1389	.1829	.2339
200	.1163	.1386	.1824	.2333
201	.1160	.1382	.1820	.2328
202	.1157	.1379	.1815	.2322
203	.1155	.1376	.1811	.2316
204	.1152	.1372	.1806	.2310
205	.1149	.1369	.1802	.2305
206	.1146	.1366	.1798	.2299
207	.1143	.1362	.1793	.2294
208	.1141	.1359	.1789	.2288
209	.1138	.1356	.1785	.2283
210	.1136	.1353	.1780	.2277
211	.1132	.1349	.1776	.2272
212	.1130	.1346	.1772	.2266
213	.1127	.1343	.1768	.2261
214	.1125	.1340	.1764	.2256
215	.1122	.1337	.1760	.2251
216	.1120	.1334	.1755	.2245
217	.1117	.1331	.1751	.2240
218	.1114	.1327	.1747	.2235
219	.1111	.1324	.1743	.2230
220	.1109	.1321	.1739	.2225
221	.1106	.1318	.1735	.2220
222	.1104	.1315	.1732	.2215
223	.1102	.1313	.1728	.2210
224	.1099	.1310	.1724	.2205
225	.1097	.1307	.1720	.2200
226	.1094	.1304	.1716	.2195
227	.1092	.1301	.1712	.2190
228	.1089	.1298	.1709	.2185
229	.1087	.1295	.1705	.2181
230	.1084	.1292	.1701	.2176
231	.1083	.1290	.1698	.2171
232	.1080	.1287	.1694	.2167
233	.1078	.1284	.1690	.2162
234	.1075	.1281	.1687	.2157
235	.1073	.1279	.1683	.2153
236	.1071	.1276	.1679	.2148
237	.1068	.1273	.1676	.2144
238	.1066	.1270	.1672	.2139
239	.1064	.1268	.1669	.2135

When Sample Size is:	For Confidence Levels (Two-sided) of: 90%	95%	99%	99.9%
	Sampling Error as Multiple of Standard Deviation			
240	±.1062	±.1265	±.1665	±.2130
241	.1060	.1263	.1662	.2126
242	.1058	.1260	.1658	.2121
243	.1055	.1257	.1655	.2117
244	.1053	.1255	.1652	.2113
245	.1051	.1252	.1648	.2108
246	.1049	.1250	.1645	.2104
247	.1047	.1247	.1642	.2100
248	.1045	.1245	.1638	.2096
249	.1042	.1242	.1635	.2091
250	.1041	.1240	.1632	.2087
251	.1038	.1237	.1628	.2083
252	.1037	.1235	.1625	.2079
253	.1034	.1232	.1622	.2075
254	.1032	.1230	.1619	.2071
255	.1030	.1227	.1616	.2067
256	.1028	.1225	.1613	.2063
257	.1026	.1223	.1609	.2058
258	.1024	.1220	.1606	.2054
259	.1022	.1218	.1603	.2051
260	.1021	.1216	.1600	.2047
261	.1018	.1213	.1597	.2043
262	.1016	.1211	.1594	.2039
263	.1015	.1209	.1591	.2035
264	.1012	.1206	.1588	.2031
265	.1011	.1204	.1585	.2027
266	.1009	.1202	.1582	.2023
267	.1007	.1200	.1579	.2020
268	.1005	.1197	.1576	.2016
269	.1003	.1195	.1573	.2012
270	.1001	.1193	1570	.2008
271	.1000	.1191	1567	.2005
272	.0997	.1188	.1564	.2001
273	.0995	.1186	.1561	.1997
274	.0994	.1184	.1559	.1994
275	.0992	.1182	.1556	.1990
276	.0990	.1180	.1553	.1984
277	.0989	.1178	.1550	.1983
278	.0987	.1176	.1547	.1979
279	.0984	.1173	.1545	.1976
280	.0983	.1171	.1542	.1972
281	.0981	.1169	.1539	.1969
282	.0979	.1167	.1536	.1965
283	.0978	.1165	.1534	.1962
284	.0976	.1163	.1531	.1958
285	.0974	.1161	.1528	.1955
286	.0973	.1159	.1526	.1951
287	.0971	.1157	.1523	.1948
288	.0969	.1155	.1520	.1945
289	.0968	.1153	.1518	.1941
290	.0966	.1151	.1515	.1938
291	.0964	.1149	.1512	.1935
292	.0963	.1147	.1510	.1931
293	.0961	.1145	.1507	.1928
294	.0959	.1143	.1505	.1925
295	.0958	.1141	.1502	.1921

H

Appendix H Sample Precision for Average Values for Random Samples Only— When Field Size Is Infinite (Continued)

When Sample Size is:	For Confidence Levels (Two-sided) of: 90%	95%	99%	99.9%
	Sampling Error as Multiple of Standard Deviation			
296	±.0956	±.1139	±.1500	±.1918
297	.0954	.1137	.1497	.1915
298	.0953	.1135	.1495	.1912
299	.0951	.1133	.1492	.1908
300	.0950	.1132	.1490	.1905
350	.0880	.1048	.1379	.1764
400	.0823	.0980	.1290	.1650
450	.0776	.0924	.1216	.1556
500	.0736	.0877	.1154	.1476
550	.0702	.0836	.1100	.1407
600	.0671	.0800	.1053	.1347
650	.0645	.0769	.1012	.1294
700	.0622	.0741	.0975	.1247
750	.0601	.0716	.0942	.1205
800	.0582	.0693	.0912	.1167
850	.0564	.0672	.0885	.1132
900	.0548	.0653	.0860	.1100
950	.0534	.0636	.0837	.1071
1000	.0520	.0620	.0816	.1044
1050	.0508	.0605	.0796	.1018
1100	.0496	.0591	.0778	.0995
1150	.0485	.0578	.0761	.0973
1200	.0475	.0566	.0745	.0953
1250	.0465	.0554	.0730	.0933
1300	.0457	.0544	.0716	.0915
1350	.0447	.0533	.0702	.0898
1400	.0440	.0524	.0690	.0882
1450	.0432	.0515	.0678	.0867
1500	.0425	.0506	.0666	.0852
1750	.0394	.0469	.0617	.0789
2000	.0368	.0438	.0577	.0738
2250	.0347	.0413	.0544	.0696
2500	.0329	.0392	.0516	.0660
2750	.0314	.0374	.0492	.0629
3000	.0300	.0358	.0471	.0603
3250	.0289	.0344	.0453	.0579
3500	.0278	.0331	.0436	.0558
3750	.0269	.0320	.0421	.0539
4000	.0260	.0310	.0408	.0522
4250	.0252	.0301	.0396	.0506
4500	.0245	.0292	.0385	.0492
4750	.0239	.0284	.0374	.0479
5000	.0233	.0277	.0365	.0467

APPENDIX I
FINITE POPULATION CORRECTION FACTOR

Proportion of Population in Sample (n/N)	Finite Correction Factor	Proportion of Population in Sample (n/N)	Finite Correction Factor
0.1%	.9995	5.2%	.9737
0.2	.9990	5.3	.9731
0.3	.9985	5.4	.9726
0.4	.9980	5.5	.9721
0.5	.9975	5.6	.9716
0.6	.9970	5.7	.9711
0.7	.9965	5.8	.9706
0.8	.9960	5.9	.9701
0.9	.9955	6.0	.9695
1.0	.9950	6.1	.9690
1.1	.9945	6.2	.9685
1.2	.9940	6.3	.9680
1.3	.9935	6.4	.9675
1.4	.9930	6.5	.9670
1.5	.9925	6.6	.9664
1.6	.9920	6.7	.9659
1.7	.9915	6.8	.9654
1.8	.9910	6.9	.9649
1.9	.9905	7.0	.9644
2.0	.9899	7.1	.9638
2.1	.9894	7.2	.9633
2.2	.9889	7.3	.9628
2.3	.9884	7.4	.9623
2.4	.9879	7.5	.9618
2.5	.9874	7.6	.9612
2.6	.9869	7.7	.9607
2.7	.9864	7.8	.9602
2.8	.9859	7.9	.9597
2.9	.9854	8.0	.9592
3.0	.9849	8.1	.9586
3.1	.9844	8.2	.9581
3.2	.9839	8.3	.9576
3.3	.9834	8.4	.9571
3.4	.9829	8.5	.9566
3.5	.9823	8.6	.9560
3.6	.9818	8.7	.9555
3.7	.9813	8.8	.9550
3.8	.9808	8.9	.9545
3.9	.9803	9.0	.9539
4.0	.9798	9.1	.9534
4.1	.9793	9.2	.9529
4.2	.9788	9.3	.9524
4.3	.9783	9.4	.9518
4.4	.9778	9.5	.9513
4.5	.9772	9.6	.9508
4.6	.9767	9.7	.9503
4.7	.9762	9.8	.9497
4.8	.9757	9.9	.9492
4.9	.9752	10.0	.9487
5.0	.9747	10.1	.9482
5.1	.9742	10.2	.9476

I

Appendix I Finite Population Correction Factor (Continued)

Proportion of Population in Sample (n/N)	Finite Correction Factor	Proportion of Population in Sample (n/N)	Finite Correction Factor
10.3%	.9471	15.8%	.9176
10.4	.9466	15.9	.9171
10.5	.9460	16.0	.9165
10.6	.9455	16.1	.9160
10.7	.9450	16.2	.9154
10.8	.9445	16.3	.9149
10.9	.9439	16.4	.9143
11.0	.9434	16.5	.9138
11.1	.9429	16.6	.9132
11.2	.9423	16.7	.9127
11.3	.9418	16.8	.9121
11.4	.9413	16.9	.9116
11.5	.9407	17.0	.9110
11.6	.9402	17.1	.9105
11.7	.9397	17.2	.9099
11.8	.9391	17.3	.9094
11.9	.9386	17.4	.9088
12.0	.9381	17.5	.9083
12.1	.9376	17.6	.9077
12.2	.9370	17.7	.9072
12.3	.9365	17.8	.9066
12.4	.9359	17.9	.9061
12.5	.9354	18.0	.9055
12.6	.9349	18.1	.9050
12.7	.9343	18.2	.9044
12.8	.9338	18.3	.9039
12.9	.9333	18.4	.9033
13.0	.9327	18.5	.9028
13.1	.9322	18.6	.9022
13.2	.9317	18.7	.9017
13.3	.9311	18.8	.9011
13.4	.9306	18.9	.9006
13.5	.9301	19.0	.9000
13.6	.9295	19.1	.8994
13.7	.9290	19.2	.8989
13.8	.9284	19.3	.8983
13.9	.9279	19.4	.8978
14.0	.9274	19.5	.8972
14.1	.9268	19.6	.8967
14.2	.9263	19.7	.8961
14.3	.9257	19.8	.8955
14.4	.9252	19.9	.8950
14.5	.9247	20.0	.8944
14.6	.9241	20.1	.8939
14.7	.9236	20.2	.8933
14.8	.9230	20.3	.8927
14.9	.9225	20.4	.8922
15.0	.9220	20.5	.8916
15.1	.9214	20.6	.8911
15.2	.9209	20.7	.8905
15.3	.9203	20.8	.8899
15.4	.9198	20.9	.8894
15.5	.9192	21.0	.8888
15.6	.9187	21.1	.8883
15.7	.9182	21.2	.8877

Proportion of Population in Sample (n/N)	Finite Correction Factor	Proportion of Population in Sample (n/N)	Finite Correction Factor
21.3%	.8871	27.1%	.8538
21.4	.8866	27.2	.8532
21.5	.8860	27.3	.8526
21.6	.8854	27.4	.8521
21.7	.8849	27.5	.8515
21.8	.8843	27.6	.8509
21.9	.8837	27.7	.8503
22.0	.8832	27.8	.8497
22.1	.8826	27.9	.8491
22.2	.8820	28.0	.8485
22.3	.8815	28.1	.8479
22.4	.8809	28.2	.8473
22.5	.8803	28.3	.8468
22.6	.8798	28.4	.8462
22.7	.8792	28.5	.8456
22.8	.8786	28.6	.8450
22.9	.8781	28.7	.8444
23.0	.8775	28.8	.8438
23.1	.8769	28.9	.8432
23.2	.8763	29.0	.8426
23.3	.8758	29.1	.8420
23.4	.8752	29.2	.8414
23.5	.8746	29.3	.8408
23.6	.8741	29.4	.8402
23.7	.8735	29.5	.8396
23.8	.8729	29.6	.8390
23.9	.8724	29.7	.8385
24.0	.8718	29.8	.8379
24.1	.8712	29.9	.8373
24.2	.8706	30.0	.8367
24.3	.8701	30.1	.8361
24.4	.8695	30.2	.8355
24.5	.8689	30.3	.8349
24.6	.8683	30.4	.8343
24.7	.8678	30.5	.8337
24.8	.8672	30.6	.8331
24.9	.8666	30.7	.8325
25.0	.8660	30.8	.8319
25.1	.8654	30.9	.8313
25.2	.8649	31.0	.8307
25.3	.8643	31.1	.8301
25.4	.8637	31.2	.8295
25.5	.8631	31.3	.8289
25.6	.8626	31.4	.8283
25.7	.8620	31.5	.8276
25.8	.8614	31.6	.8270
25.9	.8608	31.7	.8264
26.0	.8602	31.8	.8258
26.1	.8597	31.9	.8252
26.2	.8591	32.0	.8246
26.3	.8585	32.1	.8240
26.4	.8579	32.2	.8234
26.5	.8573	32.3	.8228
26.6	.8567	32.4	.8222
26.7	.8562	32.5	.8216
26.8	.8556	32.6	.8210
26.9	.8550	32.7	.8204
27.0	.8544	32.8	.8198

I

Appendix I Finite Population Correction Factor (Continued)

Proportion of Population in Sample (n/N)	Finite Correction Factor	Proportion of Population in Sample (n/N)	Finite Correction Factor
32.9%	.8191	36.5%	.7969
33.0	.8185	36.6	.7962
33.1	.8179	36.7	.7956
33.2	.8173	36.8	.7950
33.3	.8167	36.9	.7944
33.4	.8161	37.0	.7937
33.5	.8155	37.1	.7931
33.6	.8149	37.2	.7925
33.7	.8142	37.3	.7918
33.8	.8136	37.4	.7912
33.9	.8130	37.5	.7906
34.0	.8124	37.6	.7899
34.1	.8118	37.7	.7893
34.2	.8112	37.8	.7887
34.3	.8106	37.9	.7880
34.4	.8099	38.0	.7874
34.5	.8093	38.1	.7868
34.6	.8087	38.2	.7861
34.7	.8081	38.3	.7855
34.8	.8075	38.4	.7849
34.9	.8068	38.5	.7842
35.0	.8062	38.6	.7836
35.1	.8056	38.7	.7829
35.2	.8050	38.8	.7823
35.3	.8044	38.9	.7817
35.4	.8037	39.0	.7810
35.5	.8031	39.1	.7804
35.6	.8025	39.2	.7797
35.7	.8019	39.3	.7791
35.8	.8012	39.4	.7785
35.9	.8006	39.5	.7778
36.0	.8000	39.6	.7772
36.1	.7994	39.7	.7765
36.2	.7987	39.8	.7759
36.3	.7981	39.9	.7752
36.4	.7975	40.0	.7746

APPENDIX J
PROBABILITIES OF INCLUDING AT LEAST ONE OCCURRENCE IN A SAMPLE (DISCOVERY SAMPLING)

Probability Level 85%
Sample Size When Occurrence Rate Is

Field Size	0.1	0.2	0.3	0.4	0.5	0.6	0.7	0.8	0.9	1.0	1.5	2.0	2.5	3.0	4.0	5.0
200	200	198	192	181	170	159	148	139	130	123	94	76	63	54	42	35
300	299	287	264	238	215	195	178	164	151	141	103	81	67	57	44	36
400	397	363	318	278	245	219	197	179	164	151	108	84	69	58	45	36
500	489	425	359	306	266	234	209	189	172	158	112	86	70	59	45	37
600	575	477	391	328	281	246	218	196	178	163	114	88	71	60	46	37
700	653	519	416	344	293	254	225	201	182	166	116	89	72	60	46	37
800	725	556	437	358	302	261	230	205	185	169	117	89	72	61	46	37
900	791	586	454	369	310	267	234	208	188	171	118	90	73	61	46	37
1000	850	613	469	378	316	271	237	211	190	173	119	90	73	61	46	37
1500	1077	703	516	407	335	285	248	219	197	178	121	92	74	62	47	37
2000	1225	755	542	422	346	292	253	224	200	181	123	93	74	62	47	38
2500	1329	789	559	432	352	297	257	226	202	183	123	93	75	62	47	38
3000	1406	813	570	439	356	300	259	228	204	184	124	93	75	63	47	38
4000	1511	844	585	447	362	304	262	230	205	185	124	94	75	63	47	38
5000	1579	864	594	452	365	306	264	232	206	186	125	94	75	63	47	38
6000	1626	877	600	456	368	308	265	233	207	187	125	94	75	63	47	38
7000	1662	887	605	459	369	309	266	233	208	187	125	94	75	63	47	38
8000	1689	894	608	460	371	310	266	234	208	187	125	94	76	63	47	38
9000	1711	900	611	462	372	311	267	234	208	188	126	94	76	63	47	38
10000	1728	905	613	463	372	311	267	234	209	188	126	94	76	63	47	38
15000	1782	919	619	467	375	313	269	235	209	189	126	95	76	63	47	38
20000	1810	926	622	469	376	314	269	236	210	189	126	95	76	63	47	38
25000	1827	931	624	470	377	314	270	236	210	189	126	95	76	63	47	38
30000	1838	934	626	471	377	315	270	236	210	189	126	95	76	63	47	38
35000	1847	936	627	471	377	315	270	236	210	189	126	95	76	63	47	38
40000	1853	937	627	471	378	315	270	236	210	189	126	95	76	63	47	38
45000	1858	939	628	472	378	315	270	237	210	189	126	95	76	63	47	38
50000	1862	940	628	472	378	315	270	237	210	189	126	95	76	63	47	38

Appendix J
Discovery Sampling (Continued)

Probability Level 90%

Sample Size When Occurrence Rate Is

Field Size	0.1	0.2	0.3	0.4	0.5	0.6	0.7	0.8	0.9	1.0	1.5	2.0	2.5	3.0	4.0	5.0
200	200	199	196	189	180	171	161	153	144	137	107	88	74	64	50	41
300	300	294	277	256	235	217	200	185	172	161	120	96	79	68	52	43
400	399	378	341	305	274	247	224	205	189	175	127	100	82	70	54	43
500	495	450	392	342	301	268	241	219	200	185	132	103	84	71	54	44
600	587	512	433	370	322	284	253	229	208	191	135	105	85	72	55	44
700	674	565	466	392	337	295	262	236	214	196	138	106	86	73	55	45
800	755	610	494	410	350	305	270	242	219	200	140	107	87	73	56	45
900	830	650	516	425	360	312	276	246	223	203	141	108	88	74	56	45
1000	900	684	536	438	369	319	280	250	226	206	142	109	88	74	56	45
1500	1177	804	601	478	397	339	295	262	235	213	146	111	89	75	56	45
2000	1368	875	637	500	411	349	303	268	240	217	148	112	90	75	57	46
2500	1505	923	661	514	421	356	308	272	243	220	149	113	90	76	57	46
3000	1608	956	677	524	427	360	312	274	245	222	150	113	91	76	57	46
4000	1751	1000	698	536	435	366	316	278	248	224	151	113	91	76	57	46
5000	1845	1028	712	544	440	369	318	280	249	225	151	114	91	76	57	46
6000	1912	1048	720	549	443	372	320	281	250	226	152	114	91	76	57	46
7000	1962	1062	727	553	446	373	321	282	251	227	152	114	92	76	57	46
8000	2001	1072	732	555	448	375	322	283	252	227	152	114	92	76	57	46
9000	2032	1081	736	558	449	376	323	283	252	227	152	114	92	76	57	46
10000	2057	1087	739	559	450	376	324	284	253	228	152	114	92	76	57	46
15000	2135	1108	748	565	454	379	325	285	254	229	153	115	92	77	57	46
20000	2175	1119	753	567	455	380	326	286	254	229	153	115	92	77	57	46
25000	2200	1125	756	569	456	381	327	286	255	229	153	115	92	77	58	46
30000	2216	1129	758	570	457	381	327	286	255	229	153	115	92	77	58	46
35000	2228	1133	759	571	458	382	327	287	255	230	153	115	92	77	58	46
40000	2238	1135	760	572	458	382	328	287	255	230	153	115	92	77	58	46
45000	2245	1137	761	572	458	382	328	287	255	230	153	115	92	77	58	46
50000	2250	1138	762	572	458	382	328	287	255	230	153	115	92	77	58	46

Probability Level 95%
Sample Size When Occurrence Rate Is

Field Size	0.1	0.2	0.3	0.4	0.5	0.6	0.7	0.8	0.9	1.0	1.5	2.0	2.5	3.0	4.0	5.0
200	200	200	199	195	190	184	176	169	162	155	126	105	90	79	62	52
300	300	298	289	275	259	243	228	214	201	189	146	118	99	85	66	54
400	400	391	367	338	311	285	263	243	226	211	157	125	104	88	68	56
500	499	475	432	388	349	316	288	264	243	225	165	129	107	91	70	56
600	596	551	486	428	379	339	306	279	255	236	170	133	109	92	70	57
700	690	618	532	460	403	357	320	290	265	244	174	135	110	93	71	57
800	781	677	570	486	422	371	331	299	272	250	177	137	111	94	71	58
900	868	730	603	508	437	383	341	306	278	255	179	138	112	95	72	58
1000	950	776	632	527	451	393	348	312	283	259	181	139	113	95	72	58
1500	1296	947	729	590	494	425	372	331	299	272	187	143	115	97	73	59
2000	1553	1054	786	625	518	442	385	341	307	278	190	144	116	97	74	59
2500	1746	1127	823	647	533	453	393	348	312	282	192	145	117	98	74	59
3000	1895	1179	849	663	543	460	399	352	315	285	193	146	117	98	74	59
4000	2109	1249	884	683	556	469	406	357	319	289	195	147	118	99	74	59
5000	2254	1294	905	696	565	475	410	361	322	291	196	148	118	99	74	60
6000	2358	1326	920	704	570	479	413	363	324	292	196	148	119	99	74	60
7000	2437	1348	931	710	574	482	415	365	325	293	197	148	119	99	74	60
8000	2499	1366	939	715	577	484	417	366	326	294	197	148	119	99	75	60
9000	2548	1380	945	719	580	486	418	367	327	295	198	149	119	99	75	60
10000	2589	1391	950	722	582	487	419	368	327	295	198	149	119	99	75	60
15000	2716	1426	966	731	587	491	422	370	329	297	198	149	119	100	75	60
20000	2782	1443	974	735	590	493	423	371	330	297	199	149	119	100	75	60
25000	2823	1454	979	738	592	494	424	372	331	298	199	149	120	100	75	60
30000	2851	1461	982	740	593	495	425	372	331	298	199	149	120	100	75	60
35000	2871	1466	984	741	594	496	425	372	331	298	199	149	120	100	75	60
40000	2886	1470	986	742	595	496	426	373	331	298	199	150	120	100	75	60
45000	2898	1473	988	743	595	497	426	373	332	299	199	150	120	100	75	60
50000	2908	1476	989	743	596	497	426	373	332	299	199	150	120	100	75	60

J

Appendix J
Discovery Sampling (Continued)

Probability Level 99%

Sample Size When Occurrence Rate Is

Field Size	0.1	0.2	0.3	0.4	0.5	0.6	0.7	0.8	0.9	1.0	1.5	2.0	2.5	3.0	4.0	5.0
200	200	200	200	199	198	196	193	189	185	180	157	137	120	107	88	74
300	300	300	298	294	286	277	267	256	246	235	192	161	138	120	96	79
400	400	399	391	378	360	341	323	305	289	274	214	175	148	127	100	82
500	500	495	477	450	421	392	366	342	320	301	229	185	154	132	103	84
600	600	587	554	512	471	433	400	370	344	322	240	191	159	135	105	85
700	699	674	622	565	512	466	427	392	363	337	249	196	162	138	106	86
800	797	755	683	610	547	494	448	410	378	350	255	200	165	140	107	87
900	895	830	737	650	577	516	467	425	390	360	260	203	167	141	108	88
1000	990	900	785	684	602	536	482	438	401	369	264	206	168	142	109	88
1500	1430	1177	961	804	688	601	533	478	434	397	278	213	173	146	111	89
2000	1800	1368	1072	875	738	637	561	500	451	411	285	217	176	148	112	90
2500	2104	1505	1147	923	770	661	578	514	463	421	289	220	178	149	113	90
3000	2354	1608	1202	956	793	677	591	524	470	427	292	222	179	150	113	91
4000	2735	1751	1275	1000	823	698	607	536	480	435	296	224	180	151	113	91
5000	3009	1845	1322	1028	841	712	616	544	486	440	298	225	181	151	114	91
6000	3215	1912	1354	1048	854	720	623	549	490	443	299	226	181	152	114	91
7000	3374	1962	1378	1062	863	727	628	553	493	446	300	227	182	152	114	92
8000	3501	2001	1397	1072	870	732	632	555	496	448	301	227	182	152	114	92
9000	3605	2032	1411	1081	875	736	634	558	497	449	302	227	182	152	114	92
10000	3690	2057	1423	1087	880	739	637	559	499	450	302	228	183	152	114	92
15000	3965	2135	1459	1108	893	748	644	565	503	454	304	229	183	153	115	92
20000	4113	2175	1478	1119	900	753	647	567	505	455	305	229	183	153	115	92
25000	4206	2200	1489	1125	904	756	649	569	506	456	305	229	184	153	115	92
30000	4269	2216	1496	1129	907	758	651	570	507	457	305	229	184	153	115	92
35000	4315	2228	1502	1133	909	759	652	571	508	458	306	230	184	153	115	92
40000	4350	2238	1506	1135	911	760	653	572	508	458	306	230	184	153	115	92
45000	4377	2245	1509	1137	912	761	653	572	509	458	306	230	184	153	115	92
50000	4399	2250	1512	1138	913	762	654	572	509	458	306	230	184	153	115	92

APPENDIX K
ACCEPTANCE SAMPLING PLANS

Field Size 200

n Sample Size	c Acceptance Number	When Field Contains Error Rate of: .5%	1%	1.5%	2%	2.5%	When Field Contains Error Rate of: 3%	4%	5%	10%	15%
		The Probability of Acceptance is					The Probability of Acceptance is				
40	0	80.0	63.9	51.0	40.7	32.4	25.7	16.2	10.1	0.9	0.1
40	1	100.0	96.1	89.8	82.1	73.8	65.5	50.0	37.0	6.0	0.7
40	2	100.0	100.0	99.3	97.4	94.4	90.4	80.0	67.9	19.2	3.3
40	3	100.0	100.0	100.0	99.9	99.4	98.5	94.8	88.5	40.2	10.3
50	0	75.0	56.2	42.0	31.3	23.3	17.3	9.5	5.2	.2	*0.1-
50	1	100.0	93.8	84.5	73.9	63.3	53.2	36.2	23.7	1.9	.1
50	2	100.0	100.0	98.5	95.1	89.9	83.4	68.0	52.4	8.0	.7
50	3	100.0	100.0	100.0	99.7	98.6	96.5	89.1	78.0	21.1	2.7
60	0	70.0	48.9	34.1	23.7	16.4	11.4	5.4	2.6	0.1	*0.1-
60	1	100.0	91.1	78.5	65.1	52.7	41.7	25.0	14.3	0.6	*0.1-
60	2	100.0	100.0	97.4	91.7	84.0	74.7	55.1	37.8	2.9	0.1
60	3	100.0	100.0	100.0	99.1	97.1	93.3	81.0	65.2	9.5	0.6
80	0	60.0	35.9	21.4	12.7	7.5	4.4	1.5	0.5	*0.1-	*0.1-
80	1	100.0	84.1	64.9	47.4	33.4	22.9	10.2	4.2	*0.1-	*0.1-
80	2	100.0	100.0	93.8	82.3	68.4	54.4	31.1	16.1	0.2	*0.1-
80	3	100.0	100.0	100.0	97.5	91.6	82.4	59.5	37.8	1.2	*0.1-
100	0	50.0	24.9	12.3	6.1	3.0	1.4	0.3	0.1	*0.1-	*0.1-
100	1	100.0	75.1	50.0	31.1	18.4	10.6	3.2	0.9	*0.1-	*0.1-
100	2	100.0	100.0	87.7	68.9	50.0	34.1	13.9	5.0	*0.1-	*0.1-
100	3	100.0	100.0	100.0	93.9	81.6	65.9	36.0	16.6	0.1	*0.1-
100	4	100.0	100.0	100.0	100.0	97.0	98.5	63.9	37.4	0.4	*0.1-

*Less than 0.05%.

K

Appendix K Acceptance Sampling Plans (Continued)

Field Size 400

n Sample Size	c Acceptance Number	When Field Contains Error Rate of: .5%	1%	1.5%	2%	2.5%	When Field Contains Error Rate of: 3%	4%	5%	10%	15%
		The Probability of Acceptance is					The Probability of Acceptance is				
25	0	87.9	77.2	67.7	59.4	52.0	45.6	34.9	26.6	6.6	1.5
25	1	99.6	97.9	95.2	91.7	87.6	83.2	73.6	64.0	26.2	8.6
25	2	100.0	99.9	99.6	99.0	98.1	96.7	93.0	87.9	53.4	24.5
25	3		99.9+	99.9+	99.0	99.8	99.6	98.7	97.1	76.8	46.7
40	0	81.0	65.5	52.9	42.7	34.4	27.7	17.9	11.5	1.2	0.1
40	1	99.0	94.9	88.7	81.4	73.7	65.8	51.1	38.5	7.0	0.9
40	2	100.0	99.6	98.5	96.3	93.2	89.2	79.2	67.8	20.8	4.1
40	3		99.9+	99.9	99.5	98.7	97.6	93.5	87.2	41.3	11.5
50	0	76.5	58.5	44.6	34.0	25.9	19.7	11.3	6.4	0.3	*0.1-
50	1	98.5	92.2	83.5	73.7	63.8	54.5	38.3	25.9	2.6	0.2
50	2	100.0	99.3	97.2	93.5	88.3	82.0	67.8	53.3	9.6	1.0
50	3		99.9+	99.7	99.0	97.4	95.0	87.4	76.9	23.2	3.7
60	0	72.2	52.1	37.5	26.9	19.3	13.8	7.0	3.5	0.1	*0.1-
60	1	97.8	89.1	77.7	65.7	54.3	44.0	27.8	16.8	0.9	*0.1-
60	2	100.0	98.8	95.4	89.7	82.2	73.7	56.0	40.0	4.1	0.2
60	3		99.9	99.5	98.0	95.2	91.1	79.3	64.9	11.7	1.0
75	0	66.0	43.4	28.5	18.7	12.2	8.0	3.4	1.4	*0.1-	*0.1-
75	1	96.5	83.9	68.6	53.9	41.2	30.5	16.4	8.3	0.2	*0.1-
75	2	100.0	97.8	91.7	82.6	71.6	60.0	39.6	24.0	1.0	*0.1-
75	3		99.9	98.7	95.6	90.3	82.7	64.9	46.4	3.6	0.1

Field Size 400 (Cont.)

n Sample Size	c Acceptance Number	When Field Contains Error Rate of: .5%	1%	1.5%	2%	2.5%	When Field Contains Error Rate of: 3%	4%	5%	10%	15%
		The Probability of Acceptance is					The Probability of Acceptance is				
100	0	56.2	31.5	17.6	9.8	0.5	3.0	0.9	0.3	*0.1-	*0.1-
100	1	93.8	73.9	53.3	36.5	2.4	15.4	6.0	2.2	*0.1-	*0.1-
100	2	100.0	95.0	83.2	67.9	5.3	38.8	19.2	8.6	0.1	*0.1-
100	3		99.6	96.4	88.8	7.8	65.0	40.1	21.8	0.3	*0.1-
100	4		100.0	99.6	97.4	9.3	84.6	63.1	41.1	1.2	*0.1-
125	0	47.2	22.2	10.4	4.8	2.2	1.0	0.2	*0.1-	*0.1-	*0.1-
125	1	90.3	63.0	39.2	22.9	12.8	6.9	1.9	0.5	*0.1-	*0.1-
125	2	100.0	90.7	72.2	52.0	34.8	22.0	7.8	2.5	*0.1-	*0.1-
125	3		99.1	92.1	78.5	61.7	45.3	20.8	8.9	*0.1-	*0.1-
125	4		100.0	98.7	93.4	83.0	69.2	40.4	19.6	0.1	*0.1-
150	0	39.0	15.1	5.8	2.2	0.9	0.3	*0.1-	*0.1-	*0.1-	*0.1-
150	1	86.0	51.8	27.2	13.2	6.1	2.7	0.5	0.1	*0.1-	*0.1-
150	2	100.0	84.9	59.6	36.8	20.8	11.0	2.7	0.6	*0.1-	*0.1-
150	3		98.1	85.5	65.2	44.6	27.9	9.0	2.4	*0.1-	*0.1-
150	4		100.0	97.0	86.5	69.6	51.0	21.7	7.4	*0.1-	*0.1-

*Less than 0.05%.

K

Appendix K Acceptance Sampling Plans (Continued)

Field Size 500

n Sample Size	c Acceptance Number	When Field Contains Error Rate of: .2%	.4%	1%	2%	3%	When Field Contains Error Rate of: 4%	5%	10%	15%
		The Probability of Acceptance is					The Probability of Acceptance is			
25	0	95.0	90.2	77.3	59.6	45.8	35.1	26.8	6.7	1.5
25	1	100.0	99.8	97.8	91.6	83.1	73.6	64.1	26.4	8.8
25	2		100.0	99.9	99.0	96.6	92.8	87.8	53.4	24.7
25	3			99.9+	99.9	99.5	98.6	97.0	76.7	46.8
40	0	92.0	84.6	65.8	43.1	28.1	18.2	11.8	1.2	0.1
40	1	100.0	99.4	94.6	81.3	65.9	51.3	38.8	7.2	1.0
40	2		100.0	99.6	96.2	89.0	79.1	68.7	21.1	4.2
40	3			99.9+	99.5	97.5	93.7	87.0	41.5	12.0
50	0	90.0	81.0	58.9	34.5	20.1	11.6	6.7	0.4	*0.1-
50	1	100.0	99.0	91.9	73.6	54.7	38.6	26.4	2.8	0.2
50	2		100.0	99.2	93.2	81.8	67.7	53.4	9.9	1.1
50	3			99.9+	98.8	94.7	87.1	76.7	23.6	3.8
60	0	88.0	77.4	52.6	27.5	14.3	7.3	3.8	0.1	*0.1-
60	1	100.0	98.6	88.8	65.8	44.4	28.3	17.3	1.0	*0.1-
60	2		100.0	98.6	89.3	73.6	56.1	40.3	4.3	0.3
60	3			99.9	97.7	90.7	79.1	64.8	12.1	1.1
75	0	85.0	72.2	44.2	19.4	8.4	3.6	1.5	*0.1-	*0.1-
75	1	100.0	97.8	83.6	54.3	31.4	17.0	8.8	0.2	*0.1-
75	2		100.0	97.4	82.2	60.4	40.1	24.7	1.1	*0.1-
75	3			99.8	95.2	82.6	64.9	46.8	3.8	0.1

Field Size 500 (Cont.)

n Sample Size	c Acceptance Number	When Field Contains Error Rate of: .2%	.4%	1%	2%	3%	When Field Contains Error Rate of: 4%	5%	10%	15%
		The Probability of Acceptance is					The Probability of Acceptance is			
100	0	80.0	64.0	32.6	10.5	3.3	1.0	0.3	*0.1-	*0.1-
100	1	100.0	96.0	73.8	37.3	16.3	6.5	2.5	*0.1-	*0.1-
100	2		100.0	94.3	67.8	39.5	20.0	9.2	0.1	*0.1-
100	3			99.4	88.1	64.9	40.8	22.7	0.4	*0.1-
100	4			99.9+	96.9	83.9	63.1	41.7	1.4	*0.1-
125	0	75.0	56.2	23.6	5.5	1.2	0.3	0.1	*0.1-	*0.1-
125	1	100.0	93.8	63.3	24.2	7.7	2.2	0.6	*0.1-	*0.1-
125	2		100.0	89.8	52.5	24.3	8.7	2.9	*0.1-	*0.1-
125	3			98.5	77.8	48.7	22.0	9.1	*0.1-	*0.1-
125	4			99.9	92.4	73.2	41.2	20.7	0.1	*0.1-
150	0	70.0	49.0	16.7	2.7	0.4	0.1	*0.1-	*0.1-	*0.1-
150	1	100.0	91.0	52.8	14.7	3.3	0.7	0.1	*0.1-	*0.1-
150	2		100.0	83.8	38.1	12.3	3.3	0.8	*0.1-	*0.1-
150	3			97.0	65.0	29.3	10.2	3.0	*0.1-	*0.1-
150	4			99.8	85.2	51.5	23.2	8.5	*0.1-	*0.1-
175	0	65.0	42.2	11.5	1.3	0.1	*0.1-	*0.1-	*0.1-	*0.1-
175	1	100.0	87.8	42.8	8.4	1.3	0.2	*0.1-	*0.1-	*0.1-
175	2		100.0	76.6	25.9	5.9	1.1	0.2	*0.1-	*0.1-
175	3			94.7	51.3	16.9	4.1	0.8	*0.1-	*0.1-
175	4			99.5	75.3	34.9	11.3	2.9	*0.1-	*0.1-

*Less than 0.05%.

K

Appendix K Acceptance Sampling Plans (Continued)

Field Size 1,000

n Sample Size	c Acceptance Number	.1%	.2%	.3%	.4%	.5%	1%	1.5%	2%	2.5%	3%	4%	5%	10%
		When Field Contains Error Rate of: The Probability of Acceptance is							When Field Contains Error Rate of: The Probability of Acceptance is					
25	0	97.5	95.1	92.7	90.4	88.1	77.5	68.2	60.0	52.7	46.3	35.6	27.3	6.9
25	1	100.0	99.9	99.8	99.7	99.4	97.6	94.8	91.3	87.3	82.9	73.6	64.2	26.7
25	2		100.0	99.9+	99.9+	99.9+	99.9	99.5	98.8	97.8	96.4	92.6	87.5	53.6
25	3			100.0	99.9+	99.9+	99.9+	99.9+	99.9	99.7	99.5	98.5	96.8	77.0
50	0	95.0	90.2	85.7	81.4	77.3	59.7	46.1	35.5	27.3	21.0	12.3	7.2	0.4
50	1	100.0	99.8	99.3	98.6	97.8	91.5	82.8	73.6	64.0	55.1	39.4	27.2	3.1
50	2		100.0	99.9+	99.9+	99.9	98.9	96.2	92.6	87.1	81.4	67.7	53.7	10.6
50	3			100.0	99.9+	99.9+	99.9	99.1	98.5	96.2	94.2	86.6	76.4	24.3
60	0	94.0	88.4	83.0	78.0	73.3	53.7	39.3	28.7	20.9	15.2	8.0	4.2	0.1
60	1	100.0	99.7	99.0	98.0	96.9	88.3	77.2	66.0	54.9	45.2	29.7	18.3	1.2
60	2		100.0	99.9+	99.9	99.8	98.2	94.0	88.7	81.0	73.3	56.5	41.1	4.8
60	3			100.0	99.9+	99.9+	99.8	98.6	97.2	93.6	90.0	78.6	64.8	12.9
75	0	92.5	85.6	79.1	73.2	67.7	45.7	30.8	20.7	13.9	9.3	4.1	1.8	*0.1-
75	1	100.0	99.4	98.4	97.0	95.2	83.1	68.8	55.0	42.8	32.7	18.2	9.7	0.3
75	2		100.0	99.9+	99.9	99.6	96.7	90.4	81.6	71.3	60.6	41.0	25.9	1.3
75	3			100.0	99.9+	99.9+	99.6	97.9	94.4	88.9	81.8	64.8	47.4	4.4
100	0	90.0	81.0	72.9	65.6	59.0	34.7	20.3	11.9	6.9	4.0	1.3	0.4	*0.1-
100	1	100.0	99.0	97.2	94.8	91.9	73.6	54.8	38.9	26.7	17.9	7.6	3.1	*0.1-
100	2		100.0	99.9	99.6	99.2	93.1	81.7	67.7	53.6	40.8	21.7	10.6	0.1
100	3			100.0	99.9+	99.9+	98.8	94.6	86.9	76.5	64.8	41.9	24.3	0.6
100	4				100.0	99.9+	99.8	98.8	95.8	90.5	82.7	62.9	42.7	1.9
125	0	87.5	76.6	67.0	58.6	51.2	26.1	13.3	67.3	3.4	1.7	0.4	0.1	*0.1-
125	1	100.0	98.5	95.7	92.2	83.0	68.9	42.2	26.4	15.9	9.3	3.0	0.9	*0.1-
125	2		100.0	99.8	99.3	98.4	88.2	71.4	53.4	37.7	25.4	10.4	3.8	*0.1-
125	3			100.0	99.9+	99.9	97.3	89.4	76.7	61.8	47.1	24.1	10.8	0.1
125	4				100.0	99.9+	99.6	97.0	90.7	80.7	68.2	42.5	22.8	0.2

Field Size 1,000 (Cont.)

n Sample Size	c Acceptance Number	.1%	.2%	.3%	.4%	.5%	1%	1.5%	2%	2.5%	3%	4%	5%	10%
		When Field Contains Error Rate of: The Probability of Acceptance is							When Field Contains Error Rate of: The Probability of Acceptance is:					
150	0	85.0	72.2	61.4	52.1	44.3	19.5	8.6	3.7	1.6	0.7	0.1	*0.1-	*0.1-
150	1	100.0	97.8	94.0	89.0	83.6	54.4	31.7	17.3	9.0	4.6	1.1	0.2	*0.1-
150	2		100.0	99.7	98.8	97.4	82.1	60.4	40.3	25.0	14.7	4.5	1.2	*0.1-
150	3			100.0	99.9+	99.8	95.1	82.4	64.8	46.9	31.8	12.5	4.2	*0.1-
150	4				100.0	99.9+	99.0	94.0	83.2	68.3	52.3	25.8	10.6	*0.1-
200	0	80.0	64.0	51.2	40.9	32.7	10.6	3.4	1.1	0.4	0.1	*0.1-	*0.1-	*0.1-
200	1	100.0	96.0	89.6	82.0	73.8	37.6	16.5	6.7	2.6	1.0	0.1	*0.1-	*0.1-
200	2		100.0	99.2	97.3	94.3	68.3	39.7	20.3	9.5	4.2	0.7	0.1	*0.1-
200	3			100.0	99.8	99.3	88.2	64.9	41.0	23.1	11.9	2.6	0.5	*0.1-
200	4				100.0	99.9+	97.0	83.7	62.7	41.9	25.1	7.2	1.6	*0.1-
200	5					100.0	99.6	94.0	80.4	61.7	42.5	15.6	4.4	*0.1-
225	0	77.5	60.0	46.5	36.0	27.9	7.7	2.1	0.6	0.1	*0.1-	*0.1-	*0.1-	*0.1-
225	1	100.0	95.0	87.1	78.0	68.6	30.1	11.5	4.0	1.3	0.4	*0.1-	*0.1-	*0.1-
225	2		100.0	98.9	96.2	92.2	59.5	30.9	13.7	5.5	2.1	0.3	*0.1-	*0.1-
225	3			100.0	99.8	99.0	82.2	55.4	30.8	15.0	6.7	1.1	0.1	*0.1-
225	4				100.0	99.9	93.7	76.7	52.0	30.4	15.9	3.4	0.6	*0.1-
225	5					100.0	97.7	90.3	71.7	49.3	29.9	8.3	1.7	*0.1-
275	0	72.5	52.5	38.1	27.6	20.0	3.9	0.8	0.1	*0.1-	*0.1-	*0.1-	*0.1-	*0.1-
275	1	100.0	92.5	81.5	69.6	58.0	19.1	5.3	1.3	0.3	*0.1-	*0.1-	*0.1-	*0.1-
275	2		100.0	97.9	93.4	86.9	45.1	17.3	5.6	1.6	0.4	*0.1-	*0.1-	*0.1-
275	3			100.0	99.4	97.8	71.6	37.3	15.5	5.6	1.8	0.2	*0.1-	*0.1-
275	4				100.0	99.9	89.0	69.2	31.7	13.9	3.1	0.6	*0.1-	*0.1-
275	5					100.0	96.9	79.3	51.5	27.4	5.8	1.8	0.2	*0.1-
300	0	70.0	49.0	34.3	23.9	16.7	2.8	0.5	0.1	*0.1-	*0.1-	*0.1-	*0.1-	*0.1-
300	1	100.0	91.0	78.4	65.2	52.8	14.8	3.4	0.7	0.1	*0.1-	*0.1-	*0.1-	*0.1-
300	2		100.0	97.3	91.7	83.8	38.2	12.5	3.4	0.8	0.2	*0.1-	*0.1-	*0.1-
300	3			100.0	99.2	97.0	65.0	29.5	10.5	3.2	0.8	*0.1-	*0.1-	*0.1-
300	4				100.0	99.8	85.1	51.5	23.5	8.8	2.8	0.2	*0.1-	*0.1-
300	5					100.0	95.3	72.3	41.5	19.0	7.3	0.8	0.1	*0.1-

*Less than 0.05%.

K

Appendix K Acceptance Sampling Plans (Continued)

Field Size 2,000

n Sample Size	c Acceptance Number	When Field Contains Error Rate of: .05%	.1%	.2%	.3%	.4%	.5%	1%	1.5%	When Field Contains Error Rate of: 2%	2.5%	3%	4%	5%	10%
		The Probability of Acceptance is:								The Probability of Acceptance is:					
50	0	97.5	95.1	90.4	85.9	81.6	77.6	60.1	46.5	36.0	27.8	21.4	12.7	7.4	0.5
50	1	100.0	99.9	99.6	99.1	98.4	97.6	91.3	82.9	73.6	64.3	55.3	39.7	27.6	3.2
50	2		100.0	99.9+	99.9+	99.9	99.8	98.8	96.3	92.4	87.3	81.3	67.7	53.9	10.9
50	3			99.9+	99.9+	99.9+	99.9+	99.9	99.4	98.4	96.6	94.0	86.3	76.2	24.7
60	0	97.0	94.1	88.5	83.3	78.3	73.7	54.2	39.8	29.2	21.4	15.6	8.3	4.4	0.2
60	1	100.0	99.9	99.5	98.8	97.8	96.6	88.1	77.3	66.1	55.3	45.6	29.8	18.7	1.3
60	2		100.0	99.9+	99.9+	99.9	99.7	98.0	94.1	88.4	81.3	73.3	56.6	41.4	5.1
60	3			99.9+	99.9+	99.9+	99.9+	99.8	98.9	97.0	94.0	89.7	78.3	64.8	13.4
75	0	96.3	92.6	85.8	79.5	73.6	68.2	46.4	31.5	21.3	14.4	9.7	4.4	2.0	*0.1-
75	1	100.0	99.9	99.2	98.1	96.6	94.9	82.9	68.9	55.3	43.3	33.2	18.8	10.1	0.3
75	2		100.0	99.9+	99.9	99.8	99.5	96.4	90.0	81.3	71.2	60.7	41.4	26.4	1.5
75	3			99.9+	99.9+	99.9+	99.9+	99.4	94.0	94.0	88.5	81.5	64.8	4[illegible].7	4.8
90	0	95.5	91.2	83.2	75.8	69.1	63.0	39.6	24.9	15.6	9.7	6.0	2.3	0.9	*0.1-
90	1	100.0	99.8	98.9	97.3	95.3	92.9	77.4	60.6	45.5	33.2	23.7	11.5	5.3	0.1
90	2		100.0	99.9+	99.8	99.6	99.2	94.2	85.0	73.3	60.7	48.7	29.1	16.0	0.4
90	3			99.9+	99.9+	99.9+	99.9	98.9	95.7	89.8	81.5	71.7	51.0	33.0	1.5
100	0	95.0	90.2	81.4	73.5	66.3	59.8	35.7	21.2	12.6	7.4	4.4	1.5	0.5	*0.1-
100	1	100.0	99.8	98.6	96.8	94.3	91.4	73.6	55.2	39.6	27.6	18.7	8.2	3.4	*0.1-
100	2		100.0	99.9+	99.8	99.4	98.9	92.6	81.3	67.7	53.9	41.4	22.5	11.2	0.2
100	3			99.9+	99.9+	99.9+	99.9	97.9	94.1	94.1	76.2	64.8	42.5	25.1	0.7
100	4			100.0	99.9+	99.9+	99.9+	99.0	98.5	98.5	89.9	82.2	62.9	43.2	2.1
125	0	93.8	87.9	77.2	67.9	59.6	52.4	27.3	14.2	7.4	3.8	2.0	0.5	0.1	*0.1-
125	1	100.0	99.6	97.9	95.1	91.5	87.5	64.2	43.1	27.4	16.8	10.1	3.4	1.1	*0.1-
125	2		100.0	99.9	99.6	98.9	97.9	87.5	71.2	53.9	38.5	26.3	11.2	4.3	*0.1-
125	3			99.9+	99.9+	99.9	99.8	96.8	88.7	76.2	61.8	47.7	25.0	11.6	0.1
125	4			100.0	99.9+	99.9+	99.9+	99.4	96.5	90.0	80.1	68.0	43.1	23.7	0.3

Field Size 2,000 (Cont.)

n Sample Size	c Acceptance Number	.05%	.1%	.2%	.3%	.4%	.5%	1%	1.5%	2%	2.5%	3%	4%	5%	10%
		When Field Contains Error Rate of: The Probability of Acceptance is:								When Field Contains Error Rate of: The Probability of Acceptance is:					
150	0	92.5	85.6	73.2	62.6	53.5	45.8	20.9	9.5	4.3	1.7	0.9	0.2	*0.1-	*0.1-
150	1	100.0	99.4	97.0	93.1	88.4	83.1	55.1	32.9	18.5	10.0	5.2	1.3	0.3	*0.1-
150	2		100.0	99.8	99.3	98.3	96.7	81.5	60.6	41.2	26.2	15.9	5.2	1.5	*0.1-
150	3			99.9+	99.9+	99.8	99.6	94.3	81.7	64.8	47.6	32.9	13.6	4.9	*0.1-
150	4			100.0	99.9+	99.9+	99.9+	98.6	93.1	82.4	68.0	52.7	26.9	11.6	*0.1-
200	0	90.0	81.0	65.6	53.1	43.0	34.8	12.0	4.1	1.4	0.5	0.2	*0.1-	*0.1-	*0.1-
200	1	100.0	99.0	94.8	88.6	81.3	73.6	39.1	18.2	7.8	3.2	1.3	0.2	*0.1-	*0.1-
200	2		100.0	99.6	98.4	96.2	93.0	67.7	41.0	22.0	10.9	5.1	1.0	0.2	*0.1-
200	3			99.9+	99.9	99.5	98.7	86.8	64.8	42.1	24.7	13.4	3.3	0.7	*0.1-
200	4			100.0	99.9+	99.9+	99.8	95.8	82.6	62.9	42.9	26.7	8.4	2.1	*0.1-
200	5				99.9+	99.9+	99.9+	98.9	92.8	79.6	61.6	43.5	17.2	5.3	*0.1-
300	0	85.0	72.2	52.2	37.7	27.2	19.6	3.8	0.7	0.1	*0.1-	*0.1-	*0.1-	*0.1-	*0.1-
300	1	100.0	97.8	89.1	77.7	65.7	54.4	17.4	4.7	1.2	0.3	0.1	*0.1-	*0.1-	*0.1-
300	2		100.0	98.8	95.3	89.5	82.1	40.4	14.9	4.7	1.3	0.4	*0.1-	*0.1-	*0.1-
300	3			99.9+	99.4	97.9	95.1	64.8	32.0	12.8	4.4	1.4	0.1	*0.1-	*0.1-
300	4			100.0	99.9+	99.7	99.0	83.1	52.4	26.1	10.9	4.0	0.4	*0.1-	*0.1-
300	5				99.9+	99.9+	99.8	93.4	71.2	43.1	21.6	9.3	1.3	0.1	*0.1-
400	0	80.0	64.0	40.9	26.2	16.7	10.7	1.1	0.1	*0.1-	*0.1-	*0.1-	*0.1-	*0.1-	*0.1-
400	1	100.0	96.0	81.9	65.5	50.3	37.5	6.8	1.0	0.1	*0.1-	*0.1-	*0.1-	*0.1-	*0.1-
400	2		100.0	97.3	90.1	79.7	67.8	20.5	4.3	0.8	0.1	*0.1-	*0.1-	*0.1-	*0.1-
400	3			99.8	98.3	94.4	88.0	41.1	12.1	2.7	0.5	*0.1-	*0.1-	*0.1-	*0.1-
400	4			100.0	99.8	99.0	96.8	63.0	25.3	7.4	1.7	*0.1-	*0.1-	*0.1-	*0.1-
400	5				99.9+	99.9	99.4	80.5	42.6	15.9	4.6	0.1	*0.1-	*0.1-	*0.1-

*Less than 0.05%.

K

Appendix K Acceptance Sampling Plans (Continued)

Field Size 5,000

n Sample Size	c Acceptance Number	.1%	.2%	.3%	.4%	.5%	1%	1.5%	2%	2.5%	3%	4%	5%	6%	7%	8%	9%	10%
		When Field Contains Error Rate of: The Probability of Acceptance is:							When Field Contains Error Rate of: The Probability of Acceptance is:					The Probability of Acceptance is:				
50	0	95.1	90.4	86.0	81.7	77.8	60.3	46.8	36.3	28.0	21.6	12.9	7.6	4.5	2.6	1.5	0.9	0.5
50	1	99.9	99.6	99.0	98.3	97.5	91.1	82.8	73.6	64.3	55.5	39.9	27.8	18.9	12.5	8.2	5.2	3.3
50	2	99.9+	99.9+	99.9+	99.9	99.9	98.7	96.2	92.3	87.1	81.2	67.7	54.0	41.5	30.9	22.4	15.9	11.1
50	3	99.9+	99.9+	99.9+	99.9+	99.9+	99.8	99.3	98.4	96.4	93.8	86.2	76.1	64.7	53.2	42.4	32.9	24.9
100	0	90.4	81.6	73.9	66.7	60.3	36.3	21.2	13.0	7.7	4.6	1.6	0.6	0.2	0.1	*0.1-	*0.1-	*0.1-
100	1	99.7	98.3	96.5	94.1	91.2	73.6	55.5	40.1	28.0	19.2	8.5	3.6	1.5	0.6	0.2	0.1	*0.1-
100	2	99.9+	99.8	99.7	99.3	98.8	92.3	81.1	67.7	54.1	41.8	22.9	11.6	5.5	2.5	1.1	0.4	0.2
100	3	99.9+	99.9+	99.9+	99.9+	99.9	98.4	93.8	86.2	76.0	64.7	42.7	25.5	14.1	7.2	3.5	1.7	0.7
100	4	99.9+	99.9+	99.9+	99.9+	99.9+	99.8	98.4	95.2	89.6	82.0	62.9	43.4	27.4	16.1	8.8	4.6	2.3
125	0	88.1	77.6	68.4	60.2	53.0	28.0	14.8	7.7	4.1	2.1	0.6	0.2	*0.1-	*0.1-	*0.1-	*0.1-	*0.1-
125	1	99.4	97.5	94.7	91.2	87.2	64.3	43.6	28.0	17.4	10.5	3.6	1.2	0.4	0.1	*0.1-	*0.1-	*0.1-
125	2	99.9	99.8	99.4	98.7	97.7	87.2	71.1	54.1	39.0	26.9	11.6	4.6	1.7	0.6	0.2	0.1	*0.1-
125	3	99.9+	99.9+	99.9+	99.8	99.7	96.5	88.3	76.0	61.8	47.9	25.6	12.1	5.2	2.1	0.8	0.3	0.1
125	4	99.9+	99.9+	99.9+	99.9+	99.9+	99.2	96.1	89.6	79.8	67.9	43.5	24.3	12.1	5.5	2.4	0.9	0.4
150	0	85.8	73.6	63.3	54.3	46.6	21.6	10.0	.6	2.1	1.0	0.2	*0.1-	*0.1-	*0.1-	*0.1-	*0.1-	*0.1-
150	1	99.1	96.5	92.7	88.0	82.8	55.5	33.6	19.2	10.5	5.6	1.5	0.4	0.1	*0.1-	*0.1-	*0.1-	*0.1-
150	2	99.9	99.6	99.1	97.9	96.2	81.2	60.7	41.8	26.9	16.5	5.6	1.7	0.5	0.1	*0.1-	*0.1-	*0.1-
150	3	99.9+	99.9	99.9	99.7	99.4	93.8	81.2	64.7	47.9	33.4	14.2	5.2	1.7	0.5	0.2	*0.1-	*0.1-
150	4	99.9+	99.9+	99.9+	99.9	99.9	98.4	92.6	82.0	67.9	52.9	27.5	12.2	4.9	1.7	0.5	0.2	*0.1-
200	0	81.5	66.4	54.2	44.1	35.9	12.9	4.6	1.6	0.6	0.2	*0.1-	*0.1-	*0.1-	*0.1-	*0.1-	*0.1-	*0.1-
200	1	98.5	94.1	88.2	81.0	73.6	39.9	19.1	8.5	3.6	1.5	0.2	*0.1-	*0.1-	*0.1-	*0.1-	*0.1-	*0.1-
200	2	99.9	99.3	98.0	95.6	92.4	67.7	41.7	22.9	11.6	5.6	1.1	0.2	*0.1-	*0.1-	*0.1-	*0.1-	*0.1-
200	3	99.9+	99.9	99.8	99.2	98.3	86.2	64.7	42.7	25.6	14.2	3.7	0.8	0.2	*0.1-	*0.1-	*0.1-	*0.1-
200	4	99.9+	99.9+	99.9+	99.8	99.7	95.2	82.0	62.8	43.5	27.5	9.1	2.4	0.5	0.1	*0.1-	*0.1-	*0.1-
200	5	100.0	99.9+	99.9+	99.9+	99.9	98.6	92.1	78.9	61.6	43.9	18.0	5.9	1.6	0.4	0.1	*0.1-	*0.1-
300	0	73.4	53.9	39.5	28.0	21.2	4.5	0.9	0.2	*0.1-	*0.1-	*0.1-	*0.1-	*0.1-	*0.1-	*0.1-	*0.1-	*0.1-
300	1	96.9	88.3	77.5	66.0	55.2	18.9	5.5	1.5	0.4	0.1	*0.1-	*0.1-	*0.1-	*0.1-	*0.1-	*0.1-	*0.1-
300	2	99.9	98.2	94.4	88.5	81.4	41.5	16.3	5.5	1.7	0.5	*0.1-	*0.1-	*0.1-	*0.1-	*0.1-	*0.1-	*0.1-
300	3	99.9+	99.9	99.1	97.1	94.2	64.7	33.3	14.1	5.2	1.7	0.2	*0.1-	*0.1-	*0.1-	*0.1-	*0.1-	*0.1-
300	4	99.9+	99.9+	99.9+	99.4	98.6	82.2	52.9	27.4	12.1	4.8	0.6	*0.1-	*0.1-	*0.1-	*0.1-	*0.1-	*0.1-
300	5	100.0	99.9+	99.9+	99.9	99.8	92.3	70.7	44.0	23.0	10.5	1.6	0.1	*0.1-	*0.1-	*0.1-	*0.1-	*0.1-

Field Size 5,000 (Cont.)

n Sample Size	c Acceptance Number	.1%	.2%	.3%	.4%	.5%	1%	1.5%	2%	2.5%	3%	4%	5%	6%	7%	8%	9%	10%
		When Field Contains Error Rate of: The Probability of Acceptance is:							When Field Contains Error Rate of: The Probability of Acceptance is:					The Probability of Acceptance is:				
400	0	65.9	43.4	28.6	18.8	12.4	1.5	0.2	*0.1-	*0.1-	*0.1-	*0.1-	*0.1-	*0.1-	*0.1-	*0.1-	*0.1-	*0.1-
400	1	94.6	81.1	66.0	51.6	39.4	8.2	1.4	0.2	*0.1-	*0.1-	*0.1-	*0.1-	*0.1-	*0.1-	*0.1-	*0.1-	*0.1-
400	2	99.6	95.9	88.8	78.7	67.7	22.5	5.4	1.1	0.2	*0.1-	*0.1-	*0.1-	*0.1-	*0.1-	*0.1-	*0.1-	*0.1-
400	3	99.9+	99.3	97.3	92.9	86.5	42.4	13.8	3.5	0.8	0.2	*0.1-	*0.1-	*0.1-	*0.1-	*0.1-	*0.1-	*0.1-
400	4	99.9+	99.9	99.6	98.1	95.5	62.9	27.2	7.8	2.4	0.6	*0.1-	*0.1-	*0.1-	*0.1-	*0.1-	*0.1-	*0.1-
400	5	100.0	99.9+	99.9+	99.7	98.8	79.3	43.7	16.7	5.7	1.6	0.1	*0.1-	*0.1-	*0.1-	*0.1-	*0.1-	*0.1-
500	0	59.0	34.8	20.6	12.1	7.1	.5	*0.1-	*0.1-	*0.1-	*0.1-	*0.1-	*0.1-	*0.1-	*0.1-	*0.1-	*0.1-	*0.1-
500	1	91.9	73.6	54.9	39.1	27.1	3.3	0.3	*0.1-	*0.1-	*0.1-	*0.1-	*0.1-	*0.1-	*0.1-	*0.1-	*0.1-	*0.1-
500	2	99.1	93.0	81.7	67.7	53.7	11.0	1.6	0.2	*0.1-	*0.1-	*0.1-	*0.1-	*0.1-	*0.1-	*0.1-	*0.1-	*0.1-
500	3	99.9+	99.4	95.5	87.8	77.4	25.1	5.0	0.7	*0.1-	*0.1-	*0.1-	*0.1-	*0.1-	*0.1-	*0.1-	*0.1-	*0.1-
500	4	99.9+	99.9	99.3	97.2	91.9	43.6	11.8	2.3	0.1	*0.1-	*0.1-	*0.1-	*0.1-	*0.1-	*0.1-	*0.1-	*0.1-
500	5	100.0	99.9+	99.9+	99.5	98.6	62.5	22.8	5.6	0.8	*0.1-	*0.1-	*0.1-	*0.1-	*0.1-	*0.1-	*0.1-	*0.1-
600	0	52.8	27.8	14.6	7.7	4.0	0.2	*0.1-	*0.1-	*0.1-	*0.1-	*0.1-	*0.1-	*0.1	*0.1-	*0.1-	*0.1-	*0.1-
600	1	88.8	65.8	44.7	28.9	18.0	1.3	*0.1-	*0.1-	*0.1-	*0.1-	*0.1-	*0.1-	*0.1-	*0.1-	*0.1-	*0.1-	*0.1-
600	2	98.2	89.2	73.4	56.3	40.8	5.1	0.4	*0.1-	*0.1-	*0.1-	*0.1-	*0.1-	*0.1-	*0.1-	*0.1-	*0.1-	*0.1-
600	3	99.5	97.6	90.4	78.8	64.8	13.3	1.6	0.1	*0.1-	*0.1-	*0.1-	*0.1-	*0.1-	*0.1-	*0.1-	*0.1-	*0.1-
600	4	99.9+	99.6	97.3	91.8	82.7	26.7	4.4	0.5	*0.1-	*0.1-	*0.1-	*0.1-	*0.1-	*0.1-	*0.1-	*0.1-	*0.1-
600	5	100.0	99.9+	99.4	97.4	93.0	43.5	9.9	1.4	*0.1-	*0.1-	*0.1-	*0.1-	*0.1-	*0.1-	*0.1-	*0.1-	*0.1-
700	0	47.0	22.1	10.4	4.9	2.2	*0.1-	*0.1-	*0.1-	*0.1-	*0.1-	*0.1-	*0.1-	*0.1-	*0.1-	*0.1-	*0.1-	*0.1-
700	1	85.3	58.2	35.9	20.9	11.0	0.4	*0.1-	*0.1-	*0.1-	*0.1-	*0.1-	*0.1-	*0.1-	*0.1-	*0.1-	*0.1-	*0.1-
700	2	97.8	84.7	60.4	45.7	28.4	2.1	0.1	*0.1-	*0.1-	*0.1-	*0.1-	*0.1-	*0.1-	*0.1-	*0.1-	*0.1-	*0.1-
700	3	99.8	96.2	77.7	69.9	50.1	6.3	0.4	*0.1-	*0.1-	*0.1-	*0.1-	*0.1-	*0.1-	*0.1-	*0.1-	*0.1-	*0.1-
700	4	99.9+	99.5	86.1	86.6	69.5	14.4	1.4	0.1	*0.1-	*0.1-	*0.1-	*0.1-	*0.1-	*0.1-	*0.1-	*0.1-	*0.1-
700	5	100.0	99.9+	97.3	94.0	82.8	26.5	3.6	0.3	*0.1-	*0.1-	*0.1-	*0.1-	*0.1-	*0.1-	*0.1-	*0.1-	*0.1-

*Less than 0.05%.

Appendix K Acceptance Sampling Plans (Continued)

Field Size 10,000

n Sample Size	c Acceptance Number	When Field Contains Error Rate of						When Field Contains Error Rate of:						When Field Contains Error Rate of:				
		.05%	.1%	.2%	.3%	.4%	.5%	1%	1.5%	2%	3%	4%	5%	6%	7%	8%	9%	10%
		The Probability of Acceptance is:						The Probability of Acceptance is:						The Probability of Acceptance is:				
100	0	95.1	90.5	81.8	73.9	66.8	60.5	36.4	21.9	13.1	4.7	1.7	0.6	0.2	0.1	*0.1-	*0.1-	*0.1-
100	1	99.9	99.6	98.3	96.4	93.9	91.2	73.6	55.6	40.3	19.3	8.6	3.6	1.5	0.6	0.2	0.1	*0.1-
100	2	99.9+	99.9+	99.9	99.7	99.2	98.8	92.1	81.0	67.8	41.9	23.1	11.7	5.6	2.5	1.1	0.5	0.2
100	3	99.9+	99.9+	99.9+	99.9+	99.9+	99.9+	98.2	93.7	78.6	64.7	42.8	25.6	14.2	7.3	3.6	1.7	0.8
100	4	99.9+	99.9+	99.9+	99.9+	99.9+	99.9+	99.6	98.3	87.6	81.9	62.9	43.5	27.6	16.2	8.9	4.7	2.3
150	0	92.7	85.9	73.8	63.5	54.5	46.8	21.9	10.2	4.7	1.0	0.2	*0.1-	*0.1-	*0.1-	*0.1-	*0.1-	*0.1-
150	1	99.8	99.0	96.3	92.6	88.1	82.7	55.6	33.8	19.4	5.7	1.5	0.4	0.1	*0.1-	*0.1-	*0.1-	*0.1-
150	2	99.9+	99.9	99.6	99.0	98.1	96.0	81.0	60.8	41.9	16.7	5.7	1.8	0.5	0.1	*0.1-	*0.1-	*0.1-
150	3	99.9+	99.9+	99.9	99.9	99.7	99.3	93.7	81.2	64.7	33.6	14.4	5.3	1.8	0.6	0.2	*0.1-	*0.1-
150	4	99.9+	99.9+	99.9+	99.9+	99.9+	99.8	98.3	92.5	81.8	52.9	27.7	12.4	4.9	1.7	0.6	0.2	*0.1-
200	0	90.5	81.8	66.6	54.5	44.5	36.4	13.1	4.7	1.7	.2	*0.1-	*0.1-	*0.1-	*0.1-	*0.1-	*0.1-	*0.1-
200	1	99.8	98.5	93.9	88.0	81.0	73.7	40.3	19.4	8.7	1.6	0.2	*0.1-	*0.1-	*0.1-	*0.1-	*0.1-	*0.1-
200	2	99.9+	99.9	99.2	97.9	95.5	92.3	67.8	41.9	23.3	5.8	1.2	0.2	*0.1-	*0.1-	*0.1-	*0.1-	*0.1-
200	3	99.9+	99.9+	99.8	99.8	99.2	98.4	86.1	64.7	43.0	14.4	3.8	0.9	0.2	*0.1-	*0.1-	*0.1-	*0.1-
200	4	99.9+	99.9+	99.9+	99.9+	99.9	99.8	95.1	81.8	63.0	27.8	9.3	2.5	0.6	0.1	*0.1-	*0.1-	*0.1-
200	5	100.0	99.9+	99.9+	99.9+	99.9+	99.9+	99.0	92.0	79.0	44.2	18.2	6.1	1.7	0.4	*0.1-	*0.1-	*0.1-
300	0	85.8	73.7	54.2	40.0	29.5	21.7	4.7	1.0	0.2	*0.1-	*0.1-	*0.1-	*0.1-	*0.1-	*0.1-	*0.1-	*0.1-
300	1	99.0	96.5	87.8	77.3	66.1	55.5	19.3	5.7	1.6	0.1	*0.1-	*0.1-	*0.1-	*0.1-	*0.1-	*0.1-	*0.1-
300	2	99.8	99.6	97.7	94.0	88.2	81.1	41.9	16.7	5.8	0.5	*0.1-	*0.1-	*0.1-	*0.1-	*0.1-	*0.1-	*0.1-
300	3	99.9+	99.9	99.5	98.8	96.8	93.8	64.7	33.6	14.4	1.7	0.2	*0.1-	*0.1-	*0.1-	*0.1-	*0.1-	*0.1-
300	4	99.9+	99.9+	99.9	99.8	99.2	98.3	81.9	52.9	27.8	4.4	0.6	0.1	*0.1-	*0.1-	*0.1-	*0.1-	*0.1-
300	5	100.0	99.9+	99.9+	99.9+	99.8	99.6	92.0	70.3	44.2	9.7	1.7	0.2	*0.1-	*0.1-	*0.1-	*0.1-	*0.1-
400	0	81.4	66.5	44.1	29.4	19.4	12.9	1.7	0.1	*0.1-	*0.1-	*0.1-	*0.1-	*0.1-	*0.1-	*0.1-	*0.1-	*0.1-
400	1	98.4	94.2	80.9	66.2	52.0	39.9	8.6	0.8	0.2	*0.1-	*0.1-	*0.1-	*0.1-	*0.1-	*0.1-	*0.1-	*0.1-
400	2	99.8	99.4	95.5	88.4	78.4	67.6	23.1	3.1	1.2	*0.1-	*0.1-	*0.1-	*0.1-	*0.1-	*0.1-	*0.1-	*0.1-
400	3	99.9+	99.9	99.1	97.1	92.4	86.1	42.8	7.7	3.8	0.2	*0.1-	*0.1-	*0.1-	*0.1-	*0.1-	*0.1-	*0.1-
400	4	99.9+	99.9+	99.8	99.5	97.7	95.1	62.9	14.8	9.3	0.6	*0.1-	*0.1-	*0.1-	*0.1-	*0.1-	*0.1-	*0.1-
400	5	100.0	99.9+	99.9+	99.9+	99.3	98.5	71.6	23.6	18.3	1.7	0.1	*0.1-	*0.1-	*0.1-	*0.1-	*0.1-	*0.1-

Field Size 10,000 (Cont.)

n Sample Size	c Acceptance Number	.05%	.1%	.2%	.3%	.4%	.5%	1%	1.5%	2%	3%	4%	5%	6%	7%	8%	9%	10%
		When Field Contains Error Rate of: The Probability of Acceptance is:						When Field Contains Error Rate of: The Probability of Acceptance is:						When Field Contains Error Rate of: The Probability of Acceptance is:				
500	0	77.3	59.9	35.8	21.4	12.8	7.6	0.6	*0.1-	*0.1-	*0.1-	*0.1-	*0.1-	*0.1-	*0.1-	*0.1-	*0.1-	*0.1-
500	1	97.7	91.4	73.6	55.4	39.8	27.9	3.6	0.2	*0.1-	*0.1-	*0.1-	*0.1-	*0.1-	*0.1-	*0.1-	*0.1-	*0.1-
500	2	99.8	98.9	92.4	81.3	67.7	54.1	11.7	0.9	0.2	*0.1-	*0.1-	*0.1-	*0.1-	*0.1-	*0.1-	*0.1-	*0.1-
500	3	99.9+	99.9	98.4	94.0	86.2	76.1	25.6	2.9	0.9	*0.1-	*0.1-	*0.1-	*0.1-	*0.1-	*0.1-	*0.1-	*0.1-
500	4	99.9+	99.9+	99.7	98.5	95.2	89.7	43.5	6.6	2.5	0.1	*0.1-	*0.1-	*0.1-	*0.1-	*0.1-	*0.1-	*0.1-
500	5	100.0	99.9+	99.9+	99.7	98.6	96.3	61.5	12.4	6.1	0.2	*0.1-	*0.1-	*0.1-	*0.1-	*0.1-	*0.1-	*0.1-
600	0	73.4	53.9	29.0	15.6	8.4	4.5	0.2	*0.1-	*0.1-	*0.1-	*0.1-	*0.1-	*0.1-	*0.1-	*0.1-	*0.1-	*0.1-
600	1	96.9	88.3	66.1	45.6	29.9	19.0	1.5	0.1	*0.1-	*0.1-	*0.1-	*0.1-	*0.1-	*0.1-	*0.1-	*0.1-	*0.1-
600	2	99.8	98.2	88.6	73.4	56.7	41.6	5.6	0.3	*0.1-	*0.1-	*0.1-	*0.1-	*0.1-	*0.1-	*0.1-	*0.1-	*0.1-
600	3	99.9+	99.9	97.2	89.9	78.4	64.8	14.2	1.0	0.2	*0.1-	*0.1-	*0.1-	*0.1-	*0.1-	*0.1-	*0.1-	*0.1-
600	4	99.9+	99.9+	99.5	97.0	91.2	82.2	27.6	2.6	0.6	*0.1-	*0.1-	*0.1-	*0.1-	*0.1-	*0.1-	*0.1-	*0.1-
60C	5	100.0	99.9+	99.9+	99.4	97.1	92.4	44.1	5.7	1.7	*0.1-	*0.1-	*0.1-	*0.1-	*0.1-	*0.1-	*0.1-	*0.1-
700	0	69.5	48.3	23.3	11.3	5.4	2.6	0.1	*0.1-	*0.1-	*0.1-	*0.1-	*0.1-	*0.1-	*0.1-	*0.1-	*0.1-	*0.1-
700	1	95.6	84.8	58.5	36.9	21.9	12.6	0.6	*0.1-	*0.1-	*0.1-	*0.1-	*0.1-	*0.1-	*0.1-	*0.1-	*0.1-	*0.1-
700	2	99.6	97.1	83.7	64.9	46.1	31.0	2.5	0.1	*0.1-	*0.1-	*0.1-	*0.1-	*0.1-	*0.1-	*0.1-	*0.1-	*0.1-
700	3	99.9	99.6	95.1	84.6	69.2	53.3	7.3	0.3	*0.1-	*0.1-	*0.1-	*0.1-	*0.1-	*0.1-	*0.1-	*0.1-	*0.1-
700	4	99.9+	99.9	98.7	94.6	85.3	72.9	16.2	0.9	0.1	*0.1-	*0.1-	*0.1-	*0.1-	*0.1-	*0.1-	*0.1-	*0.1-
700	5	100.0	99.9+	99.6	98.5	94.0	86.6	29.0	2.3	0.4	*0.1-	*0.1-	*0.1-	*0.1-	*0.1-	*0.1-	*0.1-	*0.1-

*Less than 0.05%.

K

Field Size 50,000

n Sample Size	c Acceptance Number	When Field Contains Error Rate of: .05%	.1%	.2%	.3%	.4%	.5%	1%	1.5%	2%	2.5%	3%	4%	When Field Contains Error Rate of: 5%	6%	7%	8%	9%	10%
		The Probability of Acceptance is:												The Probability of Acceptance is:					
50	0	97.5	95.1	90.5	86.1	81.8	77.8	60.5	47.0	36.4	28.2	21.8	13.0	8.7	4.5	2.7	1.5	0.9	0.5
50	1	99.9	99.9	99.5	99.0	98.3	97.4	91.1	82.7	73.6	64.4	55.5	40.0	27.9	19.0	12.6	8.3	5.3	3.4
50	2	99.9+	99.9+	99.9+	99.9+	99.9	99.8	98.6	96.1	92.2	87.1	81.1	67.7	54.1	41.6	31.1	22.6	16.1	11.2
50	3	99.9+	99.9+	99.9+	99.9+	99.9+	99.9+	99.8	99.3	98.2	96.4	93.7	86.1	76.0	64.7	53.3	42.5	33.0	25.0
100	0	95.1	90.5	81.9	74.0	67.0	60.6	36.6	22.1	13.3	8.0	4.8	1.7	0.6	0.2	0.1	*0.1-	*0.1-	*0.1-
100	1	99.9	99.5	98.3	96.3	93.9	91.0	73.6	55.7	40.3	28.3	19.5	8.7	3.7	1.5	0.6	0.2	0.1	*0.1-
100	2	99.9+	99.9+	99.9	99.7	99.2	98.6	92.1	81.0	67.7	54.2	42.0	23.2	11.8	5.7	2.6	1.1	0.5	0.2
100	3	99.9+	99.9+	99.9+	99.9+	99.9	99.8	98.2	93.6	85.9	75.9	64.7	42.9	25.8	14.3	7.4	3.7	1.7	0.8
100	4	99.9+	99.9+	99.9+	99.9+	99.9+	99.9+	99.7	98.2	94.9	89.4	81.8	62.9	43.6	27.7	16.3	9.0	4.7	2.4
150	0	92.8	86.1	74.1	63.7	54.8	47.1	22.1	10.4	4.8	2.2	1.0	0.2	*0.1-	*0.1-	*0.1-	*0.1-	*0.1-	*0.1-
150	1	99.7	99.0	96.3	92.5	87.8	82.7	55.7	34.0	19.6	10.9	5.8	1.6	.4	0.1	*0.1-	*0.1-	*0.1-	*0.1-
150	2	99.9+	99.9+	99.6	98.9	97.7	96.0	80.9	60.9	42.1	27.3	16.9	5.8	1.8	0.5	0.1	*0.1-	*0.1-	*0.1-
150	3	99.9+	99.9+	99.9+	99.9	99.7	99.3	93.5	81.1	64.7	48.2	33.8	14.6	5.5	1.9	0.6	0.2	*0.1-	*0.1-
150	4	99.9+	99.9+	99.9+	99.9+	99.9+	99.9	98.2	92.3	81.7	67.8	53.1	28.0	12.6	5.0	1.8	0.6	0.2	0.1
200	0	90.5	81.9	67.0	54.8	44.9	36.7	13.4	4.9	1.8	0.6	0.2	*0.1-	*0.1-	*0.1-	*0.1-	*0.1-	*0.1-	*0.1-
200	1	99.5	98.3	93.9	87.8	80.9	73.6	40.5	19.7	8.9	3.9	1.6	0.3	*0.1-	*0.1-	*0.1-	*0.1-	*0.1-	*0.1-
200	2	99.9+	99.9+	99.2	97.7	95.3	92.0	67.7	42.2	23.5	12.1	5.9	1.2	0.2	*0.1-	*0.1-	*0.1-	*0.1-	*0.1-
200	3	99.9+	99.9+	99.9	99.7	99.1	98.1	85.8	64.7	43.1	26.1	14.7	4.0	0.9	0.2	*0.1-	*0.1-	*0.1-	*0.1-
200	4	99.9+	99.9+	99.9+	99.9+	99.9	99.6	94.8	81.7	62.9	43.8	28.1	9.5	2.6	0.6	0.1	*0.1-	*0.1-	*0.1-
200	5	99.9+	99.9+	99.9+	99.9+	99.9+	99.9	98.4	91.8	78.7	61.6	44.3	18.6	6.2	1.8	0.4	0.1	*0.1-	*0.1-
300	0	86.1	74.0	54.8	40.6	30.0	22.2	4.9	1.1	0.2	0.1	*0.1-	*0.1-	*0.1-	*0.1-	*0.1-	*0.1-	*0.1-	*0.1-
300	1	99.0	96.3	87.8	77.3	66.2	55.7	19.8	6.0	1.7	0.5	0.1	*0.1-	*0.1-	*0.1-	*0.1-	*0.1-	*0.1-	*0.1-
300	2	99.9+	99.6	97.7	93.7	88.0	80.9	42.2	17.1	6.0	2.0	0.6	*0.1-	*0.1-	*0.1-	*0.1-	*0.1-	*0.1-	*0.1-
300	3	99.9+	99.9+	99.7	98.2	96.7	93.5	64.7	34.0	14.9	6.0	2.0	0.2	*0.1-	*0.1-	*0.1-	*0.1-	*0.1-	*0.1-
300	4	99.9+	99.9+	99.9+	99.2	99.2	98.2	81.6	53.1	28.2	13.5	5.2	0.7	*0.1-	*0.1-	*0.1-	*0.1-	*0.1-	*0.1-
300	5	99.9+	99.9+	99.9+	99.4	99.9	99.6	91.7	70.3	44.4	25.0	11.2	1.9	0.2	*0.1-	*0.1-	*0.1-	*0.1-	*0.1-
400	0	81.9	67.0	44.9	30.1	20.1	13.5	1.8	0.2	*0.1-	*0.1-	*0.1-	*0.1-	*0.1-	*0.1-	*0.1-	*0.1-	*0.1-	*0.1-
400	1	98.3	93.9	80.9	66.3	52.5	40.5	9.0	1.7	0.2	*0.1-	*0.1-	*0.1-	*0.1-	*0.1-	*0.1-	*0.1-	*0.1-	*0.1-
400	2	99.9	99.2	95.3	88.0	78.4	67.7	23.7	6.1	1.3	0.3	*0.1-	*0.1-	*0.1-	*0.1-	*0.1-	*0.1-	*0.1-	*0.1-
400	3	99.9+	99.9	99.1	96.6	92.2	85.8	43.2	14.9	4.1	1.0	0.2	*0.1-	*0.1-	*0.1-	*0.1-	*0.1-	*0.1-	*0.1-
400	4	99.9+	99.9+	99.9	99.2	97.7	94.8	62.9	28.3	9.7	2.8	0.7	*0.1-	*0.1-	*0.1-	*0.1-	*0.1-	*0.1-	*0.1-
400	5	99.9+	99.9+	99.9+	99.8	99.4	98.4	78.6	44.4	18.8	6.5	1.9	0.1	*0.1-	*0.1-	*0.1-	*0.1-	*0.1-	*0.1-

Field Size 50,000 (Cont.)

n Sample Size	c Acceptance Number	When Field Contains Error Rate of: .05%	.1%	.2%	.3%	.4%	.5%	1%	1.5%	2%	2.5%	3%	When Field Contains Error Rate of: 4%	5%	6%	7%	8%	9%	10%
		The Probability of Acceptance is:											The Probability of Acceptance is:						
500	0	77.9	60.6	36.7	22.2	13.5	8.2	0.7	0.1	*0.1-	*0.1-	*0.1-	*0.1-	*0.1-	*0.1-	*0.1-	*0.1-	*0.1-	*0.1-
500	1	97.4	91.0	73.6	55.6	40.5	28.7	4.0	0.5	*0.1-	*0.1-	*0.1-	*0.1-	*0.1-	*0.1-	*0.1-	*0.1-	*0.1-	*0.1-
500	2	99.8	98.6	92.0	80.7	67.7	54.4	12.3	2.0	0.3	*0.1-	*0.1-	*0.1-	*0.1-	*0.1-	*0.1-	*0.1-	*0.1-	*0.1-
500	3	99.9+	99.8	98.1	93.3	85.7	75.8	26.4	5.8	1.0	0.1	*0.1-	*0.1-	*0.1-	*0.1-	*0.1-	*0.1-	*0.1-	*0.1-
500	4	99.9+	99.9+	99.6	97.9	94.8	89.2	44.0	13.0	2.8	0.5	0.1	*0.1-	*0.1-	*0.1-	*0.1-	*0.1-	*0.1-	*0.1-
500	5	99.9+	99.9+	99.9	99.3	98.4	95.8	61.6	23.9	6.5	1.4	0.3	*0.1-	*0.1-	*0.1-	*0.1-	*0.1-	*0.1-	*0.1-
600	0	74.1	54.9	30.1	16.5	9.0	4.9	0.2	*0.1-	*0.1-	*0.1-	*0.1-	*0.1-	*0.1-	*0.1-	*0.1-	*0.1-	*0.1-	*0.1-
600	1	96.3	87.8	66.3	46.3	30.8	19.8	1.7	0.1	*0.1-	*0.1-	*0.1-	*0.1-	*0.1-	*0.1-	*0.1-	*0.1-	*0.1-	*0.1-
600	2	99.6	97.7	88.0	73.1	56.9	42.3	6.1	0.6	*0.1-	*0.1-	*0.1-	*0.1-	*0.1-	*0.1-	*0.1-	*0.1-	*0.1-	*0.1-
600	3	99.9+	99.7	96.6	89.2	77.9	64.7	5.0	2.1	0.2	*0.1-	*0.1-	*0.1-	*0.1-	*0.1-	*0.1-	*0.1-	*0.1-	*0.1-
600	4	99.9+	99.9+	99.2	96.4	90.4	81.6	28.4	5.4	0.7	0.1	*0.1-	*0.1-	*0.1-	*0.1-	*0.1-	*0.1-	*0.1-	*0.1-
600	5	99.9+	99.9+	99.8	99.0	96.5	91.7	44.5	11.4	1.9	0.3	*0.1-	*0.1-	*0.1-	*0.1-	*0.1-	*0.1-	*0.1-	*0.1-
700	0	70.5	49.6	24.6	12.2	6.0	3.0	0.1	*0.1-	*0.1-	*0.1-	*0.1-	*0.1-	*0.1-	*0.1-	*0.1-	*0.1-	*0.1-	*0.1-
700	1	95.1	84.4	59.2	37.9	23.0	13.5	0.7	*0.1-	*0.1-	*0.1-	*0.1-	*0.1-	*0.1-	*0.1-	*0.1-	*0.1-	*0.1-	*0.1-
700	2	99.5	96.6	83.4	65.0	46.8	32.0	2.9	0.2	*0.1-	*0.1-	*0.1-	*0.1-	*0.1-	*0.1-	*0.1-	*0.1-	*0.1-	*0.1-
700	3	99.9+	99.4	94.6	83.9	69.0	53.6	8.1	0.7	*0.1-	*0.1-	*0.1-	*0.1-	*0.1-	*0.1-	*0.1-	*0.1-	*0.1-	*0.1-
700	4	99.9+	99.9	98.6	93.8	84.5	72.6	17.2	2.0	0.2	*0.1-	*0.1-	*0.1-	*0.1-	*0.1-	*0.1-	*0.1-	*0.1-	*0.1-
700	5	99.9+	99.9+	99.7	98.0	93.2	85.8	29.9	4.9	0.5	*0.1-	*0.1-	*0.1-	*0.1-	*0.1-	*0.1-	*0.1-	*0.1-	*0.1-
800	0	67.0	44.9	20.2	9.0	4.0	1.8	*0.1-	*0.1-	*0.1-	*0.1-	*0.1-	*0.1-	*0.1-	*0.1-	*0.1-	*0.1-	*0.1-	*0.1-
800	1	93.8	80.9	52.5	30.8	17.1	9.1	0.3	*0.1-	*0.1-	*0.1-	*0.1-	*0.1-	*0.1-	*0.1-	*0.1-	*0.1-	*0.1-	*0.1-
800	2	99.2	95.3	78.3	57.0	37.9	23.7	1.3	0.1	*0.1-	*0.1-	*0.1-	*0.1-	*0.1-	*0.1-	*0.1-	*0.1-	*0.1-	*0.1-
800	3	99.9	99.1	92.1	77.9	60.2	43.2	4.2	0.2	*0.1-	*0.1-	*0.1-	*0.1-	*0.1-	*0.1-	*0.1-	*0.1-	*0.1-	*0.1-
800	4	99.9+	99.9	97.6	90.5	78.1	62.7	9.8	0.7	*0.1-	*0.1-	*0.1-	*0.1-	*0.1-	*0.1-	*0.1-	*0.1-	*0.1-	*0.1-
800	5	99.9+	99.9+	99.4	96.5	89.5	78.4	19.0	2.0	0.1	*0.1-	*0.1-	*0.1-	*0.1-	*0.1-	*0.1-	*0.1-	*0.1-	*0.1-

*Less than 0.05%.

K

APPENDIX L
CLUSTER SAMPLING

When Number of Clusters is:	For Confidence Levels of: 90%	95%	99%
	Sampling Error as Multiple of Standard Deviation		
10	±.6100	±.7533	±1.0833
11	.5724	.7052	1.0024
12	.5427	.6633	.9377
13	.5138	.6293	.8833
14	.4909	.5991	.8348
15	.4704	.5719	.7964
16	.4518	.5500	.7617
17	.4375	.5300	.7300
18	.4220	.5118	.7034
19	.4078	.4950	.6788
20	.3969	.4795	.6561
21	.3846	.4673	.6350
22	.3753	.4539	.6176
23	.3667	.4413	.6012
24	.3566	.4316	.5859
25	.3491	.4205	.5715
26	.3420	.4120	.5580
27	.3354	.4040	.5452
28	.3272	.3945	.5331
29	.3213	.3874	.5216
30	.3157	.3788	.5125
31	.3104	.3725	.5021
32	.3053	.3664	.4939
33	.3005	.3606	.4861
34	.2959	.3551	.4787
35	.2915	.3481	.4665
36	.2857	.3431	.4598
37	.2817	.3383	.4533
38	.2778	.3337	.4472
39	.2742	.3293	.4412
40	.2706	.3235	.4339
41	.2656	.3194	.4285
42	.2624	.3155	.4232
43	.2592	.3117	.4182
44	.2562	.3080	.4133
45	.2533	.3045	.4055
46	.2504	.3011	.4010
47	.2477	.2978	.3966

TECHNICAL APPENDIXES

Technical Appendix I. An Alternative Method for Computation of Standard Deviation

When the number of observations from which the standard deviation is to be computed exceeds 10, the method of computation described in Chapter 4 becomes quite laborious. While a method of *approximating* the standard deviation which obviates the need for this method is described in Chapter 4, there are certain cases in which an exact computation is more desirable.

The standard deviation may be computed from:

$$\sigma = \sqrt{\frac{\Sigma(X^2)}{n} - \left(\frac{\Sigma X}{n}\right)^2}$$

where X = value of each observation
n = number of observations

Note that the value under the square root (radical) is merely the average square minus the square of the average. Thus, it is necessary only to square each value and total the results to calculate the standard deviation. This calculation can be performed readily on a calculating machine by using cumulative multiplication.

The computation may be illustrated as follows by using the same data as in Chapter 4 (page 54).

X	X^2
191.10	36,519.2000
251.53	63,267.3409
205.10	42,066.0100
196.86	38,753.8596
192.66	37,117.8756
1,037.25	217,724.2861

$$\sigma = \sqrt{\frac{217{,}724.2861}{5} - \left(\frac{1037.25}{5}\right)^2}$$

$$= \sqrt{43{,}544.85 - (207.45)^2}$$
$$= \sqrt{43{,}544.8500 - 43{,}035.5025}$$
$$= \sqrt{509.3475}$$
$$= \$22.57$$

While at first glance this method may seem more difficult than that indicated on page 54, these calculations are in fact simpler when numerous observations are involved. Only the sum of the squares of the values and the sum of the values are required, both of which can be readily obtained on a calculating machine. There is no need to calculate a whole series of deviations for an arithmetic mean and to square each one as in the previously described method.

Technical Appendix II. Standard Error of Arithmetic Mean

The standard error of the mean, by which the sampling error of the average is obtained, is given in the text as

$$\sigma_{\bar{X}} = \frac{\sigma}{\sqrt{n}}$$

Recall that the standard error of the mean is the standard deviation of the sampling distribution of the averages, or the standard deviation of the means of all possible samples of the specified size which might be drawn from the population.

Assume all possible samples of size n to be drawn from the population with each sample consisting of observations $X_1, X_2, X_3, \ldots, X_n$. This may be indicated as follows:

Sample #1	Sample #2	Sample #3	. . .	Sample #i
X_1	X_1	X_1	. . .	X_1
X_2	X_2	X_2	. . .	X_2
X_3	X_3	X_3	. . .	X_3
.	.	.	. . .	.
.	.	.	. . .	.
.	.	.	. . .	.
X_n	X_n	X_n	. . .	X_n

For the first observation or individual value in each sample, it is apparent that as the number of samples drawn increases, the standard deviation of all the X_1 values approaches the standard deviation of the population, since an increasing and very large number of different X_1 values will be included.

For this derivation, it is more convenient to work with the square of the standard deviation, which is known as the *variance*. If the standard deviation of the X_1 values approaches the standard deviation of the population, then the variances of the X_1 values will approach the variance of the population, or

$$\sigma^2_{X_1} \rightarrow \sigma^2$$

However, the interest lies in the standard deviation of the arithmetic averages of samples, where

$$\bar{X} = \frac{\sum X}{n}$$

It is seen, however, that

$$\sum X = n\bar{X}$$

By referring to the *total* of each sample rather than the average, the variance of the total values in the sample can be obtained by resorting to a statistical fact—that the sum of the variances equals the variances of the sums,[1] or

$$\sigma^2_{1+2+3+\cdots+n} = \sigma^2_1 + \sigma^2_2 + \sigma^2_3 + \cdots + \sigma^2_n$$

Therefore

$$\sigma^2_{X_1+X_2+X_3+\cdots+X_n} = \sigma^2_{X_1} + \sigma^2_{X_2} + \sigma^2_{X_3} \cdots + \sigma^2_{X_n}$$

where $\sigma^2_{X_1+X_2+X_3+\cdots+X_n}$ is the variance of the sample total.

But it was noted that the variance of X_1 approaches the variance of the population as the number of samples is increased. Similarly the variance of X_2 and of X_3, etc., will approach the variance of the population, and therefore

$$\sigma^2_{X_1} = \sigma^2_{X_2} = \sigma^2_{X_3} = \sigma^2_{X_n} = \sigma^2$$

and if, as shown above,

$$\sigma^2_{X_1+X_2+X_3+\cdots+X_n} = \sigma^2_{X_1} + \sigma^2_{X_2} + \sigma^2_{X_3} + \cdots + \sigma^2_{X_n}$$

then

$$\sigma^2_{X_1+X_2+X_3+\cdots+X_n} = n\sigma^2$$

where σ^2 = the variance of the population.

Remember that $X_1 + X_2 + X_3 + \cdots + X_n$ equals the sample total, and thus

$$\sigma_{\sum X}{}^2 = n\sigma^2$$

Taking the square root of the above,

$$\sigma_{\sum X} = \sqrt{n}\sigma$$

Since the average is the total divided by n, both sides of the above equation may be divided by n to obtain

$$\sigma_{\bar{X}} = \frac{\sigma}{\sqrt{n}}$$

or the standard deviation of the sampling distribution of the averages of all possible samples drawn from the population.

[1] For uncorrelated (independent) values such as those in a sample, see D. J. Cowden, *Statistical Methods in Quality Control*, Prentice-Hall, Inc., Englewood Cliffs, N.J., 1957, p. w3.

Technical Appendix III. Cluster Sampling

As indicated in Chapter 4, the sampling error of an average may be computed from

$$SE_{\bar{X}} = t\frac{\sigma}{\sqrt{n}}\sqrt{1 - \frac{n}{N}}$$

where $SE_{\bar{X}}$ = sampling error of average

t = factor required to achieve a given confidence level (number of standard deviations—see Table 4-3, i.e., 1.96 for 95% confidence level)

σ = standard deviation of values in field or population

n = sample size (number of sampling units in sample)

N = field or population size (number of sampling units in field)

If clusters of contiguous items are randomly selected with all items in the group included (no subsampling), the cluster may be looked upon as a single sampling unit, and the field consists of all such groups in the population. The observation from the sampling unit is the cluster *average.*

The sampling error of the average of the cluster averages can then be obtained from the above formula if it is remembered that in cluster sampling n equals the number of clusters in the sample, N equals the number of clusters in the field, and σ measures the cluster-to-cluster variability.

However, many cluster samples will involve a small number of clusters (often less than 30). In such circumstances, it is necessary to apply the theory of small samples.[1] The use of a small sample requires two modifications of the method previously described for large samples. First, the standard deviation[2] is computed from

$$\sigma = \sqrt{\frac{\Sigma(X - \bar{X})^2}{n - 1}}$$

rather than from

$$\sigma = \sqrt{\frac{\Sigma(X - \bar{X})^2}{n}}$$

to obtain an unbiased estimate of the standard deviation computed from the sample.[3]

Further, it is necessary to use adjusted t values. For instance, where the usual t value (number of standard deviations) for the 95 per cent confidence level is 1.96, the adjusted (Student's) t for various small size samples varies according to the size

[1] See H. Arkin and R. R. Colton, *Outline of Statistical Methods,* 4th ed., Barnes & Noble, Inc., New York, 1956, p. 126.

[2] See Chap. 4.

[3] While the $n - 1$ divisor technically is applicable to any standard deviation *computed from a sample,* in practice the difference between a division by $n - 1$ rather than n in its effect on the standard deviation is negligible for large samples. As a result, commonly, this modification is ignored for large samples.

of the sample, approaching 1.96 for large samples. A condensed table of a few t values is given below.

	95 per cent confidence level
$n - 1$	t
5	2.57
10	2.23
15	2.13
20	2.09
100	1.99
1,000	1.96

The tables for use with cluster samples incorporate these modifications so that no adjustment is necessary to the values in the table.

The values in the table (Appendix G) thus represent the solution of the formula given above, but for simplicity the formula is split into two parts.

$$SE_{\bar{X}} = \left(t\frac{\sigma}{\sqrt{n}}\right)\left(\sqrt{1 - \frac{n}{N}}\right)$$

where the second part of the formula is the finite correction factor. $(\sqrt{1 - n/N})$ is given in Appendix I.

The values in the table in Appendix H represent the equivalent of solution of the first part of the above formula:

$$t\frac{\sigma}{\sqrt{n}}$$

but in order to reduce the size of the table to reasonable proportions, the actual value in the table is

$$t\frac{1}{\sqrt{n}}$$

Multiplication of the tabular values by σ results in

$$\sigma\left(t\frac{1}{\sqrt{n}}\right) \quad \text{or} \quad t\frac{\sigma}{\sqrt{n}}$$

The adjustments for the two modifications mentioned above are incorporated in the table by a computation based on

$$SE = t'\frac{1}{\sqrt{n - 1}}$$

where t' is Student's t and the use of $\sqrt{n - 1}$ rather than $\sqrt{n}$ has the effect of changing to

$$\sigma = \sqrt{\frac{\Sigma(X - \bar{X})^2}{n}}$$

to

$$\sigma = \sqrt{\frac{\sum (X - \bar{X})^2}{n - 1}}$$

Multiplying the value in the table by the standard deviation σ results in the sampling error (or reliability) for the given sample size and the confidence level for sampling from an infinite size field. To adjust for the finite size of the field, the appropriate factor from Appendix I is used as a multiplier for the above result; remember that n equals the number of *clusters* in the sample, and N the number of clusters in the field.

Technical Appendix IV. Multistage Sampling

The technique outlined in the chapter on multistage sampling is based on the use of two-stage sampling.

The symbolism used by different authors in this area varies widely. However, after conversion to the form of notation used in this book, the formulas for the standard error of a two-stage sample given by both Cochran and Yates[1] resolve into

$$\sigma_{\bar{X}}^2 = \frac{\sigma_b^2}{m}\left(1 - \frac{m}{M}\right) + \frac{m}{M}\left(\frac{1}{m}\right)\sum\left[\frac{\bar{\sigma}w^2}{n}\left(1 - \frac{n}{N}\right)\right]$$

where σ_b^2 = square of standard deviation of averages of the primary sampling units

m = number of primary sampling units in sample

M = number of primary sampling units in field

$\bar{\sigma}w^2$ = average of squares of the standard deviations of values of secondary sampling units in each primary sampling unit

n = number of items in each primary sampling unit

N = number of secondary sampling units in field

Examining the first part of the formula,

$$\frac{\sigma_b^2}{m}\left(1 - \frac{m}{M}\right)$$

it will be seen that the square root of this value is

$$\frac{\sigma_b}{\sqrt{m}}\sqrt{1 - \frac{m}{M}}$$

which is the same as the cluster sampling error (see Technical Appendix III). The second part of the formula,

$$\frac{m}{M}\left(\frac{1}{m}\right)\sum\left[\frac{\bar{\sigma}w^2}{n}\left(1 - \frac{n}{N}\right)\right]$$

can be written

$$\sum\left[\frac{\bar{\sigma}w^2/n(1 - n/N)}{m}\right]$$

but

$$\sum\left[\frac{\sigma w^2/n(1 - n/N)}{m}\right]$$

[1] W. G. Cochran, *Sampling Techniques*, John Wiley & Sons, Inc., New York, 1953, p. 224; Frank Yates, *Sampling Methods for Censuses and Surveys*, 2nd ed., Hafner Publishing Company, Inc., New York, 1953, p. 226.

will be recognized as the average of the squares of the standard errors of the arithmetic mean of the values comprising each primary sampling unit, as averaged for all primary sampling units, since

$$\sigma_{\bar{X}} = \frac{\sigma}{\sqrt{n}}\sqrt{1 - \frac{n}{N}}$$

and

$$\sigma_{\bar{X}}^2 = \frac{\sigma^2}{n}\left(1 - \frac{n}{N}\right)$$

Thus

$$\frac{1}{m}\sum\left[\frac{\sigma_w^2}{n}\left(1 - \frac{n}{N}\right)\right] = \bar{\sigma}_{\bar{X}}^2$$

where $\bar{\sigma}_{\bar{X}}^2$ is the average standard error of the average of the items within each primary sampling unit.

Then the standard error of the overall average becomes

$$\sigma_{\bar{X}}^2 = \sigma_{\bar{X}}^2{}_{\substack{\text{cluster}\\(\text{primary})}} + \frac{m}{M}\bar{\sigma}_{\bar{X}}^2{}_{\substack{\text{within}\\\text{primary}\\(\text{secondary})}}$$

Since the sampling error is t times the standard error,

$$t^2\sigma_{\bar{X}}^2 = t^2\left[\sigma_{\bar{X}}^2{}_{\substack{\text{cluster}\\(\text{primary})}} + \frac{m}{M}t^2\bar{\sigma}_{\bar{X}}^2{}_{\substack{\text{within}\\\text{primary}\\(\text{secondary})}}\right]$$

$$SE_{\bar{X}}^2 = t^2\sigma_{\bar{X}}^2{}_{\substack{\text{cluster}\\(\text{primary})}} + \frac{m}{M}t^2\bar{\sigma}_{\bar{X}}^2{}_{\substack{\text{within}\\\text{primary}\\(\text{secondary})}}$$

and

$$SE_{\bar{X}}^2 = SE_{pri}^2 + \frac{m}{M}\overline{SE}^2{}_{\bar{X},\,sec}$$

Technical Appendix V. Basis of Computation of Tables for Estimating Sample Size for Variables

As noted in the text, the sampling precision (sample precision or sampling error) for an average can be computed from

$$SE_{\bar{X}} = t\frac{\sigma}{\sqrt{n}}\sqrt{1 - \frac{n}{N}}$$

where $SE_{\bar{X}}$ = sampling error of average
t = factor determined by confidence level
σ = standard deviation of population
n = sample size
N = field, or population, size

The above formula may be written as

$$SE_{\bar{X}} = \left(t\frac{1}{\sqrt{n}}\sqrt{1 - \frac{n}{N}}\right)\sigma$$

and thus

$$\frac{SE_{\bar{X}}}{\sigma} = t\frac{1}{\sqrt{n}}\sqrt{1 - \frac{n}{N}}$$

But

$$\frac{SE_{\bar{X}}}{\sigma} = \text{ratio of sampling error to standard deviation}$$

If this ratio is indicated as R, then

$$R = \frac{SE_{\bar{X}}}{\sigma}$$

and the formula becomes

$$R = t\frac{1}{\sqrt{n}}\sqrt{1 - \frac{n}{N}}$$

Squaring both sides,

$$R^2 = t^2\frac{1}{n}\left(1 - \frac{n}{N}\right)$$

or

$$R^2 = t^2\left(\frac{1}{n} - \frac{n}{Nn}\right) = t^2\left(\frac{1}{n} - \frac{1}{N}\right)$$

$$= t^2\frac{1}{n} - t^2\frac{1}{N}$$

thus
$$\frac{t^2}{n} = R^2 + \frac{t^2}{N}$$

and
$$\frac{1}{n} = \frac{R^2 + t^2/N}{t^2}$$

and
$$n = \frac{t^2}{R^2 + t^2/N} = \frac{1}{R^2/t^2 + 1/N}$$

The table of sample size for variables estimates was computed by means of this last formula.

Technical Appendix VI. Basis of Computation of Tables for Estimating Sample Size for Attributes (Appendix D)

In Chapter 5 the formula for the sample precision of a proportion is given as

$$\text{Sampling error} = \pm t \sqrt{\frac{p(1-p)}{n}} \sqrt{1 - \frac{n}{N}}$$

This formula may be inverted to find n when given all the other factors. The value of t is determined by the confidence level. The value of N is the field size. The value of p may be selected arbitrarily and will be a conservative estimate as long as it is closer to 50% than the actual rate of occurrence in the field. The inverse form of the formula is

$$n = \frac{p(1-p)}{(SE/t)^2 + [p(1-p)/N]}$$

where n = required sample size
t = factor determined by confidence level (see Chapter 4)
SE = desired or allowable sampling error
N = field size
p = maximum anticipated rate of occurrence
The values in the table were obtained from this formula.

Technical Appendix VII. Basis of Computation of Tables for Appraising the Sample Precision of Relative Frequencies (Appendix F)

The general concepts on which this table is founded are explained in detail in Chapter 6.

The principle is summarized in statistical terms by Fisher and Yates:[1]

> If an event is observed to occur a times out of N, a lower limit π_1 can be assigned to the probability of this event such that if the probability were actually π_1, then an observed number of occurrences as great or greater than a out of N trials would only occur by chance with a frequency of p. Similarly an upper limit π_2 can be assigned such that if the probability were actually π_2 an observed number of occurrences as small or smaller than a would occur with frequency p.

To find these limits, it is necessary to compute and cumulate the terms of the binomial distribution inward from each end for the infinite universe case. The sum of these terms would be

$$\sum\left[\frac{n!}{r!(n-r)!}p^r(1-p)^{n-r}\right]$$

where n = sample size

p = rate of occurrence in population

r = specified number of occurrences in sample

For the finite case, the hypergeometric distribution formula would have to be cumulated. This formula is

$$\sum\frac{C_r^d C_{n-r}^{N-d}}{C_n^N}$$

where d = number of occurrences in field

r = number of occurrences in sample

N = field size

n = sample size

The direct solution of either of these formulas for a set of tables as extensive as those given in this book would be a mountainous task even with a computer.

However, Table VIII(1) of Fisher and Yates[2] provides the means for the computation of the binomial expectation limits, and Mainland[3] has extended this table con-

[1] R. A. Fisher and F. Yates, *Statistical Tables for Biological, Agricultural and Medical Research,* Hafner Publishing Company, Inc., New York, 1957, p. 6.

[2] *Ibid.*

[3] D. Mainland, L. Herrera, and M. I. Sutcliffe, *Statistical Tables for Use with Binomial Samples,* New York University, College of Medicine, New York, 1956.

siderably. These tables plus some additional calculations where required provide the limits for the infinite case.

It was necessary to modify these limits for the finite case. This was done by determining the confidence interval separately for each side of the value indicated as the percentage in the sample in the table, applying the finite correction factor and adding (or subtracting) the result to the sample percentage. Extensive testing by exact calculation disclosed that this approximation gave a result with an error of not more than .1% in any case.

In addition, the values in these tables have been checked extensively against the confidence limits given graphically by Chung and De Lury[4] for population sizes 500 and 10,000 and for a wide variety of sample sizes and rates of occurrence.

[4] J. H. Chung and D. B. De Lury, *Confidence Limits for the Hypergeometric Distribution*, University of Toronto Press, Toronto, Canada, 1950.

Technical Appendix VIII. Post Stratification

The formula given in Chapter 14 for the computation of the sampling error of a post-stratified sample is based on the formula cited by Hansen, Hurwitz, and Madow,[1] converted to the symbols used in this book. The formula as given in that reference is

$$\sigma_{\bar{X}}^2 = \frac{1-f}{n} S_w^2 + \frac{1-f}{n\bar{n}} \frac{\Sigma S_h^2 Q_h}{L}$$

where $\bar{X}$ = standard error of the mean

$f = \dfrac{n}{N}$

L = number of strata

$\bar{n}$ = average sample size per stratum, or $\dfrac{n}{L}$

$Q_h = 1 - \dfrac{N_h}{N}$

$S_w^2 = \dfrac{\Sigma N_h S_h^2}{N}$ (see Hansen et al., vol. 1, p. 188)

Substituting for S_w^2 and collecting terms, the equation becomes

$$\sigma_x^2 = \left(\frac{1}{n}\frac{\Sigma N_h S_h^2}{N} + \frac{1}{n\bar{n}}\frac{\Sigma S_h^2 Q_h}{L}\right)(1-f)$$

but $\bar{n}L = n$ and $f = n/N$, and

$$\sigma_{\bar{X}}^2 = \left(\frac{\Sigma N_h S_h^2}{Nn} + \frac{\Sigma S_h^2 Q_h}{n^2}\right)\left(1 - \frac{n}{N}\right)$$

Since $Q = 1 - n/N$, and changing symbols,

$$\sigma_{\bar{X}}^2 = \left[\frac{\Sigma(N_i \sigma_i^2)}{Nn} + \frac{\Sigma(1 - N_h/N)(\sigma_i^2)}{n^2}\right]\left(1 - \frac{n}{N}\right)$$

Finally,

$$SE_X = t(\sigma_{\bar{X}})$$

[1]M. H. Hansen, W. N. Hurwitz, and W. G. Madow, *Sample Survey Methods and Theory*, John Wiley & Sons, Inc., New York, 1953. The formula is given on p. 232 of vol. 1 and its derivation on pp. 138–139 of vol. 2.

Index

Acceptable quality level (AQL), 149
Acceptance number (c), 142, 145–149
Acceptance sampling, 13, 15, 141–157
  advantages of, 142–145
  applications of, 156–157
  Dodge-Romig table for, 144, 156
  formula for, 145*n*.
  in industry, 142
  limitations of, 142–145
  Military Standard 105A, B, C, and D, 156
  operating characteristic curve, 147
  statistical principles of, 145–146
  tables for, 150–152, 489
Allocation of sample items, stratified sampling variables:
  arbitrary sample size, 168
  optimum, 170–172
  proportional, 170
AOQ (average outgoing quality), 153–154
AOQ curve, 153
AOQL (average outgoing quality limit), 154
AQL (acceptable quality level), 149
Arithmetic average (*see entries beginning with the term:* Average)
Arithmetic mean, 52
  standard error of, 72, 509
Attributes, 14, 60
Attributes sampling, 13–14, 60–71
  concepts, sample size, 83–86
Average error rates, 152–154
Average outgoing quality (AOQ), 153–154
Average outgoing quality limit (AOQL), 154
Average range ($\bar{R}$), 94–96
Averages, 52
  sample reliability of, tables, 118–122, 470, 475

Bias, 41–42
Binomial distribution, 63
  formula for, 63*n*.
  normal approximation to, 66, 83
  standard deviation of, 66
Binomial sample precision (exact method), 103

c (acceptance number), 142, 145–149
Central tendency, 52
Cluster sampling, 13, 47, 182–194
  appraisal: attributes, 191
    variables, 186
  efficiency of, 184
  reasons for, 182
  sample size determination: attributes, 193
    variables, 190
  unequal clusters, 225–228
Cochran, W. G., 43*n*.

Compliance test, 3
Confidence interval, 64
Confidence level, 64, 80–83
Confidence limits:
  for average, 72, 122
  one-sided, 110–111, 122–125
    averages, 122
    proportions, 110
  for percentage, 67, 388
Costs, sampling, 48–49
Cowden, D. J., 155*n.*

d_2 factor, 94
Difference estimates, 195–201
Discovery sampling, 13, 15, 132–140
  formula, 137
  general considerations, 140
  place in auditing, 132–135
  principles of, 135–138
  tables, 138–140, 485–488
Dispersion, measures of, 53–59
Distribution:
  frequency, 51
  left-skewed, 58
  right-skewed, 58
  skewed, 58
  (*See also* Binomial distribution; Normal distribution; Sampling distribution)
Dodge, H. F., 144*n.*, 156
Dodge-Romig table, 144, 156
Double sampling, 155

Estimation sampling, 75–131
  attributes, 13
  variables, 14
Exploratory sampling (*see* Discovery sampling)

Federal Government Accountants Association, 7
Field, 19–23, 60
Finite population correction factor, 70
  table, 481
Fisher and Yates random number table, 27*n.*
Fraud, 133
Frequency distribution, 51

Grant, E. L., 155*n.*

Hansen, M. H., 43*n.*

Independent auditor, 2
Internal auditing, 5–6
Internal control system, 2–3
Interstate Commerce Commission random number table, 29

Judgment sample, 8

Kendall and Babington-Smith random number table, 27*n.*

Left-skewed distribution, 58
LIFO index, 222
Lot size, 145
Lot tolerance per cent defective (LTPD), 147–151

Maximum expected error rate, 86
Maximum tolerable error rate (MTER), 79
Military Standard 105A, B, C, and D, 156
Million random digits table, 29
Multiple acceptance sampling plans, 155
Multipurpose samples, 24, 98
Multistage sampling, 13, 47, 210–217
  illustration, 213
  limitations, 210–211
  precision, 211–212
  standard error, 514–515

Nonsampling errors, 23–24
Normal distribution, 55
  formula for, 55*n.*
  table of values for, 56

Objective sampling, 6–7
OC (operating characteristic) curve, 146–147
One-sided confidence limits, 110–111, 122–125
  averages, 122
  proportions, 110
Operating characteristic (OC) curve, 146–147

Population, 19–23, 60
Post stratification, 13, 218–221
Precision, sampling (*see* Sample precision)
Probability sample, 8, 12, 25, 26
  methods of obtaining, 26
  (*See also* Statistical sample)

$\bar{R}$ (average range), 94–96
Rand Corporation random number table, 29
Random letters, 36
  table, 296–297
Random months, 38
  table, 298–308
Random number generators, 35
Random number grid, 32
Random number sampling, 26–27
Random number tables, 27–29, 235–295
Random sample, 8, 12, 25, 26
  special problems, 35–38
  (*See also* Statistical sample)
Range, 53, 96
Ratio estimates, 195–196, 201–209
  of a ratio, 221–228
  of a total, 201–209
Replicated sampling, 228–231
  illustration, 229
  sample precision, 228
Right-skewed distribution, 58
Romig, H. G., 144*n*., 156

Sample (*see* Statistical sample)
Sample average, precision of, 72
Sample precision, 65, 78–80, 94
  of an average, 117–131
    basis of tables for, 509–510
    finite population, tables for, 470, 475
  of a proportion, 101–116
    tables for appraisal: of attributes (relative frequency), 388
Sample size estimates, 9, 75–99
  another approach, 113–115
  formula for, proportions, 85
  general considerations, variables, 97
  multipurpose samples, 24, 98
  steps in determination: of attributes, 89
    of variables, 97
  stratified samples, variables, 168
  tables: for attributes, 86, 309ff
      basis of, 518
Sample size estimates, tables (*Cont.*):
    for variables, 94, 118, 376
      basis of, 516
Sampling costs, 48–49
Sampling distribution, 62
  of average, 72
  of proportion, 66
Sampling efficiency, 160
Sampling error, 10
Sampling plan, 13
Sampling unit, 19
Schwartz, M. A., 135*n*.
Sequential sampling plan, 155
Skewed distribution, 58
Standard deviation, 53–59, 94, 117
  computation of, average range method, 94
  direct method, 53
  short method, 507
Standard error:
  of arithmetic mean, 72, 509
  of proportion (per cent), 67
Statistical measures, 51
  averages, 52
  standard deviation, 53
Statistical sample, 8
  acceptance (*see* Acceptance sampling)
  advantages of, 8
  cluster (*see* Cluster sampling)
  discovery (*see* Discovery sampling)
  estimation, 13, 14, 75–131
  multipurpose, 24, 98
  multistage (*see* Multistage sampling)
  random, stratified (*see* Stratified random samples)
  unrestricted, 12, 26
Strata, 159
Stratified random samples, 2, 47, 158–181
  allocation of sample items, 168–174
  appraisal: attributes, 176–180
    variables estimates, 162–168
  determination of sample size, 174–176
  post stratification, 13, 218–221
Substantive test, 4
Systematic sampling, 40–47
  bias, 41–42
  mechanics of, 44–47

t values, table, 56
Tables:
  acceptance sampling, 489
  attributes sample size, 376
  attributes sampling, appraisal, 310

Tables (*Cont.*):
discovery sampling, 485–488
sample size, 376–386
variables, average, sample precision of, 470–480
Teitelbaum, L. N., 135*n*.
Test objectives, 5–6, 16
Tests, 2–6
of account balances, 5
of compliance, 5
substantive, 5
of transaction, 5
Tippett random sampling numbers, 27*n*.
Total value estimates, unknown population size, 127–131

Unequal clusters, 225–228
Universe, 19–23, 60
Unknown population size, 127–131
Unrestricted random samples, 12, 26

Variables, 14
Variables sampling, 71–74
appraisal of sample results, 116–131, 475, 481
sample size determination, 91, 376–386

Weighted average, 166

$\bar{X}$, 52

ABOUT THE AUTHOR

HERBERT ARKIN PH.D., is Professor Emeritus at Bernard M. Baruch College, City University of New York, a school with which he has been associated for many years. Dr. Arkin has been a sampling consultant to many large corporations, including public accounting firms as well as government agencies. He has conducted numerous courses in statistical sampling for auditors, for the personnel of accounting firms, internal audit departments of corporations, as well as federal, state, and local government agencies and the government of Canada. Dr. Arkin is a lecturer and a prolific author of numerous articles for professional publications, and author of many texts, including *Sampling Methods for the Auditor: An Advanced Treatment* (McGraw-Hill). He is a member of professional societies including the American Statistical Association and the Institute of Mathematical Statistics. Dr. Arkin is listed in *Who's Who in America* and *Leading Men of Science*, among others.